SECOND EDITION

Introduction to Data Compression

The Morgan Kaufmann Series in Multimedia Information and Systems
Series Editor, Edward Fox

SECOND EDITION

Introduction to Data Compression

Khalid Sayood
University of Nebraska–Lincoln

MORGAN KAUFMANN PUBLISHERS

AN IMPRINT OF ACADEMIC PRESS

A Harcourt Science and Technology Company

SAN FRANCISCO   SAN DIEGO   NEW YORK   BOSTON
LONDON   SYDNEY   TOKYO

Senior Editor	Jennifer Mann
Director of Production and Manufacturing	Yonie Overton
Production Editor	Cheri Palmer
Editorial Coordinator	Karyn Johnson
Cover Design	Ross Carron Design
Cover Photograph	Harald Sund / The Image Bank
Composition	Babel Press
Illustration	Lineworks, Inc.
Copyeditor	Ken DellaPenta
Proofreader	Jennifer McClain
Indexer	Ty Koontz
Printer	Courier Corporation

ACADEMIC PRESS
A Harcourt Science and Technology Company
525 B Street, Suite 1900, San Diego, CA 92101-4495, USA
http://www.academicpress.com

Academic Press
Harcourt Place, 32 Jamestown Road, London, NW1 7BY United Kingdom
http://www.hbuk.co.uk/ap/

Morgan Kaufmann Publishers
340 Pine Street, Sixth Floor, San Francisco, CA 94104-3205, USA
http://www.mkp.com

Library of Congress Cataloging-in-Publication Data

Sayood, Khalid.
    Introduction to data compression / Khalid Sayood.–2nd ed.
    p.   cm.
    Includes bibliographical references and index.
    ISBN 1-55860-558-4
    1. Data compression (Telecommunication) 2. Coding theory I. Title.
TK5102.92.S39 2000
005.74'6–dc21
                            99-059343
                            CIP

This book is printed on acid-free paper.

To Füsun

Contents

Preface

As we move further into the information age, the rapid advancement will continue in all aspects of information technology. As one of the enabling technologies of the multimedia revolution, data compression is no exception. Since the publication of the first edition of this book, there has been a great deal of excitement in the field. Techniques such as wavelet-based compression, which were mainly research topics just a few years ago, are now part of an increasing number of commercial products. New techniques, such as SPIHT and CALIC, have been developed, and old techniques, such as *ppm*, have been enhanced. New standards, such as JPEG 2000 and JPEG-LS, are being developed to replace old standards, some of which are barely a decade old. These developments were a major motivation for this second edition, resulting in a new chapter on wavelets, another chapter on predictive lossless compression schemes, and substantial updates in many of the other chapters.

With these modifications and additions, we have tried not to lose sight of the fact that this book is an introduction to the art or science of data compression. Various forms of compression are part of almost all multimedia applications. We describe a variety of lossless and lossy compression techniques with applications to image, speech, text, audio, and video compression.

Given the pace of developments in this area, there are bound to be new ones that are not reflected in this book. In order to keep you informed of these developments, we will periodically provide updates at *http://www.mkp.com*.

Audience

If you are designing hardware or software implementations of compression algorithms, or need to interact with individuals engaged in such design, or are involved in development of multimedia applications and have some background in either electrical or computer engineering, or computer science, this book should be useful to you. We have included a large number of examples to aid in self-study. We have also included discussion of various multimedia standards. The intent here is not to provide all the details that may be required to implement a standard but to provide information that will help you follow and understand the standards documents.

Course Use

The impetus for writing this book came from the need for a self-contained book that could be used at the senior/graduate level for a course in data compression in either electrical engineering, computer engineering, or computer science departments. We have increased the number of end-of-chapter exercises that can be used to further a student's understanding of the material. More exercises can be found at the publisher's Web site. A solutions manual is also available from the publisher. Also at the publisher's Web site we provide links to various course homepages, which can be a valuable source of project ideas and support material.

With judicious use of the starred sections, this book can be tailored to fit a number of compression courses that emphasize various aspects of compression. If the course emphasis is on lossless compression, the instructor could cover all the sections in the first six chapters and skip all the starred sections in the later chapters, using some of the techniques described in these later chapters as simply front ends for lossless compression. Similarly, if the emphasis is on lossy compression, or a particular application of lossy compression, the instructor can select a collection of starred and unstarred sections that best fit course requirements.

Approach

In this book, we cover both lossless and lossy compression techniques with applications to image, speech, text, audio, and video compression. The various lossless and lossy coding techniques are introduced with just enough theory to tie things together. The necessary theory is introduced just before we need it. Therefore, there are three *mathematical preliminaries* chapters. In each of these chapters, we present the mathematical material needed to understand and appreciate the techniques that follow.

Although this book is an introductory text, the word *introduction* may have a different meaning for different audiences. We have tried to accommodate the needs of different audiences by taking a dual-track approach. Wherever we felt there was material that could enhance the understanding of the subject being discussed but could still be skipped without seriously hindering your understanding of the technique, we marked those sections with a star ($\star$). If you are primarily interested in understanding how the various techniques function, especially if you are using this book for self-study, we recommend you skip the starred sections, at least in a first reading. Readers who require a slightly more theoretical approach should use the starred sections. Except for the starred sections, we tried to keep the mathematics to a minimum.

Learning from This Book

I have found that it is easier for me to understand things if I can see examples. Therefore, I have relied heavily on examples to explain concepts. You may find it useful to spend more time with the examples if you have difficulty with some of the concepts.

Compression is still largely an art and to gain proficiency in an art we need to get a "feel" for the process. We have included software implementations for most of the techniques discussed in this book, along with a large number of data sets. The software and data sets can be obtained from *ftp://ftp.mkp.com/pub/Sayood/*. The programs are written in C and have been tested on a number of platforms. The programs should run under most flavors of UNIX machines and, with some slight modifications, under other operating systems as well. More detailed information is contained in the README file in the *pub/Sayood* directory.

You are strongly encouraged to use and modify these programs to work with your favorite data in order to understand some of the issues involved in compression. A useful and achievable goal should be the development of your own compression package by the time you have worked through this book. This would also be a good way to learn the trade-offs involved in different approaches. We have tried to give comparisons of techniques wherever possible; however, different types of data have their own idiosyncrasies. The best way to know which scheme to use in any given situation is to try them.

Content and Organization

The organization of the chapters is as follows: We introduce the mathematical preliminaries necessary for understanding lossless compression in Chapter 2; Chapters 3 and 4 are devoted to coding algorithms, including Huffman coding, arithmetic coding, Golomb-Rice codes, and Tunstall codes. Chapters 5 and 6 describe many of the popular lossless compression schemes along with their applications. The schemes include LZW, *ppm*, CALIC, BWT, and DMC, among others. We also describe the compression algorithm used in the current JBIG standard and the Group 3 and Group 4 facsimile standards.

Chapter 7 is devoted to providing the mathematical preliminaries for lossy compression. Quantization is at the heart of most lossy compression schemes. Chapters 8 and 9 are devoted to the study of quantization. Chapter 8 deals with scalar quantization, and Chapter 9 deals with vector quantization. Chapter 10 deals with differential encoding techniques, in particular differential pulse code modulation (DPCM) and delta modulation. Included in this chapter is a discussion of the CCITT G.726 standard.

Chapter 11 is our third mathematical preliminaries chapter. The goal of this chapter is to provide the mathematical foundation necessary to understand some aspects of the transform, subband, and wavelet-based techniques that are described in the next three chapters. As in the case of the previous mathematical preliminaries chapters, not all material covered is necessary for everyone. We describe the current JPEG standard in Chapter 12, the CCITT G.722 international standard and the MPEG audio compression standard in Chapter 13, and EZW, SPIHT, and JPEG 2000 in Chapter 14.

Chapter 15 covers techniques in which the data to be compressed are analyzed, and a model for the generation of the data is transmitted to the receiver. The receiver uses this model to synthesize the data. These analysis/synthesis schemes include linear predictive schemes used for low-rate speech coding and the relatively new fractal compression technique. We describe the federal government LPC-10 standard. Although code-excited linear prediction (CELP) is an analysis by synthesis scheme rather than an analysis/synthesis scheme, we have included discussion of CELP in this chapter because of its close relationship to analysis/synthesis schemes. We also discuss two CELP-based standards, the federal standard 1016 and the CCITT G.728 international standard. We have also included a discussion of the mixed excitation linear prediction (MELP) technique, which is the new federal standard for speech coding at 2.4 kbps.

Chapter 16 is an exception to the book's general rule of organization, as it deals with an application (video coding) instead of a technique. We describe several international standards, including H.261, and the various MPEG standards.

A Personal View

For me, data compression is more than a manipulation of numbers; it is the process of discovering structures that exist in the data. In the ninth-century, the poet Omar Khayyam wrote

> The moving finger writes, and having writ,
> moves on; not all thy piety nor wit,
> shall lure it back to cancel half a line,
> nor all thy tears wash out a word of it.
> (The Rubaiyat of Omar Khayyam)

To explain these few lines would take volumes. They tap into a common human experience so that in our mind's eye, we can reconstruct what the poet was trying to convey centuries ago. To understand the words we not only need to know the language, we also need to have a model of reality that is close to that of the poet. The genius of the poet lies in identifying a model of reality that is so much a part of our humanity that centuries later and in widely diverse cultures, these few words can evoke volumes.

Data compression is much more limited in its aspirations, and it may be presumptuous to mention it in the same breath as poetry. But there is much that is similar to both endeavors. Data compression involves identifying models for the many different types of structures that exist in different types of data and then using these models, perhaps along with the perceptual framework in which these data will be used, to obtain a compact representation of the data. These structures can be in the form of patterns that we can recognize simply by plotting the data, or they might be statistical structures that require a more mathematical approach to comprehend.

In *The Long Dark Teatime of the Soul* by Douglas Adams, the protagonist finds that he can enter Valhalla (a rather shoddy one) if he tilts his head in a certain way. Appreciating the structures that exist in data sometimes require us to tilt our heads in a certain way. There are an infinite number of ways we can tilt our head and, in order not to get a pain in the neck (carrying our analogy to absurd limits), it would be nice to know some of the ways that will generally lead to a profitable result. One of the objectives of this book is to provide you with a frame of reference that can be used for further exploration. I hope this exploration will provide as much enjoyment for you as it has given to me.

Acknowledgments

It has been a lot of fun writing both the initial and the second editions of this book. My task has been made considerably easier and the end product considerably better because of the help I have received. Acknowledging that help is itself a pleasure.

The first edition benefitted from the careful and detailed criticism of Roy Hoffman from IBM, Glen Langdon from the University of California at Santa Cruz, Debra Lelewer from California Polytechnic State University, Eve Riskin from the University of Washington, Ibrahim Sezan from Kodak, and Peter Swaszek from the University of Rhode Island. They provided detailed comments on all or most of the first edition. Nasir Memon from Polytechnic University, Victor Ramamoorthy at S3, Grant Davidson at Dolby Corporation, Hakan Caglar, who was then at TÜBITAK in Istanbul, and Allen Gersho from the University of California at Santa Barbara reviewed parts of the manuscript.

Since the appearance of the first edition, various readers have sent me their comments and critiques. I am grateful to all who sent me comments and suggestions. I am especially grateful to Roberto Lopez-Hernandez, Dirk vom Stein, and Christopher A. Larrieu for pointing out errors and suggesting improvements to the book. I am also grateful to the various instructors who have sent me their critiques. In particular I would like to thank Bruce Bomar from the University of Tennessee, Mark Fowler from SUNY Binghamton, Paul Amer from the University of Delaware, K.R. Rao from the University of Texas at Arlington, Ralph Wilkerson from the University of Missouri–Rolla, and Adam Drozdek from Duquesne University.

For the second edition Steve Tate at the University of North Texas, Sheila Horan at New Mexico State University, Edouard Lamboray at Oerlikon Contraves Group, Steven Pigeon at the University of Montreal, and Jesse Olvera at Raytheon Systems reviewed the entire manuscript. Their detailed critiques pointed out areas of significant omissions as well as errors in the manuscript. They showed me many ways to improve the manuscript. I am grateful to them for sharing their knowledge and their time. I did not always take their advice, which is probably why there may still be some remaining errors.

The new subband chapter owes its origins to Emin Anarım of Boğaziçi University and Hakan Çağlar. We had planned to write a book exclusively devoted to transform, subband, and wavelet-based coding. The idea stayed, and died, in the planning stage. However, during this period, with the help of Hakan's Ph.D. dissertation, I started what is now part of Chapter 13 in this edition. Mark Fowler provided extensive comments on Chapters 11–14, correcting mistakes of both commission and omission.

Frazer Williams and Mike Hoffman, from my department at the University of Nebraska, provided reviews for the first edition of the book. Mike read the new chapters in the second edition in their raw form (no task for the fainthearted) and provided me with critiques that led to major rewrites. Tim James, Devajani Khataniar, and Lance Pérez also read and critiqued parts of the new material.

The folks at Morgan Kaufmann are the people who did the real work of actually getting the book out, and very nice people they are. Jennifer Mann, ably assisted by Karyn Johnson, who is a master of the art of gentle reminders, directed the process. Cheri Palmer, the production editor, did a marvelous job of keeping her frustration from showing at missed deadlines. Copyeditor Ken DellaPenta seemed to know more about the subject than I did and was wonderful at catching and correcting all kinds of problems.

Chloeann Nelson, along with trying to stop me from splitting infinitives, also tried to make both editions of the book more user-friendly. There are very few parts of the book that were not modified in some way based on her recommendations.

Most of the examples in this book were generated in a lab set up by Andy Hadenfeldt. James Nau helped me extricate myself out of numerous software puddles. In my times of panic, he was always just an email or voice mail away.

I would like to thank the various "models" for the data sets that accompany this book and were used as examples. The individuals in the images are Sinan Sayood, Sena Sayood, and Elif Kokceli. The female voice belongs to Pat Masek.

This book reflects what I have learned over the years. I have been very fortunate in the teachers I have had. David Farden, now at North Dakota State University, introduced me to the area of digital communication. Norm Griswold at Texas A&M University introduced me to the area of data compression. Jerry Gibson, now at Southern Methodist University, was my Ph.D. advisor and helped me get started on my professional career. The world may not thank him for that, but I certainly do.

I have also learned a lot from my students at the University of Nebraska and Boğaziçi University. Their interest and curiousity forced me to learn and kept me in touch with the broad field that is data compression today. I learned at least as much from them as they learned from me.

Much of this learning would not have been possible but for the support I received from NASA. Warner Miller and Pen-Shu Yeh at the Goddard Space Flight Center and Wayne Whyte at the Lewis Research Center have been a consistent source of support and ideas. I am truly grateful for their helpful guidance, trust, and friendship.

Our two boys, Sena and Sinan, graciously forgave my evenings and weekends at work. For that, and for being such perfect joys, I thank them and promise to read the entire discworld series to them.

Above all the person most responsible for the existence of this book is my partner and closest friend Füsun. Her support and her friendship gives me the freedom to do things I would not otherwise even consider. She centers my universe and, as with every significant endeavor that I have undertaken since I met her, this book is at least as much hers as it is mine.

Introduction

n the last decade we have been witnessing a transformation—some call it a revolution—in the way we communicate, and the process is still under way. This transformation includes the ever-present, ever-growing Internet; the explosive development of mobile communications; and the ever-increasing importance of video communication. Data compression is one of the enabling technologies for each of these aspects of the multimedia revolution. It would not be practical to put images, let alone audio and video, on websites if it were not for data compression algorithms. Cellular phones would not be able to provide communication with increasing clarity were it not for compression. The advent of digital TV would not be possible without compression. Data compression, which for a long time was the domain of a relatively small group of engineers and scientists, is now ubiquitous. Make a long-distance call and you are using compression. Use your modem, or your fax machine, and you will benefit from compression. If you use a satellite TV service, you are using compression.

So, what is data compression, and why do we need it? Many of you have probably heard of JPEG and MPEG, which are standards for representing images and video. Data compression algorithms are used in these standards to reduce the number of bits required to represent an image or a video sequence. In brief, data compression is the art or science of representing information in a compact form. We create these compact representations by identifying and using structures that exist in the data. Data can be characters in a text file, numbers that are samples of speech or image waveforms, or sequences of numbers that are generated by other processes. The reason we need data compression is that more and more of the information that we generate and use is in digital form—in the form of numbers represented by bytes of data. And the number of bytes required to represent multimedia data can be huge. For example, in order to digitally represent 1 second of video without compression (using the CCIR 601 format), we need more than 20 megabytes, or 160 megabits. If we consider the number of seconds in a movie, we can easily see why we would need compression. To represent 2 minutes of uncompressed CD-quality music (44,100 samples per second, 16 bits per sample) requires more than 84 million bits. Downloading music from a website at these rates would take a long time.

As human activity has a greater and greater impact on our environment, there is an ever-increasing need for more information about our environment, how it functions, and what we are doing to it. Various space agencies from around the world, including the European Space Agency (ESA), the National Aeronautics and Space Agency (NASA), the Canadian Space Agency (CSA), and the Japanese Space Agency (STA), are collaborating on a program to monitor global change that will generate half a terabyte of data per *day* when they are fully operational. Compare this to the 130 terabytes of data currently stored at the EROS data center in South Dakota, that is the largest archive for land mass data in the world.

Given the explosive growth of data that needs to be transmitted and stored, why not focus on developing better transmission and storage technologies? This is happening, but it is not enough. There have been significant advances that permit larger and larger volumes of information to be stored and transmitted without using compression, including CD-ROMs, optical fibers, Asymmetric Digital Subscriber Lines (ADSL), and cable modems. However, while it is true that both storage and transmission capacities are steadily increasing with new technological innovations, as a corollary to Parkinson's First Law,[1] it seems that the need for mass storage and transmission increases at least twice as fast as storage and transmission capacities improve. Then there are situations in which capacity has not increased significantly. For example, the amount of information we can transmit over the airwaves will always be limited by the characteristics of the atmosphere.

An early example of data compression is Morse code, developed by Samuel Morse in the mid-19th century. Letters sent by telegraph are encoded with dots and dashes. Morse noticed that certain letters occurred more often than others. In order to reduce the average time required to send a message, he assigned shorter sequences to letters that occur more frequently, such as e ($\cdot$) and a ($\cdot\,-$), and longer sequences to letters that occur less frequently, such as q ($-\,-\,\cdot\,-$) and j ($\cdot\,-\,-\,-$). This idea of using shorter codes for more frequently occurring characters is used in Huffman coding, which we will describe in Chapter 3.

Where Morse code uses the frequency of occurrence of single characters, a widely used form of Braille code, which was also developed in the mid-19th century, uses the frequency of occurrence of words to provide compression [20]. In Braille coding, 2×3 arrays of dots are used to represent text. Different letters can be represented depending on whether the dots are raised or flat. In Grade 1 Braille, each array of six dots represents a single character. However, given six dots with two positions for each dot, we can obtain 2^6, or 64, different combinations. If we use 26 of these for the different letters, we have 38 combinations left. In Grade 2 Braille, some of these leftover combinations are used to represent words that occur frequently, such as "and" and "for." One of the combinations is used as a special symbol indicating that the symbol that follows is a word and not a character, thusallowing a large number of words to

---

[1] Parkinson's First Law: "Work expands so as to fill the time available," in *Parkinson's Law and Other Studies in Administration*, by Cyril Northcote Parkinson, Ballantine Books, New York, 1957.

be represented by two arrays of dots. These modifications, along with contractions of some of the words, result in an average reduction in space, or compression, of about 20% [20].

Statistical structure is being used to provide compression in these examples, but that is not the only kind of structure that exists in the data. There are many other kinds of structures existing in data of different types that can be exploited for compression. Consider speech. When we speak, the physical construction of our voice box dictates the kinds of sounds that we can produce. That is, the mechanics of speech production impose a structure on speech. Therefore, instead of transmitting the speech itself, we could send information about the conformation of the voice box, which could be used by the receiver to synthesize the speech. An adequate amount of information about the conformation of the voice box can be represented much more compactly than the numbers that are the sampled values of speech. Therefore, we get compression. This compression approach is being used currently in a number of applications, including transmission of speech over mobile radios and the synthetic voice in toys that speak. An early version of this compression approach, called the *vocoder* (*voice coder*), was developed by Homer Dudley at Bell Laboratories in 1936. The vocoder was demonstrated at the New York World's Fair in 1939, where it was a major attraction. We will revisit the vocoder and this approach to compression of speech in Chapter 15.

These are only a few of the many different types of structures that can be used to obtain compression. The structure in the data is not the only thing that can be exploited to obtain compression. We can also make use of the characteristics of the user of the data. Many times, for example, when transmitting or storing speech and images, the data are intended to be perceived by a human, and humans have limited perceptual abilities. For example, we cannot hear the very high frequency sounds that dogs can hear. If something is represented in the data that cannot be perceived by the user, is there any point in preserving that information? The answer often is "no." Therefore, we can make use of the perceptual limitations of humans to obtain compression by discarding irrelevant information. This approach is used in a number of compression schemes that we will visit in Chapters 12, 13, and 14.

Before we embark on our study of data compression techniques, let's take a general look at the area and define some of the key terms and concepts we will be using in the rest of the book.

1.1 Compression Techniques

When we speak of a compression technique or compression algorithm,[2] we are actually referring to two algorithms. There is the compression algorithm that takes an input $\mathcal{X}$ and generates a representation $\mathcal{X}_c$ that requires fewer bits, and there is a reconstruction algorithm that operates on the compressed representation $\mathcal{X}_c$ to generate the reconstruction $\mathcal{Y}$. These operations

---

[2]The word *algorithm* comes from the name of an early ninth-century Arab mathematician, Al-Khwarizmi, who wrote a treatise entitled *The Compendious Book on Calculation by* al-jabr *and* al-muqabala, in which he explored (among other things) the solution of various linear and quadratic equations via rules or an "algorithm." This approach became known as the method of Al-Khwarizmi. The name was changed to *algoritni* in Latin, from which we get the word *algorithm*. The name of the treatise also gave us the word *algebra* [229].

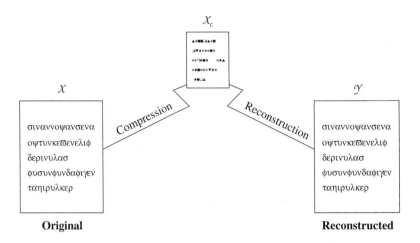

FIGURE 1.1   **Compression and reconstruction.**

are shown schematically in Figure 1.1. We will follow convention and refer to both the compression and reconstruction algorithms together to mean the compression algorithm.

Based on the requirements of reconstruction, data compression schemes can be divided into two broad classes: *lossless* compression schemes, in which $\mathcal{Y}$ is identical to $\mathcal{X}$, and *lossy* compression schemes, which generally provide much higher compression than lossless compression but allow $\mathcal{Y}$ to be different from $\mathcal{X}$.

1.1.1   Lossless Compression

Lossless compression techniques, as their name implies, involve no loss of information. If data have been losslessly compressed, the original data can be recovered exactly from the compressed data. Lossless compression is generally used for applications that cannot tolerate any difference between the original and reconstructed data.

Text compression is an important area for lossless compression. It is very important that the reconstruction is identical to the text original, as very small differences can result in statements with very different meanings. Consider the sentences "Do *not* send money" and "Do *now* send money." A similar argument holds for computer files and for certain types of data such as bank records.

If data of any kind are to be processed or "enhanced" later to yield more information, it is important that the integrity be preserved. For example, suppose we compressed a radiological image in a lossy fashion, and the difference between the reconstruction $\mathcal{Y}$ and the original $\mathcal{X}$ was visually undetectable. If this image was later enhanced, the previously undetectable differences may cause the appearance of artifacts that could seriously mislead the radiologist. Because the price for this kind of mishap may be a human life, it makes sense to be very careful about using a compression scheme that generates a reconstruction that is different from the original.

Data obtained from satellites often are processed later to obtain different numerical indicators of vegetation, deforestation, and so on. If the reconstructed data are not identical to the original data, processing may result in "enhancement" of the differences. It may not be possible to go back and obtain the same data over again. Therefore, it is not advisable to allow for any differences to appear in the compression process.

There are many situations that require compression where we want the reconstruction to be identical to the original. There are also a number of situations in which it is possible to relax this requirement in order to get more compression. In these situations we look to lossy compression techniques.

1.1.2 Lossy Compression

Lossy compression techniques involve some loss of information, and data that have been compressed using lossy techniques generally cannot be recovered or reconstructed exactly. In return for accepting this distortion in the reconstruction, we can generally obtain much higher compression ratios than is possible with lossless compression.

In many applications, this lack of exact reconstruction is not a problem. For example, when storing or transmitting speech, the exact value of each sample of speech is not necessary. Depending on the quality required of the reconstructed speech, varying amounts of loss of information about the value of each sample can be tolerated. If the quality of the reconstructed speech is to be similar to that heard on the telephone, a significant loss of information can be tolerated. However, if the reconstructed speech needs to be of the quality heard on a compact disc, the amount of information loss that can be tolerated is relatively low.

Similarly, when viewing a reconstruction of a video sequence, the fact that the reconstruction is different from the original is generally not important as long as the differences do not result in annoying artifacts. Thus, video is generally compressed using lossy compression.

Once we have developed a data compression scheme, we need to be able to measure its performance. Because of the number of different areas of application, different terms have been developed to describe and measure the performance.

1.1.3 Measures of Performance

A compression algorithm can be evaluated in a number of different ways. We could measure the relative complexity of the algorithm, the memory required to implement the algorithm, how fast the algorithm performs on a given machine, the amount of compression, and how closely the reconstruction resembles the original. In this book we will mainly be concerned with the last two criteria. Let us take each one in turn.

A very logical way of measuring how well a compression algorithm compresses a given set of data is to look at the ratio of the number of bits required to represent the data before compression to the number of bits required to represent the data after compression. This ratio is called the *compression ratio*. Suppose storing an image made up of a square array of 256×256 pixels requires 65,536 bytes. The image is compressed and the compressed version requires 16,384 bytes. We would say that the compression ratio is 4:1. We can also represent the compression ratio by expressing the reduction in the amount of data required as a percentage of the size of the original data. In this particular example the compression ratio calculated in this manner would be 75%.

Another way of reporting compression performance is to provide the average number of bits required to represent a single sample. This is generally referred to as the *rate*. For example, in the case of the compressed image described above, if we assume 8 bits per byte (or pixel), the average number of bits per pixel in the compressed representation is 2. Thus, we would say that the rate is 2 bits per pixel.

In lossy compression, the reconstruction differs from the original data. Therefore, in order to determine the efficiency of a compression algorithm, we have to have some way of quantifying the difference. The difference between the original and the reconstruction is often called the *distortion*. (We will describe several measures of distortion in Chapter 7.) Lossy techniques are generally used for the compression of data that originate as analog signals, such as speech and video. Since analog signals are often called *waveforms*, compression of analog signals is referred to as *waveform coding*. In waveform coding of speech and video, the final arbiter of quality is human. Because human responses are difficult to model mathematically, many approximate measures of distortion are used to determine the quality of the reconstructed waveforms. We will discuss this topic in more detail in Chapter 7.

Other terms that are also used when talking about differences between the reconstruction and the original are *fidelity* and *quality*. When we say that the fidelity or quality of a reconstruction is high, we mean that the difference between the reconstruction and the original is small. Whether this difference is a mathematical difference or a perceptual difference should be evident from the context.

1.2 Modeling and Coding

While reconstruction requirements may force the decision of whether a compression scheme is to be lossy or lossless, the exact compression scheme we use will depend on a number of different factors. Some of the most important factors are the characteristics of the data that need to be compressed. A compression technique that will work well for the compression of text may not work well for compressing images. Each application presents a different set of challenges.

There is a saying attributed to Bobby Knight, the basketball coach at Indiana University: "If the only tool you have is a hammer, you approach every problem as if it were a nail." Our intention in this book is to provide you with a large number of tools that you can use to solve the particular data compression problem. It should be remembered that data compression, if it is a science at all, is an experimental science. The approach that works best for a particular application will depend to a large extent on the redundancies inherent in the data.

The development of data compression algorithms for a variety of data can be divided into two phases. The first phase is usually referred to as *modeling*. In this phase we try to extract information about any redundancy that exists in the data and describe the redundancy in the form of a model. The second phase is called *coding*. A description of the model and a "description" of how the data differ from the model are encoded, generally using a binary alphabet. The difference between the data and the model is often referred to as the *residual*.

In the following three examples we will look at three different ways that data can be modeled. We will then use the model to obtain compression.

Example 1.2.1:

Consider the following sequence of numbers $\{x_1, x_2, x_3, \ldots\}$:

9	11	11	11	14	13	15	17	16	17	20	21

If we were to transmit or store the binary representations of these numbers, we would need to use 5 bits per sample. However, by exploiting the structure in the data, we can represent the sequence using fewer bits. If we plot these data as shown in Figure 1.2, we see that the data seem to fall on a straight line. A model for the data could therefore be a straight line given by the equation

$$\hat{x}_n = n + 8 \qquad n = 1, 2, \ldots$$

Thus, the structure in the data can be characterized by an equation. To make use of this structure, let's examine the difference between the data and the model. The difference (or residual) is given by the sequence

$$e_n = x_n - \hat{x}_n \; : \; 0\;1\;0\;-1\;1\;-1\;0\;1\;-1\;-1\;1\;1$$

The residual sequence consists of only three numbers $\{-1, 0, 1\}$. If we assign a code of 00 to -1, a code of 01 to 0, and a code of 10 to 1, we need to use 2 bits to represent each element of the residual sequence. Therefore, we can obtain compression by transmitting or storing the parameters of the model and the residual sequence. The encoding can be exact if the required compression is to be lossless, or approximate if the compression can be lossy.

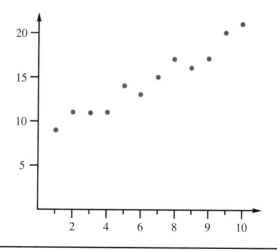

FIGURE 1.2   **A sequence of data values.**

The type of structure or redundancy that existed in these data follows a simple law. Once we recognize this law, we can make use of the structure to *predict* the value of each element in the sequence and then encode the residual. Structure of this type is only one of many types of structure. Consider the following example.

Example 1.2.2:

Consider the following sequence of numbers:

27	28	29	28	26	27	29	28	30	32	34	36	38

The sequence is plotted in Figure 1.3.

The sequence does not seem to follow a simple law as in the previous case. However, each value is close to the previous value. Suppose we send the first value, then in place of subsequent values we send the difference between it and the previous value. The sequence of transmitted values would be

27	1	1	−1	−2	1	2	−1	2	2	2	2	2

Like the previous example, the number of distinct values has been reduced. Fewer bits are required to represent each number and compression is achieved. The decoder adds each received value to the previous decoded value to obtain the reconstruction corresponding to the received value. Techniques that use the past values of a sequence to *predict* the current value and then encode the error in prediction, or residual, are called *predictive coding* schemes. We will discuss lossless predictive compression schemes in Chapter 6 and lossy predictive coding schemes in Chapter 10.

Assuming both encoder and decoder know the model being used, we would still have to send the value of the first element of the sequence.

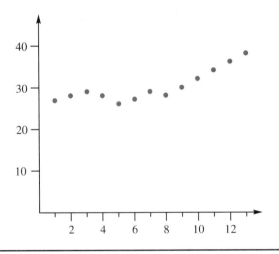

FIGURE 1.3   A sequence of data values.

A very different type of redundancy is statistical in nature. Often we will encounter sources that generate some symbols more often than others. In these situations, it will be advantageous to assign binary codes of different lengths to different symbols.

Example 1.2.3:

Suppose we have the following sequence:

$$abbarayaranbarraybranbfarbfaarbfaaarbaway$$

which is typical of all sequences generated by a source. Notice that the sequence is made up of eight different symbols. In order to represent eight symbols, we need to use 3 bits per symbol. Suppose instead we used the code shown in Table 1.1. Notice that we have assigned a code-

TABLE 1.1	A code with codewords of varying length.
a	1
b	001
b	01100
f	0100
n	0111
r	000
w	01101
y	0101

word with only a single bit to the symbol that occurs most often, and correspondingly longer codewords to symbols that occur less often. If we substitute the codes for each symbol, we will use 106 bits to encode the entire sequence. As there are 41 symbols in the sequence, this works out to approximately 2.58 bits per symbol. This means we have obtained a compression ratio of 1.16:1. We will study how to use statistical redundancy of this sort in Chapters 3 and 4. ◆

When dealing with text, along with statistical redundancy, we also see redundancy in the form of words that repeat often. We can take advantage of this form of redundancy by constructing a list of these words and then represent them by their position in the list. This type of compression scheme is called a *dictionary* compression scheme. We will study these schemes in Chapter 5.

Often the structure or redundancy in the data becomes more evident when we look at groups of symbols. We will look at compression schemes that take advantage of this in Chapters 4 and 9.

Finally, there will be situations in which it is easier to take advantage of the structure if we decompose the data into a number of components. We can then study each component separately and use a model appropriate to that component. We will look at such schemes in Chapters 12, 13, and 14.

There are a number of different ways to characterize data. Different characterizations will lead to different compression schemes. We will study these compression schemes in the upcoming chapters, and use a number of examples that should help us understand the relationship between the characterization and the compression scheme.

With the increasing use of compression, there has also been an increasing need for standards. Standards allow products developed by different vendors to communicate. Thus, we can compress something with products from one vendor and reconstruct it using the products of a different vendor. The different international standards organizations have responded to this need, and a number of standards for various compression applications have been approved. We will discuss these standards as applications of the various compression techniques.

Finally, compression is still largely an art, and to gain proficiency in an art you need to get a feel for the process. To help, we have developed software implementations of most of the techniques discussed in this book, and also provided the data sets used for developing the examples in this book. Details on how to obtain these programs and data sets are provided in the Preface. You should use these programs on your favorite data or on the data sets provided in order to understand some of the issues involved in compression. We would also encourage you to write your own software implementations of some of these techniques, as very often the best way to understand how an algorithm works is to implement the algorithm.

1.3 Summary

In this chapter we have introduced the subject of data compression. We have provided some motivation for why we need data compression and defined some of the terminology we will need in this book. Additional terminology will be introduced as needed. We have briefly introduced the two major types of compression algorithms: lossless compression and lossy compression. Lossless compression is used for applications that require an exact reconstruction of the original data, while lossy compression is used when the user can tolerate some differences between the original and reconstructed representations of the data. An important element in the design of data compression algorithms is the modeling of the data. We have briefly looked at how modeling can help us in obtaining more compact representations of the data. We have described some of the different ways we can view the data in order to model it. The more ways we have of looking at the data, the more successful we will be in developing compression schemes that take full advantage of the structures in the data.

1.4 Projects and Problems

1. If you have access to a UNIX machine, use the `compress` or the `gzip` command to compress different files. Study the effect of the original file size and file type on the ratio of compressed file size to original file size. (If you are using a DOS machine, use the compression utility available on your machine.)

To compress a file called `something.c`, type `compress something.c` or `gzip something.c`. A file called `something.c.Z` or `something.c.gz` (this is the compressed file) will be created in your directory, and the file `something.c` will be deleted. To recover your original file, type `uncompress something.c` or `gunzip something.c`.

2. Take a few paragraphs of text from a popular magazine and compress them by removing all words that are not essential for comprehension. For example, in the sentence "This is the dog that belongs to my friend," we can remove the words *is*, *the*, *that*, and *to* and still convey the same meaning. Let the ratio of the words removed to the total number of words in the original text be the measure of redundancy in the text. Repeat the experiment using paragraphs from a technical journal. Can you make any quantitative statements about the redundancy in the text obtained from different sources?

2

Mathematical Preliminaries
for Lossless Compression

2.1 Overview

The treatment of data compression in this book is not very mathematical. (For a more mathematical treatment of some of the topics covered in this book, see [55, 23, 86, 155].) However, we do need some mathematical preliminaries to appreciate the compression techniques we will discuss. Compression schemes can be divided into two classes, lossy and lossless. Lossy compression schemes involve the loss of some information, and data that have been compressed using a lossy scheme generally cannot be recovered exactly. Lossless schemes compress the data without loss of information, and the original data can be recovered exactly from the compressed data. In this chapter, some of the ideas in information theory that provide the framework for the development of lossless data compression schemes are briefly reviewed. We will also look at some ways to model the data that lead to efficient coding schemes. We have assumed some knowledge of probability concepts (see Appendix A for a brief review of probability and random processes).

2.2 A Brief Introduction to Information Theory

While the idea of a quantitative measure of information has been around for a while, the person who pulled everything together into what is now called information theory was Claude Elwood Shannon [209], an electrical engineer at Bell Labs. Shannon defined a quantity called *self-information*. Suppose we have an event A, which is a set of outcomes of some random experiment. If $P(A)$ is the probability that the event A will occur, then the self-information associated with A is given by

$$i(A) = \log_b \frac{1}{P(A)} = -\log_b P(A). \tag{2.1}$$

Note that we have not specified the base of the log function. We will discuss this in more detail later in the chapter. The use of the logarithm to obtain a measure of information was not an arbitrary choice as we shall see later in this chapter. But first let's see if the use of a logarithm in this context makes sense from an intuitive point of view. Recall that $\log(1) = 0$, and $-\log(x)$ increases as x decreases from one to zero. Therefore, if the probability of an event is low, the amount of self-information associated with it is high; if the probability of an event is high, the information associated with it is low. Even if we ignore the mathematical definition of information and simply use the definition we use in everyday language, this makes some intuitive sense. The barking of a dog during a burglary is a high-probability event and, therefore, does not contain too much information. However, if the dog did not bark during a burglary, this is a low-probability event and contains a lot of information. (Obviously, Sherlock Holmes understood information theory![1]) Although this equivalence of the mathematical and semantic definitions of information holds true most of the time, it does not hold all of the time. For example, a totally random string of letters will contain more information (in the mathematical sense) than a well-thought-out treatise on information theory.

Another property of this mathematical definition of information that makes intuitive sense is that the information obtained from the occurrence of two independent events is the sum of the information obtained from the occurrence of the individual events. Suppose A and B are two independent events. The self-information associated with the occurrence of both event A *and* event B is, by Equation (2.1),

$$i(AB) = \log_b \frac{1}{P(AB)}.$$

As A and B are independent,

$$P(AB) = P(A)P(B)$$

and

$$\begin{aligned} i(AB) &= \log_b \frac{1}{P(A)P(B)} \\ &= \log_b \frac{1}{P(A)} + \log_b \frac{1}{P(B)} \\ &= i(A) + i(B). \end{aligned}$$

The unit of information depends on the base of the log. If we use log base 2, the unit is *bits*; if we use log base e, the unit is *nats*; and if we use log base 10, the unit is *hartleys*.

Note that to calculate the information in bits, we need to take the logarithm base 2 of the probabilities. Because this probably does not appear on your calculator, let's review logarithms briefly. Recall that

$$\log_b x = a$$

---

[1] *Silver Blaze* by Arthur Conan Doyle.

means that

$$b^a = x.$$

Therefore, if we want to take the log base 2 of x

$$\log_2 x = a \Rightarrow 2^a = x,$$

we want to find the value of a. We can take the natural log (log base e) or log base 10 of both sides (which do appear on your calculator). Then

$$\ln(2^a) = \ln x \Rightarrow a \ln 2 = \ln x$$

and

$$a = \frac{\ln x}{\ln 2}$$

Example 2.2.1:

Let H and T be the outcomes of flipping a coin. If the coin is fair, then

$$P(H) = P(T) = \tfrac{1}{2}$$

and

$$i(H) = i(T) = 1 \text{ bit.}$$

If the coin is not fair, then we would expect the information associated with each event to be different. Suppose

$$P(H) = \tfrac{1}{8}, \quad P(T) = \tfrac{7}{8}.$$

Then

$$i(H) = 3 \text{ bits}, \quad i(T) = 0.193 \text{ bits.}$$

At least mathematically, the occurrence of a head conveys much more information than the occurrence of a tail. As we shall see later, this has certain consequences for how the information conveyed by these outcomes should be encoded.   ◆

If we have a set of independent events A_i, which are sets of outcomes of some experiment S, such that

$$\bigcup A_i = S$$

where S is the sample space, then the average self-information associated with the random experiment is given by

$$H = \sum P(A_i)i(A_i) = -\sum P(A_i)\log_b P(A_i).$$

This quantity is called the *entropy* associated with the experiment. One of the many contributions of Shannon was that he showed that if the experiment is a source that puts out symbols A_i from a set $\mathcal{A}$, then the entropy is a measure of the average number of binary symbols needed to code the output of the source. Shannon showed that the best that a lossless compression scheme can do is to encode the output of a source with an average number of bits equal to the entropy of the source.

The set of symbols $\mathcal{A}$ is often called the *alphabet* for the source, and the symbols are referred to as *letters*. For a general source $\mathcal{S}$ with alphabet $\mathcal{A} = \{1, 2, \ldots, m\}$ that generates a sequence $\{X_1, X_2, \ldots\}$, the entropy is given by

$$H(\mathcal{S}) = \lim_{n \to \infty} \frac{1}{n} G_n \tag{2.2}$$

where

$$G_n = - \sum_{i_1=1}^{i_1=m} \sum_{i_2=1}^{i_2=m} \cdots \sum_{i_n=1}^{i_n=m} P(X_1 = i_1, X_2 = i_2, \ldots, X_n = i_n) \log P(X_1 = i_1, X_2 = i_2, \ldots, X_n = i_n)$$

and $\{X_1, X_2, \ldots, X_n\}$ is a sequence of length n from the source. We will talk more about the reason for the limit in Equation (2.2) later in the chapter. If each element in the sequence is independent and identically distributed (*iid*), then we can show that

$$G_n = -n \sum_{i_1=1}^{i_1=m} P(X_1 = i_1) \log P(X_1 = i_1) \tag{2.3}$$

and the equation for the entropy becomes

$$H(S) = - \sum P(X_1) \log P(X_1). \tag{2.4}$$

For most sources Equations (2.2) and (2.4) are not identical. If we need to distinguish between the two, we will call the quantity computed in (2.4) the *first-order entropy* of the source, while the quantity in (2.2) will be referred to as the *entropy* of the source.

In general, it is not possible to know the entropy for a physical source, so we have to estimate the entropy. The estimate of the entropy depends on our assumptions about the structure of the source sequence.

Consider the following sequence:

$$1\ 2\ 3\ 2\ 3\ 4\ 5\ 4\ 5\ 6\ 7\ 8\ 9\ 8\ 9\ 10$$

Assuming the frequency of occurrence of each number is reflected accurately in the number of times it appears in the sequence, we can estimate the probability of occurrence of each symbol as follows:

$$P(1) = P(6) = P(7) = P(10) = \tfrac{1}{16}$$

$$P(2) = P(3) = P(4) = P(5) = P(8) = P(9) = \tfrac{2}{16}.$$

Assuming the sequence is *iid*, the entropy for this sequence is the same as the first-order entropy as defined in (2.4). The entropy can then be calculated as

$$H = - \sum_{i=1}^{10} P(i) \log_2 P(i).$$

With our stated assumptions, the entropy for this source is 3.25 bits. This means that the best scheme we could find for coding this sequence could only code it at 3.25 bits/sample.

However, if we assume that there was sample-to-sample correlation between the samples and we remove the correlation by taking differences of neighboring sample values, we arrive at the *residual* sequence

$$1\ 1\ 1\ -1\ 1\ 1\ 1\ -1\ 1\ 1\ 1\ 1\ 1\ -1\ 1\ 1$$

This sequence is constructed using only two values with probabilities $P(1) = \frac{13}{16}$ and $P(-1) = \frac{3}{16}$. The entropy in this case is 0.70 bits per symbol. Of course, knowing only this sequence would not be enough for the receiver to reconstruct the original sequence. The receiver must also know the process by which this sequence was generated from the original sequence. The process depends on our assumptions about the structure of the sequence. These assumptions are called the *model* for the sequence. In this case, the model for the sequence is

$$x_n = x_{n-1} + r_n$$

where x_n is the nth element of the original sequence and r_n is the nth element of the residual sequence. This model is called a *static* model because its parameters do not change with n. A model whose parameters change or adapt with n to the changing characteristics of the data is called an *adaptive* model.

Basically, we see that knowing something about the structure of the data can help to "reduce the entropy." We have put "reduce the entropy" in quotes because the entropy of the source is a measure of the amount of information generated by the source. As long as the information generated by the source is preserved (in whatever representation), the entropy remains the same. What we are reducing is our estimate of the entropy. The "actual" structure of the data in practice is generally unknowable, but anything we can learn about the data can help us to estimate the actual source entropy. Theoretically, as seen in Equation (2.2), we accomplish this in our definition of the entropy by picking larger and larger blocks of data to calculate the probability over, letting the size of the block go to infinity.

Consider the following contrived sequence:

$$1\ 2\ 1\ 2\ 3\ 3\ 3\ 3\ 1\ 2\ 3\ 3\ 3\ 3\ 1\ 2\ 3\ 3\ 1\ 2$$

Obviously, there is some structure to this data. However, if we look at it one symbol at a time, the structure is difficult to extract. Consider the probabilities: $P(1) = P(2) = \frac{1}{4}$, and $P(3) = \frac{1}{2}$. The entropy is 1.5 bits/symbol. This particular sequence consists of 20 symbols; therefore, the total number of bits required to represent this sequence is 30. Now let's take the same sequence and look at it in blocks of two. Obviously, there are only two symbols, 1 2, and 3 3. The probabilities are $P(1\ 2) = \frac{1}{2}$, $P(3\ 3) = \frac{1}{2}$, and the entropy is 1 bit/symbol. As there are 10 such symbols in the sequence, we need a total of 10 bits to represent the entire sequence—a reduction of a factor of three. The theory says we can always extract the structure of the data by taking larger and larger block sizes; in practice, there are limitations to this approach. To avoid these limitations, we try to obtain an accurate model for the data and code the source with respect to the model. In Section 2.3, we describe some of the models commonly used in lossless compression algorithms. But before we do that, let's make a slight detour and see a more rigorous development of the expression for average information. While the explanation is interesting, it is not really necessary for understanding much of what we will study in this book and can be skipped.

2.2.1 Derivation of Average Information ★

We start with the properties we want in our measure of average information. We will then show that requiring these properties in the information measure leads inexorably to the particular definition of average information, or entropy, that we have provided earlier.

Given a set of independent events $A_1, A_2, \ldots, A_n$ with probability $p_i = P(A_i)$, we desire the following properties in the measure of average information H:

1. We want H to be a continuous function of the probabilities p_i. That is, a small change in p_i should only cause a small change in the average information.

2. If all events are equally likely, that is, $p_i = 1/n$ for all i, then H should be a monotonically increasing function of n. The more possible outcomes there are, the more information should be contained in the occurrence of any particular outcome.

3. Suppose we divide the possible outcomes into a number of groups. We indicate the occurrence of a particular event by first indicating the group it belongs to, then indicating which particular member of the group it is. Thus, we get some information first by knowing which group the event belongs to and then we get additional information by learning which particular event (from the events in the group) has occurred. The information associated with indicating the outcome in multiple stages should not be any different than the information associated with indicating the outcome in a single stage.

For example, suppose we have an experiment with three outcomes A_1, A_2, and A_3, with corresponding probabilities p_1, p_2, and p_3. The average information associated with this experiment is simply a function of the probabilities:

$$H = H(p_1, p_2, p_3).$$

Let's group the three outcomes into two groups

$$B_1 = \{A_1\}, \quad B_2 = \{A_2, A_3\}.$$

The probabilities of the events B_i are given by

$$q_1 = P(B_1) = p_1, \quad q_2 = P(B_2) = p_2 + p_3.$$

If we indicate the occurrence of an event A_i by first declaring which group the event belongs to and then declaring which event occurred, the total amount of average information would be given by

$$H = H(q_1, q_2) + q_1 H\left(\frac{p_1}{q_1}\right) + q_2 H\left(\frac{p_2}{q_2}, \frac{p_3}{q_2}\right).$$

We require that the average information computed either way be the same.

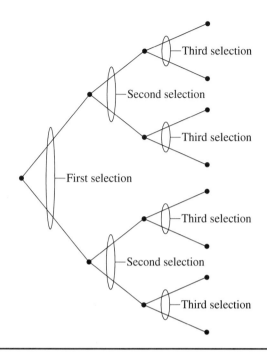

FIGURE 2.1   A possible way of identifying the occurrence of an event.

In his classic paper, Shannon showed that the only way all these conditions could be satisfied was if

$$H = -K \sum p_i \log p_i$$

where K is an arbitrary positive constant. Let's review his proof as it appears in the appendix of his paper [209].

Suppose we have an experiment with $n = k^m$ equally likely outcomes. The average information $H(\frac{1}{n}, \frac{1}{n}, \ldots, \frac{1}{n})$ associated with this experiment is a function of n. In other words,

$$H \left(\frac{1}{n}, \frac{1}{n}, \ldots, \frac{1}{n} \right) = A(n).$$

We can indicate the occurrence of an event from k^m events by a series of m choices from k equally likely possibilities. For example, consider the case of $k = 2$ and $m = 3$. There are eight equally likely events; therefore, $H(\frac{1}{8}, \frac{1}{8}, \ldots, \frac{1}{8}) = A(8)$.

We can indicate occurrence of any particular event as shown in Figure 2.1. In this case, we have a sequence of three selections. Each selection is between two equally likely possibilities. Therefore,

$$H \left(\tfrac{1}{8}, \tfrac{1}{8}, \ldots, \tfrac{1}{8} \right) = A(8)$$

$$= H(\tfrac{1}{2}, \tfrac{1}{2}) + \tfrac{1}{2} \left[H(\tfrac{1}{2}, \tfrac{1}{2}) + \tfrac{1}{2} H(\tfrac{1}{2}, \tfrac{1}{2}) \right.$$
$$+ \tfrac{1}{2} H(\tfrac{1}{2}, \tfrac{1}{2}) \big]$$
$$+ \tfrac{1}{2} \left[H(\tfrac{1}{2}, \tfrac{1}{2}) + \tfrac{1}{2} H(\tfrac{1}{2}, \tfrac{1}{2}) \right.$$
$$+ \tfrac{1}{2} H(\tfrac{1}{2}, \tfrac{1}{2}) \big] \tag{2.5}$$
$$= 3H(\tfrac{1}{2}, \tfrac{1}{2})$$
$$= 3A(2).$$

In other words,

$$A(8) = 3A(2).$$

(The rather odd way of writing the left-hand side of Equation (2.5) is to show how the terms correspond to the branches of the tree shown in Figure 2.1.) We can generalize this for the case of $n = k^m$ as

$$A(n) = A(k^m) = mA(k).$$

Similarly, for j^l choices,

$$A(j^l) = lA(j).$$

We can pick l arbitrarily large (more on this later) and then choose m so that

$$k^m \le j^l \le k^{(m+1)}.$$

Taking logarithms of all terms, we get

$$m \log k \le l \log j \le (m+1) \log k.$$

Now divide through by $l \log k$ to get

$$\frac{m}{l} \le \frac{\log j}{\log k} \le \frac{m}{l} + \frac{1}{l}.$$

Recall that we picked l arbitrarily large. If l is arbitrarily large, then $\frac{1}{l}$ is arbitrarily small. This means that the upper and lower bounds of $\frac{\log j}{\log k}$ can be made arbitrarily close to $\frac{m}{l}$ by picking l arbitrarily large. Another way of saying this is

$$\left| \frac{m}{l} - \frac{\log j}{\log k} \right| < \epsilon$$

where ϵ can be made arbitrarily small. We will use this fact to find an expression for $A(n)$ and hence for $H(\frac{1}{n}, \ldots, \frac{1}{n})$.

To do this we use our second requirement that $H(\frac{1}{n}, \ldots, \frac{1}{n})$ be a monotonically increasing function of n. As

$$H\left(\frac{1}{n}, \ldots, \frac{1}{n} \right) = A(n),$$

this means that $A(n)$ is a monotonically increasing function of n. If

$$k^m \le j^l \le k^{m+1}$$

then in order to satisfy our second requirement

$$A(k^m) \leq A(j^l) \leq A(k^{m+1})$$

or

$$mA(k) \leq lA(j) \leq (m+1)A(k).$$

Dividing through by $lA(k)$, we get

$$\frac{m}{l} \leq \frac{A(j)}{A(k)} \leq \frac{m}{l} + \frac{1}{l}.$$

Using the same arguments as before, we get

$$\left| \frac{m}{l} - \frac{A(j)}{A(k)} \right| < \epsilon$$

where ϵ can be made arbitrarily small.

Now $\frac{A(j)}{A(k)}$ is at most a distance of ϵ away from $\frac{m}{l}$, and $\frac{\log j}{\log k}$ is at most a distance of ϵ away from $\frac{m}{l}$. Therefore, $\frac{A(j)}{A(k)}$ is at most a distance of 2ϵ away from $\frac{\log j}{\log k}$.

$$\left| \frac{A(j)}{A(k)} - \frac{\log j}{\log k} \right| < 2\epsilon$$

We can pick ϵ to be arbitrarily small, and j and k are arbitrary. The only way this inequality can be satisfied for arbitrarily small ϵ and arbitrary j and k is for $A(j) = K \log(j)$, where K is an arbitrary constant. In other words,

$$H = K \log(n).$$

Up to this point we have only looked at equally likely events. We now make the transition to the more general case of an experiment with outcomes that are not equally likely. We do that by considering an experiment with $\sum n_i$ equally likely outcomes that are grouped in n unequal groups of size n_i with rational probabilities (if the probabilities are not rational, we approximate them with rational probabilities and use the continuity requirement):

$$p_i = \frac{n_i}{\sum_{j=1}^n n_j}.$$

Given that we have $\sum n_i$ equally likely events, from the development above we have

$$H = K \log \left(\sum n_j \right). \tag{2.6}$$

If we indicate an outcome by first indicating which of the n groups it belongs to, and second indicating which member of the group it is, then by our earlier development the average information H is given by

$$H = H(p_1, p_2, \ldots, p_n) + p_1 H \left(\frac{1}{n_1}, \ldots, \frac{1}{n_1} \right) + \cdots + p_n H \left(\frac{1}{n_n}, \ldots, \frac{1}{n_n} \right) \tag{2.7}$$

$$= H(p_1, p_2, \ldots, p_n) + p_1 K \log n_1 + p_2 K \log n_2 + \cdots + p_n K \log n_n \tag{2.8}$$

$$= H(p_1, p_2, \ldots, p_n) + K \sum_{i=1}^n p_i \log n_i. \tag{2.9}$$

Equating the expressions in Equations (2.6) and (2.9), we obtain

$$K \log \left(\sum n_j \right) = H(p_1, p_2, \ldots, p_n) + K \sum_{i=1}^{n} p_i \log n_i$$

or

$$
\begin{aligned}
H(p_1, p_2, \ldots, p_n) &= K \log \left(\sum n_j \right) - K \sum_{i=1}^{n} p_i \log n_i \\
&= -K \left[\sum_{i=1}^{n} p_i \log n_i - \log \left(\sum_{j=1}^{n} n_j \right) \right] \\
&= -K \left[\sum_{i=1}^{n} p_i \log n_i - \log \left(\sum_{j=1}^{n} n_j \right) \sum_{i=1}^{n} p_i \right] \qquad (2.10) \\
&= -K \left[\sum_{i=1}^{n} p_i \log n_i - \sum_{i=1}^{n} p_i \log \left(\sum_{j=1}^{n} n_j \right) \right] \\
&= -K \sum_{i=1}^{n} p_i \left[\log n_i - \log \left(\sum_{j=1}^{n} n_j \right) \right] \\
&= -K \sum_{i=1}^{n} p_i \log \frac{n_i}{\sum_{j=1}^{n} n_j} \qquad (2.11) \\
&= -K \sum p_i \log p_i \qquad (2.12)
\end{aligned}
$$

where, in Equation (2.10) we have used the fact that $\sum_{i=1}^{n} p_i = 1$. By convention we pick K to be 1, and we have the formula

$$H = -\sum p_i \log p_i.$$

Note that this formula is a natural outcome of the requirements we imposed in the beginning. It was not artificially forced in any way. Therein lies the beauty of information theory. Like the laws of physics, its laws are intrinsic in the nature of things. Mathematics is simply a tool to express these relationships.

2.3   Models

As we saw in Section 2.2, having a good model for the data can be useful in estimating the entropy of the source. As we will see in later chapters, good models for sources lead to more efficient compression algorithms. In general, in order to develop techniques that manipulate data using mathematical operations, we need to have a mathematical model for the data. Obviously, the better the model (i.e., the closer the model matches the aspects of reality that are of interest to us), the more likely it is that we will come up with a satisfactory technique. There are several approaches to building mathematical models.

2.3.1 Physical Models

If we know something about the physics of the data generation process, we can use that information to construct a model. For example, in speech-related applications, knowledge about the physics of speech production can be used to construct a mathematical model for the sampled speech process. Sampled speech can then be encoded using this model. We will discuss speech production models in more detail in Chapter 7.

Models for certain telemetry data can also be obtained through knowledge of the underlying process. For example, if residential electrical meter readings at hourly intervals were to be coded, knowledge about the living habits of the populace could be used to determine when electricity usage would be high and when the usage would be low. Then instead of the actual readings, the difference (residual) between the actual readings and those predicted by the model could be coded.

In general, however, the physics of data generation is simply too complicated to understand, let alone use to develop a model. Where the physics of the problem is too complicated, we can obtain a model based on empirical observation of the statistics of the data.

2.3.2 Probability Models

The simplest statistical model for the source is to assume that each letter that is generated by the source is independent of every other letter, and each occurs with the same probability. We could call this the *ignorance model*, as it would generally be useful only when we know nothing about the source. (Of course, that *really* might be true, in which case we have a rather unfortunate name for the model!) The next step up in complexity is to keep the independence assumption, but remove the equal probability assumption and assign a probability of occurrence to each letter in the alphabet. For a source that generates letters from an alphabet $\mathcal{A} = \{a_1, a_2, \ldots, a_M\}$, we can have a *probability model* $\mathcal{P} = \{P(a_1), P(a_2), \ldots, P(a_M)\}$.

Given a probability model (and the independence assumption), we can compute the entropy of the source using Equation (2.4). As we will see in the following chapters using the probability model, we can also construct some very efficient codes to represent the letters in $\mathcal{A}$. Of course, these codes are only efficient if our mathematical assumptions are in accord with reality.

If the assumption of independence does not fit with our observation of the data, we can generally find better compression schemes if we discard this assumption. When we discard the independence assumption, we have to come up with a way to describe the dependence of elements of the data sequence on each other.

2.3.3 Markov Models

One of the most popular ways of representing dependence in the data is through the use of Markov models, named after the Russian mathematician Andrei Andrevich Markov (1856–1922). For models used in lossless compression, we use a specific type of Markov process called a *discrete time Markov chain*. Let $\{x_n\}$ be a sequence of observations. This sequence is

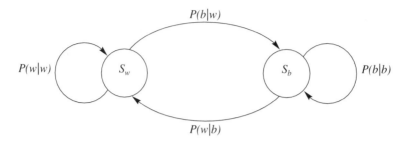

FIGURE 2.2   **A two-state Markov model for binary images.**

said to follow a kth-order Markov model if

$$P(x_n|x_{n-1},\ldots,x_{n-k}) = P(x_n|x_{n-1},\ldots,x_{n-k},\ldots). \tag{2.13}$$

In other words, knowledge of the past k symbols is equivalent to the knowledge of the entire past history of the process. The values taken on by the set $\{x_{n-1},\ldots,x_{n-k}\}$ are called the *states* of the process. If the size of the source alphabet is l, then the number of states is l^k. The most commonly used Markov model is the first-order Markov model, for which

$$P(x_n|x_{n-1}) = P(x_n|x_{n-1},x_{n-2},x_{n-3},\ldots). \tag{2.14}$$

Equations (2.13) and (2.14) indicate the existence of dependence between samples. However, they do not describe the form of the dependence. We can develop different first-order Markov models depending on our assumption about the form of the dependence between samples.

   If we assumed that the dependence was introduced in a linear manner, we could view the data sequence as the output of a linear filter driven by white noise. The output of such a filter can be given by the difference equation

$$x_n = \rho x_{n-1} + \epsilon_n \tag{2.15}$$

where ϵ_n is a white noise process. This model is often used when developing coding algorithms for speech and images.

   The use of the Markov model does not require the assumption of linearity. For example, consider a binary image. The image has only two types of pixels, white pixels and black pixels. We know that the appearance of a white pixel as the next observation depends, to some extent, on whether the current pixel is white or black. Therefore, we can model the pixel process as a discrete time Markov chain. Define two states S_w and S_b (S_w would correspond to the case where the current pixel is a white pixel, and S_b corresponds to the case where the current pixel is a black pixel). We define the transition probabilities $P(w/b)$ and $P(b/w)$, and the probability of being in each state $P(S_w)$ and $P(S_b)$. The Markov model can then be represented by the state diagram shown in Figure 2.2.

   The entropy of a finite state process with states S_i is simply the average value of the entropy at each state:

$$H = \sum_{i=1}^{M} P(S_i)H(S_i). \tag{2.16}$$

For our particular example of a binary image

$$H(S_w) = -P(b/w) \log P(b/w) - P(w/w) \log P(w/w)$$

where $P(w/w) = 1 - P(b/w)$. $H(S_b)$ can be calculated in a similar manner.

Example 2.3.1: Markov model

To see the effect of modeling on the estimate of entropy, let us calculate the entropy for a binary image, first using a simple probability model and then using the finite state model described above. Let us assume the following values for the various probabilities:

$$P(S_w) = 30/31 \quad P(S_b) = 1/31$$
$$P(w|w) = 0.99 \quad P(b|w) = 0.01 \quad P(b|b) = 0.7 \quad P(w|b) = 0.3.$$

Then the entropy using a probability model and the *iid* assumption is

$$H = -0.8 \log 0.8 - 0.2 \log 0.2 = 0.206 \text{ bits.}$$

Now using the Markov model

$$H(S_b) = -0.3 \log 0.3 - 0.7 \log 0.7 = 0.881 \text{ bits}$$

and

$$H(S_w) = -0.01 \log 0.01 - 0.99 \log 0.99 = 0.081 \text{ bits}$$

which, using Equation (2.16), results in an entropy for the Markov model of 0.107 bits, about a half of the entropy obtained using the *iid* assumption. ◆

Markov Models in Text Compression

As expected, Markov models are particularly useful in text compression, where the probability of the next letter is heavily influenced by the preceding letters. In fact, the use of Markov models for written English appears in the original work of Shannon [209]. In current text compression literature, the kth-order Markov models are more widely known as *finite context models*, with the word *context* being used for what we have earlier defined as state.

Consider the word *preceding*. Suppose we have already processed *precedin* and are going to encode the next letter. If we take no account of the context and treat each letter as a surprise, the probability of the letter g occurring is relatively low. If we use a first-order Markov model or single-letter context (that is, we look at the probability model given n), we can see that the probability of g would increase substantially. As we increase the context size (go from n to *in* to *din* and so on), the probability of the alphabet becomes more and more skewed, which results in lower entropy.

Shannon used a second-order model for English text consisting of the 26 letters and one space to obtain an entropy of 3.1 bits/letter [210]. Using a model where the output symbols were words rather than letters brought down the entropy to 2.4 bits/letter. Shannon then used predictions generated by people (rather than statistical models) to estimate the upper and lower bounds on the entropy of the 27-letter English language. For the case where the subjects knew the 100 previous letters, he estimated these bounds to be 1.3 and 0.6 bits/letter, respectively.

The longer the context, the better its predictive value. However, if we were to store the probability model with respect to all contexts of a given length, the number of contexts would grow exponentially with the length of context. Furthermore, given that the source imposes some structure on its output, many of these contexts may correspond to strings that would never occur in practice. Consider a context model of order four (the context is determined by the last four symbols). If we take an alphabet size of 95, the possible number of contexts is 95^4—more than 81 million!

This problem is further exacerbated by the fact that different realizations of the source output may vary considerably in terms of repeating patterns. Therefore, context modeling in text compression schemes tends to be an adaptive strategy in which the probabilities for different symbols in the different contexts are updated as they are encountered. However, this means that we will often encounter symbols that have not been encountered before for any of the given contexts (this is known as the *zero frequency problem*). The larger the context, the more often this will happen. This problem could be resolved by sending a code to indicate that the following symbol was being encountered for the first time, followed by a prearranged code for that symbol. This would significantly increase the length of the code for the symbol on its first occurrence (in the given context). However, if this situation did not occur too often, the overhead associated with such occurrences would be small compared to the total number of bits used to encode the output of the source. Unfortunately, in context-based encoding, the zero frequency problem is encountered often enough for overhead to be a problem, especially for longer contexts. Solutions to this problem are presented by the *ppm* (prediction with partial match) algorithm and its variants (described in detail in Chapter 6).

Briefly, the *ppm* algorithms first attempt to find if the symbol to be encoded has a nonzero probability with respect to the maximum context length. If this is so, the symbol is encoded and transmitted. If not, an escape symbol is transmitted, the context size is reduced by one, and the process is repeated. This procedure is repeated until a context is found with respect to which the symbol has a nonzero probability. To guarantee that this process converges, a null context is always included with respect to which all symbols have equal probability. Initially, only the shorter contexts are likely to be used. However, as more and more of the source output is processed, the longer contexts, which offer better prediction, will be used more often. The probability of the escape symbol can be computed in a number of different ways leading to different implementations [20].

The use of Markov models in text compression is a rich and active area of research. We describe some of these approaches in Chapter 6 (for more details, see [20]).

2.3.4 Composite Source Model

In many applications, it is not easy to use a single model to describe the source. In such cases, we can define a *composite source*, which can be viewed as a combination or composition of several sources, with only one source being *active* at any given time. A composite source can be represented as a number of individual sources S_i, each with its own model M_i, and a switch that selects a source S_i with probability P_i (as shown in Figure 2.3). This is an exceptionally

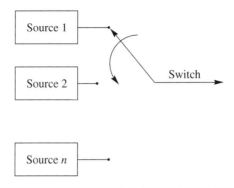

FIGURE 2.3   A composite source.

rich model and can be used to describe some very complicated processes. We will describe this model in more detail when we need it.

2.4 Coding

When we talk about *coding* in this chapter (and through most of this book), we mean the assignment of binary sequences to elements of an alphabet. The set of binary sequences is called a *code*, and the individual members of the set are called *codewords*. An *alphabet* is a collection of symbols called *letters*. For example, the alphabet used in writing most books consists of the 26 lowercase letters, 26 uppercase letters, and a variety of punctuation marks. In the terminology used in this book, a comma is a letter. The ASCII code for the letter a is 1000011, the letter A is coded as 1000001, and the letter , is coded as 0011010. Notice that the ASCII code uses the same number of bits to represent each symbol. Such a code is called a *fixed-length code*. If we want to reduce the number of bits required to represent different messages, we need to use a different number of bits to represent different symbols. If we use fewer bits to represent symbols that occur more often, on the average we would use fewer bits per symbol. The average number of bits per symbol is often called the *rate* of the code. The idea of using fewer bits to represent symbols that occur more often is the same idea that is used in Morse code: the codewords for letters that occur more frequently are shorter than for letters that occur less frequently. For example, the codeword for E is $\cdot$, while the codeword for Z is $--\cdot\cdot$ [100].

2.4.1 Uniquely Decodable Codes

The average length of the code is not the only important point in designing a "good" code. Consider the following example adapted from [178]. Suppose our source alphabet consists of four letters a_1, a_2, a_3, and a_4, with probabilities $P(a_1) = \frac{1}{2}$, $P(a_2) = \frac{1}{4}$, and $P(a_3) = P(a_4) = \frac{1}{8}$. The entropy for this source is 1.75 bits/symbol. Consider the codes for this source in Table 2.1.

T A B L E   2 . 1   **Four different codes for a four-letter alphabet.**

Letters	Probability	Code 1	Code 2	Code 3	Code 4
a_1	0.5	0	0	0	0
a_2	0.25	0	1	10	01
a_3	0.125	1	00	110	011
a_4	0.125	10	11	111	0111
Average length		1.125	1.25	1.75	1.875

The average length l for for each code is given by

$$l = \sum_{i=1}^{4} P(a_i)n(a_i)$$

where $n(a_i)$ is the number of bits in the codeword for letter a_i and the average length is given in bits/symbol. Based on the average length, Code 1 appears to be the best code. However, to be useful, a code should have the ability to transfer information in an unambiguous manner. This is obviously not the case with Code 1. Both a_1 and a_2 have been assigned the codeword 0. When a 0 is received, there is no way to know whether an a_1 was transmitted or an a_2. We would like each symbol to be assigned a *unique* codeword.

At first glance Code 2 does not seem to have the problem of ambiguity; each symbol is assigned a distinct codeword. However, suppose we want to encode the sequence a_2 a_1 a_1. Using Code 2, we would encode this with the binary string 100. However, when the string 100 is received at the decoder, there are several ways in which the decoder can decode this string. The string 100 can be decoded as a_2 a_1 a_1, or as a_2 a_3. This means that once a sequence is encoded with Code 2, the original sequence cannot be recovered with certainty. In general, this is not a desirable property for a code. We would like *unique decodability* from the code; that is, any given sequence of codewords can be decoded in one, and only one, way.

We have already seen that Code 1 and Code 2 are not uniquely decodable. How about Code 3? Notice that the first three codewords all end in a 0. In fact, a 0 always denotes the termination of a codeword. The final codeword contains no 0s and is 3 bits long. Because all other codewords have fewer than three 1s and terminate in a 0, the only way we can get three 1s in a row is as a code for a_4. The decoding rule is simple. Accumulate bits until you get a 0 or until you have three 1s. There is no ambiguity in this rule, and it is reasonably easy to see that this code is uniquely decodable. With Code 4 we have an even simpler condition. Each codeword starts with a 0, and the only time we see a 0 is in the beginning of a codeword. Therefore, the decoding rule is accumulate bits until you see a 0. The bit before the 0 is the last bit of the previous codeword.

There is a slight difference between Code 3 and Code 4. In the case of Code 3, the decoder knows the moment a code is complete. In Code 4, we have to wait till the beginning of the next codeword before we know that the current codeword is complete. Because of this property, Code 3 is called an *instantaneous* code. Although Code 4 is not an instantaneous code, it is almost that.

While this property of instantaneous or near-instantaneous decoding is a nice property to have, it is not a requirement for unique decodability. Consider the code shown in Table 2.2.

TABLE 2.2	**Code 5.**
Letter	Codeword
a_1	0
a_2	01
a_3	11

TABLE 2.3	**Code 6.**
Letter	Codeword
a_1	0
a_2	01
a_3	10

Let's decode the string 0111111111111111111. In this string, the first codeword is either 0 corresponding to a_1 or 01 corresponding to a_2. We cannot tell which one until we have decoded the whole string. Starting with the assumption that the first codeword corresponds to a_1, the next eight pairs of bits are decoded as a_3. However, after decoding eight a_3s, we are left with a single (dangling) 1 that does not correspond to any codeword. On the other hand, if we assume the first codeword corresponds to a_2, we can decode the next 16 bits as a sequence of eight a_3s, and we do not have any bits left over. The string can be uniquely decoded. In fact, Code 5, while it is certainly not instantaneous, is uniquely decodable.

We have been looking at small codes with four letters or less. Even with these, it is not immediately evident whether the code is uniquely decodable or not. In deciding whether larger codes are uniquely decodable, a systematic procedure would be useful. Actually, we should include a caveat with that last statement. Later in this chapter we will include a class of variable-length codes that are always uniquely decodable, so a test for unique decodability may not be that necessary. You might wish to skip the following discussion for now, and come back to it when you find it necessary.

Before we describe the procedure for deciding whether a code is uniquely decodable, let's take another look at our last example. We found that we had an incorrect decoding because we were left with a binary string (1) that was not a codeword. If this had not happened, we would have had two valid decodings. For example, consider the code shown in Table 2.3 Let's encode the sequence a_1 followed by eight a_3s using this code. The coded sequence is 01010101010101010. The first bit is the codeword for a_1. However, we can also decode it as the first bit of the codeword for a_2. If we use this (incorrect) decoding, we decode the next seven pairs of bits as the codewords for a_2. After decoding seven a_2s, we are left with a single 0 that we decode as a_1. Thus, the incorrect decoding is also a valid decoding, and this code is not uniquely decodable.

A Test for Unique Decodability ★

In the previous examples, in the case of the uniquely decodable code, the binary string left over after we had gone through an incorrect decoding was not a codeword. In the case of the code that was not uniquely decodable, in the incorrect decoding what was left was a valid codeword. Based on whether the dangling suffix is a codeword or not, we get the following test [79, 202].

We start with some definitions. Suppose we have two binary codewords a and b, where a is k bits long, b is n bits long, and $k < n$. If the first k bits of b are identical to a, then a is called a *prefix* of b. The last $n - k$ bits of b are called the *dangling suffix* [79]. For example, if $a = 010$ and $b = 01011$, then a is a prefix of b and the dangling suffix is 11.

Construct a list of all the codewords. Examine all pairs of codewords to see if any codeword is a prefix of another codeword. Whenever you find such a pair, add the dangling suffix to the list unless you have added the same dangling suffix to the list in a previous iteration. Now repeat the procedure using this larger list. Continue in this fashion until one of the following two things happens:

1. You get a dangling suffix that is a codeword.

2. There are no more unique dangling suffixes.

If you get the first outcome, the code is not uniquely decodable. However, if you get the second outcome, the code is uniquely decodable.

Let's see how this procedure works with a couple of examples.

Example 2.4.1:

Consider Code 5. First list the codewords

$$\{0, 01, 11\}$$

The codeword 0 is a prefix for the codeword 01. The dangling suffix is 1. There are no other pairs for which one element of the pair is the prefix of the other. Let us augment the codeword list with the dangling suffix.

$$\{0, 01, 11, 1\}$$

Comparing the elements of this list, we find 0 is a prefix of 01 with a dangling suffix of 1. But we have already included 1 in our list. Also, 1 is a prefix of 11. This gives us a dangling suffix of 1, which is already in the list. There are no other pairs that would generate a dangling suffix, so we cannot augment the list any further. Therefore, Code 5 is uniquely decodable. ◆

Example 2.4.2:

Consider Code 6. First list the codewords

$$\{0, 01, 10\}$$

The codeword 0 is a prefix for the codeword 01. The dangling suffix is 1. There are no other pairs for which one element of the pair is the prefix of the other. Augmenting the codeword list with 1, we obtain the list

$$\{0, 01, 10, 1\}$$

In this list, 1 is a prefix for 10. The dangling suffix for this pair is 0, which is the codeword for a_1. Therefore, Code 6 is not uniquely decodable. ◆

FIGURE 2.4   Binary trees for three different codes.

2.4.2 Prefix Codes

The test for unique decodability requires examining the dangling suffixes initially generated by codeword pairs in which one codeword is the prefix of the other. If the dangling suffix is itself a codeword, then the code is not uniquely decodable. One type of code in which we will never face the possibility of a dangling suffix being a codeword is a code in which no codeword is a prefix of the other. In this case, the set of dangling suffixes is the null set, and we do not have to worry about finding a dangling suffix that is identical to a codeword. A code in which no codeword is a prefix to another codeword is called a *prefix code*. A simple way to check if a code is a prefix code is to draw the rooted binary tree corresponding to the code. Draw a tree that starts from a single node (the *root node*) and has a maximum of two possible branches at each node. One of these branches corresponds to a 1 and the other branch corresponds to a 0. In this book, we will adopt the convention that when we draw a tree with the root node at the top, the left branch corresponds to a 0 and the right branch corresponds to a 1. Using this convention, we can draw the binary tree for Code 2, Code 3, and Code 4 as shown in Figure 2.4.

Note that apart from the root node, the trees have two kinds of nodes—nodes that give rise to other nodes and nodes that do not. The first kind of nodes are called *internal nodes*, and the second kind are called *external nodes* or *leaves*. In a prefix code, the codewords are only associated with the external nodes. A code that is not a prefix code, such as Code 4, will have codewords associated with internal nodes. The code for any symbol can be obtained by traversing the tree from the root to the external node corresponding to that symbol. Each branch on the way contributes a bit to the codeword: a 0 for each left branch and a 1 for each right branch.

It is nice to have a class of codes, whose members are so clearly uniquely decodable. However, are we losing something if we restrict ourselves to prefix codes? Could it be that if we do not restrict ourselves to prefix codes, we can find shorter codes? Fortunately for us the answer is no. For any nonprefix uniquely decodable code, we can always find a prefix code with the same codeword lengths. We prove this in the next section.

2.4.3 The Kraft-McMillan Inequality ★

The particular result we look at in this section consists of two parts. The first part provides a necessary condition on the codeword lengths of uniquely decodable codes. The second part shows that we can always find a prefix code that satisfies this necessary condition. Therefore, if we have a uniquely decodable code that is not a prefix code, we can always find a prefix code with the same codeword lengths.

Theorem *Let C be a code with N codewords with lengths $l_1, l_2, \ldots, l_N$. If C is uniquely decodable, then*

$$K(C) = \sum_{i=1}^{N} 2^{-l_i} \leq 1.$$

This inequality is known as the Kraft-McMillan *inequality.*

Proof The proof works by looking at the nth power of $K(C)$. If $K(C)$ is greater than one, then $K(C)^n$ should grow exponentially with n. If it does not grow exponentially with n, then this is proof that $\sum_{i=1}^{N} 2^{-l_i} \leq 1$.

Let n be an arbitrary integer. Then

$$\left[\sum_{i=1}^{N} 2^{-l_i} \right]^n = \left(\sum_{i_1=1}^{N} 2^{-l_{i_1}} \right) \left(\sum_{i_2=1}^{N} 2^{-l_{i_2}} \right) \cdots \left(\sum_{i_n=1}^{N} 2^{-l_{i_n}} \right) \qquad (2.17)$$

$$= \sum_{i_1=1}^{N} \sum_{i_2=1}^{N} \cdots \sum_{i_n=1}^{N} 2^{-(l_{i_1}+l_{i_2}+\cdots+l_{i_n})}. \qquad (2.18)$$

The exponent $l_{i_1} + l_{i_2} + \cdots + l_{i_n}$ is simply the length of n codewords from the code C. The smallest value that this exponent can take is greater than or equal to n, which would be the case if all codewords were 1 bit long. If

$$l = \max\{l_1, l_2, \ldots, l_N\}$$

then the largest value that the exponent can take is less than or equal to nl. Therefore, we can write this summation as

$$K(C)^n = \sum_{k=n}^{nl} A_k 2^{-k}$$

where A_k is the number of combinations of n codewords that have a combined length of k. Let's take a look at the size of this coefficient. The number of possible distinct binary sequences of length k is 2^k. If this code is uniquely decodable, then each sequence can represent one and only one sequence of codewords. Therefore, the number of possible combinations of codewords whose combined length is k cannot be greater than 2^k. In other words,

$$A_k \leq 2^k.$$

This means that

$$K(C)^n = \sum_{k=n}^{nl} A_k 2^{-k} \leq \sum_{k=n}^{nl} 2^k 2^{-k} = nl - n + 1. \qquad (2.19)$$

But if $K(\mathcal{C})$ is greater than one, it will grow exponentially with n, while $n(l-1)+1$ can only grow linearly. So if $K(\mathcal{C})$ is greater than one, we can always find an n large enough that the inequality (2.19) is violated. Therefore, for a uniquely decodable code $\mathcal{C}$, $K(\mathcal{C})$ is less than or equal to one. $\qquad\qquad\qquad\qquad\qquad\qquad\qquad\qquad\qquad\qquad\qquad\qquad\qquad\qquad\quad\square$

This part of the Kraft-McMillan inequality provides a necessary condition for uniquely decodable codes. That is, if a code is uniquely decodable, the codeword lengths have to satisfy the inequality. The second part of this result is that if we have a set of codeword lengths that satisfy the inequality, we can always find a prefix code with those codeword lengths. The proof of this assertion presented here is adapted from [155].

Theorem *Given a set of integers $l_1, l_2, \ldots, l_N$ that satisfy the inequality*

$$\sum_{i=1}^{N} 2^{-l_i} \leq 1$$

we can always find a prefix code with codeword lengths $l_1, l_2, \ldots, l_N$.

Proof We will prove this assertion by developing a procedure for constructing a prefix code with codeword lengths $l_1, l_2, \ldots, l_N$ that satisfy the given inequality.
    Without loss of generality, we can assume that

$$l_1 \leq l_2 \leq \cdots \leq l_N.$$

Define a sequence of numbers $w_1, w_2, \ldots, w_N$ as follows:

$$w_1 = 0$$
$$w_j = \sum_{i=1}^{j-1} 2^{l_j - l_i} \qquad j > 1.$$

The binary representation of w_j for $j > 1$ would take up $\lceil \log_2 w_j \rceil$ bits. We will use this binary representation to construct a prefix code. We first note that the number of bits in the binary representation of w_j is less than or equal to l_j. This is obviously true for w_1. For $j > 1$,

$$\log_2 w_j = \log_2 \left[\sum_{i=1}^{j-1} 2^{l_j - l_i} \right]$$
$$= \log_2 \left[2^{l_j} \sum_{i=1}^{j-1} 2^{-l_i} \right]$$
$$= l_j + \log_2 \left[\sum_{i=1}^{j-1} 2^{-l_i} \right]$$
$$\leq l_j.$$

The last inequality results from the hypothesis of the theorem that $\sum_{i=1}^{N} 2^{-l_i} \le 1$, which implies that $\sum_{i=1}^{j-1} 2^{-l_i} \le 1$. As the logarithm of a number less than one is negative, $l_j + \log_2 \left\lceil \sum_{i=1}^{j-1} 2^{-l_i} \right\rceil$ has to be less than l_j.

Using the binary representation of w_j, we can devise a binary code in the following manner: If $\lceil \log_2 w_j \rceil = l_j$, then the jth codeword c_j is the binary representation of w_j. If $\lceil \log_2 w_j \rceil < l_j$, then c_j is the binary representation of w_j, with $l_j - \lceil \log_2 w_j \rceil$ zeros appended to the right. This is certainly a code, but is it a prefix code? If we can show that the code $\mathcal{C} = \{c_1, c_2, \ldots, c_N\}$ is a prefix code, then we will have proved the theorem by construction.

Suppose that our claim is not true. Then for some $j < k$, c_j is a prefix of c_k. This means that the l_j most significant bits of w_k form the binary representation of w_j. Therefore if we right-shift the binary representation of w_k by $l_k - l_j$ bits, we should get the binary representation for w_j. We can write this as

$$w_j = \left\lfloor \frac{w_k}{2^{l_k - l_j}} \right\rfloor.$$

However,

$$w_k = \sum_{i=1}^{k-1} 2^{l_k - l_i}.$$

Therefore,

$$
\begin{aligned}
\frac{w_k}{2^{l_k - l_j}} &= \sum_{i=0}^{k-1} 2^{l_j - l_i} \\
&= w_j + \sum_{i=j}^{k-1} 2^{l_j - l_i} \\
&= w_j + 2^0 + \sum_{i=j+1}^{k-1} 2^{l_j - l_i} \\
&\ge w_j + 1.
\end{aligned}
\tag{2.20}
$$

That is, the smallest value for $\frac{w_k}{2^{l_k - l_j}}$ is $w_j + 1$. This contradicts the requirement for c_j being the prefix of c_k. Therefore, c_j cannot be the prefix for c_k. As j and k were arbitrary, this means that no codeword is a prefix of another codeword, and the code $\mathcal{C}$ is a prefix code. $\square$

Therefore, if we have a uniquely decodable code, the codeword lengths have to satisfy the Kraft-McMillan inequality. And, given codeword lengths that satisfy the Kraft-McMillan inequality, we can always find a prefix code with those codeword lengths. Thus, by restricting ourselves to prefix codes, we are not in danger of overlooking nonprefix uniquely decodable codes that have a shorter average length.

2.5 Summary

In this chapter we learned some of the basic definitions of information theory. This was a rather brief visit, and we will revisit the subject in Chapter 7. However, the coverage in this chapter will be sufficient to take us through the next four chapters. The concepts introduced in this chapter allow us to estimate the number of bits we need to represent the output of a source given the probability model for the source. The process of assigning a binary representation to the output of a source is called coding. We have introduced the concepts of unique decodability and prefix codes, which we will use in the next two chapters when we describe various coding algorithms. We also looked, rather briefly, at different approaches to modeling. If we need to understand a model in more depth later in the book, we will devote more attention to it at that time. However, for the most part, the coverage of modeling in this chapter will be sufficient to understand methods described in the next four chapters.

Further Reading

1. A very readable book on information theory and its applications in a number of fields is *Symbols, Signals, and Noise—The Nature and Process of Communications*, by J.R. Pierce [180].

2. Another good introductory source for the material in this chapter is Chapter 6 of *Coding and Information Theory*, by R.W. Hamming [100].

3. Various models for text compression are described very nicely and in more detail in *Text Compression*, by T.C. Bell, J.G. Cleary, and I.H. Witten [20].

4. For a more thorough and detailed account of information theory, the following books are especially recommended (the first two are my personal favorites): *Information Theory*, by R.B. Ash [12]; *Transmission of Information*, by R.M. Fano [70]; *Information Theory and Reliable Communication*, by R.G. Gallagher [79]; *Entropy and Information Theory*, by R.M. Gray [98]; *Elements of Information Theory*, by T.M. Cover and J.A. Thomas [55]; and *The Theory of Information and Coding*, by R.J. McEliece [155].

2.6 Projects and Problems

1. Suppose X is a random variable that takes on values from an M-letter alphabet. Show that $0 \leq H(X) \leq \log_2 M$.

2. Show that for the case where the elements of an observed sequence are *iid*, the entropy is equal to the first-order entropy.

3. Given an alphabet $\mathcal{A} = \{a_1, a_2, a_3, a_4\}$, find the first-order entropy in the following cases:

   (a) $P(a_1) = P(a_2) = P(a_3) = P(a_4) = \frac{1}{4}$

   (b) $P(a_1) = \frac{1}{2}, P(a_2) = \frac{1}{4}, P(a_3) = P(a_4) = \frac{1}{8}.$

(c) $P(a_1) = 0.505$, $P(a_2) = \frac{1}{4}$, $P(a_3) = \frac{1}{8}$, and $P(a_4) = 0.12$.

4. Suppose we have a source with a probability model $P = \{p_0, p_1, \ldots, p_m\}$ and entropy H_P. Suppose we have another source with probability model $Q = \{q_0, q_1, \ldots, q_m\}$ and entropy H_Q, where

$$q_i = p_i \qquad i = 0, 1, \ldots, j - 2, j + 1, \ldots, m$$

and

$$q_j = q_{j-1} = \frac{p_j + p_{j-1}}{2}.$$

How is H_Q related to H_P (greater, equal, or less)? Prove your answer.

5. There are several image and speech files among the accompanying data sets.

(a) Write a program to compute the first-order entropy of some of the image and speech files.

(b) Pick one of the image files and compute its second-order entropy. Comment on the difference between the first- and second-order entropies.

(c) Compute the entropy of the differences between neighboring pixels for the image you used in part (b). Comment on what you discover.

6. Conduct an experiment to see how well a model can describe a source.

(a) Write a program that randomly selects letters from the 26-letter alphabet $\{a, b, \ldots, z\}$ and forms four-letter words. Form 100 such words and see how many of these words make sense.

(b) Among the accompanying data sets is a file called 4letter.words, which contains a list of four-letter words. Using this file, obtain a probability model for the alphabet. Now repeat part (a) generating the words using the probability model. To pick letters according to a probability model, construct the cumulative density function (cdf) $F_X(x)$ (see Appendix A for the definition of cdf). Using a uniform pseudorandom number generator to generate a value r, where $0 \leq r < 1$, pick the letter x_k if $F_X(x_k - 1) \leq r < F_X(x_k)$. Compare your results with those of part (a).

(c) Repeat (b) using a single-letter context.

(d) Repeat (b) using a two-letter context.

7. Determine whether the following codes are uniquely decodable:

(a) $\{0, 01, 11, 111\}$

(b) $\{0, 01, 110, 111\}$

(c) $\{0, 10, 110, 111\}$

(d) $\{1, 10, 110, 111\}$

8. Using a text file compute the probabilities of each letter p_i.

   (a) Assume that we need a codeword of length $\lceil \frac{1}{\log_2 p_i} \rceil$ to encode the letter i. Determine the number of bits needed to encode the file.

   (b) Compute the conditional probabilities $P(i/j)$ of a letter i given that the previous letter is j. Assume that we need $\lceil \frac{1}{\log_2 P(i/j)} \rceil$ to represent a letter i that follows a letter j. Determine the number of bits needed to encode the file.

3

Huffman Coding

3.1 Overview

In this chapter we describe a very popular coding algorithm called the Huffman coding algorithm. We first present a procedure for building Huffman codes when the probability model for the source is known, then a procedure for building codes when the source statistics are unknown. We also describe a few techniques for code design that are in some sense similar to the Huffman coding approach. Finally, we give some examples of using the Huffman code for image compression, audio compression, and text compression.

3.2 The Huffman Coding Algorithm

This technique was developed by David Huffman as part of a class assignment; the class was the first ever in the area of information theory and was taught by Robert Fano at MIT [107]. The codes generated using this technique or procedure are called *Huffman codes*. These codes are prefix codes and are optimum for a given model (set of probabilities).

The Huffman procedure is based on two observations regarding optimum prefix codes.

1. In an optimum code, symbols that occur more frequently (have a higher probability of occurrence) will have shorter codewords than symbols that occur less frequently.

2. In an optimum code, the two symbols that occur least frequently will have the same length.

It is easy to see that the first observation is correct. If symbols that occur more often had codewords that were longer than the codewords for symbols that occurred less often, the average number of bits per symbol would be larger than if the conditions were reversed. Therefore, a code that assigns longer codewords to symbols that occur more frequently cannot be optimum.

To see why the second observation holds true, consider the following situation. Suppose an optimum code $\mathcal{C}$ exists in which the two codewords corresponding to the two least probable symbols do not have the same length. Suppose the longer codeword is k bits longer than the shorter codeword. Because this is a prefix code, the shorter codeword cannot be a prefix of the longer codeword. This means that even if we drop the last k bits of the longer codeword, the two codewords would still be distinct. As these codewords correspond to the least probable symbols in the alphabet, no other codeword can be longer than these codewords; therefore, there is no danger that the shortened codeword would become the prefix of some other codeword. Furthermore, by dropping these k bits we obtain a new code that has a shorter average length than $\mathcal{C}$. But this violates our initial contention that $\mathcal{C}$ is an optimal code. Therefore, for an optimal code the second observation also holds true.

The Huffman procedure is obtained by adding a simple requirement to these two observations. This requirement is that the codewords corresponding to the two lowest probability symbols differ only in the last bit. That is, if γ and δ are the two least probable symbols in an alphabet, if the codeword for γ was $\mathbf{m} * 0$, the codeword for δ would be $\mathbf{m} * 1$. Here $\mathbf{m}$ is a string of 1s and 0s, and $*$ denotes concatenation.

This requirement does not violate our two observations and leads to a very simple encoding procedure. We describe this procedure with the help of the following example.

Example 3.2.1: Design of a Huffman code

Let us design a Huffman code for a source that puts out letters from an alphabet $\mathcal{A} = \{a_1, a_2, a_3, a_4, a_5\}$ with $P(a_1) = P(a_3) = 0.2$, $P(a_2) = 0.4$, and $P(a_4) = P(a_5) = 0.1$. The entropy for this source is 2.122 bits/symbol. To design the Huffman code, we first sort the letters in a descending probability order as shown in Table 3.1. Here $c(a_i)$ denotes the codeword for a_i.

The two symbols with the lowest probability are a_4 and a_5. Therefore, we can assign their codewords as

$$c(a_4) = \alpha_1 * 0$$
$$c(a_5) = \alpha_1 * 1$$

where α_1 is a binary string, and $*$ denotes concatenation.

TABLE 3.1   **The initial five-letter alphabet.**

Letter	Probability	Codeword
a_2	0.4	$c(a_2)$
a_1	0.2	$c(a_1)$
a_3	0.2	$c(a_3)$
a_4	0.1	$c(a_4)$
a_5	0.1	$c(a_5)$

T A B L E   3 . 2   **The reduced four-letter alphabet.**

Letter	Probability	Codeword
a_2	0.4	$c(a_2)$
a_1	0.2	$c(a_1)$
a_3	0.2	$c(a_3)$
a_4'	0.2	α_1

T A B L E   3 . 3   **The reduced three-letter alphabet.**

Letter	Probability	Codeword
a_2	0.4	$c(a_2)$
a_3'	0.4	α_2
a_1	0.2	$c(a_1)$

We now define a new alphabet A' with a four-letter alphabet a_1, a_2, a_3, a_4', where a_4' is composed of a_4 and a_5 and has a probability $P(a_4') = P(a_4) + P(a_5) = 0.2$. We sort this new alphabet in descending order to obtain Table 3.2.

In this alphabet, a_3 and a_4' are the two letters at the bottom of the sorted list. We assign their codewords as

$$c(a_3) = \alpha_2 * 0$$
$$c(a_4') = \alpha_2 * 1$$

but $c(a_4') = \alpha_1$. Therefore,

$$\alpha_1 = \alpha_2 * 1$$

which means that

$$c(a_4) = \alpha_2 * 10$$
$$c(a_5) = \alpha_2 * 11.$$

At this stage, we again define a new alphabet A'' that consists of three letters a_1, a_2, a_3', where a_3' is composed of a_3 and a_4' and has a probability $P(a_3') = P(a_3) + P(a_4') = 0.4$. We sort this new alphabet in descending order to obtain Table 3.3.

In this case, the two least probable symbols are a_1 and a_3'. Therefore,

$$c(a_3') = \alpha_3 * 0$$
$$c(a_1) = \alpha_3 * 1.$$

But $c(a_3') = \alpha_2$. Therefore,

$$\alpha_2 = \alpha_3 * 0$$

which means that

$$c(a_3) = \alpha_3 * 00$$
$$c(a_4) = \alpha_3 * 010$$
$$c(a_5) = \alpha_3 * 011.$$

TABLE 3.4   **The reduced two-letter alphabet.**

Letter	Probability	Codeword
a_3''	0.6	α_3
a_2	0.4	$c(a_2)$

TABLE 3.5   **Huffman code for the original five-letter alphabet.**

Letter	Probability	Codeword
a_2	0.4	1
a_1	0.2	01
a_3	0.2	000
a_4	0.1	0010
a_5	0.1	0011

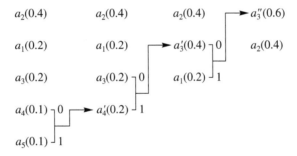

FIGURE 3.1   **The Huffman encoding procedure. The symbol probabilities are listed in parentheses.**

Again we define a new alphabet, this time with only two letters a_3'', a_2. Here a_3'' is composed of the letters a_3' and a_1 and has probability $P(a_3'') = P(a_3') + P(a_1) = 0.6$. We now have Table 3.4.

As we have only two letters, the codeword assignment is straightforward:

$$c(a_3'') = 0$$
$$c(a_2) = 1$$

which means that $\alpha_3 = 0$, which in turn means that

$$c(a_1) = 01$$
$$c(a_3) = 000$$
$$c(a_4) = 0010$$
$$c(a_5) = 0011$$

and the Huffman code is given by Table 3.5. The procedure can be summarized as shown in Figure 3.1. ◆

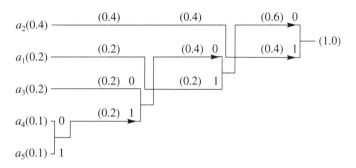

FIGURE 3.2   **Building the binary Huffman tree.**

The average length for this code is

$$l = .4 \times 1 + .2 \times 2 + .2 \times 3 + .1 \times 4 + .1 \times 4 = 2.2 \text{ bits/symbol}.$$

A measure of the efficiency of this code is its *redundancy*—the difference between the entropy and the average length. In this case, the redundancy is 0.078 bits/symbol. The redundancy is zero when the probabilities are negative powers of two.

An alternative way of building a Huffman code is to use the fact that the Huffman code, by virtue of being a prefix code, can be represented as a binary tree in which the external nodes or leaves correspond to the symbols. The Huffman code for any symbol can be obtained by traversing the tree from the root node to the leaf corresponding to the symbol, adding a 0 to the codeword every time the traversal takes us over an upper branch and a 1 every time the traversal takes us over a lower branch.

We build the binary tree starting at the leaf nodes. We know that the codewords for the two symbols with smallest probabilities are identical except for the last bit. This means that the traversal from the root to the leaves corresponding to these two symbols must be the same except for the last step. This in turn means that the leaves corresponding to the two symbols with lowest probabilities are offsprings of the same node. Once we have connected the leaves corresponding to the symbols with the lowest probabilities to a single node, we treat this node as a symbol of a reduced alphabet. The probability of this symbol is the sum of the probabilities of its offsprings. We can now sort the nodes corresponding to the reduced alphabet and apply the same rule to generate a parent node for the nodes corresponding to the two symbols in the reduced alphabet with lowest probabilities. Continuing in this manner, we end up with a single node, which is the root node. To obtain the code for each symbol, we traverse the tree from the root to each leaf node, assigning a 0 to the upper branch and a 1 to the lower branch. This procedure as applied to the alphabet of Example 3.2.1 is shown in Figure 3.2. Notice the similarity between Figures 3.1 and 3.2. This is not surprising, as they are a result of viewing the same procedure in two different ways.

3.2.1   Minimum Variance Huffman Codes

By performing the sorting procedure in a slightly different manner, we could have found a different Huffman code. In the first re-sort, we could place a_4' higher in the list, as shown in Table 3.6.

TABLE   3.6   **Reduced four-letter alphabet.**

Letter	Probability	Codeword
a_2	0.4	$c(a_2)$
a_4'	0.2	α_1
a_1	0.2	$c(a_1)$
a_3	0.2	$c(a_3)$

TABLE   3.7   **Reduced three-letter alphabet.**

Letter	Probability	Codeword
a_1'	0.4	α_2
a_2	0.4	$c(a_2)$
a_4'	0.2	α_1

TABLE   3.8   **Reduced two-letter alphabet.**

Letter	Probability	Codeword
a_2'	0.6	α_3
a_1'	0.4	α_2

TABLE   3.9   **Minimum variance Huffman code.**

Letter	Probability	Codeword
a_1	0.2	10
a_2	0.4	00
a_3	0.2	11
a_4	0.1	010
a_5	0.1	011

Now combine a_1 and a_3 into a_1', which has a probability of 0.4. Sorting the alphabet a_2, a_4', a_1' and putting a_1' as far up the list as possible, we get Table 3.7. Finally, by combining a_2 and a_4' and re-sorting, we get Table 3.8. If we go through the unbundling procedure, we get the codewords in Table 3.9. The procedure is summarized in Figure 3.3. The average length of the code is

$$l = .4 \times 2 + .2 \times 2 + .2 \times 2 + .1 \times 3 + .1 \times 3 = 2.2 \text{ bits/symbol.}$$

The two codes are identical in terms of their redundancy. However, the variance of the length of the codewords is significantly different. This can be clearly seen from Figure 3.4. Remember that in many applications, although you might be using a variable-length code, the available transmission rate is generally fixed. For example, if we were going to transmit symbols from the alphabet we have been using at 10,000 symbols per second, we might ask for transmission capacity of 22,000 bits per second. This means that during each second the channel expects to receive 22,000 bits, no more and no less. As the bit generation rate will vary around 22,000 bits per second, the output of the source coder is generally fed into a buffer. The

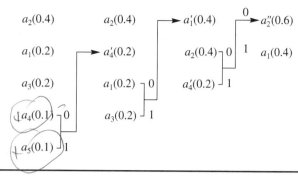

FIGURE 3.3   The minimum variance Huffman encoding procedure.

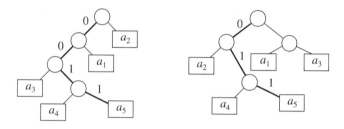

FIGURE 3.4   Two Huffman trees corresponding to the same probabilities.

purpose of the buffer is to smooth out the variations in the bit generation rate. However, the buffer has to be of finite size, and the greater the variance in the codewords, the more difficult the buffer design problem becomes. Suppose that the source we are discussing generates a string of a_4s and a_5s for several seconds. If we are using the first code, this means that we will be generating bits at a rate of 40,000 bits per second. For each second, the buffer has to store 18,000 bits. On the other hand, if we use the second code, we would be generating 30,000 bits per second, and the buffer would have to store 8,000 bits for every second this condition persisted. If we have a string of a_1s instead of a string of a_4s and a_5s, the first code would result in the generation of 10,000 bits per second. Remember that the channel will still be expecting 22,000 bits every second, so somehow we will have to make up a deficit of 12,000 bits per second. The same situation using the second code would lead to a deficit of 2000 bits per second. Thus, it seems reasonable to elect to use the second code instead of the first. To obtain the Huffman code with minimum variance, we always put the combined letter as high in the list as possible.

3.2.2 Optimality of Huffman Codes ★

The optimality of Huffman codes can be proven rather simply by first writing down the necessary conditions that an optimal code has to satisfy and then showing that satisfying these conditions necessarily leads to designing a Huffman code. The proof we present here is based on the proof shown in [70] and is obtained for the binary case (for a more general proof, see [70]).

The necessary conditions for an optimal variable-length binary code are as follows:

■ **Condition 1:** Given any two letters a_j and a_k, if $P[a_j] \geq P[a_k]$, then $l_j \leq l_k$, where l_j is the number of bits in the codeword for a_j.

■ **Condition 2:** The two least probable letters have codewords with the same maximum length l_m.

We have provided the justification for these two conditions in the opening sections of this chapter.

■ **Condition 3:** In the tree corresponding to the optimum code, there must be two branches stemming from each intermediate node.

If there were any intermediate node with only one branch coming from that node, we could remove it without affecting the decipherability of the code while reducing its average length.

■ **Condition 4:** Suppose we change an intermediate node into a leaf node by combining all the leaves descending from it into a composite word of a reduced alphabet. Then, if the original tree was optimal for the original alphabet, the reduced tree is optimal for the reduced alphabet.

If this condition were not satisfied, we could find a code with smaller average code length for the reduced alphabet and then simply expand the composite word again to get a new code tree that would have a shorter average length than our original "optimum" tree. This would contradict our statement about the optimality of the original tree.

In order to satisfy conditions 1, 2, and 3, the two least probable letters would have to be assigned codewords of maximum length l_m. Furthermore, the leaves corresponding to these letters arise from the same intermediate node. This is the same as saying that the codewords for these letters are identical except for the last bit. Consider the common prefix as the codeword for the composite letter of a reduced alphabet. Since the code for the reduced alphabet needs to be optimum for the code of the original alphabet to be optimum, we follow the same procedure again. To satisfy the necessary conditions, the procedure needs to be iterated until we have a reduced alphabet of size one. But this is exactly the Huffman procedure. Therefore, the necessary conditions above, which are all satisfied by the Huffman procedure, are also sufficient conditions.

3.2.3 Length of Huffman Codes ★

We have said that the Huffman coding procedure generates an optimum code, but we have not said what the average length of an optimum code is. The length of any code will depend on a number of things, including the size of the alphabet and the probabilities of individual letters. In this section we will show that the optimal code for a source $\mathcal{S}$, hence the Huffman code for the source $\mathcal{S}$, has an average code length $\bar{l}$ bounded below by the entropy and bounded above by the entropy plus 1 bit. In other words,

$$H(\mathcal{S}) \leq \bar{l} < H(\mathcal{S}) + 1. \tag{3.1}$$

In order for us to do this, we will need to use the Kraft-McMillan inequality introduced in Chapter 2. Recall that the first part of this result, due to McMillan, states that if we have a uniquely decodable code $\mathcal{C}$ with K codewords of length $\{l_i\}_{i=1}^K$, then the following inequality holds:

$$\sum_{i=1}^K 2^{-l_i} \le 1. \tag{3.2}$$

Example 3.2.2:

Examining the code generated in Example 3.2.1 (Table 3.5), the lengths of the codewords are $\{1, 2, 3, 4, 4\}$. Substituting these values into the left-hand side of Equation (3.2), we get

$$2^{-1} + 2^{-2} + 2^{-3} + 2^{-4} + 2^{-4} = 1$$

which satisfies the Kraft-McMillan inequality.

If we use the minimum variance code (Table 3.9), the lengths of the codewords are $\{2, 2, 2, 3, 3\}$. Substituting these values into the left-hand side of Equation (3.2), we get

$$2^{-2} + 2^{-2} + 2^{-2} + 2^{-3} + 2^{-3} = 1$$

which again satisfies the inequality. ◆

The second part of this result, due to Kraft, states that if we have a sequence of positive integers $\{l_i\}_{i=1}^K$, which satisfies (3.2), then there exists a uniquely decodable code whose codeword lengths are given by the sequence $\{l_i\}_{i=1}^K$.

Using this result, we will now show the following:

1. The average codeword length $\bar{l}$ of an optimal code for a source $\mathcal{S}$ is greater than or equal to $H(\mathcal{S})$.

2. The average codeword length $\bar{l}$ of an optimal code for a source $\mathcal{S}$ is strictly less than $H(\mathcal{S}) + 1$.

For a source $\mathcal{S}$ with alphabet $\mathcal{A} = \{a_1, a_2, \ldots a_K\}$, and probability model $\{P(a_1), P(a_2), \ldots, P(a_K)\}$, the average codeword length is given by

$$\bar{l} = \sum_{i=1}^K P(a_i) l_i.$$

Therefore, we can write the difference between the entropy of the source $H(\mathcal{S})$ and the average length as

$$H(\mathcal{S}) - \bar{l} = -\sum_{i=1}^K P(a_i) \log_2 P(a_i) - \sum_{i=1}^K P(a_i) l_i$$

$$= \sum_{i=1}^K P(a_i) \left(\log_2 \left[\frac{1}{P(a_i)} \right] - l_i \right)$$

$$= \sum_{i=1}^K P(a_i) \left(\log_2 \left[\frac{1}{P(a_i)} \right] - \log_2 [2^{l_i}] \right)$$

$$= \sum_{i=1}^{K} P(a_i) \log_2 \left[\frac{2^{-l_i}}{P(a_i)} \right]$$

$$\leq \log_2 \left[\sum_{i=1}^{K} 2^{-l_i} \right].$$

The last inequality is obtained using Jensen's inequality, which states that if $f(x)$ is a concave (convex cap, convex ∩) function, then $E[f(X)] \leq f(E[X])$. The log function is a concave function.

As the code is an optimal code $\sum_{i=1}^{K} 2^{-l_i} \leq 1$, therefore

$$H(\mathcal{S}) - \bar{l} \leq 0. \tag{3.3}$$

We will prove the upper bound by showing that there exists a uniquely decodable code with average codeword length $H(\mathcal{S}) + 1$. Therefore, if we have an optimal code, this code must have an average length that is less than or equal to $H(\mathcal{S}) + 1$.

Given a source, alphabet, and probability model as before, define

$$l_i = \left\lceil \log_2 \frac{1}{P(a_i)} \right\rceil$$

where $\lceil x \rceil$ is the smallest integer greater than or equal to x. For example, $\lceil 3.3 \rceil = 4$ and $\lceil 5 \rceil = 5$. Therefore,

$$\lceil x \rceil = x + \epsilon \qquad \text{where } 0 \leq \epsilon < 1.$$

Therefore,

$$\log_2 \frac{1}{P(a_i)} \leq l_i < \log_2 \frac{1}{P(a_i)} + 1. \tag{3.4}$$

From the left inequality of (3.4) we can see that

$$2^{-l_i} \leq P(a_i).$$

Therefore,

$$\sum_{i=1}^{K} 2^{-l_i} \leq \sum_{i=1}^{K} P(a_i) = 1$$

and by the Kraft-McMillan inequality there exists a uniquely decodable code with codeword lengths $\{l_i\}$. The average length of this code can be upper-bounded by using the right inequality of (3.4):

$$\bar{l} = \sum_{i=1}^{K} P(a_i) l_i < \sum_{i=1}^{K} P(a_i) \left[\log_2 \frac{1}{P(a_i)} + 1 \right]$$

or

$$\bar{l} < H(\mathcal{S}) + 1.$$

We can see from the way the upper bound was derived that this is a rather loose upper bound. In fact, it can be shown that if $p_{\max}$ is the largest probability in the probability model, then for $p_{\max} \geq 0.5$, the upper bound for the Huffman code is $H(\mathcal{S}) + p_{\max}$, while for $p_{\max} < 0.5$, the upper bound is $H(\mathcal{S}) + p_{\max} + 0.086$. Obviously, this is a much tighter bound than the one we derived above. The derivation of this bound takes some time (see [80] for details).

3.2.4 Extended Huffman Codes ★

In applications where the alphabet size is large, p_{max} is generally quite small, and the amount of deviation from the entropy, especially in terms of a percentage of the rate, is quite small. However, in cases where the alphabet is small and the probability of occurrence of the different letters is skewed, the value of p_{max} can be quite large and the Huffman code can become rather inefficient when compared to the entropy.

Example 3.2.3:

Consider a source that puts out *iid* letters from the alphabet $\mathcal{A} = \{a_1, a_2, a_3\}$ with the probability model $P(a_1) = 0.8$, $P(a_2) = 0.02$, and $P(a_3) = 0.18$. The entropy for this source is 0.816 bits/symbol. A Huffman code for this source is shown in Table 3.10.

TABLE 3.10   Huffman code for the alphabet $\mathcal{A}$.

Letter	Codeword
a_1	0
a_2	11
a_3	10

The average length for this code is 1.2 bits/symbol. The difference between the average code length and the entropy, or the redundancy, for this code is 0.384 bits/symbol, which is 47% of the entropy. This means that to code this sequence we would need 47% more bits than the minimum required.   ◆

We can sometimes reduce the coding rate by blocking more than one symbol together. To see how this can happen, consider a source S that emits a sequence of letters from an alphabet $\mathcal{A} = \{a_1, a_2, \ldots, a_m\}$. Each element of the sequence is generated independently of the other elements in the sequence. The entropy for this source is given by

$$H(S) = - \sum_{i=1}^{m} P(a_i) \log_2 P(a_i).$$

We know that we can generate a Huffman code for this source with rate R such that

$$H(S) \leq R < H(S) + 1. \tag{3.5}$$

We have used the looser bound here; the same argument can be made with the tighter bound. Notice that we have used "rate R" to denote the number of bits per symbol. This is a standard convention in the data compression literature. However, in the communication literature, the word "rate" often refers to the number of bits per second.

Suppose we now encode the sequence by generating one codeword for every n symbols. As there are m^n combinations of n symbols, we will need m^n codewords in our Huffman code. We could generate this code by viewing the m^n symbols as letters of an *extended alphabet*

$$\mathcal{A}^{(n)} = \{\overbrace{a_1 a_1 \ldots a_1}^{n \text{ times}}, a_1 a_1 \ldots a_2, \ldots, a_1 a_1 \ldots a_m, a_1 a_1 \ldots a_2 a_1, \ldots, a_m a_m \ldots a_m\}$$

from a source $S^{(n)}$. Let us denote the rate for the new source as $R^{(n)}$. Then we know that

$$H(S^{(n)}) \le R^{(n)} < H(S^{(n)}) + 1. \tag{3.6}$$

$R^{(n)}$ is the number of bits required to code n symbols. Therefore, the number of bits required per symbol, R, is given by

$$R = \frac{1}{n} R^{(n)}.$$

The number of bits per symbol can be bounded as

$$\frac{H(S^{(n)})}{n} \le R < \frac{H(S^{(n)})}{n} + \frac{1}{n}.$$

In order to compare this to (3.5), and see the advantage we get from encoding symbols in blocks instead of one at a time, we need to express $H(S^{(n)})$ in terms of $H(S)$. This turns out to be a relatively easy (although somewhat messy) thing to do.

$$H(S^{(n)}) = -\sum_{i_1=1}^{m}\sum_{i_2=1}^{m}\cdots\sum_{i_n=1}^{m} P(a_{i_1}, a_{i_2}, \ldots a_{i_n}) \log[P(a_{i_1}, a_{i_2}, \ldots a_{i_n})]$$

$$= -\sum_{i_1=1}^{m}\sum_{i_2=1}^{m}\cdots\sum_{i_n=1}^{m} P(a_{i_1})P(a_{i_2})\ldots P(a_{i_n}) \log[P(a_{i_1})P(a_{i_2})\ldots P(a_{i_n})]$$

$$= -\sum_{i_1=1}^{m}\sum_{i_2=1}^{m}\cdots\sum_{i_n=1}^{m} P(a_{i_1})P(a_{i_2})\ldots P(a_{i_n}) \sum_{j=1}^{n}\log[P(a_{i_j})]$$

$$= -\sum_{i_1=1}^{m} P(a_{i_1}) \log[P(a_{i_1})]\left\{\sum_{i_2=1}^{m}\cdots\sum_{i_n=1}^{m} P(a_{i_2})\ldots P(a_{i_n})\right\}$$

$$\quad -\sum_{i_2=1}^{m} P(a_{i_2}) \log[P(a_{i_2})]\left\{\sum_{i_1=1}^{m}\sum_{i_3=1}^{m}\cdots\sum_{i_n=1}^{m} P(a_{i_1})P(a_{i_3})\ldots P(a_{i_n})\right\}$$

$$\vdots$$

$$\quad -\sum_{i_n=1}^{m} P(a_{i_n}) \log[P(a_{i_n})]\left\{\sum_{i_1=1}^{m}\sum_{i_2=1}^{m}\cdots\sum_{i_{n-1}=1}^{m} P(a_{i_1})P(a_{i_2})\ldots P(a_{i_{n-1}})\right\}$$

The $n - 1$ summations in braces in each term sum to one. Therefore,

$$H(S^{(n)}) = -\sum_{i_1=1}^{m} P(a_{i_1}) \log[P(a_{i_1})] - \sum_{i_2=1}^{m} P(a_{i_2}) \log[P(a_{i_2})] - \cdots - \sum_{i_n=1}^{m} P(a_{i_n}) \log[P(a_{i_n})]$$

$$= nH(S)$$

and we can write (3.6) as

$$H(S) \leq R \leq H(S) + \frac{1}{n}. \tag{3.7}$$

Comparing this to (3.5), we can see that by encoding the output of the source in longer blocks of symbols we are *guaranteed* a rate closer to the entropy. Note that all we are talking about here is a bound or guarantee about the rate. As we have seen in the previous chapter, there are a number of situations in which we can achieve a rate *equal* to the entropy with a block length of one!

Example 3.2.4:

For the source described in the previous example, instead of generating a codeword for every symbol, we will generate a codeword for every *two* symbols. If we look at the source sequence two at a time, the number of possible symbol pairs, or size of the extended alphabet, is $3^2 = 9$. The extended alphabet, probability model, and Huffman code for this example are shown in Table 3.11.

TABLE 3.11   The extended alphabet and corresponding Huffman code.

Letter	Probability	Code
$a_1 a_1$	0.64	0
$a_1 a_2$	0.016	10101
$a_1 a_3$	0.144	11
$a_2 a_1$	0.016	101000
$a_2 a_2$	0.0004	10100101
$a_2 a_3$	0.0036	1010011
$a_3 a_1$	0.1440	100
$a_3 a_2$	0.0036	10100100
$a_3 a_3$	0.0324	1011

The average codeword length for this extended code is 1.7228 bits/symbol. However, each symbol in the extended alphabet corresponds to two symbols from the original alphabet. Therefore, in terms of the original alphabet, the average codeword length is $1.7228/2 = 0.8614$ bits/symbol. This redundancy is about 0.045 bits/symbol, which is only about 5.5% of the entropy.   ◆

We see that by coding blocks of symbols together we can reduce the redundancy of Huffman codes. In the previous example, two symbols were blocked together to obtain a rate reasonably close to the entropy. Blocking two symbols together means the alphabet size goes from m to m^2, where m was the size of the initial alphabet. In this case, m was three, so the size of the extended alphabet was nine. This size is not an excessive burden for most applications. However, if the probabilities of the symbols were more unbalanced, then it would require blocking many more symbols together before the redundancy lowered to acceptable levels. As we block more and more symbols together, the size of the alphabet grows exponentially, and the Huffman coding scheme becomes impractical. Under these conditions, we need to look at techniques other than Huffman coding. One approach that is very useful in these conditions is *arithmetic coding*. We will discuss this technique in some detail in the next chapter.

3.3 Nonbinary Huffman Codes ★

The binary Huffman coding procedure can be easily extended to the nonbinary case where the code elements come from an m-ary alphabet, and m is not equal to two. Recall that we obtained the Huffman algorithm based on the observations that in an optimum binary prefix code

1. symbols that occur more frequently (have a higher probability of occurrence) will have shorter codewords than symbols that occur less frequently, and

2. the two symbols that occur least frequently will have the same length,

and the requirement that the two symbols with the lowest probability differ only in the last position.

We can obtain a nonbinary Huffman code in almost exactly the same way. The obvious thing to do would be to modify the second observation to read: "The m symbols that occur least frequently will have the same length," and also modify the additional requirement to read "The m symbols with the lowest probability differ only in the last position."

However, we run into a small problem with this approach. Consider the design of a ternary Huffman code for a source with a six-letter alphabet. Using the rules described above, we would first combine the three letters with the lowest probability into a composite letter. This would give us a reduced alphabet with four letters. However, combining the three letters with lowest probability from this alphabet would result in a further reduced alphabet consisting of only two letters. We have three values to assign and only two letters. Instead of combining three letters at the beginning, we could have combined two letters. This would result in a reduced alphabet of size five. If we combined three letters from this alphabet, we would end up with a final reduced alphabet size of three. Finally, we could combine two letters in the second step, which would again result in a final reduced alphabet of size three. Which alternative should we choose?

Recall that the symbols with lowest probability will have the longest codeword. Furthermore, all the symbols that we combine together into a composite symbol will have codewords of the same length. This means that all letters we combine together at the very first stage will have codewords that have the same length, and these codewords will be the longest of all the codewords. This being the case, if at some stage we are allowed to combine less than m symbols, the logical place to do this would be in the very first stage.

In the general case of an m-ary code and an M-letter alphabet, how many letters should we combine in the first phase? Let m' be the number of letters that are combined in the first phase. Then m' is the number between two and m, which is equal to M modulo $(m-1)$.

Example 3.3.1:

Generate a ternary Huffman code for a source with a six-letter alphabet and a probability model $P(a_1) = P(a_3) = P(a_4) = 0.2$, $P(a_5) = 0.25$, $P(a_6) = 0.1$, and $P(a_2) = 0.05$. In this case $m = 3$, therefore m' is either 2 or 3.

$$6 \ (\text{mod} \ 2) = 0, \quad 2 \ (\text{mod} \ 2) = 0, \quad 3 \ (\text{mod} \ 2) = 1$$

Since $6 \ (\text{mod} \ 2) = 2 \ (\text{mod} \ 2)$, $m' = 2$. Sorting the symbols in probability order results in Table 3.12.

As m' is 2, we can assign the codewords of the two symbols with lowest probability as

$$c(a_6) = \alpha_1 * 0$$
$$c(a_2) = \alpha_1 * 1$$

where α_1 is a ternary string and $*$ denotes concatenation. The reduced alphabet is shown in Table 3.13.

Now we combine the three letters with the lowest probability into a composite letter a_3' and assign their codewords as

$$c(a_3) = \alpha_2 * 0$$
$$c(a_4) = \alpha_2 * 1$$
$$c(a_6') = \alpha_2 * 2.$$

But $c(a_6') = \alpha_1$. Therefore,

$$\alpha_1 = \alpha_2 * 2$$

TABLE 3.12   Sorted six-letter alphabet.

Letter	Probability	Codeword
a_5	0.25	$c(a_5)$
a_1	0.20	$c(a_1)$
a_3	0.20	$c(a_3)$
a_4	0.20	$c(a_4)$
a_6	0.10	$c(a_6)$
a_2	0.05	$c(a_2)$

TABLE 3.13   Reduced five-letter alphabet.

Letter	Probability	Codeword
a_5	0.25	$c(a_5)$
a_1	0.20	$c(a_1)$
a_3	0.20	$c(a_3)$
a_4	0.20	$c(a_4)$
a_6'	0.15	α_1

TABLE 3.14   Reduced three-letter alphabet.

Letter	Probability	Codeword
a_3'	0.45	α_2
a_5	0.25	$c(a_5)$
a_1	0.20	$c(a_1)$

TABLE 3.15   Ternary code for six-letter alphabet.

Letter	Probability	Codeword
a_1	0.20	2
a_2	0.05	021
a_3	0.20	00
a_4	0.20	01
a_5	0.25	1
a_6	0.10	020

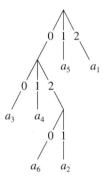

FIGURE 3.5   Code tree for the nonbinary Huffman code.

which means that

$$c(a_6) = \alpha_2 * 20$$
$$c(a_2) = \alpha_2 * 21.$$

Sorting the reduced alphabet, we have Table 3.14. Thus, $\alpha_2 = 0$, $c(a_5) = 1$, and $c(a_1) = 2$. Substituting for α_2, we get the codeword assignments in Table 3.15.

The tree corresponding to this code is shown in Figure 3.5. Notice that at the lowest level of the tree we have only two codewords. If we had combined three letters at the first step, and combined two letters at a later step, the lowest level would have contained three codewords and a longer average code length would result (see Problem 7).   ◆

3.4   Adaptive Huffman Coding

Huffman coding requires knowledge of the probabilities of the source sequence. If this knowledge is not available, Huffman coding becomes a two-pass procedure: the statistics are collected in the first pass, and the source is encoded in the second pass. In order to convert this algorithm into a one-pass procedure, Faller [69] and Gallagher [80] independently developed adaptive algorithms to construct the Huffman code based on the statistics of the symbols already encountered. These were later improved by Knuth [126] and Vitter [232].

Theoretically, if we wanted to encode the $(k+1)$-th symbol using the statistics of the first k symbols, we could recompute the code using the Huffman coding procedure each time a symbol is transmitted. However, this would not be a very practical approach due to the large amount of computation involved—hence, the adaptive Huffman coding procedures.

The Huffman code can be described in terms of a binary tree similar to the ones shown in Figure 3.4. The squares denote the external nodes or leaves and correspond to the symbols in the source alphabet. The codeword for a symbol can be obtained by traversing the tree from the root to the leaf corresponding to the symbol, where 0 corresponds to a left branch and 1 corresponds to a right branch. In order to describe how the adaptive Huffman code works, we add two other parameters to the binary tree: the *weight* of each leaf, which is written as a number inside the node, and a *node number*. The weight of each external node is simply the number of times the symbol corresponding to the leaf has been encountered. The weight of each internal node is the sum of the weights of its offspring. The node number y_i is a unique number assigned to each internal and external node. If we have an alphabet of size n, then the $2n - 1$ internal and external nodes can be numbered as $y_1, \ldots, y_{2n-1}$ such that if x_j is the weight of node y_j, we have $x_1 \leq x_2 \leq \cdots \leq x_{2n-1}$. Furthermore, the nodes y_{2j-1} and y_{2j} are offsprings of the same parent node, or siblings, for $1 \leq j < n$, and the node number for the parent node is greater than y_{2j-1} and y_{2j}. These last two characteristics are called the *sibling property*, and any tree that possesses this property is a Huffman tree [80].

In the adaptive Huffman coding procedure, neither transmitter nor receiver knows anything about the statistics of the source sequence at the start of transmission. The tree at both the transmitter and the receiver consists of a single node that corresponds to all symbols not yet transmitted (NYT) and has a weight of zero. As transmission progresses, nodes corresponding to symbols transmitted will be added to the tree, and the tree is reconfigured using an update procedure. Before the beginning of transmission, a fixed code for each symbol is agreed upon between transmitter and receiver. A simple (short) code is as follows:

If the source has an alphabet $(a_1, a_2, \ldots, a_m)$ of size m, then pick e and r such that $m = 2^e + r$ and $0 \leq r < 2^e$. The letter a_k is encoded as the $(e + 1)$-bit binary representation of $k - 1$, if $1 \leq k \leq 2r$; else, a_k is encoded as the e-bit binary representation of $k - r - 1$. For example, suppose $m = 26$, then $e = 4$, and $r = 10$. The symbol a_1 is encoded as 00000, the symbol a_2 is encoded as 00001, and the symbol a_{22} is encoded as 1011.

When a symbol is encountered for the first time, the code for the NYT node is transmitted, followed by the fixed code for the symbol. A node for the symbol is then created, and the symbol is taken out of the NYT list.

Both transmitter and receiver start with the same tree structure. The updating procedure used by both transmitter and receiver is identical. Therefore, the encoding and decoding processes remain synchronized.

3.4.1 Update Procedure

The update procedure requires that the nodes be in a fixed order. This ordering is preserved by numbering the nodes. The largest node number is given to the root of the tree, and the smallest number is assigned to the NYT node. The numbers from the NYT node to the root of the tree are assigned in increasing order from left to right, and from lower level to upper level. The set of nodes with the same weight makes up a *block*. Figure 3.6 is a flowchart of the updating procedure.

The function of the update procedure is to preserve the sibling property. In order that the update procedures at the transmitter and receiver both operate with the same information, the tree at the transmitter is updated after each symbol is encoded, and the tree at the receiver is updated after each symbol is decoded. The procedure operates as follows:

After a symbol has been encoded or decoded, the external node corresponding to the symbol is examined to see if it has the largest node number in its block. If the external node does not have the largest node number, it is exchanged with the node that has the largest node number in the block, as long as the node with the higher number is not the parent of the node being updated. The weight of the external node is then incremented. If we did not exchange the nodes before the weight of the node is incremented, it is very likely that the ordering required by the sibling property would be destroyed. Once we have incremented the weight of the node, we have adapted the Huffman tree at that level. We then turn our attention to the next level by examining the parent node of the node whose weight was incremented to see if it has the largest number in its block. If it does not, it is exchanged with the node with the largest number in the block. Again, an exception to this is when the node with the higher node number is the parent of the node under consideration. Once an exchange has taken place (or it has been determined that there is no need for an exchange), the weight of the parent node is incremented. We then proceed to a new parent node and the process is repeated. This process continues until the root of the tree is reached.

If the symbol to be encoded or decoded has occurred for the first time, a new external node is assigned to the symbol and a new NYT node is appended to the tree. Both the new external node and the new NYT node are offsprings of the old NYT node. We increment the weight of the new external node by one. As the old NYT node is the parent of the new external node, we increment its weight by one and then go on to update all the other nodes until we reach the root of the tree.

Example 3.4.1: Update procedure

Assume we are encoding the message [a a r d v a r k], where our alphabet consists of the 26 lowercase letters of the English alphabet.

The updating process is shown in Figure 3.7. We begin with only the NYT node. The total number of nodes in this tree will be $2 \times 26 - 1 = 51$, so we start numbering backwards from 51 with the number of the root node being 51. The first letter to be transmitted is a. As a does not yet exist in the tree, we send a binary code 00000 for a and then add a to the tree. The NYT node gives birth to a new NYT node and a terminal node corresponding to a. The weight of the terminal node will be higher than the NYT node, so we assign the number 49 to the NYT node and 50 to the terminal node corresponding to the letter a. The second letter to

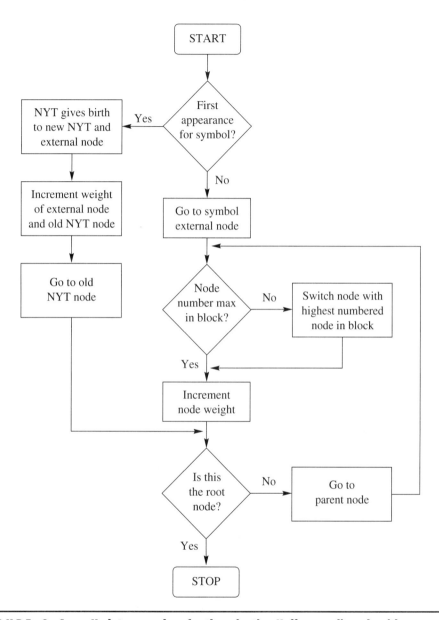

F I G U R E   3 . 6   Update procedure for the adaptive Huffman coding algorithm.

be transmitted is also a. This time the transmitted code is 1. The node corresponding to a has the highest number (if we do not consider its parent), so we do not need to swap nodes. The next letter to be transmitted is r. This letter does not have a corresponding node on the tree, so we send the codeword for the NYT node, which is 0 followed by the index of r, which is 10001. The NYT node gives birth to a new NYT node and an external node corresponding to

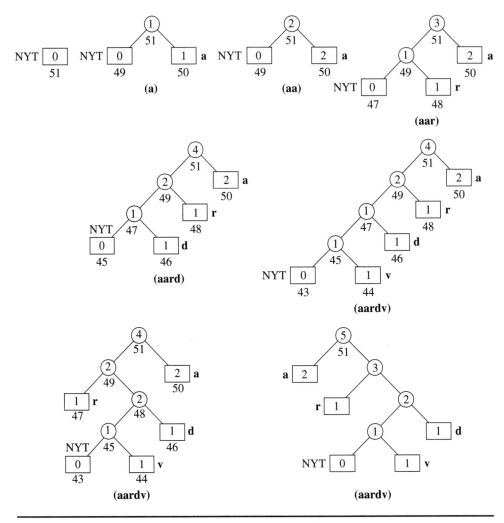

r. Again, no update is required. The next letter to be transmitted is *d*, which is also being sent for the first time. We again send the code for the NYT node, which is now 00 followed by the index for *d*, which is 00011. The NYT node again gives birth to two new nodes. However, an update is still not required. This changes with the transmission of the next letter, *v*, which has also not yet been encountered. Nodes 43 and 44 are added to the tree, with 44 as the terminal node corresponding to *v*. We examine the parent node of *v* (node 45) to see if it has the largest number in its block. As it does not, we swap it with node 48, which has the largest number in its block. We then increment node 48 and move to its parent, which is node 49. In the block containing node 49, the largest number belongs to node 50. Therefore, we swap nodes 49 and 50 and then increment node 50. We then move to the parent node of node 50, which is node 51. As this is the root node, all we do is increment node 51.   ◆

3.4.2 Encoding Procedure

The flowchart for the encoding procedure is shown in Figure 3.8. Initially, the tree at both the encoder and decoder consists of a single node, the NYT node. Therefore, the codeword for the very first symbol that appears is a previously agreed-upon fixed code. After the very first symbol, whenever we have to encode a symbol that is being encountered for the first time, we send the code for the NYT node, followed by the previously agreed-upon fixed code for the symbol. The code for the NYT node is obtained by traversing the Huffman tree from the root to the NYT node. This alerts the receiver to the fact that the symbol whose code follows does not as yet have a node in the Huffman tree. If a symbol to be encoded has a corresponding

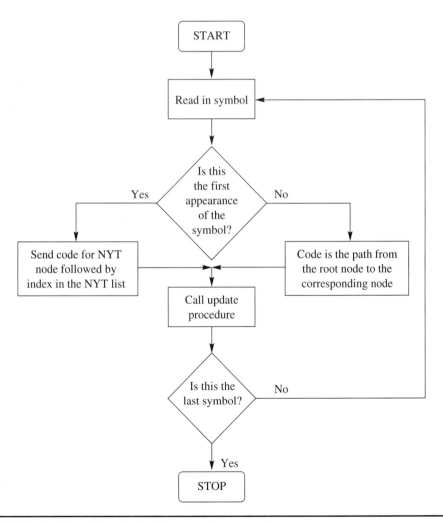

FIGURE 3.8   Flowchart of the encoding procedure.

node in the tree, then the code for the symbol is generated by traversing the tree from the root to the external node corresponding to the symbol.

To see how the coding operation functions, we use the same example that was used to demonstrate the update procedure.

Example 3.4.2: Encoding procedure

In Example 3.4.1 we used an alphabet consisting of 26 letters. In order to obtain our prearranged code, we have to find m and e such that $2^e + r = 26$, where $0 \leq r < 2^e$. It is easy to see that the values of $e = 4$ and $r = 10$ satisfy this requirement.

The first symbol encoded is the letter a. As a is the first letter of the alphabet, $k = 1$. As 1 is less than 20, a is encoded as the 5-bit binary representation of $k - 1$, or 0, which is 00000. The Huffman tree is then updated as shown in the figure. The NYT node gives birth to an external node corresponding to the element a and a new NYT node. As a has occurred once, the external node corresponding to a has a weight of one. The weight of the NYT node is zero. The internal node also has a weight of one, as its weight is the sum of the weights of its offspring. The next symbol is again a. As we have an external node corresponding to symbol a, we simply traverse the tree from the root node to the external node corresponding to a in order to find the codeword. This traversal consists of a single right branch. Therefore, the Huffman code for the symbol a is 1.

After the code for a has been transmitted, the weight of the external node corresponding to a is incremented, as is the weight of its parent. The third symbol to be transmitted is r. As this is the first appearance of this symbol, we send the code for the NYT node followed by the previously arranged binary representation for r. If we traverse the tree from the root to the NYT node, we get a code of 0 for the NYT node. The letter r is the 18th letter of the alphabet; therefore, the binary representation of r is 10001. The code for the symbol r becomes 010001. The tree is again updated as shown in the figure, and the coding process continues with symbol d. Using the same procedure for d, the code for the NYT node, which is now 00, is sent, followed by the index for d, resulting in the codeword 0000011. The next symbol v is the 22nd symbol in the alphabet. As this is greater than 20, we send the code for the NYT node followed by the 4-bit binary representation of $22 - 10 - 1 = 11$. The code for the NYT node at this stage is 000, and the 4-bit binary representation of 11 is 1011; therefore, v is encoded as 0001011. The next symbol is a, for which the code is 0, and the encoding proceeds.   ◆

3.4.3 Decoding Procedure

The flowchart for the decoding procedure is shown in Figure 3.9. As we read in the received binary string, we traverse the tree in a manner identical to that used in the encoding procedure. Once a leaf is encountered, the symbol corresponding to that leaf is decoded. If the leaf is the NYT node, then we check the next e bits to see if the resulting number is less than r. If it is less than r, we read in another bit to complete the code for the symbol. The index for the symbol is obtained by adding one to the decimal number corresponding to the e- or $e + 1$-bit binary string. Once the symbol has been decoded, the tree is updated and the next received bit is used to start another traversal down the tree. To see how this procedure works, let us decode the binary string generated in the previous example.

Example 3.4.3: Decoding procedure

The binary string generated by the encoding procedure is

$$000001010001000001100010110$$

Initially, the decoder tree consists only of the NYT node. Therefore, the first symbol to be decoded must be obtained from the NYT list. We read in the first 4 bits, 0000, as the value of e is four. The 4 bits 0000 correspond to the decimal value of 0. As this is less than the value of r, which is 10, we read in one more bit for the entire code of 00000. Adding one to the decimal value corresponding to this binary string, we get the index of the received symbol as 1. This is the index for a; therefore, the first letter is decoded as a. The tree is now updated as shown in Figure 3.7. The next bit in the string is 1. This traces a path from the root node to the external node corresponding to a. We decode the symbol a and update the tree. In this case, the update consists only of incrementing the weight of the external node corresponding to a. The next bit is a 0, which traces a path from the root to the NYT node. The next 4 bits, 1000, correspond to the decimal number 8, which is less than 10, so we read in one more bit to get the 5-bit word 10001. The decimal equivalent of this 5-bit word plus one is 18, which is the index for r. We decode the symbol r and then update the tree. The next 2 bits, 00, again trace a path to the NYT node. We read the next 4 bits, 0001. Since this corresponds to the decimal number 1, which is less than 10, we read another bit to get the 5-bit word 00011. To get the index of the received symbol in the NYT list, we add one to the decimal value of this 5-bit word. The value of the index is 4, which corresponds to the symbol d. Continuing in this fashion, we decode the sequence *aardva*.   ◆

Although the Huffman coding algorithm is one of the best-known variable-length coding algorithms, there are some other lesser-known algorithms that can be very useful in certain situations. In particular, the Golomb-Rice codes and the Tunstall codes are becoming increasingly popular. We describe these codes in the following sections.

3.5 Golomb Codes

The Golomb-Rice codes belong to a family of codes designed to encode integers with the assumption that the larger an integer, the lower its probability of occurrence. The simplest code for this situation is the *unary* code. The unary code for a positive integer n is simply n 1s followed by a 0. Thus, the code for 4 is 11110, and the code for 7 is 11111110. The unary code is the same as the Huffman code for the semi-infinite alphabet $\{1, 2, 3, \ldots\}$ with probability model

$$P[k] = \frac{1}{2^k}.$$

Because the Huffman code is optimal, the unary code is also optimal for this probability model.

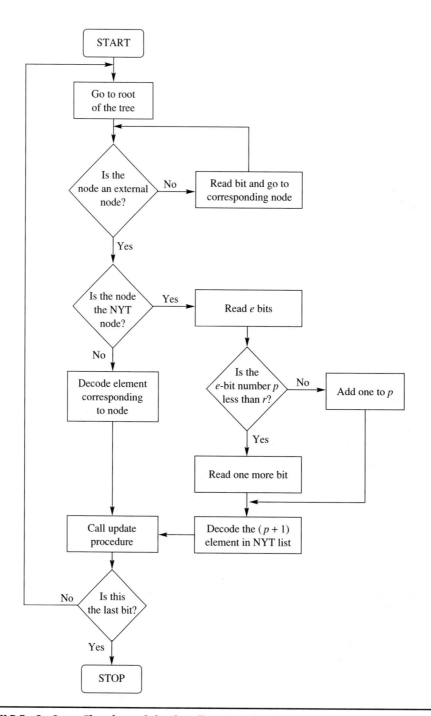

FIGURE 3.9   Flowchart of the decoding procedure.

Although the unary code is optimal in very restricted conditions, we can see that it is certainly very simple to implement. One step higher in complexity are a number of coding schemes that split the integer into two parts, representing one part with a unary code and the other part with a different code. An example of such a code is the Golomb code. Other examples can be found in [65].

The Golomb code is described in a succinct paper [95] by Solomon Golomb, which begins "Secret Agent 00111 is back at the Casino again, playing a game of chance, while the fate of mankind hangs in the balance." Agent 00111 requires a code to represent runs of success in a roulette game, and Golomb provides it! The Golomb code is actually a family of codes parameterized by an integer $m > 0$. In the Golomb code with parameter m, we represent an integer $n > 0$ using two numbers q and r, where

$$q = \left\lfloor \frac{n}{m} \right\rfloor$$

and

$$r = n - qm.$$

$\lfloor x \rfloor$ is the integer part of x. In other words, q is the quotient and r is the remainder when n is divided by m. The quotient q can take on values $0, 1, 2, \ldots$ and is represented by the unary code of q. The remainder r can take on the values $0, 1, 2, \ldots, m - 1$. If m is a power of two, we use the $\log_2 m$-bit binary representation of r. If m is not a power of two, we could still use $\lceil \log_2 m \rceil$ bits, where $\lceil x \rceil$ is the smallest integer greater than or equal to x. We can reduce the number of bits required if we use the $\lfloor \log_2 m \rfloor$-bit binary representation of r for the first $2^{\lceil \log_2 m \rceil} - m$ values, and the $\lceil \log_2 m \rceil$-bit binary representation of $r + 2^{\lceil \log_2 m \rceil} - m$ for the rest of the values.

Example 3.5.1: Golomb code

Let's design a Golomb code for $m = 5$. As

$$\lceil \log_2 5 \rceil = 3, \quad \text{and} \quad \lfloor \log_2 5 \rfloor = 2$$

the first $8 - 5 = 3$ values of r (that is, $r = 0, 1, 2$) will be represented by the 2-bit binary representation of r, and the next two values (that is, $r = 3, 4$) will be represented by the 3-bit representation of $r + 3$. The quotient q is always represented by the unary code for q. Thus, the codeword for 3 is 0110, and the codeword for 21 is 11110001. The codewords for $n = 0, \ldots, 15$ are shown in Table 3.16. $\blacklozenge$

It can be shown that the Golomb code is optimal for the probability model

$$P(n) = p^{n-1}q, \qquad q = 1 - p$$

when

$$m = \left\lceil -\frac{1}{\log_2 p} \right\rceil.$$

TABLE 3.16   Golomb code for m = 5.

n	q	r	Codeword	n	q	r	Codeword
0	0	0	000	8	1	3	10110
1	0	1	001	9	1	4	10111
2	0	2	010	10	2	0	11000
3	0	3	0110	11	2	1	11001
4	0	4	0111	12	2	2	11010
5	1	0	1000	13	2	3	110110
6	1	1	1001	14	2	4	110111
7	1	2	1010	15	3	0	111000

3.6   Rice Codes

The Rice code was originally developed by Robert F. Rice (he called it the Rice machine) [189, 190] and later extended by Pen-Shu Yeh and Warner Miller [247]. The Rice code can be viewed as an adaptive Golomb code. In the Rice code, a sequence of nonnegative integers (which might have been obtained from the preprocessing of other data) is divided into blocks of J integers apiece. Each block is then coded using one of several options, most of which are a form of Golomb codes. Each block is encoded with each of these options, and the option resulting in the least number of coded bits is selected. The particular option used is indicated by an identifier attached to the code for each block.

The easiest way to understand the Rice code is to examine one of its implementations. We will study the implementation of the Rice code in the recommendation for lossless compression from the Consultative Committee on Space Data Standards (CCSDS).

3.6.1   CCSDS Recommendation for Lossless Compression

As an application of the Rice algorithm, let's briefly look at the algorithm for lossless data compression recommended by CCSDS. The algorithm consists of a preprocessor (the modeling step) and a binary coder (coding step). The preprocessor removes correlation from the input and generates a sequence of nonnegative integers. This sequence has the property that smaller values are more probable than larger values. The binary coder generates a bitstream to represent the integer sequence. The binary coder is our main focus at this point.

The preprocessor functions as follows: Given a sequence $\{y_i\}$, for each y_i we generate a prediction $\hat{y}_i$. A simple way to generate a prediction would be to take the previous value of the sequence to be a prediction of the current value of the sequence:

$$\hat{y}_i = y_{i-1}.$$

We will look at more sophisticated ways of generating a prediction in Chapter 6. We then generate a sequence whose elements are the difference between y_i and its predicted value $\hat{y}_i$:

$$d_i = y_i - \hat{y}_i.$$

The d_i value will have a small magnitude when our prediction is good and a large value when it is not. Assuming an accurate modeling of the data, the former situation is more likely than the latter. Let y_{max} and y_{min} be the largest and smallest values that the sequence $\{y_i\}$ takes on. It is reasonable to assume that the value of $\hat{y}$ will be confined to the range $[y_{min}, y_{max}]$. Define

$$T_i = \min\{y_{max} - \hat{y}, \hat{y} - y_{min}\}. \tag{3.8}$$

The sequence $\{d_i\}$ can be converted into a sequence of nonnegative integers $\{x_i\}$ using the following mapping:

$$x_i = \begin{cases} 2d_i & 0 \leq d_i \leq T_i \\ 2|d_i| - 1 & -T_i \leq d_i < 0 \\ T_i + |d_i| & \text{otherwise.} \end{cases} \tag{3.9}$$

The value of x_i will be small whenever the magnitude of d_i is small. Therefore, the value of x_i will be small with higher probability. The sequence $\{x_i\}$ is divided into segments with each segment being further divided into blocks of size J. It is recommended by CCSDS that J have a value of 16. Each block is then coded using one of the following options. The coded block is transmitted along with an identifier that indicates which particular option was used.

- **Fundamental sequence:** This is a unary code. A number n is represented by a sequence of n 0s followed by a 1 (or a sequence of n 1s followed by a 0).

- **Split sample options:** These options consist of a set of codes indexed by a parameter m. The code for a k-bit number n using the mth split sample option consists of the m least significant bits of k followed by a unary code representing the $k - m$ most significant bits. For example, suppose we wanted to encode the 8-bit number 23 using the third split sample option. The 8-bit representation of 23 is 00010111. The three least significant bits are 111. The remaining bits (00010) correspond to the number 2, which has a unary code 001. Therefore, the code for 23 using the third split sample option is 111011. Notice that different values of m will be preferable for different values of x_i, with higher values of m used for higher-entropy sequences.

- **Second extension option:** The second extension option is useful for sequences with low entropy—when, in general, many of the values of x_i will be zero. In the second extension option the sequence is divided into consecutive pairs of samples. Each pair is used to obtain an index γ using the following transformation:

$$\gamma = \frac{1}{2}(x_i + x_{i+1})(x_i + x_{i+1} + 1) + x_{i+1} \tag{3.10}$$

and the value of γ is encoded using a unary code. The value of γ is an index to a lookup table with each value of γ corresponding to a pair of values x_i, x_{i+1}.

- **Zero block option:** The zero block option is used when one or more of the blocks of x_i are zero—generally when we have long sequences of y_i that have the same value. In this case the number of zero blocks are transmitted using the code shown in Table 3.17. The ROS code is used when the last five or more blocks in a segment are all zero.

The Rice code has been used in several space applications, and variations of the Rice code have been proposed for a number of different applications.

TABLE 3.17 **Code used for zero block option.**

Number of All-Zero Blocks	Codeword
1	1
2	01
3	001
4	0001
5	000001
6	0000001
⋮	⋮
63	$\overbrace{000\cdots0}^{63\ 0s}1$
ROS	00001

TABLE 3.18 **A 2-bit Tunstall code.**

Sequence	Codeword
AAA	00
AAB	01
AB	10
B	11

3.7 Tunstall Codes

Most of the variable-length codes that we look at in this book encode letters from the source alphabet using codewords with varying numbers of bits: codewords with fewer bits for letters that occur more frequently and codewords with more bits for letters that occur less frequently. The Tunstall code is an important exception. In the Tunstall code, all codewords are of equal length. However, each codeword represents a different number of letters. An example of a 2-bit Tunstall code for an alphabet $\mathcal{A} = \{A, B\}$ is shown in Table 3.18. The main advantage of a Tunstall code is that errors in codewords do not propagate, unlike other variable-length codes, such as Huffman codes, in which an error in one codeword will cause a series of errors to occur.

Example 3.7.1:

Let's encode the sequence *AAABAABAABAABAAA* using the code in Table 3.18. Starting at the left, we can see that the string *AAA* occurs in our codebook and has a code of 00. We then code *B* as 11, *AAB* as 01, and so on. We finally end up with coded string 001101010100. ◆

The design of a code that has a fixed codeword length but a variable number of symbols per codeword should satisfy the following conditions:

TABLE 3.19 **A 2-bit (non-Tunstall) code.**

Sequence	Codeword
AAA	00
ABA	01
AB	10
B	11

1. We should be able to parse a source output sequence into sequences of symbols that appear in the codebook.

2. We should maximize the average number of source symbols represented by each codeword.

In order to understand what we mean by the first condition, consider the code shown in Table 3.19. Let's encode the same sequence *AAABAABAABAABAAA* as in the previous example using the code in Table 3.19. We first encode *AAA* with the code 00. We then encode *B* with 11. The next three symbols are *AAB*. However, there are no codewords corresponding to this sequence of symbols. Thus, this sequence is unencodable using this particular code— not a desirable situation.

Tunstall [227] gives a simple algorithm that fulfills these conditions. The algorithm is as follows:

Suppose we want an *n*-bit Tunstall code for a source that generates *iid* letters from an alphabet of size N. The number of codewords is 2^n. We start with the N letters of the source alphabet in our codebook. Remove the entry in the codebook that has the highest probability and add the N strings obtained by concatenating this letter with every letter in the alphabet (including itself). This will increase the size of the codebook from N to $N + (N - 1)$. The probabilities of the new entries will be the product of the probabilities of the letters concatenated to form the new entry. Now look through the $N + (N - 1)$ entries in the codebook and find the entry that has the highest probability, keeping in mind that the entry with the highest probability may be a concatenation of symbols. Each time we perform this operation we increase the size of the codebook by $N - 1$. Therefore, this operation can be performed K times, where

$$N + K(N - 1) \leq 2^n.$$

Example 3.7.2: Tunstall codes

Let us design a 3-bit Tunstall code for a memoryless source with the following alphabet:

$$\mathcal{A} = \{A, B, C\}$$
$$P(A) = 0.6, \quad P(B) = 0.3, \quad P(C) = 0.1$$

We start out with the codebook and associated probabilities shown in Table 3.20. Since the letter *A* has the highest probability, we remove it from the list and add all two-letter strings beginning with *A* as shown in Table 3.21. After one iteration we have 5 entries in our

TABLE 3.20   **Source alphabet and associated probabilities.**

Letter	Probability
A	0.60
B	0.30
C	0.10

TABLE 3.21   **The codebook after one iteration.**

Sequence	Probability
B	0.30
C	0.10
AA	0.36
AB	0.18
AC	0.06

TABLE 3.22   **A 3-bit Tunstall code.**

Sequence	Probability
B	000
C	001
AB	010
AC	011
AAA	100
AAB	101
AAC	110

codebook. Going through one more iteration will increase the size of the codebook by 2, and we will have 7 entries, which is still less than the final codebook size. Going through another iteration after that would bring the codebook size to 10, which is greater than the maximum size of 8. Therefore, we will go through just one more iteration. Looking through the entries in Table 3.21, the entry with the highest probability is *AA*. Therefore, at the next step we re-move *AA* and add all extensions of *AA* as shown in Table 3.22. The final 3-bit Tunstall code is shown in Table 3.22.   ◆

3.8   Applications of Huffman Coding

In this section we describe some applications of Huffman coding. As we progress through the book, we will describe more applications, since Huffman coding is often used in conjunction with other coding techniques.

FIGURE 3.10   Test images.

3.8.1 Lossless Image Compression

A simple application of Huffman coding to image compression would be to generate a Huffman code for the set of values that any pixel may take. For monochrome images, this set usually consists of integers from 0 to 255. Examples of such images are contained in the accompanying data sets. The four that we will use in the examples in this book are shown in Figure 3.10.

We will make use of one of the programs from the accompanying software (see Preface) to generate a Huffman code for each image, and then encode the image using the Huffman code. The results for the four images in Figure 3.10 are shown in Table 3.23. The Huffman

TABLE 3.23   **Compression using Huffman codes on pixel values.**

Image Name	Bits/Pixel	Total Size (bytes)	Compression Ratio
Sena	7.01	57,504	1.14
Sensin	7.49	61,430	1.07
Earth	4.94	40,534	1.62
Omaha	7.12	58,374	1.12

TABLE 3.24   **Compression using Huffman codes on pixel difference values.**

Image Name	Bits/Pixel	Total Size (bytes)	Compression Ratio
Sena	4.02	32,968	1.99
Sensin	4.70	38,541	1.70
Earth	4.13	33,880	1.93
Omaha	6.42	52,643	1.24

code is stored along with the compressed image as the code will be required by the decoder to reconstruct the image.

The original (uncompressed) image representation uses 8 bits/pixel. The image consists of 256 rows of 256 pixels, so the uncompressed representation uses 65,536 bytes. The compression ratio is simply the ratio of the number of bytes in the uncompressed representation to the number of bytes in the compressed representation. The number of bytes in the compressed representation includes the number of bytes needed to store the Huffman code. Notice that the compression ratio is different for different images. This can cause some problems in certain applications where it is necessary to know in advance how many bytes will be needed to represent a particular data set.

The results in Table 3.23 are somewhat disappointing because we get a reduction of only about $\frac{1}{2}$ to 1 bit/pixel after compression. For some applications this reduction is acceptable. For example, if we were storing thousands of images in an archive, a reduction of 1 bit/pixel saves many megabytes in disk space. However, we can do better. Recall that when we first talked about compression, we said that the first step for any compression algorithm was to model the data so as to make use of the structure in the data. In this case, we have made absolutely no use of the structure in the data.

From a visual inspection of the test images, we can clearly see that the pixels in an image are heavily correlated with their neighbors. We could represent this structure with the crude model $\hat{x}_n = x_{n-1}$. The residual would be the difference between neighboring pixels. If we carry out this differencing operation and use the Huffman coder on the residuals, the results are as shown in Table 3.24. As we can see, using the structure in the data resulted in substantial improvement.

The results in Tables 3.23 and 3.24 were obtained using a two-pass system, in which the statistics were collected in the first pass and a Huffman table was generated. Instead of using a two-pass system, we could have used a one-pass adaptive Huffman coder. The results for this are given in Table 3.25.

T A B L E   3 . 2 5   **Compression using adaptive Huffman codes on pixel difference values.**

Image Name	Bits/Pixel	Total Size (bytes)	Compression Ratio
Sena	3.93	32,261	2.03
Sensin	4.63	37,896	1.73
Earth	4.82	39,504	1.66
Omaha	6.39	52,321	1.25

Notice that there is little difference between the performance of the adaptive Huffman code and the two-pass Huffman coder. In addition, the fact that the adaptive Huffman coder can be used as an on-line or real-time coder makes the adaptive Huffman coder a more attractive option in many applications. However, the adaptive Huffman coder is more vulnerable to errors and may also be more difficult to implement. In the end, the particular application will determine which approach is more suitable.

3.8.2   Text Compression

Text compression seems natural for Huffman coding. In text, we have a discrete alphabet that, in a given class, has relatively stationary probabilities. For example, the probability model for a particular novel will not differ significantly from the probability model for another novel. Similarly, the probability model for a set of FORTRAN programs is not going to be much different than the probability model for a different set of FORTRAN programs. The probabilities in Table 3.26 are the probabilities of the 26 letters (upper- and lowercase) obtained for the U.S. Constitution and are representative of English text. The probabilities in Table 3.27 were obtained by counting the frequency of occurrences of letters in an earlier version of this chapter. While the two documents are substantially different, the two sets of probabilities are very much alike.

We encoded the earlier version of this chapter using Huffman codes that were created using the probabilities of occurrence obtained from the chapter. The file size dropped from about 70,000 bytes to about 43,000 bytes with Huffman coding.

While this reduction in file size is useful, we could have obtained better compression if we first removed the structure existing in the form of correlation between the symbols in the file. Obviously, there is a substantial amount of correlation in this text. For example, *Huf* is always followed by *fman*! Unfortunately, this correlation is not amenable to simple numerical models, as was the case for the image files. However, there are other somewhat more complex techniques that can be used to remove the correlation in text files. We will look more closely at these in Chapters 5 and 6.

3.8.3   Audio Compression

Another class of data that is very suitable for compression is CD-quality audio data. The audio signal for each stereo channel is sampled at 44.1 kHz, and each sample is represented by 16 bits. This means that the amount of data stored on one CD is enormous. If we want to transmit this data, the amount of channel capacity required would be significant. Compression

TABLE 3.26 Probabilities of occurrence of the letters in the English alphabet in the U.S. Constitution.

Letter	Probability	Letter	Probability
A	0.057305	N	0.056035
B	0.014876	O	0.058215
C	0.025775	P	0.021034
D	0.026811	Q	0.000973
E	0.112578	R	0.048819
F	0.022875	S	0.060289
G	0.009523	T	0.078085
H	0.042915	U	0.018474
I	0.053475	V	0.009882
J	0.002031	W	0.007576
K	0.001016	X	0.002264
L	0.031403	Y	0.011702
M	0.015892	Z	0.001502

TABLE 3.27 Probabilities of occurrence of the letters in the English alphabet in this chapter.

Letter	Probability	Letter	Probability
A	0.049855	N	0.048039
B	0.016100	O	0.050642
C	0.025835	P	0.015007
D	0.030232	Q	0.001509
E	0.097434	R	0.040492
F	0.019754	S	0.042657
G	0.012053	T	0.061142
H	0.035723	U	0.015794
I	0.048783	V	0.004988
J	0.000394	W	0.012207
K	0.002450	X	0.003413
L	0.025835	Y	0.008466
M	0.016494	Z	0.001050

is definitely useful in this case. In Table 3.28 we show for a variety of audio material the file size, the entropy, the estimated compressed file size if a Huffman coder is used, and the resulting compression ratio.

The three segments used in this example represent a wide variety of audio material, from a symphonic piece by Mozart to a folk rock piece by Cohn. Even though the material is varied, Huffman coding can lead to some reduction in the capacity required to transmit this material.

Note that we have only provided the *estimated* compressed file sizes. The estimated file size in bits was obtained by multiplying the entropy by the number of samples in the file. We used this approach because the samples of 16-bit audio can take on 65,536 distinct values, and therefore the Huffman coder would require 65,536 distinct (variable-length) codewords. In

TABLE 3.28   Huffman coding of 16-bit CD-quality audio.

File Name	Original File Size (bytes)	Entropy (bits)	Estimated Compressed File Size (bytes)	Compression Ratio
Mozart	939,862	12.8	725,420	1.30
Cohn	402,442	13.8	349,300	1.15
Mir	884,020	13.7	759,540	1.16

TABLE 3.29   Huffman coding of differences of 16-bit CD-quality audio.

File Name	Original File Size (bytes)	Entropy of Differences (bits)	Estimated Compressed File Size (bytes)	Compression Ratio
Mozart	939,862	9.7	569,792	1.65
Cohn	402,442	10.4	261,590	1.54
Mir	884,020	10.9	602,240	1.47

most applications, a codebook of this size would not be practical. There is a way of handling large alphabets, called recursive indexing, that we will describe in Chapter 8. There is also some recent work [180] on using a Huffman tree in which leaves represent sets of symbols with the same probability. The codeword consists of a prefix that specifies the set followed by a suffix that specifies the symbol within the set. This approach can accommodate relatively large alphabets.

As with the other applications, we can obtain an increase in compression if we first remove the structure from the data. Audio data can be modeled numerically. In later chapters we will examine more sophisticated modeling approaches. For now, let us use the very simple model that was used in the image-coding example; that is, each sample has the same value as the previous sample. Using this model we obtain the difference sequence. The entropy of the difference sequence is shown in Table 3.29.

Note that there is a further reduction in the file size: the compressed file sizes are about 60% of the original files. Further reductions can be obtained by using more sophisticated models.

3.9 Summary

In this chapter we began our exploration of data compression techniques with a description of the Huffman coding technique and several other related techniques. The Huffman coding technique and its variants are some of the most commonly used coding approaches. We will encounter modified versions of Huffman codes when we look at compression techniques for text, image, and video. In this chapter we described how to design Huffman codes and discussed some of the issues related to Huffman codes. We also described how adaptive Huffman codes work and looked briefly at some of the places where Huffman codes are used. We will see more of these in future chapters.

To explore further applications of Huffman coding, you can use the programs huff_enc, huff_dec, and adap_huff to generate your own Huffman codes for your favorite applications.

Further Reading

1. Details about nonbinary Huffman codes and a much more theoretical and rigorous description of variable-length codes can be found in *The Theory of Information and Coding*, volume 3 of *Encyclopedia of Mathematic and Its Application*, by R.J. McEliece [155].

2. The tutorial article "Data Compression" in the September 1987 issue of *ACM Computing Surveys*, by D.A. Lelewer and D.S. Hirschberg [136], along with other material, provides a very nice brief coverage of the material in this chapter.

3. A somewhat different approach to describing Huffman codes can be found in *Data Compression—Methods and Theory*, by J.A. Storer [219].

4. A more theoretical but very readable account of variable-length coding can be found in *Elements of Information Theory*, by T.M. Cover and J.A. Thomas [55].

5. Although the book *Coding and Information Theory*, by R.W. Hamming [100], is mostly about channel coding, Huffman codes are described in some detail in Chapter 4.

3.10 Projects and Problems

1. The probabilities in Tables 3.26 and 3.27 were obtained using the program countalpha from the accompanying software. Use this program to compare probabilities for different types of text, C programs, messages on Usenet, and so on. Comment on any differences you might see and describe how you would tailor your compression strategy for each type of text.

2. Use the programs huff_enc and huff_dec to do the following (in each case use the codebook generated by the image being compressed):

   (a) Code the Sena, Sinan, and Omaha images.

   (b) Write a program to take the difference between adjoining pixels, and then use huff_enc to code the difference images.

   (c) Repeat (a) and (b) using adap_huff_enc and adap_huff_dec.

   Report the resulting file sizes for each of these experiments and comment on the differences.

3. Using the program huff_enc, code the Bookshelf1 and Sena images using the codebook generated by the Sinan image. Compare the results with the case where the codebook was generated by the image being compressed.

4. A source emits letters from an alphabet $\mathcal{A} = \{a_1, a_2, a_3, a_4, a_5\}$ with probabilities $P(a_1) = 0.15$, $P(a_2) = 0.04$, $P(a_3) = 0.26$, $P(a_4) = 0.05$, and $P(a_5) = 0.50$.

(a) Calculate the entropy of this source.

(b) Find a Huffman code for this source.

(c) Find the average length of the code in (b) and its redundancy.

5. For an alphabet $\mathcal{A} = \{a_1, a_2, a_3, a_4\}$ with probabilities $P(a_1) = 0.1$, $P(a_2) = 0.3$, $P(a_3) = 0.25$, and $P(a_4) = 0.35$, find a Huffman code

(a) using the first procedure outlined in this chapter, and

(b) using the minimum variance procedure.

Comment on the difference in the Huffman codes.

6. In many communication applications, it is desirable that the number of 1s and 0s transmitted over the channel are about the same. However, if we look at Huffman codes, many of them seem to have many more 1s than 0s or vice versa. Does this mean that Huffman coding will lead to inefficient channel usage? For the Huffman code obtained in Problem 4, find the probability that a 0 will be transmitted over the channel. What does this probability say about the question posed above?

7. For the source in Example 3.3.1, generate a ternary code by combining three letters in the first and second steps and two letters in the third step. Compare with the ternary code obtained in the example.

8. In Example 3.4.1 we have shown how the tree develops when the sequence $a\ a\ r\ d\ v$ is transmitted. Continue this example with the next letters in the sequence, $a\ r\ k$.

9. The Monte Carlo approach is often used for studying problems that are difficult to solve analytically. Let's use this approach to study the problem of buffering when using variable-length codes. We will simulate the situation in Example 3.2.1, and study the time to overflow and underflow as a function of the buffer size. In our program, we will need a random number generator, a set of seeds to initialize the random number generator, a counter B to simulate the buffer occupancy, a counter T to keep track of the time, and a value N, which is the size of the buffer. Input to the buffer is simulated by using the random number generator to select a letter from our alphabet. The counter B is then incremented by the length of the codeword for the letter. The output to the buffer is simulated by decrementing B by 2 except when T is divisible by 5. For values of T divisible by 5, decrement B by 3 instead of 2 (why?). Keep incrementing T, each time simulating an input and an output, until either $B \geq N$, corresponding to a buffer overflow, or $B < 0$, corresponding to a buffer underflow. When either of these events happens, record what happened and when, and restart the simulation with a new seed. Do this with at least 100 seeds.

Perform this simulation for a number of buffer sizes ($N = 100, 1000, 10,000$), and the two Huffman codes obtained for the source in Example 3.2.1. Describe your results in a report.

10. While the variance of lengths is an important consideration when choosing between two Huffman codes that have the same average lengths, it is not the only consideration. Another consideration is the ability to recover from errors in the channel. In this problem we will explore the effect of error on two equivalent Huffman codes.

(a) For the source and Huffman code of Example 3.2.1 (Table 3.5), encode the sequence

$$a_2\ a_1\ a_3\ a_2\ a_1\ a_2$$

Suppose there was an error in the channel and the first bit was received as a 0 instead of a 1. Decode the received sequence of bits. How many characters are received in error before the first correctly decoded character?

(b) Repeat using the code in Table 3.9.

(c) Repeat parts (a) and (b) with the error in the third bit.

11. (This problem was suggested by P.F. Swaszek.)

(a) For a binary source with probabilities $P(0) = 0.9$, $P(1) = 0.1$, design a Huffman code for the source obtained by blocking m bits together, $m = 1, 2, \ldots, 8$. Plot the average lengths versus m. Comment on your result.

(b) Repeat for $P(0) = 0.99$, $P(1) = 0.01$.

You can use the program huff_enc to generate the Huffman codes.

12. Encode the following sequence of 16 values using the Rice code with $J = 8$ and one split sample option.

$$32, 33, 35, 39, 37, 38, 39, 40, 40, 40, 40, 39, 40, 40, 41, 40$$

For prediction use the previous value in the sequence

$$\hat{y}_i = y_{i-1}$$

and assume a prediction of zero for the first element of the sequence.

13. For an alphabet $\mathcal{A} = \{a_1, a_2, a_3\}$ with probabilities $P(a_1) = 0.7$, $P(a_2) = 0.2$, $P(a_3) = 0.1$, design a 3-bit Tunstall code.

14. Write a program for encoding images using the Rice algorithm. Use eight options, including the fundamental sequence, five split sample options, and the two low-entropy options. Use $J = 16$. For prediction use either the pixel to the left or the pixel above. Encode the Sena image using your program. Compare your results with the results obtained by Huffman coding the differences between pixels.

4

Arithmetic Coding

4.1 Overview

n the previous chapter we saw one approach to generating variable-length codes. In this chapter we see another, increasingly popular, method of generating variable-length codes called *arithmetic coding*. Arithmetic coding is especially useful when dealing with sources with small alphabets, such as binary sources, and alphabets with highly skewed probabilities. It is also a very useful approach when, for various reasons, the modeling and coding aspects of lossless compression are to be kept separate. In this chapter, we look at the basic ideas behind arithmetic coding, study some of the properties of arithmetic codes, and describe an implementation. A variation of the arithmetic code is the coding method used in the Joint Bi-level Experts Group (JBIG) standard for encoding binary images. We describe the relevant portions of the standard and briefly compare arithmetic coding with Huffman coding.

4.2 Introduction

In the last chapter we studied the Huffman coding method, which guarantees a coding rate R within 1 bit of the entropy H. Recall that the coding rate is the average number of bits used to represent a symbol from a source and, for a given probability model, the entropy is the lowest rate at which the source can be coded. We can tighten this bound somewhat. It has been shown [80] that the Huffman algorithm will generate a code whose rate is within $p_{max} + 0.086$ of the entropy, where p_{max} is the probability of the most frequently occurring symbol. We noted in the last chapter that, in applications where the alphabet size is large, p_{max} is generally quite small, and the amount of deviation from the entropy, especially in terms of a percentage of the rate, is quite small. However, in cases where the alphabet is small and the probability of occurrence of the different letters is skewed, the value of p_{max} can be quite large and the Huffman code can become rather inefficient when compared to the entropy. One way to avoid this problem is to block more than one symbol together and generate an extended Huffman code. Unfortunately, this approach does not always work.

Example 4.2.1:

Consider a source that puts out independent, identically distributed (*iid*) letters from the alphabet $\mathcal{A} = \{a_1, a_2, a_3\}$ with the probability model $P(a_1) = 0.95$, $P(a_2) = 0.02$, and $P(a_3) = 0.03$. The entropy for this source is 0.335 bits/symbol. A Huffman code for this source is given in Table 4.1.

The average length for this code is 1.05 bits/symbol. The difference between the average code length and the entropy, or the redundancy, for this code is 0.715 bits/symbol, which is 213% of the entropy. This means that to code this sequence we would need more than twice the number of bits promised by the entropy.

Recall Example 3.2.4. Here also we can group the symbols in blocks of two. The extended alphabet, probability model, and code can be obtained as shown in Table 4.2. The average rate for the extended alphabet is 1.222 bits/symbol, which in terms of the original alphabet is 0.611 bits/symbol. As the entropy of the source is 0.335 bits/symbol, the additional rate over the entropy is still about 72% of the entropy! By continuing to block symbols together, we find that the redundancy drops to acceptable values when we block eight symbols together. The corresponding alphabet size for this level of blocking is 6561! A code of this size is impractical for a number of reasons. Storage of a code like this requires memory that may not be available for

TABLE 4.1   Huffman code for three-letter alphabet.

Letter	Codeword
a_1	0
a_2	11
a_3	10

TABLE 4.2   Huffman code for extended alphabet.

Letter	Probability	Code
$a_1 a_1$	0.9025	0
$a_1 a_2$	0.0190	111
$a_1 a_3$	0.0285	100
$a_2 a_1$	0.0190	1101
$a_2 a_2$	0.0004	110011
$a_2 a_3$	0.0006	110001
$a_3 a_1$	0.0285	101
$a_3 a_2$	0.0006	110010
$a_3 a_3$	0.0009	110000

many applications. While it may be possible to design reasonably efficient encoders, decoding a Huffman code of this size would be a highly inefficient and time-consuming procedure. Finally, if there were some perturbation in the statistics, and some of the assumed probabilities changed slightly, this would have a major impact on the efficiency of the code. ◆

We can see that it is more efficient to generate codewords for groups or sequences of symbols rather than generating a separate codeword for each symbol in a sequence. However, this approach becomes impractical when we try to obtain Huffman codes for long sequences of symbols. In order to find the Huffman codeword for a particular sequence of length m, we need codewords for all possible sequences of length m. This fact causes an exponential growth in the size of the codebook. We need a way of assigning codewords to *particular* sequences without having to generate codes for all sequences of that length. The arithmetic coding technique fulfills this requirement.

In arithmetic coding a unique identifier or tag is generated for the sequence to be encoded. This tag corresponds to a binary fraction, which becomes the binary code for the sequence. In practice the generation of the tag and the binary code are the same process. However, the arithmetic coding approach is easier to understand if we conceptually divide the approach into two phases. In the first phase a unique identifier or tag is generated for a given sequence of symbols. This tag is then given a unique binary code. A unique arithmetic code can be generated for a sequence of length m without the need for generating codewords for all sequences of length m. This is unlike the situation for Huffman codes. In order to generate a Huffman code for a sequence of length m, where the code is not a concatenation of the codewords for the individual symbols, we need to obtain the Huffman codes for all sequences of length m.

4.3 Coding a Sequence

In order to distinguish a sequence of symbols from another sequence of symbols we need to tag it with a unique identifier. One possible set of tags for representing sequences of symbols are the numbers in the unit interval $[0, 1)$. Because the number of numbers in the unit interval is infinite, it should be possible to assign a unique tag to each distinct sequence of symbols. In order to do this we need a function that will map sequences of symbols into the unit interval. A function that maps random variables, and sequences of random variables, into the unit interval is the cumulative distribution function (*cdf*) of the random variable associated with the source. This is the function we will use in developing the arithmetic code. (If you are not familiar with random variables and cumulative distribution functions, or need to refresh your memory, you may wish to look at Appendix A.)

The use of the cumulative distribution function to generate a binary code for a sequence has a rather interesting history. Shannon, in his original 1948 paper [209], mentioned an approach using the cumulative distribution function when describing what is now known as the Shannon-Fano code. Peter Elias, another member of Fano's first information theory class at MIT (this class also included Huffman), came up with a recursive implementation for this idea. However, he never published it, and we only know about it through a mention in a 1963 book on information theory by Abramson [2]. Abramson described this coding approach in a note to a chapter. In another book on information theory by Jelinek [120] in 1968, the idea of arithmetic coding is further developed, this time in an appendix, as an example of variable-length coding. Modern arithmetic coding owes its birth to the independent discoveries in 1976 of Pasco [174] and Rissanen [192] that the problem of finite precision could be resolved. Finally, several papers appeared that provided practical arithmetic coding algorithms, the most well known of which is the paper by Rissanen and Langdon [193].

Before we begin our development of the arithmetic code, we need to establish some notation. Recall that a random variable maps the outcomes, or sets of outcomes, of an experiment to values on the real number line. For example, in a coin-tossing experiment, the random variable could map a head to zero and a tail to one (or it could map a head to 2367.5 and a tail to -192). To use this technique, we need to map the source symbols or letters to numbers. For convenience, in the discussion in this chapter we will use the mapping

$$X(a_i) = i \qquad a_i \in \mathcal{A} \tag{4.1}$$

where $\mathcal{A} = \{a_1, a_2, \ldots, a_m\}$ is the alphabet for a discrete source and X is a random variable. This mapping means that given a probability model $\mathcal{P}$ for the source, we also have a probability density function for the random variable

$$P(X = i) = P(a_i)$$

and the cumulative density function can be defined as

$$F_X(i) = \sum_{k=1}^{i} P(X = k).$$

Notice that for each symbol a_i with a nonzero probability we have a distinct value of $F_X(i)$. We will use this fact in what follows to develop the arithmetic code. Our development may be more detailed than what you are looking for, at least on the first reading. If so, skip or skim Sections 4.3.1–4.4.1 and go directly to Section 4.4.2.

4.3.1 Generating a Tag

The procedure for generating the tag works by reducing the size of the interval in which the tag resides as more and more elements of the sequence are received.

We start out by first dividing the unit interval into subintervals of the form $[F_X(i-1), F_X(i))$, $i = 1, \ldots, m$. Because the minimum value of the *cdf* is zero and the maximum value is one, this exactly partitions the unit interval. We associate the subinterval $[F_X(i-1), F_X(i))$ with the symbol a_i. The appearance of the first symbol in the sequence restricts the interval containing the tag to one of these subintervals. Suppose the first symbol was a_k. Then the interval containing the tag value will be the subinterval $[F_X(k-1), F_X(k))$. This subinterval is now partitioned in exactly the same proportions as the original interval. That is, the jth interval corresponding to the symbol a_j is given by $[F_X(k-1) + F_X(j-1)/(F_X(k) - F_X(k-1))$, $F_X(k-1) + F_X(j)/(F_X(k) - F_X(k-1)))$. So if the second symbol in the sequence is a_j, then the interval containing the tag value becomes $[F_X(k-1) + F_X(j-1)/(F_X(k) - F_X(k-1))$, $F_X(k-1) + F_X(j)/(F_X(k) - F_X(k-1)))$. Each succeeding symbol causes the tag to be restricted to a subinterval that is further partitioned in the same proportions. This process can be more clearly understood through an example.

Example 4.3.1:

Consider a three-letter alphabet $\mathcal{A} = \{a_1, a_2, a_3\}$ with $P(a_1) = 0.7, P(a_2) = 0.1$, and $P(a_3) = 0.2$. Using the mapping of Equation (4.1), $F_X(1) = 0.7$, $F_X(2) = 0.8$, and $F_X(3) = 1$. This partitions the unit interval as shown in Figure 4.1.

The partition in which the tag resides depends on the first symbol of the sequence being encoded. For example, if the first symbol is a_1, the tag lies in the interval $[0.0, 0.7)$; if the first symbol is a_2, the tag lies in the interval $[0.7, 0.8)$; and if the first symbol is a_3, the tag lies in the interval $[0.8, 1.0)$. Once the interval containing the tag has been determined, the rest of the unit interval is discarded, and this restricted interval is again divided in the same proportions as the original interval. Suppose the first symbol was a_1. The tag would be contained in the subinterval $[0.0, 0.7)$. This subinterval is then subdivided in exactly the same proportions as the original interval, yielding the subintervals $[0.0, 0.49)$, $[0.49, 0.56)$, and $[0.56, 0.7)$. The first partition as before corresponds to the symbol a_1, the second partition corresponds to the symbol a_2, and the third partition $[0.56, 0.7)$ corresponds to the symbol a_3. Suppose the second symbol in the sequence is a_2. The tag value is then restricted to lie in the interval $[0.49, 0.56)$. We now partition this interval in the same proportion as the original interval to obtain the subintervals $[0.49, 0.539)$ corresponding to the symbol a_1, $[0.539, 0.546)$ corresponding to the symbol a_2, and $[0.546, 0.56)$ corresponding to the symbol a_3. If the third symbol is a_3, the tag will be restricted to the interval $[0.546, 0.56)$, which can then be subdivided further. This process is described graphically in Figure 4.1.

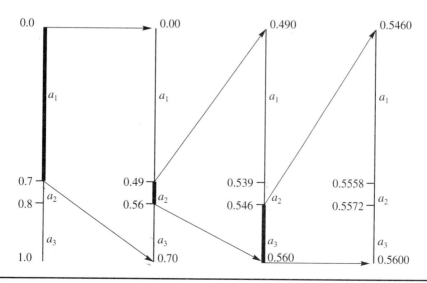

FIGURE 4.1   **Restricting the interval containing the tag for the input sequence $\{a_1, a_2, a_3, \ldots\}$.**

Notice that the appearance of each new symbol restricts the tag to a subinterval that is disjoint from any other subinterval that may have been generated using this process. For the sequence beginning with $\{a_1, a_2, a_3, \ldots\}$, by the time the third symbol a_3 is received, the tag has been restricted to the subinterval $[0.546, 0.56)$. If the third symbol had been a_1 instead of a_3, the tag would have resided in the subinterval $[0.49, 0.539)$, which is disjoint from the subinterval $[0.546, 0.56)$. Even if the two sequences are identical from this point on (one starting with a_1, a_2, a_3 and the other beginning with a_1, a_2, a_1), the tag interval for the two sequences will always be disjoint. $\blacklozenge$

As we can see, the interval in which the tag for a particular sequence resides is disjoint from all intervals in which the tag for any other sequence may reside. As such, any member of this interval can be used as a tag. One popular choice is the lower limit of the interval; another possibility is the midpoint of the interval. For the moment, let's use the midpoint of the interval as the tag.

In order to see how the tag generation procedure works mathematically, we start with sequences of length one. Suppose we have a source that puts out symbols from some alphabet $\mathcal{A} = \{a_1, a_2, \ldots, a_m\}$. We can map the symbols $\{a_i\}$ to real numbers $\{i\}$. Define $\bar{T}_X(a_i)$ as

$$\bar{T}_X(a_i) = \sum_{k=1}^{i-1} P(X = k) + \frac{1}{2}P(X = i) \tag{4.2}$$

$$= F_X(i - 1) + \frac{1}{2}P(X = i). \tag{4.3}$$

For each a_i, $\bar{T}_X(a_i)$ will have a unique value. This value can be used as a unique tag for a_i.

Example 4.3.2:

Consider a simple dice-throwing experiment with a fair die. The outcomes of a roll of the die can be mapped into the numbers $\{1, 2, \ldots, 6\}$. For a fair die

$$P(X = k) = \frac{1}{6} \qquad \text{for } k = 1, 2, \ldots, 6.$$

Therefore, using (4.3) we can find the tag for $X = 2$ as

$$\bar{T}_X(2) = P(X = 1) + \frac{1}{2}P(X = 2) = \frac{1}{6} + \frac{1}{12} = 0.25$$

and the tag for $X = 5$ as

$$\bar{T}_X(5) = \sum_{k=1}^{4} P(X = k) + \frac{1}{2}P(X = 5) = 0.75.$$

The tags for all other outcomes are shown in Table 4.3.

TABLE 4.3   Toss for outcomes in a dice-throwing experiment.

Outcome	Tag
1	$0.08\overline{33}$
3	$0.41\overline{66}$
4	$0.58\overline{33}$
6	$0.91\overline{66}$

◆

As we can see from the example above, giving a unique tag to a sequence of length one is an easy task. This approach can be extended to longer sequences by imposing an order on the sequences. We need an ordering on the sequences because we will assign a tag to a particular sequence $\mathbf{x}_i$ as

$$\bar{T}_{\mathbf{X}}^{(m)}(\mathbf{x}_i) = \sum_{\mathbf{y} < \mathbf{x}_i} P(\mathbf{y}) + \frac{1}{2}P(\mathbf{x}_i) \tag{4.4}$$

where $\mathbf{y} < \mathbf{x}$ means that $\mathbf{y}$ precedes $\mathbf{x}$ in the ordering, and the superscript denotes the length of the sequence.

An easy ordering to use is *lexicographic ordering*. In lexicographic ordering, the ordering of letters in an alphabet induces an ordering on the words constructed from this alphabet. The ordering of words in a dictionary is a good (maybe the original) example of lexicographic ordering. *Dictionary order* is sometimes used as a synonym for lexicographic order.

Example 4.3.3:

We can extend Example 4.3.2 so that the sequence consists of two rolls of a die. Using the ordering scheme described above, the outcomes (in order) would be 11 12 13 ... 66. The tags can then be generated using Equation (4.4). For example, the tag for the sequence 13 would be

$$\bar{T}_X(13) = P(\mathbf{x} = 11) + P(\mathbf{x} = 12) + 1/2P(\mathbf{x} = 13) \tag{4.5}$$

$$= 1/36 + 1/36 + 1/2(1/36) \tag{4.6}$$

$$= 5/72. \tag{4.7}$$

◆

Notice that to generate the tag for 13 we did not have to generate a tag for every other possible message. However, based on Equation (4.4) and Example 4.3.3, we need to know the probability of every sequence that is "less than" the sequence for which the tag is being generated. The requirement that the probability of all sequences of a given length be explicitly calculated can be as prohibitive as the requirement that we have codewords for all sequences of a given length. Fortunately, we shall see that to compute a tag for a given sequence of symbols, all we need is the probability of individual symbols, or the probability model.

Recall that, given our construction, the interval containing the tag value for a given sequence is disjoint from the intervals containing the tag values of all other sequences. This means that any value in this interval would be a unique identifier for x_i. Therefore, to fulfill our initial objective of uniquely identifying each sequence, it would be sufficient to compute the upper and lower limits of the interval containing the tag and select any value in that interval. The upper and lower limits can be computed recursively as shown in the following example.

Example 4.3.4:

We will use the alphabet of Example 4.3.2 and find the upper and lower limits of the interval containing the tag for the sequence 322. Assume that we are observing 3 2 2 in a sequential manner; that is, first we see 3, then 2, and then 2 again. After each observation we will compute the upper and lower limits of the interval containing the tag of the sequence observed to that point. We will denote the upper limit by $u^{(n)}$ and the lower limit by $l^{(n)}$, where n denotes the length of the sequence.

We first observe 3. Therefore,

$$u^{(1)} = F_X(3), \qquad l^{(1)} = F_X(2).$$

We then observe 2 and the sequence is $\mathbf{x} = 32$. Therefore,

$$u^{(2)} = F_X^{(2)}(32), \qquad l^{(2)} = F_X^{(2)}(31).$$

We can compute these values as follows:

$$\begin{aligned} F_X^{(2)}(32) = {} & P(\mathbf{x} = 11) + P(\mathbf{x} = 12) + \cdots + P(\mathbf{x} = 16) \\ & + P(\mathbf{x} = 21) + P(\mathbf{x} = 22) + \cdots + P(\mathbf{x} = 26) \\ & + P(\mathbf{x} = 31) + P(\mathbf{x} = 32). \end{aligned}$$

But,

$$\sum_{i=1}^{i=6} P(\mathbf{x} = ki) = \sum_{i=1}^{i=6} P(x_1 = k, x_2 = i) = P(x_1 = k)$$

where $\mathbf{x} = x_1 x_2$. Therefore,

$$\begin{aligned} F_X^{(2)}(32) &= P(x_1 = 1) + P(x_1 = 2) + P(\mathbf{x} = 31) + P(\mathbf{x} = 32) \\ &= F_X(2) + P(\mathbf{x} = 31) + P(\mathbf{x} = 32). \end{aligned}$$

However, assuming each roll of the dice is independent of the others,

$$P(\mathbf{x} = 31) = P(x_1 = 3)P(x_2 = 1)$$

and

$$P(\mathbf{x} = 32) = P(x_1 = 3)P(x_2 = 2).$$

Therefore,

$$P(\mathbf{x} = 31) + P(\mathbf{x} = 32) = P(x_1 = 3)(P(x_2 = 1) + P(x_2 = 2))$$
$$= P(x_1 = 3)F_X(2).$$

Noting that

$$P(x_1 = 3) = F_X(3) - F_X(2)$$

we can write

$$P(\mathbf{x} = 31) + P(\mathbf{x} = 32) = (F_X(3) - F_X(2))F_X(2)$$

and

$$F_X^{(2)}(32) = F_X(2) + (F_X(3) - F_X(2))F_X(2).$$

We can also write this as

$$u^{(2)} = l^{(1)} + (u^{(1)} - l^{(1)})F_X(2).$$

We can similarly show that

$$F_X^{(2)}(31) = F_X(2) + (F_X(3) - F_X(2))F_X(1)$$

or

$$l^{(2)} = l^{(1)} + (u^{(1)} - l^{(1)})F_X(1).$$

The third element of the observed sequence is 2, and the sequence is $\mathbf{x} = 322$. The upper and lower limits of the interval containing the tag for this sequence are

$$u^{(3)} = F_X^{(3)}(322), \qquad l^{(3)} = F_X^{(3)}(321).$$

Using the same approach as above we find that

$$F_X^{(3)}(322) = F_X^{(2)}(31) + (F_X^{(2)}(32) - F_X^{(2)}(31))F_X(2) \tag{4.8}$$
$$F_X^{(3)}(321) = F_X^{(2)}(31) + (F_X^{(2)}(32) - F_X^{(2)}(31))F_X(1)$$

or

$$u^{(3)} = l^{(2)} + (u^{(2)} - l^{(2)})F_X(2)$$
$$l^{(3)} = l^{(2)} + (u^{(2)} - l^{(2)})F_X(1). \qquad \blacklozenge$$

In general, we can show that for any sequence $\mathbf{x} = (x_1 x_2 \ldots x_n)$

$$l^{(n)} = l^{(n-1)} + (u^{(n-1)} - l^{(n-1)})F_X(x_n - 1) \tag{4.9}$$
$$u^{(n)} = l^{(n-1)} + (u^{(n-1)} - l^{(n-1)})F_X(x_n). \tag{4.10}$$

Notice that throughout this process we did not explicitly need to compute any joint probabilities.

If we are using the midpoint of the interval for the tag, then

$$\bar{T}_X(\mathbf{x}) = \frac{u^{(n)} + l^{(n)}}{2}.$$

Therefore, the tag for any sequence can be computed in a sequential fashion. The only information required by the tag generation procedure is the *cdf* of the source, which can be obtained directly from the probability model.

Example 4.3.5: Generating a tag

Consider the source in Example 3.2.3. Define the random variable $X(a_i) = i$. Suppose we wish to encode the sequence **1 3 2 1**. From the probability model we know that

$$F_X(k) = 0, \ k \leq 0, \quad F_X(1) = 0.8, \quad F_X(2) = 0.82, \quad F_X(3) = 1, \quad F_X(k) = 1, \ k > 3.$$

We can use Equations (4.9) and (4.10) sequentially to determine the lower and upper limits of the interval containing the tag. Initializing $u^{(0)}$ to 1, and $l^{(0)}$ to 0, the first element of the sequence **1** results in the following update:

$$l^{(1)} = 0 + (1 - 0)0 = 0$$
$$u^{(1)} = 0 + (1 - 0)(0.8) = 0.8.$$

That is, the tag is contained in the interval $[0, 0.8)$. The second element of the sequence is **3**. Using the update equations we get

$$l^{(2)} = 0 + (0.8 - 0)F_X(2) = 0.8 \times 0.82 = 0.656$$
$$u^{(2)} = 0 + (0.8 - 0)F_X(3) = 0.8 \times 1.0 = 0.8.$$

Therefore, the interval containing the tag for the sequence **1 3** is $[0.656, 0.8)$. The third element, **2**, results in the following update equations:

$$l^{(3)} = 0.656 + (0.8 - 0.656)F_X(1) = 0.656 + 0.144 \times 0.8 = 0.7712$$
$$u^{(3)} = 0.656 + (0.8 - 0.656)F_X(2) = 0.656 + 0.144 \times 0.82 = 0.77408$$

and the interval for the tag is $[0.7712, 0.77408)$. Continuing with the last element, the upper and lower limits of the interval containing the tag are

$$l^{(4)} = 0.7712 + (0.77408 - 0.7712)F_X(0) = 0.7712 + 0.00288 \times 0.0 = 0.7712$$
$$u^{(4)} = 0.7712 + (0.77408 - 0.1152)F_X(1) = 0.7712 + 0.00288 \times 0.8 = 0.773504$$

and the tag for the sequence **1 3 2 1** can be generated as

$$\bar{T}_X(1321) = \frac{0.7712 + 0.773504}{2} = 0.772352. \qquad \blacklozenge$$

Notice that each succeeding interval is contained in the preceding interval. If we examine the equations used to generate the intervals, we see that this will always be the case. This property will be used to decipher the tag. An undesirable consequence of this process is that the intervals get smaller and smaller and require higher precision as the sequence gets longer. To combat this problem, a rescaling strategy needs to be adopted. In Section 4.4.2, we will describe a simple rescaling approach that takes care of this problem.

4.3.2 Deciphering the Tag

We have spent a considerable amount of time showing how a sequence can be assigned a unique tag, given a minimal amount of information. However, the tag is useless unless we can also decipher it with minimal computational cost. Fortunately, deciphering the tag is as simple as generating it. We can see this most easily through an example.

Example 4.3.6: Deciphering a tag

Given the tag obtained in Example 4.3.5, let's try to obtain the sequence represented by the tag. We will try to mimic the encoder in order to do the decoding. The tag value is 0.772352. The interval containing this tag value is a subset of every interval obtained in the encoding process. Our decoding strategy will be to decode the elements in the sequence in such a way that the upper and lower limits $u^{(k)}$ and $l^{(k)}$ will always contain the tag value for each k. We start with $l^{(0)} = 0$ and $u^{(0)} = 1$. After decoding the first element of the sequence x_1, the upper and lower limits become

$$l^{(1)} = 0 + (1 - 0)F_X(x_1 - 1) = F_X(x_1 - 1)$$
$$u^{(1)} = 0 + (1 - 0)F_X(x_1) = F_X(x_1).$$

In other words, the interval containing the tag is $[F_X(x_1 - 1), F_X(x_1))$. We need to find the value of x_1 for which 0.772352 lies in the interval $[F_X(x_1 - 1), F_X(x_1))$. If we pick $x_1 = 1$, the interval is $[0, 0.8)$. If we pick $x_1 = 2$, the interval is $[0.8, 0.82)$, and if we pick $x_1 = 3$, the interval is $[0.82, 1.0)$. As 0.772352 lies in the interval $[0.0, 0.8]$, we choose $x_1 = 1$. We now repeat this procedure for the second element x_2, using the updated values of $l^{(1)}$ and $u^{(1)}$:

$$l^{(2)} = 0 + (0.8 - 0)F_X(x_2 - 1) = 0.8F_X(x_2 - 1)$$
$$u^{(2)} = 0 + (0.8 - 0)F_X(x_2) = 0.8F_X(x_2).$$

If we pick $x_2 = 1$, the updated interval is $[0, 0.64)$, which does not contain the tag. Therefore, x_2 cannot be 1. If we pick $x_2 = 2$, the updated interval is $[0.64, 0.656)$, which also does not contain the tag. If we pick $x_2 = 3$, the updated interval is $[0.656, 0.8)$, which does contain the tag value of 0.772352. Therefore, the second element in the sequence is 3. Knowing the second element of the sequence, we can update the values of $l^{(2)}$ and $u^{(2)}$ and find the element x_3, which will give us an interval containing the tag:

$$l^{(3)} = 0.656 + (0.8 - 0.656)F_X(x_3 - 1) = 0.656 + 0.144 \times F_X(x_3 - 1)$$
$$u^{(3)} = 0.656 + (0.8 - 0.656)F_X(x_3) = 0.656 + 0.144 \times F_X(x_3).$$

However, the expressions for $l^{(3)}$ and $u^{(3)}$ are cumbersome in this form. To make the comparisons more easily, we could subtract the value of $l^{(2)}$ from both the limits and the tag. That is, we find the value of x_3 for which the interval $[0.144 \times F_X(x_3 - 1), 0.144 \times F_X(x_3))$ contains $0.772352 - 0.656 = 0.116352$. Or, we could make this even simpler and divide the residual tag value of 0.116352 by 0.144 to get 0.808, and find the value of x_3 for which 0.808 falls in the interval $[F_X(x_3 - 1), F_X(x_3))$. We can see that the only value of x_3 for which this is possible is 2. Substituting 2 for x_3 in the update equations, we can update the values of $l^{(3)}$ and $u^{(3)}$. We can now find the element x_4 by computing the upper and lower limits as

$$l^{(4)} = 0.7712 + (0.77408 - 0.7712)F_X(x_4 - 1) = 0.7712 + 0.00288 \times F_X(x_4 - 1)$$
$$u^{(4)} = 0.7712 + (0.77408 - 0.1152)F_X(x_4) = 0.7712 + 0.00288 \times F_X(x_4).$$

Again we can subtract $l^{(3)}$ from the tag to get $0.772352 - 0.7712 = 0.001152$ and find the value of x_4 for which the interval $[0.00288 \times F_X(x_4 - 1), 0.00288 \times F_X(x_4))$ contains 0.001152.

To make the comparisons simpler, we can divide the residual value of the tag by 0.00288 to get 0.4, and find the value of x_4 for which 0.4 is contained in $[F_X(x_4 - 1), F_X(x_4))$. We can see that the value is $x_4 = 1$, and we have decoded the entire sequence. Note that we knew the length of the sequence beforehand and, therefore, we knew when to stop.   ◆

From the example above, we can deduce an algorithm that can decipher the tag.

1. Initialize $l^{(0)} = 0$ and $u^{(0)} = 1$.

2. For each k find $t^* = (tag - l^{(k-1)})/(u^{(k-1)} - l^{(k-1)})$.

3. Find the value of x_k for which $F_X(x_k - 1) \le t^* < F_X(x_k)$.

4. Update $u^{(k)}$ and $l^{(k)}$.

5. Continue until the entire sequence has been decoded.

There are two ways to know when the entire sequence has been decoded. The decoder may know the length of the sequence, in which case the deciphering process is stopped when that many symbols have been obtained. The second way to know if the entire sequence has been decoded is that a particular symbol is denoted as an end-of-transmission symbol. The decoding of this symbol would bring the decoding process to a close.

4.4   Generating a Binary Code

Using the algorithm described in the previous section, we can obtain a tag for a given sequence **x**. However, the *binary code* for the sequence is what we really want to know. We want to find a binary code that will represent the sequence **x** in a unique and efficient manner.

   We have said that the tag forms a unique representation for the sequence. This means that the binary representation of the tag forms a unique binary code for the sequence. However, we have placed no restrictions on what values in the unit interval the tag can take. The binary representation of some of these values would be infinitely long, in which case, although the code is unique, it may not be efficient. To make the code efficient, the binary representation has to be truncated. But if we truncate the representation, is the resulting code still unique? Finally, is the resulting code efficient? How far or how close is the average number of bits per symbol from the entropy? We will examine all these questions in the next section.

   Even if we show the code to be unique and efficient, the method described to this point is highly impractical. In Section 4.4.2, we will describe a more practical algorithm for generating the arithmetic code for a sequence. We will give an integer implementation of this algorithm in Section 4.4.3.

4.4.1   Uniqueness and Efficiency of the Arithmetic Code

$\bar{T}_X(x)$ is a number in the interval $[0, 1)$. A binary code for $\bar{T}_X(x)$ can be obtained by taking the binary representation of this number and truncating it to $l(x) = \lceil \log \frac{1}{P(x)} \rceil + 1$ bits.

Example 4.4.1:

Consider a source $\mathcal{A}$ that generates letters from an alphabet of size four,

$$\mathcal{A} = \{a_1, a_2, a_3, a_4\}$$

with probabilities

$$P(a_1) = \frac{1}{2}, \quad P(a_2) = \frac{1}{4}, \quad P(a_3) = \frac{1}{8}, \quad P(a_4) = \frac{1}{8}.$$

A binary code for this source can be generated as shown in Table 4.4. The quantity $\bar{T}_x$ is obtained using Equation (4.3). The binary representation of $\bar{T}_x$ is truncated to $\lceil \log \frac{1}{P(x)} \rceil + 1$ bits to obtain the binary code.

TABLE 4.4   A binary code for a four-letter alphabet.

Symbol	F_X	$\bar{T}_X$	In Binary	$\lceil \log \frac{1}{P(x)} \rceil + 1$	Code
1	.5	.25	.010	2	01
2	.75	.625	.101	3	101
3	.875	.8125	.1101	4	1101
4	1.0	.9375	.1111	4	1111

♦

We will show that a code obtained in this fashion is a uniquely decodable code. We first show that this code is unique, and then we will show that it is uniquely decodable.

Recall that while we have been using $\bar{T}_X(x)$ as the tag for a sequence $\mathbf{x}$, any number in the interval $[F_X(\mathbf{x} - 1), F_X(\mathbf{x}))$ would be a unique identifier. Therefore, to show that the code $\lfloor \bar{T}_X(\mathbf{x}) \rfloor_{l(\mathbf{x})}$ is unique, all we need to do is show that it is contained in the interval $[F_X(\mathbf{x} - 1), F_X(\mathbf{x}))$. Because we are truncating the binary representation of $\bar{T}_X(\mathbf{x})$ to obtain $\lfloor \bar{T}_X(\mathbf{x}) \rfloor_{l(\mathbf{x})}$, $\lfloor \bar{T}_X(\mathbf{x}) \rfloor_{l(\mathbf{x})}$ is less than or equal to $\bar{T}_X(\mathbf{x})$. More specifically,

$$0 \leq \bar{T}_X(\mathbf{x}) - \lfloor \bar{T}_X(\mathbf{x}) \rfloor_{l(\mathbf{x})} < \frac{1}{2^{l(\mathbf{x})}}. \tag{4.11}$$

As $\bar{T}_X(\mathbf{x})$ is strictly less than $F_X(\mathbf{x})$,

$$\lfloor \bar{T}_X(\mathbf{x}) \rfloor_{l(\mathbf{x})} < F_X(\mathbf{x}).$$

To show that $\lfloor \bar{T}_X(\mathbf{x}) \rfloor_{l(\mathbf{x})} \geq F_X(\mathbf{x} - 1)$, note that

$$\frac{1}{2^{l(\mathbf{x})}} = \frac{1}{2^{\lceil \log \frac{1}{P(x)} \rceil + 1}}$$

$$\leq \frac{1}{2^{\log \frac{1}{P(x)} + 1}}$$

$$= \frac{1}{2 \frac{1}{P(x)}}$$

$$= \frac{P(\mathbf{x})}{2}.$$

From (4.3) we have

$$\frac{P(\mathbf{x})}{2} = \bar{T}_X(\mathbf{x}) - F_X(\mathbf{x} - 1).$$

Therefore,

$$\bar{T}_X(\mathbf{x}) - F_X(\mathbf{x} - 1) > \frac{1}{2^{l(\mathbf{x})}}. \tag{4.12}$$

Combining (4.11) and (4.12), we have

$$\lfloor \bar{T}_X(\mathbf{x}) \rfloor_{l(\mathbf{x})} > F_X(\mathbf{x} - 1). \tag{4.13}$$

Therefore, the code $\lfloor \bar{T}_X(\mathbf{x}) \rfloor_{l(\mathbf{x})}$ is a unique representation of $\bar{T}_X(\mathbf{x})$.

To show that this code is uniquely decodable, we will show that the code is a prefix code; that is, no codeword is a prefix of another codeword. Because a prefix code is always uniquely decodable, by showing that an arithmetic code is a prefix code, we automatically show that it is uniquely decodable. Given a number a in the interval $[0, 1)$ with an n-bit binary representation $[b_1 b_2 \ldots b_n]$, for any other number b to have a binary representation with $[b_1 b_2 \ldots b_n]$ as the prefix, b has to lie in the interval $[a, a + \frac{1}{2^n})$. (See Problem 1.)

If $\mathbf{x}$ and $\mathbf{y}$ are two distinct sequences, we know that $\lfloor \bar{T}_X(\mathbf{x}) \rfloor_{l(\mathbf{x})}$ and $\lfloor \bar{T}_X(\mathbf{y}) \rfloor_{l(\mathbf{y})}$ lie in two *disjoint* intervals, $[F_X(\mathbf{x} - 1), F_X(\mathbf{x}))$ and $[F_X(\mathbf{y} - 1), F_X(\mathbf{y}))$. Therefore, if we can show that for any sequence $\mathbf{x}$, the interval $[\lfloor \bar{T}_X(\mathbf{x}) \rfloor_{l(\mathbf{x})}, \lfloor \bar{T}_X(\mathbf{x}) \rfloor_{l(\mathbf{x})} + \frac{1}{2^{l(\mathbf{x})}})$ lies entirely within the interval $[F_X(\mathbf{x} - 1), F_X(\mathbf{x}))$, this will mean that the code for one sequence cannot be the prefix for the code for another sequence.

We have already shown that $\lfloor \bar{T}_X(\mathbf{x}) \rfloor_{l(\mathbf{x})} > F_X(\mathbf{x} - 1)$. Therefore, all we need to do is show that

$$F_X(\mathbf{x}) - \lfloor \bar{T}_X(\mathbf{x}) \rfloor_{l(\mathbf{x})} > \frac{1}{2^{l(\mathbf{x})}}.$$

This is true because

$$F_X(\mathbf{x}) - \lfloor \bar{T}_X(\mathbf{x}) \rfloor_{l(\mathbf{x})} > F_X(\mathbf{x}) - \bar{T}_X(\mathbf{x})$$
$$= \frac{P(\mathbf{x})}{2}$$
$$> \frac{1}{2^{l(\mathbf{x})}}.$$

This code is prefix free, and by taking the binary representation of $\bar{T}_X(\mathbf{x})$ and truncating it to $l(x) = \lceil \log \frac{1}{P(x)} \rceil + 1$ bits, we obtain a uniquely decodable code.

Although the code is uniquely decodable, how efficient is it? We have shown that the number of bits $l(\mathbf{x})$ required to represent $F_X(\mathbf{x})$ with enough accuracy such that the code for different values of $\mathbf{x}$ are distinct is

$$l(\mathbf{x}) = \left\lceil \log \frac{1}{P(\mathbf{x})} \right\rceil + 1.$$

Remember that $l(\mathbf{x})$ is the number of bits required to encode the *entire* sequence $\mathbf{x}$. So, the average length of an arithmetic code for a sequence of length m is given by

$$l_{A^m} = \sum P(\mathbf{x}) l(\mathbf{x}) \tag{4.14}$$

$$= \sum P(\mathbf{x}) \left[\left\lceil \log \frac{1}{P(\mathbf{x})} \right\rceil + 1 \right] \tag{4.15}$$

$$\leq \sum P(\mathbf{x}) \left[\log \frac{1}{P(\mathbf{x})} + 1 + 1 \right] \tag{4.16}$$

$$= - \sum P(\mathbf{x}) \log P(\mathbf{x}) + 2 \sum P(\mathbf{x}) \tag{4.17}$$

$$= H(X^m) + 2. \tag{4.18}$$

Given that the average length is always greater than the entropy, the bounds on $l_{A^{(m)}}$ are

$$H(X^{(m)}) \leq l_{A^{(m)}} \leq H(X^{(m)}) + 2.$$

The length per symbol, l_A, or rate of the arithmetic code is $\frac{l_{A^{(m)}}}{m}$. Therefore, the bounds on l_A are

$$\frac{H(X^{(m)})}{m} \leq l_A \leq \frac{H(X^{(m)})}{m} + \frac{2}{m}. \tag{4.19}$$

We have shown in Chapter 3 that for *iid* sources

$$H(X^{(m)}) = mH(X). \tag{4.20}$$

Therefore,

$$H(X) \leq l_A \leq H(X) + \frac{2}{m}. \tag{4.21}$$

By increasing the length of the sequence, we can guarantee a rate as close to the entropy as we desire.

4.4.2 Algorithm Implementation

In Section 4.3.1 we developed a recursive algorithm for the boundaries of the interval containing the tag for the sequence being encoded as

$$l^{(n)} = l^{(n-1)} + (u^{(n-1)} - l^{(n-1)})F_X(x_n - 1) \tag{4.22}$$

$$u^{(n)} = l^{(n-1)} + (u^{(n-1)} - l^{(n-1)})F_X(x_n) \tag{4.23}$$

where x_n is the value of the random variable corresponding to the nth observed symbol, $l^{(n)}$ is the lower limit of the tag interval at the nth iteration, and $u^{(n)}$ is the upper limit of the tag interval at the nth iteration.

Before we can implement this algorithm, there is one major problem we have to resolve. Recall that the rationale for using numbers in the interval $[0, 1)$ as a tag was that there are an infinite number of numbers in this interval. However, in practice the number of numbers that can be uniquely represented on a machine is limited by the maximum number of digits (or bits) we can use for representing the number. Consider the values of $l^{(n)}$ and $u^{(n)}$ in Example 4.3.5. As n gets larger, these values come closer and closer together. This means that in order to represent all the subintervals uniquely we need increasing precision as the length of the sequence increases. In a system with finite precision, the two values are bound to converge, and we will lose all information about the sequence from the point at which the two values converged. To avoid this situation, we need to rescale the interval. However, we have to do it in a way that will preserve the information that is being transmitted. We would also like to perform the encoding *incrementally*—that is, to transmit portions of the code as the sequence is being observed, rather than wait until the entire sequence has been observed before transmitting the first bit. The algorithm we describe in this section takes care of the problems of synchronized rescaling and incremental encoding.

As the interval becomes narrower, we have three possibilities:

1. The interval is entirely confined to the lower half of the unit interval $[0, 0.5)$.

2. The interval is entirely confined to the upper half of the unit interval $[0.5, 1.0)$.

3. The interval straddles the midpoint of the unit interval.

We will look at the third case a little later in this section. First, let us examine the first two cases. Once the interval is confined to either the upper or lower half of the unit interval, it is forever confined to that half of the unit interval. The most significant bit of the binary representation of all numbers in the interval $[0, 0.5)$ is 0, and the most significant bit of the binary representation of all numbers in the interval $[0.5, 1]$ is 1. Therefore, once the interval gets restricted to either the upper or lower half of the unit interval, the most significant bit of the tag is fully determined. Therefore, without waiting to see what the rest of the sequence looks like, we can indicate to the decoder whether the tag is confined to the upper or lower half of the unit interval by sending a 1 for the upper half and a 0 for the lower half. The bit that we send is also the first bit of the tag.

Once the encoder and decoder know which half contains the tag, we can ignore the half of the unit interval not containing the tag and concentrate on the half containing the tag. As our arithmetic is of finite precision, we can do this best by mapping the half interval containing the tag to the full $[0, 1)$ interval. The mappings required are

$$E_1 : [0, 0.5) \rightarrow [0, 1); \qquad E_1(x) = 2x \qquad\qquad (4.24)$$
$$E_2 : [0.5, 1) \rightarrow [0, 1); \qquad E_2(x) = 2(x - 0.5). \qquad\qquad (4.25)$$

As soon as we perform either of these mappings, we lose all information about the most significant bit. However, this should not matter because we have already sent that bit to the decoder. We can now continue with this process, generating another bit of the tag every time the tag interval is restricted to either half of the unit interval. This process of generating the bits of the tag without waiting to see the entire sequence is called incremental encoding.

Example 4.4.2: Tag generation with scaling

Let's revisit Example 4.3.5. Recall that we wish to encode the sequence **1 3 2 1**. The probability model for the source is $P(a_1) = 0.8$, $P(a_2) = 0.02$, $P(a_3) = 0.18$. Initializing $u^{(0)}$ to 1, and $l^{(0)}$ to 0, the first element of the sequence, **1**, results in the following update:

$$l^{(1)} = 0 + (1 - 0)0 = 0$$
$$u^{(1)} = 0 + (1 - 0)(0.8) = 0.8.$$

The interval $[0, 0.8)$ is not confined to either the upper or lower half of the unit interval, so we proceed.

The second element of the sequence is **3**. This results in the update

$$l^{(2)} = 0 + (0.8 - 0)F_X(2) = 0.8 \times 0.82 = 0.656$$
$$u^{(2)} = 0 + (0.8 - 0)F_X(3) = 0.8 \times 1.0 = 0.8.$$

The interval $[0.656, 0.8)$ is contained entirely in the upper half of the unit interval, so we send the binary code 1 and rescale:

$$l^{(2)} = 2 \times (0.656 - 0.5) = 0.312$$
$$u^{(2)} = 2 \times (0.8 - 0.5) = 0.6.$$

The third element, **2**, results in the following update equations:

$$l^{(3)} = 0.312 + (0.6 - 0.312)F_X(1) = 0.312 + 0.288 \times 0.8 = 0.5424$$
$$u^{(3)} = 0.312 + (0.8 - 0.312)F_X(2) = 0.312 + 0.288 \times 0.82 - 0.54816.$$

The interval for the tag is $[0.5424, 0.54816)$, which is contained entirely in the upper half of the unit interval. We transmit a 1 and go through another rescaling:

$$l^{(3)} = 2 \times (0.5424 - 0.5) = 0.0848$$
$$u^{(3)} = 2 \times (0.54816 - 0.5) = 0.09632.$$

This interval is contained entirely in the lower half of the unit interval, so we send a 0 and use the E_1 mapping to rescale:

$$l^{(3)} = 2 \times (0.0848) = 0.1696$$
$$u^{(3)} = 2 \times (0.09632) = 0.19264.$$

The interval is still contained entirely in the lower half of the unit interval, so we send another 0 and go through another rescaling:

$$l^{(3)} = 2 \times (0.1696) = 0.3392$$
$$u^{(3)} = 2 \times (0.19264) = 0.38528.$$

Because the interval containing the tag remains in the lower half of the unit interval, we send another 0 and rescale one more time:

$$l^{(3)} = 2 \times 0.3392 = 0.6784$$
$$u^{(3)} = 2 \times 0.38528 = 0.77056.$$

Now the interval containing the tag is contained entirely in the upper half of the unit interval. Therefore, we transmit a 1 and rescale using the E_2 mapping:

$$l^{(3)} = 2 \times (0.6784 - 0.5) = 0.3568$$
$$u^{(3)} = 2 \times (0.77056 - 0.5) = 0.54112.$$

At each stage we are transmitting the most significant bit that is the same in both the upper and lower limit of the tag interval. If the most significant bits in the upper and lower limit are the same, then the value of this bit will be identical to the most significant bit of the tag. Therefore, by sending the most significant bits of the upper and lower endpoint of the tag whenever they are identical, we are actually sending the binary representation of the tag. The rescaling operations can be viewed as left shifts, which make the second most significant bit the most significant bit.

Continuing with the last element, the upper and lower limits of the interval containing the tag are

$$l^{(4)} = 0.3568 + (0.54112 - 0.3568)F_X(0) = 0.3568 + 0.18422 \times 0.0 = 0.3568$$
$$u^{(4)} = 0.3568 + (0.54112 - 0.3568)F_X(1) = 0.3568 + 0.18422 \times 0.8 = 0.504256.$$

At this point, if we wished to stop encoding, all we need to do is inform the receiver of the final status of the tag value. We can do so by sending the binary representation of any value in the final tag interval. Generally, this value is taken to be $l^{(n)}$. In this particular example, it is convenient to use the value of 0.5. The binary representation of 0.5 is .10 . . . . Thus, we would transmit a 1 followed by as many 0s as required by the word length of the implementation being used.   ◆

Notice that the tag interval size at this stage is approximately 64 times the size it was when we were using the unmodified algorithm. Therefore, this technique solves the finite precision problem. As we shall soon see, the bits that we have been sending with each mapping constitute the tag itself, which satisfies our desire for incremental encoding. The binary sequence generated during the encoding process in the previous example is 1100011. We could simply treat this as the binary expansion of the tag. A binary number .1100011 corresponds to the decimal number 0.7734375. Looking back to Example 4.3.5, notice that this number lies within the final tag interval. Therefore, we could use this to decode the sequence.

However, we would like to do incremental decoding as well as incremental encoding. This raises three questions:

1. How do we start decoding?

2. How do we continue decoding?

3. How do we stop decoding?

The second question is the easiest to answer. Once we have started decoding, all we have to do is mimic the encoder algorithm. That is, once we have started decoding, we know how to continue decoding. To begin the decoding process, we need to have enough information to decode the first symbol unambiguously. In order to guarantee unambiguous decoding, the number of bits received should point to an interval smaller than the smallest tag interval. The number of bits needed for this can only be determined when we have a finite word length. Therefore, we defer discussion of this to a later section.

Example 4.4.3:

Let's decode the message generated in Example 4.4.2. We will use a word length of 6 bits. As in the encoder, we start with initializing $u^{(0)}$ to 1, and $l^{(0)}$ to 0. The sequence of received bits is $110001100\ldots0$. The first 6 bits correspond to a tag value of 0.765625, which means that the first element of the sequence is **1**, resulting in the following update:

$$l^{(1)} = 0 + (1 - 0)0 = 0$$
$$u^{(1)} = 0 + (1 - 0)(0.8) = 0.8.$$

The interval $[0, 0.8)$ is not confined to either the upper or lower half of the unit interval, so we proceed. The tag 0.765625 lies in the top 18% of the interval $[0, 0.8)$; therefore, the second element of the sequence is **3**. Updating the tag interval we get

$$l^{(2)} = 0 + (0.8 - 0)F_X(2) = 0.8 \times 0.82 = 0.656$$
$$u^{(2)} = 0 + (0.8 - 0)F_X(3) = 0.8 \times 1.0 = 0.8.$$

The interval $[0.656, 0.8)$ is contained entirely in the upper half of the unit interval. At the encoder, we sent the bit 1 and rescaled. At the decoder, we will shift 1 out of the receive buffer and move the next bit in to make up the 6 bits in the tag. We will also update the tag interval, resulting in

$$l^{(2)} = 2 \times (0.656 - 0.5) = 0.312$$
$$u^{(2)} = 2 \times (0.8 - 0.5) = 0.6$$

while shifting a bit to give us a tag of 0.546875. When we compare this value with the tag interval, we can see that this value lies in the 80–82% range of the tag interval, so we decode the next element of the sequence as **2**. We can then update the equations for the tag interval as

$$l^{(3)} = 0.312 + (0.6 - 0.312)F_X(1) = 0.312 + 0.288 \times 0.8 = 0.5424$$
$$u^{(3)} = 0.312 + (0.8 - 0.312)F_X(2) = 0.312 + 0.288 \times 0.82 = 0.54816.$$

As the tag interval is now contained entirely in the upper half of the unit interval, we rescale using E_2 to obtain

$$l^{(3)} = 2 \times (0.5424 - 0.5) = 0.0848$$
$$u^{(3)} = 2 \times (0.54816 - 0.5) = 0.09632.$$

We also shift out a bit from the tag and shift in the next bit. The tag is now 000110. The interval is contained entirely in the lower half of the unit interval. Therefore, we apply E_1 and shift another bit. The lower and upper limits of the tag interval become

$$l^{(3)} = 2 \times (0.0848) = 0.1696$$
$$u^{(3)} = 2 \times (0.09632) = 0.19264$$

and the tag becomes 001100. The interval is still contained entirely in the lower half of the unit interval, so we shift out another 0 to get a tag of 011000 and go through another rescaling:

$$l^{(3)} = 2 \times (0.1696) = 0.3392$$
$$u^{(3)} = 2 \times (0.19264) = 0.38528.$$

Because the interval containing the tag remains in the lower half of the unit interval, we shift out another 0 from the tag to get 110000 and rescale one more time:

$$l^{(3)} = 2 \times 0.3392 = 0.6784$$
$$u^{(3)} = 2 \times 0.38528 = 0.77056.$$

Now the interval containing the tag is contained entirely in the upper half of the unit interval. Therefore, we shift out a 1 from the tag and rescale using the E_2 mapping:

$$l^{(3)} = 2 \times (0.6784 - 0.5) = 0.3568$$
$$u^{(3)} = 2 \times (0.77056 - 0.5) = 0.54112.$$

Now we compare the tag value to the the tag interval to decode our final element. The tag is 100000, which corresponds to 0.5. This value lies in the first 80% of the interval, so we decode this element as **1**.   ◆

If the tag interval is entirely contained in the upper or lower half of the unit interval, the scaling procedure described will prevent the interval from continually shrinking. Now we consider the case where the diminishing tag interval straddles the midpoint of the unit interval. As our trigger for rescaling, we check to see if the tag interval is contained in the interval $[0.25, 0.75)$. This will happen when $l^{(n)}$ is greater than 0.25 and $u^{(n)}$ is less than 0.75. When this happens, we double the tag interval using the following mapping:

$$E_3 : [0.25, 0.75) \to [0, 1); \qquad E_3(x) = 2(x - 0.25). \qquad \text{(4.26)}$$

We have used a 1 to transmit information about an E_2 mapping, and a 0 to transmit information about an E_1 mapping. How do we transfer information about an E_3 mapping to the decoder? We use a somewhat different strategy in this case. At the time of the E_3 mapping, we do not send any information to the decoder; instead, we simply record the fact that we have used the E_3 mapping at the encoder. Suppose that after this, the tag interval gets confined to the upper half of the unit interval. At this point we would use an E_2 mapping and send a 1 to the receiver. Note that the tag interval at this stage is at least twice what it would have been if we had not used the E_3 mapping. Furthermore, the upper limit of the tag interval would have been less than 0.75. Therefore, if the E_3 mapping had not taken place right before the E_2 mapping, the tag interval would have been contained entirely in the lower half of the unit interval. At this point we would have used an E_1 mapping and transmitted a 0 to the receiver. In fact, the effect of the earlier E_3 mapping can be mimicked at the decoder by following the E_2 mapping with an E_1 mapping. At the encoder, right after we send a 1 to announce the E_2 mapping, we send a 0 to help the decoder track the changes in the tag interval at the decoder. If the first rescaling after the E_3 mapping happens to be an E_1 mapping, we do exactly the opposite. That is, we follow the 0 announcing an E_1 mapping with a 1 to mimic the effect of the E_3 mapping at the encoder.

What happens if we have to go through a series of E_3 mappings at the encoder? We simply keep track of the number of E_3 mappings and then send that many bits of the opposite variety after the first E_1 or E_2 mapping. If we went through three E_3 mappings at the encoder, followed by an E_2 mapping, we would transmit a 1 followed by three 0s. On the other hand, if we went through an E_1 mapping after the E_3 mappings, we would transmit a 0 followed by three 1s. Since the decoder mimics the encoder, the E_3 mappings are also applied at the decoder when the tag interval is contained in the interval $[0.25, 0.75)$.

4.4.3 Integer Implementation

We have described a floating-point implementation of arithmetic coding. Let us now repeat the procedure using integer arithmetic and generate the binary code in the process.

Encoder Implementation

The first thing we have to do is decide on the word length to be used. Given a word length of m, we map the important values in the $[0, 1)$ interval to the range of 2^m binary words. The point 0 gets mapped to

$$\overbrace{00\ldots0}^{m \text{ times}},$$

1 gets mapped to

$$\overbrace{11\ldots1}^{m \text{ times}}.$$

The value of 0.5 gets mapped to

$$1\overbrace{00\ldots0}^{m-1 \text{ times}}.$$

The update equations remain almost the same as Equations (4.9) and (4.10). As we are going to do integer arithmetic, we need to replace $F_X(x)$ in these equations.

Define n_j as the number of times the symbol j occurs in a sequence of length *Total Count*. Then $F_X(k)$ can be estimated by

$$F_X(k) = \frac{\sum_{i=1}^{k} n_i}{Total\ Count}. \tag{4.27}$$

If we now define

$$Cum\_Count(k) = \sum_{i=1}^{k} n_i$$

we can write Equations (4.9) and (4.10) as

$$l^{(n)} = l^{(n-1)} + \left\lfloor \frac{(u^{(n-1)} - l^{(n-1)} + 1) \times Cum\_Count(x_n - 1)}{Total\ Count} \right\rfloor \tag{4.28}$$

$$u^{(n)} = l^{(n-1)} + \left\lfloor \frac{(u^{(n-1)} - l^{(n-1)} + 1) \times Cum\_Count(x_n)}{Total\ Count} \right\rfloor - 1 \qquad (4.29)$$

where x_n is the nth symbol to be encoded, $\lfloor x \rfloor$ is the largest integer less than or equal to x, and where the addition and subtraction of one is to handle the effects of the integer arithmetic.

Because of the way we mapped the endpoints and the halfway points of the unit interval, when both $l^{(n)}$ and $u^{(n)}$ are in either the upper half or lower half of the interval, the leading bit of $u^{(n)}$ and $l^{(n)}$ will be the same. If the leading or most significant bit (MSB) is 1, then the tag interval is contained entirely in the upper half of the $[00\ldots0, 11\ldots1]$ interval. If the MSB is 0, then the tag interval is contained entirely in the lower half. Applying the E_1 and E_2 mappings is a simple matter. All we do is shift out the MSB and then shift in a 1 into the integer code for $u^{(n)}$ and a 0 into the code for $l^{(n)}$. For example, suppose m was 6, $u^{(n)}$ was 54, and $l^{(n)}$ was 33. The binary representations of $u^{(n)}$ and $l^{(n)}$ are 110110 and 100001, respectively. Notice that the MSB for both endpoints is 1. Following the procedure above, we would shift out (and transmit or store) the 1, and shift in 1 for $u^{(n)}$ and 0 for $l^{(n)}$, obtaining the new value for $u^{(n)}$ as 101101, or 45, and a new value for $l^{(n)}$ as 000010, or 2. This is equivalent to performing the E_2 mapping. We can see how the E_1 mapping would also be performed using the same operation.

To see if the E_3 mapping needs to be performed, we monitor the second most significant bit of $u^{(n)}$ and $l^{(n)}$. When the second most significant bit of $u^{(n)}$ is 0 and the second most significant bit of $l^{(n)}$ is 1, this means that the tag interval lies in the middle half of the $[00\ldots0, 11\ldots1]$ interval. To implement the E_3 mapping, we complement the second most significant bit in $u^{(n)}$ and $l^{(n)}$, and shift left, shifting in a 1 in $u^{(n)}$ and a 0 in $l^{(n)}$. We also keep track of the number of E_3 mappings in Scale3.

We can summarize the encoding algorithm using the following pseudocode:

Initialize l and u.
Get symbol.

$$l \longleftarrow l + \left\lfloor \frac{(u - l + 1) \times Cum\_Count(x - 1)}{Total Count} \right\rfloor$$

$$u \longleftarrow l + \left\lfloor \frac{(u - l + 1) \times Cum\_Count(x)}{Total Count} \right\rfloor - 1$$

while(MSB of u and l are both equal to b or E_3 condition holds)
if(MSB of u and l are both equal to b)

```
{
send b
shift l to the left by 1 bit and shift 0 into LSB
shift u to the left by 1 bit and shift 1 into LSB
while(Scale3 > 0)
        {
        send complement of b
        decrement Scale3
        }
}
```

if(E_3 condition holds)

{

shift l to the left by 1 bit and shift 0 into LSB

shift u to the left by 1 bit and shift 1 into LSB

complement (new) MSB of l and u

increment Scale3

}

To see how all this functions together, let's look at an example.

Example 4.4.4:

We will encode the sequence **1 3 2 1** with parameters shown in Table 4.5. First we need to select the word length m. Note that $Cum\_Count(1)$ and $Cum\_Count(2)$ differ by only 1. Recall that the values of Cum_Count will get translated to the endpoints of the subintervals. We want to make sure that the value we select for the word length will allow enough range for it to be possible to represent the smallest difference between the endpoints of intervals. We always rescale whenever the interval gets small. In order to make sure that the endpoints of the intervals always remain distinct, we need to make sure that all values in the range from 0 to $Total\_Count$, which is the same as $Cum\_Count(3)$, are uniquely represented in the smallest range an interval under consideration can be without triggering a rescaling. The interval is smallest without triggering a rescaling when $l^{(n)}$ is just below the midpoint of the interval and $u^{(n)}$ is at three-quarters of the interval, or when $u^{(n)}$ is right at the midpoint of the interval and $l^{(n)}$ is just below a quarter of the interval. That is, the smallest the interval $[l^{(n)}, u^{(n)}]$ can be is one-quarter of the total available range of 2^m values. Thus, m should be large enough to accommodate uniquely the set of values between 0 and $Total\_Count$.

For this example, this means that the total interval range has to be greater than 200. A value of $m = 8$ satisfies this requirement.

With this value of m we have

$$l^{(0)} = 0 = (00000000)_2 \tag{4.30}$$
$$u^{(0)} = 255 = (11111111)_2 \tag{4.31}$$

where $(\cdots)_2$ is the binary representation of a number.

The first element of the sequence to be encoded is **1**. Using Equations (4.28) and (4.29),

$$l^{(1)} = 0 + \left\lfloor \frac{256 \times Cum\_Count(0)}{50} \right\rfloor = 0 = (00000000)_2 \tag{4.32}$$

TABLE 4.5 **Values of some of the parameters for arithmetic coding example.**

$Count(1) = 40$	$Cum\_Count(0) = 0$	Scale3 $= 0$
$Count(2) = 1$	$Cum\_Count(1) = 40$	
$Count(3) = 9$	$Cum\_Count(2) = 41$	
$Total\_Count = 50$	$Cum\_Count(3) = 50$	

$$u^{(1)} = 0 + \left\lfloor \frac{256 \times Cum\_Count(1)}{50} \right\rfloor - 1 = 203 = (11001011)_2. \qquad \text{(4.33)}$$

The next element of the sequence is **3**.

$$l^{(2)} = 0 + \left\lfloor \frac{204 \times Cum\_Count(2)}{50} \right\rfloor = 167 = (10100111)_2 \qquad \text{(4.34)}$$

$$u^{(2)} = 0 + \left\lfloor \frac{204 \times Cum\_Count(3)}{50} \right\rfloor - 1 = 203 = (11001011)_2 \qquad \text{(4.35)}$$

The MSBs of $l^{(2)}$ and $u^{(2)}$ are both 1. Therefore, we shift this value out and send it to the decoder. All other bits are shifted left by 1 bit, giving

$$l^{(2)} = (01001110)_2 = 78 \qquad \text{(4.36)}$$

$$u^{(2)} = (10010111)_2 = 151. \qquad \text{(4.37)}$$

Notice that while the MSBs of the limits are different, the second MSB of the upper limit is 0, while the second MSB of the lower limit is 1. This is the condition for the E_3 mapping. We complement the second MSB of both limits and shift 1 bit to the left, shifting in a 0 as the LSB of $l^{(2)}$ and a 1 as the LSB of $u^{(2)}$. This gives us

$$l^{(2)} = (00011100)_2 = 28 \qquad \text{(4.38)}$$

$$u^{(2)} = (10101111)_2 = 175. \qquad \text{(4.39)}$$

We also increment Scale3 to a value of 1.

The next element in the sequence is **2**. Updating the limits, we have

$$l^{(3)} = 28 + \left\lfloor \frac{148 \times Cum\_Count(1)}{50} \right\rfloor = 146 = (10010010)_2 \qquad \text{(4.40)}$$

$$u^{(3)} = 28 + \left\lfloor \frac{148 \times Cum\_Count(2)}{50} \right\rfloor - 1 = 148 = (10010100)_2. \qquad \text{(4.41)}$$

The two MSBs are identical, so we shift out a 1 and shift left by 1 bit:

$$l^{(3)} = (00100100)_2 = 36 \qquad \text{(4.42)}$$

$$u^{(3)} = (00101001)_2 = 41. \qquad \text{(4.43)}$$

As Scale3 is 1, we transmit a 0 and decrement Scale3 to 0. The MSBs of the upper and lower limits are both 0, so we shift out and transmit 0:

$$l^{(3)} = (01001000)_2 = 72 \qquad \text{(4.44)}$$

$$u^{(3)} = (01010011)_2 = 83. \qquad \text{(4.45)}$$

Both MSBs are again 0, so we shift out and transmit 0:

$$l^{(3)} = (10010000)_2 = 144 \qquad \text{(4.46)}$$

$$u^{(3)} = (10100111)_2 = 167. \qquad \text{(4.47)}$$

Now both MSBs are 1, so we shift out and transmit a 1. The limits become

$$l^{(3)} = (00100000)_2 = 32 \tag{4.48}$$
$$u^{(3)} = (01001111)_2 = 79. \tag{4.49}$$

Once again the MSBs are the same. This time we shift out and transmit a 0.

$$l^{(3)} = (01000000)_2 = 64 \tag{4.50}$$
$$u^{(3)} = (10011111)_2 = 159. \tag{4.51}$$

Now the MSBs are different. However, the second MSB for the lower limit is 1 while the second MSB for the upper limit is 0. This is the condition for the E_3 mapping. Applying the E_3 mapping by complementing the second MSB and shifting 1 bit to the left, we get

$$l^{(3)} = (00000000)_2 = 0 \tag{4.52}$$
$$u^{(3)} = (10111111)_2 = 191. \tag{4.53}$$

We also increment Scale3 to 1.

The next element in the sequence to be encoded is **1**. Therefore,

$$l^{(4)} = 0 + \left\lfloor \frac{192 \times Cum\_Count(0)}{50} \right\rfloor = 0 = (00000000)_2 \tag{4.54}$$

$$u^{(4)} = 0 + \left\lfloor \frac{192 \times Cum\_Count(1)}{50} \right\rfloor - 1 = 152 = (10011000)_2. \tag{4.55}$$

The encoding continues in this fashion. To this point we have generated the binary sequence 1100010. If we wished to terminate the encoding at this point, we have to send the current status of the tag. This can be done by sending the value of the lower limit $l^{(4)}$. As $l^{(4)}$ is 0, we will end up sending eight 0s. However, Scale3 at this point is 1. Therefore, after we send the first 0 from the value of $l^{(4)}$, we need to send a 1 before sending the remaining seven 0s. The final transmitted sequence is 1100010010000000. ◆

Decoder Implementation

Once we have the encoder implementation, the decoder implementation is easy to describe. As mentioned earlier, once we have started decoding all we have to do is mimic the encoder algorithm. Let us first describe the decoder algorithm using pseudocode and then study its implementation using Example 4.4.5.

Decoder Algorithm

Initialize l and u.
Read the first m bits of the received bitstream into tag t.
$k = 0$
$\text{while} \left(\left\lfloor \frac{(t - l + 1) \times TotalCount - 1}{u - l + 1} \right\rfloor \geq Cum\_Count(k) \right)$

$$k \longleftarrow k + 1$$

decode symbol x.

$$l \longleftarrow l + \left\lfloor \frac{(u - l + 1) \times Cum\_Count(x - 1)}{TotalCount} \right\rfloor$$

$$u \longleftarrow l + \left\lfloor \frac{(u - l + 1) \times Cum\_Count(x)}{TotalCount} \right\rfloor - 1$$

while(MSB of u and l are both equal to b or E_3 condition holds)
if(MSB of u and l are both equal to b)

> {
> shift l to the left by 1 bit and shift 0 into LSB
> shift u to the left by 1 bit and shift 1 into LSB
> shift t to the left by 1 bit and read next bit from received bitstream into LSB
> }

if(E_3 condition holds)

> {
> shift l to the left by 1 bit and shift 0 into LSB
> shift u to the left by 1 bit and shift 1 into LSB
> shift t to the left by 1 bit and read next bit from received bitstream into LSB
> complement (new) MSB of l, u, and t
> }

Example 4.4.5:

After encoding the sequence in Example 4.4.4, we ended up with the following binary sequence: 1100010010000000. Treating this as the received sequence and using the parameters from Table 4.5, let us decode this sequence. Using the same word length, eight, we read in the first 8 bits of the received sequence to form the tag t:

$$t = (11000100)_2 = 196.$$

We initialize the lower and upper limits as

$$l = (00000000)_2 = 0$$
$$u = (11111111)_2 = 255.$$

To begin decoding, we compute

$$\left\lfloor \frac{(t - l + 1) \times TotalCount - 1}{u - l + 1} \right\rfloor = \left\lfloor \frac{197 \times 50 - 1}{255 - 0 + 1} \right\rfloor = 38$$

and compare this value to

$$Cum\_Count = \begin{bmatrix} 0 \\ 40 \\ 41 \\ 50 \end{bmatrix}$$

Since

$$0 \le 38 < 40,$$

we decode the first symbol as **1**. Once we have decoded a symbol, we update the lower and upper limits:

$$l = 0 + \left\lfloor \frac{256 \times Cum\_Count(0)}{TotalCount} \right\rfloor = 0 + \left\lfloor 256 \times \frac{0}{50} \right\rfloor = 0$$

$$u = 0 + \left\lfloor \frac{256 \times Cum\_Count(1)}{TotalCount} \right\rfloor - 1 = 0 + \left\lfloor 256 \times \frac{40}{50} \right\rfloor - 1 = 203$$

or

$$l = (00000000)_2$$
$$u = (11001011)_2.$$

The MSB of the limits are different and the E_3 condition does not hold. Therefore, we continue decoding without modifying the tag value. To obtain the next symbol, we compare

$$\left\lfloor \frac{(t - l + 1) \times TotalCount - 1}{u - l + 1} \right\rfloor$$

which is 48, against the *Cum_Count* array:

$$Cum\_Count(2) \le 48 < Cum\_Count(3).$$

Therefore, we decode **3** and update the limits:

$$l = 0 + \left\lfloor \frac{204 \times Cum\_Count(2)}{TotalCount} \right\rfloor = 0 + \left\lfloor 204 \times \frac{41}{50} \right\rfloor = 167 = (10100111)_2$$

$$u = 0 + \left\lfloor \frac{204 \times Cum\_Count(3)}{TotalCount} \right\rfloor - 1 = 0 + \left\lfloor 204 \times \frac{50}{50} \right\rfloor - 1 = 203 = (11001011)_2.$$

As the MSB of u and l are the same, we shift the MSB out and read in a 0 for the LSB of l and a 1 for the LSB of u. We mimic this action for the tag as well, shifting the MSB out and reading in the next bit from the received bitstream as the LSB:

$$l = (01001110)_2$$
$$u = (10010111)_2$$
$$t = (10001001)_2.$$

Examining l and u we can see we have an E_3 condition. Therefore, for l, u, and t, we shift the MSB out, complement the new MSB, and read in a 0 as the LSB of l, a 1 as the LSB of u, and the next bit in the received bitstream as the LSB of t. We now have

$$l = (00011100)_2 = 28$$
$$u = (10101111)_2 = 175$$
$$t = (10010010)_2 = 146.$$

To decode the next symbol, we compute

$$\left\lfloor \frac{(t - l + 1) \times TotalCount - 1}{u - l + 1} \right\rfloor = 40.$$

Since $40 \le 40 < 41$, we decode **2**.

Updating the limits using this decoded symbol, we get

$$l = 28 + \left\lfloor \frac{(175 - 28 + 1) \times 40}{50} \right\rfloor = 146 = (10010010)_2$$
$$u = 28 + \left\lfloor \frac{(175 - 28 + 1) \times 41}{50} \right\rfloor - 1 = 148 = (10010100)_2.$$

We can see that we have quite a few bits to shift out. However, notice that the lower limit l has the same value as the tag t. Furthermore, the remaining received sequence consists entirely of 0s. Therefore, we will be performing identical operations on numbers that are the same, resulting in identical numbers. This will result in the final decoded symbol being **1**. We knew this was the final symbol to be decoded because only four symbols had been encoded. In practice this information has to be conveyed to the decoder. ◆

4.5 Comparison of Huffman and Arithmetic Coding

We have described a new coding scheme that, although more complicated than Huffman coding, allows us to code *sequences* of symbols. How well this coding scheme works depends on how it is used. Let's first try to use this code for encoding sources for which we know the Huffman code.

Looking at Example 4.4.1, the average length for this code is

$$l = 2 \times 0.5 + 3 \times 0.25 + 4 \times 0.125 + 4 \times 0.125 \qquad (4.56)$$
$$= 2.75 \text{ bits/symbol}. \qquad (4.57)$$

Recall from Section 2.4 that the entropy of this source was 1.75 bits/symbol and the Huffman code achieved this entropy. Obviously, arithmetic coding is not a good idea if you are going to encode your message one symbol at a time. Let's repeat the example with messages consisting of two symbols. (Note that we are only doing this to demonstrate a point. In practice, we would not code sequences this short using an arithmetic code.)

Example 4.5.1:

If we encode two symbols at a time, the resulting code is shown in Table 4.6.

TABLE 4.6   Arithmetic code for two-symbol sequences.

Message	$P(x)$	$\bar{T}_X(x)$	$\bar{T}_X(x)$ in Binary	$\lceil \log \frac{1}{P(x)} \rceil + 1$	Code
11	.25	.125	.001	3	001
12	.125	.3125	.0101	4	0101
13	.0625	.40625	.01101	5	01101
14	.0625	.46875	.01111	5	01111
21	.125	.5625	.1001	4	1001
22	.0625	.65625	.10101	5	10101
23	.03125	.703125	.101101	6	101101
24	.03125	.734375	.101111	6	101111
31	.0625	.78125	.11001	5	11001
32	.03125	.828125	.110101	6	110101
33	.015625	.8515625	.1101101	7	1101101
34	.015625	.8671875	.1101111	7	1101111
41	.0625	.90625	.11101	5	11101
42	.03125	.953125	.111101	6	111101
43	.015625	.9765625	.1111101	7	1111101
44	.015625	.984375	.1111111	7	1111111

The average length per message is 4.5 bits. Therefore, using two symbols at a time we get a rate of 2.25 bits/symbol (certainly better than 2.75 bits/symbol, but still not as good as the best rate of 1.75 bits/symbol). However, we see that as we increase the number of symbols per message, our results get better and better. ◆

How many samples do we have to group together to make the arithmetic coding scheme perform better than the Huffman coding scheme? We can get some idea by looking at the bounds on the coding rate.

Recall that the bounds on the average length l_A of the arithmetic code are

$$H(X) \leq l_A \leq H(X) + \frac{2}{m}.$$

It does not take many symbols in a sequence before the coding rate for the arithmetic code becomes quite close to the entropy. However, recall that for Huffman codes, if we block m symbols together, the coding rate is

$$H(X) \leq l_H \leq H(X) + \frac{1}{m}.$$

The advantage seems to lie with the Huffman code, although the advantage decreases with increasing m. However, remember that to generate a codeword for a sequence of length m, using the Huffman procedure requires building the entire code for all possible sequences of length m. If the original alphabet size was k, then the size of the codebook would be k^m.

Taking relatively reasonable values of $k = 16$ and $m = 20$ gives a codebook size of 16^{20}! This is obviously not a viable option. For the arithmetic coding procedure, we do not need to build the entire codebook. Instead, we simply obtain the code for the tag corresponding to a given sequence. Therefore, it is entirely feasible to code sequences of length 20 or much more. In practice, we can make m large for the arithmetic coder and not for the Huffman coder. This means that for most sources we can get rates closer to the entropy using arithmetic coding than by using Huffman coding. The exceptions are sources whose probabilities are powers of two. In these cases, the single-letter Huffman code achieves the entropy, and we cannot do any better with arithmetic coding, no matter how long a sequence we pick.

The amount of gain also depends on the source. Recall that for Huffman codes we are guaranteed to obtain rates within $0.086 + p_{max}$ of the entropy, where p_{max} is the probability of the most probable letter in the alphabet. If the alphabet size is relatively large and the probabilities are not too skewed, the maximum probability p_{max} is generally small. In these cases, the advantage of arithmetic coding over Huffman coding is small, and it might not be worth the extra complexity to use arithmetic coding rather than Huffman coding. However, there are many sources, such as facsimile, in which the alphabet size is small, and the probabilities are highly unbalanced. In these cases, the use of arithmetic coding is generally worth the added complexity.

Another major advantage of arithmetic coding is that it is easy to implement a system with multiple arithmetic codes. This may seem contradictory, as we have claimed that arithmetic coding is more complex than Huffman coding. However, it is the computational machinery that causes the increase in complexity. Once we have the computational machinery to implement one arithmetic code, all we need to implement more than a single arithmetic code is the availability of more probability tables. If the alphabet size of the source is small, as in the case of a binary source, there is very little added complexity indeed. In fact, as we shall see in the next section, it is possible to develop multiplication-free arithmetic coders that are quite simple to implement (nonbinary multiplication-free arithmetic coders are described in [195]).

Finally, it is much easier to adapt arithmetic codes to changing input statistics. All we need to do is estimate the probabilities of the input alphabet. This can be done by keeping a count of the letters as they are coded. There is no need to preserve a tree, as with adaptive Huffman codes. Furthermore, there is no need to generate a code a priori, as in the case of Huffman coding. This property allows us to separate the modeling and coding procedures in a manner that is not very feasible with Huffman coding. This separation permits greater flexibility in the design of compression systems, which can be used to great advantage.

4.6 Applications

Arithmetic coding is used in a variety of lossless and lossy compression applications. In this section we describe two of the more well-known applications.

4.6.1 Bi-level Image Compression—The JBIG Standard

Arithmetic coding is the coding scheme recommended by the Joint Bi-level Image Processing Group (JBIG) as part of the standard for coding binary images. JBIG is a joint experts group of the International Standards Organization (ISO), International Electrotechnical Commission (IEC), and the Consultative Committee on International Telephone and Telegraph (CCITT). The first two are industry groups, while CCITT is a committee of the International Telecommunications Union (ITU), which is part of the United Nations. This group of experts was formed in 1988 to establish a standard for the progressive encoding of bi-level images.

In progressive transmission of an image, a low-resolution representation of the image is sent first. This low-resolution representation requires very few bits to encode. The image is then updated, or refined, to the desired fidelity by transmitting more and more information. The JBIG standard can be viewed as a combination of two algorithms, a progressive transmission algorithm and a lossless compression algorithm. Each of these can be understood independently of the other. Let's first look at the lossless compression algorithm.

Lossless Compression

Many bi-level images have a lot of local structure. Consider a digitized page of text. In large portions of the image we will encounter white pixels with a probability approaching one. In other parts of the image there will be a high probability of encountering a black pixel. We can make a reasonable guess of the situation for a particular pixel by looking at values of the pixel in the neighborhood of the pixel being encoded. For example, if the pixels in the neighborhood of the pixel being encoded are mostly white, then there is a high probability that the pixel to be encoded is also white. On the other hand, if most of the pixels in the neighborhood are black, there is a high probability that the pixel being encoded is also black. Each case gives us a skewed probability—a situation ideally suited for arithmetic coding. If we treat each case separately using a different arithmetic coder for each of the two situations, we should be able to obtain improvement over the case where we use the same arithmetic coder for all pixels. Consider the following example.

Suppose the probability of encountering a black pixel is 0.2 and the probability of encountering a white pixel is 0.8. The entropy for this source is given by

$$H = -0.2 \log_2 0.2 - 0.8 \log_2 0.8 = 0.722. \tag{4.58}$$

If we use a single arithmetic coder to encode this source, we will get an average bit rate close to 0.722 bits per pixel. Now suppose, based on the neighborhood of the pixels, we can divide the pixels into two sets, one comprising 80% of the pixels and the other 20%. In the first set, the probability of encountering a white pixel is 0.95, and in the second set the probability of encountering a black pixel is 0.7. The entropy of these sets is 0.286 and 0.881, respectively. If we used two different arithmetic coders for the two sets with frequency tables matched to the probabilities, we would get rates close to 0.286 bits per pixel about 80% of the time, and close to 0.881 bits per pixel about 20% of the time. The average rate would be about 0.405 bits per pixel, which is almost half the rate required if we used a single arithmetic coder. If we use only those pixels in the neighborhood that had already been transmitted to the receiver to make our decision as to which arithmetic coder to use, the decoder can keep track of which encoder was used to encode a particular pixel.

As we have mentioned before, the arithmetic coding approach is particularly amenable to the use of multiple coders. All coders use the same computational machinery, with each coder using a different set of probabilities. The JBIG algorithm makes full use of this feature

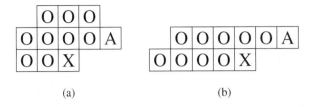

FIGURE   4.2   (a) Three-line and (b) two-line neighborhoods.

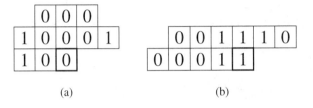

FIGURE   4.3   (a) Three-line and (b) two-line contexts.

of arithmetic coding. Instead of checking to see if most of the pixels in the neighborhood are white or black, the JBIG encoder uses the pattern of pixels in the neighborhood or *context* to decide which set of probabilities to use in encoding a particular pixel. If the neighborhood consists of 10 pixels, with each pixel capable of taking on two different values, the number of possible patterns is 1024. The JBIG coder uses 1024 to 4096 coders, depending on whether a low- or high-resolution layer is being encoded.

For the low-resolution layer the JBIG encoder uses one of the two different neighborhoods shown in Figure 4.2. The pixel to be coded is marked **X**, while the pixels to be used for templates are marked **O** or **A**. The **A** and **O** pixels are previously encoded pixels and are available to both encoder and decoder. The **A** pixel can be thought of as a floating member of the neighborhood. Its placement is dependent on the input being encoded. Suppose the image has vertical lines 30 pixels apart. The **A** pixel would be placed 30 pixels to the left of the pixel being encoded. The **A** pixel can be moved around in order to capture any structure that might exist in the image. This is especially useful in halftone images in which the **A** pixels are used to capture the periodic structure. The location and movement of the **A** pixel are transmitted to the decoder as side information.

In Figure 4.3, the symbols in the neighborhoods have been replaced by 0s and 1s. We take 0 to correspond to white pixels, while 1 corresponds to black pixels. The pixel to be encoded is enclosed by the heavy box. The pattern of 0s and 1s is interpreted as a binary number, which is used as an index to the set of probabilities. The context in the case of the three-line neighborhood (reading left to right, top to bottom) is 0001000110, which corresponds to an index of 70. For the two-line neighborhood, the context is 0011100001, or 225. As there are 10 bits in these templates, we will have 1024 different arithmetic coders.

In the JBIG standard, the 1024 arithmetic coders are a variation of the arithmetic coder known as the QM coder. The QM coder is a modification of an adaptive binary arithmetic coder called the Q coder [179, 159, 177], which in turn is an extension of another binary adaptive arithmetic coder called the skew coder [133].

In our description of arithmetic coding, we have been updating the tag interval by updating the endpoints of the interval, $u^{(n)}$ and $l^{(n)}$. We could just as well have kept track of one endpoint and the size of the interval. This is the approach adopted in the QM coder, which tracks the lower end of the tag interval $l^{(n)}$ and the size of the interval $A^{(n)}$, where

$$A^{(n)} = u^{(n)} - l^{(n)}. \tag{4.59}$$

The tag for a sequence is the binary representation of $l^{(n)}$.

We can obtain the update equation for $A^{(n)}$ by subtracting Equation (4.9) from Equation (4.10):

$$A^{(n)} = A^{(n-1)}(F_X(x_n) - F_X(x_n - 1)) \tag{4.60}$$
$$= A^{(n-1)}P(x_n). \tag{4.61}$$

Substituting $A^{(n)}$ for $u^{(n)} - l^{(n)}$ in Equation (4.9), we get the update equation for $l^{(n)}$:

$$l^{(n)} = l^{(n-1)} + A^{(n-1)}F_X(x_n - 1). \tag{4.62}$$

Instead of dealing directly with the 0s and 1s put out by the source, the QM coder maps them into a More Probable Symbol (MPS) and Less Probable Symbol (LPS). If 0 represents black pixels and 1 represents white pixels, then in a mostly black image, 0 will be the MPS, while in an image with mostly white regions, 1 will be the MPS. Denoting the probability of occurrence of the LPS for the context C by q_c, and mapping the MPS to the lower subinterval, the occurrence of an MPS symbol results in the following update equations:

$$l^{(n)} = l^{(n-1)} \tag{4.63}$$
$$A^{(n)} = A^{(n-1)}(1 - q_c) \tag{4.64}$$

while the occurrence of an LPS symbol results in the following update equations:

$$l^{(n)} = l^{(n-1)} + A^{(n-1)}(1 - q_c) \tag{4.65}$$
$$A^{(n)} = A^{(n-1)}q_c. \tag{4.66}$$

Until this point, the QM coder looks very much like the arithmetic coder described earlier in this chapter. In order to make the implementation simpler, the JBIG committee recommended several deviations from the standard arithmetic coding algorithm. The update equations involve multiplications, which are expensive in both hardware and software. In the QM coder, the multiplications are avoided by assuming that $A^{(n)}$ has a value close to one, and multiplication with $A^{(n)}$ can be approximated by multiplication with one. Therefore, the update equations become

For MPS:
$$l^{(n)} = l^{(n-1)} \tag{4.67}$$
$$A^{(n)} = 1 - q_c \tag{4.68}$$

For LPS:
$$l^{(n)} = l^{(n-1)} + (1 - q_c) \tag{4.69}$$
$$A^{(n)} = q_c \tag{4.70}$$

In order not to violate the assumption on $A^{(n)}$ whenever the value of $A^{(n)}$ drops below 0.75, the QM coder goes through a series of rescalings until the value of $A^{(n)}$ is greater than or equal to 0.75. The rescalings take the form of repeated doubling, which corresponds to a left shift in the binary representation of $A^{(n)}$. In order to keep all parameters in sync, the same scaling is also applied to $l^{(n)}$. The bits shifted out of the buffer containing the value of $l^{(n)}$ make up the encoder output. Looking at the update equations for the QM coder, we can see that a rescaling will occur every time an LPS occurs. Occurrence of an MPS may or may not result in a rescale, depending on the value of $A^{(n)}$.

The probability q_c of the LPS for context C is updated each time a rescaling takes place and the context C is active. An ordered list of values for q_c is listed in a table. Every time a rescaling occurs, the value of q_c is changed to the next lower or next higher value in the table, depending on whether the rescaling was caused by the occurrence of an LPS or an MPS.

In a nonstationary situation, it may happen that the symbol assigned to LPS actually occurs more often than the symbol assigned to MPS. This condition is detected when $q_c > (A^{(n)} - q_c)$. In this situation, the assignments are reversed; the symbol assigned the LPS label is assigned the MPS label and vice versa. The test is conducted every time a rescaling takes place.

The decoder for the QM coder operates in much the same way as the decoder described in this chapter, mimicking the encoder operation.

Progressive Transmission

In some applications we may not always need to view an image at full resolution. For example, if we were looking at the layout of a page, we may not need to know what each word or letter on the page is. The JBIG standard allows for the generation of progressively lower-resolution images. If the user is interested in some gross patterns in the image, for example, if they were interested in seeing if there were any figures on a particular page, they can request a lower-resolution image, which could be transmitted using fewer bits. Once the lower-resolution image was available, the user could decide if a higher-resolution image was necessary. The JBIG specification recommends generating one lower-resolution pixel for each 2×2 block in the higher-resolution image. The number of lower-resolution images (called layers) is not specified by JBIG.

A straightforward method for generating lower-resolution images is to replace every 2×2 block of pixels with the average value of the four pixels, thus reducing the resolution by two in both the horizontal and vertical directions. This approach works well as long as three of the four pixels are either black or white. However, when we have two pixels of each kind, we run into trouble; consistently replacing the four pixels with either a white or black pixel causes a severe loss of detail, and randomly replacing with a black or white pixel introduces a considerable amount of noise into the image [241].

Instead of simply taking the average of every 2×2 block, the JBIG specification provides a table-based method for resolution reduction. The table is indexed by the neighboring pixels shown in Figure 4.4, in which the circles represent the lower-resolution layer pixels and the squares represent the higher-resolution layer pixels.

Each pixel contributes a bit to the index. The table is formed by computing the expression

$$4e + 2(b + d + f + h) + (a + c + g + i) - 3(B + C) - A.$$

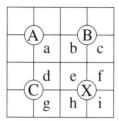

FIGURE 4.4 **Pixels used to determine the value of a lower-level pixel.**

If the value of this expression is greater than 4.5, the pixel X is tentatively declared to be 1. The table has certain exceptions to this rule to reduce the amount of edge smearing, generally encountered in a filtering operation. There are also exceptions that preserve periodic patterns and dither patterns.

As the lower-resolution layers are obtained from the higher-resolution images, we can use them when encoding the higher-resolution images. The JBIG specification makes use of the lower-resolution images when encoding the higher-resolution images by using the pixels of the lower-resolution images as part of the context for encoding the higher-resolution images. The contexts used for coding the lowest-resolution layer are those shown in Figure 4.2. The contexts used in coding the higher-resolution layer are shown in Figure 4.5.

Ten pixels are used in each context. If we include the 2 bits required to indicate which context template is being used, 12 bits will be used to indicate the context. This means that we can have 4096 different contexts.

4.6.2 JBIG2

At the writing of this book, the JBIG2 standard is in the working draft stage and is very likely to become a standard in the near future. The standard only provides specifications for the decoder, leaving the encoder design open. This means that the encoder design can be constantly refined, subject only to compatibility with the decoder specifications. This also allows for lossy compression as the encoder can incorporate lossy transformations to the data that enhance the level of compression.

The compression algorithm in JBIG provides excellent compression of a generic bi-level image. The compression algorithm proposed for JBIG2 uses the same arithmetic coding scheme as JBIG. However, it takes advantage of the fact that a significant number of bi-level images contain structure that can be used to enhance the compression performance. A large percentage of bi-level images consist of text on some background, while another significant percentage of bi-level images are, or contain, halftone images. The JBIG2 approach allows the encoder to select the compression technique that would provide the best performance for the type of data. In order to do this, the encoder divides the page to be compressed into three types of regions called *symbol regions*, *halftone regions*, and *generic regions*. The symbol regions are the regions containing text data, the halftone regions are the regions containing halftone images, and the generic regions are all the regions that do not fit into either category.

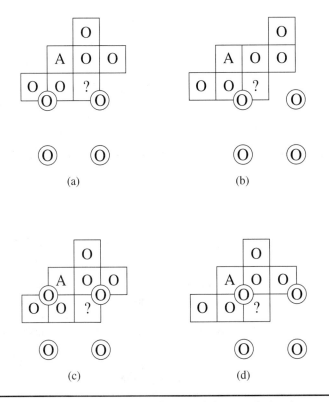

FIGURE 4.5   **Contexts used in the coding of higher-resolution layers.**

The partitioning information has to be supplied to the decoder. The decoder requires that all information provided to it be organized in *segments* that are made up of a segment header, a data header, and segment data. The page information segment contains information about the page, including the size and resolution. The decoder uses this information to set up the page buffer. It then decodes the various regions using the appropriate decoding procedure and places the different regions in their appropriate location.

Generic Decoding Procedures

There are two procedures used for decoding the generic regions: the generic region decoding procedure and the generic refinement region decoding procedure. The generic region decoding procedure uses either the MMR technique used in the Group 3 and Group 4 fax standards or a variation of the technique used to encode the lowest resolution layer in the JBIG recommendation. We describe the operation of the MMR algorithm in Chapter 6. The latter procedure is described below.

The second generic region decoding procedure is a procedure called *typical prediction*. In a bi-level image, a line of pixels is often identical to the line above. In typical prediction, if the current line is the same as the line above, a bit flag called $LNTP_n$ is set to 0, and the line is not transmitted. If this is not the case, the flag is set to 1, and the line is coded using the contexts currently used for the low-resolution layer in JBIG. The value of $LNTP_n$ is encoded by generating another bit $SLNTP_n$ according to the rule

$$SLNTP_n = !(LNTP_n \oplus LNTP_{n-1})$$

which is treated as a virtual pixel to the left of each row. If the decoder decodes an $LNTP$ value of 0, it copies the line above. If it decodes an $LNTP$ value of 1, the following bits in the segment data are decoded using an arithmetic decoder and the contexts described previously.

The generic refinement decoding procedure assumes the existence of a *reference* layer and decodes the segment data with reference to this layer. The standard leaves open the specification of the reference layer.

Symbol Region Decoding

The symbol region decoding procedure is a dictionary-based decoding procedure. The symbol region segment is decoded with the help of a symbol dictionary contained in the symbol dictionary segment. The data in the symbol region segment contains the location where a symbol is to be placed as well as the index to an entry in the symbol dictionary. The symbol dictionary consists of a set of bitmaps and is decoded using the generic decoding procedures. Note that as JBIG2 allows for lossy compression, the symbols do not have to exactly match the symbols in the original document. This feature can significantly increase the compression performance when the original document contains noise that may preclude exact matches with the symbols in the dictionary.

Halftone Region Decoding

The halftone region decoding procedure is also a dictionary-based decoding procedure. The halftone region segment is decoded with the help of a halftone dictionary contained in the halftone dictionary segment. The halftone dictionary segment is decoded using the generic decoding procedures. The data in the halftone region segment consists of the location of the halftone region and indices to the halftone dictionary. The dictionary is a set of fixed-size halftone patterns. As in the case of the symbol region, if lossy compression is allowed, the halftone patterns do not have to exactly match the patterns in the original document. By allowing for nonexact matches, the dictionary can be kept small, resulting in higher compression.

4.6.3 Image Compression

The JBIG standard has been designed for encoding bi-level images. It can also be used to code images that use more bits per pixel, or gray-scale images, by operating on the bit planes. However, when encoding gray-scale images, the structure in the images is captured better when operating at the gray-scale pixel level. In Tables 4.7 and 4.8, we show the results of using adaptive arithmetic coding to encode the same set of test images that were previously encoded using Huffman coding. We have included the compression ratios obtained using Huffman code from the previous chapter for comparison.

TABLE 4.7   **Compression using adaptive arithmetic coding of pixel values.**

Image Name	Bits/Pixel	Total Size (bytes)	Compression Ratio (arithmetic)	Compression Ratio (Huffman)
Sena	6.52	53,431	1.23	1.16
Sensin	7.12	58,306	1.12	1.27
Earth	4.67	38,248	1.71	1.67
Omaha	6.84	56,061	1.17	1.14

TABLE 4.8   **Compression using adaptive arithmetic coding of pixel differences.**

Image Name	Bits/Pixel	Total Size (bytes)	Compression Ratio (arithmetic)	Compression Ratio (Huffman)
Sena	3.89	31,847	2.06	2.08
Sensin	4.56	37,387	1.75	1.73
Earth	3.92	32,137	2.04	2.04
Omaha	6.27	51,393	1.28	1.26

Comparing these values to those obtained in the previous chapter, we can see very little change. The reason is that as the alphabet size for the images is quite large, the value of p_{max} is quite small, and the Huffman coder performs very close to the entropy.

As we mentioned before, a major advantage of arithmetic coding over Huffman coding is the ability to separate the modeling and coding aspects of the compression approach. In terms of image coding, this allows us to use a number of different models that take advantage of local properties. For example, we could use different decorrelation strategies in regions of the image that are quasi-constant and will, therefore, have differences that are small, and regions where there is a lot of activity, causing the presence of larger difference values.

4.7   Summary

In this chapter we introduced the basic ideas behind arithmetic coding. We have shown that the arithmetic code is a uniquely decodable code that provides a rate close to the entropy for long stationary sequences. This ability to encode sequences directly instead of as a concatenation of the codes for the elements of the sequence makes this approach more efficient than Huffman coding for alphabets with highly skewed probabilities. We have looked in some detail at the implementation of the arithmetic coding approach. As an example of the applications of arithmetic coding, we have described the compression aspects of the JBIG standard.

The arithmetic coding results in this chapter were obtained by using the program provided by Witten, Neal, and Cleary [242]. This code can be used (with some modifications) for exploring different aspects of arithmetic coding (see problems).

Further Reading

1. The book *Text Compression*, by T.C. Bell, J.G. Cleary, and I.H. Witten [20], contains a very readable section on arithmetic coding, complete with pseudocode and C code.

2. There is an excellent tutorial article by G.G. Langdon [131] in the March 1984 issue of the *IBM Journal on Research and Development*.

3. The separate model and code paradigm is explored in a precise manner in the context of arithmetic coding in a paper by J.J. Rissanen and G.G. Langdon [194].

4. The separation of modeling and coding is exploited in a very nice manner in an early paper by G.G. Langdon and J.J. Rissanen [132].

5. Various models for text compression that can be used effectively with arithmetic coding are described by T.G. Bell, I.H. Witten, and J.G. Cleary [21] in an article in the *ACM Computing Surveys*.

6. The coder used in the JBIG algorithm is a descendant of the Q coder, described in some detail in several papers [179, 159, 177] in the November 1988 issue of the *IBM Journal of Research and Development*.

7. The book *JPEG Still Image Data Compression Standard*, by W.B. Pennebaker and J.L. Mitchell [178], is a good source for more information about the JBIG algorithm.

8. An excellent discussion of the progressive transmission aspects of the JBIG algorithm can be found in *Managing Gigabytes: Compressing and Indexing Documents and Images*, by I.H. Witten, A. Moffat, and T.C. Bell [241].

4.8 Projects and Problems

1. Given a number a in the interval $[0, 1)$ with an n-bit binary representation $[b_1 b_2 \ldots b_n]$, show that for any other number b to have a binary representation with $[b_1 b_2 \ldots b_n]$ as the prefix, b has to lie in the interval $[a, a + \frac{1}{2^n})$.

2. The binary arithmetic coding approach specified in the JBIG standard can be used for coding gray-scale images via *bit plane encoding*. In bit plane encoding, we combine the most significant bits for each pixel into one bit plane, the next most significant bits into another bit plane, and so on. Use the function `extrctbp` to obtain eight bit planes for the `sena.img` and `omaha.img` test images, and encode them using arithmetic coding. Use the low-resolution contexts shown in Figure 4.3.

3. Bit plane encoding is more effective when the pixels are encoded using a *Gray code*. The Gray code assigns numerically adjacent values binary codes that differ by only 1 bit. To convert from the standard binary code $b_0 b_1 b_2 \ldots b_7$ to the Gray code $g_0 g_1 g_2 \ldots g_7$, we can use the equations

$$g_0 = b_0$$
$$g_k = b_k \oplus b_{k-1}.$$

TABLE 4.9   Probability model for Problems
                 5 and 6.

Letter	Probability
a_1	.2
a_2	.3
a_3	.5

TABLE 4.10   Frequency counts for
                 Problem 7.

Letter	Count
a	37
b	38
c	25

Convert the test images `sena.img` and `omaha.img` to a Gray code representation, and bit plane encode. Compare with the results for the non-Gray-coded representation.

4. In Example 4.4.4, repeat the encoding using $m = 6$. Comment on your results.

5. Given the probability model in Table 4.9, find the real valued tag for the sequence $a_1\, a_1\, a_3\, a_2\, a_3\, a_1$.

6. For the probability model in Table 4.9, decode a sequence of length 10 with the tag 0.63215699.

7. Given the frequency counts shown in Table 4.10:

(a) What is the word length required for unambiguous encoding?

(b) Find the binary code for the sequence *abacabb*.

(c) Decode the code you obtained to verify that your encoding was correct.

8. Generate a binary sequence of length L with $P(0) = 0.8$, and use the arithmetic coding algorithm to encode it. Plot the difference of the rate in bits/symbol and the entropy as a function of L. Comment on the effect of L on the rate.

5

Dictionary Techniques

5.1 Overview

I n the previous two chapters we looked at coding techniques that assume a source that generates a sequence of independent symbols. As most sources are correlated to start with, the coding step is generally preceded by a decorrelation step. In this chapter we will look at techniques that incorporate the structure in the data in order to increase the amount of compression. These techniques—both static and adaptive (or dynamic)—build a list of commonly occurring patterns and encode these patterns by transmitting their index in the list. They are most useful with sources that generate a relatively small number of patterns quite frequently, such as text sources and computer commands. We discuss two applications in these areas: the UNIX compress command and the V.42 bis specifications. A discussion of the Graphics Interchange Format (GIF) highlights the limitations of this approach.

5.2 Introduction

In many applications, the output of the source consists of recurring patterns. A classic example is a text source in which certain patterns or words recur constantly. Also, there are certain patterns that simply do not occur, or if they do, occur with great rarity. For example, we can be reasonably sure that the word *Limpopo*[1] occurs in a very small fraction of the text sources in existence.

A very reasonable approach to encoding such sources is to keep a list, or *dictionary*, of frequently occurring patterns. When these patterns appear in the source output, they are

---

[1] "How the Elephant Got Its Trunk" in *Just So Stories* by Rudyard Kipling.

encoded with a reference to the dictionary. If the pattern does not appear in the dictionary, then it can be encoded using some other, less efficient, method. In effect we are splitting the input into two classes, frequently occurring patterns and infrequently occurring patterns. For this technique to be effective, the class of frequently occurring patterns, and hence the size of the dictionary, must be much smaller than the number of all possible patterns.

Suppose we have a particular text that consists of four-character words, three characters from the 26 lowercase letters of the English alphabet followed by a punctuation mark. Suppose our source alphabet consists of the 26 lowercase letters of the English alphabet and the punctuation marks comma, period, exclamation mark, question mark, semicolon, and colon. In other words, the size of the input alphabet is 32. If we were to encode the text source one character at a time, treating each character as an equally likely event, we would need 5 bits per character. Treating all 32^4 ($= 2^{20} = 1,048,576$) four-character patterns as equally likely, we have a code that assigns 20 bits to each four-character pattern. Let us now put the 256 most likely four-character patterns into a dictionary. The transmission scheme works as follows: Whenever we want to send a pattern that exists in the dictionary, we will send a 1-bit flag, say, a 0, followed by an 8-bit index corresponding to the entry in the dictionary. If the pattern is not in the dictionary, we will send a 1 followed by the 20-bit encoding of the pattern. If the pattern we encounter is not in the dictionary, we will actually use more bits than in the original scheme, 21 instead of 20. But if it is in the dictionary, we will send only 9 bits. The utility of our scheme will depend on the percentage of the words we encounter that are in the dictionary. We can get an idea about the utility of our scheme by calculating the average number of bits per pattern. If the probability of encountering a pattern from the dictionary is p, then the average number of bits per pattern R is given by

$$R = 9p + 21(1 - p) = 21 - 12p. \tag{5.1}$$

For our scheme to be useful, R should have a value less than 20. This happens when $p \geq 0.084$. This does not seem like a very large number. However, note that if all patterns were occurring in an equally likely manner, the probability of encountering a pattern from the dictionary would be less than 0.00025!

We do not simply want a coding scheme that performs slightly better than the simple-minded approach of coding each pattern as equally likely; we would like to improve the performance as much as possible. In order for this to happen, p should be as large as possible. This means that we should carefully select patterns that are most likely to occur as entries in the dictionary. To do this, we have to have a pretty good idea about the structure of the source output. If we do not have information of this sort available to us prior to the encoding of a particular source output, we need to acquire this information somehow when we are encoding. If we feel we have sufficient prior knowledge, we can use a *static* approach; if not, we can take an *adaptive* approach. We will look at both these approaches in this chapter.

5.3 Static Dictionary

Choosing a static dictionary technique is most appropriate when considerable prior knowledge about the source is available. This technique is especially suitable for use in specific applications. For example, if the task were to compress the student records at a university, a static dictionary approach may be the best. This is because we know ahead of time that certain words such as "Name" and "Student ID" are going to appear in almost all of the records. Other words such as "Sophomore," "credits," and so on will occur quite often. Depending on the location of the university, certain digits in social security numbers are more likely to occur. For example, in Nebraska most student ID numbers begin with the digits 505. In fact, most entries will be of a recurring nature. In this situation, it is highly efficient to design a compression scheme based on a static dictionary containing the recurring patterns. Similarly, there could be a number of other situations in which an application-specific or data-specific static-dictionary-based coding scheme would be the most efficient. It should be noted that these schemes would work well only for the applications and data they were designed for. If these schemes were to be used with different applications, they may cause an expansion of the data instead of compression.

A static dictionary technique that is less specific to a single application is *digram coding*. We describe this in the next section.

5.3.1 Digram Coding

One of the more common forms of static dictionary coding is digram coding. In this form of coding, the dictionary consists of all letters of the source alphabet followed by as many pairs of letters, called *digrams*, as can be accommodated by the dictionary. For example, suppose we were to construct a dictionary of size 256 for digram coding of all printable ASCII characters. The first 95 entries of the dictionary would be the 95 printable ASCII characters. The remaining 161 entries would be the most frequently used pairs of characters.

The digram encoder reads a two-character input and searches the dictionary to see if this input exists in the dictionary. If it does, the corresponding index is encoded and transmitted. If it does not, the first character of the pair is encoded. The second character in the pair then becomes the first character of the next digram. The encoder reads another character to complete the digram, and the search procedure is repeated.

Example 5.3.1:

Suppose we have a source with a five-letter alphabet $\mathcal{A} = \{a, b, c, d, r\}$. Based on knowledge about the source, we build the dictionary shown in Table 5.1.

Suppose we wish to encode the sequence

abracadabra

TABLE 5.1   A sample dictionary.

Code	Entry	Code	Entry
000	*a*	100	*r*
001	*b*	101	*ab*
010	*c*	110	*ac*
011	*d*	111	*ad*

The encoder reads the first two characters *ab* and checks to see if this pair of letters exists in the dictionary. It does and is encoded using the codeword 101. The encoder then reads the next two characters *ra* and checks to see if this pair occurs in the dictionary. It does not, so the encoder sends out the code for *r*, which is 100, then reads in one more character, *c*, to make the two-character pattern *ac*. This does exist in the dictionary and is encoded as 110. Continuing in this fashion, the remainder of the sequence is coded. The output string for the given input sequence is 101100110111101100000.   ◆

A list of the 30 most frequently occurring pairs of characters in an earlier version of this chapter is shown in Table 5.2. For comparison, the 30 most frequently occurring pairs of characters in a set of C programs is shown in Table 5.3.

In these tables, *b̸* corresponds to a space and *nl* corresponds to a new line. Notice how different the two tables are. It is easy to see that a dictionary designed for compressing LaTeX documents would not work very well when compressing C programs. However, generally we want techniques that will be able to compress a variety of source outputs. If we wanted to compress computer files, we do not want to change techniques based on the content of the file. Rather, we would like the technique to *adapt* to the characteristics of the source output. We discuss adaptive-dictionary-based techniques in the next section.

5.4 Adaptive Dictionary

Most adaptive-dictionary-based techniques have their roots in two landmark papers by Jacob Ziv and Abraham Lempel in 1977 [248] and 1978 [249]. These papers provide two different approaches to adaptively building dictionaries, and each approach has given rise to a number of variations. The approaches based on the 1977 paper are said to belong to the LZ77 family (also known as LZ1), while the approaches based on the 1978 paper are said to belong to the LZ78, or LZ2, family. The transposition of the initials is a historical accident and is a convention we will observe in this book. In the following sections, we first describe an implementation of each approach followed by some of the more well-known variations.

5.4.1 The LZ77 Approach

In the LZ77 approach, the dictionary is simply a portion of the previously encoded sequence. The encoder examines the input sequence through a sliding window as shown in Figure 5.1. The window consists of two parts, a *search buffer* that contains a portion of the recently encoded sequence, and a *look-ahead buffer* that contains the next portion of the sequence to be encoded. In Figure 5.1, the search buffer contains eight symbols, while the look-ahead buffer contains seven symbols. In practice, the sizes of the buffers are significantly larger; however, for the purpose of explanation, we will keep the buffer sizes small.

To encode the sequence in the look-ahead buffer, the encoder moves a search pointer back through the search buffer until it encounters a match to the first symbol in the look-ahead buffer. The distance of the pointer from the look-ahead buffer is called the *offset*. The encoder then examines the symbols following the symbol at the pointer location to see if they

TABLE 5.2　　Thirty most frequently occurring pairs of characters in a 41,364-character-long LaTeX document.

Pair	Count	Pair	Count
eþ	1128	*ar*	314
þt	838	*at*	313
þþ	823	*þw*	309
th	817	*te*	296
he	712	*þs*	295
in	512	*dþ*	272
sþ	494	*þo*	266
er	433	*io*	257
þa	425	*co*	256
tþ	401	*re*	247
en	392	*þ$*	246
on	385	*rþ*	239
nþ	353	*di*	230
ti	322	*ic*	229
þi	317	*ct*	226

TABLE 5.3　　Thirty most frequently occurring pairs of characters in a collection of C programs containing 64,983 characters.

Pair	Count	Pair	Count
þþ	5728	*st*	442
nlþ	1471	*le*	440
; nl	1133	*ut*	440
in	985	*f (*	416
nt	739	*ar*	381
= þ	687	*or*	374
þi	662	*rþ*	373
tþ	615	*en*	371
þ =	612	*er*	358
);	558	*ri*	357
,þ	554	*at*	352
nlnl	506	*pr*	351
þf	505	*te*	349
eþ	500	*an*	348
þ∗	444	*lo*	347

Match pointer

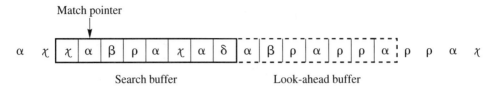

FIGURE   5.1   **Encoding using the LZ77 approach.**

match consecutive symbols in the look-ahead buffer. The number of consecutive symbols in the search buffer that match consecutive symbols in the look-ahead buffer, starting with the first symbol, is called the length of the match. The encoder searches the search buffer for the longest match. Once the longest match has been found, the encoder encodes it with a triple $\langle o, l, c \rangle$, where o is the offset, l is the length of the match, and c is the codeword corresponding to the symbol in the look-ahead buffer that follows the match. For example, in Figure 5.1 the pointer is pointing to the beginning of the longest match. The offset o in this case is 7, the length of the match l is 4, and the symbol in the look-ahead buffer following the match is ρ.

The reason for sending the third element in the triple is to take care of the situation where no match for the symbol in the look-ahead buffer can be found in the search buffer. In this case, the offset and match-length values are set to 0, and the third element of the triple is the code for the symbol itself.

If the size of the search buffer is S, the size of the window (search and look-ahead buffers) is W, and the size of the source alphabet is A, then the number of bits needed to code the triple using fixed-length codes is $\lceil \log_2 S \rceil + \lceil \log_2 W \rceil + \lceil \log_2 A \rceil$. Notice that the second term is $\lceil \log_2 W \rceil$, not $\lceil \log_2 S \rceil$. The reason for this is that the length of the match can actually exceed the length of the search buffer. We will see how this happens in Example 5.4.1.

In the following example, we will look at three different possibilities that may be encountered during the coding process:

1. There is no match for the next character to be encoded in the window.

2. There is a match.

3. The matched string extends inside the look-ahead buffer.

Example   5.4.1:   The   LZ77   approach

Suppose the sequence to be encoded is

$$\ldots cabracadabrarrarrad \ldots$$

Suppose the length of the window is 13, the size of the look-ahead buffer is six, and the current condition is as follows:

cabraca	dabrar

with *dabrar* in the look-ahead buffer. We look back in the already encoded portion of the window to find a match for *d*. As we can see, there is no match, so we transmit the triple

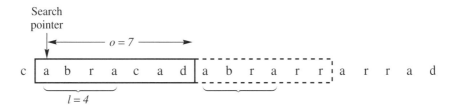

FIGURE 5.2   The encoding process.

$\langle 0, 0, C(d) \rangle$. The first two elements of the triple show that there is no match to d in the search buffer, while $C(d)$ is the code for the character d. This seems like a wasteful way to encode a single character, and we will have more to say about this later.

For now, let's continue with the encoding process. As we have encoded a single character, we move the window by one character. Now the contents of the buffer are

| abracad | abrarr |

with *abrarr* in the look-ahead buffer. Looking back from the current location, we find a match to *a* at an offset of two. The length of this match is one. Looking further back, we have another match for *a* at an offset of four; again the length of the match is one. Looking back even further in the window, we have a third match for *a* at an offset of seven. However, this time the length of the match is four (see Figure 5.2). So we encode the string *abra* with the triple $\langle 7, 4, C(r) \rangle$, and move the window forward by five characters. The window now contains the following characters:

| adabrar | rarrad |

Now the look-ahead buffer contains the string *rarrad*. Looking back in the window, we find a match for *r* at an offset of one and a match length of one, and a second match at an offset of three with a match length of what at first appears to be three. It turns out we can use a match length of five instead of three.

Why this is so will become clearer when we decode the sequence. To see how the decoding works, let us assume that we have decoded the sequence *cabraca* and we receive the triples $\langle 0, 0, C(d) \rangle$, $\langle 7, 4, C(r) \rangle$, and $\langle 3, 5, C(d) \rangle$. The first triple is easy to decode; there was no match within the previously decoded string, and the next symbol is d. The decoded string is now *cabracad*. The first element of the next triple tells the decoder to move the copy pointer back seven characters, and copy four characters from that point. The decoding process works as shown in Figure 5.3.

Finally, let's see how the triple $\langle 3, 5, C(d) \rangle$ gets decoded. We move back three characters and start copying. The first three characters we copy are *rar*. The copy pointer moves once again, as shown in Figure 5.4, to copy the recently copied character *r*. Similarly, we copy the next character *a*. Even though we started copying only three characters back, we end up decoding five characters. Notice that the match only has to *start* in the search buffer; it can extend into the look-ahead buffer. In fact, if the last character in the look-ahead buffer had been *r* instead of *d*, followed by several more repetitions of *rar*, the entire sequence of repeated *rars* could have been encoded with a single triple.

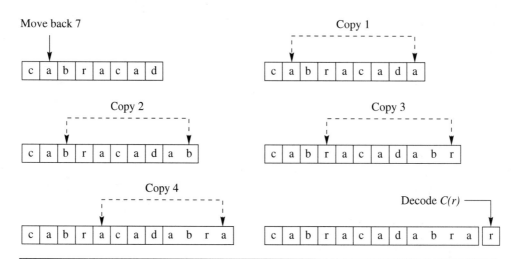

FIGURE 5.3   Decoding of the triple ⟨7, 4, C(r)⟩.

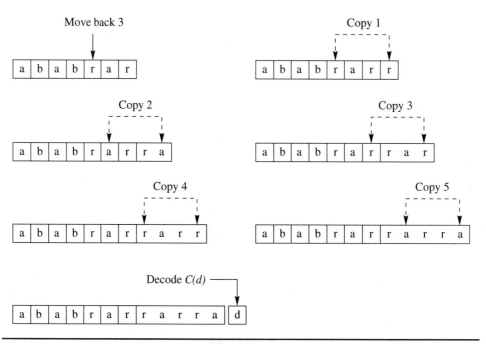

FIGURE 5.4   Decoding the triple ⟨3, 5, C(d)⟩.   ◆

As we can see, the LZ77 scheme is a very simple adaptive scheme that requires no prior knowledge of the source and seems to require no assumptions about the characteristics of the source. The authors of this algorithm showed that asymptotically the performance of this algorithm approached the best that could be obtained by using a scheme that had full knowledge about the statistics of the source. While this may be true asymptotically, in practice there are a number of ways of improving the performance of the LZ77 algorithm as described here. Furthermore, by using the recent portions of the sequence, there is an assumption of sorts being used here—that is, that patterns recur "close" together. As we shall see, in LZ78 the authors removed this "assumption" and came up with an entirely different adaptive-dictionary-based scheme. Before we get to that, let us look at the different variations of the LZ77 algorithm.

Variations on the LZ77 Theme

There are a number of ways that the LZ77 scheme can be made more efficient, and most of these have appeared in the literature. Many of the improvements deal with the efficient encoding of the triples. In the description of the LZ77 algorithm, we assumed that the triples were encoded using a fixed-length code. However, if we were willing to accept more complexity, we could encode the triples using variable-length codes. As we saw in earlier chapters, these codes can be adaptive or, if we were willing to use a two-pass algorithm, they can be semi-adaptive. Popular compression packages, such as PKZip, Zip, LHarc, PNG, gzip, and ARJ, all use an LZ77-based algorithm followed by a variable-length coder.

Other variations on the LZ77 algorithm include varying the size of the search and look-ahead buffers. To make the search buffer large requires the development of more effective search strategies. Such strategies can be implemented more effectively if the contents of the search buffer are stored in a manner conducive to fast searches.

The simplest modification to the LZ77 algorithm, and one that is used by most variations of the LZ77 algorithm, is to eliminate the situation where we use a triple to encode a single character. Use of a triple is highly inefficient, especially if a large number of characters occur infrequently. The modification to get rid of this inefficiency is simply the addition of a flag bit, to indicate whether what follows is the codeword for a single symbol. By using this flag bit we also get rid of the necessity for the third element of the triple. Now all we need to do is to send a pair of values corresponding to the offset and length of match. This modification to the LZ77 algorithm is referred to as LZSS [220, 19].

5.4.2 The LZ78 Approach

The LZ77 approach implicitly assumes that like patterns will occur close together. It makes use of this structure by using the recent past of the sequence as the dictionary for encoding. However, this means that any pattern that recurs over a period longer than that covered by the coder window will not be captured. The worst-case situation would be where the sequence to be encoded was periodic with a period longer than the search buffer. Consider Figure 5.5.

This is a periodic sequence with a period of nine. If the search buffer had been just one symbol longer, this sequence could have been significantly compressed. As it stands, none of the new symbols will have a match in the search buffer and will have to be represented by separate codewords. As this involves sending along overhead (a 1-bit flag for LZSS and

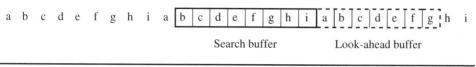

Search buffer   Look-ahead buffer

FIGURE 5.5   *The Achilles' heel of LZ77.*

a triple for the original LZ77 algorithm), the net result will be an expansion rather than a compression.

Although this is an extreme situation, there are less drastic circumstances in which the finite view of the past would be a drawback. The LZ78 algorithm solves this problem by dropping the reliance on the search buffer and keeping an explicit dictionary. This dictionary has to be built at both the encoder and decoder, and care must be taken that the dictionaries are built in an identical manner. The inputs are coded as a double $\langle i, c \rangle$, with i being an index corresponding to the dictionary entry that was the longest match to the input, and c being the code for the character in the input following the matched portion of the input. As in the case of LZ77, the index value of 0 is used in the case of no match. This double then becomes the newest entry in the dictionary. Thus, each new entry into the dictionary is one new symbol concatenated with an existing dictionary entry. To see how the LZ78 algorithm works, consider the following example.

Example 5.4.2: The LZ78 approach

Let us encode the following sequence using the LZ78 approach:

$$wabba\flat wabba\flat wabba\flat wabba\flat woo\flat woo\flat woo^2$$

where $\flat$ stands for space. Initially, the dictionary is empty, so the first few symbols encountered are encoded with the index value set to 0. The first three encoder outputs are $\langle 0, C(w) \rangle$, $\langle 0, C(a) \rangle$, $\langle 0, C(b) \rangle$, and the dictionary looks like Table 5.4.

The fourth symbol is a b, which is the third entry in the dictionary. If we append the next symbol, we would get the pattern ba, which is not in the dictionary, so we encode these two symbols as $\langle 3, C(a) \rangle$, and add the pattern ba as the fourth entry in the dictionary. Continuing in this fashion, the encoder output and the dictionary develop as in Table 5.5. Notice that the entries in the dictionary generally keep getting longer, and if this particular sentence was

TABLE 5.4   **The initial dictionary.**

Index	Entry
1	w
2	a
3	b

---

[2]"The Monster Song" from *Sesame Street*.

TABLE 5.5   **Development of dictionary.**

| | Dictionary | |
Encoder Output	Index	Entry
$\langle 0, C(w) \rangle$	1	w
$\langle 0, C(a) \rangle$	2	a
$\langle 0, C(b) \rangle$	3	b
$\langle 3, C(a) \rangle$	4	ba
$\langle 0, C(\flat) \rangle$	5	$\flat$
$\langle 1, C(a) \rangle$	6	wa
$\langle 3, C(b) \rangle$	7	bb
$\langle 2, C(\flat) \rangle$	8	$a\flat$
$\langle 6, C(b) \rangle$	9	wab
$\langle 4, C(\flat) \rangle$	10	$ba\flat$
$\langle 9, C(b) \rangle$	11	$wabb$
$\langle 8, C(w) \rangle$	12	$a\flat w$
$\langle 0, C(o) \rangle$	13	o
$\langle 13, C(\flat) \rangle$	14	$o\flat$
$\langle 1, C(o) \rangle$	15	wo
$\langle 14, C(w) \rangle$	16	$o\flat w$
$\langle 13, C(o) \rangle$	17	oo

repeated often, as it is in the song, after a while the entire sentence would be an entry in the dictionary.   ◆

While the LZ78 algorithm has the ability to capture patterns and hold them indefinitely, it also has a rather serious drawback. As seen from the example, the dictionary keeps growing without bound. In a practical situation, we would have to stop the growth of the dictionary at some stage, and then either prune it back or treat the encoding as a fixed dictionary scheme. We will discuss some possible approaches when we study applications of dictionary coding.

Variations on the LZ78 Theme—The LZW Algorithm

There are a number of ways the LZ78 algorithm can be modified, and as is the case with the LZ77 algorithm, anything that can be modified probably has been. The most well-known modification, one that initially sparked much of the interest in the LZ algorithms, is a modification by Terry Welch known as LZW [237]. Welch proposed a technique for removing the necessity of encoding the second element of the pair $\langle i, c \rangle$. That is, the encoder would only send the index to the dictionary. In order to do this, the dictionary has to be primed with all the letters of the source alphabet. The input to the encoder is accumulated in a pattern p as long as p is contained in the dictionary. If the addition of another letter a results in a pattern $p * a$ (* denotes concatenation) that is not in the dictionary, then the index of p is transmitted to the receiver, the pattern $p * a$ is added to the dictionary, and we start another pattern with the letter a. The LZW algorithm is best understood with an example. In the following two examples, we will look at the encoder and decoder operations for the same sequence used to explain the LZ78 algorithm.

Example 5.4.3: The LZW algorithm—encoding

We will use the sequence previously used to demonstrate the LZ78 algorithm as our input sequence:

$$wabba\flat wabba\flat wabba\flat wabba\flat woo\flat woo\flat woo$$

Assuming that the alphabet for the source is $\{\flat, a, b, o, w\}$, the LZW dictionary initially looks like Table 5.6.

The encoder first encounters the letter w. This "pattern" is in the dictionary so we concatenate the next letter to it, forming the pattern wa. This pattern is not in the dictionary, so we encode w with its dictionary index 5, add the pattern wa to the dictionary as the sixth element of the dictionary, and begin a new pattern starting with the letter a. As a is in the dictionary, we concatenate the next element b to form the pattern ab. This pattern is not in the dictionary, so we encode a with its dictionary index value 2, add the pattern ab to the dictionary as the seventh element of the dictionary, and start constructing a new pattern with the letter b. We continue in this manner, constructing two-letter patterns, until we reach the letter w in the second $wabba$. At this point the output of the encoder consists entirely of indices from the initial dictionary: 5 2 3 3 2 1. The dictionary at this point looks like Table 5.7. (The 12th entry in the dictionary is still under construction.) The next symbol in the sequence is a. Concatenating this to w, we get the pattern wa. This pattern already exists in the dictionary (item 6), so we read the next symbol, which is b. Concatenating this to wa, we get the pattern wab. This pattern does not exist in the dictionary, so we include it as the 12th entry in the dictionary and start a new pattern with the symbol b. We also encode wa with its index value of 6. Notice that after a series of two-letter entries, we now have a three-letter entry. As the encoding progresses, the length of the entries keeps increasing. The longer entries in the dictionary indicate that the dictionary is capturing more of the structure in the sequence. The dictionary at the end of the encoding process is shown in Table 5.8. Notice that the 12th through the 19th entries are all either three or four letters in length. Then we encounter the pattern woo for the first time and we drop back to two-letter patterns for three more entries, after which we go back to entries of increasing length.

The encoder output sequence is 5 2 3 3 2 1 6 8 10 12 9 11 7 16 5 4 4 11 21 23 4.

TABLE 5.6   Initial LZW dictionary.

Index	Entry
1	$\flat$
2	a
3	b
4	o
5	w

TABLE 5.7	Constructing the 12th entry of the LZW dictionary.
Index	**Entry**
1	þ
2	a
3	b
4	o
5	w
6	wa
7	ab
8	bb
9	ba
10	aþ
11	þw
12	w ...

TABLE 5.8 The LZW dictionary for encoding wabbaþwabbaþwabbaþwabbaþwooþwooþwoo.

Index	Entry	Index	Entry
1	þ	14	aþw
2	a	15	wabb
3	b	16	baþ
4	o	17	þwa
5	w	18	abb
6	wa	19	baþw
7	ab	20	wo
8	bb	21	oo
9	ba	22	oþ
10	aþ	23	þwo
11	þw	24	ooþ
12	wab	25	þwoo
13	bba		

◆

Example 5.4.4: The LZW algorithm—decoding

In this example we will take the encoder output from the previous example and decode it using the LZW algorithm. The encoder output sequence in the previous example was

$$5\ 2\ 3\ 3\ 2\ 1\ 6\ 8\ 10\ 12\ 9\ 11\ 7\ 16\ 5\ 4\ 4\ 11\ 21\ 23\ 4$$

This becomes the decoder input sequence. The decoder starts with the same initial dictionary as the encoder (Table 5.6).

The index value 5 corresponds to the letter *w*, so we decode *w* as the first element of our sequence. At the same time, in order to mimic the dictionary construction procedure of the encoder, we begin construction of the next element of the dictionary. We start with the letter

TABLE 5.9   **Constructing the 11th entry of the LZW dictionary while decoding.**

Index	Entry
1	b
2	a
3	b
4	o
5	w
6	wa
7	ab
8	bb
9	ba
10	ab
11	$b\ldots$

w. This pattern exists in the dictionary, so we do not add it to the dictionary and continue with the decoding process. The next decoder input is 2, which is the index corresponding to the letter a. We decode an a and concatenate it with our current pattern to form the pattern wa. As this does not exist in the dictionary, we add it as the sixth element of the dictionary and start a new pattern beginning with the letter a. The next four inputs 3 3 2 1 correspond to the letters $bbab$ and generate the dictionary entries ab, bb, ba, and ab. The dictionary now looks like Table 5.9, where the 11th entry is under construction.

The next input is 6, which is the index of the pattern wa. Therefore, we decode a w and an a. We first concatenate w to the existing pattern, which is b, and form the pattern bw. As bw does not exist in the dictionary, it becomes the 11th entry. The new pattern now starts with the letter w. We had previously decoded the letter a, which we now concatenate to w to obtain the pattern wa. This pattern is contained in the dictionary, so we decode the next input, which is 8. This corresponds to the entry bb in the dictionary. We decode the first b and concatenate it to the pattern wa to get the pattern wab. This pattern does not exist in the dictionary, so we add it as the 12th entry in the dictionary and start a new pattern with the letter b. Decoding the second b and concatenating it to the new pattern, we get the pattern bb. This pattern exists in the dictionary, so we decode the next element in the sequence of encoder outputs. Continuing in this fashion, we can decode the entire sequence. Notice that the dictionary being constructed by the decoder is identical to that constructed by the encoder.   ◆

There is one particular situation in which the method of decoding the LZW algorithm described above breaks down. Suppose we had a source with an alphabet $\mathcal{A} = \{a, b\}$, and we were to encode the sequence beginning with *abababab*.... The encoding process is still the same. We begin with the initial dictionary shown in Table 5.10 and end up with the final dictionary shown in Table 5.11.

TABLE 5.10 **Initial dictionary for ababab.**

Index	Entry
1	*a*
2	*b*

TABLE 5.11 **Final dictionary for ababab.**

Index	Entry
1	*a*
2	*b*
3	*ab*
4	*ba*
5	*aba*
6	*abab*
7	*b* . . .

TABLE 5.12 **Constructing the fourth entry of the dictionary while decoding.**

Index	Entry
1	*a*
2	*b*
3	*ab*
4	*b* . . .

The transmitted sequence is 1 2 3 5 .... This looks like a relatively straightforward sequence to decode. However, when we try to do so, we run into a snag. Let us go through the decoding process and see what happens.

We begin with the same initial dictionary as the encoder (Table 5.10). The first two elements in the received sequence 1 2 3 5 ... are decoded as *a* and *b*, giving rise to the third dictionary entry *ab*, and the beginning of the next pattern to be entered in the dictionary, *b*. The dictionary at this point is shown in Table 5.12.

The next input to the decoder is 3. This corresponds to the dictionary entry *ab*. Decoding each in turn, we first concatenate *a* to the pattern under construction to get *ba*. This pattern is not contained in the dictionary, so we add this to the dictionary (keep in mind, we have not used the *b* from *ab* yet), which now looks like Table 5.13.

The new entry starts with the letter *a*. We have only used the first letter from the pair *ab*. Therefore, we now concatenate *b* to *a* to obtain the pattern *ab*. This pattern is contained in the dictionary, so we continue with the decoding process. The dictionary at this stage looks like Table 5.14.

The first four entries in the dictionary are complete, while the fifth entry is still under construction. However, the very next input to the decoder is 5, which corresponds to the

TABLE 5.13 **Constructing the fifth entry (stage one).**

Index	Entry
1	*a*
2	*b*
3	*ab*
4	*ba*
5	*a* ...

TABLE 5.14 **Constructing the fifth entry (stage two).**

Index	Entry
1	*a*
2	*b*
3	*ab*
4	*ba*
5	*ab* ...

TABLE 5.15 **Completion of the fifth entry.**

Index	Entry
1	*a*
2	*b*
3	*ab*
4	*ba*
5	*aba*
6	*a* ...

incomplete entry! How do we decode an index for which we do not as yet have a complete dictionary entry?

The situation is actually not as bad as it looks. (Of course, if it were, we would not now be studying LZW.) While we may not have a fifth entry for the dictionary, we do have the beginnings of the fifth entry, which is *ab*.... Let us, for the moment, pretend that we do indeed have the fifth entry and continue with the decoding process. If we had a fifth entry, the first two letters of the entry would be *a* and *b*. Concatenating *a* to the partial new entry we get the pattern *aba*. This pattern is not contained in the dictionary, so we add this to our dictionary, which now looks like Table 5.15. Notice that we now have the fifth entry in the dictionary, which is *aba*. We have already decoded the *ab* portion of *aba*. We can now decode the last letter *a* and continue on our merry way.

This means that the LZW decoder has to contain an exception handler to handle the special case of decoding an index that does not have a corresponding complete entry in the decoder dictionary.

5.5 Applications

Since the publication of Terry Welch's article [237], there has been a steadily increasing number of applications that use some variant of the LZ78 algorithm. Among the LZ78 variants, by far the most popular is the LZW algorithm. Lately, there has been renewed interest in the LZ77 approach and its variants as well. However, for now, the LZ78 approach, or more specifically, the LZW algorithm, is one of the most widely used compression algorithms. In this section we describe three of the best-known applications of LZW: UNIX compress, GIF, and V.42 bis.

5.5.1 File Compression—UNIX compress

The UNIX compress command is one of the earlier applications of LZW. The size of the dictionary is adaptive. We start with a dictionary of size 512. This means that the transmitted codewords are 9 bits long. Once the dictionary has filled up, the size of the dictionary is doubled to 1024 entries. The codewords transmitted at this point have 10 bits. The size of the dictionary is progressively doubled as it fills up. In this way, during the earlier part of the coding process when the strings in the dictionary are not very long, the codewords used to encode them also have fewer bits. The maximum size of the codeword, $b_{\max}$, can be set by the user to between 9 and 16, with 16 bits being the default. Once the dictionary contains $2^{b_{\max}}$ entries, compress becomes a static dictionary coding technique. At this point the algorithm monitors the compression ratio. If the compression ratio falls below a threshold, the dictionary is flushed, and the dictionary building process is restarted. This way, the dictionary always reflects the local characteristics of the source.

5.5.2 Image Compression—The Graphics Interchange Format (GIF)

The Graphics Interchange Format (GIF) was developed by Compuserve Information Service to encode graphical images. It is another implementation of the LZW algorithm and is very similar to the compress command. The compressed image is stored with the first byte being the minimum number of bits b per pixel in the original image. For the images we have been using as examples, this would be eight. The binary number 2^b is defined to be the *clear code*. This code is used to reset all compression and decompression parameters to a start-up state. The initial size of the dictionary is 2^{b+1}. When this fills up, the dictionary size is doubled, as was done in the compress algorithm, until the maximum dictionary size of 4096 is reached. At this point the compression algorithm behaves like a static dictionary algorithm. The codewords from the LZW algorithm are stored in blocks of characters. The characters are 8 bits long, and the maximum block size is 255. Each block is preceded by a header that contains the block size. The block is terminated by a block terminator consisting of eight 0s. The end of the compressed image is denoted by an end-of-information code with a value of $2^b + 1$. This codeword should appear before the block terminator.

GIF has become quite popular for encoding all kinds of images, both computer-generated and "natural" images. While GIF works well with computer-generated graphical images, and

TABLE 5.16   **Comparison of GIF with arithmetic coding.**

Image	GIF	Arithmetic Coding of Pixel Values	Arithmetic Coding of Pixel Differences
Sena	51,085	53,431	31,847
Sensin	60,649	58,306	37,126
Earth	34,276	38,248	32,137
Omaha	61,580	56,061	51,393

pseudocolor or color-mapped images, it is generally not the most efficient way to losslessly compress images of natural scenes, photographs, satellite images, and so on. In Table 5.16 we give the file sizes for the GIF-encoded test images. For comparison, we also include the file sizes for arithmetic coding the original images and arithmetic coding the differences.

Notice that even if we account for the extra overhead in the GIF files, for these images GIF barely holds its own even with simple arithmetic coding of the original pixels. While this might seem odd at first, if we examine the image on a pixel level, we see that there are very few repetitive patterns compared to a text source. Some images, like the Earth image, contain large regions of constant values. In the dictionary coding approach, these regions become single entries in the dictionary. Therefore, for images like these, the dictionary coding approach does hold its own. However, for most other images, it would probably be preferable to use some other approach. We will revisit this subject in Chapter 6.

5.5.3   Compression over Modems—V.42 bis

The CCITT (now called ITU-T) Recommendation V.42 bis is a compression standard to be used over a telephone network along with error-correcting procedures described in CCITT Recommendation V.42. This algorithm is used in modems connecting computers to remote users. The algorithm described in this recommendation operates in two modes, a transparent mode and a compressed mode. In the transparent mode, the data are transmitted in uncompressed form, while in the compressed mode an LZW algorithm is used to provide compression.

The reason for the existence of two modes is that at times the data being transmitted do not have repetitive structure and therefore cannot be compressed using the LZW algorithm. In this case, the use of a compression algorithm may even result in expansion. In these situations, it is better to send the data in an uncompressed form. A random data stream would cause the dictionary to grow without any long patterns as elements of the dictionary. This means that most of the time the transmitted codeword would represent a single letter from the source alphabet. As the dictionary size is much larger than the source alphabet size, the number of bits required to represent an element in the dictionary is much more than the number of bits required to represent a source letter. Therefore, if we tried to compress a sequence that does not contain repeating patterns, we would end up with more bits to transmit than if we had not performed any compression. Data without repetitive structure are often encountered when a previously compressed file is transferred over the telephone lines.

TABLE 5.17   Control codewords in compressed mode.

Codeword	Name	Description
0	ETM	Enter transparent mode
1	FLUSH	Flush data
2	STEPUP	Increment codeword size

The V.42 bis recommendation suggests periodic testing of the output of the compression algorithm to see if data expansion is taking place. The exact nature of the test is not specified in the recommendation.

In the compressed mode, the system uses LZW compression with a variable-size dictionary. The initial dictionary size is negotiated at the time a link is established between the transmitter and receiver. The V.42 bis recommendation suggests a value of 2048 for the dictionary size. It specifies that the minimum size of the dictionary is to be 512. Suppose the initial negotiations result in a dictionary size of 512. This means that our codewords that are indices into the dictionary will be 9 bits long. Actually, the entire 512 indices do not correspond to input strings; three entries in the dictionary are reserved for control codewords. These codewords in the compressed mode are shown in Table 5.17.

When the numbers of entries in the dictionary exceed a prearranged threshold C_3, the encoder sends the STEPUP control code, and the codeword size is incremented by 1 bit. At the same time, the threshold C_3 is also doubled. When all available dictionary entries are filled, the algorithm initiates a reuse procedure. The location of the first string entry in the dictionary is maintained in a variable N_5. Starting from N_5, a counter C_1 is incremented until it finds a dictionary entry that is not a prefix to any other dictionary entry. The fact that this entry is not a prefix to another dictionary entry means that this pattern has not been encountered since it was created. Furthermore, because of the way it was located, among patterns of this kind this pattern has been around the longest. This reuse procedure enables the algorithm to prune the dictionary of strings that may have been encountered in the past but have not been encountered recently, on a continual basis. In this way the dictionary is always matched to the current source statistics.

To reduce the effect of errors, the CCITT recommends setting a maximum string length. This maximum length is negotiated at link setup. The CCITT recommends a range of 6–250, with a default value of 6.

The V.42 bis recommendation avoids the need for an exception handler for the case where the decoder receives a codeword corresponding to an incomplete entry by forbidding the use of the last entry in the dictionary. Instead of transmitting the codeword corresponding to the last entry, the recommendation requires the sending of the codewords corresponding to the constituents of the last entry. In the example used to demonstrate this quirk of the LZW algorithm, instead of transmitting the codeword 5, the V.42 bis recommendation would have forced us to send the codewords 3 and 1.

5.6 Summary

In this chapter we have introduced techniques that keep a dictionary of recurring patterns and transmit the index of those patterns instead of the patterns themselves in order to achieve compression. There are a number of ways the dictionary can be constructed.

- In applications where certain patterns consistently recur, we can build application-specific static dictionaries. Care should be taken not to use these dictionaries outside their area of intended application. Otherwise, we may end up with data expansion instead of data compression.

- The dictionary can be the source output itself. This is the approach used by the LZ77 algorithm. When using this algorithm, there is an implicit assumption that recurrence of a pattern is a local phenomenon.

- This assumption is removed in the LZ78 approach, which dynamically constructs a dictionary from patterns observed in the source output.

Dictionary-based algorithms are being used to compress all kinds of data; however, care should be taken with their use. This approach is most useful when structural constraints restrict the frequently occurring patterns to a small subset of all possible patterns. This is the case with text, as well as computer-to-computer communication. However, this is not the case with images.

Further Reading

1. *Text Compression*, by T.C. Bell, J.G. Cleary, and I.H. Witten [20], provides an excellent exposition of dictionary-based coding techniques.

2. *The Data Compression Book*, by M. Nelson and J.-L. Gailley [167], also does a good job of describing the Ziv-Lempel algorithms. There is also a very nice description of some of the software implementation aspects.

3. *Data Compression*, by G. Held and T.R. Marshall [101], contains a description of digram coding under the name "diatomic coding." The book also includes BASIC programs that help in the design of dictionaries.

5.7 Projects and Problems

1. To study the effect of dictionary size on the efficiency of a static dictionary technique, we can modify Equation (5.1) so that it gives the rate as a function of both p and the dictionary size M. Plot the rate as a function of p for different values of M, and discuss the trade-offs involved in selecting larger or smaller values of M.

2. Design and implement a digram coder for text files of interest to you.

TABLE 5.18   Initial dictionary for Problem 4.

Index	Entry
1	*a*
2	*þ*
3	*h*
4	*i*
5	*s*
6	*t*

TABLE 5.19   Initial dictionary for Problem 5.

Index	Entry
1	*a*
2	*þ*
3	*r*
4	*t*

(a) Study the effect of the dictionary size, and the size of the text file being encoded on the amount of compression.

(b) Use the digram coder on files that are not similar to the ones you used to design the digram coder. How much does this affect your compression?

3. Given an initial dictionary consisting of the letters *a b r y þ*, encode the following message using the LZW algorithm: *aþbarþarrayþbyþbarrayarþbay*.

4. A sequence is encoded using the LZW algorithm and the initial dictionary shown in Table 5.18.

(a) The output of the LZW encoder is the following sequence:

6	3	4	5	2	3	1	6	2	9	11	16	12	14	4	20	10	8	23	13

Decode this sequence.

(b) Encode the decoded sequence using the same initial dictionary. Does your answer match the sequence given above?

5. A sequence is encoded using the LZW algorithm and the initial dictionary shown in Table 5.19.

(a) The output of the LZW encoder is the following sequence:

3	1	4	6	8	4	2	1	2	5	10	6	11	13	6

Decode this sequence.

(b) Encode the decoded sequence using the same initial dictionary. Does your answer match the sequence given above?

6. Encode the following sequence using the LZ77 algorithm:

$$barrayar\flat bar\flat by\flat barrayar\flat bay$$

Assume you have a window size of 30 with a look-ahead buffer of size 15. Furthermore, assume that $C(a) = 1$, $C(b) = 2$, $C(\flat) = 3$, $C(r) = 4$, and $C(y) = 5$.

7. A sequence is encoded using the LZ77 algorithm. Given that $C(a) = 1$, $C(\flat) = 2$, $C(r) = 3$, and $C(t) = 4$, decode the following sequence of triples:

$$\langle 0, 0, 3 \rangle \ \langle 0, 0, 1 \rangle \ \langle 0, 0, 4 \rangle \ \langle 2, 8, 2 \rangle \ \langle 3, 1, 2 \rangle \ \langle 0, 0, 3 \rangle \ \langle 6, 4, 4 \rangle \ \langle 9, 5, 4 \rangle$$

Assume that the size of the window is 20 and the size of the look-ahead buffer is 10. Encode the decoded sequence and make sure you get the same sequence of triples.

8. The program diffim, available on the publisher's website, can be used to generate various types of difference images. Use this program in conjunction with huff_enc to encode several of the Sena, Sinan, and Earth images. Look at the compressed file size, and compare with the file size obtained when you use the compress command on these images. Why do you not get much improvement (if any) when you use compress on the difference images?

6.1 Overview

n this chapter we present a number of techniques that make use of the past history of the data being encoded to provide more efficient compression. We will look at a number of schemes principally used for the compression of text and images.

6.2 Introduction

In Chapters 3 and 4 we learned that we get more compression when the message that is being coded has a more skewed set of probabilities. By "skewed" we mean that, in the sequence to be encoded, certain symbols occur with much higher probability than others. There are several ways to achieve this situation. We can transform the sequence (in an invertible fashion) into another sequence that has the desired property. Or, we can use a different probability distribution for each symbol, such that in the probability distribution used, with high likelihood the symbol being coded is a high-probability symbol. In both approaches we also need to let the decoder know the transformation or the distribution function being used. If the transformation or distribution is based on the history of the sequence, history that is available to both encoder and decoder, then there might not be any need to transmit the additional information. Because we use the history of the sequence in a predictive manner to determine its encoding, such schemes are called *predictive coding schemes*.

There are a number of ways we can transform a sequence using its history to generate a sequence with a skewed distribution. For example, consider the following sequence:

1	2	5	7	2	−2	0	−5	−3	−1	1	−2	−7	−4	−2	1	3	4

If we consider this sample to be fairly typical of the sequence, we can see that the probability of any given number being in the range from -7 to 7 is about the same. If we were to encode this sequence using a Huffman or arithmetic code, we would use almost 4 bits per symbol.

Instead of encoding this sequence directly, we could do the following: add two to the previous number in the sequence and send the difference between the current element in the sequence and this *predicted* value. The transmitted sequence would be

1	-1	1	0	-7	-4	0	-7	0	0	0	-5	-7	1	0	1	0	-1

This method uses a rule (add two) and the history (value of the previous symbol) to generate the new sequence. If the rule by which this *residual sequence* was generated is known to the decoder, it can recover the original sequence from the residual sequence. The length of the residual sequence is the same as the original sequence. However, notice that the residual sequence is much more likely to contain 0s, 1s, and -1s than other values. That is, the probability of 0, 1, and -1 will be significantly higher than the probabilities of other numbers. This, in turn, means that the entropy of the residual sequence will be low and, therefore, provide more compression.

We used a particular method of prediction in this example (add two to the previous element of the sequence) that was specific to this sequence. In order to get the best possible performance, we need to find the prediction approach that is best suited to the particular data we are dealing with. We will look at several prediction schemes used for lossless image compression in Sections 6.5 and 6.6.

A different kind of prediction is used when encoding nonnumerical data such as text. Recall that high-probability symbols require fewer bits to encode. Therefore, when encoding a particular symbol, we would like to use the probability distribution in which the symbol we are trying to encode has a high probability. We can then use adaptive arithmetic coding to encode that symbol at a low rate. However, if we are going to use a different probability model to encode each symbol, for each symbol we need to let the receiver know which probability model is being used. One way to do this with no cost is to use the preceding symbols to predict the probability model. In other words, the preceding symbols form the *context* in which the symbol is being encoded.

Consider the encoding of the word *probability*. Suppose we have already encoded the first four letters, and we want to code the fifth letter, *a*. If we ignore the first four letters, the probability of the letter *a* is about 0.06. If we use the information that the previous letter is *b*, this reduces the probability of several letters such as *q* and *z* occurring and boosts the probability of an *a* occurring. In this example, *b* would be the first-order context for *a*, *ob* would be the second-order context for *a*, and so on. Using more letters to define the context in which *a* occurs, or higher-order contexts, will generally increase the probability of the occurrence of *a* in this example, and hence reduce the number of bits required to encode its occurrence. Therefore, what we would like to do is to encode each letter using the probability of its occurrence with respect to a context of high order.

If we want to have probabilities with respect to all possible high-order contexts, this might be an overwhelming amount of information. Consider an alphabet of size M. The number of first-order contexts is M, the number of second-order contexts is M^2, and so on. Therefore, if we wanted to encode a sequence from an alphabet of size 256 using contexts of order 5, we would need 256^5, or about 1.09951×10^{12} probability distributions! This is not a practical alternative. A set of algorithms that resolve this problem in a very simple and elegant way is based on the *prediction with partial match (ppm)* approach. We will describe this in the next section.

Predictive coding in its various forms has enjoyed a resurgence in recent years. Some of the best-performing text compression algorithms are variants of the *ppm* algorithm. The new JPEG standard for lossless image compression is a predictive coding algorithm. This is not to say that the idea of predictive coding has not been around for a very long time. In fact, one of the earliest compression algorithms that is still used in facsimile transmission has predictive elements in it. We will discuss several of these algorithms in this chapter.

We begin with algorithms that use the context of the symbol being encoded to obtain the probability distribution to be used in the encoding. We then turn our attention to predictive coding schemes that try to predict the value of the symbol being encoded, then code the prediction error.

6.3 Prediction with Partial Match (*ppm*)

The best-known context-based algorithm is the *ppm* algorithm, first proposed by Cleary and Witten [50] in 1984. It has not been as popular as the various Ziv-Lempel-based algorithms mainly because of the faster execution speeds of the latter algorithms. Lately, with the development of more efficient variants, *ppm*-based algorithms are becoming increasingly more popular.

The idea of the *ppm* algorithm is elegantly simple. We would like to use large contexts to determine the probability of the symbol being encoded. However, the use of large contexts would require us to estimate and store an extremely large number of conditional probabilities, which might not be feasible. Instead of estimating these probabilities ahead of time, we can reduce the burden by estimating the probabilities as the coding proceeds. This way we only need to store those contexts that have occurred in the sequence being encoded. This is a much smaller number than the number of all possible contexts. While this mitigates the problem of storage, it also means that, especially at the beginning of an encoding, we will need to code letters that have not occurred previously in this context. In order to handle this situation, the source coder alphabet always contains an escape symbol, which is used to signal that the letter to be encoded has not been seen in this context.

6.3.1 The Basic Algorithm

The basic algorithm initially attempts to use the largest context. The size of the largest context is predetermined. If the symbol to be encoded has not previously been encountered in this context, an escape symbol is encoded and the algorithm attempts to use the next smaller context. If the symbol has not occurred in this context either, the size of the context is further reduced. This process continues until either we obtain a context that has previously been encountered with this symbol, or we arrive at the conclusion that the symbol has not been encountered previously in *any* context. In this case, we use a probability of $1/M$ to encode the symbol, where M is the size of the source alphabet. For example, when coding the *a* of *probability*, we would first attempt to see if the string *proba* has previously occurred—that is, if *a* had previously occurred in the context of *prob*. If not, we would encode an escape and see if *a* had occurred in the context of *rob*. If the string *roba* had not occurred previously, we would again send an escape symbol and try the context *ob*. Continuing in this manner, we would try the context *b*, and failing that, we would see if the letter *a* (with a zero-order context) had occurred previously. If *a* was being encountered for the first time, we would use a model in which all letters occur with equal probability to encode *a*. This equiprobable model is sometimes referred to as the context of order -1.

As the development of the probabilities with respect to each context is an adaptive process, each time a symbol is encountered, the count corresponding to that symbol is updated. The number of counts to be assigned to the escape symbol is not obvious, and a number of different approaches have been used. One approach used by Cleary and Witten is to give the escape symbol a count of one, thus inflating the total count by one. Cleary and Witten call this method of assigning counts Method A, and the resulting algorithm *ppma*. We will describe some of the other ways of assigning counts to the escape symbol later in this section.

Before we delve into some of the details, let's work through an example to see how all this works together. As we will be using arithmetic coding to encode the symbols, you might wish to refresh your memory of the arithmetic coding algorithms.

Example 6.3.1:

Let's encode the sequence

$$thisþisþtheþtithe$$

Assuming we have already encoded the initial seven characters *thisþis*, the various counts and *Cum_Count* arrays to be used in the arithmetic coding of the symbols are shown in Tables 6.1–6.4. In this example, we are assuming that the longest context length is two. This is a rather small value and is used here to keep the size of the example reasonably small. A more common value for the longest context length is five.

We will assume that the word length for arithmetic coding is four. Thus, $l = 0000$ and $u = 1111$. As *thisþis* has already been encoded, the next letter to be encoded is *þ*. The second-order context for this letter is *is*. Looking at Table 6.4, we can see that the letter *þ* is the first letter in this context with a *Cum_Count* value of 1. As the *Total_Count* in this case is 2, the update equations for the lower and upper limits are

$$l = 0 + \left\lfloor (15 - 0 + 1) \times \frac{0}{2} \right\rfloor = 0 = 0000$$

$$u = 0 + \left\lfloor (15 - 0 + 1) \times \frac{1}{2} \right\rfloor - 1 = 7 = 0111.$$

As the MSBs of both *l* and *u* are the same, we shift that bit out, shift a 0 into the LSB of *l*, and a 1 into the LSB of *u*. The transmitted sequence, lower limit, and upper limit after the update are

Transmitted sequence: 0

l: 0000

u: 1111

TABLE 6.1   **Count array for –1 order context.**

Letter	Count	Cum_Count
t	1	1
h	1	2
i	1	3
s	1	4
e	1	5
♭	1	6
Total Count		6

TABLE 6.2   **Count array for zero-order context.**

Letter	Count	Cum_Count
t	1	1
h	1	2
i	2	4
s	1	5
♭	1	6
⟨Esc⟩	1	7
Total Count		7

We also update the counts in Tables 6.2–6.4.

The next letter to be encoded in the sequence is t. The second-order context is $s♭$. Looking at Table 6.4, we can see that t has not appeared before in this context. We therefore encode an escape symbol. Using the counts listed in Table 6.4, we update the lower and upper limits:

$$l = 0 + \left\lfloor (15 - 0 + 1) \times \frac{1}{2} \right\rfloor = 8 = 1000$$

$$u = 0 + \left\lfloor (15 - 0 + 1) \times \frac{2}{2} \right\rfloor - 1 = 15 = 1111.$$

Again, the MSBs of l and u are the same, so we shift the bit out and shift 0 into the LSB of l, and 1 into u, restoring l to a value of 0 and u to a value of 15. The transmitted sequence is now 01. After transmitting the escape, we look at the first-order context of t, which is $♭$. Looking at Table 6.3, we can see that t has not previously occurred in this context. To let the decoder know this, we transmit another escape. Updating the limits, we get

$$l = 0 + \left\lfloor (15 - 0 + 1) \times \frac{1}{2} \right\rfloor = 8 = 1000$$

$$u = 0 + \left\lfloor (15 - 0 + 1) \times \frac{2}{2} \right\rfloor - 1 = 15 = 1111.$$

As the MSBs of l and u are the same, we shift the MSB out and shift 0 into the LSB of l and 1 into the LSB of u. The transmitted sequence is now 011. Having escaped out of the first-order

TABLE 6.3   **Count array for first-order contexts.**

Context	Letter	Count	Cum_Count
t	h	1	1
	⟨Esc⟩	1	2
	Total Count		2
h	i	1	1
	⟨Esc⟩	1	2
	Total Count		2
i	s	2	2
	⟨Esc⟩	1	3
	Total Count		3
♭	i	1	1
	⟨Esc⟩	1	2
	Total Count		2
s	♭	1	1
	⟨Esc⟩	1	2
	Total Count		2

TABLE 6.4   **Count array for second-order contexts.**

Context	Letter	Count	Cum_Count
th	i	1	1
	⟨Esc⟩	1	2
	Total Count		2
hi	s	1	1
	⟨Esc⟩	1	2
	Total Count		2
is	♭	1	1
	⟨Esc⟩	1	2
	Total Count		2
s♭	i	1	1
	⟨Esc⟩	1	2
	Total Count		2
♭i	s	1	1
	⟨Esc⟩	1	2
	Total Count		2

TABLE 6.5 **Count array for zero-order context.**

Letter	Count	*Cum_Count*
t	2	2
h	1	3
i	2	5
s	1	6
Þ	1	7
⟨Esc⟩	1	8
Total Count		8

contexts, we examine Table 6.2 to see if we can encode *t* using a zero-order context. Indeed we can, and using the *Cum_Count* array, we can update *l* and *u*:

$$l = 0 + \left\lfloor (15 - 0 + 1) \times \frac{0}{7} \right\rfloor = 0 = 0000$$

$$u = 0 + \left\lfloor (15 - 0 + 1) \times \frac{1}{7} \right\rfloor - 1 = 1 = 0001.$$

The three most significant bits of both *l* and *u* are the same, so we shift them out. After the update we get

Transmitted sequence: 011000

l: 0000

u: 1111

The next letter to be encoded is *h*. The second-order context *Þt* has not occurred previously, so we move directly to the first-order context *t*. The letter *h* has occurred previously in this context, so we update *l* and *u* and obtain

Transmitted sequence: 0110000

l: 0000

u: 1111

The method of encoding should now be clear. At this point the various counts are as shown in Tables 6.5–6.7. ◆

Now that we have an idea of how the *ppm* algorithm works, let's examine some of the variations.

6.3.2 The Escape Symbol

In our example we used a count of one for the escape symbol, thus inflating the total count in each context by one. Cleary and Witten call this Method A, and the corresponding algorithm

TABLE 6.6   Count array for first-order contexts.

Context	Letter	Count	Cum_Count
t	h	2	2
	⟨Esc⟩	1	3
	Total Count		3
h	i	1	1
	⟨Esc⟩	1	2
	Total Count		2
i	s	2	2
	⟨Esc⟩	1	3
	Total Count		3
♭	i	1	1
	t	1	2
	⟨Esc⟩	1	3
	Total Count		3
s	♭	1	1
	⟨Esc⟩	1	2
	Total Count		2

TABLE 6.7   Count array for second-order contexts.

Context	Letter	Count	Cum_Count
th	i	1	1
	⟨Esc⟩	1	2
	Total Count		2
hi	s	1	1
	⟨Esc⟩	1	2
	Total Count		2
is	♭	2	2
	⟨Esc⟩	1	3
	Total Count		3
s♭	i	1	1
	t	1	2
	⟨Esc⟩	1	3
	Total Count		3
♭i	s	1	1
	⟨Esc⟩	1	2
	Total Count		2
♭t	h	1	1
	⟨Esc⟩	1	2
	Total Count		2

TABLE 6.8   **Counts using Method A.**

Context	Symbol	Count
prob	*a*	10
	l	9
	o	3
	⟨*Esc*⟩	1
Total Count		23

TABLE 6.9   **Counts using Method B.**

Context	Symbol	Count
prob	*a*	9
	l	8
	o	2
	⟨*Esc*⟩	3
Total Count		22

is referred to as *ppma*. There is really no obvious justification for assigning a count of one to the escape symbol. For that matter, there is no obvious method of assigning counts to the escape symbol. There have been various methods reported in the literature.

Another method described by Cleary and Witten is to reduce the counts of each symbol by one and assign these counts to the escape symbol. For example, suppose in a given sequence *a* occurs 10 times in the context of *prob*, *l* occurs 9 times, and *o* occurs 3 times in the same context (e.g., *problem*, *proboscis*, etc.). In Method A we assign a count of one to the escape symbol, resulting in a total count of 23, which is one more than the number of times *prob* has occurred. The situation is shown in Table 6.8.

In this second method, known as Method B, we reduce the count of each of the symbols *a*, *l*, and *o* by one and give the escape symbol a count of three, resulting in the counts shown in Table 6.9.

The reasoning behind this approach is that if in a particular context more symbols can occur, there is a greater likelihood that there is a symbol in this context that has not occurred before. This increases the likelihood that the escape symbol will be used. Therefore, we should assign a higher probability to the escape symbol.

A variant of Method B, appropriately named Method C, was proposed by Moffat [163]. In Method C, the count assigned to the escape symbol is the number of symbols that have occurred in that context. In this respect, Method C is similar to Method B. The difference comes in the fact that, instead of "robbing" this from the counts of individual symbols, the total count is inflated by this amount. This situation is shown in Table 6.10.

While there is some variation in the performance depending on the characteristics of the data being encoded, of the three methods for assigning counts to the escape symbol, on the average, Method C seems to provide the best performance.

TABLE 6.10   Counts using Method C.

Context	Symbol	Count
prob	*a*	10
	l	9
	o	3
	⟨*Esc*⟩	3
Total Count		25

6.3.3 Length of Context

It would seem that as far as the maximum length of the contexts is concerned, more is better. However, this is not necessarily true. A longer maximum length will usually result in a higher probability if the symbol to be encoded has a nonzero count with respect to that context. However, a long maximum length also means a higher probability of long sequences of escapes, which in turn can increase the number of bits used to encode the sequence. If we plot the compression performance versus maximum context length, we see an initial sharp increase in performance until some value of the maximum length, followed by a steady drop as the maximum length is further increased. The value at which we see a downturn in performance changes depending on the characteristics of the source sequence.

An alternative to the policy of a fixed maximum length is used in the algorithm *ppm** [49]. This algorithm uses the fact that long contexts that give only a single prediction are seldom followed by a new symbol. If *mike* has always been followed by *y* in the past, it will probably not be followed by *b̸* the next time it is encountered. Contexts that are always followed by the same symbol are called *deterministic* contexts. The *ppm** algorithm first looks for the longest deterministic context. If the symbol to be encoded does not occur in that context, an escape symbol is encoded and the algorithm defaults to the maximum context length. This approach seems to provide a small but significant amount of improvement over the basic algorithm. Currently, the best variant of the *ppm** algorithm is the *ppmz* algorithm by Charles Bloom. Details of the *ppmz* algorithm as well as implementations of the algorithm can be found at *http://www.its.caltech.edu/˜bloom/src/ppmz.html*.

6.3.4 The Exclusion Principle

The basic idea behind arithmetic coding is the division of the unit interval into subintervals, each of which represents a particular letter. The smaller the subinterval, the more bits are required to distinguish it from other subintervals. If we can reduce the number of symbols to be represented, the number of subintervals goes down as well. This in turn means that the sizes of the subintervals increase, leading to a reduction in the number of bits required for encoding. The exclusion principle used in *ppm* provides this kind of reduction in rate. Suppose we have been compressing a text sequence and come upon the sequence *proba*, and suppose we are trying to encode the letter *a*. Suppose also that the state of the two-letter context *ob* and the one-letter context *b* are as shown in Table 6.11.

First we attempt to encode *a* with the two-letter context. As *a* does not occur in this context, we issue an escape symbol and reduce the size of the context. Looking at the table for the one-letter context *b*, we see that *a* does occur in this context with a count of 4 out of

TABLE 6.11 Counts for exclusion example.

Context	Symbol	Count
ob	*l*	10
	o	3
	⟨*Esc*⟩	2
Total Count		15
b	*l*	5
	o	3
	a	4
	r	2
	e	2
	⟨*Esc*⟩	5
Total Count		21

TABLE 6.12 Modified table used for exclusion example.

Context	Symbol	Count
b	*a*	4
	r	2
	e	2
	⟨*Esc*⟩	3
Total Count		11

a total possible count of 21. Notice that other letters in this context include *l* and *o*. However, by sending the escape symbol in the context of *ob*, we have already signalled to the decoder that the symbol being encoded is not any of the letters that have previously been encountered in the context of *ob*. Therefore, we can increase the size of the subinterval corresponding to *a* by temporarily removing *l* and *o* from the table. Instead of using Table 6.11, we use Table 6.12 to encode *a*. This exclusion of symbols from contexts on a temporary basis can result in cumulatively significant savings in terms of rate.

You may have noticed that we keep talking about small but significant savings. In lossless compression schemes, there is usually a basic principle, such as the idea of prediction with partial match, followed by a host of relatively small modifications. The importance of these modifications should not be underestimated because often together they provide the margin of compression that makes a particular scheme competitive.

6.4 The Burrows-Wheeler Transform

The Burrows-Wheeler Transform (BWT) algorithm also uses the context of the symbol being encoded, but in a very different way, for lossless compression. The transform that is a major part of this algorithm was developed by Wheeler in 1983. However, the BWT compression algorithm, which uses this transform, saw the light of day in 1994 [32]. Unlike most of the previous algorithms we have looked at, the BWT algorithm requires that the entire sequence to be coded be available to the encoder before the coding takes place. Also, unlike most of the previous algorithms, the decoding procedure is not immediately evident once we know the encoding procedure. We will first describe the encoding procedure. If it is not clear how this particular encoding can be reversed, bear with us and we will get to it.

The algorithm can be summarized as follows. Given a sequence of length N, we create $N - 1$ other sequences where each of these $N - 1$ sequences is a cyclic shift of the original sequence. These N sequences are arranged in lexicographic order. The encoder then transmits the sequence of length N created by taking the last letter of each sorted, cyclically shifted, sequence. This sequence of last letters L, and the position of the original sequence in the sorted list, are coded and sent to the decoder. As we shall see, this information is sufficient to recover the original sequence.

We start with a sequence of length N and end with a representation that contains $N + 1$ elements. However, this sequence has a structure that makes it highly amenable to compression. In particular we will use a method of coding called move-to-front (*mtf*), which is particularly effective on the type of structure exhibited by the sequence L.

Before we describe the *mtf* approach, let us work through an example to generate the L sequence.

Example 6.4.1:

Let's encode the sequence

$$thisþisþthe$$

We start with all the cyclic permutations of this sequence. As there are a total of 11 characters, there are 11 permutations, shown in Table 6.13.

Now let's sort these sequences in lexicographic (dictionary) order (Table 6.14). The sequence L in this case is

$$L : sshtthþiiþe$$

Notice how like letters have come together. If we had a longer sequence of letters, the *runs* of like letters would have been even longer. The *mtf* algorithm takes advantage of these runs.

TABLE 6.13   Permutations of *thisþisþthe*.

0	t	h	i	s	þ	i	s	þ	t	h	e
1	h	i	s	þ	i	s	þ	t	h	e	t
2	i	s	þ	i	s	þ	t	h	e	t	h
3	s	þ	i	s	þ	t	h	e	t	h	i
4	þ	i	s	þ	t	h	e	t	h	i	s
5	i	s	þ	t	h	e	t	h	i	s	þ
6	s	þ	t	h	e	t	h	i	s	þ	i
7	þ	t	h	e	t	h	i	s	þ	i	s
8	t	h	e	t	h	i	s	þ	i	s	þ
9	h	e	t	h	i	s	þ	i	s	þ	t
10	e	t	h	i	s	þ	i	s	þ	t	h

TABLE 6.14　Sequences sorted into lexicographic order.

0	þ	i	s	þ	t	h	e	t	h	i	s
1	þ	t	h	e	t	h	i	s	þ	i	s
2	e	t	h	i	s	þ	i	s	þ	t	h
3	h	e	t	h	i	s	þ	i	s	þ	t
4	h	i	s	þ	i	s	þ	t	h	e	t
5	i	s	þ	i	s	þ	t	h	e	t	h
6	i	s	þ	t	h	e	t	h	i	s	þ
7	s	þ	i	s	þ	t	h	e	t	h	i
8	s	þ	t	h	e	t	h	i	s	þ	i
9	t	h	e	t	h	i	s	þ	i	s	þ
10	t	h	i	s	þ	i	s	þ	t	h	e

The original sequence appears as sequence number 10 in the sorted list, so the encoding of the sequence consists of the sequence L and the index value 10. ◆

Now that we have an encoding of the sequence, let's see how we can decode the original sequence by using the sequence L and the index to the original sequence in the sorted list. The important thing to note is that all the elements of the initial sequence are contained in L. We just need to figure out the permutation that will let us recover the original sequence.

The first step in obtaining the permutation is to generate the sequence F consisting of the first element of each row. That is simple to do because we lexicographically ordered the sequences. Therefore, the sequence F is simply the sequence L in lexicographic order. In our example this means that F is given as

$$F : þþehhiisstt$$

We can use L and F to generate the transformation T that will tell us in which order to read the elements of the sequence L to generate the original sequence. In order to see how T is generated, let us take a look at our example sequence. Let's write the sorted array and the array obtained by cyclically shifting each row of the sorted array once (Table 6.15).

Let's call the sorted array A and the cyclically shifted array A^s. The first elements of each line of A form the sequence F, while the first elements of each line of A^s is the sequence L. The 11 rows in each array are all the cyclical shifts of the original sequence. Therefore, each row in A^s also appears in A. For example, row 0 in A^s corresponds to row 7 of A. Let's store this information in the array T. That is, the row $T[j]$ in A is the same as the jth row in A^s. Thus, $T[0] = 7$, and

$$T = [7\ 8\ 3\ 9\ 10\ 4\ 0\ 5\ 6\ 1\ 2].$$

Let's now define two operators $\mathcal{F}$ and $\mathcal{L}$, where $\mathcal{F}[j]$ is the first element in the jth row of A and $\mathcal{L}[j]$ is the last element in the jth row of A. As the row $T[j]$ of A is the same as the row j of A^s, and as the first element of the row j in A^s is the last element of the row j in A,

$$\mathcal{F}[T[j]] = \mathcal{L}[j].$$

TABLE 6.15 **The sorted array (A) and the cyclically shifted array (A^s).**

	A	A^s
0	þisþthethis	sþisþthethi
1	þthethisþis	sþthethisþi
2	ethisþisþth	hethisþisþt
3	hethisþisþt	thethisþisþ
4	hisþisþthet	thisþisþthe
5	isþisþtheth	hisþisþthet
6	isþthethisþ	þisþthethis
7	sþisþthethi	isþisþtheth
8	sþthethisþi	isþthethisþ
9	thethisþisþ	þthethisþis
10	thisþisþthe	ethisþisþth

Note that as each row is a cyclical rotation of the original sequence, $\mathcal{L}[j]$ cyclicly precedes $\mathcal{F}[j]$ in the original sequence. Therefore, $\mathcal{L}[T[j]]$ precedes $\mathcal{F}[T[j]]$. And because $\mathcal{F}[T[j]] = \mathcal{L}[j]$, $\mathcal{L}[T[j]]$ precedes $\mathcal{L}[j]$ in the original sequence. We will use this fact to recover the original sequence.

Recall we only have the sequence L available to the decoder and the index to the original sequence in A. Given this index I and L, we know the last element of the original sequence, $\mathcal{L}[I]$. The element immediately preceding this is $\mathcal{L}[T[I]]$. The element immediately preceding that is $\mathcal{L}[T[T[I]]]$, and so on.

We can write this procedure as follows for a sequence of length N.

$$D[N] = L[I]$$
$$k \leftarrow I$$
$$\text{for } j = 1 \text{ to } N - 1$$
$$\{$$
$$\quad k \leftarrow T[k]$$
$$\quad D[N - j] = L[k]$$
$$\}$$

where D contains the decoded sequence.

Note that we have not yet shown how the decoder can obtain T. We will do so later in this section. For now let's assume that T is available to us and look at an example of the operation of the decoding algorithm.

Example 6.4.2:

Let's use the decoding algorithm to recover the original sequence from the sequence L in the previous example using

$$T = [7\ 8\ 3\ 9\ 10\ 4\ 0\ 5\ 6\ 1\ 2].$$

Note that

$$L = [s\ s\ h\ t\ t\ h\ þ\ i\ i\ þ\ e],$$

Example 6.4.4:

Let's encode $L = sshtth\flat ii\flat e$. Let's assume that the source alphabet is given by

$$\mathcal{A} = \{\flat, e, h, i, s, t\}.$$

We start out with the assignment

0	1	2	3	4	5
$\flat$	e	h	i	s	t

The first element of L is s, which gets encoded as a 4. We then move s to the top of the list, which gives us

0	1	2	3	4	5
s	$\flat$	e	h	i	t

The next s is encoded as 0. Because s is already at the top of the list, we do not need to make any changes. The next letter is h, which we encode as 3. We then move h to the top of the list:

0	1	2	3	4	5
h	s	$\flat$	e	i	t

The next letter is t, which gets encoded as 5. Moving t to the top of the list, we get

0	1	2	3	4	5
t	h	s	$\flat$	e	i

The next letter is also a t, so that gets encoded as a 0.

Continuing in this fashion, we get the sequence

$$4\ 0\ 3\ 5\ 0\ 1\ 3\ 5\ 0\ 1\ 5$$

As we warned, the results are not too impressive with this small sequence, but we can see how we would get large numbers of 0s and small values if the sequence to be encoded was longer. ◆

6.5 CALIC

We have been looking at schemes that use the context of the symbol being encoded to obtain the distribution of the symbol being encoded. However, as we pointed out earlier, we can also use the previous values of the sequence to obtain a prediction of the actual value of the symbol being encoded. The Context Adaptive Lossless Image Compression (CALIC) scheme, which came into being in response to a call for proposal for a new lossless image compression scheme in 1994 [245, 244], uses both context and prediction of the pixel values. The CALIC scheme actually functions in two modes, one for gray-scale images and another for bi-level images. In this section, we will concentrate on the compression of gray-scale images.

		NN	NNE
	NW	N	NE
WW	W	X	

FIGURE 6.1   Labeling the neighbors of pixel X.

In an image, a given pixel generally has a value close to one of its neighbors. Which neighbor has the closest value depends on the local structure of the image. Depending on whether there is a horizontal or vertical edge in the neighborhood of the pixel being encoded, the pixel above, or the pixel to the left, or some weighted average of neighboring pixels may give the best prediction. How close the prediction is to the pixel being encoded depends on the surrounding texture. In a region of the image with a great deal of variability, the prediction is likely to be further from the pixel being encoded than in the regions with less variability.

In order to take into account all these factors, the algorithm has to make a determination of the environment of the pixel to be encoded. The only information that can be used to make this determination has to be available to both encoder and decoder.

Let's take up the question of the presence of vertical or horizontal edges in the neighborhood of the pixel being encoded. To help our discussion, we will refer to Figure 6.1. In this figure, the pixel to be encoded has been marked with an X. The pixel above is called the north pixel, the pixel to the left is the west pixel, and so on. Note that when pixel X is being encoded, all other marked pixels (N, W, NW, NE, WW, NN, NE, and NNE) are available to both encoder and decoder.

We can get an idea of what kinds of boundaries may or may not be in the neighborhood of X by computing

$$d_h = |W - WW| + |N - NW| + |NE - N|$$
$$d_v = |W - NW| + |N - NN| + |NE - NNE|.$$

The relative values of d_h and d_v are used to obtain the initial prediction of the pixel X. This initial prediction is then refined by taking other factors into account. If the value of d_h is much higher than the value of d_v, this will mean there is a large amount of horizontal variation, and it would be better to pick N to be the initial prediction. If, on the other hand, d_v is much larger than d_h, this would mean that there is a large amount of vertical variation, and the initial prediction is taken to be W. If the differences are more moderate or smaller, the predicted value is a weighted average of the neighboring pixels.

The exact algorithm used by CALIC to form the initial prediction is given by the following pseudocode:

```
if dh − dv > 80
    X̂ ← N
else if dv − dh > 80
    X̂ ← W
```

```
else
{
    X̂ ← (N + W)/2 + (NE − NW)/4
    if d_h − d_v > 32
        X̂ ← (X̂ + N)/2
    else if d_v − d_h > 32
        X̂ ← (X̂ + W)/2
    else if d_h − d_v > 8
        X̂ ← (3X̂ + N)/4
    else if d_v − d_h > 8
        X̂ ← (3X̂ + W)/4
}
```

Using the information about whether the pixel values are changing by large or small amounts in the vertical or horizontal direction in the neighborhood of the pixel being encoded provides a good initial prediction. In order to refine this prediction, we need some information about the interrelationships of the pixels in the neighborhood. Using this information, we can generate an offset or refinement to our initial prediction. We quantify the information about the neighborhood by first forming the vector

$$[N, W, NW, NE, NN, WW, 2N − NN, 2W − WW]$$

We then compare each component of this vector with our initial prediction $\hat{X}$. If the value of the component is less than the prediction, we replace the value with a 1; otherwise we replace it with a 0. Thus, we end up with an eight-component binary vector. If each component of the binary vector was independent, we would end up with 256 possible vectors. However, because of the dependence of various components, we actually have 144 possible configurations. We also compute a quantity that incorporates the vertical and horizontal variations and the previous error in prediction by

$$\delta = d_h + d_v + 2\,|N − \hat{N}| \tag{6.1}$$

where $\hat{N}$ is the predicted value of N. This range of values of δ is divided into four intervals, each being represented by 2 bits. These four possibilities, along with the 144 texture descriptors, create $144 \times 4 = 576$ contexts for X. As the encoding proceeds, we keep track of how much prediction error is generated in each context and offset our initial prediction by that amount. This results in the final predicted value.

Once the prediction is obtained, the difference between the pixel value and the prediction (the prediction error, or residual) has to be encoded. While the prediction process outlined above removes a lot of the structure that was in the original sequence, there is still some structure left in the residual sequence. We can take advantage of some of this structure by coding the residual in terms of its context. The context of the residual is taken to be the value of δ defined in Equation (6.1). In order to reduce the complexity of the encoding, rather than using the actual value as the context, CALIC uses the range of values in which δ lies as the context. Thus:

$$0 \le \delta < q_1 \Rightarrow \text{Context 1}$$

$$q_1 \leq \delta < q_2 \Rightarrow \text{Context } 2$$
$$q_2 \leq \delta < q_3 \Rightarrow \text{Context } 3$$
$$q_3 \leq \delta < q_4 \Rightarrow \text{Context } 4$$
$$q_4 \leq \delta < q_5 \Rightarrow \text{Context } 5$$
$$q_5 \leq \delta < q_6 \Rightarrow \text{Context } 6$$
$$q_6 \leq \delta < q_7 \Rightarrow \text{Context } 7$$
$$q_7 \leq \delta < q_8 \Rightarrow \text{Context } 8$$

The values of q_1-q_8 can be prescribed by the user.

If the original pixel values lie between 0 and $M - 1$, the differences or prediction residuals will lie between $-(M - 1)$ and $M - 1$. Even though most of the differences will have a magnitude close to zero, for arithmetic coding we still have to assign a count to all possible symbols. This means a reduction in the size of the intervals assigned to values that do occur, which in turn means using a larger number of bits to represent these values. The CALIC algorithm attempts to resolve this problem in a number of ways. Let's describe these using an example.

Consider the sequence

$$x_n : 0,\ 7,\ 4,\ 3,\ 5,\ 2,\ 1,\ 7$$

We can see that all the numbers lie between 0 and 7, a range of values that would require 3 bits to represent. Now suppose we predict a sequence element by the previous element in the sequence. The sequence of differences

$$r_n = x_n - x_{n-1}$$

is given by

$$r_n : 0,\ 7,\ -3,\ -1,\ 2,\ -3,\ -1,\ 6$$

If we were given this sequence, we could easily recover the original sequence by using

$$x_n = x_{n-1} + r_n.$$

However, the prediction residual values r_n lie in the $[-7, 7]$ range. That is, the alphabet required to represent these values is almost twice the size of the original alphabet. However, if we look closely we can see that the value of r_n actually lies between $-x_{n-1}$ and $7 - x_{n-1}$. The smallest value that r_n can take on occurs when x_n has a value of 0, in which case r_n will have a value of $-x_{n-1}$. The largest value that r_n can take on occurs when x_n is 7, in which case r_n has a value of $7 - x_{n-1}$. In other words, given a particular value for x_{n-1}, the number of different values that r_n can take on is the same as the number of values that x_n can take on. Generalizing from this, we can see that if a pixel takes on values between 0 and $M - 1$, then given a predicted value $\hat{X}$, the difference $X - \hat{X}$ will take on values in the range $-\hat{X}$ to $M - 1 - \hat{X}$. We can use this fact to map the difference values into the range $[0, M - 1]$, using the following mapping:

$$0 \rightarrow 0$$
$$1 \rightarrow 1$$

$$-1 \rightarrow 2$$
$$2 \rightarrow 3$$
$$\vdots \quad \vdots$$
$$-\hat{X} \rightarrow 2\hat{X}$$
$$\hat{X} + 1 \rightarrow 2\hat{X} + 1$$
$$\hat{X} + 2 \rightarrow 2\hat{X} + 2$$
$$\vdots \quad \vdots$$
$$M - 1 - \hat{X} \rightarrow M - 1$$

where we have assumed that $\hat{X} \leq (M - 1)/2$.

Another approach used by CALIC to reduce the size of its alphabet is to use a modification of a technique called *recursive indexing* [206]. Recursive indexing is a technique for representing a large range of numbers using only a small set. It is easiest to explain using an example. Suppose we want to represent positive integers using only the integers between 0 and 7—that is, a representation alphabet of size 8. Recursive indexing works as follows: If the number to be represented lies between 0 and 6, we simply represent it by that number. If the number to be represented is greater than or equal to 7, we first send the number 7, subtract 7 from the original number, and repeat the process. We keep repeating the process until the remainder is a number between 0 and 6. Thus, for example, 9 would be represented by 7 followed by a 2, and 17 would be represented by two 7s followed by a 3. The decoder, when it sees a number between 0 and 6, would decode it at its face value, and when it saw 7, would keep accumulating the values until a value between 0 and 6 was received. This method of representation followed by entropy coding has been shown to be optimal for sequences that follow a geometric distribution [165].

In CALIC, the representation alphabet is different for different coding contexts. For each coding context k, we use an alphabet $A_k = \{0, 1, \ldots, N_k\}$. Furthermore, if the residual occurs in context k, then the first number that is transmitted is coded with respect to context k; if further recursion is needed, we use the $k + 1$ context.

We can summarize the CALIC algorithm as follows:

1. Find initial prediction $\hat{X}$.

2. Compute prediction context.

3. Refine prediction by removing the estimate of the bias in that context.

4. Update bias estimate.

5. Obtain the residual and remap it so the residual values lie between 0 and $M - 1$, where M is the size of the initial alphabet.

6. Find the coding context k.

7. Code the residual using the coding context.

All these components working together have kept CALIC as the state of the art in lossless image compression. However, we can get almost as good a performance if we simplify some of the more involved aspects of CALIC. We study such a scheme in the next section.

6.6 JPEG-LS

The Joint Photographic Experts Group (JPEG) is a joint ISO/ITU committee responsible for developing standards for continuous-tone still-picture coding. The more famous standard produced by this group is the lossy image compression standard. However, the group also has a lossless standard for image compression. At the time of this writing, the current standard is in the process of being superseded by a new standard. Both standards are based on predictive coding. We describe them in the following. They are referred to as the "current" and "new" standards. The reason for the quotes is that by the time you are reading this, the "current" standard may have become the old standard, and the "new" standard may be the "current" standard.

6.6.1 "Current" Standard

The "current" JPEG lossless still compression standard [233] provides eight different predictive schemes from which the user can select. The first scheme makes no prediction. The next seven are listed below. Three of the seven are one-dimensional predictors, and four are two-dimensional prediction schemes. Here, $I(i,j)$ is the (i,j)th pixel of the original image, and $\hat{I}(i,j)$ is the predicted value for the (i,j)th pixel.

$$\textbf{1}\quad \hat{I}(i,j) = I(i-1,j) \tag{6.2}$$

$$\textbf{2}\quad \hat{I}(i,j) = I(i,j-1) \tag{6.3}$$

$$\textbf{3}\quad \hat{I}(i,j) = I(i-1,j-1) \tag{6.4}$$

$$\textbf{4}\quad \hat{I}(i,j) = I(i,j-1) + I(i-1,j) - I(i-1,j-1) \tag{6.5}$$

$$\textbf{5}\quad \hat{I}(i,j) = I(i,j-1) + \left(I(i-1,j) - I(i-1,j-1)\right)/2 \tag{6.6}$$

$$\textbf{6}\quad \hat{I}(i,j) = I(i-1,j) + \left(I(i,j-1) - I(i-1,j-1)\right)/2 \tag{6.7}$$

$$\textbf{7}\quad \hat{I}(i,j) = \left(I(i,j-1) + I(i-1,j)\right)/2 \tag{6.8}$$

Different images can have different structures that can be best exploited by one of these eight modes of prediction. If compression is performed in a non-real-time environment—for example, for the purposes of archiving—all eight modes of prediction can be tried and the one that gives the most compression is used. The mode used to perform the prediction can be stored in a 3-bit header along with the compressed file. We encoded our four test images using the various JPEG modes. The residual images were encoded using adaptive arithmetic coding. The results are shown in Table 6.17.

The best results, that is, the smallest compressed file sizes, are indicated in bold in the table. From these we can see that a different JPEG predictor is the best for the different images. In Table 6.18, we compare the best JPEG results with the file sizes obtained using GIF.

TABLE 6.17 Compressed file size in bytes of the residual images obtained using the various JPEG prediction modes.

Image	JPEG 0	JPEG 1	JPEG 2	JPEG 3	JPEG 4	JPEG 5	JPEG 6	JPEG 7
Sena	53,431	37,220	31,559	38,261	31,055	**29,742**	33,063	32,179
Sensin	58,306	41,298	37,126	43,445	**32,429**	33,463	35,965	36,428
Earth	38,248	32,295	**32,137**	34,089	33,570	33,057	33,072	32,672
Omaha	56,061	**48,818**	51,283	53,909	53,771	53,520	52,542	52,189

TABLE 6.18 Comparison of the file sizes obtained using JPEG lossless compression and GIF.

Image	Best JPEG	GIF
Sena	31,055	51,085
Sensin	32,429	60,649
Earth	32,137	34,276
Omaha	48,818	61,341

Even if we take into account the overhead associated with GIF, from this comparison we can see that the predictive approach is generally much more suited to lossless image compression than the dictionary-based approach when the images are "natural" gray-scale images. The situation is different when the images are graphic images or pseudocolor images. A possible exception could be the Earth image. The best compressed file size using the second JPEG mode and adaptive arithmetic coding is 32,137 bytes, compared to 34,276 bytes using GIF. The difference between the file sizes is not significant. We can see the reason by looking at the Earth image. Note that a significant portion of the image is the background, which is of a constant value. In dictionary coding, this would result in some very long entries that would provide significant compression. We can see that if the ratio of background to foreground were just a little different in this image, the dictionary method might have outperformed the predictive approach.

6.6.2 "New" Standard

The "new" standard looks more like CALIC than the "current" standard. When the initial proposals for the new lossless compression standard were compared, CALIC was rated first in six of the seven categories of images tested. Motivated by some aspects of CALIC, a team from Hewlett-Packard proposed a much simpler predictive coder, under the name LOCO-I (for low complexity), that still performed close to CALIC [157].

As in CALIC, the standard has both a lossless and a lossy mode. We will not describe the lossy coding procedures.

The initial prediction is obtained using the following algorithm:

$$\text{if } NW \geq \max(W,N)$$
$$\hat{X} = \max(W,N)$$

```
else
{

    if NW ≤ min(W, N)
    X̂ = min(W, N)
    else
    X̂ = W + N − NW


}
```

This prediction approach is a variation of Median Adaptive Prediction [151], in which the predicted value is the median of the N, W, and NW pixels. The initial prediction is then refined using the average value of the prediction error in that particular context.

The contexts in JPEG-LS also reflect the local variations in pixel values. However, they are computed differently from CALIC. First, measures of differences D_1, D_2, and D_3 are computed as follows:

$$D_1 = NE - N$$
$$D_2 = N - NW$$
$$D_3 = NW - W.$$

The values of these differences define a three-component context vector $\mathbf{Q}$. The components of $\mathbf{Q}$ (Q_1, Q_2, and Q_3) are defined by the following mappings:

$$D_i \leq -T_3 \Rightarrow Q_i = -4$$
$$-T_3 < D_i \leq -T_2 \Rightarrow Q_i = -3$$
$$-T_2 < D_i \leq -T_1 \Rightarrow Q_i = -2$$
$$-T_1 < D_i \leq 0 \Rightarrow Q_i = -1$$
$$D_i = 0 \Rightarrow Q_i = 0$$
$$0 < D_i \leq T_1 \Rightarrow Q_i = 1$$
$$T_1 < D_i \leq T_2 \Rightarrow Q_i = 2$$
$$T_2 < D_i \leq T_3 \Rightarrow Q_i = 3$$
$$T_3 < D_i \Rightarrow Q_i = 4 \tag{6.9}$$

where T_1, T_2, and T_3 are positive coefficients that can be defined by the user. Given nine possible values for each component of the context vector, this results in $9 \times 9 \times 9 = 729$ possible contexts. In order to simplify the coding process, the number of contexts is reduced by replacing any context vector $\mathbf{Q}$ whose first nonzero element is negative by $-\mathbf{Q}$. Whenever this happens, a variable $SIGN$ is also set to -1; otherwise, it is set to $+1$. This reduces the number of contexts to 365. The vector $\mathbf{Q}$ is then mapped into a number between 0 and 364. (The standard does not specify the particular mapping to use.)

The variable $SIGN$ is used in the prediction refinement step. The correction is first multiplied by $SIGN$ and then added to the initial prediction.

TABLE 6.19 Comparison of the file sizes obtained using new and old JPEG lossless compression standard and CALIC.

Image	Old JPEG	New JPEG	CALIC
Sena	31,055	27,339	26,433
Sensin	32,429	30,344	29,213
Earth	32,137	26,088	25,280
Omaha	48,818	50,765	48,249

The prediction error r_n is mapped into an interval that is the same size as the range occupied by the original pixel values. The mapping used in JPEG-LS is as follows:

$$r_n < -\frac{M}{2} \Rightarrow r_n \leftarrow r_n + M$$

$$r_n > \frac{M}{2} \Rightarrow r_n \leftarrow r_n - M$$

Finally, the prediction errors are encoded using adaptively selected codes based on Golomb codes, which have also been shown to be optimal for sequences with a geometric distribution. In Table 6.19 we compare the performance of the old and new JPEG standards and CALIC. The results for the new JPEG scheme were obtained using a software implementation courtesy of HP.

We can see that for most of the images the new JPEG standard performs very close to CALIC and outperforms the old standard by 6% to 18%. The only case where the performance is not as good is for the Omaha image. While the performance improvement in these examples may not be very impressive, we should keep in mind that for the old JPEG we are picking the best result out of eight. In practice, this would mean trying all eight JPEG predictors and picking the best. On the other hand, both CALIC and the new JPEG standard are single-pass algorithms. Furthermore, because of the ability of both CALIC and the new standard to function in multiple modes, both perform very well on compound documents, which may contain images along with text.

6.7 Multiresolution Approaches

Our final predictive image compression scheme is perhaps not as competitive as the other schemes. However, it is an interesting algorithm because it approaches the problem from a slightly different point of view.

Multiresolution models generate representations of an image with varying spatial resolution. This usually results in a pyramidlike representation of the image, with each layer of the pyramid serving as a prediction model for the layer immediately below.

One of the more popular of these techniques is known as HINT (Hierarchical INTerpolation) [185]. The specific steps involved in HINT are as follows. First, residuals corresponding to the pixels labeled Δ in Figure 6.2 are obtained using linear prediction and transmitted. Then, the intermediate pixels (∘) are estimated by linear interpolation, and the error in estimation is then transmitted. Then, the pixels X are estimated from Δ and ∘, and the estimation

Δ	•	X	•	Δ	•	X	•	Δ
•	*	•	*	•	*	•	*	•
X	•	○	•	X	•	○	•	X
•	*	•	*	•	*	•	*	•
Δ	•	X	•	Δ	•	X	•	Δ
•	*	•	*	•	*	•	*	•
X	•	○	•	X	•	○	•	X
•	*	•	*	•	*	•	*	•
Δ	•	X	•	Δ	•	X	•	Δ

FIGURE 6 . 2   The HINT scheme for hierarchical prediction.

error is transmitted. Finally, the pixels labeled ⋆ and then • are estimated from known neighbors, and the errors are transmitted. The reconstruction process proceeds in a similar manner.

One use of a multiresolution approach is in progressive image transmission. We describe this application in the next section.

6.7.1 Progressive Image Transmission

The last few years have seen a very rapid increase in the amount of information stored as images, especially remotely sensed images (such as images from weather and other satellites) and medical images (such as CAT scans, magnetic resonance images, and mammograms). It is not enough to have information. We also need to make these images accessible to individuals who can make use of them. There are many issues involved with making large amounts of information accessible to a large number of people. In this section we will look at one particular issue—transmitting these images to remote users. (For a more general look at the problem of managing large amounts of information, see [241].)

Suppose a user wants to browse through a number of images in a remote database. The user is connected to the database via a 56 kbits per second (kbps) modem. Suppose the images are of size 1024×1024, and on the average users have to look through 30 images before finding the image they are looking for. If these images were monochrome with 8 bits per pixel, this process would take close to an hour and 15 minutes, which is not very practical. Even if we compressed these images before transmission, lossless compression on average gives us about a two-to-one compression. This would only cut the transmission in half, which still makes the approach cumbersome. A better alternative is to send an approximation of each image first, which does not require too many bits but still is sufficiently accurate to give users an idea of what the image looks like. If users find the image to be of interest, they can request a further refinement of the approximation, or the complete image. This approach is called *progressive image transmission*.

Example 6.7.1:

A simple progressive transmission scheme is to divide the image into blocks and then send a representative pixel for the block. The receiver replaces each pixel in the block with the representative value. In this example, the representative value is the value of the pixel in the top-left corner. Depending on the size of the block, the amount of data that would need to be transmitted could be substantially reduced. For example, to transmit a 1024×1024 image at 8 bits per pixel over a 56 kbps line takes about two and a half minutes. Using a block size of 8×8, and using the top-left pixel in each block as the representative value, means we approximate the 1024×1024 image with a 128×128 subsampled image. Using 8 bits per pixel and a 56 kbps line, the time required to transmit this approximation to the image takes less than two and a half seconds. Assuming that this approximation was sufficient to let the user decide whether a particular image was the desired image, the time required now to look through 30 images becomes a minute and a half instead of the hour and a half mentioned earlier. If the approximation using a block size of 8×8 does not provide enough resolution to make a decision, the user can ask for a refinement. The transmitter can then divide the 8×8 block into four 4×4 blocks. The pixel at the upper-left corner of the upper-left block was already transmitted as the representative pixel for the 8×8 block, so we need to send three more pixels for the other three 4×4 blocks. This takes about seven seconds, so even if the user had to request a finer approximation every third image, this would only increase the total search time by a little more than a minute. To see what these approximations look like, we have taken the Sena image and encoded it using different block sizes. The results are shown in Figure 6.3. The lowest-resolution image, shown in the top left, is a 32×32 image. The top-left image is a 64×64 image. The bottom-left image is a 128×128 image, and the bottom-right image is the 256×256 original.

Notice that even with a block size of 8 the image is clearly recognizable as a person. Therefore, if the user was looking for a house, they would probably skip over this image after seeing the first approximation. If the user was looking for a picture of a person, they could still make decisions based on the second approximation.

Finally, when an image is built line by line, the eye tends to follow the scan line. With the progressive transmission approach, the user gets a more global view of the image very early in the image formation process. Consider the images in Figure 6.4. The images on the left are the 8×8, 4×4, and 2×2 approximations of the Sena image. On the right, we show how much of the image we would see in the same amount of time if we used the standard line-by-line raster scan order.   ◆

We would like the first approximations that we transmit to use as few bits as possible yet be accurate enough to allow the user to make a decision to accept or reject the image with a certain degree of confidence. As these approximations are lossy, many progressive transmission schemes use well-known lossy compression schemes in the first pass.

The more popular lossy compression schemes, such as transform coding, tend to require a significant amount of computation. As the decoders for most progressive transmission

FIGURE 6.3   Sena image coded using different block sizes for progressive transmission. Top row: block size 8 × 8 and block size 4 × 4. Bottom row: block size 2 × 2 and original image.

schemes have to function on a wide variety of platforms, they are generally implemented in software and need to be simple and fast. This requirement has led to the development of a number of progressive transmission schemes that do not use lossy compression schemes for their initial approximations. Most of these schemes have a form similar to the one described in Example 6.7.1, and they are generally referred to as *pyramid schemes* because of the manner in which the approximations are generated and the image is reconstructed.

When we use the pyramid form, we still have a number of ways to generate the approximations. One of the problems with the simple approach described in Example 6.7.1 is that if the pixel values vary a lot within a block, the "representative" value may not be very representative. To prevent this from happening, we could represent the block by some sort of an average or composite value. For example, suppose we start out with a 512×512 image. We first divide the image into 2×2 blocks and compute the integer value of the average of each block [223, 214]. The integer values of the averages would constitute the penultimate

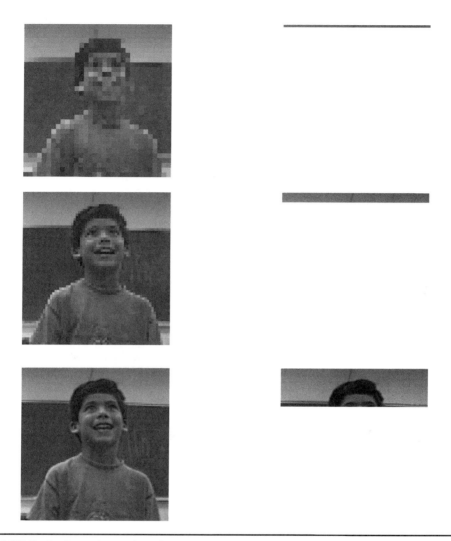

FIGURE 6.4 **Comparison between the received image using progressive transmission and using the standard raster scan order.**

approximation. The approximation to be transmitted prior to that can be obtained by taking the average of 2×2 averages and so on, as shown in Figure 6.5.

Using the simple technique in Example 6.7.1, we ended up transmitting the same number of values as the original number of pixels. However, when we use the mean of the pixels as our approximation, after we have transmitted the mean values at each level, we still have to transmit the actual pixel values. The reason is that when we take the integer part of the average we end up throwing away information that cannot be retrieved. To avoid this problem of data expansion, we can transmit the sum of the values in the 2×2 block. Then we only need to transmit three more values to recover the original four values. With this approach, although

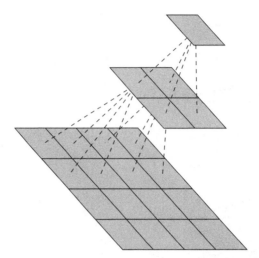

FIGURE 6.5   **The pyramid structure for progressive transmission.**

we would be transmitting the same number of values as the number of pixels in the image, we might still end up sending more bits because representing all possible values of the sum would require transmitting 2 more bits than was required for the original value. For example, if the pixels in the image can take on values between 0 and 255, which can be represented by 8 bits, their sum will take on values between 0 and 1024, which would require 10 bits. If we are allowed to use entropy coding, we can remove the problem of data expansion by using the fact that the neighboring values in each approximation are heavily correlated, as are values in different levels of the pyramid. This means that differences between these values can be efficiently encoded using entropy coding. By doing so, we end up getting compression instead of expansion.

Instead of taking the arithmetic average, we could also form some sort of weighted average. The general procedure would be similar to that described above. (For one of the more well-known weighted average techniques, see [34].)

The representative value does not have to be an average. We could use the pixel values in the approximation at the lower levels of the pyramid as indices into a lookup table. The lookup table can be designed to preserve important information such as edges. The problem with this approach would be the size of the lookup table. If we were using 2×2 blocks of 8-bit values, the lookup table would have 2^{32} values, which is too large for most applications. The size of the table could be reduced if the number of bits per pixel was lower or if, instead of taking 2×2 blocks, we used rectangular blocks of size 2×1 and 1×2 [125].

Finally, we do not have to build the pyramid one layer at a time. After sending the lowest-resolution approximations, we can use some measure of information contained in a block to decide whether it should be transmitted [60]. One possible measure could be the difference between the largest and smallest intensity values in the block. Another might be to look at the maximum number of similar pixels in a block. Using an information measure to guide the progressive transmission of images allows the user to see portions of the image first that are visually more significant.

6.8 Facsimile Encoding

One of the earliest applications of lossless compression in the modern era has been the compression of facsimile, or fax. In facsimile transmission, a page is scanned and converted into a sequence of black or white pixels. The requirements of how fast the facsimile of an A4 document (210×297 mm) must be transmitted have changed over the last two decades. The CCITT (now ITU-T) has issued a number of recommendations based on the speed requirements at a given time. The CCITT classifies the apparatus for facsimile transmission into four groups. Although several considerations are used in this classification, if we only consider the time to transmit an A4-size document over phone lines, the four groups can be described as follows:

■ **Group 1:** This apparatus is capable of transmitting an A4-size document in about six minutes over phone lines using an analog scheme. The apparatus is standardized in recommendation T.2.

■ **Group 2:** This apparatus is capable of transmitting an A4-size document over phone lines in about three minutes. A Group 2 apparatus also uses an analog scheme and, therefore, does not use data compression. The apparatus is standardized in recommendation T.3.

■ **Group 3:** This apparatus uses a digitized binary representation of the facsimile. Because it is a digital scheme, it can and does use data compression and is capable of transmitting an A4-size document in about a minute. The apparatus is standardized in recommendation T.4.

■ **Group 4:** This apparatus has the same speed requirement as Group 3. The apparatus is standardized in recommendations T.6, T.503, T.521, and T.563.

In this chapter, we will look at the compression schemes described in the CCITT recommendations T.4 and T.6. Before we do that, we will look at an earlier technique for facsimile called *run-length coding*, which still survives as part of the T.4 recommendation.

6.8.1 Run-Length Coding

The model that gives rise to run-length coding is the Capon model [40], a two-state Markov model with states S_w and S_b (S_w corresponds to the case where the pixel that has just been encoded is a white pixel, and S_b corresponds to the case where the pixel that has just been encoded is a black pixel). The transition probabilities $P(w|b)$ and $P(b|w)$, and the probability of being in each state $P(S_w)$ and $P(S_b)$, completely specify this model. For facsimile images, $P(w|w)$ and $P(w|b)$ are generally significantly higher than $P(b|w)$ and $P(b|b)$. The Markov model is represented by the state diagram shown in Figure 6.6.

The entropy of a finite state process with states S_i is given by Equation (2.16). Recall that in Example 2.3.1, the entropy using a probability model and the *iid* assumption was significantly more than the entropy using the Markov model.

Let us try to interpret what the model says about the structure of the data. The highly skewed nature of the probabilities $P(b|w)$ and $P(w|w)$, and to a lesser extent $P(w|b)$ and

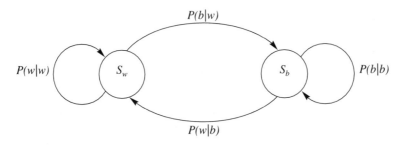

FIGURE 6.6   **The Capon model for binary images.**

$P(b|b)$, says that once a pixel takes on a particular color (black or white), it is highly likely that the following pixels will also be of the same color. So, rather than code the color of each pixel separately, we can simply code the length of the runs of each color. For example, if we had 190 white pixels followed by 30 black pixels, followed by another 210 white pixels, instead of coding the 430 pixels individually, we would code the sequence 190, 30, 210, along with an indication of the color of the first string of pixels. Coding the lengths of runs instead of coding individual values is called run-length coding.

6.8.2 CCITT Group 3 and 4—Recommendations T.4 and T.6

The recommendations for Group 3 facsimile include two coding schemes. One is a one-dimensional scheme in which the coding on each line is performed independently of any other line. The other is two-dimensional; the coding of one line is performed using the line-to-line correlations.

The one-dimensional coding scheme is a run-length coding scheme in which each line is represented as a series of alternating white runs and black runs. The first run is always a white run. If the first pixel is a black pixel, then we assume that we have a white run of length zero.

Runs of different lengths occur with different probabilities; therefore, they are coded using a variable-length code. The approach taken in the CCITT standards T.4 and T.6 is to use a Huffman code to encode the run lengths. However, the number of possible lengths of runs is extremely large, and it is simply not feasible to build a codebook that large. Therefore, instead of generating a Huffman code for each run length r_l, the run length is expressed in the form

$$r_l = 64 \times m + t \qquad \text{for } t = 0, 1, \ldots, 63, \text{ and } m = 1, 2, \ldots, 27. \qquad (6.10)$$

When we have to represent a run length r_l, instead of finding a code for r_l, we use the corresponding codes for m and t. The codes for t are called the *terminating codes*, and the codes for m are called the *make-up codes*. If $r_l < 63$, we only need to use a terminating code. Otherwise, both a make-up code and a terminating code are used. For the range of m and t given here, we can represent lengths of 1728, which is the number of pixels per line in an A4-size document. However, if the document is wider, the recommendations provide for those with an optional set of 13 codes. Except for the optional codes, there are separate codes for black and white run lengths. This coding scheme is generally referred to as a *modified Huffman (MH)* scheme.

FIGURE 6.7   **Two rows of an image. The transition pixels are marked with a dot.**

In the two-dimensional scheme, instead of reporting the run lengths, which in terms of our Markov model is the length of time we remain in one state, we report the transition times when we move from one state to another state. Look at Figure 6.7. We can encode this in two ways. We can say that the first row consists of a sequence of runs $0, 2, 3, 3, 8$, and the second row consists of runs of length $0, 1, 8, 3, 4$ (notice the first runs of length zero). Or, we can encode the location of the pixel values that occur at a transition from white to black or black to white. The first pixel is an imaginary white pixel assumed to be to the left of the first actual pixel. Therefore, if we were to code transition locations, we would encode the first row as $1, 3, 6, 9$ and the second row as $1, 2, 10, 13$.

Generally, rows of a facsimile image are heavily correlated. Therefore, it would be easier to code the transition points with reference to the previous line than to code each one in terms of its absolute location, or even its distance from the previous transition point. This is the basic idea behind the recommended two-dimensional coding scheme. This scheme is a modification of a two-dimensional coding scheme called the *Relative Element Address Designate* (READ) code [246, 108] and is often referred to as *Modified READ* (MR). The READ code was the Japanese proposal to the CCITT for the Group 3 standard.

To understand the two-dimensional coding scheme, we need some definitions.

a_0: This is the last pixel whose value is known to both encoder and decoder. At the beginning of encoding each line, a_0 refers to an imaginary white pixel to the left of the first actual pixel. While it is often a transition pixel, it does not have to be.

a_1: This is the first transition pixel to the right of a_0. By definition its color should be the opposite of a_0. The location of this pixel is known only to the encoder.

a_2: This is the second transition pixel to the right of a_0. Its color should be the opposite of a_1, which means it has the same color as a_0. The location of this pixel is also known only to the encoder.

b_1: This is the first transition pixel on the line above the line currently being encoded to the right of a_0 whose color is the opposite of a_0. As the line above is known to both encoder and decoder, as is the value of a_0, the location of b_1 is also known to both encoder and decoder.

b_2: This is the first transition pixel to the right of b_1 in the line above the line currently being encoded.

For the pixels in Figure 6.7, if the second row is the one being currently encoded, and if we have encoded the pixels up to the second pixel, the assignment of the different pixels is shown in Figure 6.8. The pixel assignments for a slightly different arrangement of black and white pixels are shown in Figure 6.9.

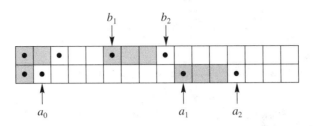

FIGURE 6.8   **Two rows of an image. The transition pixels are marked with a dot.**

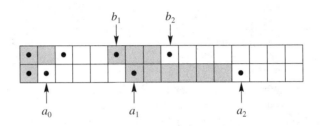

FIGURE 6.9   **Two rows of an image. The transition pixels are marked with a dot.**

If b_1 and b_2 lie between a_0 and a_1, we call the coding mode used the *pass mode*. The transmitter informs the receiver about the situation by sending the code 0001. Upon receipt of this code, the receiver knows that from the location of a_0 to the pixel right below b_2, all pixels are of the same color. If this had not been true, we would have encountered a transition pixel. As the first transition pixel to the right of a_0 is a_1, and as b_2 occurs before a_1, no transitions have occurred and all pixels from a_0 to right below b_2 are the same color. At this time, the last pixel known to both the transmitter and receiver is the pixel below b_2. Therefore, this now becomes the new a_0, and we find the new positions of b_1 and b_2 by examining the row above the one being encoded and continue with the encoding process.

If a_1 is detected before b_2 by the encoder, we do one of two things. If the distance between a_1 and b_1 (the number of pixels from a_1 to right under b_1) is less than or equal to three, then we send the location of a_1 with respect to b_1, move a_0 to a_1, and continue with the coding process. This coding mode is called the *vertical mode*. If the distance between a_1 and b_1 is large, we essentially revert to the one-dimensional technique and send the distances between a_0 and a_1, and a_1 and a_2, using the modified Huffman code. Let us look at exactly how this is accomplished.

In the vertical mode, if the distance between a_1 and b_1 is zero (that is, a_1 is exactly under b_1), we send the code 1. If the a_1 is to the right of b_1 by one pixel (as in Figure 6.9), we send the code 011. If a_1 is to the right of b_1 by two or three pixels, we send the codes 000011 or 0000011, respectively. If a_1 is to the left of b_1 by one, two, or three pixels, we send the codes 010, 000010, or 0000010, respectively.

In the horizontal mode, we first send the code 001 to inform the receiver about the mode, and then send the modified Huffman codewords corresponding to the run length from a_0 to a_1, and a_1 to a_2.

TABLE 6.20   Comparison of binary image coding schemes. Data from [11].

Source Description	Original Size (pixels)	MH (bytes)	MR (bytes)	MMR (bytes)	JBIG (bytes)
Letter	4352 × 3072	20,605	14,290	8,531	6,682
Sparse text	4352 × 3072	26,155	16,676	9,956	7,696
Dense text	4352 × 3072	135,705	105,684	92,100	70,703

As the encoding of a line in the two-dimensional algorithm is based on the previous line, an error in one line could conceivably propagate to all other lines in the transmission. To prevent this from happening, the T.4 recommendations contain the requirement that after each line is coded with the one-dimensional algorithm, at most $K - 1$ lines will be coded using the two-dimensional algorithm. For standard vertical resolution, $K = 2$, and for high resolution, $K = 4$.

The Group 4 encoding algorithm, as standardized in CCITT recommendation T.6, is identical to the two-dimensional encoding algorithm in recommendation T.4. The main difference between T.6 and T.4 from the compression point of view is that T.6 does not have a one-dimensional coding algorithm, which means that the restriction described in the previous paragraph is also not present. This slight modification of the modified READ algorithm has earned the name *modified modified READ* (MMR)!

6.8.3 Comparison of MH, MR, MMR, and JBIG

In this chapter we have seen three facsimile coding algorithms: modified Huffman, modified READ, and modified modified READ. In Chapter 4, we saw another algorithm designed for coding binary images, the JBIG algorithm, which has been standardized in CCITT recommendation T.62. As we might expect, the JBIG algorithm performs better than the MMR algorithm, which performs better than the MR algorithm, which in turn performs better than the MH algorithm. The level of complexity also follows the same trend, although we could argue that MMR is actually less complex than MR.

A comparison of the schemes for some facsimile sources is shown in Table 6.20. The modified READ algorithm was used with $K = 4$, while the JBIG algorithm was used with an adaptive three-line template and adaptive arithmetic coder to obtain the results in this table. As we go from the one-dimensional MH coder to the two-dimensional MMR coder, we get a factor of two reduction in file size for the sparse text sources. We get even more reduction when we use an adaptive coder and an adaptive model, as is true for the JBIG coder. When we come to the dense text, the advantage of the two-dimensional MMR over the one-dimensional MH is not as significant, as the amount of two-dimensional correlation becomes substantially less.

The compression schemes specified in T.4 and T.6 break down when we try to use them to encode halftone images. In halftone images, gray levels are represented using binary pixel patterns. A gray level closer to black would be represented by a pattern that contains more black pixels, while a gray level closer to white would be represented by a pattern with fewer black pixels. Thus, the model that was used to develop the compression schemes specified in

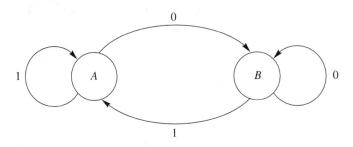

FIGURE 6.10   **A two-state model for binary sequences.**

T.4 and T.6 is not valid for halftone images. The JBIG algorithm, with its adaptive model and coder, suffers from no such drawbacks and performs well for halftone images also [11].

6.9 Dynamic Markov Compression

In the Capon model, the probability of the next symbol being white or black depends only on the value of the current symbol. However, we know that quite often the probabilities of the value that the next symbol in a sequence takes on depend not only on the current value but on the past values as well. The *ppm* scheme relies on this longer-range correlation. Dynamic Markov compression (DMC), introduced by Cormack and Horspool [54], generalizes the Capon model in order to take advantage of relationships and correlations that extend beyond a single symbol.

Consider the sequence of pixels in a scanned document. The sequence consists of runs of black and white pixels. If we represent black by 0 and white by 1, we have runs of 0s and 1s. If the current value is 0, the probability that the next value is 0 is higher than if the current value was 1. The fact that we have two different sets of probabilities is reflected in the two-state model shown in Figure 6.10. Consider state A. The probability of the next value being 1 changes depending on whether we reached state A from state B or from state A itself. We can have the model reflect this by *cloning* state A, as shown in Figure 6.11, to create state A'. Now if we see a white pixel after a run of black pixels, we go to state A'. The probability that the next value will be 1 is very high in this state. This way, when we estimate probabilities for the next pixel value, we take into account not only the value of the current pixel but also the value of the previous pixel.

This process can be continued as long as we wish to take into account longer and longer histories. "As long as we wish" is a rather vague statement when it comes to implementing the algorithm. In fact, we have been rather vague about a number of implementation issues. We will attempt to rectify the situation.

There are a number of issues that need to be addressed in order to implement this algorithm:

1. What is the initial number of states?

2. How do we estimate probabilities?

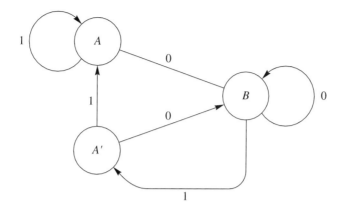

FIGURE 6.11 **A three-state model obtained by cloning.**

3. How do we decide when a state needs to be cloned?

4. What do we do when the number of states becomes too large?

Let's answer each question in turn.

We can start the encoding process with a single state with two self-loops for 0 and 1. This state can be cloned to two and then a higher number of states. In practice it has been found that, depending on the particular application, it is more efficient to start with a larger number of states than one.

The probabilities from a given state can be estimated by simply counting the number of times a 0 or a 1 occurs in that state divided by the number of times the particular state is occupied. For example, if in state V the number of times a 0 occurs is denoted by n_0^V and the number of times a 1 occurs is denoted by n_1^V, then

$$P(0|V) = \frac{n_0^V}{n_0^V + n_1^V}$$

$$P(1|V) = \frac{n_1^V}{n_0^V + n_1^V}.$$

What if a 1 has never previously occurred in this state? This approach would assign a probability of zero to the occurrence of a 1. This means that there will be no subinterval assigned to the possibility of a 1 occurring, and when it does occur, we will not be able to represent it. In order to avoid this, instead of counting from zero, we start the count of 1s and 0s with a small number c and estimate the probabilities as

$$P(0|V) = \frac{n_0^V + c}{n_0^V + n_1^V + 2c}$$

$$P(1|V) = \frac{n_1^V + c}{n_0^V + n_1^V + 2c}.$$

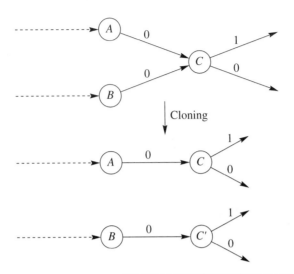

FIGURE 6.12   The cloning process.

Whenever we have two branches leading to a state, it can be cloned. And, theoretically, cloning is never harmful. By cloning we are providing additional information to the encoder. This might not reduce the rate, but it should never result in an increase in the rate. However, cloning does increase the complexity of the coding, and hence the decoding, process. In order to control the increase in the number of states, we should only perform cloning when there is a reasonable expectation of reduction in rate. We can do this by making sure that both paths leading to the state being considered for cloning are used often enough. Consider the situation shown in Figure 6.12. Suppose the current state is A and the next state is C. As there are two paths entering C, C is a candidate for cloning. Cormack and Horspool suggest that C be cloned if $n_0^A > T_1$ and $n_0^B > T_2$, where T_1 and T_2 are threshold values set by the user. If there are more than three paths leading to a candidate for cloning, then we check that both the number of transitions from the current state is greater than T_1 and the number of transitions from all other states to the candidate state is greater than T_2.

Finally, what do we do when, for practical reasons, we cannot accommodate any more states? A simple solution is to restart the algorithm. In order to make sure that we do not start from ground zero every time, we can train the initial state configuration using a certain number of past inputs.

6.10   Summary

The past history of a sequence provides information that can be used in a variety of ways to provide efficient compression. The past values of the sequence can be used to predict the actual value of the current source output. The prediction error can then be encoded and transmitted. The past history of the sequence can also be used to predict a probability model for the source output being encoded. In this chapter we have looked at a number of creative ways of using the past history of the sequence to predictively encode the source output. Predictive coding schemes are currently among the best for encoding text and for losslessly encoding images.

Further Reading

1. A survey of lossless image compression techniques can be found in "Lossless Image Compression—A Comparative Study" by N.D. Memon and K. Sayood [156], which appears in the *Proceedings of the 1995 Conference on Electronic Imaging*.

2. The basic *ppm* algorithm is described in detail in *Text Compression*, by T.C. Bell, J.G. Cleary, and I.H. Witten [20].

3. For a detailed description of the LOCO-I and JPEG-LS compression algorithm, see "The LOCO-I Lossless Image Compression Algorithm: Principles and Standardization into JPEG-LS," Hewlett-Packard Laboratories Technical Report HPL-98-193, November 1998 [236].

4. A comparative study of the various lossless image compression standards can be found in a paper by R.B. Arps and T.K. Truong, entitled "Comparison of International Standards for Lossless Still Image Compression," which appeared in the June 1994 issue of the *Proceedings of the IEEE* [11].

5. The area of lossless image compression is a very active one, and new schemes are being published all the time. These articles appear in a number of journals, including *Journal of Electronic Imaging, Optical Engineering, IEEE Transactions on Image Processing, IEEE Transactions on Communications, Communications of the ACM, IEEE Transactions on Computers*, and *Image Communication*, among others.

6.11 Projects and Problems

1. Decode the bitstream generated in Example 6.3.1. Assume you have already decoded *thisþis* and Tables 6.1–6.4 are available to you.

2. Given the sequence *theþbetaþcatþateþtheþcetaþhat*:

    (a) Encode the sequence using the *ppma* algorithm and an adaptive arithmetic coder. Assume a six-letter alphabet $\{h, e, t, a, c, þ\}$.

    (b) Decode the encoded sequence.

3. Given the sequence *etaþcetaþandþbetaþceta*:

    (a) Encode using the Burrows-Wheeler transform and move-to-front coding.

    (b) Decode the encoded sequence.

4. Encode the binary image shown in Figure 6.13 using the modified Huffman scheme.

5. Encode the binary image shown in Figure 6.13 using the modified READ scheme.

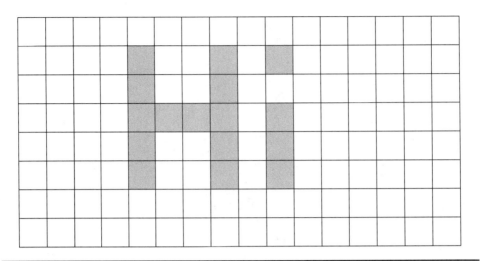

FIGURE 6.13   An 8 × 16 binary image.

6. Encode the binary image shown in Figure 6.13 using the modified modified READ scheme.

7. Suppose we want to transmit a 512 × 512, 8-bits-per-pixel image over a 9600 bits per second line.

   (a) If we were to transmit this image using raster scan order, after 15 seconds how many rows of the image will the user have received? To what fraction of the image does this correspond?

   (b) If we were to transmit the image using the method of Example 6.7.1, how long would it take the user to receive the first approximation? How long would it take to receive the first two approximations?

8. An implementation of the progressive transmission example (Example 6.7.1) is included in the programs accompanying this book. The program is called `prog_tran1.c`. Using this program as a template, experiment with different ways of generating approximations (you could use various types of weighted averages) and comment on the qualitative differences (or lack thereof) with using various schemes. Try different block sizes and comment on the practical effects in terms of quality and rate.

9. The program `jpegll_enc.c` generates the residual image for the different JPEG prediction modes, while the program `jpegll_dec.c` reconstructs the original image from the residual image. The output of the encoder program can be used as the input to the public domain arithmetic coding program mentioned in Chapter 4 and the Huffman coding programs mentioned in Chapter 3. Study the performance of different combinations of prediction mode and entropy coder using three images of your choice. Account for any differences you see.

10. Extend `jpegll_enc.c` and `jpegll_dec.c` with an additional prediction mode—be creative! Compare the performance of your predictor with the JPEG predictors.

11. Implement the portions of the CALIC algorithm described in this chapter. Encode the Sena image using your implementation.

7

Mathematical Preliminaries
for Lossy Coding

7.1 Overview

Before we discussed lossless compression, we presented some of the mathematical background necessary for understanding and appreciating the compression schemes that followed. We will try to do the same here for lossy compression schemes. In lossless compression schemes, rate is the general concern. With lossy compression schemes, the loss of information associated with such schemes is also a concern. We will look at different ways of assessing the impact of the loss of information. We will also briefly revisit the subject of information theory, mainly to get an understanding of the part of the theory that deals with the trade-offs involved in reducing the rate, or number of bits per sample, at the expense of the introduction of distortion in the decoded information. This aspect of information theory is also known as rate distortion theory. We will also look at some of the models used in the development of lossy compression schemes.

7.2 Introduction

This chapter will provide some mathematical background that is necessary for discussing lossy compression techniques. Most of the material covered in this chapter is common to many of the compression techniques described in the later chapters. Material that is specific to a particular technique is described in the chapter in which the technique is presented. Some of the material presented in this chapter is not essential for understanding the techniques described in this book. However, to follow some of the literature in this area, familiarity with these topics is necessary. We have marked these sections with a ⋆. If you are primarily interested in the techniques, you may wish to skip these sections, at least on first reading. On the other hand, if you wish to delve more deeply into these topics, we have included a list of resources at the end of this chapter that provide a more mathematically rigorous treatment of this material.

When we were looking at lossless compression, one thing we never had to worry about was how the reconstructed sequence would differ from the original sequence. By definition, the reconstruction of a losslessly constructed sequence is identical to the original sequence. However, there is only a limited amount of compression that can be obtained with lossless compression. There is a floor (a hard one) defined by the entropy of the source, below which we cannot drive the size of the compressed sequence. As long as we wish to preserve all of the information in the source, the entropy, like the speed of light, is a fundamental limit.

The limited amount of compression available from using lossless compression schemes may be acceptable in several circumstances. The storage or transmission resources available to us may be sufficient to handle our data requirements after lossless compression. Or the possible consequences of a loss of information may be much more expensive than the cost of additional storage and/or transmission resources. This would be the case with the storage and archiving of bank records; an error in the records could turn out to be much more expensive than the cost of buying additional storage media.

If neither of these conditions hold—that is, resources are limited and we do not require absolute integrity—we can improve the amount of compression by accepting a certain degree of loss during the compression process. Performance measures are necessary to determine the efficiency of our *lossy* compression schemes. For the lossless compression schemes we essentially used only the rate as the performance measure. That would not be feasible for lossy compression. If rate were the only criterion for lossy compression schemes, where loss of information is permitted, the best lossy compression scheme would be simply to throw away all the data! Therefore, we need some additional performance measure, such as some measure of the difference between the original and reconstructed data, which we will refer to as the *distortion* in the reconstructed data. In the next section, we will look at some of the more well-known measures of difference and discuss their advantages and shortcomings.

In the best of all possible worlds we would like to incur the minimum amount of distortion while compressing to the lowest rate possible. Obviously, there is a trade-off between minimizing the rate and keeping the distortion small. The extreme cases are when we transmit no information, in which case the rate is zero, or keep all the information, in which case the distortion is zero. The rate for a discrete source is simply the entropy. The study of the situations between these two extremes is called *rate distortion theory*. In this chapter we will take a brief look at some important concepts related to this theory.

Finally, we need to expand the dictionary of models available for our use, for several reasons. First, because we are now able to introduce distortion, we need to determine how to add distortion intelligently. For this, we often need to look at the sources somewhat differently than we have done previously. Another reason is that we will be looking at compression schemes for sources that are analog in nature, even though we have treated them as discrete sources in the past. We need models that more precisely describe the true nature of these sources. We will describe several different models that are widely used in the development of lossy compression algorithms.

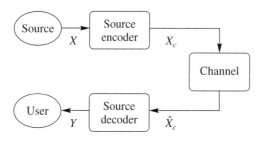

FIGURE 7.1   **Block diagram of a generic compression scheme.**

We will use the block diagram and notation used in Figure 7.1 throughout our discussions. The output of the source is modeled as a random variable X. The *source coder* takes the source output and produces the compressed representation X_c. The channel block represents all transformations the compressed representation undergoes before the source is reconstructed. Usually, we will take the channel to be the identity mapping, which means $X_c = \hat{X}_c$. The source decoder takes the compressed representation and produces a reconstruction of the source output for the user.

7.3 Distortion Criteria

How do we measure the closeness or fidelity of a reconstructed source sequence to the original? The answer frequently depends on what is being compressed and who is doing the answering. Suppose we were to compress and then reconstruct an image. If the image is a work of art and the resulting reconstruction is to be part of a book on art, the best way to find out how much distortion was introduced and in what manner is to ask a person familiar with the work to look at the image and provide an opinion. If the image is that of a house and is to be used in an advertisement, the best way to evaluate the quality of the reconstruction is probably to ask a real estate agent. However, if the image is from a satellite and is to be processed by a machine to obtain information about the objects in the image, the best measure of fidelity is to see how the introduced distortion affects the functioning of the machine. Similarly, if we were to compress and then reconstruct an audio segment, the judgment of how close the reconstructed sequence is to the original depends on the type of material being examined as well as the manner in which the judging is done. An audiophile is much more likely to perceive distortion in the reconstructed sequence, and distortion is much more likely to be noticed in a musical piece than in a politician's speech.

In the best of all worlds we would always use the end user of a particular source output to assess quality and provide the feedback required for the design. In practice this is not often possible, especially when the end user is a human, because it is difficult to incorporate the human response into mathematical design procedures. Also, there is difficulty in objectively reporting the results. The people asked to assess one person's design may be more easygoing than the people who were asked to assess another person's design. Even though the reconstructed output using one person's design is rated "excellent" and the reconstructed output using the other person's design is only rated "acceptable," switching observers may change the ratings. We could reduce this kind of bias by recruiting a large number of observers in the hope that the various biases will cancel each other out. This is often the option used, especially in the final stages of the design of compression systems. However, the rather cumbersome nature of this process is limiting. We generally need a more practical method for looking at how close the reconstructed signal is to the original.

A natural thing to do when looking at the fidelity of a reconstructed sequence is to look at the differences between the original and reconstructed values—in other words, the distortion introduced in the compression process. Two popular measures of distortion or difference between the original and reconstructed sequences are the squared error measure and the absolute difference measure. These are called *difference distortion measures*. If $\{x_n\}$ is the source output and $\{y_n\}$ is the reconstructed sequence, then the squared error measure is given by

$$d(x, y) = (x - y)^2 \tag{7.1}$$

and the absolute difference measure is given by

$$d(x, y) = |x - y|. \tag{7.2}$$

In general, it is difficult to examine the difference on a term-by-term basis. Therefore, a number of average measures are used to summarize the information in the difference sequence. The most often used average measure is the average of the squared error measure. This is called the *mean squared error* (mse) and is often represented by the symbol σ^2 or σ_d^2:

$$\sigma^2 = \frac{1}{N} \sum_{n=1}^{N} (x_n - y_n)^2. \tag{7.3}$$

If we are interested in the size of the error relative to the signal, we can find the ratio of the average squared value of the source output and the mse. This is called the *signal-to-noise ratio* (SNR).

$$\text{SNR} = \frac{\sigma_x^2}{\sigma_d^2} \tag{7.4}$$

where σ_x^2 is the average squared value of the source output, or signal, and σ_d^2 is the mse. The SNR is often measured on a logarithmic scale and the units of measurement are *decibels* (abbreviated to dB).

$$\text{SNR(dB)} = 10 \log_{10} \frac{\sigma_x^2}{\sigma_d^2} \tag{7.5}$$

Sometimes we are more interested in the size of the error relative to the peak value of the signal x_{peak} than with the size of the error relative to the average squared value of the signal. This ratio is called the *peak-signal-to-noise-ratio* (PSNR) and is given by

$$\text{PSNR(dB)} = 10 \log_{10} \frac{x_{\text{peak}}^2}{\sigma_d^2}. \tag{7.6}$$

Another difference distortion measure that is used quite often, although not as often as the mse, is the average of the absolute difference, or

$$d_1 = \frac{1}{N} \sum_{n=1}^{N} |x_n - y_n|. \tag{7.7}$$

This measure seems especially useful for evaluating image compression algorithms.

In some applications, the distortion is not perceptible as long as it is below some threshold. In these situations we might be interested in the maximum value of the error magnitude,

$$d_\infty = \max_n |x_n - y_n|. \tag{7.8}$$

We have looked at two approaches to measuring the fidelity of a reconstruction. The first method involving humans may provide a very accurate measure of perceptible fidelity, but it is not practical and not useful in mathematical design approaches. The second is mathematically tractable, but it usually does not provide a very accurate indication of the perceptible fidelity of the reconstruction. A middle ground is to find a mathematical model for human perception, transform both the source output and the reconstruction to this perceptual space, and then measure the difference in the perceptual space. For example, suppose we could find a transformation $\mathcal{V}$ that represented the actions performed by the human visual system (HVS) on the light intensity impinging on the retina before it is "perceived" by the cortex. We could then find $\mathcal{V}(x)$ and $\mathcal{V}(y)$ and examine the difference between them. There are two problems with this approach. First, the process of human perception is very difficult to model, and accurate models of perception are yet to be discovered. Second, even if we could find a mathematical model for perception, the odds are that it would be so complex that it would be mathematically intractable.

In spite of these disheartening prospects, the study of perception mechanisms is still important from the perspective of design and analysis of compression systems. Even if we cannot obtain a transformation that accurately models perception, we can learn something about the properties of perception that may come in handy in the design of compression systems. In the following, we will look at some of the properties of the human visual system and the perception of sound. Our review will be far from thorough, but the intent here is to present some properties that will be useful in later chapters when we talk about compression of images, video, speech, and audio.

7.3.1 The Human Visual System

The eye is a globe-shaped object with a lens in the front that focuses objects onto the retina in the back of the eye. The retina contains two kinds of receptors, called *rods* and *cones*. The rods are more sensitive to light than cones, and in low light most of our vision is due to the operation of rods. There are three kinds of cones, each of which are most sensitive at different wavelengths of the visible spectrum. The peak sensitivities of the cones are in the red, blue, and green regions of the visible spectrum [182]. The cones are mostly concentrated in a very small area of the retina called the *fovea*. Although the rods are more numerous than the cones, the cones provide better resolution because they are more closely packed in the fovea. The

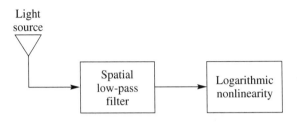

FIGURE 7.2   A model of monochromatic vision.

muscles of the eye move the eyeball, positioning the image of the object on the fovea. This becomes a drawback in low light. One way to improve what you see in low light is to focus to one side of the object. This way the object is imaged on the rods, which are more sensitive to light.

The eye is sensitive to light over an enormously large range of intensities; the upper end of the range is about 10^{10} times the lower end of the range. However, at a given instant we cannot perceive the entire range of brightness. Instead, the eye adapts to an average brightness level. The range of brightness levels that the eye can perceive at any given instant is much smaller than the total range it is capable of perceiving.

If we illuminate a screen with a certain intensity I and shine a spot on it with different intensity, the spot becomes visible when the difference in intensity is ΔI. This is called the *just noticeable difference* (jnd). The ratio $\frac{\Delta I}{I}$ is known as the *Weber fraction* or *Weber ratio*. This ratio is known to be constant at about 0.02 over a wide range of intensities in the absence of background illumination. However, if the background illumination is changed, the range over which the Weber ratio remains constant becomes relatively small. The constant range is centered around the intensity level to which the eye adapts.

If $\frac{\Delta I}{I}$ is constant, then we can infer that the sensitivity of the eye to intensity is a logarithmic function ($d(\log I) = dI/I$). Thus, we can model the eye as a receptor whose output goes to a logarithmic nonlinearity. We also know that the eye acts as a spatial low-pass filter [37, 148]. Putting all of this information together, we can develop a model for monochromatic vision, shown in Figure 7.2.

How does this description of the human visual system relate to coding schemes? Notice that the mind does not perceive everything the eye sees. We can use this knowledge to design compression systems such that the distortion introduced by our lossy compression scheme is not noticeable.

7.3.2 Auditory Perception

The ear is divided into three parts, creatively named the outer ear, the middle ear, and the inner ear. The outer ear consists of the structure that directs the sound waves, or pressure waves, to the *tympanic membrane*, or eardrum. This membrane separates the outer ear from the middle ear. The middle ear is an air-filled cavity containing three small bones that provide coupling between the tympanic membrane and the *oval window*, which leads into the inner ear. The tympanic membrane and the bones convert the pressure waves in the air to acoustical vibrations. The inner ear contains, among other things, a snail-shaped passage called the *cochlea* that contains the transducers that convert the acoustical vibrations to nerve impulses.

The human ear can hear sounds from approximately 20 Hz to 20 kHz, a 1000:1 range of frequencies. The range decreases with age; older people are usually unable to hear the higher frequencies. As in vision, auditory perception has several nonlinear components. One is that loudness is a function not only of the sound level, but also of the frequency. Thus, for example, a pure 1 kHz tone presented at a 20 dB intensity level will have the same apparent loudness as a 50 Hz tone presented at a 50 dB intensity level. By plotting the amplitude of tones at different frequencies that sound equally loud, we get a series of curves called the *Fletcher-Munson curves* [77].

Another very interesting audio phenomenon is that of *masking*, where one sound blocks out or masks the perception of another sound. The fact that one sound can drown out another seems reasonable. What is not so intuitive about masking is that if we were to try to mask a pure tone with noise, only the noise in a small frequency range around the tone being masked contributes to the masking. This range of frequencies is called the *critical band*. For most frequencies, when the noise just masks the tone, the ratio of the power of the tone divided by the power of the noise in the critical band is a constant [164]. The width of the critical band varies with frequency. This fact has led to the modeling of auditory perception as a bank of band-pass filters. There are a number of other, more complicated masking phenomena that also lend support to this theory (see [164, 218] for more information).

7.4 Information Theory Revisited ★

In order to study the trade-offs between rate and the distortion of lossy compression schemes, we would like to have rate defined explicitly as a function of the distortion for a given distortion measure. Unfortunately, this is generally not possible, and we have to go about it in a more roundabout way. Before we head down this path, we need a few more concepts from information theory.

In Chapter 2, when we talked about information, we were referring to letters from a single alphabet. In the case of lossy compression, we have to deal with two alphabets, the source alphabet and the reconstruction alphabet. These two alphabets are generally different from each other.

Example 7.4.1:

A simple lossy compression approach is to drop a certain number of the least significant bits from the source output. We might use such a scheme between a source that generates monochrome images at 8 bits per pixel and a user whose display facility can display only 64 different shades of gray. We could drop the two least significant bits from each pixel before transmitting the image to the user. There are other methods we can use in this situation that are much more effective, but this is certainly simple.

Suppose our source output consists of 4-bit words $\{0, 1, 2, \ldots, 15\}$. The source encoder encodes each value by shifting out the least significant bit. The output alphabet for the source coder is $\{0, 1, 2, \ldots, 7\}$. At the receiver we cannot recover the original value exactly.

However, we can get an approximation by shifting in a 0 as the least significant bit, or in other words, multiplying the source encoder output by two. Thus, the reconstruction alphabet is $\{0, 2, 4, \ldots, 14\}$, and the source and reconstruction do not take values from the same alphabet. ◆

As the source and reconstruction alphabets can be distinct, we need to be able to talk about the information relationships between two random variables that take on values from two different alphabets.

7.4.1 Conditional Entropy

Let X be a random variable that takes values from the source alphabet $\mathcal{X} = \{x_0, x_1, \ldots, x_{N-1}\}$. Let Y be a random variable that takes on values from the reconstruction alphabet $\mathcal{Y} = \{y_0, y_1, \ldots, y_{M-1}\}$. From Chapter 2 we know that the entropy of the source and the reconstruction are given by

$$H(X) = - \sum_{i=0}^{N-1} P(x_i) \log_2 P(x_i)$$

and

$$H(Y) = - \sum_{j=0}^{M-1} P(y_j) \log_2 P(y_j).$$

A measure of the relationship between two random variables is the *conditional entropy* (the average value of the conditional self-information). Recall that the self-information for an event A was defined as

$$i(A) = \log \frac{1}{P(A)} = - \log P(A).$$

In a similar manner, the conditional self-information of an event A, given that another event B has occurred, can be defined as

$$i(A|B) = \log \frac{1}{P(A|B)} = - \log P(A|B).$$

Suppose B is the event "Frazer has not drunk anything in two days," and A is the event "Frazer is thirsty." Then $P(A|B)$ should be close to one, which means that the conditional self-information $i(A|B)$ would be close to zero. This makes sense from an intuitive point of view as well. If we know that Frazer has not drunk anything in two days, then the statement that Frazer is thirsty would not be at all surprising to us and would contain very little information.

As in the case of self-information, we are generally interested in the average value of the conditional self-information. This average value is called the conditional entropy. The conditional entropies of the source and reconstruction alphabets are given as

$$H(X|Y) = - \sum_{i=0}^{N-1} \sum_{j=0}^{M-1} P(x_i|y_j) P(y_j) \log_2 P(x_i|y_j) \tag{7.9}$$

and

$$H(Y|X) = -\sum_{i=0}^{N-1}\sum_{j=0}^{M-1} P(x_i|y_j)P(y_j) \log_2 P(y_j|x_i). \qquad (7.10)$$

The conditional entropy $H(X|Y)$ can be interpreted as the amount of uncertainty remaining about the random variable X, or the source output, given that we know what value the reconstruction Y took. The additional knowledge of Y should reduce the uncertainty about X, and we can show that

$$H(X|Y) \leq H(X) \qquad (7.11)$$

(see Problem 5).

Example 7.4.2:

Suppose we have the 4-bits-per-symbol source and compression scheme described in Example 7.4.1. Assume that the source is equally likely to select any letter from its alphabet. Let us calculate the various entropies for this source and compression scheme.

As the source outputs are all equally likely, $P(X = i) = \frac{1}{16}$ for all $i \in \{0, 1, 2, \ldots, 15\}$, and therefore

$$H(X) = -\sum_{i} \frac{1}{16} \log \frac{1}{16} = \log 16 = 4 \text{ bits.} \qquad (7.12)$$

We can calculate the probabilities of the reconstruction alphabet:

$$P(Y = j) = P(X = j) + P(X = j + 1) = \frac{1}{16} + \frac{1}{16} = \frac{1}{8}. \qquad (7.13)$$

Therefore, $H(Y) = 3$ bits. To calculate the conditional entropy $H(X|Y)$, we need the conditional probabilities $\{P(x_i|y_j)\}$. From our construction of the source encoder, we see that

$$P(X = i|Y = j) = \begin{cases} \frac{1}{2} & \text{if } i = j \text{ or } i = j + 1, \text{ for } j = 0, 2, 4, \ldots, 14 \\ 0 & \text{otherwise.} \end{cases} \qquad (7.14)$$

Substituting this in the expression for $H(X|Y)$ in Equation (7.9), we get

$$H(X|Y) = -\sum_{i}\sum_{j} P(X = i|Y = j)P(Y = j) \log P(X = i|Y = j)$$

$$= -\sum_{j} [P(X = j|Y = j)P(Y = j) \log P(X = j|Y = j)$$

$$+ P(X = j + 1|Y = j)P(Y = j) \log P(X = j + 1|Y = j)]$$

$$= -8 \left[\frac{1}{2} \cdot \frac{1}{8} \log \frac{1}{2} + \frac{1}{2} \cdot \frac{1}{8} \log \frac{1}{2} \right] \qquad (7.15)$$

$$= 1. \qquad (7.16)$$

Let us compare this answer to what we would have intuitively expected the uncertainty to be, based on our knowledge of the compression scheme. With the coding scheme described here, knowledge of Y means that we know the first 3 bits of the input X. The only thing about the input that we are uncertain about is the value of the last bit. In other words, if we know the value of the reconstruction, our uncertainty about the source output is 1 bit. Therefore, at least in this case, our intuition matches the mathematical definition.

To obtain $H(Y|X)$, we need the conditional probabilities $\{P(y_j|x_i)\}$. From our knowledge of the compression scheme, we see that

$$P(Y = j|X = i) = \begin{cases} 1 & \text{if } i = j \text{ or } i = j+1, \text{ for } j = 0, 2, 4, \ldots, 14 \\ 0 & \text{otherwise.} \end{cases} \tag{7.17}$$

If we substitute these values into Equation (7.10), we get $H(Y|X) = 0$ bits (note that $0 \log 0 = 0$). This also makes sense. For the compression scheme described here, if we know the source output, we know 4 bits, the first 3 of which are the reconstruction. Therefore, in this example, knowledge of the source output at a specific time completely specifies the corresponding reconstruction. ◆

7.4.2   Average   Mutual   Information

We make use of one more quantity that relates the uncertainty or entropy of two random variables. This quantity is called the *mutual information* and is defined as

$$i(x_k; y_j) = \log \left[\frac{P(x_k|y_j)}{P(x_k)} \right]. \tag{7.18}$$

We will use the average value of this quantity, appropriately called the *average mutual information*, which is given by

$$I(X; Y) = \sum_{i=0}^{N-1} \sum_{j=0}^{M-1} P(x_i, y_j) \log \left[\frac{P(x_i|y_j)}{P(x_i)} \right] \tag{7.19}$$

$$= \sum_{i=0}^{N-1} \sum_{j=0}^{M-1} P(x_i|y_j) P(y_j) \log \left[\frac{P(x_i|y_j)}{P(x_i)} \right]. \tag{7.20}$$

We can write the average mutual information in terms of the entropy and the conditional entropy by expanding the argument of the logarithm in Equation (7.20).

$$I(X; Y) = \sum_{i=0}^{N-1} \sum_{j=0}^{M-1} P(x_i, y_j) \log \left[\frac{P(x_i|y_j)}{P(x_i)} \right] \tag{7.21}$$

$$= \sum_{i=0}^{N-1} \sum_{j=0}^{M-1} P(x_i, y_j) \log P(x_i|y_j) - \sum_{i=0}^{N-1} \sum_{j=0}^{M-1} P(x_i, y_j) \log P(x_i) \tag{7.22}$$

$$= H(X) - H(X|Y) \tag{7.23}$$

where the second term in Equation (7.22) is $H(X)$, and the first term is $-H(X|Y)$. Thus, the average mutual information is the entropy of the source minus the uncertainty that remains about the source output after the reconstructed value has been received. The average mutual information can also be written as

$$I(X; Y) = H(Y) - H(Y|X) = I(Y; X). \qquad (7.24)$$

Example 7.4.3:

For the source coder of Example 7.4.2, $H(X) = 4$ bits, and $H(X|Y) = 1$ bit. Therefore, using Equation (7.23), the average mutual information $I(X; Y)$ is 3 bits. If we wish to use Equation (7.24) to compute $I(X; Y)$, we would need $H(Y)$ and $H(Y|X)$, which from Example 7.4.2 are 3 and 0, respectively. Thus, the value of $I(X; Y)$ still works out to be 3 bits. ◆

7.4.3 Differential Entropy

Up to this point we have assumed that the source picks its outputs from a discrete alphabet. When we study lossy compression techniques, we will see that for many sources of interest to us this assumption is not true. In this section, we will extend some of the information theoretic concepts defined for discrete random variables to the case of random variables with continuous distributions.

Unfortunately, we run into trouble from the very beginning. Recall that the first quantity we defined was self-information, which was given by $\log \frac{1}{P(x_i)}$, where $P(x_i)$ is the probability that the random variable will take on the value x_i. For a random variable with a continuous distribution, this probability is zero. Therefore, if the random variable has a continuous distribution, the "self-information" associated with any value is infinity.

If we do not have the concept of self-information, how do we go about defining entropy, which is the average value of the self-information? We know that many continuous functions can be written as limiting cases of their discretized version. We will try to take this route in order to define the entropy of a continuous random variable X with probability density function *(pdf)* $f_X(x)$.

While the random variable X cannot generally take on a particular value with nonzero probability, it can take on a value in an *interval* with nonzero probability. Therefore, let us divide the range of the random variable into intervals of size Δ. Then, by the mean value theorem, in each interval $[(i - 1)\Delta, i\Delta)$, there exists a number x_i, such that

$$f_X(x_i)\Delta = \int_{(i-1)\Delta}^{i\Delta} f_X(x)\, dx. \qquad (7.25)$$

Let us define a discrete random variable X_d with *pdf*

$$P(X_d = x_i) = f_X(x_i)\Delta. \qquad (7.26)$$

Then we can obtain the entropy of this random variable as

$$H(X_d) = - \sum_{i=-\infty}^{\infty} P(x_i) \log P(x_i) \qquad (7.27)$$

$$= - \sum_{i=-\infty}^{\infty} f_X(x_i)\Delta \log f_X(x_i)\Delta \tag{7.28}$$

$$= - \sum_{i=-\infty}^{\infty} f_X(x_i)\Delta \log f_X(x_i) - \sum_{i=-\infty}^{\infty} f_X(x_i)\Delta \log \Delta \tag{7.29}$$

$$= - \sum_{i=-\infty}^{\infty} [f_X(x_i)\log f_X(x_i)]\,\Delta - \log \Delta. \tag{7.30}$$

Taking the limit as $\Delta \to 0$ of Equation (7.30), the first term goes to $-\int_{-\infty}^{\infty} f_X(x) \log f_X(x)\,dx$, which looks like the analog to our definition of entropy for discrete sources. However, the second term is $-\log \Delta$, which goes to plus infinity when Δ goes to zero. It seems there is not an analog to entropy as defined for discrete sources. However, the first term in the limit serves some functions similar to that served by entropy in the discrete case and is a useful function in its own right. We call this term the *differential entropy* of a continuous source and denote it by $h(X)$.

Example 7.4.4:

Suppose we have a random variable X that is uniformly distributed in the interval $[a, b)$. The differential entropy of this random variable is given by

$$h(X) = - \int_{-\infty}^{\infty} f_X(x)\log f_X(x)\,dx \tag{7.31}$$

$$= - \int_a^b \frac{1}{b-a} \log \frac{1}{b-a}\,dx \tag{7.32}$$

$$= \log(b-a). \tag{7.33}$$

Notice that when $b - a$ is less than one, the differential entropy will become negative—in contrast to the entropy, which never takes on negative values. ◆

   Later in this chapter, we will find particular use for the differential entropy of the Gaussian source.

Example 7.4.5:

Suppose we have a random variable X that has a Gaussian *pdf*,

$$f_X(x) = \frac{1}{\sqrt{2\pi\sigma^2}} \exp - \frac{(x-\mu)^2}{2\sigma^2}. \tag{7.34}$$

The differential entropy is given by

$$h(X) = - \int_{-\infty}^{\infty} \frac{1}{\sqrt{2\pi\sigma^2}} \exp - \frac{(x-\mu)^2}{2\sigma^2} \log \left[\frac{1}{\sqrt{2\pi\sigma^2}} \exp - \frac{(x-\mu)^2}{2\sigma^2} \right] dx \tag{7.35}$$

$$= -\log \frac{1}{\sqrt{2\pi\sigma^2}} \int_{-\infty}^{\infty} f_X(x)dx + \int_{-\infty}^{\infty} \frac{(x-\mu)^2}{2\sigma^2} \log e f_X(x)dx \qquad (7.36)$$

$$= \frac{1}{2} \log 2\pi\sigma^2 + \frac{1}{2} \log e \qquad (7.37)$$

$$= \frac{1}{2} \log 2\pi e \sigma^2. \qquad (7.38)$$

Thus, the differential entropy of a Gaussian random variable is directly proportional to its variance. ◆

The differential entropy for the Gaussian distribution has the added distinction that it is larger than the differential entropy for any other continuously distributed random variable with the same variance. That is, for any random variable X, with variance σ^2

$$h(X) \le \frac{1}{2} \log 2\pi e \sigma^2. \qquad (7.39)$$

The proof of this statement depends on the fact that for any two continuous distributions $f_X(X)$ and $g_X(X)$

$$-\int_{-\infty}^{\infty} f_X(x) \log f_X(x)dx \le -\int_{-\infty}^{\infty} f_X(x) \log g_X(x)dx. \qquad (7.40)$$

We will not prove Equation (7.40) here, but you may refer to [149] for a simple proof. To obtain Equation (7.39), we substitute the expression for the Gaussian distribution for $g_X(x)$. Noting that the left-hand side of Equation (7.40) is simply the differential entropy of the random variable X, we have

$$h(X) \le -\int_{-\infty}^{\infty} f_X(x) \log \frac{1}{\sqrt{2\pi\sigma^2}} \exp -\frac{(x-\mu)^2}{2\sigma^2} dx$$

$$= \frac{1}{2} \log (2\pi\sigma^2) + \log e \int_{-\infty}^{\infty} f_X(x) \frac{(x-\mu)^2}{2\sigma^2} dx$$

$$= \frac{1}{2} \log (2\pi\sigma^2) + \frac{\log e}{2\sigma^2} \int_{-\infty}^{\infty} f_X(x)(x-\mu)^2 dx$$

$$= \frac{1}{2} \log (2\pi e \sigma^2). \qquad (7.41)$$

We seem to be striking out with continuous random variables. There is no analog for self-information and really none for entropy either. However, the situation improves when we look for an analog for the average mutual information. Let us define the random variable Y_d in a manner similar to the random variable X_d, as the discretized version of a continuous valued random variable Y. Then we can show (see Problem 4)

$$H(X_d|Y_d) = -\sum_{i=-\infty}^{\infty} \sum_{j=-\infty}^{\infty} \left[f_{X|Y}(x_i|y_j) f_Y(y_j) \log f_{X|Y}(x_i|y_j) \right] \Delta\Delta - \log \Delta. \qquad (7.42)$$

Therefore, the average mutual information for the discretized random variables is given by

$$I(X_d; Y_d) = H(X_d) - H(X_d|Y_d) \tag{7.43}$$

$$= -\sum_{i=-\infty}^{\infty} f_X(x_i)\Delta \log f_X(x_i) \tag{7.44}$$

$$-\sum_{i=-\infty}^{\infty}\left[\sum_{j=-\infty}^{\infty} f_{X|Y}(x_i|y_j)f_Y(y_j) \log f_{X|Y}(x_i|y_j)\Delta\right]\Delta. \tag{7.45}$$

Notice that the two $\log \Delta$s in the expression for $H(X_d)$ and $H(X_d|Y_d)$ cancel each other out, and as long as $h(X)$ and $h(X|Y)$ are not equal to infinity, when we take the limit as $\Delta \to 0$ of $I(X_d; Y_d)$ we get

$$I(X; Y) = h(X) - h(X|Y). \tag{7.46}$$

The average mutual information in the continuous case can be obtained as a limiting case of the average mutual information for the discrete case and has the same physical significance.

   We have gone through a lot of mathematics in this section. But the information will be used immediately to define the rate distortion function for a random source.

7.5   Rate Distortion Theory ★

Rate distortion theory is concerned with the trade-offs between distortion and rate in lossy compression schemes. Rate is defined as the average number of bits used to represent each sample value. One way of representing the trade-offs is via a *rate distortion function R(D)*. The rate distortion function $R(D)$ specifies the lowest rate at which the output of a source can be encoded while keeping the distortion less than or equal to D. On our way to mathematically defining the rate distortion function, let us look at the rate and distortion for some different lossy compression schemes.

   In Example 7.4.2, knowledge of the value of the input at time k completely specifies the reconstructed value at time k. In this situation,

$$P(y_j|x_i) = \begin{cases} 1 & \text{for some } j = j_i \\ 0 & \text{otherwise.} \end{cases} \tag{7.47}$$

Therefore,

$$D = \sum_{i=0}^{N-1}\sum_{j=0}^{M-1} P(y_j|x_i)P(x_i)d(x_i, y_j) \tag{7.48}$$

$$= \sum_{i=0}^{N-1} P(x_i)d(x_i, y_{j_i}) \tag{7.49}$$

where we used the fact that $P(x_i, y_j) = P(y_j|x_i)P(x_i)$ in Equation (7.48). The rate for this source coder is the output entropy $H(Y)$ of the source decoder. If this were always the case, the task of obtaining a rate distortion function would be relatively simple. Given a distortion constraint D^*, we could look at all encoders with distortion less than D^* and pick the one with the lowest output entropy. This entropy would be the rate corresponding to the distortion D^*. However, the requirement that knowledge of the input at time k completely specifies the reconstruction at time k is very restrictive, and there are many efficient compression techniques that would have to be excluded under this requirement. Consider the following example.

Example 7.5.1:

With a data sequence that consists of height and weight measurements, obviously height and weight are quite heavily correlated. In fact, after studying a long sequence of data, we find that if we plot the height along the x axis and the weight along the y axis, the data points cluster along the line $y = 2.5x$. In order to take advantage of this correlation, we devise the following compression scheme. For a given pair of height and weight measurements, we find the orthogonal projection on the $y = 2.5x$ line as shown in Figure 7.3. The point on this line can be represented as the distance to the nearest integer from the origin. Thus, we encode a pair of values into a single value. At the time of reconstruction, we simply map this value back into a pair of height and weight measurements.

For instance, suppose somebody is 72 inches tall and weighs 200 pounds (point A in Figure 7.3). This corresponds to a point at a distance of 212 along the $y = 2.5x$ line. The

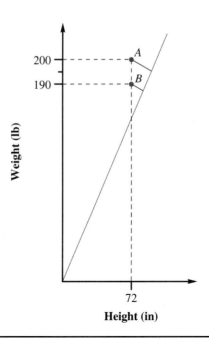

FIGURE 7.3   **Compression scheme for encoding height-weight pairs.**

reconstructed values of the height and weight corresponding to this value are 79 and 197. Notice that the reconstructed values differ from the original values. Suppose we now have another individual who is also 72 inches tall but weighs 190 pounds (point B in Figure 7.3). The source coder output for this pair would be 203, and the reconstructed values for height and weight are 75 and 188, respectively. Notice that while the height value in both cases was the same, the reconstructed value is different. The reason for this is that the reconstructed value for the height depends on the weight. Thus, for this particular source coder, we do not have a conditional probability density function $\{P(y_j|x_i)\}$ of the form shown in Equation (7.47).   ◆

Let us examine the distortion for this scheme a little more closely. As the conditional probability for this scheme is not of the form of Equation (7.47), we can no longer write the distortion in the form of Equation (7.49). Recall that the general form of the distortion is

$$D = \sum_{i=0}^{N-1} \sum_{j=0}^{M-1} d(x_i, y_j) P(x_i) P(y_j|x_i). \tag{7.50}$$

Each term in the summation consists of three factors: the distortion measure $d(x_i, y_j)$, the source density $P(x_i)$, and the conditional probability $P(y_j|x_i)$. The distortion measure is a measure of closeness of the original and reconstructed versions of the signal and is generally determined by the particular application. The source probabilities are solely determined by the source. The third factor, the set of conditional probabilities, can be seen as a description of the compression scheme.

Therefore, for a given source with some *pdf* $\{P(x_i)\}$ and a specified distortion measure $d(\cdot, \cdot)$, the distortion is a function only of the conditional probabilities $\{P(y_j|x_i)\}$; that is,

$$D = D(\{P(y_j|x_i)\}). \tag{7.51}$$

Therefore, we can write the constraint that the distortion D be less than some value D^* as a requirement that the conditional probabilities for the compression scheme belong to a set of conditional probabilities Γ that have the property that

$$\Gamma = \{\{P(y_j|x_i\} \text{ such that } D(\{P(y_j|x_i)\}) \leq D^*\}. \tag{7.52}$$

Once we know the set of compression schemes to which we have to confine ourselves, we can start to look at the rate of these schemes. In Example 7.4.2, the rate was the entropy of Y. However, that was a result of the fact that the conditional probability describing that particular source coder took on only the values 0 and 1. Consider the following trivial situation.

Example 7.5.2:

Suppose we have the same source as in Example 7.4.2 and the same reconstruction alphabet. Suppose the distortion measure is

$$d(x_i, y_j) = (x_i - y_j)^2$$

and $D^* = 225$. One compression scheme that satisfies the distortion constraint randomly maps the input to any one of the outputs; that is,

$$P(y_j|x_i) = \frac{1}{8} \qquad \text{for } i = 0, 1, \ldots, 15 \text{ and } j = 0, 2, \ldots, 14.$$

We can see that this conditional probability assignment satisfies the distortion constraint. As each of the eight reconstruction values is equally likely, $H(Y)$ is 3 bits. However, we are not transmitting *any* information. We could get exactly the same results by transmitting 0 bits and randomly picking Y at the receiver. ◆

Therefore, the entropy of the reconstruction $H(Y)$ cannot be a measure of the rate. In his 1959 paper on source coding [211], Shannon showed that the minimum rate for a given distortion is given by

$$R(D) = \min_{\{P(y_j|x_i)\}\in\Gamma} I(X;Y). \tag{7.53}$$

To prove this is beyond the scope of this book. (Further information can be found in [55] and [23].) However, we can at least convince ourselves that defining the rate as an average mutual information gives sensible answers when used for the examples shown here. Consider Example 7.4.2. The average mutual information in this case is 3 bits, which is what we said the rate was. In fact, notice that whenever the conditional probabilities are constrained to be of the form of Equation (7.47),

$$H(Y|X) = 0,$$

then

$$I(X;Y) = H(Y),$$

which had been our measure of rate.

In Example 7.5.2, the average mutual information is 0 bits, which accords with our intuitive feeling of what the rate should be. Again, whenever

$$H(Y|X) = H(Y),$$

that is, knowledge of the source gives us no knowledge of the reconstruction,

$$I(X;Y) = 0,$$

which seems entirely reasonable. We should not have to transmit any bits when we are not sending any information.

At least for the examples here, it seems that the average mutual information does represent the rate. However, earlier we had said that the average mutual information between the source output and the reconstruction is a measure of the information conveyed by the reconstruction about the source output. Why are we then looking for compression schemes that *minimize* this value? To understand this, we have to remember that the process of finding the performance of the optimum compression scheme had two parts. In the first part we specified the desired distortion. The entire set of conditional probabilities over which the average mutual information is minimized satisfies the distortion constraint. Therefore, we can leave the question of distortion, or fidelity, aside and concentrate on minimizing the rate.

Finally, how do we find the rate distortion function? There are two ways: one is a computational approach developed by Arimoto [10] and Blahut [25]. While the derivation of the algorithm is beyond the scope of this book, the algorithm itself is relatively simple. The other approach is to find a lower bound for the average mutual information and then show that we can achieve this bound. We use this approach to find the rate distortion functions for two important sources.

Example 7.5.3: Rate distortion function for the binary source

Suppose we have a source alphabet $\{0, 1\}$, with $P(0) = p$. The reconstruction alphabet is also binary. Given the distortion measure

$$d(x_i, y_j) = x_i \oplus y_j, \tag{7.54}$$

where $\oplus$ is modulo 2 addition, let us find the rate distortion function. Assume for the moment that $p < \frac{1}{2}$. For $D > p$ an encoding scheme that would satisfy the distortion criterion would be not to transmit anything and fix $Y = 1$. So for $D \geq p$

$$R(D) = 0. \tag{7.55}$$

We will find the rate distortion function for the distortion range $0 \leq D < p$.

Find a lower bound for the average mutual information:

$$I(X; Y) = H(X) - H(X|Y) \tag{7.56}$$
$$= H(X) - H(X \oplus Y|Y) \tag{7.57}$$
$$\geq H(X) - H(X \oplus Y) \qquad \text{from Equation (7.11).} \tag{7.58}$$

In the second step we have used the fact that if we know Y, then knowing X we can obtain $X \oplus Y$ and vice versa as $X \oplus Y \oplus Y = X$.

Let us look at the terms on the right-hand side of (7.11):

$$H(X) = -p \log_2 p - (1 - p) \log_2(1 - p) = H_b(p), \tag{7.59}$$

where $H_b(p)$ is called the *binary entropy function* and is plotted in Figure 7.4. Note that $H_b(p) = H_b(1 - p)$.

Given that $H(X)$ is completely specified by the source probabilities, our task now is to find the conditional probabilities $\{P(x_i|y_j)\}$ such that $H(X \oplus Y)$ is maximized while the average distortion $E[d(x_i, y_j)] \leq D$. $H(X \oplus Y)$ is simply the binary entropy function $H_b(P(X \oplus Y = 1))$, where

$$P(X \oplus Y = 1) = P(X = 0, Y = 1) + P(X = 1, Y = 0). \tag{7.60}$$

Therefore, to maximize $H(X \oplus Y)$, we would want $P(X \oplus Y = 1)$ to be as close as possible to one-half. However, the selection of $P(X \oplus Y)$ also has to satisfy the distortion constraint. The distortion is given by

$$E[d(x_i, y_j)] = 0 \times P(X = 0, Y = 0) + 1 \times P(X = 0, Y = 1)$$

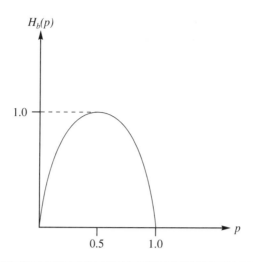

FIGURE 7.4 **The binary entropy function.**

$$+ 1 \times P(X = 1, Y = 0) + 0 \times P(X = 1, Y = 1)$$
$$= P(X = 0, Y = 1) + P(X = 1, Y = 0)$$
$$= P(Y = 1|X = 0)p + P(Y = 0|X = 1)(1 - p). \tag{7.61}$$

But this is simply the probability that $X \oplus Y = 1$. Therefore, the maximum value that $P(X \oplus Y = 1)$ can have is D. Our assumptions were that $D < p$ and $p \leq \frac{1}{2}$, which means that $D < \frac{1}{2}$. Therefore, $P(X \oplus Y = 1)$ is closest to $\frac{1}{2}$ while being less than or equal to D when $P(X \oplus Y = 1) = D$. Therefore,

$$I(X; Y) \geq H_b(p) - H_b(D). \tag{7.62}$$

We can show that for $P(X = 0|Y = 1) = P(X = 1|Y = 0) = D$, this bound is achieved. That is, if $P(X = 0|Y = 1) = P(X = 1|Y = 0) = D$, then

$$I(X; Y) = H_b(p) - H_b(D). \tag{7.63}$$

Therefore, for $D < p$ and $p \leq \frac{1}{2}$,

$$R(D) = H_b(p) - H_b(D). \tag{7.64}$$

Finally, if $p > \frac{1}{2}$, then we simply switch the roles of p and $1 - p$. Putting all this together, the rate distortion function for a binary source is

$$R(D) = \begin{cases} H_b(p) - H_b(D) & \text{for } D < \min\{p, 1 - p\} \\ 0 & \text{otherwise.} \end{cases} \tag{7.65}$$

◆

Example 7.5.4: Rate distortion function for the Gaussian source

Suppose we have a continuous amplitude source that has a zero mean Gaussian *pdf* with variance σ^2. If our distortion measure is given by

$$d(x, y) = (x - y)^2, \tag{7.66}$$

our distortion constraint is given by

$$E\left[(X - Y)^2\right] \leq D. \tag{7.67}$$

Our approach to finding the rate distortion function will be the same as in the previous example; that is, find a lower bound for $I(X; Y)$ given a distortion constraint, and then show that this lower bound can be achieved.

First we find the rate distortion function for $D < \sigma^2$.

$$I(X; Y) = h(X) - h(X|Y) \tag{7.68}$$
$$= h(X) - h(X - Y|Y) \tag{7.69}$$
$$\geq h(X) - h(X - Y) \tag{7.70}$$

In order to minimize the right-hand side of Equation (7.70), we have to maximize the second term subject to the constraint given by Equation (7.67). This term is maximized if $X - Y$ is Gaussian, and the constraint can be satisfied if $E\left[(X - Y)^2\right] = D$. Therefore, $h(X - Y)$ is the differential entropy of a Gaussian random variable with variance D, and the lower bound becomes

$$I(X; Y) \geq \frac{1}{2}\log(2\pi e\sigma^2) - \frac{1}{2}\log(2\pi eD) \tag{7.71}$$

$$= \frac{1}{2}\log\frac{\sigma^2}{D}. \tag{7.72}$$

This average mutual information can be achieved if Y is zero mean Gaussian with variance $\sigma^2 - D$, and

$$f_{X|Y}(x|y) = \frac{1}{\sqrt{2\pi D}}\exp\frac{-x^2}{2D}. \tag{7.73}$$

For $D > \sigma^2$, if we set $Y = 0$, then

$$I(X; Y) = 0 \tag{7.74}$$

and

$$E\left[(X - Y)^2\right] = \sigma^2 < D. \tag{7.75}$$

Therefore, the rate distortion function for the Gaussian source can be written as

$$R(D) = \begin{cases} \frac{1}{2}\log\frac{\sigma^2}{D} & \text{for } D < \sigma^2 \\ 0 & \text{for } D > \sigma^2. \end{cases} \tag{7.76}$$

◆

Like the differential entropy for the Gaussian source, the rate distortion function for the Gaussian source also has the distinction of being larger than the rate distortion function for any other source with a continuous distribution and the same variance. This is especially valuable because for many sources it can be very difficult to calculate the rate distortion function. In these situations, it is helpful to have an upper bound for the rate distortion function. It would be very nice if we also had a lower bound for the rate distortion function of a continuous random variable. Shannon described such a bound in his 1948 paper [209], and it is appropriately called the *Shannon lower bound*. We will simply state the bound here without derivation (for more information, see [23]).

The Shannon lower bound for a random variable X and the magnitude error criterion

$$d(x, y) = |x - y| \tag{7.77}$$

is given by

$$R_{SLB}(D) = h(X) - \log(2eD). \tag{7.78}$$

If we used the squared error criterion, the Shannon lower bound is given by

$$R_{SLB}(D) = h(X) - \frac{1}{2} \log(2\pi eD). \tag{7.79}$$

In this section we have defined the rate distortion function and obtained the rate distortion function for two important sources. We have also obtained upper and lower bounds on the rate distortion function for an arbitrary *iid* source. These functions and bounds are especially useful when we want to know if it is possible to design compression schemes to provide a specified rate and distortion given a particular source. They are also useful in determining the amount of performance improvement that we could obtain by designing a better compression scheme. In these ways the rate distortion function plays the same role for lossy compression that entropy plays for lossless compression.

7.6 Models

As in the case of lossless compression, models play an important role in the design of lossy compression algorithms; there are a variety of approaches available. The set of models we can draw on for lossy compression is much wider than the set of models we studied for lossless compression. We will look at some of these models in this section. What is presented here is by no means an exhaustive list of models. Our only intent is to describe those models that will be useful in the following chapters.

7.6.1 Probability Models

An important method for characterizing a particular source is through the use of probability models. As we shall see later, knowledge of the probability model is important for the design of a number of compression schemes.

Probability models used for the design and analysis of lossy compression schemes differ from those used in the design and analysis of lossless compression schemes. When developing models in the lossless case, we tried for an exact match. The probability of each symbol was estimated as part of the modeling process. When modeling sources in order to design or analyze lossy compression schemes, we look more to the general rather than exact correspondence. The reasons are more pragmatic than theoretical. Certain probability distribution functions are more analytically tractable than others, and we try to match the distribution of the source with one of these "nice" distributions.

Uniform, Gaussian, Laplacian, and Gamma distribution are four probability models commonly used in the design and analysis of lossy compression systems:

■ **Uniform Distribution:** As for lossless compression, this is again our ignorance model. If we do not know anything about the distribution of the source output, except possibly the range of values, we can use the uniform distribution to model the source. The probability density function for a random variable uniformly distributed between a and b is

$$f_X(x) = \begin{cases} \frac{1}{b-a} & \text{for } a \leq x \leq b \\ 0 & \text{otherwise.} \end{cases} \tag{7.80}$$

■ **Gaussian Distribution:** The Gaussian distribution is one of the most commonly used probability models for two reasons: it is mathematically tractable and, by virtue of the central limit theorem, it can be argued that in the limit the distribution of interest goes to a Gaussian distribution. The probability density function for a random variable with a Gaussian distribution and mean μ and variance σ^2 is

$$f_X(x) = \frac{1}{\sqrt{2\pi\sigma^2}} \exp -\frac{(x-\mu)^2}{2\sigma^2}. \tag{7.81}$$

■ **Laplacian Distribution:** Many sources that we deal with have distributions that are quite peaked at zero. For example, speech consists mainly of silence. Therefore, samples of speech will be zero or close to zero with high probability. Image pixels themselves do not have any attraction to small values. However, there is a high degree of correlation among pixels. Therefore, a large number of the pixel-to-pixel differences will have values close to zero. In these situations, a Gaussian distribution is not a very close match to the data. A closer match is the Laplacian distribution, which is peaked at zero. The distribution function for a zero mean random variable with Laplacian distribution and variance σ^2 is

$$f_X(x) = \frac{1}{\sqrt{2\sigma^2}} \exp \frac{-\sqrt{2}\,|x|}{\sigma}. \tag{7.82}$$

■ **Gamma Distribution:** A distribution that is even more peaked, though considerably less tractable, than the Laplacian distribution is the Gamma distribution. The distribution function for a Gamma distributed random variable with zero mean and variance σ^2 is given by

$$f_X(x) = \frac{\sqrt[4]{3}}{\sqrt{8\pi\sigma\,|x|}} \exp \frac{-\sqrt{3}\,|x|}{2\sigma}. \tag{7.83}$$

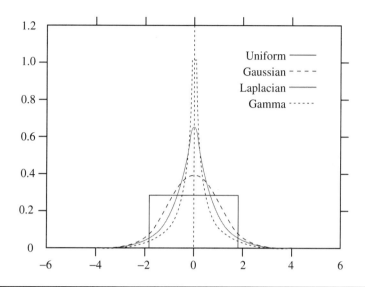

FIGURE 7.5   **Uniform, Gaussian, Laplacian, and Gamma distributions.**

The shapes of these four distributions, assuming a mean of zero and a variance of one, are shown in Figure 7.5.

One way of obtaining the estimate of the distribution of a particular source is to divide the range of outputs into "bins" or intervals I_k. We can then find the number of values n_k that fall into each interval. A plot of $\frac{n_k}{n_T}$, where n_T is the total number of source outputs being considered, should give us some idea of what the input distribution looks like. Be aware that this is a rather crude method and can at times be misleading. For example, if we were not careful in our selection of the source output, we might end up modeling some local peculiarities of the source. If the bins are too large, we might effectively filter out some important properties of the source. If the bin sizes are too small, we may miss out on some of the gross behavior of the source.

Once we have decided on some candidate distributions, we can select between them using a number of sophisticated tests. These tests are beyond the scope of this book but are described in [135].

Many of the sources that we deal with when we design lossy compression schemes have a great deal of structure in the form of sample-to-sample dependencies. The probability models described here capture none of these dependencies. Fortunately, we have a lot of models that can capture most of this structure. We describe some of these models in the next section.

7.6.2 Linear System Models

A large class of processes can be modeled in the form of the following difference equation:

$$x_n = \sum_{i=1}^{N} a_i x_{n-i} + \sum_{j=1}^{M} b_j \epsilon_{n-j} + \epsilon_n, \tag{7.84}$$

where $\{x_n\}$ are samples of the process we wish to model, and $\{\epsilon_n\}$ is a white noise sequence. We will assume throughout this book that we are dealing with real valued samples. Recall that a zero-mean wide-sense-stationary noise sequence $\{\epsilon_n\}$ is a sequence with autocorrelation function

$$R_{\epsilon\epsilon}(k) = \begin{cases} \sigma_\epsilon^2 & \text{for } k = 0 \\ 0 & \text{otherwise.} \end{cases} \tag{7.85}$$

In digital signal-processing terminology, Equation (7.84) represents the output of a linear discrete time invariant filter with N poles and M zeros. In the statistical literature, this model is called an autoregressive moving average model of order (N,M), or an ARMA (N,M) model. The autoregressive label is because of the first summation in Equation (7.84), while the second summation gives us the moving average portion of the name.

If all the b_j were zero in Equation (7.84), only the autoregressive part of the ARMA model would remain:

$$x_n = \sum_{i=1}^{N} a_i x_{n-i} + \epsilon_n. \tag{7.86}$$

This model is called an Nth-order autoregressive model and is denoted by AR(N). In digital signal-processing terminology, this is an *all pole filter*. The AR(N) model is the most popular of all the linear models, especially in speech compression, where it arises as a natural consequence of the speech production model. We will look at it a bit more closely.

First notice that for the AR(N) process, knowing all the past history of the process gives no more information than knowing the last N samples of the process; that is,

$$P(x_n|x_{n-1}, x_{n-2}, \ldots) = P(x_n|x_{n-1}, x_{n-2}, \ldots, x_{n-N}), \tag{7.87}$$

which means that the AR(N) process is a Markov model of order N.

The autocorrelation function of a process can tell us a lot about the sample-to-sample behavior of a sequence. A slowly decaying autocorrelation function indicates a high sample-to-sample correlation, while a fast decaying autocorrelation denotes low sample-to-sample correlation. In the case of *no* sample-to-sample correlation, such as white noise, the autocorrelation function is zero for lags greater than zero, as seen in Equation (7.85). The autocorrelation function for the AR(N) process can be obtained as follows:

$$R_{xx}(k) = E[x_n x_{n-k}] \tag{7.88}$$

$$= E\left[\left(\sum_{i=1}^{N} a_i x_{n-i} + \epsilon_n\right)(x_{n-k})\right] \tag{7.89}$$

$$= E\left[\sum_{i=1}^{N} a_i x_{n-i} x_{n-k}\right] + E[\epsilon_n x_{n-k}] \tag{7.90}$$

$$= \begin{cases} \sum_{i=1}^{N} a_i R_{xx}(k-i) & \text{for } k > 0 \\ \sum_{i=1}^{N} a_i R_{xx}(i) + \sigma_\epsilon^2 & \text{for } k = 0. \end{cases} \tag{7.91}$$

Example 7.6.1:

Suppose we have an AR(3) process. Let us write out the equations for the autocorrelation coefficient for lags 1, 2, 3:

$$R_{xx}(1) = a_1 R_{xx}(0) + a_2 R_{xx}(1) + a_3 R_{xx}(2)$$
$$R_{xx}(2) = a_1 R_{xx}(1) + a_2 R_{xx}(0) + a_3 R_{xx}(1)$$
$$R_{xx}(3) = a_1 R_{xx}(2) + a_2 R_{xx}(1) + a_3 R_{xx}(0).$$

If we know the values of the autocorrelation function $R_{xx}(k)$, for $k = 0, 1, 2, 3$, we can use this set of equations to find the AR(3) coefficients $\{a_1, a_2, a_3\}$. On the other hand, if we know the model coefficients and σ_ϵ^2, we can use the above equations along with the equation for $R_{xx}(0)$ to find the first four autocorrelation coefficients. All the other autocorrelation values can be obtained by using Equation (7.91). ◆

To see how the autocorrelation function is related to the temporal behavior of the sequence, let us look at the behavior of a simple AR(1) source.

Example 7.6.2:

An AR(1) source is defined by the equation

$$x_n = a_1 x_{n-1} + \epsilon_n. \tag{7.92}$$

The autocorrelation function for this source (see Problem 8) is given by

$$R_{xx}(k) = \frac{1}{1 - a_1^2} a_1^k \sigma_\epsilon^2. \tag{7.93}$$

From this we can see that the autocorrelation will decay more slowly for larger values of a_1. Remember that the value of a_1 in this case is an indicator of how closely the current sample is related to the previous sample. The autocorrelation function is plotted for two values of a_1 in Figure 7.6. Notice that for a_1 close to 1, the autocorrelation function decays extremely slowly. As the value of a_1 moves farther away from 1, the autocorrelation function decays much faster.

Sample waveforms for $a_1 = 0.99$ and $a_1 = 0.6$ are shown in Figures 7.7 and 7.8. Notice the slower variations in the waveform for the process with a higher value of a_1. Because the waveform in Figure 7.7 varies more slowly than the waveform in Figure 7.8, samples of this waveform are much more likely to be close in value than the samples of the waveform of Figure 7.8.

Let's look at what happens when the AR(1) coefficient is negative. The sample waveforms are plotted in Figures 7.9 and 7.10. The sample-to-sample variation in these waveforms is much higher than in the waveforms shown in Figures 7.7 and 7.8. However, if we were to look at the variation in magnitude, we can see that the higher value of a_1 results in magnitude values that are closer together.

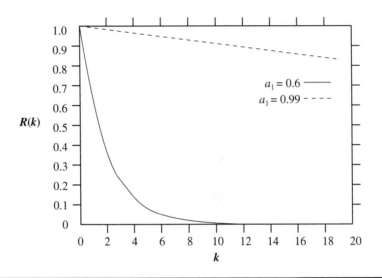

FIGURE 7.6   Autocorrelation function of an AR(1) process with two values of a_1.

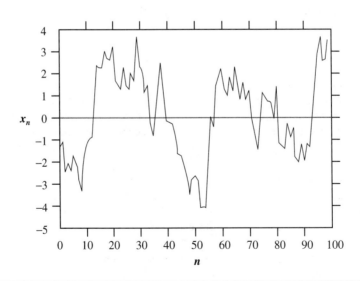

FIGURE 7.7   Sample function of an AR(1) process with $a_1 = 0.99$.

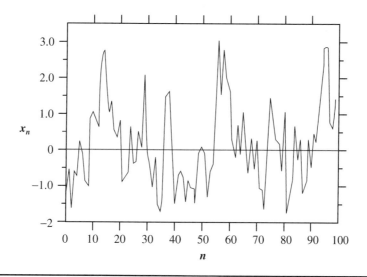

FIGURE 7.8   Sample function of an AR(1) process with $a_1 = 0.6$.

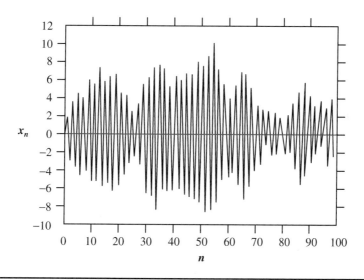

FIGURE 7.9   Sample function of an AR(1) process with $a_1 = -0.99$.

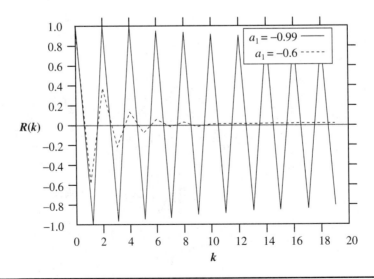

FIGURE 7.11   Autocorrelation function of an AR(1) process with two negative values of a_1.

This behavior is also reflected in the autocorrelation function, shown in Figure 7.11, as we might expect from looking at Equation (7.93). ◆

In Equation (7.84), instead of setting all the $\{b_j\}$ coefficients to zero, if we set all the $\{a_i\}$ coefficients to zero, we are left with the moving average part of the ARMA process:

$$x_n = \sum_{j=1}^{M} b_j \epsilon_{n-j} + \epsilon_n. \tag{7.94}$$

This process is called an Mth-order moving average process. This is a weighted average of the current and M past samples. Because of the form of this process, it is most useful when modeling slowly varying processes.

7.6.3 Physical Models

Physical models are based on the physics of the source output production. The physics are generally complicated and not amenable to a reasonable mathematical approximation. An exception to this rule is speech generation.

Speech Production

There has been a significant amount of research conducted in the area of speech production [186], and volumes have been written about it. We will try to summarize some of the pertinent aspects in this section.

Speech is produced by forcing air first through an elastic opening, the vocal cords, and then through cylindrical tubes with nonuniform diameter (the laryngeal, oral, nasal, and pharynx passages), and finally through cavities with changing boundaries such as the mouth and the nasal cavity. Everything past the vocal cords is generally referred to as the *vocal tract*. The first action generates the sound, which is then modulated into speech as it traverses through the vocal tract.

We will often be talking about filters in the coming chapters. We will try to describe filters more precisely at that time. For our purposes at present, a filter is a system that has an input and an output, and a rule for converting the input to the output, which we will call the *transfer function*. If we think of speech as the output of a filter, the sound generated by the air rushing past the vocal cords can be viewed as the input, while the rule for converting the input to the output is governed by the shape and physics of the vocal tract.

The output depends on the input and the transfer function. Let's look at each in turn. There are several different forms of input that can be generated by different conformations of the vocal cords and the associated cartilages. If the vocal cords are stretched shut and we force air through, the vocal cords vibrate, providing a periodic input. If a small aperture is left open, the input resembles white noise. By opening an aperture at different locations along the vocal cords, we can produce a white-noise–like input with certain dominant frequencies that depend on the location of the opening. The vocal tract can be modeled as a series of tubes of unequal diameter. If we now examine how an acoustic wave travels through this series of tubes, we find that the mathematical model that best describes this process is an autoregressive model. We will often encounter the autoregressive model when we discuss speech compression algorithms.

7.7 Summary

In this chapter we have looked at a variety of topics that will be useful to us when we study various lossy compression techniques, including distortion and its measurement, some new concepts from information theory, average mutual information and its connection to the rate of a compression scheme, and the rate distortion function. We have also briefly looked at some of the properties of the human visual system and the auditory system—most importantly, visual and auditory masking. The masking phenomena allow us to incur distortion in such a way that the distortion is not perceptible to the human observer. We also presented a model for speech production.

Further Reading

There are a number of excellent books available that delve more deeply in the area of information theory:

1. *Information Theory*, by R.B. Ash [12].

2. *Information Transmission*, by R.M. Fano [70].

3. *Information Theory and Reliable Communication*, by R.G. Gallagher [79].

4. *Entropy and Information Theory*, by R.M. Gray [98].

5. *Elements of Information Theory*, by T.M. Cover and J.A. Thomas [55].

6. *The Theory of Information and Coding*, by R.J. McEliece [155].

   The subject of rate distortion theory is discussed in very clear terms in *Rate Distortion Theory*, by T. Berger [23].
   For an introduction to the concepts behind speech perception, see *Voice and Speech Processing*, by T. Parsons [173].

7.8 Projects and Problems

1. Although SNR is a widely used measure of distortion, it often does not correlate with perceptual quality. In order to see this we conduct the following experiment. Using one of the images provided, generate two "reconstructed" images. For one of the recon-

structions add a value of 10 to each pixel. For the other reconstruction, randomly add either $+10$ or -10 to each pixel.

(a) What is the SNR for each of the reconstructions? Do the relative values reflect the difference in the perceptual quality?

(b) Devise a mathematical measure that will better reflect the difference in perceptual quality for this particular case.

2. Consider the following lossy compression scheme for binary sequences. We divide the binary sequence into blocks of size M. For each block we count the number of 0s. If this number is greater than or equal to $M/2$, we send a 0; otherwise, we send a 1.

(a) If the sequence is random with $P(0) = 0.8$, compute the rate and distortion (use Equation (7.54)) for $M = 1, 2, 4, 8, 16$. Compare your results with the rate distortion function for binary sources.

(b) Repeat assuming that the output of the encoder is encoded at a rate equal to the entropy of the output.

3. Write a program to implement the compression scheme described in the previous problem.

(a) Generate a random binary sequence with $P(0) = 0.8$, and compare your simulation results with the analytical results.

(b) Generate a binary first-order Markov sequence with $P(0|0) = 0.9$, and $P(1|1) = 0.9$. Encode it using your program. Discuss and comment on your results.

4. Show that

$$H(X_d|Y_d) = - \sum_{j=-\infty}^{\infty} \sum_{i=-\infty}^{\infty} f_{X|Y}(x_i|y_j)f_Y(y_j)\Delta\Delta \log f_{X|Y}(x_i|y_j) - \log \Delta. \qquad (7.95)$$

5. For two random variables X and Y, show that

$$H(X|Y) \leq H(X)$$

with equality if X is independent of Y.

Hint: $E[\log(f(x))] \leq \log\{E[f(x)]\}$ (Jensen's inequality).

6. Given two random variables X and Y, show that $I(X; Y) = I(Y; X)$.

7. For a binary source with $P(0) = p$, $P(X = 0|Y = 1) = P(X = 1|Y = 0) = D$, and distortion measure

$$d(x_i, y_j) = x_i \oplus y_j, \qquad (7.96)$$

show that

$$I(X; Y) = H_b(p) - H_b(D). \qquad (7.97)$$

8. Find the autocorrelation function in terms of the model coefficients and σ_ϵ^2 for

    (a) an AR(1) process,

    (b) an MA(1) process, and

    (c) an AR(2) process.

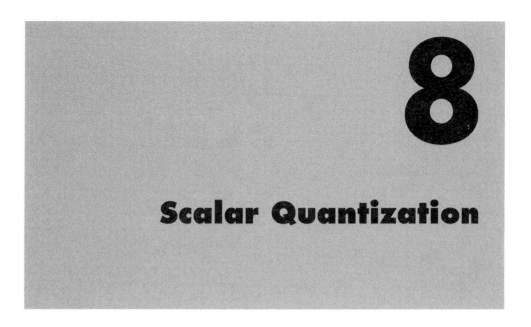

Scalar Quantization

8.1 Overview

n this chapter we begin our study of quantization, one of the simplest and most general ideas in lossy compression. We will look at scalar quantization in this chapter and continue with vector quantization in the next chapter. First, the general quantization problem is stated, then various solutions are examined, starting with the simpler solutions, which require the most assumptions, and proceeding to more complex solutions that require fewer assumptions. We describe uniform quantization with fixed-length codewords, first assuming a uniform source, then a source with a known probability density function (*pdf*) that is not necessarily uniform, and finally a source with unknown or changing statistics. We then look at *pdf*-optimized nonuniform quantization, followed by companded quantization. Finally, we return to the more general statement of the quantizer design problem and study entropy-coded quantization.

8.2 Introduction

In many lossy compression applications we are required to represent each source output using one of a small number of codewords. The number of possible distinct source output values is generally much larger than the number of codewords available to represent them. The process of representing a large—possibly infinite—set of values with a much smaller set is called *quantization*.

Consider a source that generates numbers between −10.0 and 10.0. A simple quantization scheme would be to represent each output of the source with the integer value closest to it. (If the source output is equally close to two integers, we will randomly pick one of them.) For example, if the source output is 2.47, we would represent it as 2, and if the source output is 3.1415926, we would represent it as 3.

This approach reduces the size of the alphabet required to represent the source output; the infinite number of values between -10.0 and 10.0 are represented with a set that contains only 21 values ($\{-10, \ldots, 0, \ldots, 10\}$). At the same time we have also forever lost the original value of the source output. If we are told that the reconstruction value is 3, we cannot tell whether the source output was 2.95, 3.16, 3.057932, or any other of an infinite set of values. In other words, we have lost some information. This loss of information is the reason for the use of the word "lossy" in many lossy compression schemes.

The set of inputs and outputs of a quantizer can be scalars or vectors. If they are scalars, we call the quantizers *scalar quantizers*. If they are vectors, we call the quantizers *vector quantizers*. We will study scalar quantizers in this chapter and vector quantizers in Chapter 9.

8.3   The Quantization Problem

Quantization is a very simple process. However, the design of the quantizer has a significant impact on the amount of compression obtained and loss incurred in a lossy compression scheme. Therefore, we will devote a lot of attention to issues related to the design of quantizers.

In practice, the quantizer consists of two mappings: an encoder mapping and a decoder mapping. The encoder divides the range of values that the source generates into a number of intervals. Each interval is represented by a distinct codeword. The encoder represents all the source outputs that fall into a particular interval by the codeword representing that interval. As there could be many—possibly infinitely many—distinct sample values that can fall in any given interval, the encoder mapping is irreversible. Knowing the code only tells us the interval to which the sample value belongs. It does not tell us which of the many values in the interval is the actual sample value. When the sample value comes from an analog source, the encoder is called an analog-to-digital (A/D) converter.

The encoder mapping for a quantizer with eight reconstruction values is shown in Figure 8.1. For this encoder, all samples with values between -1 and 0 would be assigned the code 011. All values between 0 and 1.0 would be assigned the codeword 100, and so on. On the two boundaries, all inputs with values greater than 3 would be assigned the code 111, and all inputs with values less than -3.0 would be assigned the code 000. Thus, any input that we receive will be assigned a codeword depending on the interval in which it falls. As we are using 3 bits to represent each value, we refer to this quantizer as a 3-bit quantizer.

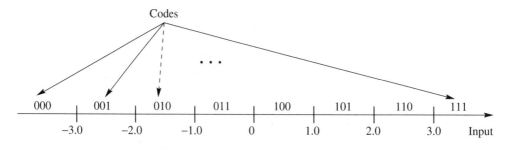

FIGURE 8.1   Mapping for a 3-bit encoder.

Input Codes	Output
000	−3.5
001	−2.5
010	−1.5
011	−0.5
100	0.5
101	1.5
110	2.5
111	3.5

FIGURE 8.2   **Mapping for a 3-bit D/A converter.**

For every codeword generated by the encoder, the decoder generates a reconstruction value. Because a codeword represents an entire interval, and there is no way of knowing which value in the interval was actually generated by the source, the decoder puts out a value that, in some sense, best represents all the values in the interval. Later, we will see how to use information we may have about the distribution of the input in the interval to obtain a representative value. For now, we simply use the midpoint of the interval as the representative value generated by the decoder. If the reconstruction is analog, the decoder is often referred to as a digital-to-analog (D/A) converter. A decoder mapping corresponding to the 3-bit encoder shown in Figure 8.1 is shown in Figure 8.2.

Example 8.3.1:

Suppose a sinusoid $4\cos(2\pi t)$ was sampled every 0.05 second. The sample was digitized using the A/D mapping shown in Figure 8.1 and reconstructed using the D/A mapping shown in Figure 8.2. The first few inputs, codewords, and reconstruction values are given in Table 8.1.

TABLE 8.1   **Digitizing a sine wave.**

t	$4\cos(2\pi t)$	A/D Output	D/A Output	Error
0.05	3.804	111	3.5	0.304
0.10	3.236	111	3.5	−0.264
0.15	2.351	110	2.5	−0.149
0.20	1.236	101	1.5	−0.264

Notice the first two samples in Table 8.1. Although the two input values are distinct, they both fall into the same interval in the quantizer. The encoder, therefore, represents both inputs with the same codeword, which in turn leads to identical reconstruction values.   ◆

Construction of the intervals (their location, etc.) can be viewed as part of the design of the encoder. Selection of reconstruction values is part of the design of the decoder. However,

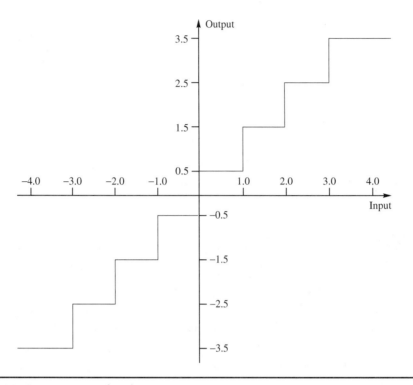

FIGURE 8.3   Quantizer input-output map.

the fidelity of the reconstruction depends on both the intervals and the reconstruction values. Therefore, when designing or analyzing encoders and decoders, it is reasonable to view them as a pair. We call this encoder-decoder pair a *quantizer*. The quantizer mapping for the 3-bit encoder-decoder pair shown in Figures 8.1 and 8.2 can be represented by the input-output map shown in Figure 8.3. The quantizer accepts sample values, and depending on the interval in which the sample values fall, it provides an output codeword and a representation value. Using the map of Figure 8.3, we can see that an input to the quantizer of 1.7 will result in an output of 1.5, and an input of -0.3 will result in an output of -0.5.

From Figures 8.1–8.3 we can see that we need to know how to divide the input range into intervals, assign binary codes to these intervals, and find representation or output values for these intervals in order to specify a quantizer. We need to do all of this while satisfying distortion and rate criteria. In this chapter we will define distortion to be the average squared difference between the quantizer input and output. We call this the mean squared quantization error (msqe) and denote it by σ_q^2. The rate of the quantizer is the average number of bits required to represent a single quantizer output. We would like to get the lowest distortion for a given rate, or the lowest rate for a given distortion.

Let us pose the design problem in precise terms. Suppose we have an input modeled by a random variable X with $pdf\ f_X(x)$. If we wished to quantize this source using a quantizer with M intervals, we would have to specify $M + 1$ endpoints for the intervals, and a representative

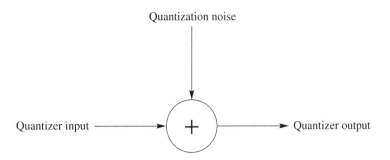

FIGURE 8.4 **Additive noise model of a quantizer.**

value for each of the M intervals. The endpoints of the intervals are known as *decision boundaries*, while the representative values are called *reconstruction levels*. We will often model discrete sources with continuous distributions. For example, the difference between neighboring pixels is often modeled using a Laplacian distribution even though the differences can only take on a limited number of discrete values. Discrete processes are modeled with continuous distributions because it can simplify the design process considerably, and the resulting designs perform well in spite of the incorrect assumption. Several of the continuous distributions used to model source outputs are unbounded—that is, the range of values is infinite. In these cases, the first and last endpoints are generally chosen to be $\pm\infty$.

Let us denote the decision boundaries by $\{b_i\}_{i=0}^M$, the reconstruction levels by $\{y_i\}_{i=1}^M$, and the quantization operation by $Q(\cdot)$. Then

$$Q(x) = y_i \quad \text{iff} \quad b_{i-1} < x \le b_i. \tag{8.1}$$

The mean squared quantization error is then given by

$$\sigma_q^2 = \int_{-\infty}^{\infty} (x - Q(x))^2 f_X(x)dx \tag{8.2}$$

$$= \sum_{i=1}^M \int_{b_{i-1}}^{b_i} (x - y_i)^2 f_X(x)dx. \tag{8.3}$$

The difference between the quantizer input x and output $y = Q(x)$, besides being referred to as the quantization error, is also called the *quantizer distortion* or *quantization noise*. But the word "noise" is somewhat of a misnomer. Generally, when we talk about noise we mean a process external to the source process. Because of the manner in which the quantization error is generated, it is dependent on the source process and, therefore, cannot be regarded as external to the source process. One reason for the use of the word "noise" in this context is that from time to time we will find it useful to model the quantization process as an additive noise process as shown in Figure 8.4.

If we use fixed-length codewords to represent the quantizer output, then the size of the output alphabet immediately specifies the rate. If the number of quantizer outputs is M, then the rate is given by

$$R = \lceil \log_2 M \rceil. \tag{8.4}$$

TABLE 8.2   **Codeword assignment for an eight-level quantizer.**

y_1	1110
y_2	1100
y_3	100
y_4	00
y_5	01
y_6	101
y_7	1101
y_8	1111

For example, if $M = 8$, then $R = 3$. In this case, we can pose the quantizer design problem as follows:

> Given an input *pdf* $f_X(x)$ and the number of levels M in the quantizer, find the decision boundaries $\{b_i\}$ and the reconstruction levels $\{y_i\}$ so as to minimize the mean squared quantization error given by Equation (8.3).

However, if we are allowed to use variable-length codes, such as Huffman codes or arithmetic codes, along with the size of the alphabet, the selection of the decision boundaries will also affect the rate of the quantizer. Consider the codeword assignment for the output of an eight-level quantizer shown in Table 8.2.

According to this codeword assignment, if the output y_4 occurs, we use 2 bits to encode it, while if the output y_1 occurs, we need 4 bits to encode it. Obviously, the rate will depend on how often we have to encode y_4 versus how often we have to encode y_1. In other words, the rate will depend on the probability of occurrence of the outputs. If l_i is the length of the codeword corresponding to the output y_i, and $P(y_i)$ is the probability of occurrence of y_i, then the rate is given by

$$R = \sum_{i=1}^{M} l_i P(y_i). \tag{8.5}$$

However, the probabilities $\{P(y_i)\}$ depend on the decision boundaries $\{b_i\}$. For example, the probability of y_i occurring is given by

$$P(y_i) = \int_{b_{i-1}}^{b_i} f_X(x)dx.$$

Therefore, the rate R is a function of the decision boundaries and is given by the expression

$$R = \sum_{i=1}^{M} l_i \int_{b_{i-1}}^{b_i} f_X(x)dx. \tag{8.6}$$

From this discussion and Equations (8.3) and (8.6), we see that for a given source input, the partitions we select and the representation for those partitions will determine the distortion incurred during the quantization process. The partitions we select and the binary codes for the partitions will determine the rate for the quantizer. Thus, the problem of finding the optimum partitions, codes, and representation levels are all linked. In light of this information, we can restate our problem statement:

Given a distortion constraint

$$\sigma_q^2 \leq D^* \tag{8.7}$$

find the decision boundaries, reconstruction levels, and binary codes that minimize the rate given by Equation (8.6), while satisfying Equation (8.7).

Or, given a rate constraint

$$R \leq R^* \tag{8.8}$$

find the decision boundaries, reconstruction levels, and binary codes that minimize the distortion given by Equation (8.3), while satisfying Equation (8.8).

This problem statement of quantizer design, while more general than our initial statement, is substantially more complex. Fortunately, in practice there are situations in which we can simplify the problem. We often use fixed-length codewords to encode the quantizer output. In this case, the rate is simply the number of bits used to encode each output, and we can use our initial statement of the quantizer design problem. We start our study of quantizer design by looking at this simpler version of the problem, and later use what we have learned in this process to attack the more complex version.

8.4 Uniform Quantizer

The simplest type of quantizer is the uniform quantizer. All intervals are the same size in the uniform quantizer, except possibly for the two outer intervals. In other words, the decision boundaries are spaced evenly. The reconstruction values are also spaced evenly, with the same spacing as the decision boundaries; in the inner intervals, they are the midpoints of the intervals. This constant spacing is usually referred to as the step size and is denoted by Δ. The quantizer shown in Figure 8.3 is a uniform quantizer with $\Delta = 1$. It does not have zero as one of its representation levels. Such a quantizer is called a *midrise quantizer*. An alternative uniform quantizer could be the one shown in Figure 8.5. This is called a *midtread quantizer*. As the midtread quantizer has zero as one of its output levels, it is especially useful in situations where it is important that the zero value be represented—for example, control systems in which it is important to represent a zero value accurately, and audio coding schemes in which we need to represent silence periods. Notice that the midtread quantizer has only seven intervals or levels. That means that if we were using a fixed-length 3-bit code, we would have one codeword left over.

Usually, we use a midrise quantizer if the number of levels is even and a midtread quantizer if the number of levels is odd. For the remainder of this chapter, unless we specifically mention otherwise, we will assume that we are dealing with midrise quantizers. We will also generally assume that the input distribution is symmetric around the origin and the quantizer is also symmetric. (The optimal minimum mean squared error quantizer for a symmetric distribution need not be symmetric [1].) Given all these assumptions, the design of a uniform quantizer consists of finding the step size Δ that minimizes the distortion for a given input process and number of decision levels.

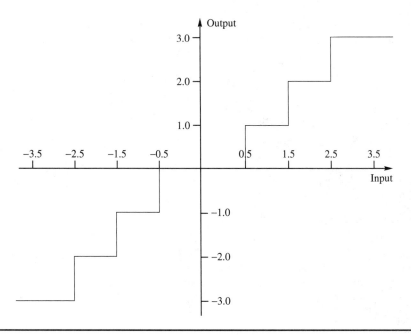

FIGURE 8.5   **A midtread quantizer.**

Uniform Quantization of a Uniformly Distributed Source

We start our study of quantizer design with the simplest of all cases: design of a uniform quantizer for a uniformly distributed source. Suppose we want to design an M-level uniform quantizer for an input that is uniformly distributed in the interval $[-X_{max}, X_{max}]$. This means we need to divide the $[-X_{max}, X_{max}]$ interval into M equally sized intervals. In this case, the step size Δ is given by

$$\Delta = \frac{2X_{max}}{M}. \tag{8.9}$$

The distortion in this case becomes

$$\sigma_q^2 = 2\sum_{i=1}^{\frac{M}{2}} \int_{(i-1)\Delta}^{i\Delta} (x - \frac{2i-1}{2}\Delta)^2 \frac{1}{2X_{max}} dx. \tag{8.10}$$

If we evaluate this integral (after some suffering), we find that the msqe is $\Delta^2/12$.

The same result can be more easily obtained if we examine the behavior of the quantization error q given by

$$q = x - Q(x). \tag{8.11}$$

In Figure 8.6 we plot the quantization error versus the input signal for an eight-level uniform quantizer, with an input that lies in the interval $[-X_{max}, X_{max}]$. Notice that the quantization error lies in the interval $[-\frac{\Delta}{2}, \frac{\Delta}{2}]$. As the input is uniform, it is not difficult to establish that the quantization error is also uniform over this interval. Thus, the mean squared quantization error

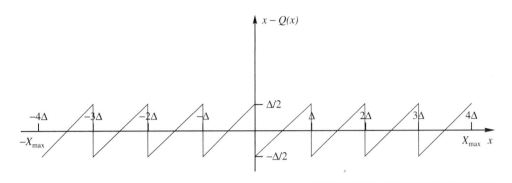

FIGURE 8.6   **Quantization error for a uniform midrise quantizer with a uniformly distributed input.**

is the second moment of a random variable uniformly distributed in the interval $[-\frac{\Delta}{2}, \frac{\Delta}{2}]$:

$$\sigma_q^2 = \frac{1}{\Delta} \int_{-\frac{\Delta}{2}}^{\frac{\Delta}{2}} q^2 dq \tag{8.12}$$

$$= \frac{\Delta^2}{12}. \tag{8.13}$$

Let us also calculate the signal-to-noise ratio for this case. The signal variance σ_s^2 for a uniform random variable, which takes on values in the interval $[-X_{max}, X_{max}]$, is $\frac{(2X_{max})^2}{12}$. The value of the step size Δ is related to X_{max} and the number of levels M by

$$\Delta = \frac{2X_{max}}{M}.$$

For the case where we use a fixed-length code, with each codeword being made up of n bits, the number of codewords or the number of reconstruction levels M is 2^n. Combining all this, we have

$$\text{SNR(dB)} = 10 \log_{10} \left(\frac{\sigma_s^2}{\sigma_q^2} \right) \tag{8.14}$$

$$= 10 \log_{10} \left(\frac{(2X_{max})^2}{12} \cdot \frac{12}{\Delta^2} \right) \tag{8.15}$$

$$= 10 \log_{10} \left(\frac{(2X_{max})^2}{12} \frac{12}{(\frac{2X_{max}}{M})^2} \right) \tag{8.16}$$

$$= 10 \log_{10}(M^2)$$

$$= 20 \log_{10}(2^n)$$

$$= 6.02n \text{ dB}. \tag{8.17}$$

This equation says that for every additional bit in the quantizer, we get an increase in the signal-to-noise ratio of 6.02 dB. This is a well-known result and is often used to get an indication of the maximum gain available if we increase the rate. However, remember that we obtained this result under some assumptions about the input. If the assumptions are not true, this result will not hold true either.

Example 8.4.1: Image compression

A probability model for the variations of pixels in an image is almost impossible to obtain because of the great variety of images available. A common approach is to declare the pixel values to be uniformly distributed between 0 and $2^b - 1$, where b is the number of bits per pixel. For most of the images we deal with, the number of bits per pixel is 8; therefore, the pixel values would be assumed to vary uniformly between 0 and 255. Let us quantize our test image Sena using a uniform quantizer.

If we wanted to use only 1 bit per pixel, we would divide the range $[0, 255]$ into two intervals, $[0, 127]$ and $[128, 255]$. The first interval would be represented by the value 64, the midpoint of the first interval; the pixels in the second interval would be represented by the pixel value 196, the midpoint of the second interval. In other words, the boundary values are $\{0, 128, 255\}$, while the reconstruction values are $\{64, 196\}$. The quantized image is shown in Figure 8.7. As expected, almost all the details in the image have disappeared. If we were to use a 2-bit quantizer, with boundary values $\{0, 64, 128, 196, 255\}$ and reconstruction levels $\{32, 96, 160, 224\}$, we get considerably more detail. The level of detail increases as the use of bits increases until at 6 bits per pixel, the reconstructed image is indistinguishable from the original, at least to a casual observer. The 1-, 2-, and 3-bit images are shown in Figure 8.7.

Looking at the lower-rate images, we notice a couple of things. First, the lower-rate images are darker than the original, and the lowest-rate reconstructions are the darkest. The reason for this is that the quantization process usually results in scaling down of the dynamic range of the input. For example, in the 1-bit-per-pixel reproduction, the highest pixel value is 196, as opposed to 255 for the original image. As higher gray values represent lighter shades, there is a corresponding darkening of the reconstruction. The other thing to notice in the low-rate reconstruction is that wherever there were smooth changes in gray values there are now abrupt transitions. This is especially evident in the face and neck area, where gradual shading has been transformed to blotchy regions of constant values. This is because a range of values is being mapped to the same value, as was the case for the first two samples of the sinusoid in Example 8.3.1. For obvious reasons, this effect is called *contouring*. The perceptual effect of contouring can be reduced by a procedure called *dithering* [119].   ◆

Uniform Quantization of Nonuniform Sources

Quite often the sources we deal with do not have a uniform distribution; however, we still want the simplicity of a uniform quantizer. In these cases, even if the sources are bounded, simply dividing the range of the input by the number of quantization levels does not produce a very good design.

FIGURE 8.7 Top left: original Sena image; top right: 1 bit/pixel image; bottom left: 2 bits/pixel; bottorm right: 3 bits/pixel.

Example 8.4.2:

Suppose our input fell within the interval $[-1, 1]$ with probability 0.95, and fell in the intervals $[-100, 1), (1, 100]$ with probability 0.05. Suppose we wanted to design an eight-level uniform quantizer. If we followed the procedure of the previous section, the step size would be 25. This means that inputs in the $[-1, 0)$ interval would be represented by the value -12.5, and inputs in the interval $[0, 1)$ would be represented by the value 12.5. The maximum quantization error that can be incurred is 12.5. However, at least 95% of the time, the *minimum* error that will be incurred is 11.5. Obviously, this is not a very good design. A much better approach would be to use a smaller step size, which would result in better representation of the values in the

$[-1, 1]$ interval, even if it meant a larger maximum error. Suppose we pick a step size of 0.3. In this case, the maximum quantization error goes from 12.5 to 98.95. However, 95% of the time the quantization error will be less than 0.15. Therefore, the average distortion, or msqe, for this quantizer would be substantially less than the msqe for the first quantizer.   ◆

We can see that when the distribution is no longer uniform, it is not a good idea to obtain the step size by simply dividing the range of the input by the number of levels. This approach becomes totally impractical when we model our sources with distributions that are unbounded, such as the Gaussian distribution. Therefore, we include the *pdf* of the source in the design process.

Our objective is to find the step size that, for a given value of M, will minimize the distortion. The simplest way to do this is to write the distortion as a function of the step size, and then minimize this function. An expression for the distortion, or msqe, for an M-level uniform quantizer as a function of the step size can be found by replacing the b_is and y_is in Equation (8.3) with functions of Δ. As we are dealing with a symmetric condition, we need only compute the distortion for positive values of x; the distortion for negative values of x will be the same.

From Figure 8.8, we see that the decision boundaries are integral multiples of Δ, and the representation level for the interval $[(k-1)\Delta, k\Delta)$ is simply $\frac{2k-1}{2}\Delta$. Therefore, the expression

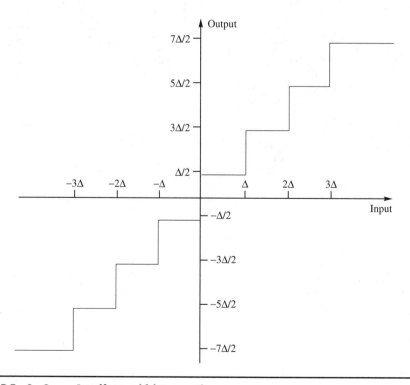

FIGURE 8.8   A uniform midrise quantizer.

TABLE 8.3 Optimum step size and SNR for uniform quantizers for different distributions and alphabet sizes [153, 4].

| Alphabet | Uniform | | Gaussian | | Laplacian | |
Size	Step Size	SNR	Step Size	SNR	Step Size	SNR
2	1.732	6.02	1.596	4.40	1.414	3.00
4	0.866	12.04	0.9957	9.24	1.0873	7.05
6	0.577	15.58	0.7334	12.18	0.8707	9.56
8	0.433	18.06	0.5860	14.27	0.7309	11.39
10	0.346	20.02	0.4908	15.90	0.6334	12.81
12	0.289	21.60	0.4238	17.25	0.5613	13.98
14	0.247	22.94	0.3739	18.37	0.5055	14.98
16	0.217	24.08	0.3352	19.36	0.4609	15.84
32	0.108	30.10	0.1881	24.56	0.2799	20.46

for msqe becomes

$$\sigma_q^2 = 2 \sum_{i=1}^{\frac{M}{2}-1} \int_{(i-1)\Delta}^{i\Delta} \left(x - \frac{2i-1}{2}\Delta \right)^2 f_X(x)dx$$

$$+ 2 \int_{(\frac{M}{2}-1)\Delta}^{\infty} \left(x - \frac{M-1}{2}\Delta \right)^2 f_X(x)dx. \tag{8.18}$$

To find the optimal value of Δ, we simply take a derivative of this equation and set it equal to zero [153] (see Problem 1).

$$\frac{\delta\sigma_q^2}{\delta\Delta} = - \sum_{i=1}^{\frac{M}{2}-1} (2i-1) \int_{(i-1)\Delta}^{i\Delta} (x - \frac{2i-1}{2}\Delta) f_X(x)dx$$

$$- (M-1) \int_{(\frac{M}{2}-1)\Delta}^{\infty} \left(x - \frac{M-1}{2}\Delta \right) f_X(x)dx = 0. \tag{8.19}$$

This is a rather messy-looking expression, but given the *pdf* $f_X(x)$, it is easy to solve using any one of a number of numerical techniques (see Problem 2). In Table 8.3, we list step sizes found by solving (8.19) for nine different alphabet sizes and three different distributions.

Before we discuss the results in Table 8.3, let's take a look at the quantization noise for the case of nonuniform sources. Nonuniform sources are often modeled by *pdf*s with unbounded support. That is, there is a nonzero probability of getting an unbounded input. In practical situations, we are not going to get inputs that are unbounded, but often it is very convenient to model the source process with an unbounded distribution. The classic example of this is measurement error, which is often modeled as having a Gaussian distribution, even when the measurement error is known to be bounded. If the input is unbounded, the quantization error is no longer bounded either. The quantization error as a function of input is shown in Figure 8.9. We can see that in the inner intervals the error is still bounded by $\frac{\Delta}{2}$; however, the quantization error in the outer intervals is unbounded. These two types of quantization errors are given different names. The bounded error is called *granular error* or *granular noise*,

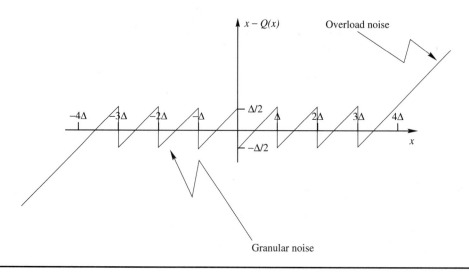

FIGURE 8.9   **Quantization error for a uniform midrise quantizer.**

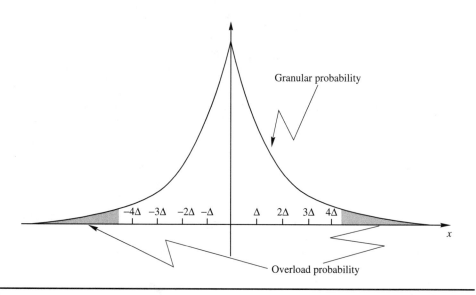

FIGURE 8.10   **Overload and granular regions for a 3-bit uniform quantizer.**

while the unbounded error is called *overload error* or *overload noise*. In the expression for the msqe in Equation (8.18), the first term represents the granular noise, while the second term represents the overload noise. The probability that the input will fall into the overload region is called the *overload probability* (Figure 8.10).

The nonuniform sources we deal with have probability density functions that are generally peaked at zero and decay as we move away from the origin. Therefore, the overload probability is generally much smaller than the probability of the input falling in the granular region.

As we see from Equation (8.19), an increase in the size of the step size Δ will result in an increase in the value of $(\frac{M}{2} - 1)\Delta$, which in turn will result in a decrease in the overload probability and the second term in Equation (8.19). However, an increase in the step size Δ will also increase the granular noise, which is the first term in Equation (8.19). The design process for the uniform quantizer is a balancing of these two effects. An important parameter that describes this trade-off is the loading factor f_l, defined as the ratio of the maximum value the input can take in the granular region to the standard deviation. A common value of the loading factor is 4. This is also referred to as 4σ *loading*.

Recall that when quantizing an input with a uniform distribution, the SNR and bit rate are related by Equation (8.17), which says that for each bit increase in the rate there is an increase of 6.02 dB in the SNR. In Table 8.3, along with the step sizes, we have also listed the SNR obtained when a million input values with the appropriate *pdf* are quantized using the indicated quantizer.

From this table, we can see that, although the SNR for the uniform distribution follows the rule of a 6.02 dB increase in the signal-to-noise ratio for each additional bit, this is not true for the other distributions. Remember that we made some assumptions when we obtained the $6.02n$ rule that are only valid for the uniform distribution. Notice that the more peaked a distribution is (that is, the further away from uniform it is), the more it seems to vary from the 6.02 dB rule.

We also said that the selection of Δ is a balance between the overload and granular errors. The Laplacian distribution has more of its probability mass away from the origin in its tails than the Gaussian distribution. This means that for the same step size and number of levels there is a higher probability of being in the overload region if the input has a Laplacian distribution than if the input has a Gaussian distribution. The uniform distribution is the extreme case, where the overload probability is zero. For the same number of levels, if we increase the step size, the size of the overload region (and hence the overload probability) is reduced at the expense of granular noise. Therefore, for a given number of levels, if we were picking the step size to balance the effects of the granular and overload noise, distributions that have heavier tails will tend to have larger step sizes. This effect can be seen in Table 8.3. For example, for eight levels the step size for the uniform quantizer is 0.433. The step size for the Gaussian quantizer is larger (0.586), while the step size for the Laplacian quantizer is larger still (0.7309).

Mismatch Effects

We have seen that for a result to hold, the assumptions we used to obtain the result have to hold. When we obtain the optimum step size for a particular uniform quantizer using Equation (8.19), we make some assumptions about the statistics of the source. We assume a certain distribution and certain parameters of the distribution. What happens when our assumptions do not hold? Let's try to answer this question empirically.

We will look at two types of mismatches. The first is when the assumed distribution type matches the actual distribution type, but the variance of the input is different from the assumed variance. The second mismatch is when the actual distribution type is different from the distribution type assumed when obtaining the value of the step size. Throughout our discussion, we will assume that the mean of the input distribution is zero.

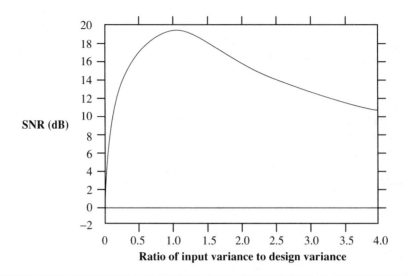

In Figure 8.11, we have plotted the signal-to-noise ratio as a function of the ratio of the actual to assumed variance of a 4-bit Gaussian uniform quantizer, with a Gaussian input. (To see the effect under different conditions, see Problem 5.) Remember that for a distribution with zero mean, the variance is given by $\sigma_x^2 = E[X^2]$, which is also a measure of the power in the signal X. As we can see from the figure, the signal-to-noise ratio is maximum when the input signal variance matches the variance assumed when designing the quantizer. From the plot we also see that there is an asymmetry; the SNR is considerably worse when the input variance is lower than the assumed variance. This is because the SNR is a ratio of the input variance and the mean squared quantization error. When the input variance is smaller than the assumed variance, the mean squared quantization error actually drops because there is less overload noise. However, because the input variance is low, the ratio is small. When the input variance is higher than the assumed variance, the msqe increases substantially, but because the input power is also increasing, the ratio does not decrease as dramatically. To see this more clearly, we have plotted the mean squared error versus the signal variance separately in Figure 8.12. We can see from these figures that the decrease in signal-to-noise ratio does not always correlate directly with an increase in msqe.

The second kind of mismatch is where the input distribution does not match the distribution assumed when designing the quantizer. In Table 8.4 we have listed the SNR when inputs with different distributions are quantized using several different eight-level quantizers. The quantizers were designed assuming a particular input distribution.

Notice that as we go from left to right in the table, the designed step size becomes progressively larger than the "correct" step size. This is similar to the situation where the input variance is smaller than the assumed variance. As we can see when we have a mismatch that results in a smaller step size relative to the optimum step size, there is a greater drop in performance than when the quantizer step size is larger than its optimum value.

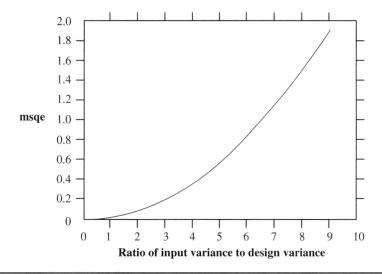

FIGURE 8.12   **The msqe as a function of variance mismatch with a 4-bit uniform quantizer.**

TABLE 8.4   **Demonstration of the effect of mismatch using eight-level quantizers (dB).**

Input Distribution	Uniform Quantizer	Gaussian Quantizer	Laplacian Quantizer	Gamma Quantizer
Uniform	18.06	15.56	13.29	12.41
Gaussian	12.40	14.27	13.37	12.73
Laplacian	8.80	10.79	11.39	11.28
Gamma	6.98	8.06	8.64	8.76

8.5 Adaptive Quantization

One way to deal with the mismatch problem is to adapt the quantizer to the statistics of the input. Several things might change in the input relative to the assumed statistics, including the mean, the variance, and the *pdf*. The strategy for handling each of these variations can be different, though certainly not exclusive. If more than one aspect of the input statistics changes, it is possible to combine the strategies for handling each case separately. If the mean of the input is changing with time, the best strategy is to use some form of differential encoding (discussed in some detail in Chapter 10). For changes in the other statistics, the common approach is to adapt the quantizer parameters to the input statistics.

There are two main approaches to adapting the quantizer parameters: an *off-line* or *forward adaptive* approach, and an *on-line* or *backward adaptive* approach. In forward adaptive quantization, the source output is divided into blocks of data. Each block is analyzed before quantization, and the quantizer parameters are set accordingly. The settings of the quantizer are then transmitted to the receiver as *side information*. In backward adaptive quantization, the adaptation is performed based on the quantizer output. As this is available to both transmitter and receiver, there is no need for side information.

8.5.1   Forward Adaptive Quantization

Let us first look at approaches for adapting to changes in input variance using the forward adaptive approach. This approach necessitates a delay of at least the amount of time required to process a block of data. The insertion of side information in the transmitted data stream may also require the resolution of some synchronization problems. The size of the block of data processed also affects a number of other things. If the size of the block is too large, then the adaptation process may not capture the changes taking place in the input statistics. Furthermore, large block sizes mean more delay, which may not be tolerable in certain applications. On the other hand, small block sizes mean that the side information has to be transmitted more often, which in turn means the amount of overhead per sample increases. The selection of the block size is a trade-off between the increase in side information necessitated by small block sizes and the loss of fidelity due to large block sizes (see Problem 7).

The variance estimation procedure is rather simple. At time n we use a block of N future samples to compute an estimate of the variance

$$\hat{\sigma}_q^2 = \frac{1}{N} \sum_{i=0}^{N-1} x_{n+i}^2. \tag{8.20}$$

Note that we are assuming that our input has a mean of zero. The variance information also needs to be quantized so that it can be transmitted to the receiver. Usually, the number of bits used to quantize the value of the variance is significantly larger than the number of bits used to quantize the sample values.

Example 8.5.1:

In Figure 8.13 we show a segment of speech quantized using a fixed 3-bit quantizer. The step size of the quantizer was adjusted based on the statistics of the entire sequence. The sequence was the `testm.raw` sequence from the sample data sets, consisting of about 4000 samples of a male speaker saying the word "test." The speech signal was sampled at 8000 samples per second and digitized using a 16-bit A/D.

We can see from the figure that, as in the case of the example of the sinusoid earlier in this chapter, there is a considerable loss in amplitude resolution. Sample values that are close together have been quantized to the same value.

The same sequence quantized with a forward adaptive quantizer is shown in Figure 8.14. For this example, we divided the input into blocks of 128 samples. Before quantizing the samples in a block, the standard deviation for the samples in the block was obtained. This value was quantized using an 8-bit quantizer and sent to both the transmitter and receiver. The samples in the block were then normalized using this value of the standard deviation. Notice that the reconstruction follows the input much more closely, though there seems to be room for improvement, especially in the latter half of the displayed samples.

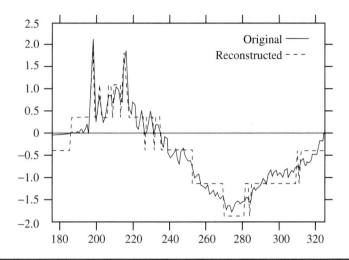

FIGURE   8.13   **Original 16-bit speech and compressed 3-bit speech sequences.**

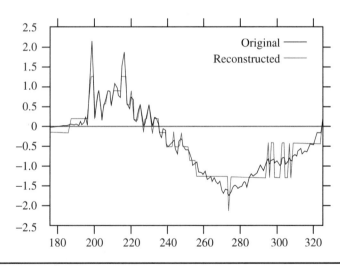

FIGURE   8.14   **Original 16-bit speech sequence and sequence obtained using an eight-level forward adaptive quantizer.**   ◆

Example   8.5.2:

In Example 8.4.1, we used a uniform quantizer with the assumption that the input is uniformly distributed. Let us refine this source model a bit and say that while the source is uniformly distributed over different regions, the range of the input changes. In a forward adaptive quantization scheme, we would obtain the minimum and maximum values for each block of data, which would be transmitted as side information. In Figure 8.15, we see the Sena image quantized with a block size of 8×8 using 3-bit forward adaptive uniform quantization. The side

FIGURE 8.15   **Sena image quantized to 3.25 bits per pixel using forward adaptive quantization.**

information consists of the minimum and maximum values in each block, which require 8 bits each. Therefore, the overhead in this case is $\frac{16}{8\times8}$ or 0.25 bits per pixel, which is quite small compared to the number of bits per sample used by the quantizer.

The resulting image is hardly distinguishable from the original. Certainly at higher rates, forward adaptive quantization seems to be a very good alternative.   ◆

8.5.2 Backward Adaptive Quantization

In backward adaptive quantization, only the past quantized samples are available for use in adapting the quantizer. The values of the input are only known to the encoder; therefore, this information cannot be used to adapt the quantizer. How can we get information about mismatch simply by examining the output of the quantizer without knowing what the input was? If we studied the output of the quantizer for a long period of time, we could get some idea about mismatch from the distribution of output values. If the quantizer step size Δ is well matched to the input, the probability that an input to the quantizer would land in a particular interval would be consistent with the *pdf* assumed for the input. However, if the actual *pdf* differs from the assumed *pdf*, the number of times the input falls in the different quantization intervals will be inconsistent with the assumed *pdf*. If Δ is smaller than what it should be, the input will fall in the outer levels of the quantizer an excessive number of times. On the other hand, if Δ is larger than it should be for a particular source, the input will fall in the inner levels an excessive number of times. Therefore, it seems that we should observe the output of the quantizer for a long period of time, then expand the quantizer step size if the input falls in the outer levels an excessive number of times, and contract the step size if the input falls in the inner levels an excessive number of times.

Nuggehally S. Jayant at Bell Labs showed that we did not need to observe the quantizer output over a long period of time [117]. In fact, we could adjust the quantizer step size after observing a single output. Jayant named this quantization approach "quantization with one word memory." The quantizer is better known as the *Jayant quantizer*. The idea behind the Jayant quantizer is very simple. If the input falls in the outer levels, the step size needs to be expanded, and if the input falls in the inner quantizer levels, the step size needs to be reduced. The expansions and contractions should be done in such a way that once the quantizer is matched to the input, the product of the expansions and contractions is unity.

The expansion and contraction of the step size is accomplished in the Jayant quantizer by assigning a *multiplier* M_k to each interval. If the $(n - 1)$th input falls in the kth interval, the step size to be used for the nth input is obtained by multiplying the step size used for the $(n - 1)$th input with M_k. The multiplier values for the inner levels in the quantizer are less than one, and the multiplier values for the outer levels of the quantizer are greater than one. Therefore, if an input falls into the inner levels, the quantizer used to quantize the next input will have a smaller step size. Similarly, if an input falls into the outer levels, the step size will be multiplied with a value greater than one, and the next input will be quantized using a larger step size. Notice that the step size for the current input is modified based on the previous quantizer output. The previous quantizer output is available to both the transmitter and receiver, so there is no need to send any additional information to inform the receiver about the adaptation. Mathematically, the adaptation process can be represented as

$$\Delta_n = M_{l(n-1)}\Delta_{n-1} \tag{8.21}$$

where $l(n - 1)$ is the quantization interval at time $n - 1$.

In Figure 8.16 we show a 3-bit uniform quantizer. We have eight intervals represented by the different quantizer outputs. However, the multipliers for symmetric intervals are identical because of symmetry:

$$M_0 = M_4 \quad M_1 = M_5 \quad M_2 = M_6 \quad M_3 = M_7$$

Therefore, we only need four multipliers. To see how the adaptation proceeds, let us work through a simple example using this quantizer.

Example 8.5.3: Jayant quantizer

For the quantizer in Figure 8.16, suppose the multiplier values are $M_0 = M_4 = 0.8$, $M_1 = M_5 = 0.9$, $M_2 = M_6 = 1$, $M_3 = M_7 = 1.2$; the initial value of the step size, Δ_0, is 0.5; and the sequence to be quantized is $0.1, -0.2, 0.2, 0.1, -0.3, 0.1, 0.2, 0.5, 0.9, 1.5, \ldots$. When the first input is received, the quantizer step size is 0.5. Therefore, the input falls into level 0, and the output value is 0.25, resulting in an error of 0.15. As this input fell into the quantizer level 0, the new step size Δ_1 is $M_0 \times \Delta_0 = 0.8 \times 0.5 = 0.4$. The next input is -0.2, which falls into level 4. As the step size at this time is 0.4, the output is -0.2. To update, we multiply the current step size with M_4. Continuing in this fashion, we get the sequence of step sizes and outputs shown in Table 8.5.

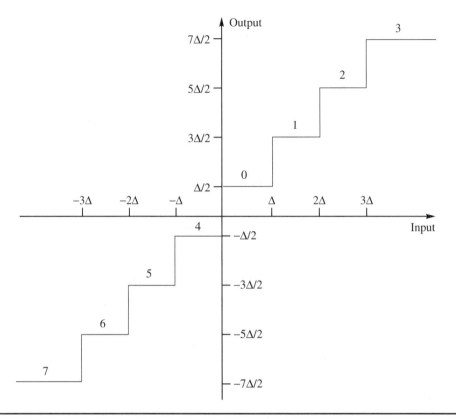

FIGURE   8.16   *Output levels for the Jayant quantizer.*

Notice how the quantizer adapts to the input. In the beginning of the sequence, the input values are mostly small, and the quantizer step size becomes progressively smaller, providing better and better estimates of the input. At the end of the sample sequence, the input values are large and the step size becomes progressively bigger. However, the size of the error is quite large during the transition. This means that if the input was changing rapidly, which would happen if we had a high-frequency input, such transition situations would be much more likely to occur, and the quantizer would not function very well. However, in cases where the statistics of the input change slowly, the quantizer could adapt to the input. As most natural sources such as speech and images tend to be correlated, their values do not change drastically from sample to sample. Even when some of this structure is removed through some transformation, the residual structure is generally enough for the Jayant quantizer (or some variation of it) to function quite effectively.   ◆

The step size in the initial part of the sequence in this example is progressively getting smaller. We can easily conceive of situations where the input values would be small for a long period. Such a situation could occur during a silence period in speech-encoding systems, or while encoding a dark background in image-encoding systems. If the step size continues to

TABLE 8.5   **Operation of a Jayant quantizer.**

n	Δ_n	Input	Output Level	Output	Error	Update Equation		
0	0.5	0.1	0	0.25	0.15	Δ_1	$=$	$M_0 \times \Delta_0$
1	0.4	−0.2	4	−0.2	0.0	Δ_2	$=$	$M_4 \times \Delta_1$
2	0.32	0.2	0	0.16	0.04	Δ_3	$=$	$M_0 \times \Delta_2$
3	0.256	0.1	0	0.128	0.028	Δ_4	$=$	$M_0 \times \Delta_3$
4	0.2048	−0.3	5	−0.3072	−0.0072	Δ_5	$=$	$M_5 \times \Delta_4$
5	0.1843	0.1	0	0.0922	−0.0078	Δ_6	$=$	$M_0 \times \Delta_5$
6	0.1475	0.2	1	0.2212	0.0212	Δ_7	$=$	$M_1 \times \Delta_6$
7	0.1328	0.5	3	0.4646	−0.0354	Δ_8	$=$	$M_3 \times \Delta_7$
8	0.1594	0.9	3	0.5578	−0.3422	Δ_9	$=$	$M_3 \times \Delta_8$
9	0.1913	1.5	3	0.6696	−0.8304	Δ_{10}	$=$	$M_3 \times \Delta_9$
10	0.2296	1.0	3	0.8036	0.1964	Δ_{11}	$=$	$M_3 \times \Delta_{10}$
11	0.2755	0.9	3	0.9643	0.0643	Δ_{12}	$=$	$M_3 \times \Delta_{11}$

shrink for an extended period of time, in a finite precision system it would result in a value of zero. This would be catastrophic, effectively replacing the quantizer with a zero output device. Usually, a minimum value $\Delta_{\min}$ is defined, and the step size is not allowed to go below this value to prevent this from happening. Similarly, if we get a sequence of large values, the step size could increase to a point that, when we started getting smaller values, the quantizer would not be able to adapt fast enough. To prevent this from happening, a maximum value $\Delta_{\max}$ is defined, and the step size is not allowed to increase beyond this value.

The adaptivity of the Jayant quantizer depends on the values of the multipliers. The further the multiplier values are from unity, the more adaptive the quantizer. However, if the adaptation algorithm reacts too fast, this could lead to instability. So how do we go about selecting the multipliers?

First of all, we know that the multipliers correpponding to the inner levels are less than one, and the multipliers for the outer levels are greater than one. If the input process is stationary and P_k represents the probability of being in quantizer interval k (generally estimated by using a fixed quantizer for the input data), then we can impose a stability criterion for the Jayant quantizer based on our requirement that once the quantizer is matched to the input, the product of the expansions and contractions are equal to unity. That is, if n_k is the number of times the input falls in the kth interval,

$$\prod_{k=0}^{M} M_k^{n_k} = 1. \tag{8.22}$$

Taking the Nth root of both sides (where N is the total number of inputs) we obtain

$$\prod_{k=0}^{M} M_k^{\frac{n_k}{N}} = 1,$$

or

$$\prod_{k=0}^{M} M_k^{P_k} = 1 \tag{8.23}$$

where we have assumed that $P_k = n_k/N$.

There are an infinite number of multiplier values that would satisfy Equation (8.23). One way to restrict this number is to impose some structure on the multipliers by requiring them to be of the form

$$M_k = \gamma^{l_k} \tag{8.24}$$

where γ is a number greater than one and l_k takes on only integer values [161, 85]. If we substitute this expression for M_k into Equation (8.23), we get

$$\prod_{k=0}^{M} \gamma^{l_k P_k} = 1, \tag{8.25}$$

which implies that

$$\sum_{k=0}^{M} l_k P_k = 0. \tag{8.26}$$

The final step is the selection of γ, which involves a significant amount of creativity. The value we pick for γ determines how fast the quantizer will respond to changing statistics. A large value of γ will result in faster adaptation, while a smaller value of γ will result in greater stability.

Example 8.5.4:

Suppose we have to obtain the multiplier functions for a 2-bit quantizer with input probabilities $P_0 = 0.8$, $P_1 = 0.2$. First, note that the multiplier value for the inner level has to be less than 1. Therefore, l_0 is less than 0. If we pick $l_0 = -1$ and $l_1 = 4$, this would satisfy Equation (8.26), while making M_0 less than 0 and M_1 greater than 1. Finally, we need to pick a value for γ.

In Figure 8.17 we see the effect of using different values of γ in a rather extreme example. The input is a square wave that switches between 0 and 1 every 30 samples. The input is quantized using a 2-bit Jayant quantizer. We have used $l_0 = -1$ and $l_1 = 2$. Notice what happens when the input switches from 0 to 1. At first the input falls in the outer level of the quantizer, and the step size increases. This process continues until Δ is just greater than 1. If γ is close to 1, Δ has been increasing quite slowly and should have a value close to 1 right before its value increases to greater than 1. Therefore, the output at this point is close to 1.5. When Δ becomes greater than 1, the input falls in the inner level, and if γ is close to 1, the output suddenly drops to about 0.5. The step size now decreases until it is just below 1, and the process repeats, causing the "ringing" seen in Figure 8.17. As γ increases, the quantizer adapts more rapidly, and the magnitude of the ringing effect decreases. The reason for the decrease is that right before the value of Δ increases above 1, its value is much smaller than 1, and subsequently the output value is much smaller than 1.5. When Δ increases beyond 1, it may increase by a significant amount, so the inner level may be much greater than 0.5. These two effects together compress the ringing phenomenon. Looking at this phenomenon, we can

FIGURE 8.17   **Effect of γ on the performance of the Jayant quantizer.**

see that it may have been better to have two adaptive strategies, one for when the input is changing rapidly, as in the case of the transitions between 0 and 1, and one for when the input is constant, or nearly so. We will explore this approach further when we describe the quantizer used in the CCITT standard G.726.   ◆

When selecting multipliers for a Jayant quantizer, the best quantizers expand more rapidly than they contract. This makes sense when we consider that, when the input falls into the outer levels of the quantizer, it is incurring overload error, which is essentially unbounded. This situation needs to be mitigated with dispatch. On the other hand, when the input falls in the inner levels, the noise incurred is granular noise, which is bounded and therefore may be more tolerable. Finally, the discussion of the Jayant quantizer was motivated by the need for robustness in the face of changing input statistics. Let us repeat the earlier experiment with changing input variance and distributions and see the performance of the Jayant quantizer compared to the *pdf*-optimized quantizer. The results for these experiments are presented in Figure 8.18.

Notice how flat the performance curve is. While the performance of the Jayant quantizer is much better than the nonadaptive uniform quantizer over a wide range of input variances, at the point where the input variance and design variance agree, the performance of the nonadaptive quantizer is significantly better than the performance of the Jayant quantizer. This means that if we know the input statistics and we are reasonably certain that the input statistics will not change over time, it is better to design for those statistics than to design an adaptive system.

FIGURE 8.18   **Performance of the Jayant quantizer for different input variances.**

8.6 Nonuniform Quantization

As we can see from Figure 8.10, if the input distribution has more mass near the origin, the input is more likely to fall in the inner levels of the quantizer. Recall that in lossless compression, in order to minimize the *average* number of bits per input symbol, we assigned shorter codewords to symbols that occurred with higher probability and longer codewords to symbols that occurred with lower probability. In an analogous fashion, in order to decrease the average distortion, we can try to approximate the input better in regions of high probability, perhaps at the cost of worse approximations in regions of lower probability. We can do this by making the quantization intervals smaller in those regions that have more probability mass. If the source distribution is like the distribution shown in Figure 8.10, we would have smaller intervals near the origin. If we wanted to keep the number of intervals constant, this would mean we would have larger intervals away from the origin. A quantizer that has nonuniform intervals is called a *nonuniform quantizer*. An example of a nonuniform quantizer is shown in Figure 8.19.

Notice that the intervals closer to zero are smaller. Hence the maximum value that the quantizer error can take on is also smaller, resulting in a better approximation. We pay for this improvement in accuracy at lower input levels by incurring larger errors when the input falls in the outer intervals. However, as the probability of getting smaller input values is much higher than getting larger signal values, on the average the distortion will be lower than if we had a uniform quantizer. While a nonuniform quantizer provides lower average distortion, the design of nonuniform quantizers is also somewhat more complex. However, the basic idea is quite straightforward: find the decision boundaries and reconstruction levels that minimize the mean squared quantization error. We look at the design of nonuniform quantizers in more detail in the following sections.

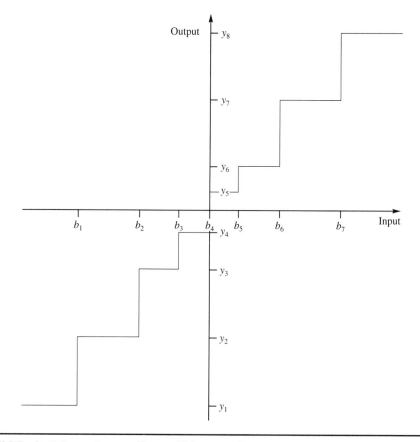

FIGURE 8.19   **A nonuniform midrise quantizer.**

8.6.1 *pdf*-Optimized Quantization

A direct approach for locating the best nonuniform quantizer, if we have a probability model for the source, is to find the $\{b_i\}$ and $\{y_i\}$ that minimize Equation (8.3). Setting the derivative of Equation (8.3) with respect to y_j to zero, and solving for y_j, we get

$$y_j = \frac{\int_{b_{j-1}}^{b_j} x f_X(x)dx}{\int_{b_{j-1}}^{b_j} f_X(x)dx}. \tag{8.27}$$

The output point for each quantization interval is the centroid of the probability mass in that interval. Taking the derivative with respect to b_j and setting it equal to zero, we get an expression for b_j as

$$b_j = \frac{y_{j+1} + y_j}{2}. \tag{8.28}$$

The decision boundary is simply the midpoint of the two neighboring reconstruction levels. Solving these two equations will give us the values for the reconstruction levels and decision boundaries that minimize the mean squared quantization error. Unfortunately, to solve

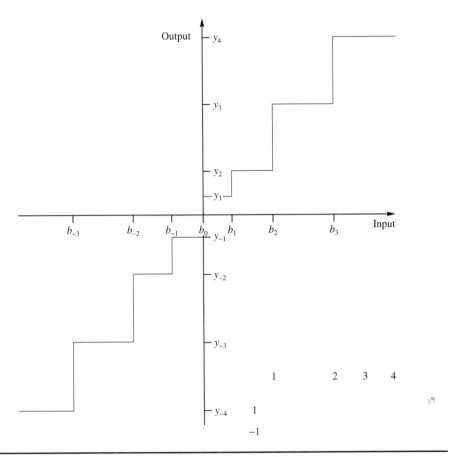

FIGURE 8.20   **A nonuniform midrise quantizer.**

for y_j, we need the values of b_j and b_{j-1}, and to solve for b_j, we need the values of y_{j+1} and y_j. In a 1960 paper, Joel Max [153] showed how to solve the two equations iteratively. The same approach was described by Stuart P. Lloyd in a 1957 internal Bell Labs memorandum. Generally, credit goes to whomever publishes first, but in this case, because much of the early work in quantization was done at Bell Labs, Lloyd's work was given due credit and the algorithm became known as the Lloyd-Max algorithm. However, the story does not end (begin?) there. Allen Gersho [82] points out that the same algorithm was published by Lukaszewicz and Steinhaus in a Polish journal in 1955 [143]! Lloyd's paper remained unpublished until 1982, when it was finally published in a special issue of the *IEEE Transactions on Information Theory* devoted to quantization [140].

   To see how this algorithm works, let us apply it to a specific situation. Suppose we want to design an *M*-level symmetric midrise quantizer. To define our symbols, we will use Figure 8.20. From the figure, we see that in order to design this quantizer, we need to obtain the reconstruction levels $\{y_1, y_2, \ldots, y_{\frac{M}{2}}\}$ and the decision boundaries $\{b_1, b_2, \ldots, b_{\frac{M}{2}-1}\}$. The reconstruction levels $\{y_{-1}, y_{-2}, \ldots, y_{-\frac{M}{2}}\}$ and the decision boundaries $\{b_{-1}, b_{-2}, \ldots,$

$b_{-(\frac{M}{2}-1)}\}$ can be obtained through symmetry, the decision boundary b_0 is zero, and the decision boundary $b_{\frac{M}{2}}$ is simply the largest value the input can take on (for unbounded inputs this would be ∞).

Let us set j equal to 1 in Equation (8.27):

$$y_1 = \frac{\int_{b_0}^{b_1} x f_X(x) dx}{\int_{b_0}^{b_1} f_X(x) dx}. \tag{8.29}$$

As b_0 is known to be 0, we have two unknowns in this equation, b_1 and y_1. We make a guess at y_1 and later we will try to refine this guess. Using this guess in Equation (8.29), we numerically find the value of b_1 that satisfies Equation (8.29). Setting j equal to 1 in Equation (8.28), and rearranging things slightly, we get

$$y_2 = 2b_1 + y_1 \tag{8.30}$$

from which we can compute y_2. This value of y_2 can then be used in Equation (8.27) with $j = 2$ to find b_2, which in turn can be used to find y_3. We continue this process, until we obtain a value for $\{y_1, y_2, \ldots, y_{\frac{M}{2}}\}$ and $\{b_1, b_2, \ldots, b_{\frac{M}{2}-1}\}$. Note that the accuracy of all the values obtained to this point depends on the quality of our initial estimate of y_1. We can check this by noting that $y_{\frac{M}{2}}$ is the centroid of the probability mass of the interval $[b_{\frac{M}{2}-1}, b_{\frac{M}{2}}]$. We know $b_{\frac{M}{2}}$ from our knowledge of the data. Therefore, we can compute the integral

$$y_{\frac{M}{2}} = \frac{\int_{b_{\frac{M}{2}-1}}^{b_{\frac{M}{2}}} x f_X(x) dx}{\int_{b_{\frac{M}{2}-1}}^{b_{\frac{M}{2}}} f_X(x) dx} \tag{8.31}$$

and compare it with the previously computed value of $y_{\frac{M}{2}}$. If the difference is less than some tolerance threshold, we can stop. Otherwise, we adjust the estimate of y_1 in the direction indicated by the sign of the difference and repeat the procedure.

Decision boundaries and reconstruction levels for various distributions and number of levels generated using this procedure are shown in Table 8.6. Notice that the distributions that have heavier tails also have larger outer step sizes. However, these same quantizers have smaller inner step sizes because they are more heavily peaked. The SNR for these quantizers is also listed in the table. Comparing these values with those for the *pdf*-optimized uniform quantizers, we can see a significant improvement, especially for distributions further away from the uniform distribution. Both uniform and nonuniform *pdf*-optimized, or Lloyd-Max, quantizers have a number of interesting properties. We list these properties here (their proofs can be found in [30, 31, 204]):

■ **Property 1:** The mean values of the input and output of a Lloyd-Max quantizer are equal.

■ **Property 2:** For a given Lloyd-Max quantizer, the variance of the output is always less than or equal to the variance of the input.

TABLE 8.6   **Quantizer boundary and reconstruction levels for nonuniform Gaussian and Laplacian quantizers.**

Levels	Gaussian			Laplacian		
	b_i	y_i	SNR	b_i	y_i	SNR
4	0.0	0.4528		0.0	0.4196	
	0.9816	1.510	9.3 dB	1.1269	1.8340	7.54 dB
6	0.0	0.3177		0.0	0.2998	
	0.6589	1.0		0.7195	1.1393	
	1.447	1.894	12.41 dB	1.8464	2.5535	10.51 dB
8	0.0	0.2451		0.0	0.2334	
	0.7560	0.6812		0.5332	0.8330	
	1.050	1.3440		1.2527	1.6725	
	1.748	2.1520	14.62 dB	2.3796	3.0867	12.64 dB

■ **Property 3:** The mean squared quantization error for a Lloyd-Max quantizer is given by

$$\sigma_q^2 = \sigma_x^2 - \sum_{j=1}^{M} y_j^2 P[b_{j-1} \le X < b_j] \tag{8.32}$$

where σ_x^2 is the variance of the quantizer input, and the second term on the right-hand side is the second moment of the output (or variance if the input is zero mean).

■ **Property 4:** Let N be the random variable corresponding to the quantization error. Then for a given Lloyd-Max quantizer,

$$E[XN] = -\sigma_q^2. \tag{8.33}$$

■ **Property 5:** For a given Lloyd-Max quantizer, the quantizer output and the quantization noise are orthogonal:

$$E[Q(X)N \mid b_0, b_1, \ldots, b_M] = 0. \tag{8.34}$$

Mismatch Effects

As in the case of uniform quantizers, the *pdf*-optimized nonuniform quantizers also have problems when the assumptions underlying their design are violated. In Figure 8.21 we show the effects of variance mismatch on a 4-bit Laplacian nonuniform quantizer.

This mismatch effect is a serious problem because in most communication systems the input variance can change considerably over time. A common example of this is the telephone system. Different people speak with differing amounts of loudness into the telephone. The quantizer used in the telephone system needs to be quite robust to the wide range of input variances in order to provide satisfactory service.

One solution to this problem is the use of adaptive quantization to match the quantizer to the changing input characteristics. We have already looked at adaptive quantization for the

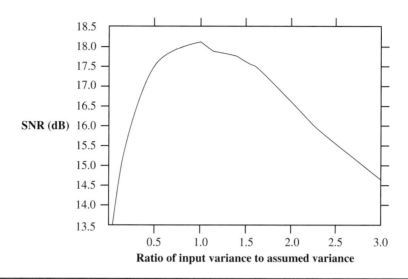

F I G U R E   8 . 2 1   **Effect of mismatch on nonuniform quantization.**

uniform quantizer. Generalizing the uniform adaptive quantizer to the nonuniform case is relatively straightforward, and we leave that as a practice exercise (see Problem 8). A somewhat different approach is to use a nonlinear mapping to flatten the performance curve shown in Figure 8.21. In order to study this approach, we need to view the nonuniform quantizer in a slightly different manner.

8.6.2   Companded Quantization

Instead of making the step size small, we could make the interval in which the input lies with high probability large—that is, expand the region in which the input lands with high probability in proportion to the probability with which the input lands in this region. This is the idea behind companded quantization. This quantization approach can be represented by the block diagram shown in Figure 8.22. The input is first mapped through a *compressor* function. This function "stretches" the high-probability regions close to the origin, and correspondingly "compresses" the low-probability regions away from the origin. Thus, regions close to the origin in the input to the compressor occupy a greater fraction of the total region covered by the compressor. If the output of the compressor function is quantized using a uniform quantizer, and the quantized value transformed via an *expander* function, the overall effect is the same as using a nonuniform quantizer. To see this, we devise a simple compander and see how the process functions.

Example 8.6.1:

Suppose we have a source that can be modeled as a random variable taking values in the interval $[-4, 4]$ with more probability mass near the origin than away from it. We want to

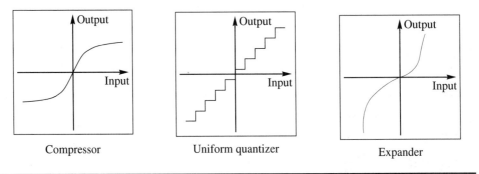

FIGURE 8.22   **Block diagram for log companded quantization.**

quantize this using the quantizer of Figure 8.3. Let us try to flatten out this distribution using the following compander, and then compare the companded quantization with straightforward uniform quantization. The compressor characteristic we will use is given by the following equation:

$$c(x) = \begin{cases} 2x & \text{if } -1 \leq x \leq 1 \\ \frac{2x}{3} + \frac{4}{3} & x > 1 \\ \frac{2x}{3} - \frac{4}{3} & x < -1. \end{cases} \tag{8.35}$$

The mapping is shown graphically in Figure 8.23. The inverse mapping is given by

$$c^{-1}(x) = \begin{cases} \frac{x}{2} & \text{if } -2 \leq x \leq 2 \\ \frac{3x}{2} - 2 & x > 2 \\ \frac{3x}{2} + 2 & x < -2. \end{cases} \tag{8.36}$$

The inverse mapping is shown graphically in Figure 8.24.

Let's see how using these mappings affects the quantization error both near and far from the origin. Suppose we had an input of 0.9. If we quantize directly with the uniform quantizer, we get an output of 0.5, resulting in a quantization error of 0.4. If we use the companded quantizer, we first use the compressor mapping, mapping the input value of 0.9 to 1.8. Quantizing this with the same uniform quantizer results in an output of 1.5, with an apparent error of 0.3. The expander then maps this to the final reconstruction value of 0.75, which is 0.15 away from the input. Comparing 0.15 with 0.4, we can see that relative to the input we get a substantial reduction in the quantization error. In fact, for all values in the interval $[-1, 1]$, we will not get any increase in the quantization error, and for most values we will get a decrease in the quantization error (see Problem 6 at the end of this chapter). Of course, this will not be true for the values outside the $[-1, 1]$ interval. Suppose we have an input of 2.7. If we quantized this directly with the uniform quantizer, we would get an output of 2.5, with a corresponding error of 0.2. Applying the compressor mapping, the value of 2.7 would be mapped to 3.13, resulting in a quantized value of 3.5. Mapping this back through the expander, we get a reconstructed value of 3.25, which differs from the input by 0.55.

As we can see, the companded quantizer effectively works like a nonuniform quantizer with smaller quantization intervals in the interval $[-1, 1]$ and larger quantization intervals

FIGURE 8.23 Compressor mapping.

FIGURE 8.24 Expander mapping.

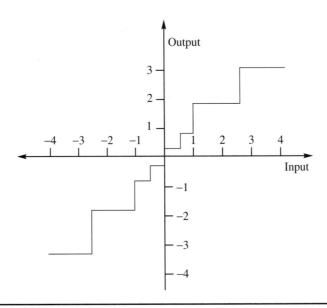

FIGURE 8.25   **Nonuniform companded quantizer.**

outside this interval. What is the effective input-output map of this quantizer? Notice that all inputs in the interval $[0, 0.5]$ get mapped into the interval $[0, 1]$, for which the quantizer output is 0.5, which in turn corresponds to the reconstruction value of 0.25. Essentially, all values in the interval $[0, 0.5]$ are represented by the value 0.25. Similarly, all values in the interval $[0.5, 1]$ are represented by the value 0.75, and so on. The effective quantizer input-output map is shown in Figure 8.25.   ◆

If we bound the source output by some value $x_{\max}$, any nonuniform quantizer can always be represented as a companding quantizer. Let us see how we can use this fact to come up with quantizers that are robust to mismatch. First we need to look at some of the properties of high-rate quantizers, or quantizers with a large number of levels.
    Define

$$\Delta_k = b_k - b_{k-1}. \tag{8.37}$$

If the number of levels is high, then the size of each quantization interval will be small, and we can assume that the *pdf* of the input $f_X(x)$ is essentially constant in each quantization interval. Then

$$f_X(x) = f_X(y_k) \qquad \text{if } b_{k-1} \le x < b_k. \tag{8.38}$$

Using this we can rewrite Equation (8.3) as

$$\sigma_q^2 = \sum_{i=1}^{M} f_X(y_i) \int_{b_{i-1}}^{b_i} (x - y_i)^2 dx \tag{8.39}$$

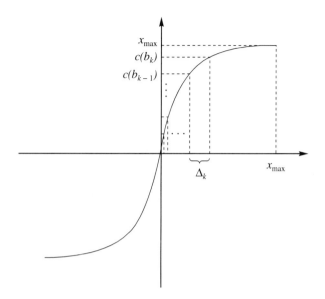

FIGURE 8.26   **A compressor function.**

$$= \frac{1}{12} \sum_{i=1}^{M} f_X(y_i) \Delta_i^3. \tag{8.40}$$

Armed with this result, let us return to companded quantization. Let $c(x)$ be a companding characteristic for a symmetric quantizer, and let $c'(x)$ be the derivative of the compressor characteristic with respect to x. If the rate of the quantizer is high, that is, if there are a large number of levels, then within the kth interval, the compressor characteristic can be approximated by a straight line segment (see Figure 8.26), and we can write

$$c'(y_k) = \frac{c(b_k) - c(b_{k-1})}{\Delta_k}. \tag{8.41}$$

From Figure 8.26 we can also see that $c(b_k) - c(b_{k-1})$ is the step size of a uniform M-level quantizer. Therefore,

$$c(b_k) - c(b_{k-1}) = \frac{2x_{max}}{M}. \tag{8.42}$$

Substituting this into Equation (8.41) and solving for Δ_k, we get

$$\Delta_k = \frac{2x_{max}}{Mc'(y_k)}. \tag{8.43}$$

Finally, substituting this expression for Δ_k into Equation (8.40), we get the following relationship between the quantizer distortion, the *pdf* of the input, and the compressor characteristic:

$$\sigma_q^2 = \frac{1}{12} \sum_{i=1}^{M} f_X(y_i) \left(\frac{2x_{max}}{Mc'(y_i)} \right)^3$$

$$= \frac{x_{max}^2}{3M^2} \sum_{i=1}^{M} \frac{f_X(y_i)}{c'^2(y_i)} \cdot \frac{2x_{max}}{Mc'(y_i)}$$

$$= \frac{x_{max}^2}{3M^2} \sum_{i=1}^{M} \frac{f_X(y_i)}{c'^2(y_i)} \Delta_i \tag{8.44}$$

which for small Δ_i can be written as

$$\sigma_q^2 = \frac{x_{max}^2}{3M^2} \int_{-x_{max}}^{x_{max}} \frac{f_X(x)}{(c'(x))^2} dx. \tag{8.45}$$

This is a famous result, known as the Bennett integral after its discoverer, W.R. Bennett [22], and it has been widely used to analyze quantizers. We can see from this integral that the quantizer distortion is dependent on the *pdf* of the source sequence. However, it also tells us how to get rid of this dependence. Define

$$c'(x) = \frac{x_{max}}{\alpha |x|}, \tag{8.46}$$

where α is a constant. From the Bennett integral we get

$$\sigma_q^2 = \frac{x_{max}^2}{3M^2} \frac{\alpha^2}{x_{max}^2} \int_{-x_{max}}^{x_{max}} x^2 f_X(x) dx \tag{8.47}$$

$$= \frac{\alpha^2}{3M^2} \sigma_x^2 \tag{8.48}$$

where

$$\sigma_x^2 = \int_{-x_{max}}^{x_{max}} x^2 f_X(x) dx. \tag{8.49}$$

Substituting the expression for σ_q^2 into the expression for SNR, we get

$$SNR = 10 \log_{10} \frac{\sigma_x^2}{\sigma_q^2} \tag{8.50}$$

$$= 10 \log_{10}(3M^2) - 20 \log_{10} \alpha \tag{8.51}$$

which is independent of the input *pdf*. This means that if we use a compressor characteristic whose derivative satisfies Equation (8.46), then regardless of the input variance, the signal-to-noise ratio will remain constant. This is an impressive result. However, we do need some caveats.

Notice that we are not saying that the mean squared quantization error is independent of the quantizer input. It is not, as is clear from Equation (8.48). Remember also that this result is valid as long as the underlying assumptions are valid. When the input variance is very small, our assumption about the *pdf* being constant over the quantization interval is no longer valid, and when the variance of the input is very large, our assumption about the input being bounded by x_{max} may no longer hold.

With fair warning, let us look at the resulting compressor characteristic. We can obtain the compressor characteristic by integrating Equation (8.46):

$$c(x) = x_{\max} + \beta \log \frac{|x|}{x_{\max}} \tag{8.52}$$

where β is a constant. The only problem with this compressor characteristic is that it becomes very large for small x. Therefore, in practice we approximate this characteristic with a function that is linear around the origin and logarithmic away from it.

Two companding characteristics that are widely used today are μ-law companding and A-law companding. The μ-law compressor function is given by

$$c(x) = x_{\max} \frac{\ln(1 + \mu \frac{|x|}{x_{\max}})}{\ln(1 + \mu)} \operatorname{sgn}(x). \tag{8.53}$$

The expander function is given by

$$c^{-1}(x) = \frac{x_{\max}}{\mu} [(1 + \mu)^{\frac{|x|}{x_{\max}}} - 1] \operatorname{sgn}(x). \tag{8.54}$$

This companding characteristic with $\mu = 255$ is used in the telephone systems in North America and Japan. The rest of the world uses the A-law characteristic, which is given by

$$c(x) = \begin{cases} \frac{A|x|}{1 + \ln A} \operatorname{sgn}(x) & 0 \le \frac{|x|}{x_{\max}} \le \frac{1}{A} \\ x_{\max} \frac{1 + \ln \frac{A|x|}{x_{\max}}}{1 + \ln A} \operatorname{sgn}(x) & \frac{1}{A} \le \frac{|x|}{x_{\max}} \le 1 \end{cases} \tag{8.55}$$

and

$$c^{-1}(x) = \begin{cases} \frac{|x|}{A}(1 + \ln A) & 0 \le \frac{|x|}{x_{\max}} \le \frac{1}{1 + \ln A} \\ \frac{x_{\max}}{A} \exp\left[\frac{|x|}{x_{\max}}(1 + \ln A) - 1\right] & \frac{1}{1 + \ln A} \le \frac{|x|}{x_{\max}} \le 1. \end{cases} \tag{8.56}$$

8.7 Entropy-Coded Quantization

In Section 8.3 we mentioned three tasks: selection of boundary values, selection of reconstruction levels, and selection of codewords. Up to this point we have talked about accomplishment of the first two tasks, with the performance measure being the mean squared quantization error. In this section we will look at accomplishing the third task, assigning codewords to the quantization interval. Recall that this becomes an issue when we use variable-length codes. In this section we will be looking at the latter situation, with the rate being the performance measure.

We can take two approaches to the variable-length coding of quantizer outputs. We can redesign the quantizer by taking into account the fact that the selection of the decision boundaries will affect the rate, or we can keep the design of the quantizer the same (i.e., Lloyd-Max quantization) and simply entropy-code the quantizer output. Since the latter approach is by far the simpler one, let's look at it first.

TABLE 8.7   **Output entropies in bits per sample for**
                 minimum mean squared error quantizers.

Number of Levels	Gaussian		Laplacian	
	Uniform	Nonuniform	Uniform	Nonuniform
4	1.904	1.911	1.751	1.728
6	2.409	2.442	2.127	2.207
8	2.759	2.824	2.394	2.479
16	3.602	3.765	3.063	3.473
32	4.449	4.730	3.779	4.427

8.7.1 Entropy Coding of Lloyd-Max Quantizer Outputs

The process of trying to find the optimum quantizer for a given number of levels and rate is a rather difficult task. An easier approach to incorporating entropy coding is to design a quantizer that minimizes the msqe, that is, a Lloyd-Max quantizer, then entropy-code its output.

In Table 8.7 we list the output entropies of uniform and nonuniform Lloyd-Max quantizers. Notice that while the difference in rate for lower levels is relatively small, for a larger number of levels, there can be a substantial difference between the fixed-rate and entropy-coded cases. For example, for 32 levels a fixed-rate quantizer would require 5 bits per sample. However, the entropy of a 32-level uniform quantizer for the Laplacian case is 3.779 bits per sample, which is more than 1 bit less. Notice that the difference between the fixed rate and the uniform quantizer entropy is generally greater than the difference between the fixed rate and the entropy of the output of the nonuniform quantizer. This is because the nonuniform quantizers have smaller step sizes in high-probability regions and larger step sizes in low-probability regions. This brings the probability of an input falling into a low-probability region and the probability of an input falling in a high-probability region closer together. This, in turn, raises the output entropy of the nonuniform quantizer with respect to the uniform quantizer. Finally, the closer the distribution is to being uniform, the less difference in the rates. Thus, the difference in rates is much less for the quantizer for the Gaussian source than the quantizer for the Laplacian source.

8.7.2 Entropy-Constrained Quantization ★

Although entropy coding the Lloyd-Max quantizer output is certainly simple, it is easy to see that we could probably do better if we take a fresh look at the problem of quantizer design, this time with the entropy as a measure of rate rather than the alphabet size. The entropy of the quantizer output is given by

$$H(Q) = -\sum_{i=1}^{M} P_i \log_2 P_i \tag{8.57}$$

where P_i is the probability of the input to the quantizer falling in the ith quantization interval and is given by

$$P_i = \int_{b_{i-1}}^{b_i} f_X(x)dx. \tag{8.58}$$

Notice that the selection of the representation values $\{y_j\}$ has no effect on the rate. This means that we can select the representation values solely to minimize the distortion. However, the selection of the boundary values affects both the rate and the distortion. Initially, we found the reconstruction levels and decision boundaries that minimized the distortion, while keeping the rate fixed by fixing the quantizer alphabet size and assuming fixed-rate coding. In an analogous fashion, we can now keep the entropy fixed and try to minimize the distortion. Or, more formally:

For a given R_o, find the decision boundaries $\{b_j\}$ that minimize σ_q^2 given by Equation (8.3), subject to $H(Q) \leq R_o$.

The solution to this problem involves the solution of the following $M - 1$ nonlinear equations [24]:

$$\ln \frac{P_{l+1}}{P_l} = \lambda(y_{k+1} - y_k)(y_{k+1} + y_k - 2b_k) \tag{8.59}$$

where λ is adjusted to obtain the desired rate, and the reconstruction levels are obtained using Equation (8.27). A generalization of the method used to obtain the minimum mean squared error quantizers can be used to obtain solutions for this equation [73]. The process of finding optimum entropy-constrained quantizers looks complex. Fortunately, at higher rates we can show that the optimal quantizer is a uniform quantizer, simplifying the problem. Furthermore, while these results are derived for the high-rate case, it has been shown that the results also hold for lower rates [73].

8.7.3 High-Rate Optimum Quantization ★

At high rates, the design of optimum quantizers becomes simple, at least in theory. Gish and Pierce's work [92] says that at high rates the optimum entropy-coded quantizer is a uniform quantizer. Recall that any nonuniform quantizer can be represented by a compander and a uniform quantizer. Let us try to find the optimum compressor function at high rates that minimizes the entropy for a given distortion. Using the calculus of variations approach, we will construct the functional

$$J = H(Q) + \lambda \sigma_q^2, \tag{8.60}$$

then find the compressor characteristic to minimize it.

For the distortion σ_q^2, we will use the Bennett integral shown in Equation (8.45). The quantizer entropy is given by Equation (8.57). For high rates, we can assume (as we did before) that the *pdf* $f_X(x)$ is constant over each quantization interval Δ_i, and we can replace Equation (8.58) by

$$P_i = f_X(y_i)\Delta_i. \tag{8.61}$$

Substituting this into Equation (8.57), we get

$$H(Q) = -\sum f_X(y_i)\Delta_i \log[f_X(y_i)\Delta_i] \tag{8.62}$$

$$= -\sum f_X(y_i) \log[f_X(y_i)]\Delta_i - \sum f_X(y_i) \log[\Delta_i]\Delta_i \tag{8.63}$$

$$= -\sum f_X(y_i) \log[f_X(y_i)]\Delta_i - \sum f_X(y_i) \log \frac{2x_{\max}/M}{c'(y_i)} \Delta_i \tag{8.64}$$

where we have used Equation (8.43) for Δ_i. For small Δ_i we can write this as

$$H(Q) = -\int f_X(x) \log f_X(x) dx - \int f_X(x) \log \frac{2x_{\max}/M}{c'(x)} dx \tag{8.65}$$

$$= -\int f_X(x) \log f_X(x) dx - \log \frac{2x_{\max}}{M} + \int f_X(x) \log c'(x) dx \tag{8.66}$$

where the first term is the differential entropy of the source $h(X)$. Let's define $g = c'(x)$. Then substituting the value of $H(Q)$ into Equation (8.60) and differentiating with respect to g, we get

$$\int f_X(x)[g^{-1} - 2\lambda \frac{x_{\max}^2}{3M^2} g^{-3}]dx = 0. \tag{8.67}$$

This equation is satisfied if the integrand is zero, which gives us

$$g = \sqrt{\frac{2\lambda}{3} \frac{x_{\max}}{M}} = K(constant). \tag{8.68}$$

Therefore,

$$c'(x) = K \tag{8.69}$$

and

$$c(x) = Kx + \alpha. \tag{8.70}$$

If we now use the boundary conditions $c(0) = 0$ and $c(x_{\max}) = x_{\max}$, we get $c(x) = x$, which is the compressor characteristic for a uniform quantizer. Thus, at high rates the optimum quantizer is a uniform quantizer.

Substituting this expression for the optimum compressor function in the Bennett integral, we get an expression for the distortion for the optimum quantizer:

$$\sigma_q^2 = \frac{x_{\max}^2}{3M^2}. \tag{8.71}$$

Substituting the expression for $c(x)$ in Equation (8.66), we get the expression for the entropy of the optimum quantizer:

$$H(Q) = h(X) - \log \frac{2x_{\max}}{M}. \tag{8.72}$$

Note that while this result provides us with an easy method for designing optimum quantizers, our derivation is only valid if the source *pdf* is entirely contained in the interval $[-x_{\max}, x_{\max}]$, and if the step size is small enough that we can reasonably assume the *pdf* to be constant over a quantization interval. Generally, these conditions can only be satisfied if we have an extremely large number of quantization intervals. While theoretically this is not much of a problem, most of these reconstruction levels will be rarely used. In practice, as mentioned in Chapter 3, entropy coding a source with a large output alphabet is very problematic. One way we can get around this is through the use of a technique called *recursive indexing*.

Recursive indexing is a mapping of a countable set to a collection of sequences of symbols from another set with finite size [206]. Given a countable set $A = \{a_0, a_1, \ldots\}$ and a finite set $B = \{b_0, b_1, \ldots, b_M\}$ of size $M + 1$, we can represent any element in A by a sequence of elements in B in the following manner:

1. Take the index i of element a_i of A.

2. Find the quotient m and remainder r of the index i such that

$$i = mM + r.$$

3. Generate the sequence: $\underbrace{b_M b_M \cdots b_M}_{m \text{ times}} b_r.$

B is called the representation set. We can see that given any element in A we will have a unique sequence from B representing it. Furthermore, no representative sequence is a prefix of any other sequence. Therefore, recursive indexing can be viewed as a trivial, uniquely decodable prefix code. The inverse mapping is given by

$$\underbrace{b_M b_M \cdots b_M}_{m \text{ times}} b_r \mapsto a_{mM+r}.$$

Since it is one-to-one, if it is used at the output of the quantizer to convert the index sequence of the quantizer output into the sequence of the recursive indices, the former can be recovered without error from the latter. Furthermore, when the size $M + 1$ of the representation set B is chosen appropriately, in effect we can achieve the reduction in the size of the output alphabets that are used for entropy coding.

Example 8.7.1:

Suppose we want to represent the set of nonnegative integers $A = \{0, 1, 2, \ldots\}$ with the representation set $B = \{0, 1, 2, 3, 4, 5\}$. Then the value 12 would be represented by the sequence $5, 5, 2$, and the value 16 would be represented by the sequence $5, 5, 5, 1$. Whenever the decoder sees the value 5, it simply adds on the next value until the next value is smaller than 5. For example, the sequence $3, 5, 1, 2, 5, 5, 1, 5, 0$ would be decoded as $3, 6, 2, 11, 5$. ◆

Recursive indexing is applicable to any representation of a large set by a small set. One way of applying recursive indexing to the problem of quantization is as follows: For a given step size $\Delta > 0$ and a positive integer K, define x_l and x_h as follows:

$$x_l = -\left\lfloor \frac{K-1}{2} \right\rfloor \Delta$$
$$x_h = x_l + (K - 1)\Delta$$

where $\lfloor x \rfloor$ is the largest integer not exceeding x. We define a recursively indexed quantizer of size K to be a uniform quantizer with step size Δ and with x_l and x_h being its smallest and largest output levels. (Q defined this way also has 0 as its output level.) The quantization rule Q, for a given input value x, is as follows:

1. If x falls in the interval $(x_l + \frac{\Delta}{2}, x_h - \frac{\Delta}{2})$, then $Q(x)$ is the nearest output level.

2. If x is greater than $x_h - \frac{\Delta}{2}$, see if $x_1 \stackrel{\Delta}{=} x - x_h \in (x_l + \frac{\Delta}{2}, x_h - \frac{\Delta}{2})$. If so, $Q(x) = (x_h, Q(x_1))$. If not, form $x_2 = x - 2x_h$ and do the same as for x_1. This process continues until for some m, $x_m = x - mx_h$ falls in $(x_l + \frac{\Delta}{2}, x_h - \frac{\Delta}{2})$, which will be quantized into

$$Q(x) = (\underbrace{x_h, x_h, \ldots, x_h}_{m \text{ times}}, Q(x_m)). \tag{8.73}$$

3. If x is smaller than $x_l + \frac{\Delta}{2}$, a similar procedure to the above is used; that is, form $x_m = x + mx_l$ so that it falls in $(x_l + \frac{\Delta}{2}, x_h - \frac{\Delta}{2})$, and quantize it to $(x_l, x_l, \ldots, x_l, Q(x_m))$.

In summary, the quantizer operates in two modes: one when the input falls in the range (x_l, x_h), the other when it falls outside of the specified range. The recursive nature in the second mode gives it the name.

We pay for the advantage of encoding a larger set by a smaller set in several ways. If we get a large input to our quantizer, the representation sequence may end up being intolerably large. We also get an increase in the rate. If $H(Q)$ is the entropy of the quantizer output, and γ is the average number of representation symbols per input symbol, then the minimum rate for the recursively indexed quantizer is $\gamma H(Q)$.

In practice, neither cost is too large. We can avoid the problem of intolerably large sequences by adopting some simple strategies for representing these sequences, and the value of γ is quite close to one for reasonable values of M. For Laplacian and Gaussian quantizers, a typical value for M would be 15 [206].

8.8　Summary

The area of quantization is a well-researched area and much is known about the subject. In this chapter, we looked at the design and performance of uniform and nonuniform quantizers for a variety of sources, and how the performance is affected when the assumptions used in the design process are not correct. When the source statistics are not well known or change with time, we can use an adaptive strategy. One of the more popular approaches to adaptive quantization is the Jayant quantizer. We also looked at the issues involved with entropy-coded quantization.

Further Reading

With an area as broad as quantization, we had to keep some of the coverage rather cursory. However, there is a wealth of information on quantization available in the published literature. The following sources are especially useful for a general understanding of the area:

1. A very thorough coverage of quantization can be found in *Digital Coding of Waveforms*, by N.S. Jayant and P. Noll [118].

2. The paper "Quantization," by A. Gersho, in *IEEE Communication Magazine*, September 1977 [82], provides an excellent tutorial coverage of many of the topics listed here.

3. The original paper by J. Max, "Quantization for Minimum Distortion," *IRE Transactions on Information Theory* [153], contains a very accessible description of the design of *pdf*-optimized quantizers.

4. A thorough study of the effects of mismatch is provided by W. Mauersberger in [152].

8.9 Projects and Problems

1. Show that the derivative of the distortion expression in Equation (8.18) results in the expression in Equation (8.19). You will have to use a result called Leibnitz's rule and the idea of a telescoping series. Leibnitz's rule states that if $a(t)$ and $b(t)$ are monotonic, then

$$\frac{\delta}{\delta t}\int_{a(t)}^{b(t)} f(x,t)dx = \int_{a(t)}^{b(t)} \frac{\delta f(x,t)}{\delta t}dx + f(b(t),t)\frac{\delta b(t)}{\delta t} - f(a(t),t)\frac{\delta a(t)}{\delta t}. \quad (8.74)$$

2. Use the program `falspos` to solve Equation (8.19) numerically for the Gaussian and Laplacian distributions. You may have to modify the function `func` in order to do this.

3. Design a 3-bit uniform quantizer (specify the decision boundaries and representation levels) for a source with a Laplacian *pdf*, with a mean of 3 and a variance of 4.

4. The pixel values in the Sena image are not really distributed uniformly. Obtain a histogram of the image (you can use the `hist_image` routine), and using the fact that the quantized image should be as good an approximation as possible for the original, design 1-, 2-, and 3-bit quantizers for this image. Compare these with the results displayed in Figure 8.7. (For better comparison, you can reproduce the results in the book using the program `uqimg_enc` and `uqimg_dec`.)

5. Use the program `misuquan` to study the effect of mismatch between the input and assumed variances. How do these effects change with the quantizer alphabet size and the distribution type?

6. For the companding quantizer of Example 8.6.1, what are the outputs for the following inputs: $-0.8, 1.2, 0.5, 0.6, 3.2, -0.3$? Compare your results with the case when the input is directly quantized with a uniform quantizer with the same number of levels. Comment on your results.

7. Use the test images Sena and Bookshelf1 to study the trade-offs involved in the selection of block sizes in the forward adaptive quantization scheme described in Example 8.5.2. Compare this with a more traditional forward adaptive scheme in which the variance

is estimated and transmitted. The variance information should be transmitted using a uniform quantizer with differing number of bits.

8. Generalize the Jayant quantizer to the nonuniform case. Assume that the input is from a known distribution with unknown variance. Simulate the performance of this quantizer over the same range of ratio of variances as we have done for the uniform case. Compare your results to the fixed nonuniform quantizer and the adaptive uniform quantizer. To get a start on your program, you may wish to use `misnuq.c` and `juquan.c`.

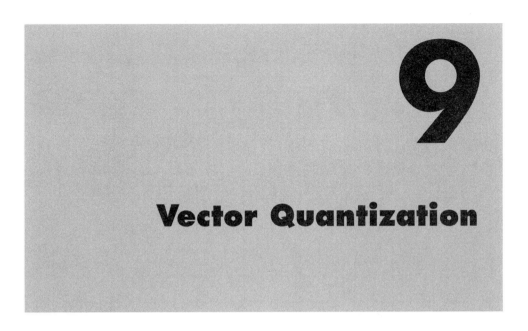

9.1 Overview

By grouping source outputs together and encoding them as a single block, we can obtain efficient lossy as well as lossless compression algorithms. Many of the lossless compression algorithms that we looked at took advantage of this fact. We can do the same with quantization. In this chapter, several quantization techniques that operate on blocks of data are described. We can view these blocks as vectors, hence the name "vector quantization." We will describe several different approaches to vector quantization. We will explore how to design vector quantizers and how these quantizers can be used for compression.

9.2 Introduction

In the last chapter, we looked at different ways of quantizing the output of a source. In all cases the quantizer inputs were scalar values, and each quantizer codeword represented a single sample of the source output. In Chapter 2 we saw that, by taking longer and longer sequences of input samples, it is possible to extract the structure in the source coder output. In Chapter 4 we saw that, even when the input is random, encoding sequences of samples instead of encoding individual samples separately provides a more efficient code. Encoding sequences of samples is more advantageous in the lossy compression framework as well. By "advantageous" we mean a lower distortion for a given rate, or a lower rate for a given distortion. As in the previous chapter, by "rate" we mean the average number of bits per input sample, and the measures of distortion will generally be the mean squared error and the signal-to-noise ratio.

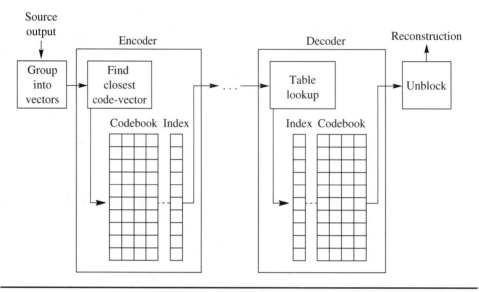

FIGURE 9.1   **The vector quantization procedure.**

The idea that encoding sequences of outputs can provide an advantage over the encoding of individual samples was first put forward by Shannon, and the basic results in information theory were all proved by taking longer and longer sequences of inputs. This indicates that a quantization strategy that works with sequences or blocks of output would provide some improvement in performance over scalar quantization. In other words, we wish to generate a representative set of sequences. Given a source output sequence, we would represent it with one of the elements of the representative set.

In vector quantization we group the source output into blocks or vectors. For example, we can treat L consecutive samples of speech as the components of an L-dimensional vector. Or, we can take a block of L pixels from an image and treat each pixel value as a component of a vector of size or dimension L. This vector of source outputs forms the input to the vector quantizer. At both the encoder and decoder of the vector quantizer, we have a set of L-dimensional vectors called the *codebook* of the vector quantizer. The vectors in this codebook, known as *code-vectors*, are selected to be representative of the vectors we generate from the source output. Each code-vector is assigned a binary index. At the encoder, the input vector is compared to each code-vector in order to find the code-vector closest to the input vector. The elements of this code-vector are the quantized values of the source output. In order to inform the decoder about which code-vector was found to be the closest to the input vector, we transmit or store the binary index of the code-vector. Because the decoder has exactly the same codebook, it can retrieve the code-vector given its binary index. A pictorial representation of this process is shown in Figure 9.1.

Although the encoder may have to perform a considerable amount of computations in order to find the closest reproduction vector to the vector of source outputs, the decoding consists of a table lookup. This makes vector quantization a very attractive encoding scheme for applications in which the resources available for decoding are considerably less than the resources available for encoding. For example, in multimedia applications, considerable computational resources may be available for the encoding operation. However, if the decoding is to be done in software, the amount of computational resources available to the decoder may be quite limited.

Even though vector quantization is a relatively new area, it has developed very rapidly, and now even some of the subspecialties are broad areas of research. In this chapter we will try to introduce you to as much of this fascinating area as we can. If your appetite is whetted by what is available here and you wish to explore further, there is an excellent book by Gersho and Gray [86] devoted to the subject of vector quantization.

Our approach in this chapter is as follows: First, we try to answer the question of why we would want to use vector quantization over scalar quantization. There are several answers to this question, each illustrated through examples. In our discussion, we assume that you are familiar with the material in Chapter 8. We will then turn to one of the most important elements in the design of a vector quantizer, the generation of the codebook. While there are a number of ways of obtaining the vector quantizer codebook, most of them are based on one particular approach, popularly known as the Linde-Buzo-Gray (LBG) algorithm. We devote a considerable amount of time in describing some of the details of this algorithm. Our intent here is to provide you with enough information so that you can write your own programs for design of vector quantizer codebooks. In the software accompanying this book, we have also included programs for designing codebooks that are based on the descriptions in this chapter. If you are not currently thinking of implementing vector quantization routines, you may wish to skip these sections (Sections 9.4.1 and 9.4.2.) We follow our discussion of the LBG algorithm with some examples of image compression using codebooks designed with this algorithm, and then with a brief sampling of the many different kinds of vector quantizers. Finally, we describe another quantization strategy, called trellis-coded quantization (TCQ), which, though different in implementation from the vector quantizers, also makes use of the advantage to be gained from operating on sequences.

Before we begin our discussion of vector quantization, let us define some of the terminology we will be using. The amount of compression will be described in terms of the rate, which will be measured in bits per sample. Suppose we have a codebook of size K, and the input vector is of dimension L. In order to inform the decoder of which code-vector was selected, we need to use $\lceil \log_2 K \rceil$ bits. For example, if the codebook contained 256 code-vectors, we would need 8 bits to specify which of the 256 code-vectors had been selected at the encoder. Thus, the number of bits *per vector* is $\lceil \log_2 K \rceil$ bits. As each code-vector contains the reconstruction values for L source output samples, the number of bits *per sample* would be $\frac{\lceil \log_2 K \rceil}{L}$. Thus, the rate for an L-dimensional vector quantizer with a codebook of size K is $\frac{\lceil \log_2 K \rceil}{L}$. As our measure of distortion we will use the mean squared error. When we say that in a codebook $\mathcal{C}$, containing the K code-vectors $\{Y_i\}$, the input vector X is closest to Y_j, we will mean that

$$\|X - Y_j\|^2 \leq \|X - Y_i\|^2 \qquad \text{for all } Y_i \in \mathcal{C} \tag{9.1}$$

where $X = (x_1 \ x_2 \ \cdots \ x_L)$ and

$$\|X\|^2 = \sum_{i=1}^{L} x_i^2. \tag{9.2}$$

The term *sample* will always refer to a scalar value. Thus, when we are discussing compression of images, a sample refers to a single pixel. Finally, the output points of the quantizer are often referred to as *levels*. Thus, when we wish to refer to a quantizer with K output points or code-vectors, we may refer to it as a K-level quantizer.

9.3 Advantages of Vector Quantization over Scalar Quantization

For a given rate (in bits per sample), use of vector quantization results in a lower distortion than when scalar quantization is used at the same rate, for several reasons. In this section we will explore these reasons with examples (for a more theoretical explanation, see [55, 23, 98]).

If the source output is correlated, vectors of source output values will tend to fall in clusters. By selecting the quantizer output points to lie in these clusters, we have a more accurate representation of the source output. Consider the following example.

Example 9.3.1:

In Example 7.5.1, we introduced a source that generates the height and weight of individuals. Suppose the height of these individuals varied uniformly between 40 and 80 inches, and the weight varied uniformly between 40 and 240 pounds. Suppose we were allowed a total of 6 bits to represent each pair of values. We could use 3 bits to quantize the height and 3 bits to quantize the weight. Thus, the weight range between 40 and 240 pounds would be divided into eight intervals of equal width of 25 and with reconstruction values $\{52, 77, \ldots, 227\}$. Similarly, the height range between 40 and 80 inches can be divided into eight intervals of width five, with reconstruction levels $\{42, 47, \ldots, 77\}$. When we look at the representation of height and weight separately, this approach seems reasonable. But let's look at this quantization scheme in two dimensions. We will plot the height values along the x-axis and the weight values along the y-axis. Note that we are not changing anything in the quantization process. The height values are still being quantized to the same eight different values, as are the weight values. The two-dimensional representation of these two quantizers is shown in Figure 9.2.

From the figure we can see that we effectively have a quantizer output for a person who is 80 inches (6 feet 8 inches) tall and weighs 40 pounds, as well as a quantizer output for an individual whose height is 42 inches but weighs more than 200 pounds. Obviously, these outputs will never be used, as is the case for many of the other outputs. A more sensible approach would be to use a quantizer like the one shown in Figure 9.3, where we take account of the fact that the height and weight are correlated. This quantizer has exactly the same number of output points as the quantizer in Figure 9.2; however, the output points are clustered in the area occupied by the input. Using this quantizer, we can no longer quantize the height and weight separately. We have to consider them as the coordinates of a point in two dimensions in order to find the closest quantizer output point. However, this method provides a much finer quantization of the input.

Note that we have not said how we would obtain the locations of the quantizer outputs shown in Figure 9.3. These output points make up the codebook of the vector quantizer, and we will be looking at codebook design in some detail later in this chapter. ◆

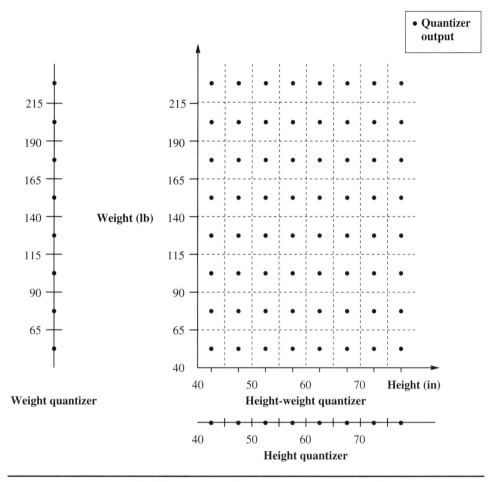

FIGURE 9.2   **The height/weight scalar quantizers when viewed in two dimensions.**

We can see from this example that, as in lossless compression, looking at longer sequences of inputs brings out the structure in the source output. This structure can then be used to provide more efficient representations.

We can easily see how structure in the form of correlation between source outputs can make it more efficient to look at sequences of source outputs rather than looking at each sample separately. However, the vector quantizer is also more efficient than the scalar quantizer when the source output values are not correlated. The reason for this is actually quite simple. As we look at longer and longer sequences of source outputs, we are afforded more flexibility in terms of our design. This flexibility in turn allows us to match the design of the quantizer to the source characteristics. Consider the following example.

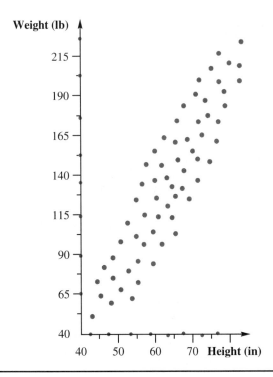

FIGURE 9.3   The height-weight vector quantizer.

Example 9.3.2:

Suppose we have to design a uniform quantizer with eight output values for a Laplacian input. Using the information from Table 8.3 in Chapter 8, we would obtain the quantizer shown in Figure 9.4, where Δ is equal to 0.7309. As the input has a Laplacian distribution, the probability of the source output falling in the different quantization intervals is not the same. For example, the probability that the input will fall in the interval $[0, \Delta)$ is 0.3242, while the probability that a source output will fall in the interval $[3\Delta, \infty)$ is 0.0225. Let's look at how this quantizer will quantize two consecutive source outputs. As we did in the previous example, let's plot the first sample along the x-axis and the second sample along the y-axis. We can represent this two-dimensional view of the quantization process as shown in Figure 9.5. Note that, as in the previous example, we have not changed the quantization process; we are simply representing it differently. The first quantizer input, which we have represented in the figure as x_1, is quantized to the same eight possible output values as before. The same is true for the second quantizer input, which we have represented in the figure as x_2. This two-dimensional representation allows us to examine the quantization process in a slightly different manner. Each filled-in circle in the figure represents a sequence of two quantizer outputs. For example, the top rightmost circle represents the two quantizer outputs that would be obtained if we had two consecutive source outputs with a value greater than 3Δ. We computed the probability of a single source output greater than 3Δ to be 0.0225. The

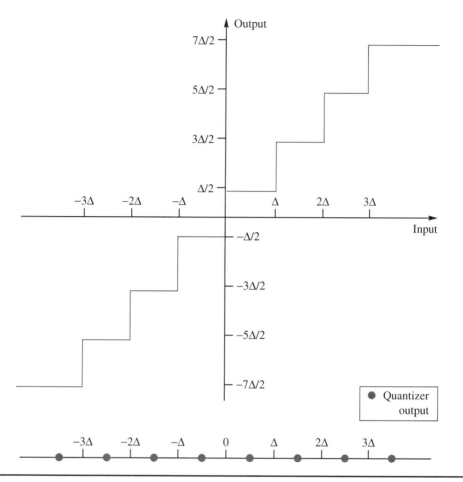

FIGURE 9.4   **Two representations of an eight-level scalar quantizer.**

probability of two consecutive source outputs greater than 2.193 is simply $0.0225 \times 0.0225 = 0.0005$, which is quite small. Given that we do not use this output point very often, we could simply place it somewhere else where it would be of more use. Let us move this output point to the origin, as shown in Figure 9.6. We have now modified the quantization process. Now if we get two consecutive source outputs with values greater than 3Δ, the quantizer output corresponding to the second source output may not be the same as the first source output.

   If we compare the rate distortion performance of the two vector quantizers, the SNR for the first vector quantizer is 11.44 dB, which agrees with the result in Chapter 8 for the uniform quantizer with a Laplacian input. The SNR for the modified vector quantizer, however, is 11.73 dB, an increase of about 0.3 dB. Recall that the SNR is a measure of the average squared value of the source output samples and the mean squared error. As the average squared value of the source output is the same in both cases, an increase in SNR means a decrease in the mean squared error. Whether this increase in SNR is significant will depend on the particular

FIGURE 9.5   **Input-output map for consecutive quantization of two inputs using an eight-level scalar quantizer.**

application. What is important here is that by treating the source output in groups of two we could effect a positive change with only a minor modification. We could argue that this modification is really not that minor since the uniform characteristic of the original quantizer has been destroyed. However, if we begin with a nonuniform quantizer and modify it in a similar way, we get similar results.

Could we do something similar with the scalar quantizer? If we move the output point at $\frac{7\Delta}{2}$ to the origin, the SNR *drops* from 11.44 dB to 10.8 dB. What is it that permits us to make modifications in the vector case, but not in the scalar case? This advantage is caused by the added flexibility we get by viewing the quantization process in higher dimensions. Consider the effect of moving the output point from $\frac{7\Delta}{2}$ to the origin in terms of two consecutive inputs. This one change in one dimension corresponds to moving 15 output points in two dimensions. Thus, modifications at the scalar quantizer level are gross modifications when viewed from the point of view of the vector quantizer. Remember that in this example we have only looked at two-dimensional vector quantizers. As we block the input into larger and larger blocks or

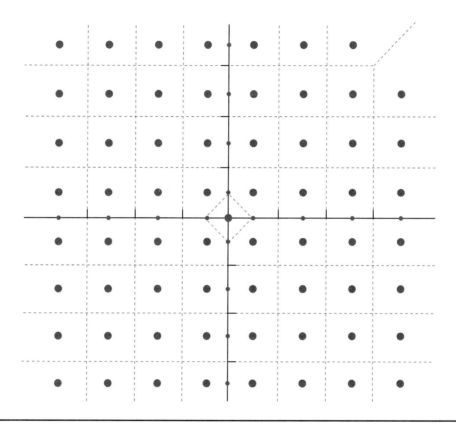

FIGURE 9.6 **Modified two-dimensional vector quantizer.**

vectors, these higher dimensions provide even greater flexibility and the promise of further gains to be made. ◆

In Figure 9.6, notice how the quantization regions have changed for the outputs around the origin, as well as for the two neighbors of the output point that were moved. The decision boundaries between the reconstruction levels can no longer be described as easily as in the case for the scalar quantizer. However, if we know the distortion measure, simply knowing the output points gives us suffcient information to implement the quantization process. Instead of defining the quantization rule in terms of the decision boundary, we can define the quantization rule as follows:

$$Q(X) = Y_j \quad \text{iff} \quad d(X, Y_j) < d(X, Y_i) \; \forall i \neq j. \tag{9.3}$$

For the case where the input X is equidistant from two output points, we can use a simple tie-breaking rule such as "use the output point with the smaller index." The quantization regions V_j can then be defined as

$$V_j = \{X : d(X, Y_j) < d(X, Y_i) \; \forall i \neq j\}. \tag{9.4}$$

Thus, the quantizer is completely defined by the output points and a distortion measure.

From a multidimensional point of view, using a scalar quantizer for each input restricts the output points to a rectangular grid. Observing several source output values at once allows us to move the output points around. Another way of looking at this is that in one dimension the quantization intervals are restricted to be intervals, and the only parameter that we can manipulate is the size of these intervals. When we divide the input into vectors of some length n, the quantization regions are no longer restricted to be rectangles or squares. We have the freedom to divide the range of the inputs in an infinite number of ways.

These examples have shown two ways in which the vector quantizer can be used to improve performance. In the first case, we exploited the sample-to-sample dependence of the input. In the second case, there was no sample-to-sample dependence; the samples were independent. However, looking at two samples together still improved performance.

These two examples can be used to motivate two somewhat different approaches toward vector quantization. One approach is a pattern-matching approach, similar to the process used in Example 9.3.1, while the other approach deals with the quantization of random inputs. We will look at both of these approaches in this chapter.

9.4 The Linde-Buzo-Gray Algorithm

In Example 9.3.1 we saw that one way of exploiting the structure in the source output is to place the quantizer output points where the source output (blocked into vectors) are most likely to congregate. The set of quantizer output points is called the *codebook* of the quantizer, and the process of placing these output points is often referred to as *codebook design*. When we group the source output in two-dimensional vectors, as in the case of Example 9.3.1, we might be able to obtain a good codebook design by plotting a representative set of source output points and then visually locate where the quantizer output points should be. However, this approach to codebook design breaks down when we design higher-dimensional vector quantizers. Consider designing the codebook for a 16-dimensional quantizer. Obviously, a visual placement approach will not work in this case. We need an automatic procedure for locating where the source outputs are clustered.

This is a familiar problem in the field of pattern recognition. It is no surprise, therefore, that the most popular approach to designing vector quantizers is similar to a clustering procedure known as the k-means algorithm, which was developed for pattern recognition applications.

The k-means algorithm functions as follows: Given a large set of output vectors from the source, known as the *training set*, and an initial set of k representative patterns, assign each element of the training set to the closest representative pattern. After an element is assigned, the representative pattern is updated by computing the centroid of the training set vectors assigned to it. When the assignment process is complete, we will have k groups of vectors clustered around each of the output points.

Stuart Lloyd [140] used a similar approach to generate the *pdf*-optimized scalar quantizer, except that instead of using a training set, he assumed that the distribution was known. The Lloyd algorithm functions as follows:

1. Start with an initial set of reconstruction values $\{y_i^{(0)}\}_{i=1}^{M}$. Set $k = 0$, $D^{(0)} = 0$. Select threshold ϵ.

2. Find decision boundaries

$$b_j^{(k)} = \frac{y_{j+1}^{(k)} + y_j^{(k)}}{2} \qquad j = 1, 2, \ldots, M - 1.$$

3. Compute the distortion

$$D^{(k)} = \sum_{i=1}^{M} \int_{b_{i-1}^{(k)}}^{b_i^{(k)}} (x - y_i)^2 f_X(x) dx.$$

4. If $D^{(k)} - D^{(k-1)} < \epsilon$, stop; otherwise, continue.

5. $k = k + 1$. Compute new reconstruction values

$$y_j^{(k)} = \frac{\int_{b_{j-1}^{(k-1)}}^{b_j^{(k-1)}} x f_X(x) dx}{\int_{b_{j-1}^{(k-1)}}^{b_j^{(k-1)}} f_X(x) dx}.$$

Go to Step 2.

Linde, Buzo, and Gray generalized this algorithm to the case where the inputs are no longer scalars [139]. For the case where the distribution is known, the algorithm looks very much like the Lloyd algorithm described above.

1. Start with an initial set of reconstruction values $\{Y_i^{(0)}\}_{i=1}^{M}$. Set $k = 0$, $D^{(0)} = 0$. Select threshold ϵ.

2. Find quantization regions

$$V_i^{(k)} = \{X : d(X, Y_i) < d(X, Y_j) \ \forall j \neq i\} \qquad i = 1, 2, \ldots, M - 1.$$

3. Compute the distortion

$$D^{(k)} = \sum_{i=1}^{M} \int_{V_i^{(k)}} \|X - Y_i^{(k)}\|^2 f_X(X) dX.$$

4. If $\frac{(D^{(k)} - D^{(k-1)})}{D^{(k)}} < \epsilon$, stop; otherwise, continue.

5. $k = k + 1$. Find new reconstruction values $\{Y_i^{(k)}\}_{i=1}^{M}$ that are the centroids of $\{V_i^{(k-1)}\}$. Go to Step 2.

This algorithm is not very practical because the integrals required to compute the distortions and centroids are over odd-shaped regions in n dimensions, where n is the dimension of the input vectors. Generally, these integrals are extremely difficult to compute, making this particular algorithm more of an academic interest.

Of more practical interest is the algorithm for the case where we have a training set available. In this case, the algorithm looks very much like the k-means algorithm.

1. Start with an initial set of reconstruction values $\{Y_i^{(0)}\}_{i=1}^M$ and a set of training vectors $\{X_n\}_{n=1}^N$. Set $k = 0$, $D^{(0)} = 0$. Select threshold ϵ.

2. The quantization regions $\{V_i^{(k)}\}_{i=1}^M$ are given by

$$V_i^{(k)} = \{X_n : d(X_n, Y_i) < d(X_n, Y_j) \ \forall j \neq i\} \qquad i = 1, 2, \ldots, M.$$

   We assume that none of the quantization regions are empty. (Later we will deal with the case where $V_i^{(k)}$ is empty for some i and k.)

3. Compute the average distortion $D^{(k)}$ between the training vectors and the representative reconstruction value.

4. If $\frac{(D^{(k)} - D^{(k-1)})}{D^{(k)}} < \epsilon$, stop; otherwise, continue.

5. $k = k + 1$. Find new reconstruction values $\{Y_i^{(k)}\}_{i=1}^M$ that are the average value of the elements of each of the quantization regions $V_i^{(k-1)}$. Go to Step 2.

   This algorithm forms the basis of most vector quantizer designs. It is popularly known as the Linde-Buzo-Gray or LBG algorithm, or the generalized Lloyd algorithm (GLA) [139]. Although the paper of Linde, Buzo, and Gray [139] is a starting point for most of the work on vector quantization, the latter algorithm had been used several years prior by Edward E. Hilbert at the NASA Jet Propulsion Laboratories in Pasadena, California. Hilbert's starting point was the idea of clustering, and although he arrived at the same algorithm as described above, he called it the *cluster compression algorithm* [103].
   In order to see how this algorithm functions, consider the following example of a two-dimensional vector quantizer codebook design.

Example 9.4.1:

Suppose our training set consists of the height and weight values shown in Table 9.1. The initial set of output points is shown in Table 9.2. (For ease of presentation, we will always round the coordinates of the output points to the nearest integer.) The inputs, outputs, and quantization regions are shown in Figure 9.7.
   The input $(44, 41)$ has been assigned to the first output point; the inputs $(56, 91)$, $(57, 88)$, $(59, 119)$, and $(60, 110)$ have been assigned to the second output point; the inputs $(62, 114)$, and $(65, 120)$ have been assigned to the third output; and the five remaining vectors from the training set have been assigned to the fourth output. The distortion for this assignment is 387.25. We now find the new output points. There is only one vector in the first quantization region, so the first output point is $(44, 41)$. The average of the four vectors in the second quantization region (rounded up) is the vector $(58, 102)$, which is the new second output point. In a similar manner, we can compute the third and fourth output points as $(64, 117)$ and $(69, 168)$. The new output points and the corresponding quantization regions are shown in Figure 9.8. From Figure 9.8, we can see that, while the training vectors that were initially part of the first and fourth quantization regions are still in the same quantization regions, the training vectors $(59, 115)$ and $(60, 120)$, which were in quantization region 2, are now in quantization

TABLE 9.1   Training set for designing vector quantizer codebook.

Height	Weight
72	180
65	120
59	119
64	150
65	162
57	88
72	175
44	41
62	114
60	110
56	91
70	172

TABLE 9.2   Initial set of output points for codebook design.

Height	Weight
45	50
75	117
45	117
80	180

region 3. The distortion corresponding to this assignment of training vectors to quantization regions is 89, considerably less than the original 387.25. Given the new assignments, we can obtain a new set of output points. The first and fourth output points do not change because the training vectors in the corresponding regions have not changed. However, the training vectors in regions 2 and 3 have changed. Recomputing the output points for these regions, we get $(57, 90)$ and $(62, 116)$. The final form of the quantizer is shown in Figure 9.9. The distortion corresponding to the final assignments is 60.17.   ◆

The LBG algorithm is conceptually simple, and as we shall see later, the resulting vector quantizer is remarkably effective in the compression of a wide variety of inputs, both by itself and in conjunction with other schemes. In the next two sections we will look at some of the details of the codebook design process. While these details are important to consider when designing codebooks, they are not necessary for the understanding of the quantization process. If you are not currently interested in these details, you may wish to proceed directly to Section 9.4.3.

9.4.1 Initializing the LBG Algorithm

The LBG algorithm guarantees that the distortion from one iteration to the next will not increase. However, there is no guarantee that the procedure will converge to the optimal solution.

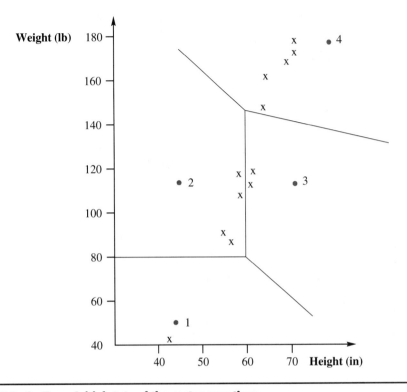

FIGURE 9.7   **Initial state of the vector quantizer.**

The solution to which the algorithm converges is heavily dependent on the initial conditions. For example, if our initial set of output points in Example 9.4.1 had been those shown in Table 9.3 instead of the set in Table 9.2, by using the LBG algorithm we would get the final codebook shown in Table 9.4.

The resulting quantization regions and their membership are shown in Figure 9.10. This is a very different quantizer than the one we had previously obtained. Given this heavy dependence on initial conditions, the selection of the initial codebook is a matter of some importance. We will look at some of the better-known methods of initialization in the following section.

Linde, Buzo, and Gray described a technique in their original paper [139] called the *splitting technique* for initializing the design algorithm. In this technique, we begin by designing a vector quantizer with a single output point; in other words, a codebook of size one, or a one-level vector quantizer. With a one-element codebook, the quantization region is the entire input space, and the output point is the average value of the entire training set. From this output point, the initial codebook for a two-level vector quantizer can be obtained by including the output point for the one-level quantizer and a second output point obtained by adding a fixed perturbation vector ϵ. We then use the LBG algorithm to obtain the two-level vector quantizer. Once the algorithm has converged, the two codebook vectors are used to obtain the

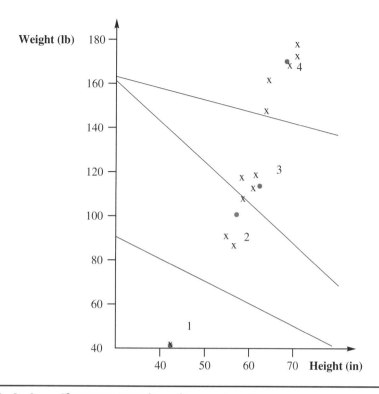

FIGURE 9.8   *The vector quantizer after one iteration.*

initial codebook of a four-level vector quantizer. This initial four-level codebook consists of the two codebook vectors from the final codebook of the two-level vector quantizer and another two vectors obtained by adding ϵ to the two codebook vectors. The LBG algorithm can then be used until this four-level quantizer converges. In this manner we keep doubling the number of levels until we reach the desired number of levels. By including the final codebook of the previous stage at each "splitting," we guarantee that the codebook after splitting will be at least as good as the codebook prior to splitting.

Example 9.4.2:

Let's revisit Example 9.4.1. This time, instead of using the initial codewords used in Example 9.4.1, we will use the splitting technique. For the perturbations, we will use a fixed vector $\epsilon = (10, 10)$. The perturbation vector is usually selected randomly; however, for purposes of explanation it is more useful to use a fixed perturbation vector.

We begin with a single-level codebook. The codeword is simply the average value of the training set. The progression of codebooks is shown in Table 9.5.

The perturbed vectors are used to initialize the LBG design of a two-level vector quantizer. The resulting two-level vector quantizer is shown in Figure 9.11. The resulting distortion is

468.58. These two vectors are perturbed to get the initial output points for the four-level design. Using the LBG algorithm, the final quantizer obtained is shown in Figure 9.12. The distortion is 156.17. The average distortion for the training set for this quantizer using the splitting algorithm is higher than the average distortion obtained previously. However, because the sample size used in this example is rather small, this is no indication of relative merit. ◆

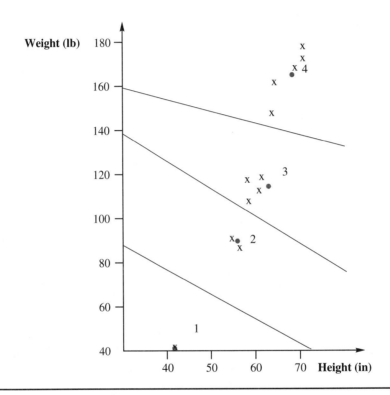

FIGURE 9.9   **Final state of the vector quantizer.**

TABLE 9.3   **An alternate initial set of output points.**

Height	Weight
75	50
75	117
75	127
80	180

TABLE 9.4   Final codebook obtained using the alternative initial codebook.

Height	Weight
44	41
60	107
64	150
70	172

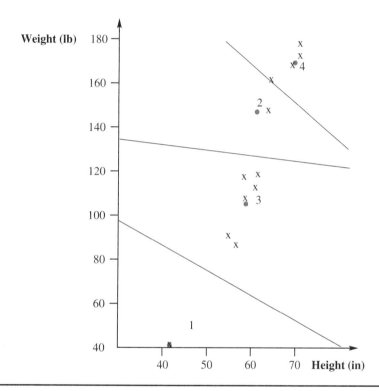

FIGURE 9.10   Final state of the vector quantizer.

If the desired number of levels is not a power of two, then in the last step, instead of generating two initial points from each of the output points of the vector quantizer designed previously, we can perturb as many vectors as necessary to obtain the desired number of vectors. For example, if we needed an eleven-level vector quantizer, we would generate a one-level vector quantizer first, then a two-level, then a four-level, and then an eight-level vector quantizer. At this stage, we would perturb only three of the eight vectors to get the eleven initial output points of the eleven-level vector quantizer. The three points should be those with the largest number of training set vectors, or the largest distortion.

TABLE 9.5   **Progression of codebooks using splitting.**

Codebook	Height	Weight
One-level	62	127
Initial two-level	62	127
	72	137
Final two-level	58	98
	69	168
Initial four-level	58	98
	68	108
	69	168
	79	178
Final four-level	52	73
	62	116
	65	156
	71	176

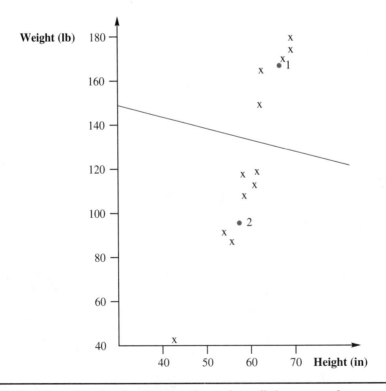

FIGURE 9.11   **Two-level vector quantizer using splitting approach.**

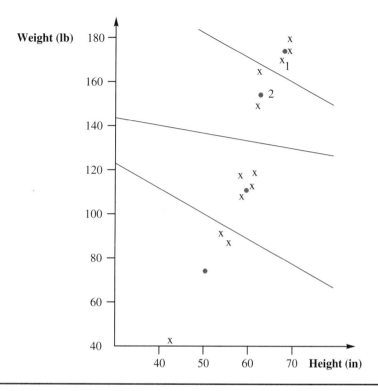

FIGURE 9.12 **Final design using the splitting approach.**

The approach used by Hilbert [103] to obtain the initial output points of the vector quantizer was to pick the output points randomly from the training set. This approach guarantees that, in the initial stages, there will always be at least one vector from the training set in each quantization region. However, we can still get different codebooks if we use different subsets of the training set as our initial codebook.

Example 9.4.3:

Using the training set of Example 9.4.1, we selected different vectors of the training set as the initial codebook. The results are summarized in Table 9.6. If we pick the codebook labeled "Initial Codebook 1," we obtain the codebook labeled "Final Codebook 1." This codebook is identical to the one obtained using the split algorithm. The set labeled "Initial Codebook 2" results in the codebook labeled "Final Codebook 2." This codebook is identical to the quantizer we obtained in Example 9.4.1. In fact, most of the other selections result in one of these two quantizers.

TABLE 9.6   **Effect of using different subsets of the training sequence as the initial codebook.**

Codebook	Height	Weight
Initial Codebook 1	72	180
	72	175
	65	120
	59	119
Final Codebook 1	71	176
	65	156
	62	116
	52	73
Initial Codebook 2	65	120
	44	41
	59	119
	57	88
Final Codebook 2	69	168
	44	41
	62	116
	57	90

Notice that by picking different subsets of the input as our initial codebook, we can generate different vector quantizers. A good approach to codebook design is to initialize the codebook randomly several times, and pick the one that generates the least distortion in the training set from the resulting quantizers.

In 1989, Equitz [67] introduced a method for generating the initial codebook called the *pairwise nearest neighbor* (PNN) algorithm. In the PNN algorithm, we start with as many clusters as there are training vectors and end with the initial codebook. At each stage, we combine the two closest vectors into a single cluster and replace the two vectors by their mean. The idea is to merge those clusters that would result in the smallest increase in distortion. Equitz showed that when we combine two clusters C_i and C_j, the increase in distortion is

$$\frac{n_i n_j}{n_i + n_j} \|Y_i - Y_j\|^2 , \tag{9.5}$$

where n_i is the number of elements in the cluster C_i, and Y_i is the corresponding output point. In the PNN algorithm, we combine clusters that cause the smallest increase in the distortion.

Example 9.4.4:

Using the PNN algorithm, we combine the elements in the training set as shown in Figure 9.13. At each step we combine the two clusters that are closest in the sense of Equation

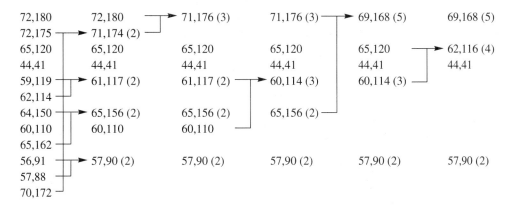

FIGURE 9.13   **Obtaining initial output points using the PNN approach.**

(9.5). If we use these values to initialize the LBG algorithm, we get a vector quantizer shown with output points $(70, 172)$, $(60, 107)$, $(44, 41)$, $(64, 150)$, and a distortion of 104.08.   ◆

Although it was a relatively easy task to generate the initial codebook using the PNN algorithm in Example 9.4.4, we can see that, as the size of the training set increases, this procedure becomes progressively more time-consuming. In order to avoid this cost, we can use a fast PNN algorithm that does not attempt to find the absolute smallest cost at each step (see [67] for details).

Finally, a simple initial codebook is the set of output points from the corresponding scalar quantizers. In the beginning of this chapter we saw how scalar quantization of a sequence of inputs can be viewed as vector quantization using a rectangular vector quantizer. We can use this rectangular vector quantizer as the initial set of outputs.

Example 9.4.5:

Return once again to the quantization of the height-weight data set. If we assume that the heights are uniformly distributed between 40 and 180, then a two-level scalar quantizer would have reconstruction values 75 and 145. Similarly, if we assume that the weights are uniformly distributed between 40 and 80, the reconstruction values would be 50 and 70. The initial reconstruction values for the vector quantizer are $(50, 75)$, $(50, 145)$, $(70, 75)$, and $(70, 145)$. The final design for this initial set is the same as the one obtained in Example 9.4.1 with a distortion of 60.17.   ◆

We have looked at four different ways of initializing the LBG algorithm. Each has its own advantages and drawbacks. The PNN initialization has been shown to result in better designs, producing a lower distortion for a given rate than the splitting approach [67]. However, the procedure for obtaining the initial codebook is much more involved and complex. We cannot make any general claims regarding the superiority of any one of these initialization techniques.

Even the PNN approach cannot be proven to be optimal. In practice, if we are dealing with a wide variety of inputs, the effect of using different initialization techniques appears to be insignificant.

9.4.2   The Empty Cell Problem

Let's take a closer look at the progression of the design in Example 9.4.5. When we assign the inputs to the initial output points, no input point gets assigned to the output point at $(70, 75)$. This is a problem because in order to update an output point, we need to take the average value of the input vectors. Obviously, some strategy is needed. The strategy that we actually used in Example 9.4.5 was not to update the output point if there were no inputs in the quantization region associated with it. This strategy seems to have worked in this particular example; however, there is a danger that we will end up with an output point that is never used. A common approach to avoid this is to remove an output point that has no inputs associated with it, and replace it with a point from the quantization region with the most output points. This can be done by selecting a point at random from the region with the highest population of training vectors, or the highest associated distortion. A more systematic approach is to design a two-level quantizer for the training vectors in the most heavily populated quantization region. This approach is computationally expensive and provides no significant improvement over the simpler approach. In the program accompanying this book, we have used the first approach. (To compare the two approaches, see Problem 3.)

9.4.3   Use of LBG for Image Compression

One application for which the vector quantizer described in this section has been extremely popular is image compression. For image compression, the vector is formed by taking blocks of pixels of size $N \times M$ and treating them as an $L = NM$ dimensional vector. Generally, we take $N = M$. Instead of forming vectors in this manner, we could form the vector by taking L pixels in a row of the image. However, this does not allow us to take advantage of the two-dimensional correlations in the image. Recall that correlation between the samples provides the clustering of the input, and the LBG algorithm takes advantage of this clustering.

Example 9.4.6:

Let us quantize the Sinan image shown in Figure 9.14 using a 16-dimensional quantizer. The input vectors are constructed using 4×4 blocks of pixels. The codebook was trained on the Sinan image.

The results of the quantization using codebooks of size 16, 64, 256, and 1024 are shown in Figure 9.15. The rates and compression ratios are summarized in Table 9.7. To see how these quantities were calculated, recall that if we have K vectors in a codebook, we need $\lceil \log_2 K \rceil$ bits to inform the receiver which of the K vectors is the quantizer output. This quantity is listed in the second column of Table 9.7 for the different values of K. If the vectors are of dimension L, this means that we have used $\lceil \log_2 K \rceil$ bits to send the quantized value of L pixels. Therefore, the rate in bits per pixel is $\frac{\lceil \log_2 K \rceil}{L}$. (We have assumed that the codebook

FIGURE 9.14   Original Sinan image.

is available to both transmitter and receiver, and therefore we do not have to use any bits to transmit the codebook from the transmitter to the receiver.) This quantity is listed in the third column of Table 9.7. Finally, the compression ratio, given in the last column of Table 9.7, is the ratio of the number of bits per pixel in the original image to the number of bits per pixel in the compressed image. The Sinan image was digitized using 8 bits per pixel. Using this information and the rate after compression, we can obtain the compression ratios.

Looking at the images, we see that reconstruction using a codebook of size 1024 is very close to the original. At the other end, the image obtained using a codebook with 16 reconstruction vectors contains a lot of visible artifacts. The utility of each reconstruction depends on the demands of the particular application. ◆

In this example, we used codebooks trained on the image itself. Generally, this is not the preferred approach because the receiver has to have the same codebook in order to reconstruct the image. Either the codebook must be transmitted along with the image, or the receiver has the same training image so that it can generate an identical codebook. This is impractical because, if the receiver already has the image in question, much better compression can be obtained by simply sending the name of the image to the receiver. Sending the codebook with the image is not unreasonable. However, the transmission of the codebook is overhead that could be avoided if a more generic codebook, one that is available to both transmitter and receiver, were to be used.

In order to compute the overhead, we need to calculate the number of bits required to transmit the codebook to the receiver. If each codeword in the codebook is a vector with L

FIGURE 9.15   Top left: codebook size 16; top right: codebook size 64; bottom left: codebook size 256; bottom right: codebook size 1024.

TABLE 9.7   Summary of compression measures for image compression example.

Codebook Size (# of codewords)	Bits Needed to Select a Codeword	Bits per Pixel	Compression Ratio
16	4	0.25	32:1
64	6	0.375	21.33:1
256	8	0.50	16:1
1024	10	0.625	12.8:1

TABLE 9.8 **Overhead in bits per pixel for codebooks of different sizes.**

Codebook Size K	Overhead in Bits per Pixel
16	0.03125
64	0.125
256	0.50
1024	2.0

elements and if we use B bits to represent each element, then in order to transmit the codebook of a K-level quantizer we need $B \times L \times K$ bits. In our example, $B = 8$ and $L = 16$. Therefore, we need $K \times 128$ bits to transmit the codebook. As our image consists of 256×256 pixels, the overhead in bits per pixel is $128 \times K/65{,}536$. The overhead for different values of K is summarized in Table 9.8. We can see that while the overhead for a codebook of size 16 seems reasonable, the overhead for a codebook of size 1024 is over three times the rate required for quantization.

Given the excessive amount of overhead required for sending the codebook along with the vector quantized image, there has been substantial interest in the design of codebooks that are more generic in nature and, therefore, can be used to quantize a number of images. To investigate the issues that might arise, we quantized the Sinan image using four different codebooks generated by the Sena, Sensin, Earth, and Omaha images. The results are shown in Figure 9.16.

As expected, the reconstructed images from this approach are not of the same quality as when the codebook is generated from the image to be quantized. However, this is only true as long as the overhead required for storage or transmission of the codebook is ignored. If we include the extra rate required to encode and transmit the codebook of output points, using the codebook generated by the image to be quantized seems unrealistic. Although using the codebook generated by another image to perform the quantization may be realistic, the quality of the reconstructions is quite poor. Later in this chapter we will take a closer look at the subject of vector quantization of images and consider a variety of ways to improve this performance.

You may have noticed that the bit rates for the vector quantizers used in the examples are quite low. The reason is that the size of the codebook increases exponentially with the rate. Suppose we want to encode a source using R bits per sample; that is, the average number of bits per sample in the compressed source output is R. By "sample" we mean a scalar element of the source output sequence. If we wanted to use an L-dimensional quantizer, we would group L samples together into vectors. This means that we would have RL bits available to represent each vector. With RL bits, we can represent 2^{RL} different output vectors. In other words, the size of the codebook for an L-dimensional R-bits-per-sample quantizer is 2^{RL}. From Table 9.7, we can see that when we quantize an image using 0.25 bits per pixel and 16-dimensional quantizers, we have $16 \times 0.25 = 4$ bits available to represent each vector. Hence, the size of the codebook is $2^4 = 16$. The quantity RL is often called the *rate dimension product*. Note that the size of the codebook grows exponentially with this product.

FIGURE 9.16   **Sinan image quantized at the rate of 0.5 bits per pixel. The images used to obtain the codebook were (clockwise from top left) Sensin, Sena, Earth, Omaha.**

Consider the problems. The codebook size for a 16-dimensional, 2-bits-per-sample vector quantizer would be $2^{16\times2}$! (If the source output was originally represented using 8 bits per sample, a rate of 2 bits per sample for the compressed source corresponds to a compression ratio of 4:1.) This large size causes problems both with storage and with the quantization process. To store 2^{32} sixteen-dimensional vectors, assuming that we can store each component of the vector in a single byte, requires $2^{32} \times 16$ bytes—approximately 64 gigabytes of storage. Furthermore, to quantize a single input vector would require over four billion vector comparisons to find the closest output point. Obviously, neither the storage requirements nor the computational requirements are realistic. Because of this problem, most vector quantization applications operate at low bit rates. In many applications, such as low-rate speech coding, we want to operate at very low rates; therefore, this is not a drawback. However, for applications such as high-quality video coding, which requires higher rates, this is definitely a problem.

There are several approaches to solving these problems. Each entails the introduction of some structure in the codebook and/or the quantization process. While the introduction of structure mitigates some of the storage and computational problems, there is generally a trade-off in terms of the distortion performance. We will look at some of these approaches in the following sections.

9.5 Tree-Structured Vector Quantizers

One way we can introduce structure is to organize our codebook in such a way that it is easy to pick which part contains the desired output vector. Consider the two-dimensional vector quantizer shown in Figure 9.17. Note that the output points in each quadrant are the mirror image of the output points in neighboring quadrants. Given an input to this vector quantizer, we can reduce the number of comparisons necessary for finding the closest output point by using the sign on the components of the input. The sign on the components of the input vector will tell us in which quadrant the input lies. Because all the quadrants are mirror images of the neighboring quadrants, the closest output point to a given input will lie in the same quadrant as the input itself. Therefore, we only need to compare the input to the output points that lie in the same quadrant, thus reducing the number of required comparisons by a factor of four. This approach can be extended to L dimensions, where the signs on the L components of the input vector can tell us in which of the 2^L hyperquadrants the input lies, which in turn would reduce the number of comparisons by 2^L.

This approach works well when the output points are distributed in a symmetrical manner. However, it breaks down as the distribution of the output points becomes less symmetrical.

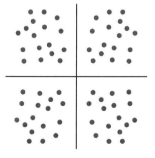

FIGURE 9.17   A symmetrical vector quantizer in two dimensions.

Example 9.5.1:

Consider the vector quantizer shown in Figure 9.18. This is different from the output points in Figure 9.17; we have dropped the mirror image requirement of the previous example. The output points are shown as filled circles, and the input point is the X. It is obvious from the figure that while the input is in the first quadrant, the closest output point is in the fourth quadrant. However, the quantization approach described above will force the input to be represented by an output in the first quadrant.

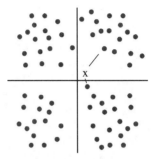

FIGURE 9.18   **Breakdown of the method using the quadrant approach.**

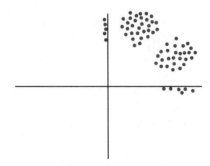

FIGURE 9.19   **Breakdown of the method using the quadrant approach.**

The situation gets worse as we lose more and more of the symmetry. Consider the situation in Figure 9.19. In this quantizer, not only will we get an incorrect output point when the input is close to the boundaries of the first quadrant, but also there is no significant reduction in the amount of computation required.

Most of the output points are in the first quadrant. Therefore, whenever the input falls in the first quadrant, which it will do quite often if the quantizer design is reflective of the distribution of the input, knowing that it is in the first quadrant does not lead to a great reduction in the number of comparisons. ◆

The idea of using the L-dimensional equivalents of quadrants to partition the output points in order to reduce the computational load can be extended to nonsymmetrical situations, like those shown in Figure 9.19, in the following manner. Divide the set of output points into two groups, *group0* and *group1*, and assign to each group a test vector such that output points in each group are closer to the test vector assigned to that group than to the test vector assigned to the other group (Figure 9.20). Label the two test vectors 0 and 1. When we get an input vector, we compare it against the test vectors. Depending on the outcome, the input is compared to the output points associated with the test vector closest to the input. After these two comparisons, we can discard half of the output points. Comparison with the test vectors takes the place of looking at the signs of the components to decide which set of output points to discard from contention. If the total number of output points is K, with this approach we have to make $\frac{K}{2}+2$ comparisons instead of K comparisons.

This process can be continued by splitting the output points in each group into two groups and assigning a test vector to the subgroups. So *group0* would be split into *group00* and *group01*, with associated test vectors labeled 00 and 01, and *group1* would be split into *group10* and *group11*, with associated test vectors labeled 10 and 11. Suppose the result of the first set of comparisons was that the output point would be searched for in *group1*. The input would be compared to the test vectors 10 and 11. If the input was closer to the test vector 10, then the output points in *group11* would be discarded, and the input would be compared to the output points in *group10*. We can continue the procedure by successively dividing each group of output points into two, until finally, if the number of output points is a power of two, the last set of groups would consist of single points. The number of comparisons required to obtain the final output point would be $2 \log K$ instead of K. Thus, for a codebook of size 4096 we would need 24 vector comparisons instead of 4096 vector comparisons.

This is a remarkable decrease in computational complexity. However, we pay for this decrease in two ways. The first penalty is a possible increase in distortion. It is possible at some stage that the input is closer to one test vector while at the same time being closest to an output belonging to the rejected group. This is similar to the situation shown in Figure 9.18. The other penalty is an increase in storage requirements. Now we not only have to store the output points from the vector quantizer codebook, we also must store the test vectors.

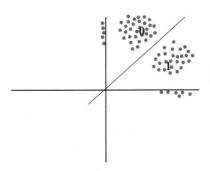

FIGURE 9.20 **Division of output points into two groups.**

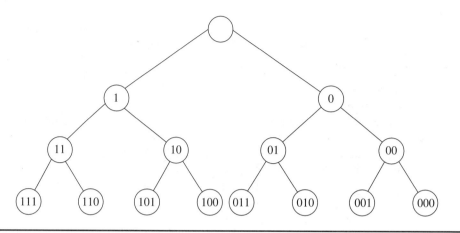

FIGURE 9.21   **Decision tree for quantization.**

The comparisons that must be made at each step are shown in Figure 9.21. The label inside each node is the label of the test vector that we compare the input against. This tree of decisions is what gives tree-structured vector quantizers (TSVQ) their name. Notice also that, as we are progressing down a tree, we are also building a binary string. As the leaves of the tree are the output points, by the time we reach a particular leaf or, in other words, select a particular output point, we have obtained the binary codeword corresponding to that output point.

This process of building the binary codeword as we progress through the series of decisions required to find the final output can result in some other interesting properties of tree-structured vector quantizers. For instance, even if a partial codeword is transmitted, we can still get an approximation of the input vector. In Figure 9.21, if the quantized value was the codebook vector 5, the binary codeword would be 011. However, if only the first two bits 01 were received by the decoder, the input can be approximated by the test vector labeled 01.

9.5.1   Design of Tree-Structured Vector Quantizers

In the last section we saw how we could reduce the computational complexity of the design process by imposing a tree structure on the vector quantizer. Rather than imposing this structure after the vector quantizer has been designed, it makes sense to design the vector quantizer within the framework of the tree structure. We can do this by a slight modification of the splitting design approach proposed by Linde et al. [139].

We start the design process in a manner identical to the splitting technique. First, obtain the average of all the training vectors, perturb it to obtain a second vector, and use these vectors to form a two-level vector quantizer. Let us label these two vectors 0 and 1, and the groups of training set vectors that would be quantized to each of these two vectors *group0* and *group1*. We will later use these vectors as test vectors. We perturb these output points to get the initial vectors for a four-level vector quantizer. At this point, the design procedure for the tree-structured vector quantizer deviates from the splitting technique. Instead of using the entire training set to design a four-level vector quantizer, we use the training set vectors in *group0* to design a two-level vector quantizer with output points labeled 00 and 01. We use the training set vectors in *group1* to design a two-level vector quantizer with output points labeled 10 and 11. We also split the training set vectors in *group0* and *group1* into two groups each. The vectors in *group0* are split, based on their proximity to the vectors labeled 00 and 01, into *group00* and *group01*, and the vectors in *group1* are divided in a like manner into the groups *group10* and *group11*. The vectors labeled 00, 01, 10, and 11 will act as test vectors at this level. To get an eight-level quantizer, we use the training set vectors in each of the four groups to obtain four two-level vector quantizers. We continue in this manner until we have the required number of output points. Notice that in the process of obtaining the output points, we have also obtained the test vectors required for the quantization process.

9.5.2 Pruned Tree-Structured Vector Quantizers

Once we have built a tree-structured codebook, we can sometimes improve its rate distortion performance by removing carefully selected subgroups. Removal of a subgroup, referred to as *pruning*, will reduce the size of the codebook and hence the rate. It may also result in an increase in distortion. Therefore, the objective of the pruning is to remove those subgroups that will result in the best trade-off of rate and distortion. Chou, Lookabaugh, and Gray [48] have developed an optimal pruning algorithm called the *generalized BFOS algorithm*. The name of the algorithm derives from the fact that it is an extension of an algorithm originally developed by Brieman, Freidman, Olshen, and Stone [29] for classification applications. (See [48] and [86] for description and discussion of the algorithm.)

Pruning output points from the codebook has the unfortunate effect of removing the structure that was previously used to generate the binary codeword corresponding to the output points. If we used the structure to generate the binary codewords, the pruning would cause the codewords to be of variable length. As the variable-length codes would correspond to the leaves of a binary tree, this code would be a prefix code and, therefore, certainly usable. However, it would not require a large increase in complexity to assign fixed-length codewords to the output points using another method. This increase in complexity is generally offset by the improvement in performance that results from the pruning [191].

9.6 Structured Vector Quantizers

The tree-structured vector quantizer solves the complexity problem, but acerbates the storage problem. We now take an entirely different tacks and develop vector quantizers that do not have these storage problems; however, we pay for this relief in other ways.

Example 9.3.1 was our motivation for the quantizer obtained by the LBG algorithm. This example showed that the correlation between samples of the output of a source leads to clustering. This clustering is exploited by the LBG algorithm by placing output points at the location of these clusters. However, in Example 9.3.2, we saw that even when there is no correlation between samples, there is a kind of probabilistic structure that becomes more evident as we group the random inputs of a source into larger and larger blocks or vectors.

In Example 9.3.2, we changed the position of the output point in the top-right corner. All four corner points have the same probability, so we could have chosen any of these points. In the case of the two-dimensional Laplacian distribution in Example 9.3.2, all points that lie on the contour described by $|x| + |y| = constant$ have equal probability. These are called *contours of constant probability*. For spherically symmetrical distributions like the Gaussian distribution, the contours of constant probability are circles in two dimensions, spheres in three dimensions, and hyperspheres in higher dimensions.

We mentioned in Example 9.3.2 that the points away from the origin have very little probability mass associated with them. Based on what we have said about the contours of constant probability, we can be a little more specific and say that the points on constant probability contours farther away from the origin have very little probability mass associated with them. Therefore, we can get rid of all of the points outside some contour of constant probability without incurring much of a distortion penalty. However, as the number of reconstruction points is reduced, there is a decrease in rate, thus improving the rate distortion performance.

Example 9.6.1:

Let us design a two-dimensional uniform quantizer by keeping only the output points in the quantizer of Example 9.3.2 that lie on or within the contour of constant probability given by $|x_1| + |x_2| = 5\Delta$. If we count all the points that are retained, we get 60 points. This is close enough to 64 that we can compare it with the eight-level uniform scalar quantizer. If we simulate this quantization scheme with a Laplacian input, and the same step size as the scalar quantizer, that is, $\Delta = 0.7309$, we get an SNR of 12.22 dB. Comparing this to the 11.44 dB obtained with the scalar quantizer, we see that there is a definite improvement. We can get slightly more improvement in performance if we modify the step size.   ◆

Notice that the improvement in the previous example is obtained only by restricting the outer boundary of the quantizer. Unlike Example 9.3.2, we did not change the shape of any of the inner quantization regions. This gain is referred to in the quantization literature as *boundary gain*. In terms of the description of quantization noise in Chapter 8, we reduced the overload error by reducing the overload probability, without a commensurate increase in the granular noise. In Figure 9.22, we have marked the 12 output points that belonged to the original 64-level quantizer, but do not belong to the 60-level quantizer, by drawing circles around them. Removal of these points results in an increase in overload probability. We also marked the eight output points that belong to the 60-level quantizer, but were not part of the original 64-level quantizer, by drawing squares around them. Adding these points results in a decrease in the overload probability. If we calculate the increases and decreases (Problem 5), we find that the net result is a decrease in overload probability. This overload probability is further reduced as the dimension of the vector is increased.

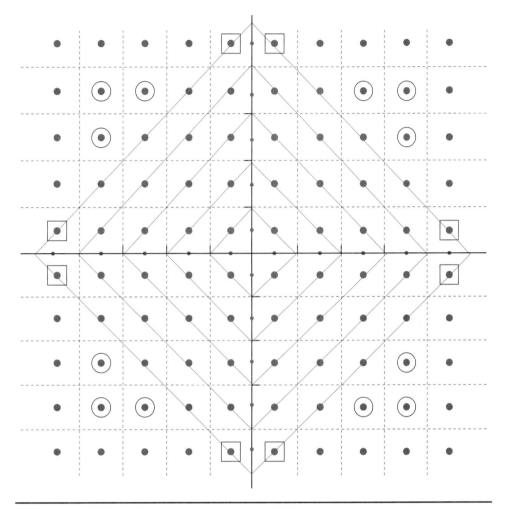

FIGURE 9.22   **Contours of constant probability.**

9.6.1 Pyramid Vector Quantization

As the dimension of the input vector increases, something interesting happens. Suppose we are quantizing a random variable X with *pdf* $f_X(X)$ and differential entropy $h(X)$. Suppose we block samples of this random variable into a vector $\mathbf{X}$. A result of Shannon's, called the *asymptotic equipartition property* (AEP), states that for sufficiently large L and arbitrarily small ϵ

$$\left| \frac{\log f_{\mathbf{X}}(\mathbf{X})}{L} + h(X) \right| < \epsilon \tag{9.6}$$

for all but a set of vectors with a vanishingly small probability [209]. This means that almost all the L-dimensional vectors will lie on a contour of constant probability given by

$$\left| \frac{\log f_{\mathbf{X}}(\mathbf{X})}{L} \right| = -h(X). \tag{9.7}$$

Given that this is the case, Sakrison [200] suggested that an optimum manner to encode the source would be to distribute 2^{RL} points uniformly in this region. Fischer [75] used this insight to design a vector quantizer called the *pyramid vector quantizer* for the Laplacian source that looks quite similar to the quantizer described in Example 9.6.1. The vector quantizer consists of points of the rectangular quantizer that fall on the hyperpyramid given by

$$\sum_{i=1}^{L} |x_i| = C$$

where C is a constant depending on the variance of the input. Shannon's result is asymptotic, and for realistic values of L, the input vector is generally not localized to a single hyperpyramid.

For this case, Fischer first finds the distance

$$r = \sum_{i=1}^{L} |x_i|.$$

This value is quantized and transmitted to the receiver. The input is normalized by this gain term and quantized using a single hyperpyramid. The quantization process for the shape term consists of two stages: finding the output point on the hyperpyramid closest to the scaled input, and finding a binary codeword for this output point. (See [75] for details about the quantization and coding process.) This approach is quite successful, and for a rate of 3 bits per sample and a vector dimension of 16, we get an SNR value of 16.32 dB. If we increase the vector dimension to 64, we get an SNR value of 17.03. Compared to the SNR obtained from using a nonuniform scalar quantizer, this is an improvement of more than 4 dB.

Notice that in this approach we separated the input vector into a *gain* term and a pattern or *shape* term. Quantizers of this form are called *gain-shape vector quantizers*, or *product code vector quantizers* [197].

9.6.2   Polar and Spherical Vector Quantizers

For the Gaussian distribution, the contours of constant probability are circles in two dimensions and spheres and hyperspheres in three and higher dimensions. In two dimensions, we can quantize the input vector by first transforming it into polar coordinates r and θ:

$$r = \sqrt{x_1^2 + x_2^2} \tag{9.8}$$

and

$$\theta = \tan^{-1} \frac{x_2}{x_1}. \tag{9.9}$$

r and θ can then be either quantized independently [176], or we can use the quantized value of r as an index to a quantizer for θ [239]. The former is known as a polar quantizer; the latter, an unrestricted polar quantizer. The advantage to quantizing r and θ independently is

FIGURE 9.23   Possible quantization regions.

one of simplicity. The quantizers for r and θ are independent scalar quantizers. However, the performance of the polar quantizers is not significantly higher than that of scalar quantization of the components of the two-dimensional vector. The unrestricted polar quantizer has a more complex implementation, as the quantization of θ depends on the quantization of r. However, the performance is also somewhat better than the polar quantizer. The polar quantizer can be extended to three or more dimensions [222].

9.6.3 Lattice Vector Quantizers

Recall that quantization error is composed of two kinds of error, overload error and granular error. The overload error is determined by the location of the quantization regions furthest from the origin, or the boundary. We have seen how we can design vector quantizers to reduce the overload probability and thus the overload error. We called this the boundary gain of vector quantization. In scalar quantization, the granular error was determined by the size of the quantization interval. In vector quantization, the granular error is affected by the size and shape of the quantization interval.

Consider the square and circular quantization regions shown in Figure 9.23. We show only the quantization region at the origin. These quantization regions need to be distributed in a regular manner over the space of source outputs. However, for now, let us simply consider the quantization region at the origin. Let's assume they both have the same area so that we can compare them. This way it would require the same number of quantization regions to cover a given area. That is, we will be comparing two quantization regions of the same "size." To have an area of one, the square has to have sides of length one. As the area of a circle is given by πr^2, the radius of the circle is $\frac{1}{\sqrt{\pi}}$. The maximum quantization error possible with the square quantization region is when the input is at one of the four corners of the square. In this case, the error is $\frac{1}{\sqrt{2}}$, or about 0.707. For the circular quantization region, the maximum error occurs when the input falls on the boundary of the circle. In this case, the error is $\frac{1}{\sqrt{\pi}}$, or about 0.56. Thus, the maximum granular error is larger for the square region than the circular region.

In general, we are more concerned with the average squared error than the maximum error. If we compute the average squared error for the square region, we obtain

$$\int_{\text{Square}} \|X\|^2 \, dX = 0.166\bar{6}.$$

For the circle, we obtain

$$\int_{\text{Circle}} \|X\|^2 \, dX = 0.159.$$

Thus, the circular region would introduce less granular error than the square region.

Our choice seems to be clear; we will use the circle as the quantization region. Unfortunately, a basic requirement for the quantizer is that for every possible input vector there should be a unique output vector. In order to satisfy this requirement and have a quantizer with sufficient structure that can be used to reduce the storage space, a union of translates of the quantization region should cover the output space of the source. In other words, the quantization region should *tile* space. A two-dimensional region can be tiled by squares, but it cannot be tiled by circles. If we tried to tile the space with circles, we would either get overlaps or holes.

Apart from squares, other shapes that tile space include rectangles and hexagons. It turns out that the best shape to pick for a quantization region in two dimensions is a hexagon [168].

In two dimensions, it is relatively easy to find the shapes that tile space, then select the one that gives the smallest amount of granular error. However, when we start looking at higher dimensions, it is difficult, if not impossible, to visualize different shapes, let alone find which ones tile space. An easy way out of this dilemma is to remember that a quantizer can be completely defined by its output points. In order for this quantizer to possess structure, these points should be spaced in some regular manner.

Regular arrangements of output points in space are called *lattices*. Mathematically, we can define a lattice as follows:

Let $\{\mathbf{a_1}, \mathbf{a_2}, \ldots, \mathbf{a_L}\}$ be L independent L-dimensional vectors. Then the set

$$\mathcal{L} = \left\{ \mathbf{x} : \mathbf{x} = \sum_{i=1}^{L} u_i \mathbf{a}_i \right\} \qquad (9.10)$$

is a lattice if $\{u_i\}$ are all integers.

When a subset of lattice points is used as the output points of a vector quantizer, the quantizer is known as a *lattice vector quantizer*. From this definition, the pyramid vector quantizer described earlier can be viewed as a lattice vector quantizer. Basing a quantizer on a lattice solves the storage problem. As any lattice point can be regenerated if we know the basis set, there is no need to store the output points. Further, the highly structured nature of lattices makes finding the closest output point to an input relatively simple. Note that what we give up when we use lattice vector quantizers is the clustering property of LBG quantizers.

Let's take a look at a few examples of lattices in two dimensions. If we pick $a_1 = (1, 0)$ and $a_2 = (0, 1)$, we obtain the integer lattice—the lattice that contains all points in two dimensions whose coordinates are integers.

If we pick $a_1 = (1, 1)$ and $a_2 = (1, -1)$, we get the lattice shown in Figure 9.24. This lattice has a rather interesting property. Any point in the lattice is given by $na_1 + ma_2$, where n and m are integers. But

$$na_1 + ma_2 = \begin{bmatrix} n + m \\ n - m \end{bmatrix}$$

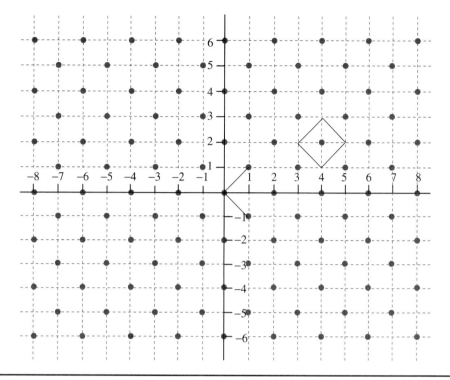

FIGURE 9.24   The D_2 lattice.

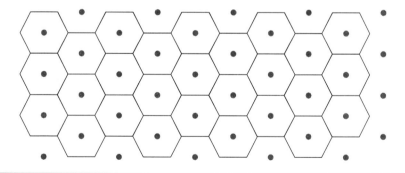

FIGURE 9.25   The A_2 lattice.

and the sum of the coefficients is $n + m + n - m = 2n$, which is even for all n. Therefore, all points in this lattice have an even coordinate sum. Lattices with these properties are called D *lattices*.

Finally, if $a_1 = (1, 0)$ and $a_2 = (-\frac{1}{2}, \frac{\sqrt{3}}{2})$, we get the hexagonal lattice shown in Figure 9.25. This is an example of an *A lattice*.

There are a large number of lattices that can be used to obtain lattice vector quantizers. In fact, given a dimension L, there are an infinite number of possible sets of L independent vectors. Among these, we would like to pick the lattice that produces the greatest reduction in granular noise. When comparing the square and circle as candidates for quantization regions, we used the integral over the shape of $\|X\|^2$. This is simply the second moment of the shape. The shape with the smallest second moment for a given volume is known to be the circle in two dimensions and the sphere and hypersphere in higher dimensions [52]. Unfortunately, circles and spheres cannot tile space; either there will be overlap or there will be holes. As the ideal case is unattainable, we can try to approximate it. We can look for ways of arranging spheres so that they cover space with minimal overlap [205], or look for ways of packing spheres with the least amount of space left over [52]. The centers of these spheres can then be used as the output points. The quantization regions will not be spheres, but they may be close approximations to spheres.

The problems of sphere covering and sphere packing are widely studied in a number of different areas. Lattices discovered in these studies have also been useful as vector quantizers [52]. Some of these lattices, such as the A_2 and D_2 lattices described earlier, are based on the root systems of Lie algebras [91]. The study of Lie algebras is beyond the scope of this book; however, we have included a brief discussion of the root systems and how to obtain the corresponding lattices in Appendix C.

One of the nice things about root lattices is that we can use their structural properties to obtain fast quantization algorithms. For example, consider building a quantizer based on the D_2 lattice. Because of the way in which we described the D_2 lattice, the size of the lattice is fixed. We can change the size by picking the basis vectors as (Δ, Δ) and $(\Delta, -\Delta)$, instead of $(1, 1)$ and $(1, -1)$. We can have exactly the same effect by dividing each input by Δ before quantization, and then multiplying the reconstruction values by Δ. Suppose we pick the latter approach and divide the components of the input vector by Δ. If we wanted to find the closest lattice point to the input, all we need to do is find the closest integer to each coordinate of the scaled input. If the sum of these integers is even, we have a lattice point. If not, find the coordinate that incurred the largest distortion during conversion to an integer and then find the next closest integer. The sum of coordinates of this new vector differs from the sum of coordinates of the previous vector by one. Therefore, if the sum of coordinates of the previous vector was odd, the sum of the coordinates of the current vector will be even, and we have the closest lattice point to the input.

Example 9.6.2:

Suppose the input vector is given by $(2.3, 1.9)$. Rounding each coefficient to the nearest integer, we get the vector $(2, 2)$. The sum of the coordinates is even; therefore, this is the closest lattice point to the input.

Suppose the input was $(3.4, 1.8)$. Rounding the components to the nearest integer, we get $(3, 2)$. The sum of the components is 5, which is odd. The differences between the components of the input vector and the nearest integer are 0.4 and 0.2. The largest difference was incurred by the first component, so we round it up to the next closest integer, and the resulting vector is $(4, 2)$. The sum of the coordinates is 6, which is even; therefore, this is the closest lattice point.   ◆

Many of the lattices have similar properties that can be used to develop fast algorithms for finding the closest output point to a given input [51, 91].

To review our coverage of lattice vector quantization, overload error can be reduced by careful selection of the boundary, and we can reduce the granular noise by selection of the lattice. The lattice also provides us with a way to avoid storage problems. Finally, we can use the structural properties of the lattice to find the closest lattice point to a given input.

Now we need two things: to know how to find the closest *output* point (remember, not all lattice points are output points), and to find a way of assigning a binary codeword to the output point and recovering the output point from the binary codeword. This can be done by again making use of the specific structures of the lattices. While the procedures necessary are simple, explanations of the procedures are lengthy and involved (see [53] and [91] for details).

9.7 Variations on the Theme

Because of its capability to provide high compression with relatively low distortion, vector quantization has been one of the more popular lossy compression techniques over the last decade in such diverse areas as video compression and low-rate speech compression. During this period, several people have come up with variations on the basic vector quantization approach. We briefly look at a few of the more well-known variations here, but this is by no means an exhaustive list. For more information, see [86] and [3].

9.7.1 Gain-Shape Vector Quantization

In some applications such as speech, the dynamic range of the input is quite large. One effect of this is that, in order to be able to represent the various vectors from the source, we need a very large codebook. This requirement can be reduced by normalizing the source output vectors, then quantizing the normalized vector and the normalization factor separately [35, 197]. In this way, the variation due to the dynamic range is represented by the normalization factor or *gain*, while the vector quantizer is free to do what it does best, which is to capture the structure in the source output. Vector quantizers that function in this manner are called *gain-shape vector quantizers*. The pyramid quantizer discussed earlier is an example of a gain-shape vector quantizer.

9.7.2 Mean-Removed Vector Quantization

If we were to generate a codebook from an image, differing amounts of background illumination would result in vastly different codebooks. This effect can be significantly reduced if we remove the mean from each vector before quantization. The mean and the mean-removed vector can then be quantized separately. The mean can be quantized using a scalar quantization scheme, while the mean-removed vector can be quantized using a vector quantizer. Of course, if this strategy is used, the vector quantizer should be designed using mean-removed vectors as well.

Example 9.7.1:

Let us encode the Sinan image using a codebook generated by the Sena image, as we did in Figure 9.16. However, this time we will use a mean-removed vector quantizer. The result is shown in Figure 9.26. For comparison we have also included the reconstructed image from Figure 9.16. Notice the annoying blotches on the shoulder have disappeared. However, the reconstructed image also suffers from more blockiness. The blockiness increases because adding the mean back into each block accentuates the discontinuity at the block boundaries.

FIGURE 9.26   **Left: Reconstructed image using mean-removed vector quantization and the Sena image as the training set. Right: LBG vector quantization with the Sena image as the training set.**

Each approach has its advantages and disadvantages. Which approach we use in a particular application depends very much on the application.   ◆

9.7.3 Classified Vector Quantization

We can sometimes divide the source output into separate classes with different spatial properties. In these cases, it can be very beneficial to design separate vector quantizers for the different classes. This approach, referred to as *classified vector quantization*, is especially useful in image compression, where edges and nonedge regions form two distinct classes. We can separate the training set into vectors that contain edges and vectors that do not. A separate vector quantizer can be developed for each class. During the encoding process, the vector is first tested to see if it contains an edge. A simple way to do this is to check the variance of the pixels in the vector. A large variance will indicate the presence of an edge. More sophisticated techniques for edge detection can also be used. Once the vector is classified, the corresponding codebook can be used to quantize the vector. The encoder transmits both the label for the codebook used and the label for the vector in the codebook [188].

A slight variation of this strategy is to use different kinds of quantizers for the different classes of vectors. For example, if certain classes of source outputs require quantization at a higher rate than is possible using LBG vector quantizers, we can use lattice vector quantizers. An example of this approach can be found in [187].

9.7.4 Multistage Vector Quantization

Multistage vector quantization [122] is an approach that reduces both the encoding complexity and the memory requirements for vector quantization, especially at high rates. In this approach, the input is quantized in several stages. In the first stage, a low-rate vector quantizer is used to generate a coarse approximation of the input. This coarse approximation, in the form of the label of the output point of the vector quantizer, is transmitted to the receiver. The error between the original input and the coarse representation is quantized by the second-stage quantizer, and the label of the output point is transmitted to the receiver. In this manner, the input to the nth-stage vector quantizer is the difference between the original input and the reconstruction obtained from the outputs of the preceding $n - 1$ stages. The difference between the input to a quantizer and the reconstruction value is often called the *residual*, and the multistage vector quantizers are also known as *residual vector quantizers* [16]. The reconstructed vector is the sum of the output points of each of the stages. Suppose we have a three-stage vector quantizer, with the three quantizers represented by $\mathbf{Q}_1, \mathbf{Q}_2$, and $\mathbf{Q}_3$. Then for a given input $\mathbf{X}$, we find

$$
\begin{aligned}
\mathbf{Y}_1 &= \mathbf{Q}_1(\mathbf{X}) \\
\mathbf{Y}_2 &= \mathbf{Q}_2(\mathbf{X} - \mathbf{Q}_1(\mathbf{X})) \\
\mathbf{Y}_3 &= \mathbf{Q}_3(\mathbf{X} - \mathbf{Q}_1(\mathbf{X}) - \mathbf{Q}_2(\mathbf{X} - \mathbf{Q}_1(\mathbf{X}))).
\end{aligned}
\tag{9.11}
$$

The reconstruction $\hat{\mathbf{X}}$ is given by

$$
\hat{\mathbf{X}} = \mathbf{Y}_1 + \mathbf{Y}_2 + \mathbf{Y}_3.
\tag{9.12}
$$

This process is shown in Figure 9.27.

If we have K stages, and the codebook size of the nth-stage vector quantizer is L_n, then the effective size of the overall codebook is $L_1 \times L_2 \times \cdots \times L_K$. However, we need to store only $L_1 + L_2 + \cdots + L_K$ vectors, which is also the number of comparisons required. Suppose we have a five-stage vector quantizer, each with a codebook size of 32, meaning that we would have to store 160 codewords. This would provide an effective codebook size of $32^5 = 33{,}554{,}432$. The computational savings are also of the same order.

This approach allows us to use vector quantization at much higher rates than we could otherwise. However, at rates at which it is feasible to use LBG vector quantizers, the performance of the multistage vector quantizers is generally lower than the LBG vector quantizers [86]. The reason for this is that after the first few stages, much of the structure used by the vector quantizer has been removed, and the vector quantization advantage that depends on this structure is not available. Details on the design of residual vector quantizers can be found in [16, 17].

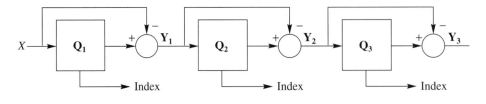

FIGURE 9.27   A three-stage vector quantizer.

There may be some vector inputs that can be well represented by fewer stages than others. A multistage vector quantizer with a variable number of stages can be implemented by extending the idea of recursively indexed scalar quantization to vectors. It is not possible to do this directly because there are some fundamental differences between scalar and vector quantizers. The input to a scalar quantizer is assumed to be *iid*. On the other hand, the vector quantizer can be viewed as a pattern-matching algorithm [84]. The input is assumed to be one of a number of different patterns. The scalar quantizer is used after the redundancy has been removed from the source sequence, while the vector quantizer takes advantage of the redundancy in the data.

With these differences in mind, the recursively indexed vector quantizer (RIVQ) can be described as a two-stage process. The first stage performs the normal pattern-matching function, while the second stage recursively quantizes the residual if the magnitude of the residual is greater than some prespecified threshold. The codebook of the second stage is ordered so that the magnitude of the codebook entries is a nondecreasing function of its index. We then choose an index I that will determine the mode in which the RIVQ operates.

The quantization rule Q, for a given input value $\mathbf{X}$, is as follows:

■ Quantize $\mathbf{X}$ with the first-stage quantizer Q_1.

■ If the residual $\|\mathbf{X} - \mathbf{Q}_1(\mathbf{X})\|$ is below a specified threshold, then $\mathbf{Q}_1(\mathbf{X})$ is the nearest output level.

■ Otherwise, generate $\mathbf{X}_1 = \mathbf{X} - \mathbf{Q}_1(\mathbf{X})$ and quantize using the second-stage quantizer $\mathbf{Q}_2$. Check if the index J_1 of the output is below the index I. If so,

$$\mathbf{Q}(\mathbf{X}) = \mathbf{Q}_1(\mathbf{X}) + \mathbf{Q}_2(\mathbf{X}_1).$$

If not, form

$$\mathbf{X}_2 = \mathbf{X}_1 - \mathbf{Q}(\mathbf{X}_1)$$

and do the same for $\mathbf{X}_2$ as we did for $\mathbf{X}_1$.

This process is repeated until for some m, the index J_m falls below the index I, in which case $\mathbf{X}$ will be quantized to

$$\mathbf{Q}(\mathbf{X}) = \mathbf{Q}_1(\mathbf{X}) + \mathbf{Q}_2(\mathbf{X}_1) + \cdots + \mathbf{Q}_2(\mathbf{X}_M).$$

Thus, the RIVQ operates in two modes: when the index J of the quantized input falls below a given index I and when the index J falls above the index I.

Details on the design and performance of the recursively indexed vector quantizer can be found in [9, 8].

9.7.5 Adaptive Vector Quantization

While LBG vector quantizers function by using the structure in the source output, this reliance on the use of the structure can also be a drawback when the characteristics of the source change over time. For situations like these, we would like to have the quantizer adapt to the changes in the source output.

For mean-removed and gain-shape vector quantizers, we can adapt the scalar aspect of the quantizer, that is, the quantization of the mean or the gain using the techniques discussed in the previous chapter. In this section, we look at a few approaches to adapting the codebook of the vector quantizer to changes in the characteristics of the input.

One way of adapting the codebook to changing input characteristics is to start with a very large codebook designed to accommodate a wide range of source characteristics [170]. This large codebook can be ordered in some manner known to both transmitter and receiver. Given a sequence of input vectors to be quantized, the encoder can select a subset of the larger codebook to be used. Information about which vectors from the large codebook were used can be transmitted as a binary string. For example, if the large codebook contained 10 vectors, and the encoder was to use the second, third, fifth, and ninth vectors, we would send the binary string 0110100010, with a 1 representing the position of the codeword used in the large codebook. This approach permits the use of a small codebook that is matched to the local behavior of the source.

This approach can be used with particular effectiveness with the recursively indexed vector quantizer [9]. Recall that in the recursively indexed vector quantizer, the quantized output is always within a prescribed distance of the inputs, determined by the index I. This means that the set of output values of the RIVQ can be viewed as an accurate representation of the inputs and their statistics. Therefore, we can treat a subset of the output set of the previous intervals as our large codebook. We can then use the method described in [170] to inform the receiver of which elements of the previous outputs form the codebook for the next interval. This method (while not the most efficient) is quite simple. Suppose an output set, in order of first appearance, is $\{p, a, q, s, l, t, r\}$, and the desired codebook for the interval to be encoded is $\{a, q, l, r\}$. Then we would transmit the binary string 0110101 to the receiver. The 1s correspond to the letters in the output set, which would be elements of the desired codebook. We select the subset for the current interval by finding the closest vectors from our collection of past outputs to the input vectors of the current set. This means that there is an inherent delay of one interval imposed by this approach. The overhead required to send the codebook selection is M/N, where M is the number of vectors in the output set and N is the interval size.

Another approach to updating the codebook is to check the distortion incurred while quantizing each input vector. Whenever this distortion is above some specified threshold, a different higher-rate mechanism is used to encode the input. The higher-rate mechanism might be the scalar quantization of each component, or the use of a high-rate lattice vector quantizer. This quantized representation of the input is transmitted to the receiver and, at the same time, added to both the encoder and decoder codebooks. In order to keep the size of the codebook the same, an entry must be discarded when a new vector is added to the codebook. Selecting an entry to discard is handled in a number of different ways. Variations of this approach have been used for speech coding, image coding, and video coding (see [175, 87, 94, 43, 234] for more details).

9.8 Trellis-Coded Quantization

Finally, we look at a quantization scheme that appears to be somewhat different from other vector quantization schemes. In fact, some may argue that it is not a vector quantizer at all. However, the trellis-coded quantization (TCQ) algorithm gets its performance advantage by exploiting the statistical structure exploited by the lattice vector quantizer. Therefore, we can argue that it should be classified as a vector quantizer.

The trellis-coded quantization algorithm was inspired by the appearance of a revolutionary concept in modulation called trellis-coded modulation (TCM). The TCQ algorithm and its entropy-constrained variants provide some of the best performance when encoding random sources. This quantizer can be viewed as a vector quantizer with very large dimension, but a restricted set of values for the components of the vectors.

Like a vector quantizer, the TCQ quantizes sequences of source outputs. Each element of a sequence is quantized using 2^R reconstruction levels selected from a set of 2^{R+1} reconstruction levels, where R is the number of bits per sample used by a trellis-coded quantizer. The 2^R element subsets are predefined; which particular subset is used is based on the reconstruction level used to quantize the previous quantizer input. However, the TCQ algorithm allows us to postpone a decision on which reconstruction level to use until we can look at a sequence of decisions. This way we can select the sequence of decisions that gives us the lowest amount of average distortion.

Let's take the case of a 2-bit quantizer. As described above, this means that we will need 2^3, or 8, reconstruction levels. Let's label these reconstruction levels as shown in Figure 9.28. The set of reconstruction levels is partitioned into two subsets: one consisting of the reconstruction values labeled $Q_{0,i}$ and $Q_{2,i}$, and the remainder comprising the second set. We use the first set to perform the quantization if the previous quantization level was one labeled $Q_{0,i}$ or $Q_{1,i}$; otherwise, we use the second set. Because the current reconstructed value defines the subset that can be used to perform the quantization on the next input, sometimes it may be advantageous to actually accept more distortion than necessary for the current sample in order to have less distortion in the next quantization step. In fact, at times it may be advantageous to accept poor quantization for several samples so that several samples down the line the quantization can result in less distortion. If you have followed this reasoning, you can see how we might be able to get lower overall distortion by looking at the quantization of an entire sequence of source outputs. The problem with delaying a decision is that the number of choices increases exponentially with each sample. In the 2-bit example, for the first sample we have four choices; for each of these four choices we have four choices for the second sample. For each of these 16 choices we have four choices for the third sample, and so on. Luckily, there is a technique that can be used to keep this explosive growth of choices under control. The technique, called the *Viterbi algorithm* [231], is widely used in error control coding.

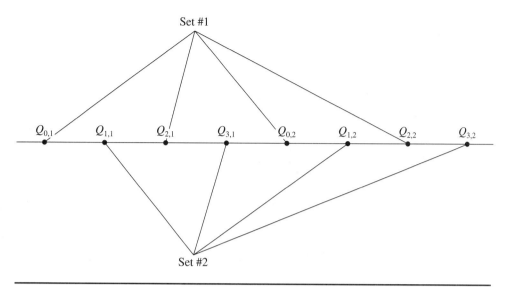

FIGURE 9.28   **Reconstruction levels for a 2-bit trellis-coded quantizer.**

In order to explain how the Viterbi algorithm works, we will need to formalize some of what we have been discussing. The sequence of choices can be viewed in terms of a state diagram. Let's suppose we have four states: S_0, S_1, S_2, and S_3. We will say we are in state S_k if we use the reconstruction levels $Q_{k,1}$ or $Q_{k,2}$. Thus, if we use the reconstruction levels $Q_{0,i}$, we are in state S_0. We have said that we use the elements of Set #1 if the previous quantization levels were $Q_{0,i}$ or $Q_{1,i}$. As Set #1 consists of the quantization levels $Q_{0,i}$ and $Q_{2,i}$, this means that we can go from state S_0 and S_1 to states S_0 and S_2. Similarly, from states S_2 and S_3 we can only go to states S_1 and S_3. The state diagram can be drawn as shown in Figure 9.29.

Let's suppose we go through two sequences of choices that converge to the same state, after which both sequences are identical. This means that the sequence of choices that had incurred a higher distortion at the time the two sequences converged will have a higher distortion from then on. In the end we will select the sequence of choices that results in the lowest distortion; therefore, there is no point in continuing to keep track of a sequence that we will discard anyway. This means that whenever two sequences of choices converge, we can discard one of them. How often does this happen? In order to see this, let's introduce time into our state diagram. The state diagram with the element of time introduced into it is called a *trellis diagram*. The trellis for this particular example is shown in Figure 9.30. At each time instant, we can go from one state to two other states. And, at each step we have two sequences that converge to each state. If we discard one of the two sequences that converge to each state, we can see that, no matter how long a sequence of decisions we use, we will always end up with four sequences.

Notice that, assuming the initial state is known to the decoder, any path through this particular trellis can be described to the decoder using 1 bit per sample. From each state we can only go to two other states. In Figure 9.31, we have marked the branches with the bits used to signal that transition. Given that each state corresponds to two quantization levels, specifying

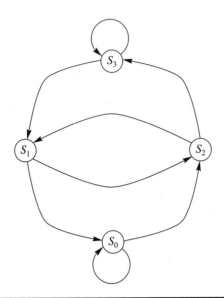

FIGURE 9.29   State diagram for the selection process.

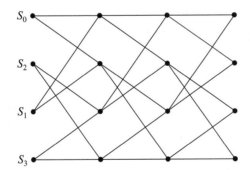

FIGURE 9.30   Trellis diagram for the selection process.

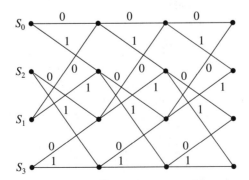

FIGURE 9.31   Trellis diagram for the selection process with binary labels for the state transitions.

the quantization level for each sample would require an additional bit, resulting in a total of 2 bits per sample. Let's see how all this works together in an example.

Example 9.8.1:

Using the quantizer whose quantization levels are shown in Figure 9.32, we will quantize the sequence of values 0.2, 1.6, 2.3. For the distortion measure we will use the sum of absolute differences. If we simply used the quantization levels marked as Set #1 in Figure 9.28, we would quantize 0.2 to the reconstruction value 0.5, for a distortion of 0.3. The second sample value of 1.6 would be quantized to 2.5, and the third sample value of 2.3 would also be quantized to 2.5, resulting in a total distortion of 1.4. If we used Set #2 to quantize these values, we would end up with a total distortion of 1.6. Let's see how much distortion results when using the TCQ algorithm.

We start by quantizing the first sample using the two quantization levels $Q_{0,1}$ and $Q_{0,2}$. The reconstruction level $Q_{0,2}$, or 0.5, is closer and results in an absolute difference of 0.3. We mark this on the first node corresponding to S_0. We then quantize the first sample using $Q_{1,1}$ and $Q_{1,2}$. The closest reconstruction value is $Q_{1,2}$, or 1.5, which results in a distortion value of 1.3. We mark the first node corresponding to S_1. Continuing in this manner, we get a distortion value of 1.7 when we use the reconstruction levels corresponding to state S_2 and a distortion value of 0.7 when we use the reconstruction levels corresponding to state S_3. At this point the trellis looks like Figure 9.33. Now we move on to the second sample. Let's first quantize the second sample value of 1.6 using the quantization levels associated with state S_0. The reconstruction levels associated with state S_0 are -3.5 and 0.5. The closest value to 1.6 is 0.5. This results in an absolute difference for the second sample of 1.1. We can reach S_0 from S_0 and from S_1. If we accept the first sample reconstruction corresponding to S_0, we will end up with an accumulated distortion of 1.4. If we accept the reconstruction corresponding to state S_1, we get an accumulated distortion of 2.4. Since the accumulated distortion is less if we accept the transition from state S_0, we do so and discard the transition from state S_1. Continuing in this fashion for the remaining states, we end up with the situation depicted in Figure 9.34. The sequence of decisions that have been terminated are shown by an X on the branch corresponding to the particular transition. The accumulated distortion is listed at each node. Repeating this procedure for the third sample value of 2.3, we obtain the trellis shown in Figure 9.35. If we wanted to terminate the algorithm at this time, we could pick the sequence of decisions with the smallest accumulated distortion. In this particular example, the sequence would be S_3, S_1, S_2. The accumulated distortion is 1.0, which is less than what we would have obtained using either Set #1 or Set #2.

$Q_{0,1}$	$Q_{1,1}$	$Q_{2,1}$	$Q_{3,1}$	$Q_{0,2}$	$Q_{1,2}$	$Q_{2,2}$	$Q_{3,2}$
-3.5	-2.5	-1.5	-0.5	0.5	1.5	2.5	3.5

FIGURE 9.32 **Reconstruction levels for a 2-bit trellis-coded quantizer.**

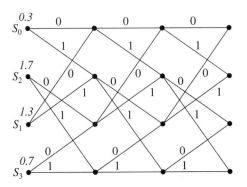

FIGURE 9.33   Quantizing the first sample.

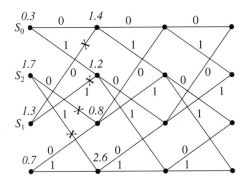

FIGURE 9.34   Quantizing the second sample.

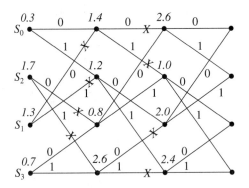

FIGURE 9.35   Quantizing the third sample.   ◆

9.9   Summary

In this chapter we introduced the technique of vector quantization. We have seen how we can make use of the structure exhibited by groups, or vectors, of values to obtain compression. Because there are different kinds of structure in different kinds of data, there are a number of different ways to design vector quantizers. Because data from many sources, when viewed as vectors, tend to form clusters, we can design quantizers that essentially consist of representations of these clusters. We also described aspects of the design of vector quantizers and looked at some applications. Recent literature in this area is substantial, and we have barely skimmed the surface of the large number of interesting variations of this technique.

Further Reading

The subject of vector quantization is dealt with extensively in the book *Vector Quantization and Signal Compression*, by A. Gersho and R.M. Gray [86]. There is also an excellent collection of papers called *Vector Quantization*, edited by H. Abut and published by IEEE Press [3].

There are a number of excellent tutorial articles on this subject:

1. "Vector Quantization," by R.M. Gray, in the April 1984 issue of *IEEE Transactions on Acoustics, Speech, and Signal Processing* [97].

2. "Vector Quantization: A Pattern Matching Technique for Speech Coding," by A. Gersho and V. Cuperman, in the December 1983 issue of *IEEE Communications Magazine* [84].

3. "Vector Quantization in Speech Coding," by J. Makhoul, S. Roucos, and H. Gish, in the November 1985 issue of the *Proceedings of the IEEE* [146].

4. "Vector Quantization," by P.F. Swaszek, in *Communications and Networks*, edited by I.F. Blake and H.V. Poor [221].

5. A survey of various image-coding applications of vector quantization can be found in "Image Coding Using Vector Quantization: A Review," by N.M. Nasrabadi and R.A. King, in the August 1988 issue of the *IEEE Transactions on Communications* [166].

6. A thorough review of lattice vector quantization can be found in "Lattice Quantization," by J.D. Gibson and K. Sayood, in *Advances in Electronics and Electron Physics* [91].

The area of vector quantization is an active one, and new techniques that use vector quantization are continually being developed. The journals that report work in this area include *IEEE Transactions on Information Theory, IEEE Transactions on Communications, IEEE Transactions on Signal Processing*, and *IEEE Transactions on Image Processing*, among others.

9.10 Projects and Problems

1. In Example 9.3.2 we increased the SNR by about 0.3 dB by moving the top-left output point to the origin. What would happen if we moved the output points at the four corners to the positions $(\pm\Delta, 0)$, $(0, \pm\Delta)$. As in the example, assume the input has a Laplacian distribution with mean zero and variance one, and $\Delta = 0.7309$. You can obtain the answer analytically or through simulation.

2. For the quantizer of the previous problem, rather than moving the output points to $(\pm\Delta, 0)$ and $(0, \pm\Delta)$, we could have moved them to other positions that might have provided a larger increase in SNR. Write a program to test different (reasonable) possibilities and report on the best and worst cases.

3. In the program `trainvq.c` the empty cell problem is resolved by replacing the vector with no associated training set vectors with a training set vector from the quantization region with the largest number of vectors. In this problem, we will investigate some possible alternatives.

Generate a sequence of pseudorandom numbers with a triangular distribution between 0 and 2. (You can obtain a random number with a triangular distribution by adding two uniformly distributed random numbers.) Design an eight-level, two-dimensional vector quantizer with the initial codebook shown in Table 9.9.

(a) Use the `trainvq` program to generate a codebook with 10,000 random numbers as the training set. Comment on the final codebook you obtain. Plot the elements of the codebook and discuss why they ended up where they did.

(b) Modify the program so that the empty cell vector is replaced with a vector from the quantization region with the largest distortion. Comment on any changes in the distortion (or lack of change). Is the final codebook different from the one you obtained earlier?

(c) Modify the program so that whenever an empty cell problem arises, a two-level quantizer is designed for the quantization region with the largest number of output points. Comment on any differences in the codebook and distortion from the previous two cases.

TABLE 9.9   **Initial codebook for Problem 3.**

1	1
1	2
1	0.5
0.5	1
0.5	0.5
1.5	1
2	5
3	3

4. Generate a 16-dimensional codebook of size 64 for the Sena image. Construct the vector as a 4×4 block of pixels, an 8×2 block of pixels, and a 16×1 block of pixels. Comment on the differences in the mean squared errors and the quality of the reconstructed images. You can use the program `trvqsp_img` to obtain the codebooks.

5. In Example 9.6.1 we designed a 60-level two-dimensional quantizer by taking the two-dimensional representation of an 8-level scalar quantizer, removing 12 output points from the 64 output points, and adding 8 points in other locations. Assume the input is Laplacian with zero mean and unit variance, and $\Delta = 0.7309$.

(a) Calculate the increase in the probability of overload by the removal of the 12 points from the original 64.

(b) Calculate the decrease in overload probability when we added the 8 new points to the remaining 52 points.

6. In this problem we will compare the performance of a 16-dimensional pyramid vector quantizer and a 16-dimensional LBG vector quantizer for two different sources. In each case the codebook for the pyramid vector quantizer consists of 272 elements:

- 32 vectors with 1 element equal to $\pm\Delta$, and the other 15 equal to zero, and
- 240 vectors with 2 elements equal to $\pm\Delta$ and the other 14 equal to zero.

The value of Δ should be adjusted to give the best performance. The codebook for the LBG vector quantizer will be obtained by using the program `trvqsp_img` on the source output. You will have to modify `trvqsp_img` slightly to give you a codebook that is not a power of two.

(a) Use the two quantizers to quantize a sequence of 10,000 zero mean unit variance Laplacian random numbers. Using either the mean squared error or the SNR as a measure of performance, compare the performance of the two quantizers.

(b) Use the two quantizers to quantize the Sinan image. Compare the two quantizers using either the mean squared error or the SNR and the reconstructed image. Compare the difference between the performance of the two quantizers with the difference when the input was random.

10

Differential Encoding

10.1 Overview

Sources such as speech and images have a great deal of correlation from sample to sample. We can use this fact to predict each sample based on its past and only encode and transmit the differences between the prediction and the sample value. Differential encoding schemes are built around this premise. Because the prediction techniques are rather simple, these schemes are much easier to implement than other compression schemes. In this chapter, we will look at various components of differential encoding schemes and study how they are used to encode sources—in particular, speech. We will also look at a widely used international differential encoding standard for speech encoding.

10.2 Introduction

In the last chapter we looked at vector quantization—a rather complex scheme requiring a significant amount of computational resources—as one way of taking advantage of the structure in the data to perform lossy compression. In this chapter, we look at a different approach that uses the structure in the source output in a slightly different manner, resulting in a significantly less complex system.

When we design a quantizer for a given source, the size of the quantization interval depends on the variance of the input. If we assume the input is uniformly distributed, the variance depends on the dynamic range of the input. In turn, the size of the quantization interval determines the amount of quantization noise incurred during the quantization process.

In many sources of interest, the sampled source output $\{x_n\}$ does not change a great deal from one sample to the next. This means that both the dynamic range and the variance of the sequence of differences $\{d_n = x_n - x_{n-1}\}$ are significantly smaller than that of the source output sequence. Furthermore, for correlated sources the distribution of d_n is highly peaked at zero. We made use of this skew, and resulting loss in entropy, for the lossless compression of images in Chapter 6. Given the relationship between the variance of the quantizer input and the incurred quantization error, it is also useful, in terms of lossy compression, to look at ways to encode the difference from one sample to the next rather than encoding the actual sample value. Techniques that transmit information by encoding differences are called *differential encoding techniques*.

Example 10.2.1:

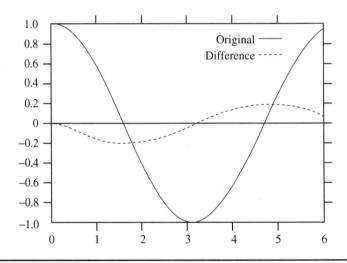

FIGURE 10.1   Sinusoid and sample-to-sample differences.

Consider the half cycle of a sinusoid shown in Figure 10.1 that has been sampled at the rate of 30 samples per cycle. The value of the sinusoid ranges between 1 and -1. If we wanted to quantize the sinusoid using a uniform four-level quantizer, we would use a step size of 0.5, which would result in quantization errors in the range $[-0.25, 0.25]$. If we take the sample-to-sample differences (excluding the first sample), the differences lie in the range $[-0.2, 0.2]$. To quantize this range of values with a four-level quantizer requires a step size of 0.1, which results in quantization noise in the range $[-0.05, 0.05]$.   ◆

The sinusoidal signal in the previous example is somewhat contrived. However, if we look at some of the real-world sources that we want to encode, we see that the dynamic range that contains most of the differences is significantly smaller than the dynamic range of the source output.

Example 10.2.2:

Figure 10.2 is the histogram of the Sinan image. Notice that the pixel values vary over almost the entire range of 0 to 255. To represent these values exactly, we need 8 bits per pixel. To represent these values in a lossy manner to within an error in the least significant bit, we need 7 bits per pixel. Figure 10.3 is the histogram of the differences.

More than 99% of the pixel values lie in the range −31 to 31. Therefore, if we were willing to accept distortion in the least significant bit, for more than 99% of the difference values we need 5 bits per pixel rather than 7. In fact, if we were willing to have a small percentage of the differences with a larger error, we could get by with 4 bits for each difference value.   ◆

FIGURE 10.2   Histogram of the Sinan image.

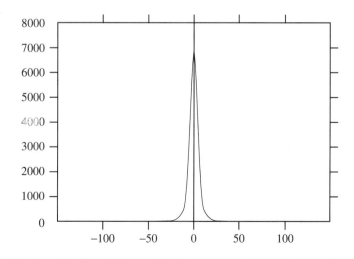

FIGURE 10.3   Histogram of pixel-to-pixel differences of the Sinan image.

In both examples, we have shown that the dynamic range of the differences between samples is substantially less than the dynamic range of the source output. In the following sections we describe encoding schemes that take advantage of this fact to provide improved compression performance.

10.3 The Basic Algorithm

Although it takes fewer bits to encode differences than it takes to encode the original pixel, we have not said whether it is possible to recover an acceptable reproduction of the original sequence from the quantized difference value. When we were looking at lossless compression schemes, we found that if we encoded and transmitted the first value of a sequence, followed by the encoding of the differences between samples, we could losslessly recover the original sequence. Unfortunately, a strictly analogous situation does not exist for lossy compression.

Example 10.3.1:

Suppose a source puts out the sequence

$$6.2 \ 9.7 \ 13.2 \ 5.9 \ 8 \ 7.4 \ 4.2 \ 1.8$$

We could generate the following sequence by taking the difference between samples (assume that the first sample value is zero):

$$6.2 \ 3.5 \ 3.5 \ -7.3 \ 2.1 \ -0.6 \ -3.2 \ -2.4$$

If we losslessly encoded these values, we could recover the original sequence at the receiver by adding back the difference values. For example, to obtain the second reconstructed value, we add the difference 3.5 to the first received value 6.2 to obtain a value of 9.7. The third reconstructed value can be obtained by adding the received difference value of 3.5 to the second reconstructed value of 9.7, resulting in a value of 13.2, which is the same as the third value in the original sequence. Thus, by adding the nth received difference value to the $(n-1)$th reconstruction value, we can recover the original sequence exactly.

Now let us look at what happens if these difference values are encoded using a lossy scheme. Suppose we had a seven-level quantizer with output values $-6, -4, -2, 0, 2, 4, 6$. The quantized sequence would be

$$6 \ 4 \ 4 \ -6 \ 2 \ 0 \ -4 \ -2$$

If we follow the same procedure for reconstruction as we did for the lossless compression scheme, we get the sequence

$$6 \ 10 \ 14 \ 8 \ 10 \ 10 \ 6 \ 4$$

The difference or error between the original sequence and the reconstructed sequence is

$$0.2 \ -0.3 \ -0.8 \ -2.1 \ -2 \ -2.6 \ -1.8 \ -2.2$$

Notice that initially the magnitudes of the error are quite small $(0.2, 0.3)$. As the reconstruction progresses, the magnitudes of the error become significantly larger $(2.6, 1.8, 2.2)$. ◆

To see what is happening, consider a sequence $\{x_n\}$. A difference sequence $\{d_n\}$ is generated by taking the differences $x_n - x_{n-1}$. This difference sequence is quantized to obtain the sequence $\{\hat{d}_n\}$:

$$\hat{d}_n = Q[d_n] = d_n + q_n$$

where q_n is the quantization error. At the receiver, the reconstructed sequence $\{\hat{x}_n\}$ is obtained by adding $\hat{d}_n$ to the previous reconstructed value $\hat{x}_{n-1}$:

$$\hat{x}_n = \hat{x}_{n-1} + \hat{d}_n.$$

Let us assume that both transmitter and receiver start with the same value x_0, that is, $\hat{x}_0 = x_0$. Follow the quantization and reconstruction process for the first few samples:

$$d_1 = x_1 - x_0 \tag{10.1}$$
$$\hat{d}_1 = Q[d_1] = d_1 + q_1 \tag{10.2}$$
$$\hat{x}_1 = x_0 + \hat{d}_1 = x_0 + d_1 + q_1 = x_1 + q_1 \tag{10.3}$$
$$d_2 = x_2 - x_1 \tag{10.4}$$
$$\hat{d}_2 = Q[d_2] = d_2 + q_2 \tag{10.5}$$
$$\hat{x}_2 = \hat{x}_1 + \hat{d}_2 = x_1 + q_1 + d_2 + q_2 \tag{10.6}$$
$$= x_2 + q_1 + q_2. \tag{10.7}$$

Continuing this process, at the nth iteration we get

$$\hat{x}_n = x_n + \sum_{k=1}^{n} q_k. \tag{10.8}$$

We can see that the quantization error accumulates as the process continues. Theoretically, if the quantization error process is zero mean, the errors will cancel each other out in the long run. In practice, often long before that can happen, the finite precision of the machines causes the reconstructed value to overflow.

Notice that the encoder and decoder are operating with different pieces of information. The encoder generates the difference sequence based on the original sample values, while the decoder adds back the quantized difference onto a distorted version of the original signal. We can solve this problem by forcing both encoder and decoder to use the same information during the differencing and reconstruction operations. The only information available to the receiver about the sequence $\{x_n\}$ is the reconstructed sequence $\{\hat{x}_n\}$. As this information is also available to the transmitter, we can modify the differencing operation to use the reconstructed value of the previous sample, instead of the previous sample itself, that is,

$$d_n = x_n - \hat{x}_{n-1}. \tag{10.9}$$

Using this new differencing operation, let's repeat our examination of the quantization and reconstruction process. We again assume that $\hat{x}_0 = x_0$.

$$d_1 = x_1 - x_0 \tag{10.10}$$
$$\hat{d}_1 = Q[d_1] = d_1 + q_1 \tag{10.11}$$
$$\hat{x}_1 = x_0 + \hat{d}_1 = x_0 + d_1 + q_1 = x_1 + q_1 \tag{10.12}$$
$$d_2 = x_2 - \hat{x}_1 \tag{10.13}$$
$$\hat{d}_2 = Q[d_2] = d_2 + q_2 \tag{10.14}$$
$$\hat{x}_2 = \hat{x}_1 + \hat{d}_2 = \hat{x}_1 + d_2 + q_2 \tag{10.15}$$
$$= x_2 + q_2 \tag{10.16}$$

At the nth iteration we have

$$\hat{x}_n = x_n + q_n, \tag{10.17}$$

and there is no accumulation of the quantization noise. In fact, the quantization noise in the nth reconstructed sequence is the quantization noise incurred by the quantization of the nth difference. The quantization error for the difference sequence is substantially less than the quantization error for the original sequence. Therefore, this procedure leads to an overall reduction of the quantization error. If we are satisfied with the quantization error for a given number of bits per sample, then we can use fewer bits with a differential encoding procedure to attain the same distortion.

Example 10.3.2:

Let us try to quantize and then reconstruct the sinusoid of Example 10.2.1 using the two different differencing approaches. Using the first approach, we get a dynamic range of differences from -0.2 to 0.2. Therefore, we use a quantizer step size of 0.1. In the second approach, the differences lie in the range $[-0.4, 0.4]$. In order to cover this range, we use a step size in the quantizer of 0.2. The reconstructed signals are shown in Figure 10.4.

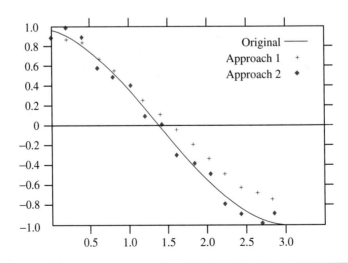

FIGURE 10.4   **Sinusoid and reconstructions.**

Notice in the first case that the reconstruction diverges from the signal as we process more and more of the signal. Although the second differencing approach uses a larger step size, this approach provides a more accurate representation of the input. ◆

A block diagram of the differential encoding system as we have described it to this point is shown in Figure 10.5. We have drawn a dotted box around the portion of the encoder that mimics the decoder. The encoder must mimic the decoder in order to obtain a copy of the reconstructed sample used to generate the next difference.

We would like our difference value to be as small as possible. For this to happen, given the system we have described to this point, $\hat{x}_{n-1}$ should be as close to x_n as possible. However, $\hat{x}_{n-1}$ is the reconstructed value of x_{n-1}; therefore, we would like $\hat{x}_{n-1}$ to be close to x_{n-1}. Unless x_{n-1} is always very close to x_n, some function of past values of the reconstructed sequence can often provide a better prediction of x_n. We will look at some of these *predictor* functions later in this chapter. For now, let's modify Figure 10.5 and replace the delay block with a predictor block to obtain our basic differential encoding system as shown in Figure 10.6. The output of the predictor is the prediction sequence $\{p_n\}$ given by

$$p_n = f(\hat{x}_{n-1}, \hat{x}_{n-2}, \ldots, \hat{x}_0). \tag{10.18}$$

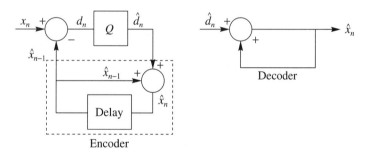

FIGURE 10.5   A simple differential encoding system.

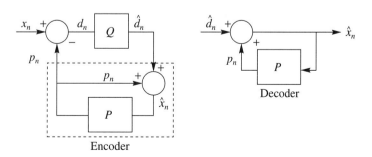

FIGURE 10.6   The basic algorithm.

This basic differential encoding system is known as the differential pulse code modulation (DPCM) system. The DPCM system was developed at Bell Laboratories a few years after World War II [57]. It is most popular as a speech-encoding system and is widely used in telephone communications.

As we can see from Figure 10.6, the DPCM system consists of two major components, the predictor and the quantizer. The study of DPCM is basically the study of these two components. In the following sections, we will look at various predictor and quantizer designs and see how they function together in a differential encoding system.

10.4 Prediction in DPCM

Differential encoding systems like DPCM gain their advantage by the reduction in the variance and dynamic range of the difference sequence. How much the variance is reduced depends on how well the predictor can predict the next symbol based on the past reconstructed symbols. In this section we will mathematically formulate the prediction problem. The analytical solution to this problem will give us one of the more widely used approaches to the design of the predictor. In order to follow this development, some familiarity with the mathematical concepts of expectation and correlation is needed. These concepts are described in Appendix A.

Define σ_d^2, the variance of the difference sequence, as

$$\sigma_d^2 = E[(x_n - p_n)^2] \qquad (10.19)$$

where $E[\ ]$ is the expectation operator. As the predictor outputs p_n are given by (10.18), the design of a good predictor is essentially the selection of the function $f(\cdot)$ that minimizes σ_d^2. One problem with this formulation is that $\hat{x}_n$ is given by

$$\hat{x}_n = x_n + q_n$$

and q_n depends on the variance of d_n. Thus, by picking $f(\cdot)$, we affect σ_d^2, which in turn affects the reconstruction $\hat{x}_n$, which then affects the selection of $f(\cdot)$. This coupling makes an explicit solution extremely difficult for even the most well-behaved source [81]. As most real sources are far from well behaved, the problem becomes computationally intractable in most applications.

We can avoid this problem by making an assumption known as the *fine quantization assumption*. We assume that quantizer step sizes are so small that we can replace $\hat{x}_n$ by x_n, and therefore

$$p_n = f(x_{n-1}, x_{n-2}, \ldots, x_0). \qquad (10.20)$$

Once the function $f(\cdot)$ has been found, we can use it with the reconstructed values $\hat{x}_n$ to obtain p_n. If we now assume that the output of the source is a stationary process, from the study of random processes [216], we know that the function that minimizes σ_d^2 is the conditional expectation $E[x_n \mid x_{n-1}, x_{n-2}, \ldots, x_0]$. Unfortunately, the assumption of stationarity is generally not true, and even if it were, finding this conditional expectation requires the knowledge of nth-order conditional probabilities, which would generally not be available.

Given the difficulty of finding the best solution, in many applications we simplify the problem by restricting the predictor function to be linear. That is, the prediction p_n is given by

$$p_n = \sum_{i=1}^{N} a_i \hat{x}_{n-i}. \tag{10.21}$$

The value of N specifies the order of the predictor. Using the fine quantization assumption, we can now write the predictor design problem as follows: Find the $\{a_i\}$ so as to minimize σ_d^2.

$$\sigma_d^2 = E\left[\left(x_n - \sum_{i=1}^{N} a_i x_{n-i}\right)^2\right] \tag{10.22}$$

where we assume that the source sequence is a realization of a real valued wide sense stationary process. Take the derivative of σ_d^2 with respect to each of the a_i and set this equal to zero. We get N equations and N unknowns:

$$\frac{\delta \sigma_d^2}{\delta a_1} = -2E\left[\left(x_n - \sum_{i=1}^{N} a_i x_{n-i}\right) x_{n-1}\right] = 0 \tag{10.23}$$

$$\frac{\delta \sigma_d^2}{\delta a_2} = -2E\left[\left(x_n - \sum_{i=1}^{N} a_i x_{n-i}\right) x_{n-2}\right] = 0 \tag{10.24}$$

$$\vdots \quad \vdots$$

$$\frac{\delta \sigma_d^2}{\delta a_N} = -2E\left[\left(x_n - \sum_{i=1}^{N} a_i x_{n-i}\right) x_{n-N}\right] = 0. \tag{10.25}$$

Taking the expectations, we can rewrite these equations as

$$\sum_{i=1}^{N} a_i R_{xx}(i-1) = R_{xx}(1) \tag{10.26}$$

$$\sum_{i=1}^{N} a_i R_{xx}(i-2) = R_{xx}(2) \tag{10.27}$$

$$\vdots \quad \vdots$$

$$\sum_{i=1}^{N} a_i R_{xx}(i-N) = R_{xx}(N) \tag{10.28}$$

where $R_{xx}(k)$ is the autocorrelation function of x_n:

$$R_{xx}(k) = E[x_n x_{n+k}]. \tag{10.29}$$

We can write these equations in matrix form as

$$\mathbf{RA} = \mathbf{P} \tag{10.30}$$

where

$$\mathbf{R} = \begin{bmatrix} R_{xx}(0) & R_{xx}(1) & R_{xx}(2) & \cdots & R_{xx}(N-1) \\ R_{xx}(1) & R_{xx}(0) & R_{xx}(1) & \cdots & R_{xx}(N-2) \\ R_{xx}(2) & R_{xx}(1) & R_{xx}(0) & \cdots & R_{xx}(N-3) \\ \vdots & \vdots & & & \vdots \\ R_{xx}(N-1) & R_{xx}(N-2) & R_{xx}(N-3) & \cdots & R_{xx}(0) \end{bmatrix} \tag{10.31}$$

$$\mathbf{A} = \begin{bmatrix} a_1 \\ a_2 \\ a_3 \\ \vdots \\ a_N \end{bmatrix} \tag{10.32}$$

$$\mathbf{P} = \begin{bmatrix} R_{xx}(1) \\ R_{xx}(2) \\ R_{xx}(3) \\ \vdots \\ R_{xx}(N) \end{bmatrix} \tag{10.33}$$

where we have used the fact that $R_{xx}(-k) = R_{xx}(k)$ for real valued wide sense stationary processes. These equations are referred to as the discrete form of the Wiener-Hopf equations. If we know the autocorrelation values $\{R_{xx}(k)\}$ for $k = 0, 1, \ldots, N$, then we can find the predictor coefficients as

$$\mathbf{A} = \mathbf{R}^{-1}\mathbf{P}. \tag{10.34}$$

Example 10.4.1:

For the speech sequence shown in Figure 10.7, let us find predictors of orders one, two, and three and examine their performance. We begin by estimating the autocorrelation values from the data. Given M data points, we use the following average to find the value for $R_{xx}(k)$:

$$R_{xx}(k) = \frac{1}{M-k} \sum_{i=1}^{M-k} x_i x_{i+k}. \tag{10.35}$$

Using these autocorrelation values, we obtain the following coefficients for the three different predictors. For $N = 1$, the predictor coefficient is $a_1 = 0.66$; for $N = 2$, the coefficients are $a_1 = 0.596$, $a_2 = 0.096$; and for $N = 3$, the coefficients are $a_1 = 0.577$, $a_2 = -0.025$, and $a_3 = 0.204$. We used these coefficients to generate the residual sequence. In order to see the reduction in variance, we computed the ratio of the source output variance to the variance of the residual sequence. For comparison, we also computed this ratio for the case where the residual sequence is obtained by taking the difference of neighboring samples. The sample-to-sample differences resulted in a ratio of 1.63. Compared to this, the ratio of the input variance to the variance of the residuals from the first-order predictor was 2.04. With a second-order predictor, this ratio rose to 3.37, and with a third-order predictor, the ratio was 6.28.

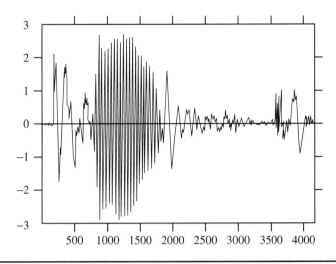

FIGURE 10.7   **A segment of speech: a male speaker saying the word "test."**

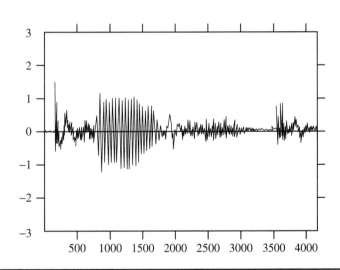

FIGURE 10.8   **The residual sequence using a third-order predictor.**

The residual sequence for the third-order predictor is shown in Figure 10.8. Notice that although there has been a reduction in the dynamic range, there is still substantial structure in the residual sequence, especially in the range of samples from about the 700th sample to the 2000th sample. We will look at ways of removing this structure when we discuss speech coding.

Let us now introduce a quantizer into the loop and look at the performance of the DPCM system. For simplicity, we will use a uniform quantizer. If we look at the histogram of the residual sequence, we find that it is highly peaked. Therefore, we will assume that the input to the quantizer will be Laplacian. We will also adjust the step size of the quantizer based on

TABLE 10.1   **Performance of DPCM system with different predictors and quantizers.**

Quantizer	Predictor Order	SNR (dB)	SPER (dB)
Four-level	None	2.43	0
	1	3.37	2.65
	2	8.35	5.9
	3	8.74	6.1
Eight-level	None	3.65	0
	1	3.87	2.74
	2	9.81	6.37
	3	10.16	6.71

the variance of the residual. The step sizes provided in Chapter 8 are based on the assumption that the quantizer input has a unit variance. It is easy to show that when the variance differs from unity, the optimal step size can be obtained by multiplying the step size for a variance of one with the standard deviation of the input. Using this approach for a four-level Laplacian quantizer, we obtain step sizes of 0.75, 0.59, and 0.43 for the first-, second-, and third-order predictors, and step sizes of 0.3, 0.4, and 0.5 for an eight-level Laplacian quantizer. We measure the performance using two different measures, the signal-to-noise ratio (SNR) and the signal-to-prediction-error ratio. These are defined as follows:

$$SNR(dB) = \frac{\sum_{i=1}^{M} x_i^2}{\sum_{i=1}^{M} (x_i - \hat{x}_i)^2} \tag{10.36}$$

$$SPER(dB) = \frac{\sum_{i=1}^{M} x_i^2}{\sum_{i=1}^{M} (x_i - p_i)^2}. \tag{10.37}$$

The results are tabulated in Table 10.1. For comparison we have also included the results when no prediction is used; that is, we directly quantize the input. Notice the large difference between using a first-order predictor and a second-order predictor, and then the relatively minor increase when going from a second-order predictor to a third-order predictor. This is fairly typical when using a fixed quantizer.

Finally, let's take a look at the reconstructed speech signal. The speech coded using a third-order predictor and an eight-level quantizer is shown in Figure 10.9. Although the reconstructed sequence looks like the original, notice that there is significant distortion in areas where the source output values are small. This is because in these regions the input to the quantizer is close to zero. Because the quantizer does not have a zero output level, the output of the quantizer flips between the two inner levels. If we listened to this signal, we would hear a hissing sound in the reconstructed signal.

The speech signal used to generate this example is contained among the data sets accompanying this book in the file `testm.raw`. The function `readau.c` can be used to read the file. You are encouraged to reproduce the results in this example and listen to the resulting reconstructions.   ◆

If we look at the speech sequence in Figure 10.7, we can see that there are several distinct segments of speech. Between sample number 700 and sample number 2000, the speech looks

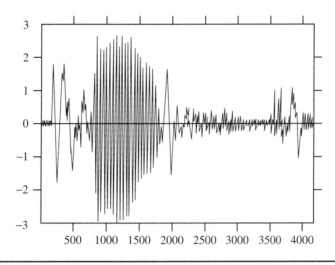

FIGURE 10.9   **The reconstructed sequence using a third-order predictor and an eight-level uniform quantizer.**

periodic. Between sample number 2200 and sample number 3500, the speech is low amplitude and noiselike. Given the distinctly different characteristics in these two regions, it would make sense to use different approaches to encode these segments. Some approaches to dealing with these issues are specific to speech coding, and we will discuss these approaches when we specifically discuss encoding speech using DPCM. However, the problem is also much more widespread than when encoding speech. A general response to the nonstationarity of the input is the use of adaptation in prediction. We will look at some of these approaches in the next section.

10.5   Adaptive DPCM

As DPCM consists of two main components, the quantizer and the predictor, making DPCM adaptive means making the quantizer and the predictor adaptive. Recall that we can adapt a system based on its input or output. The former approach is called forward adaptation; the latter, backward adaptation. In the case of forward adaptation, the parameters of the system are updated based on the input to the encoder, which is not available to the decoder. Therefore, the updated parameters have to be sent to the decoder as side information. In the case of backward adaptation, the adaptation is based on the output of the encoder. As this output is also available to the decoder, there is no need for transmission of side information.

In cases where the predictor is adaptive, especially when it is backward adaptive, we generally use adaptive quantizers (forward or backward). The reason for this is that the backward adaptive predictor is adapted based on the quantized outputs. If for some reason the predictor does not adapt properly at some point, this results in predictions that are far from the input, and the residuals will be large. In a fixed quantizer, these large residuals will tend to fall in the overload regions with consequently unbounded quantization errors. The reconstructed values with these large errors will then be used to adapt the predictor, which will result in the predictor moving further and further from the input.

The same constraint is not present for quantization, and we can have adaptive quantization with fixed predictors.

10.5.1 Adaptive Quantization in DPCM

In forward adaptive quantization, the input is divided into blocks. The quantizer parameters are estimated for each block. These parameters are transmitted to the receiver as side information. In DPCM, the quantizer is in a feedback loop, which means that the input to the quantizer is not conveniently available in a form that can be used for forward adaptive quantization. Therefore, most DPCM systems use backward adaptive quantization.

The backward adaptive quantization used in DPCM systems is basically a variation of the backward adaptive Jayant quantizer described in Chapter 8. In Chapter 8, the Jayant algorithm was used to adapt the quantizer to a stationary input. In DPCM, the algorithm is used to adapt the quantizer to the local behavior of nonstationary inputs. Consider the speech segment shown in Figure 10.7 and the residual sequence shown in Figure 10.8. Obviously, the quantizer used around the 3000th sample should not be the same quantizer that was used around the 1000th sample. The Jayant algorithm provides an effective approach to adapting the quantizer to the variations in the input characteristics.

Example 10.5.1:

Let's encode the speech sample shown in Figure 10.7 using a DPCM system with a backward adaptive quantizer. We will use a third-order predictor and an eight-level quantizer. We will also use the following multipliers [117]:

$$M_0 = 0.90, \quad M_1 = 0.90, \quad M_2 = 1.25, \quad M_3 = 1.75.$$

The results are shown in Figure 10.10. Notice the region at the beginning of the speech sample and between the 3000th and 3500th sample, where the DPCM system with the fixed quantizer had problems. Because the step size of the adaptive quantizer can become quite small, these regions have been nicely reproduced. However, right after this region, the speech output has a larger spike than the reconstructed waveform. This is an indication that the quantizer is not expanding rapidly enough. This can be remedied by increasing the value of M_3. The program used to generate this example is dpcm_aqb. You can use this program to study the behavior of the system for different configurations.   ◆

10.5.2 Adaptive Prediction in DPCM

The equations used to obtain the predictor coefficients were derived based on the assumption of stationarity. However, we see from Figure 10.7 that this assumption is not true. In the speech segment shown in Figure 10.7, different segments have different characteristics. This is true for most sources we deal with; while the source output may be locally stationary over any significant length of the output, the statistics may vary considerably. In this situation, it

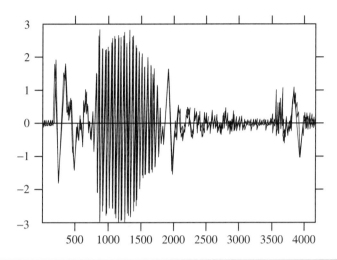

FIGURE 10.10   **The reconstructed sequence using a third-order predictor and an eight-level Jayant quantizer.**

is better to adapt the predictor to match the local statistics. This adaptation can be forward adaptive or backward adaptive.

DPCM with Forward Adaptive Prediction (DPCM-APF)

In forward adaptive prediction, the input is divided into segments or blocks. In speech coding this block consists of about 16 ms of speech. At a sampling rate of 8000 samples per second, this corresponds to 128 samples per block [118, 89]. In image coding, we use an 8×8 block [150].

The autocorrelation coefficients are computed for each block. The predictor coefficients are obtained from the autocorrelation coefficients and quantized using a relatively high-rate quantizer. If the coefficient values are to be quantized directly, we need to use at least 12 bits per coefficient [118]. This number can be reduced considerably if we represent the predictor coefficients in terms of *parcor coefficients*; we will describe how to obtain the parcor coefficients in Chapter 15. For now, let's assume that the coefficients can be transmitted with an expenditure of about 6 bits per coefficient.

In order to estimate the autocorrelation for each block, we generally assume that the sample values outside each block are zero. Therefore, for a block length of M, the autocorrelation function for the lth block would be estimated by

$$R_{xx}^{(l)}(k) = \frac{1}{M-k} \sum_{i=(l-1)M+1}^{lM-k} x_i x_{i+k} \tag{10.38}$$

for k positive, or

$$R_{xx}^{(l)}(k) = \frac{1}{M+k} \sum_{i=(l-1)M+1-k}^{lM} x_i x_{i+k} \tag{10.39}$$

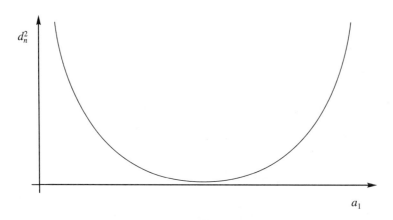

FIGURE 10.11   A plot of the residual squared versus the predictor coefficient.

for k negative. Notice that $R_{xx}^{(l)}(k) = R_{xx}^{(l)}(-k)$, which agrees with our initial assumption.

DPCM with Backward Adaptive Prediction (DPCM-APB)

Forward adaptive prediction requires that we buffer the input. This introduces delay in the transmission of the speech. As the amount of buffering is small, the use of forward adaptive prediction when there is only one encoder and decoder is not a big problem. However, in the case of speech, the connection between two parties may be several links, each of which may consist of a DPCM encoder and decoder. In such tandem links, the amount of delay can become large enough to be a nuisance. Furthermore, the need to transmit side information makes the system more complex. In order to avoid these problems, we can adapt the predictor based on the output of the encoder, which is also available to the decoder. The adaptation is done in a sequential manner [90, 89].

In our derivation of the optimum predictor coefficients, we took the derivative of the statistical average of the squared prediction error or residual sequence. In order to do this, we had to assume that the input process was stationary. Let us now remove that assumption and try to figure out how to adapt the predictor to the input algebraically. To keep matters simple, we will start with a first-order predictor and then generalize the result to higher orders.

For a first-order predictor, the value of the residual squared at time n would be given by

$$d_n^2 = (x_n - a_1\hat{x}_{n-1})^2. \tag{10.40}$$

If we could plot the value of d_n^2 against a_1, we would get a graph similar to the one shown in Figure 10.11. Let's take a look at the derivative of d_n^2 as a function of whether the current value of a_1 is to the left or right of the optimal value of a_1—that is, the value of a_1 for which d_n^2 is minimum. When a_1 is to the left of the optimal value, the derivative is negative. Furthermore, the derivative will have a larger magnitude when a_1 is further away from the optimal value. If we were asked to adapt a_1, we would add to the current value of a_1. The amount to add would be large if a_1 was far from the optimal value, and small if a_1 was close to the optimal value. If the current value was to the right of the optimal value, the derivative would be positive, and we would subtract some amount from a_1 to adapt it. The amount to subtract would be larger if we were further from the optimal, and as before, the derivative would have a larger magnitude if a_1 were further from the optimal value.

At any given time, in order to adapt the coefficient at time $n + 1$, we add an amount proportional to the magnitude of the derivative with a sign that is opposite to that of the derivative of d_n^2 at time n:

$$a_1^{(n+1)} = a_1^{(n)} - \alpha \frac{\delta d_n^2}{\delta a_1} \tag{10.41}$$

where α is some proportionality constant.

$$\frac{\delta d_n^2}{\delta a_1} = -2(x_n - a_1 \hat{x}_{n-1}) \hat{x}_{n-1} \tag{10.42}$$

$$= -2 d_n \hat{x}_{n-1}. \tag{10.43}$$

Substituting this into (10.41), we get

$$a_1^{(n+1)} = a_1^{(n)} + \alpha d_n \hat{x}_{n-1} \tag{10.44}$$

where we have absorbed the 2 into α. The residual value d_n is available only to the encoder. Therefore, in order for both the encoder and decoder to use the same algorithm, we replace d_n by $\hat{d}_n$ in (10.44) to obtain

$$a_1^{(n+1)} = a_1^{(n)} + \alpha \hat{d}_n \hat{x}_{n-1}. \tag{10.45}$$

Extending this adaptation equation for a first-order predictor to an Nth-order predictor is relatively easy. The equation for the squared prediction error is given by

$$d_n^2 = \left(x_n - \sum_{i=1}^{N} a_i \hat{x}_{n-i} \right)^2. \tag{10.46}$$

Taking the derivative with respect to a_j will give us the adaptation equation for the jth predictor coefficient:

$$a_j^{(n+1)} = a_j^{(n)} + \alpha \hat{d}_n \hat{x}_{n-j}. \tag{10.47}$$

We can combine all N equations in vector form to get

$$\mathbf{A}^{(n+1)} = \mathbf{A}^{(n)} + \alpha \hat{d}_n \hat{X}_{n-1} \tag{10.48}$$

where

$$\hat{X}_n = \begin{bmatrix} \hat{x}_n \\ \hat{x}_{n-1} \\ \vdots \\ \hat{x}_{n-N+1} \end{bmatrix}. \tag{10.49}$$

This particular adaptation algorithm is called the least mean squared (LMS) algorithm [238].

10.6 Delta Modulation

A very simple form of DPCM that has been widely used in a number of speech-coding applications is the delta modulator (DM). The DM can be viewed as a DPCM system with a 1-bit (two-level) quantizer. With a two-level quantizer with output values $\pm\Delta$, we can only represent a sample-to-sample difference of Δ. If, for a given source sequence, the sample-to-sample difference is often very different from Δ, then we may incur substantial distortion. One way to limit the difference is to sample more often. In Figure 10.12 we see a signal that has been sampled at two different rates. The lower-rate samples are shown by open circles, while the higher-rate samples are represented by +. It is apparent that the lower-rate samples are further apart in value.

The rate at which a signal is sampled is governed by the highest frequency component of a signal. If the highest frequency component in a signal is W, then in order to obtain an exact reconstruction of the signal, we need to sample it at least at twice the highest frequency, or $2W$. In systems that use delta modulation, we usually sample the signal at much more than twice the highest frequency. If F_s is the sampling frequency, then the ratio of F_s to $2W$ can range from almost 1 to almost 100 [118]. The higher sampling rates are used for high-quality A/D converters, while the lower rates are more common for low-rate speech coders.

If we look at a block diagram of a delta modulation system, we see that, while the block diagram of the encoder is identical to that of the DPCM system, the standard DPCM decoder is followed by a filter. The reason for the existence of the filter is evident from Figure 10.13, where we show a source output and the unfiltered reconstruction. The samples of the source output are represented by the filled circles. As the source is sampled at several times the highest frequency, the staircase shape of the reconstructed signal results in distortion in frequency bands outside the band of frequencies occupied by the signal. The filter can be used to remove these spurious frequencies.

The reconstruction shown in Figure 10.13 was obtained with a delta modulator using a fixed quantizer. Delta modulation systems that use a fixed step size are often referred to as linear delta modulators. Notice that the reconstructed signal shows one of two behaviors. In regions where the source output is relatively constant, the output alternates up or down by Δ; these regions are called the *granular regions*. In the regions where the source output rises or falls fast, the reconstructed output cannot keep up; these regions are called the *slope overload regions*. If we want to reduce the granular error, we need to make the step size Δ small. However, this will make it more difficult for the reconstruction to follow rapid changes in the

FIGURE 10.12   *A signal sampled at two different rates.*

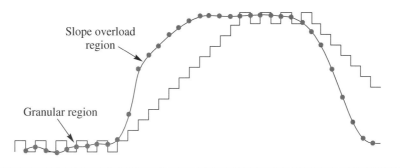

FIGURE 10.13   **A source output sampled and coded using delta modulation.**

FIGURE 10.14   **A source output sampled and coded using adaptive delta modulation.**

input. In other words, it will result in an increase in the overload error. To avoid the overload condition, we need to make the step size large so that the reconstruction can quickly catch up with rapid changes in the input. However, this will increase the granular error.

One way to avoid this impasse is to adapt the step size to the characteristics of the input, as shown in Figure 10.14. In quasi-constant regions, make the step size small in order to reduce the granular error. In regions of rapid change, increase the step size in order to reduce overload error. There are various ways of adapting the delta modulator to the local characteristics of the source output. We describe two of the more popular ways here.

10.6.1 Constant Factor Adaptive Delta Modulation (CFDM)

The objective of adaptive delta modulation is clear: increase the step size in overload regions and decrease it in granular regions. The problem lies in knowing when the system is in each of these regions. Looking at Figure 10.13, we see that in the granular region the output of the quantizer changes sign with almost every input sample; in the overload region, the sign of the quantizer output is the same for a string of input samples. Therefore, we can define an overload or granular condition based on whether the output of the quantizer has been changing signs.

A very simple system [116] uses a history of one sample to decide whether the system is in overload or granular condition and whether to expand or contract the step size. If s_n denotes the sign of the quantizer output $\hat{d}_n$,

$$s_n = \begin{cases} 1 & \text{if } \hat{d}_n > 0 \\ -1 & \text{if } \hat{d}_n < 0 \end{cases} \qquad (10.50)$$

the adaptation logic is given by

$$\Delta_n = \begin{cases} M_1 \Delta_{n-1} & s_n = s_{n-1} \\ M_2 \Delta_{n-1} & s_n \neq s_{n-1} \end{cases} \qquad (10.51)$$

where $M_1 = \frac{1}{M_2} = M > 1$. In general, $M < 2$.

By increasing the memory, we can improve the response of the CFDM system. For example, if we looked at two past samples, we could decide that the system was moving from overload to granular condition if the sign had been the same for the past two samples and then changed with the current sample:

$$s_n \neq s_{n-1} = s_{n-2}. \qquad (10.52)$$

In this case it would be reasonable to assume that the step size had been expanding previously and, therefore, needed a sharp contraction. If

$$s_n = s_{n-1} \neq s_{n-2}, \qquad (10.53)$$

then it would mean that the system was probably entering the overload region, while

$$s_n = s_{n-1} = s_{n-2} \qquad (10.54)$$

would mean the system was in overload and the step size should be expanded rapidly.

For the encoding of speech, the following multipliers M_i are recommended by [217] for a CFDM system with two-sample memory:

$$s_n \neq s_{n-1} = s_{n-2} \quad M_1 = 0.4 \qquad (10.55)$$
$$s_n \neq s_{n-1} \neq s_{n-2} \quad M_2 = 0.9 \qquad (10.56)$$
$$s_n = s_{n-1} \neq s_{n-2} \quad M_3 = 1.5 \qquad (10.57)$$
$$s_n = s_{n-1} = s_{n-2} \quad M_4 = 2.0. \qquad (10.58)$$

The amount of memory can be increased further with a concurrent increase in complexity. The space shuttle used a delta modulator with a memory of seven [15].

10.6.2 Continuously Variable Slope Delta Modulation

The CFDM systems described use a rapid adaptation scheme. For low-rate speech coding, it is more pleasing if the adaptation is over a longer period of time. This slower adaptation results in a decrease in the granular error and generally an increase in overload error. Delta modulation systems that adapt over longer periods of time are referred to as *syllabically* companded.

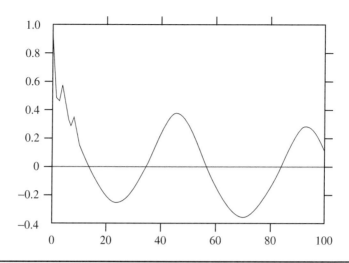

FIGURE 10.15 **Autocorrelation function for** test.snd.

A popular class of syllabically companded delta modulation systems is the continuously variable slope delta modulation systems.

The adaptation logic used in CVSD systems is as follows [118]:

$$\Delta_n = \beta\Delta_{n-1} + \alpha_n\Delta_0 \tag{10.59}$$

where β is a number less than but close to one, and α_n is equal to one if J of the last K quantizer outputs were of the same sign. That is, we look in a window of length K to obtain the behavior of the source output. If this condition is not satisfied, then α_n is equal to zero. Standard values for J and K are $J = 3$ and $K = 3$.

10.7 Speech Coding

Differential encoding schemes are immensely popular for speech encoding. They are used in the telephone system, voice messaging, and multimedia applications, among others. Adaptive DPCM is a part of several international standards (ITU-T G.721, ITU G.723, ITU G.726, ITU-T G.722), which we will look at here and in later chapters.

Before we do that, let's take a look at one issue specific to speech coding. In Figure 10.7, we see that there is a segment of speech that looks highly periodic. We can see this periodicity if we plot the autocorrelation function of the speech segment (Figure 10.15).

The autocorrelation peaks at a lag value of 47 and multiples of 47. This indicates a periodicity of 47 samples. This period is called the *pitch period*. The predictor we originally designed did not take advantage of this periodicity, as the largest predictor was a third-order predictor, and this periodic structure takes 47 samples to show up. We can take advantage of this periodicity by constructing an outer prediction loop around the basic DPCM structure as shown in Figure 10.16. This can be a simple single coefficient predictor of the form $b\hat{x}_{n-\tau}$, where τ is the pitch period. Using this system on testm.raw, we get the residual sequence shown in Figure 10.17. Notice the decrease in amplitude in the periodic portion of the speech.

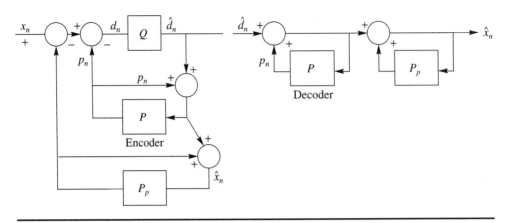

FIGURE 10.16   **The DPCM structure with a pitch predictor.**

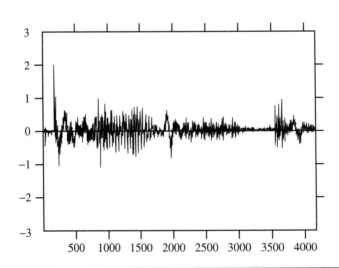

FIGURE 10.17   **The residual sequence using the DPCM system with a pitch predictor.**

Finally, remember that we have been using mean squared error as the distortion measure in all of our discussions. However, perceptual tests do not always correlate with the mean squared error. The level of distortion we perceive is often related to the level of the speech signal. In regions where the speech signal is of higher amplitude, we have a harder time perceiving the distortion, but the same amount of distortion in a different frequency band might be very perceptible. We can take advantage of this by shaping the quantization error so that most of the error lies in the region where the signal has a higher amplitude. This variation of DPCM is called *noise feedback coding* (NFC) (see [118] for details).

TABLE 10.2 Recommended input-output characteristics of the quantizer for 24-kbits-per-second operation.

Input Range	Label	Output
$\log_2 \frac{d_k}{\alpha_k}$	$|I_k|$	$\log_2 \frac{d_k}{\alpha_k}$
$[2.58, \infty)$	3	2.91
$[1.70, 2.58)$	2	2.13
$[0.06, 1.70)$	1	1.05
$(-\infty, -0.06)$	0	$-\infty$

10.7.1 G.726

The International Telecommunications Union has published recommendations for a standard ADPCM system, including recommendations G.721, G.723, and G.726. G.726 supersedes G.721 and G.723. In this section we will describe the G.726 recommendation for ADPCM systems at rates of 40, 32, 24, and 16 kbits.

The Quantizer

The recommendation assumes that the speech output is sampled at the rate of 8000 samples per second, so the rates of 40, 32, 24, and 16 kbits per second translate to 5 bits per sample, 4 bits per sample, 3 bits per sample, and 2 bits per sample. Comparing this to the PCM rate of 8 bits per sample, this would mean compression ratios of 1.6:1, 2:1, 2.67:1, and 4:1. Except for the 16 kbits per second system, the number of levels in the quantizer are $2^{nb} - 1$, where nb is the number of bits per sample. Thus, the number of levels in the quantizer is odd, which means that for the higher rates we use a midtread quantizer.

The quantizer is a backward adaptive quantizer with an adaptation algorithm that is similar to the Jayant quantizer. The recommendation describes the adaptation of the quantization interval in terms of the adaptation of a scale factor. The input d_k is normalized by a scale factor α_k. This normalized value is quantized, and the normalization removed by multiplying with α_k. In this way the quantizer is kept fixed and α_k is adapted to the input. Therefore, for example, instead of expanding the step size, we would increase the value of α_k.

The fixed quantizer is a nonuniform midtread quantizer. The recommendation describes the quantization boundaries and reconstruction values in terms of the log of the scaled input. The input-output characteristics for the 24 kbit system are shown in Table 10.2. An output value of $-\infty$ in the table corresponds to a reconstruction value of 0.

The adaptation algorithm is described in terms of the logarithm of the scale factor

$$y(k) = \log_2 \alpha_k. \tag{10.60}$$

The adaptation of the scale factor α_k or its log $y(k)$ depends on whether the input is speech or speechlike, where the sample-to-sample difference can fluctuate considerably, or whether the input is voice-band data, which might be generated by a modem, where the sample-to-sample fluctuation is quite small. In order to handle both these situations, the scale factor is composed of two values, a *locked* slow scale factor for when the sample-to-sample differences are quite small, and an *unlocked* value for when the input is more dynamic:

$$y(k) = a_l(k)y_u(k-1) + (1 - a_l(k))y_l(k-1). \qquad (10.61)$$

The value of $a_l(k)$ depends on the variance of the input. It will be close to one for speech inputs and close to zero for tones and voice band data.

The unlocked scale factor is adapted using the Jayant algorithm with one slight modification. If we were to use the Jayant algorithm, the unlocked scale factor could be adapted as

$$\alpha_u(k) = \alpha_{k-1}M[I_{k-1}] \qquad (10.62)$$

where $M[\cdot]$ is the multiplier. In terms of logarithms, this becomes

$$y_u(k) = y(k-1) + \log M[I_{k-1}]. \qquad (10.63)$$

The modification consists of introducing some memory into the adaptive process so that the encoder and decoder converge following transmission errors:

$$y_u(k) = (1 - \epsilon)y(k-1) + \epsilon W[I_{k-1}] \qquad (10.64)$$

where $W[\cdot] = \log M[\cdot]$, and $\epsilon = 2^{-5}$.

The locked scale factor is obtained from the unlocked scale factor through

$$y_l(k) = (1 - \gamma)y_l(k-1) + \gamma y_u(k), \qquad \gamma = 2^{-6}. \qquad (10.65)$$

The Predictor

The recommended predictor is a backward adaptive predictor that uses a linear combination of the past two reconstructed values as well as the six past quantized differences to generate the prediction

$$p_k = \sum_{i=1}^{2} a_i^{(k-1)}\hat{x}_{k-i} + \sum_{i=1}^{6} b_i^{(k-1)}\hat{d}_{k-i}. \qquad (10.66)$$

The set of predictor coefficients is updated using a simplified form of the LMS algorithm.

$$a_1^{(k)} = (1 - 2^{-8})a_1^{(k-1)} + 3 \times 2^{-8}\operatorname{sgn}[z(k)]\operatorname{sgn}[z(k-1)] \qquad (10.67)$$

$$a_2^{(k)} = (1 - 2^{-7})a_2^{(k-1)} + 2^{-7}(\operatorname{sgn}[z(k)]\operatorname{sgn}[z(k-2)]$$
$$-f(a_1^{(k-1)}\operatorname{sgn}[z(k)]\operatorname{sgn}[z(k-1)])) \qquad (10.68)$$

where

$$z(k) = \hat{d}_k + \sum_{i=1}^{6} b_i^{(k-1)}\hat{d}_{k-i} \qquad (10.69)$$

$$f(\beta) = \begin{cases} 4\beta & |\beta| \le \frac{1}{2} \\ 2\operatorname{sgn}(\beta) & |\beta| > \frac{1}{2}. \end{cases} \qquad (10.70)$$

The coefficients $\{b_i\}$ are updated using the following equation:

$$b_i^{(k)} = (1 - 2^{-8})b_i^{(k-1)} + 2^{-7}\,\text{sgn}[\hat{d}_k]\,\text{sgn}[\hat{d}_{k-i}].\qquad(10.71)$$

Notice that in the adaptive algorithms we have replaced products of reconstructed values and products of quantizer outputs with products of their signs. This is computationally much simpler and does not lead to any significant degradation of the adaptation process. Furthermore, the values of the coefficients are selected such that multiplication with these coefficients can be accomplished using shifts and adds. The predictor coefficients are all set to zero when the input moves from tones to speech.

10.8 Image Coding

We saw in Chapter 6 that differential encoding provided an efficient approach to the lossless compression of images. The case for using differential encoding in the lossy compression of images has not been made as clearly. In the early days of image compression, both differential encoding and transform coding were popular forms of lossy image compression. At the current time differential encoding has a much more restricted role as part of other compression strategies. Several currently popular approaches to image compression decompose the image into lower and higher frequency components. As low-frequency signals have high sample-to-sample correlation, several schemes use differential encoding to compress the low-frequency components. We will see this use of differential encoding when we look at subband- and wavelet-based compression schemes and, to a lesser extent, when we study transform coding.

For now let us look at the performance of a couple of stand-alone differential image compression schemes. We will compare the performance of these schemes with the performance of the JPEG compression standard.

Consider a simple differential encoding scheme in which the predictor $p[j, k]$ for the pixel in the jth row and the kth column is given by

$$p[j,k] = \begin{cases} \hat{x}[j, k-1] & \text{for } k > 0 \\ \hat{x}[j-1, k] & \text{for } k = 0 \text{ and } j > 0 \\ 128 & \text{for } j = 0 \text{ and } k = 0 \end{cases}$$

where $\hat{x}[j, k]$ is the reconstructed pixel in the jth row and kth column. We use this predictor in conjunction with a fixed four-level uniform quantizer and code the quantizer output using an arithmetic coder. The coding rate for the compressed image is approximately 1 bit per pixel. We compare this reconstructed image with a JPEG-coded image at the same rate in Figure 10.18. The signal-to-noise ratio for the differentially encoded image is 22.33 dB (PSNR 31.42 dB) and for the JPEG-encoded image is 32.52 dB (PSNR 41.60 dB), a difference of more than 10 dB!

However, this is an extremely simple system compared to the JPEG standard, which has been fine-tuned for encoding images. Let's make our differential encoding system slightly more complicated by replacing the uniform quantizer with a recursively indexed quantizer and the predictor by a somewhat more complicated predictor. For each pixel (except for the

FIGURE 10.18   **Left: Reconstructed image using differential encoding at 1 bit per pixel. Right: Reconstructed image using JPEG at 1 bit per pixel.**

boundary pixels) we compute the following three values:

$$
\begin{aligned}
p_1 &= 0.5 \times \hat{x}[j-1,k] + 0.5 \times \hat{x}[j,k-1] \\
p_2 &= 0.5 \times \hat{x}[j-1,k-1] + 0.5 \times \hat{x}[j,k-1] \\
p_3 &= 0.5 \times \hat{x}[j-1,k-1] + 0.5 \times \hat{x}[j-1,k]
\end{aligned}
\tag{10.72}
$$

then obtain the predicted value as

$$
p[j,k] = \text{median}\{p_1, p_2, p_3\}.
$$

For the boundary pixels we use the simple prediction scheme. At a coding rate of 1 bit per pixel, we obtain the image shown in Figure 10.19. For reference we show it next to the JPEG-coded image at the same rate. The signal-to-noise ratio for this reconstruction is 29.20 dB (PSNR 38.28 dB). We have made up two-thirds of the difference using some relatively minor modifications. We can see that it might be feasible to develop differential encoding schemes that are competitive with other image compression techniques. Therefore, it makes sense not to dismiss differential encoding out of hand when we need to develop image compression systems.

10.9 Summary

In this chapter we described some of the more well-known differential encoding techniques. Although differential encoding does not provide compression as high as vector quantization, it is very simple to implement. This approach is especially suited to the encoding of speech, where it has found broad application. The DPCM system consists of two main components,

FIGURE 10.19   **Left: Reconstructed image using differential encoding at 1 bit per pixel using median predictor and recursively indexed quantizer. Right: Reconstructed image using JPEG at 1 bit per pixel.**

the quantizer and the predictor. We spent a considerable amount of time discussing the quantizer in Chapter 8, so most of the discussion in this chapter focused on the predictor. We have seen different ways of making the predictor adaptive, and looked at some of the improvements to be obtained from source-specific modifications to the predictor design.

Further Reading

1. *Digital Coding of Waveforms*, by N.S. Jayant and P. Noll [118], contains some very detailed and highly informative chapters on differential encoding.

2. "Adaptive Prediction in Speech Differential Encoding Systems," by J.D. Gibson [89], is a comprehensive treatment of the subject of adaptive prediction.

3. A real-time video coding system based on DPCM has been developed by NASA. Details can be found in [208].

10.10   Projects and Problems

1. Generate an AR(1) process using the relationship

$$x_n = 0.9 \times x_{n-1} + \epsilon_n$$

where ϵ_n is the output of a Gaussian random number generator (this is option 2 in rangen).

(a) Encode this sequence using a DPCM system with a one-tap predictor with predictor coefficient 0.9 and a three-level Gaussian quantizer. Compute the variance of the prediction error. How does this compare with the variance of the input? How does the variance of the prediction error compare with the variance of the $\{\epsilon_n\}$ sequence?

(b) Repeat using predictor coefficient values of 0.5, 0.6, 0.7, 0.8, and 1.0. Comment on the results.

2. Generate an AR(5) process using the following coefficients: 1.381, 0.6, 0.367, −0.7, 0.359.

(a) Encode this with a DPCM system with a 3-bit Gaussian nonuniform quantizer and a first-, second-, third-, fourth-, and fifth-order predictor. Obtain these predictors by solving (10.30). For each case compute the variance of the prediction error and the SNR in dB. Comment on your results.

(b) Repeat using a 3-bit Jayant quantizer.

3. DPCM can also be used for encoding images. Encode the Sinan image using a one-tap predictor of the form

$$\hat{x}_{i,j} = a \times x_{i,j-1}$$

and a 2-bit quantizer. Experiment with quantizers designed for different distributions. Comment on your results.

4. Repeat the image-coding experiment of the previous problem using a Jayant quantizer.

5. DPCM-encode the Sinan, Elif, and bookshelf1 images using a one-tap predictor and a four-level quantizer followed by a Huffman coder. Repeat using a five-level quantizer. Compute the SNR for each case, and compare the rate distortion performances.

6. We want to DPCM-encode images using a two-tap predictor of the form

$$\hat{x}_{i,j} = a \times x_{i,j-1} + b \times x_{i-1,j}$$

and a four-level quantizer followed by a Huffman coder. Find the equations we need to solve to obtain coefficients a and b that minimize the mean squared error.

7. **(a)** DPCM-encode the Sinan, Elif, and bookshelf1 images using a two-tap predictor and a four-level quantizer followed by a Huffman coder.

(b) Repeat using a five-level quantizer. Compute the SNR and rate (in bits per pixel) for each case.

(c) Compare the rate distortion performances with the one-tap case.

(d) Repeat using a five-level quantizer. Compute the SNR for each case, and compare the rate distortion performances using a one-tap and two-tap predictor.

11

Mathematical Preliminaries for Transforms, Subbands, and Wavelets

11.1 Overview

n this chapter we will review some of the mathematical background necessary for the study of transforms, subbands, and wavelets. The topics include Fourier series, Fourier transforms, and their discrete counterparts. We will also look at sampling and briefly review some linear system concepts.

11.2 Introduction

The roots of many of the techniques we will study can be found in the mathematical literature. Therefore, in order to understand the techniques, we will need some mathematical background. Our approach in general will be to introduce the mathematical tools just prior to when they are needed. However, there is a certain amount of background that is required for most of what we will be looking at. In this chapter we will present only that material that is a common background to all the techniques we will be studying. Our approach will be rather utilitarian; more sophisticated coverage of these topics can be found in [142]. We will be introducing a rather large number of concepts, many of which depend on each other. In order to make it easier for you to find a particular concept, we will identify the paragraph in which the concept is first introduced.

We will begin our coverage with a brief introduction to the concept of vector spaces, and in particular the concept of the inner product. We will use these concepts in our description of Fourier series and Fourier transforms. Next is a brief overview of linear systems, then a look at the issues involved in sampling a function. Finally, we will revisit the Fourier concepts in the context of sampled functions and provide a brief introduction to Z-transforms. Throughout, we will try to get a physical feel for the various concepts.

11.3 Vector Spaces

The techniques we will be using to obtain compression will involve manipulations and decompositions of (sampled) functions of time. In order to do this we need some sort of mathematical framework. This framework is provided through the concept of vector spaces.

We are very familiar with vectors in two- or three-dimensional space. An example of a vector in two-dimensional space is shown in Figure 11.1. This vector can be represented in a number of different ways: we can represent it in terms of its magnitude and direction, or we can represent it as a weighted sum of the unit vectors in the x and y directions, or we can represent it as an array whose components are the coefficients of the unit vectors. Thus, the vector $\mathbf{v}$ in Figure 11.1 has a magnitude of 5 and an angle of 36.86 degrees,

$$\mathbf{v} = 4u_x + 3u_y$$

and

$$\mathbf{v} = \begin{bmatrix} 4 \\ 3 \end{bmatrix}.$$

We can view the second representation as a decomposition of V into simpler building blocks, namely, the *basis vectors*. The nice thing about this is that any vector in two dimensions can be decomposed in exactly the same way. Given a particular vector $\mathbf{A}$ and a basis set (more on this later), decomposition means finding the coefficients with which to weight the unit vectors of the basis set. In our simple example it is easy to see what these coefficients

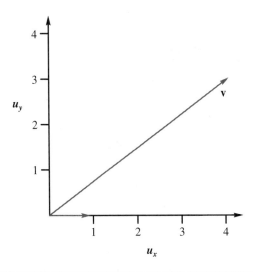

FIGURE 11.1   A vector.

should be. However, we will encounter situations where it is not a trivial task to find the coefficients that constitute the decomposition of the vector. We therefore need some machinery to extract these coefficients. The particular machinery we will use here is called the *dot product* or the *inner product*.

11.3.1 Dot or Inner Product

Given two vectors **a** and **b** such that

$$\mathbf{a} = \left[\begin{array}{c} a_1 \\ a_2 \end{array} \right], \quad \mathbf{b} = \left[\begin{array}{c} b_1 \\ b_2 \end{array} \right]$$

the inner product between **a** and **b** is defined as

$$\mathbf{a} \cdot \mathbf{b} = a_1 b_1 + a_2 b_2.$$

Two vectors are said to be *orthogonal* if their inner product is zero. A set of vectors is said to be orthogonal if each vector in the set is orthogonal to every other vector in the set. The inner product between a vector and a unit vector from an orthogonal basis set will give us the coefficient corresponding to that unit vector. It is easy to see that this is indeed so. We can write u_x and u_y as

$$u_x = \left[\begin{array}{c} 1 \\ 0 \end{array} \right], \quad u_y = \left[\begin{array}{c} 0 \\ 1 \end{array} \right].$$

These are obviously orthogonal. Therefore, the coefficient a_1 can be obtained by

$$\mathbf{a} \cdot u_x = a_1 \times 1 + a_2 \times 0 = a_1$$

and the coefficient of u_y can be obtained by

$$\mathbf{a} \cdot u_y = a_1 \times 0 + a_2 \times 1 = a_2.$$

The inner product between two vectors is in some sense a measure of how "similar" they are, but we have to be a bit careful in how we define "similarity." For example, consider the vectors in Figure 11.2. The vector **a** is closer to u_x than to u_y. Therefore $\mathbf{a} \cdot u_x$ will be greater than $\mathbf{a} \cdot u_y$. The reverse is true for **b**.

11.3.2 Vector Space

In order to handle not just two- or three-dimensional vectors but general sequences and functions of interest to us, we need to generalize these concepts. Let us begin with a more general definition of vectors and the concept of a vector space.

A *vector space* consists of a set of elements called vectors that have the operations of vector addition and scalar multiplication defined on them. Furthermore, the results of these operations are also elements of the vector space.

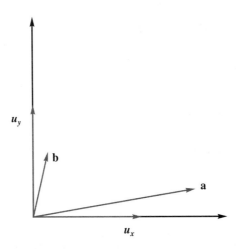

FIGURE 11.2   Example of different vectors.

By *vector addition* of two vectors, we mean the vector obtained by the pointwise addition of the components of the two vectors. For example, given two vectors **a** and **b**:

$$\mathbf{a} = \begin{bmatrix} a_1 \\ a_2 \\ a_3 \end{bmatrix}, \quad \mathbf{b} = \begin{bmatrix} b_1 \\ b_2 \\ b_3 \end{bmatrix} \tag{11.1}$$

the vector addition of these two vectors is given as

$$\mathbf{a} + \mathbf{b} = \begin{bmatrix} a_1 + b_1 \\ a_2 + b_2 \\ a_3 + b_3 \end{bmatrix}. \tag{11.2}$$

By *scalar multiplication*, we mean the multiplication of a vector with a real or complex number. For this set of elements to be a vector space it has to satisfy certain axioms.

Suppose V is a vector space; $\mathbf{x}$, $\mathbf{y}$, $\mathbf{z}$ are vectors; and α and β are scalars. Then the following axioms are satisfied:

1. $\mathbf{x} + \mathbf{y} = \mathbf{y} + \mathbf{x}$ (commutativity).

2. $(\mathbf{x} + \mathbf{y}) + \mathbf{z} = \mathbf{x} + (\mathbf{y} + \mathbf{z})$ and $(\alpha\beta)\mathbf{x} = \alpha(\beta\mathbf{x})$ (associativity).

3. There exists an element θ in V such that $\mathbf{x} + \theta = \mathbf{x}$ for all $\mathbf{x}$ in V. θ is called the additive identity.

4. $\alpha(\mathbf{x} + \mathbf{y}) = \alpha\mathbf{x} + \alpha\mathbf{y}$, and $(\alpha + \beta)\mathbf{x} = \alpha\mathbf{x} + \beta\mathbf{x}$ (distributivity).

5. $1 \cdot \mathbf{x} = \mathbf{x}$, and $0 \cdot \mathbf{x} = \theta$.

6. For every $\mathbf{x}$ in V, there exists a $(-\mathbf{x})$ such that $\mathbf{x} + (-\mathbf{x}) = \theta$.

A simple example of a vector space is the set of real numbers. In this set zero is the additive identity. We can easily verify that the set of real numbers with the standard operations of addition and multiplication obey the axioms stated above. See if you can verify that the set of real numbers is a vector space. One of the advantages of this exercise is to emphasize the fact that a vector is more than a line with an arrow at its end.

Example 11.3.1:

Another example of a vector space that is of more practical interest to us is the set of all functions $f(t)$ with finite energy. That is,

$$\int_{-\infty}^{\infty} |f(t)|^2 \, dt < \infty. \tag{11.3}$$

Let's see if this set constitutes a vector space. If we define additions as pointwise addition and scalar multiplication in the usual manner, the set of functions $f(t)$ obviously satisfies axioms 1, 2, and 4.

- If $f(t)$ and $g(t)$ are functions with finite energy, and α is a scalar, then the functions $f(t) + g(t)$ and $\alpha f(t)$ also have finite energy.

- If $f(t)$ and $g(t)$ are functions with finite energy, then $f(t) + g(t) = g(t) + f(t)$ (axiom 1).

- If $f(t)$, $g(t)$, and $h(t)$ are functions with finite energy, and α and β are scalars, then $(f(t) + g(t)) + h(t) = f(t) + (g(t) + h(t))$ and $(\alpha\beta)f(t) = \alpha(\beta f(t))$ (axiom 2).

- If $f(t)$, $g(t)$, and $h(t)$ are functions with finite energy, and α is a scalar, then $\alpha(f(t) + g(t)) = \alpha f(t) + \alpha g(t)$ and $(\alpha + \beta)f(t) = \alpha f(t) + \beta f(t)$ (axiom 4).

Let us define the additive identity function $\theta(t)$ as the function that is identically zero for all t. This function satisfies the requirement of finite energy, and we can see that axioms 3 and 5 are also satisfied. Finally, if a function $f(t)$ has finite energy, then from Equation (11.3), the function $-f(t)$ also has finite energy, and axiom 6 is satisfied. Therefore, the set of all functions with finite energy constitutes a vector space. This space is denoted by $L_2(f)$, or simply L_2. ◆

11.3.3 Subspace

A *subspace* S of a vector space V is a subset of V whose members satisfy all the axioms of the vector space and has the additional property that if $\mathbf{x}$ and $\mathbf{y}$ are in S, and α is a scalar, then $\mathbf{x} + \mathbf{y}$ and $\alpha\mathbf{x}$ are also in S.

Example 11.3.2:

Consider the set S of continuous bounded functions on the interval $[0,1]$. Then S is a subspace of the vector space L_2. ◆

11.3.4 Basis

One way we can generate a subspace is by taking linear combinations of a set of vectors. If this set of vectors is *linearly independent*, then the set is called a *basis* for the subspace.

> A set of vectors $\{\mathbf{x}_1, \mathbf{x}_2, \ldots\}$ is said to be linearly independent if no vector of the set can be written as a linear combination of the other vectors in the set.

A direct consequence of this definition is the following theorem:

Theorem *A set of vectors* $\mathbf{X} = \{\mathbf{x}_1, \mathbf{x}_2, \ldots, \mathbf{x}_N\}$ *is linearly independent if and only if the expression* $\sum_{i=1}^{N} \alpha_i \mathbf{x}_i = \theta$ *implies that* $\alpha_i = 0$ *for all* $i = 1, 2, \ldots, N$.

Proof The proof of this theorem can be found in most books on linear algebra [142]. $\square$

The set of vectors formed by all possible linear combinations of vectors from a linearly independent set $\mathbf{X}$ forms a vector space (Problem 1). The set $\mathbf{X}$ is said to be the *basis* for this vector space. The basis set contains the smallest number of linearly independent vectors required to represent each element of the vector space. More than one set can be the basis for a given space.

Example 11.3.3:

Consider the vector space consisting of vectors $[a\ b]^T$, where a and b are real numbers. Then the set

$$\mathbf{X} = \left\{ \begin{bmatrix} 1 \\ 0 \end{bmatrix}, \begin{bmatrix} 0 \\ 1 \end{bmatrix} \right\}$$

forms a basis for this space, as does the set

$$\mathbf{X} = \left\{ \begin{bmatrix} 1 \\ 1 \end{bmatrix}, \begin{bmatrix} 1 \\ 0 \end{bmatrix} \right\}.$$

In fact, any two vectors that are not scalar multiples of each other form a basis for this space. ◆

The number of basis vectors required to generate the space is called the *dimension* of the vector space. In the previous example the dimension of the vector space is two. The dimension of the space of all continuous functions on the interval $[0, 1]$ is infinity.

Given a particular basis, we can find a representation with respect to this basis for any vector in the space.

Example 11.3.4:

If $\mathbf{a} = [3\ 4]^T$, then

$$\mathbf{a} = 3 \begin{bmatrix} 1 \\ 0 \end{bmatrix} + 4 \begin{bmatrix} 0 \\ 1 \end{bmatrix}$$

and

$$\mathbf{a} = 4 \begin{bmatrix} 1 \\ 1 \end{bmatrix} + (-1) \begin{bmatrix} 1 \\ 0 \end{bmatrix}$$

so the representation of $\mathbf{a}$ with respect to the first basis set is $(3, 4)$, and the representation of $\mathbf{a}$ with respect to the second basis set is $(4, -1)$.   ◆

In the beginning of this section we had described a mathematical machinery for finding the components of a vector that involved taking the dot product or inner product of the vector to be decomposed with basis vectors. In order to use the same machinery in more abstract vector spaces we need to generalize the notion of inner product.

11.3.5   Inner Product—Formal Definition

An inner product between two vectors $\mathbf{x}$ and $\mathbf{y}$, denoted by $\langle \mathbf{x}, \mathbf{y} \rangle$, associates a scalar value with each pair of vectors. The inner product satisfies the following axioms:

1. $\langle \mathbf{x}, \mathbf{y} \rangle = \langle \mathbf{y}, \mathbf{x} \rangle^*$, where * denotes complex conjugate.

2. $\langle \mathbf{x} + \mathbf{y}, \mathbf{z} \rangle = \langle \mathbf{x}, \mathbf{z} \rangle + \langle \mathbf{y}, \mathbf{z} \rangle$.

3. $\langle \alpha \mathbf{x}, \mathbf{y} \rangle = \alpha \langle \mathbf{x}, \mathbf{y} \rangle$.

4. $\langle \mathbf{x}, \mathbf{x} \rangle \geq 0$, with equality if and only if $\mathbf{x} = \theta$. The quantity $\sqrt{\langle \mathbf{x}, \mathbf{x} \rangle}$ denoted by $\|\mathbf{x}\|$ is called the *norm* of $\mathbf{x}$ and is analogous to our usual concept of distance.

11.3.6   Orthogonal and Orthonormal Sets

As in the case of Euclidean space, two vectors are said to be *orthogonal* if their inner product is zero. If we select our basis set to be orthogonal (that is, each vector is orthogonal to every other vector in the set) and further require that the norm of each vector be one (that is, the basis vectors are unit vectors), such a basis set is called an *orthonormal basis set*. Given an orthonormal basis, it is easy to find the representation of any vector in the space in terms of the basis vectors using the inner product. Suppose we have a vector space S_N with an orthonormal basis set $\{\mathbf{x}_i\}_{i=1}^N$. Given a vector $\mathbf{y}$ in the space S_N, by definition of the basis set we can write $\mathbf{y}$ as a linear combination of the vectors $\mathbf{x}_i$:

$$\mathbf{y} = \sum_{i=1}^N \alpha_i \mathbf{x}_i.$$

To find the coefficient α_k, we find the inner product of both sides of this equation with $\mathbf{x}_k$:

$$\langle \mathbf{y}, \mathbf{x}_k \rangle = \sum_{i=1}^N \alpha_i \langle \mathbf{x}_i, \mathbf{x}_k \rangle.$$

Because of orthonormality,

$$\langle \mathbf{x}_i, \mathbf{x}_k \rangle = \begin{cases} 1 & i = k \\ 0 & i \neq k \end{cases}$$

and

$$\langle \mathbf{y}, \mathbf{x}_k \rangle = \alpha_k.$$

By repeating this with each $\mathbf{x}_i$, we can get all the coefficients α_i. Note that in order to use this machinery, the basis set has to be orthonormal.

We now have sufficient information in hand to begin looking at some of the well-known techniques for representing functions of time. This was somewhat of a crash course in vector spaces, and you might, with some justification, be feeling somewhat dazed. Basically, the important ideas that we would like you to remember are the following:

■ Vectors are not simply points in two- or three-dimensional space. In fact, functions of time can be viewed as elements in a vector space.

■ Collections of vectors that satisfy certain axioms make up a vector space.

■ All members of a vector space can be represented as linear, or weighted, combinations of the basis vectors (keep in mind that you can have many different basis sets for the same space). If the basis vectors have unit magnitude and are orthogonal, they are known as an *orthonormal basis set*.

■ If a basis set is orthonormal, the weights, or coefficients, can be obtained by taking the inner product of the vector with the corresponding basis vector.

In the next section we use these concepts to show how we can represent periodic functions as linear combinations of sines and cosines.

11.4   Fourier   Series

The representation of periodic functions in terms of a series of sines and cosines was discovered by Jean Baptiste Joseph Fourier. Although he came up with this idea in order to help him solve equations describing heat diffusion, this work has since become indispensable in the analysis and design of systems. The work was awarded the grand prize for mathematics in 1812 and has been called one of the most revolutionary contributions of the last century. A very readable account of the life of Fourier and the impact of his discovery can be found in [106].

Fourier showed that any periodic function, no matter how awkward looking, could be represented as the sum of smooth, well-behaved sines and cosines. Given a periodic function $f(t)$ with period T,

$$f(t) = f(t + nT) \qquad n = \pm 1, \pm 2, \ldots$$

we can write $f(t)$ as

$$f(t) = a_0 + \sum_{n=1}^{\infty} a_n \cos nw_0 t + \sum_{n=1}^{\infty} b_n \sin nw_0 t, \qquad w_0 = \frac{2\pi}{T}. \qquad (11.4)$$

This form is called the *trigonometric Fourier series representation* of $f(t)$.

A more useful form of the Fourier series representation from our point of view is the exponential form of the Fourier series:

$$f(t) = \sum_{n=-\infty}^{\infty} c_n e^{jnw_0 t}. \tag{11.5}$$

We can easily move between the exponential and trigonometric representations by using Euler's identity

$$e^{j\phi} = \cos\phi + j\sin\phi$$

where $j = \sqrt{-1}$.

In the terminology of the previous section, all periodic functions with period T form a vector space. The complex exponential functions $\{e^{jn\omega_0 t}\}$ constitute a basis for this space. The parameters $\{c_n\}_{n=-\infty}^{\infty}$ are the representations of a given function $f(t)$ with respect to this basis set. Therefore, by using different values of $\{c_n\}_{n=-\infty}^{\infty}$, we can build different periodic functions. If we wanted to inform somebody what a particular periodic function looked like, we could send the values of $\{c_n\}_{n=-\infty}^{\infty}$ and they could synthesize the function.

We would like to see if this basis set is orthonormal. If it is, we want to be able to obtain the coefficients that make up the Fourier representation using the approach described in the previous section. In order to do all this, we need a definition of the inner product on this vector space. If $f(t)$ and $g(t)$ are elements of this vector space, the inner product is defined as

$$\langle f(t), g(t) \rangle = \frac{1}{T} \int_{t_0}^{t_0+T} f(t)g(t)^* dt \tag{11.6}$$

where t_0 is an arbitrary constant and * denotes complex conjugate. For convenience we will take t_0 to be zero.

Using this inner product definition, let us check to see if the basis set is orthonormal.

$$\langle e^{jn\omega_0 t}, e^{jm\omega_0 t} \rangle = \frac{1}{T} \int_0^T e^{jn\omega_0 t} e^{-jm\omega_0 t} dt \tag{11.7}$$

$$= \frac{1}{T} \int_0^T e^{j(n-m)\omega_0 t} dt \tag{11.8}$$

When $n = m$, Equation (11.7) becomes the norm of the basis vector, which is clearly one. When $n \neq m$, let us define $k = n - m$. Then

$$\langle e^{jn\omega_0 t}, e^{jm\omega_0 t} \rangle = \frac{1}{T} \int_0^T e^{jk\omega_0 t} dt \tag{11.9}$$

$$= \frac{1}{jk\omega_0} (e^{jk\omega_0 T} - 1) \tag{11.10}$$

$$= \frac{1}{jk\omega_0} (e^{jk2\pi} - 1) \tag{11.11}$$

$$= 0 \tag{11.12}$$

where we have used the facts that $\omega_0 = \frac{2\pi}{T}$ and

$$e^{jk2\pi} = \cos(2k\pi) + j\sin(2k\pi) = 1.$$

Thus, the basis set is orthonormal.

Using this fact, we can find the coefficient c_n by taking the inner product of $f(t)$ with the basis vector $e^{jn\omega_0 t}$:

$$c_n = \langle f(t), e^{jn\omega_0 t} \rangle = \frac{1}{T}\int_0^T f(t)e^{-jn\omega_0 t}\, dt. \qquad (11.13)$$

What do we gain from obtaining the Fourier representation $\{c_n\}_{n=-\infty}^{\infty}$ of a function $f(t)$? Before we answer this question, let us examine the context in which we generally use Fourier analysis. We start with some signal generated by a source. If we wish to look at how this signal changes its amplitude over a period of time (or space), we represent it as a function of time $f(t)$ (or a function of space $f(x)$). Thus, $f(t)$ (or $f(x)$) is a representation of the signal that brings out how this signal varies in time (or space). The sequence $\{c_n\}_{n=-\infty}^{\infty}$ is a different representation of the same signal. However, this representation brings out a different aspect of the signal. The basis functions are sinusoids that differ from each other in how fast they fluctuate in a given time interval. The basis vector $e^{2j\omega_0 t}$ fluctuates twice as fast as the basis vector $e^{j\omega_0 t}$. The coefficients of the basis vectors $\{c_n\}_{n=-\infty}^{\infty}$ give us a measure of the different amounts of fluctuation present in the signal. Fluctuation of this sort is usually measured in terms of frequency. A frequency of 1 Hz denotes the completion of one period in one second, a frequency of 2 Hz denotes the completion of two cycles in one second, and so on. Thus, the coefficients $\{c_n\}_{n=-\infty}^{\infty}$ provide us with a frequency profile of the signal: how much of the signal changes at the rate of $\frac{\omega_0}{2\pi}$ Hz, how much of the signal changes at the rate of $\frac{2\omega_0}{2\pi}$ Hz, and so on. This information cannot be obtained by looking at the time representation $f(t)$. On the other hand, the use of the $\{c_n\}_{n=-\infty}^{\infty}$ representation tells us little about how the signal changes with time. Each representation emphasizes a different aspect of the signal. The ability to view the same signal in different ways helps us to better understand the nature of the signal, and thus develop tools for manipulation of the signal. Later, when we talk about wavelets, we will look at representations that provide information about both the time profile and the frequency profile of the signal.

The Fourier series provides us with a frequency representation of *periodic* signals. However, many of the signals we will be dealing with are not periodic. Fortunately, the Fourier series concepts can be extended to nonperiodic signals.

11.5 Fourier Transform

Consider the function $f(t)$ shown in Figure 11.3. Let us define a function $f_P(t)$ as

$$f_P(t) = \sum_{n=-\infty}^{\infty} f(t - nT) \qquad (11.14)$$

where $T > t_1$. This function, which is obviously periodic $(f_P(t + T) = f_P(t))$, is called the *periodic extension* of the function $f(t)$. Because the function $f_P(t)$ is periodic, we can define a

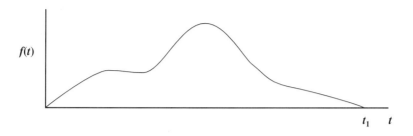

FIGURE 11.3   A function of time.

Fourier series expansion for it:

$$c_n = \frac{1}{T} \int_{-\frac{T}{2}}^{\frac{T}{2}} f_P(t) e^{-jn\omega_0 t} \, dt \tag{11.15}$$

$$f_P(t) = \sum_{n=-\infty}^{\infty} c_n e^{jn\omega_0 t}. \tag{11.16}$$

Define

$$C(n, T) = c_n T$$

and

$$\Delta\omega = \omega_0,$$

and let us slightly rewrite the Fourier series equations:

$$C(n, T) = \int_{-\frac{T}{2}}^{\frac{T}{2}} f_P(t) e^{-jn\Delta\omega t} \, dt \tag{11.17}$$

$$f_P(t) = \sum_{n=-\infty}^{\infty} \frac{C(n, T)}{T} e^{jn\Delta\omega t}. \tag{11.18}$$

We can recover $f(t)$ from $f_P(t)$ by taking the limit of $f_P(t)$ as T goes to infinity. Because $\Delta\omega = \omega_0 = \frac{2\pi}{T}$, this is the same as taking the limit as $\Delta\omega$ goes to zero. As $\Delta\omega$ goes to zero, $n\Delta\omega$ goes to a continuous variable ω. Therefore,

$$\lim_{T \to \infty \, \Delta\omega \to 0} \int_{-\frac{T}{2}}^{\frac{T}{2}} f_P(t) e^{-jn\Delta\omega t} \, dt = \int_{-\infty}^{\infty} f(t) e^{-j\omega t} \, dt. \tag{11.19}$$

From the right-hand side, we can see that the resulting function is a function only of ω. We call this function the Fourier transform of $f(t)$, and we will denote it by $F(\omega)$. To recover $f(t)$ from $F(w)$, we apply the same limits to Equation (11.18):

$$f(t) = \lim_{T \to \infty} f_P(t) = \lim_{T \to \infty \, \Delta\omega \to 0} \sum_{n=-\infty}^{\infty} C(n, T) \frac{\Delta\omega}{2\pi} e^{jn\Delta\omega t} \tag{11.20}$$

$$= \frac{1}{2\pi} \int_{-\infty}^{\infty} F(\omega) e^{j\omega t} \, d\omega. \tag{11.21}$$

The equation

$$F(\omega) = \int_{-\infty}^{\infty} f(t)e^{-j\omega t} dt \qquad (11.22)$$

is generally called the *Fourier transform*. The function $F(\omega)$ tells us how the signal fluctuates at different frequencies. The equation

$$f(t) = \frac{1}{2\pi} \int_{-\infty}^{\infty} F(w)e^{j\omega t} d\omega \qquad (11.23)$$

is called the *inverse Fourier transform*, and it shows us how we can construct a signal using components that fluctuate at different frequencies. We will denote the operation of the Fourier transform by the symbol $\mathcal{F}$. Thus, in the preceding, $F(\omega) = \mathcal{F}[f(t)]$.

There are several important properties of the Fourier transform, three of which will be of particular use to us. We state them here and leave the proof to the problems (Problems 2, 4, and 3).

11.5.1 Parseval's Theorem

The Fourier transform is an energy-preserving transform; that is, the total energy when we look at the time representation of the signal is the same as the total energy when we look at the frequency representation of the signal. This makes sense because the total energy is a physical property of the signal and should not change when we look at it using different representations. Mathematically, this is stated as

$$\int_{-\infty}^{\infty} |f(t)|^2 = \frac{1}{2\pi} \int_{-\infty}^{\infty} |F(\omega)|^2 d\omega. \qquad (11.24)$$

The $\frac{1}{2\pi}$ factor is a result of using units of radians (ω) for frequency instead of Hertz (f). If we substitute $\omega = 2\pi f$ in Equation (11.24), the 2π factor will go away. This property applies to any vector space representation obtained using an orthonormal basis set.

11.5.2 Modulation Property

If $f(t)$ has the Fourier transform $F(\omega)$, then the Fourier transform of $f(t)e^{j\omega_0 t}$ is $F(w - w_0)$. That is, multiplication with a complex exponential in the time domain corresponds to a shift in the frequency domain. As a sinusoid can be written as a sum of complex exponentials, multiplication of $f(t)$ by a sinusoid will also correspond to shifts of $F(\omega)$. For example,

$$\cos(\omega_0 t) = \frac{e^{j\omega_0 t} + e^{-j\omega_0 t}}{2}.$$

Therefore,

$$\mathcal{F}[f(t)\cos(\omega_0 t)] = \frac{1}{2}\left(F(\omega - \omega_0) + F(\omega + \omega_0)\right).$$

11.5.3 Convolution Theorem

When we examine the relationships between the input and output of linear systems, we will encounter integrals of the following forms:

$$f(t) = \int_{-\infty}^{\infty} f_1(\tau)f_2(t-\tau)d\tau$$

or

$$f(t) = \int_{-\infty}^{\infty} f_1(t-\tau)f_2(\tau)d\tau.$$

These are called convolution integrals. The convolution operation is often denoted as

$$f(t) = f_1(t) \otimes f_2(t).$$

The convolution theorem states that if $F(\omega) = \mathcal{F}[f(t)] = \mathcal{F}[f_1(t) \otimes f_2(t)]$, $F_1(\omega) = \mathcal{F}[f_1(t)]$, and $F_2(\omega) = \mathcal{F}[f_2(t)]$, then

$$F(\omega) = F_1(\omega)F_2(\omega).$$

We can also go in the other direction. If

$$F(\omega) = F_1(\omega) \otimes F_2(\omega) = \int F_1(\sigma)F_2(\omega - \sigma)d\sigma$$

then

$$f(t) = f_1(t)f_2(t).$$

As mentioned earlier, this property of the Fourier transform is important because the convolution integral relates the input and output of linear systems, which brings us to one of the major reasons for the popularity of the Fourier transform. We have claimed that the Fourier series and Fourier transform provide us with an alternative frequency profile of a signal. Although sinusoids are not the only basis set that can provide us with a frequency profile, they do, however, have an important property that helps us study linear systems, which we describe in the next section.

11.6 Linear Systems

A linear system is a system that has the following two properties:

■ **Homogeneity:** Suppose we have a linear system L with input $f(t)$ and output $g(t)$:

$$g(t) = L[f(t)].$$

If we have two inputs, $f_1(t)$ and $f_2(t)$, with corresponding outputs, $g_1(t)$ and $g_2(t)$, then the output of the sum of the two inputs is simply the sum of the two outputs:

$$L[f_1(t) + f_2(t)] = g_1(t) + g_2(t).$$

■ **Scaling:** Given a linear system L with input $f(t)$ and output $g(t)$, if we multiply the input with a scalar α, then the output will be multiplied by the same scalar:

$$L[\alpha f(t)] = \alpha L[f(t)] = \alpha g(t).$$

The two properties together are referred to as *superposition*.

11.6.1   Time Invariance

Of specific interest to us are linear systems that are *time invariant*. A time-invariant system has the property that the shape of the response of this system does not depend on the time at which the input was applied. If the response of a linear system L to an input $f(t)$ is $g(t)$,

$$L[f(t)] = g(t),$$

and we delay the input by some interval t_0, then if L is a time-invariant system, the output will be $g(t)$ delayed by the same amount:

$$L[f(t - t_0)] = g(t - t_0). \tag{11.25}$$

11.6.2   Transfer Function

Linear time-invariant systems have a very interesting (and useful) response when the input is a sinusoid. If the input to a linear system is a sinusoid of a certain frequency ω_0, then the output is also a sinusoid of the same frequency that has been scaled and delayed; that is,

$$L[\cos(\omega_0 t)] = \alpha \cos(\omega_0 (t - t_d))$$

or in terms of the complex exponential

$$L[e^{j\omega_0 t}] = \alpha e^{j\omega_0 (t - t_d)}.$$

Thus, given a linear system, we can characterize its response to sinusoids of a particular frequency by a pair of parameters, the gain α and the delay t_d. In general, we use the phase $\phi = \omega_0 t_d$ in place of the delay. The parameters α and ϕ will generally be a function of the frequency, so in order to characterize the system for all frequencies, we will need a pair of functions $\alpha(\omega)$ and $\phi(\omega)$. As the Fourier transform allows us to express the signal as coefficients of sinusoids, given an input $f(t)$, all we need to do is, for each frequency ω, multiply the Fourier transform of $f(t)$ with some $\alpha(\omega)e^{j\phi(\omega)}$, where $\alpha(\omega)$ and $\phi(\omega)$ are the gain and phase terms of the linear system for that particular frequency.

This pair of functions $\alpha(\omega)$ and $\phi(\omega)$ constitute the *transfer function* of the linear time-invariant system $H(\omega)$:

$$H(\omega) = |H(\omega)| e^{j\phi(\omega)}$$

where $|H(\omega)| = \alpha(\omega)$.

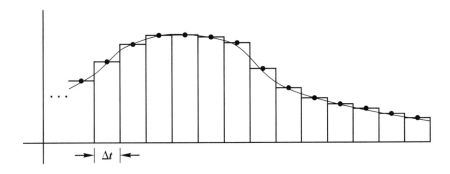

FIGURE 11.4 **A function of time.**

Because of the specific way in which a linear system responds to a sinusoidal input, given a linear system with transfer function $H(\omega)$, input $f(t)$, and output $g(t)$, the Fourier transforms of the input and output $F(\omega)$ and $G(\omega)$ are related by

$$G(\omega) = H(\omega)F(\omega).$$

Using the convolution theorem, $f(t)$ and $g(t)$ are related by

$$g(t) = \int_{-\infty}^{\infty} f(\tau)h(t-\tau)d\tau$$

or

$$g(t) = \int_{-\infty}^{\infty} f(t-\tau)h(\tau)d\tau$$

where $H(\omega)$ is the Fourier transform of $h(t)$.

11.6.3 Impulse Response

To see what $h(t)$ is, let us look at the input-output relationship of a linear time-invariant system from a different point of view. Let us suppose we have a linear system L with input $f(t)$. We can obtain a staircase approximation $f_S(t)$ to the function $f(t)$, as shown in Figure 11.4:

$$f_S(t) = \sum f(n\Delta t) \, \text{rect}\left(\frac{t-n\Delta t}{\Delta t}\right) \tag{11.26}$$

where

$$\text{rect}\left(\frac{t}{T}\right) = \begin{cases} 1 & |t| < \frac{T}{2} \\ 0 & \text{otherwise.} \end{cases} \tag{11.27}$$

The response of the linear system can be written as

$$L[f_S(t)] = L\left[\sum f(n\Delta t) \, \text{rect}\left(\frac{t-n\Delta t}{\Delta t}\right)\right] \tag{11.28}$$

$$= L\left[\sum f(n\Delta t)\frac{\text{rect}\left(\frac{t-n\Delta t}{\Delta t}\right)}{\Delta t}\Delta t\right]. \tag{11.29}$$

For a given value of Δt, we can use the superposition property of linear systems to obtain

$$L[f_S(t)] = \sum f(n\Delta t) L \left[\frac{\text{rect}(\frac{t-n\Delta t}{\Delta t})}{\Delta t} \right] \Delta t. \tag{11.30}$$

If we now take the limit as Δt goes to zero in this equation, on the left-hand side $f_S(t)$ will go to $f(t)$. To see what happens on the right-hand side of the equation, first let's look at the effect of this limit on the function $\text{rect}(\frac{t}{\Delta t})/\Delta t$. As Δt goes to zero, this function becomes narrower and taller. However, at all times the integral of this function is equal to one. The limit of this function as Δt goes to zero is called the *Dirac delta function*, or *impulse function*, and is denoted by $\delta(t)$:

$$\lim_{\Delta t \to 0} \frac{\text{rect}(\frac{t-n\Delta t}{\Delta t})}{\Delta t} = \delta(t). \tag{11.31}$$

Therefore,

$$L[f(t)] = \lim_{\Delta t \to 0} L[f_S(t)] = \int f(\tau) L[\delta(t-\tau)] d\tau. \tag{11.32}$$

Denote the response of the system L to an impulse, or the *impulse response*, by $h(t)$:

$$h(t) = L[\delta(t)]. \tag{11.33}$$

Then, if the system is also time invariant,

$$L[f(t)] = \int f(\tau) h(t-\tau) d\tau. \tag{11.34}$$

Using the convolution theorem, we can see that the Fourier transform of the impulse response $h(t)$ is the transfer function $H(\omega)$.

The Dirac delta function is an interesting function. In fact, it is not clear that it is a function at all. It has an integral that is clearly one, but at the only point where it is not zero, it is undefined! One property of the delta function that makes it very useful is the *sifting* property:

$$\int_{t_1}^{t_2} f(t)\delta(t-t_0) dt = \begin{cases} f(t_0) & t_1 \leq t_0 \leq t_2 \\ 0 & \text{otherwise.} \end{cases} \tag{11.35}$$

11.6.4 Filter

The linear systems of most interest to us will be systems that permit certain frequency components of the signal to pass through, while attenuating all other components of the signal. Such systems are called *filters*. If the filter allows only frequency components below a certain frequency W Hz to pass through, the filter is called a *low-pass filter*. The transfer function of an ideal low-pass filter is given by

$$H(\omega) = \begin{cases} e^{-j\alpha\omega} & |\omega| < 2\pi W \\ 0 & \text{otherwise .} \end{cases} \tag{11.36}$$

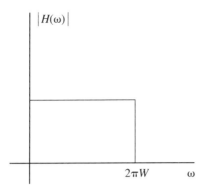

FIGURE 11.5   Magnitude of the transfer function of an ideal low-pass filter.

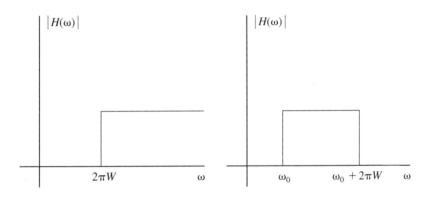

FIGURE 11.6   Magnitudes of the transfer functions of ideal high-pass (left) and ideal band-pass (right) filters.

This filter is said to have a *bandwidth* of W Hz. The magnitude of this filter is shown in Figure 11.5. A low-pass filter will produce a smoothed version of the signal by blocking higher-frequency components that correspond to fast variations in the signal.

A filter that attenuates the frequency components below a certain frequency W and allows the frequency components above this frequency to pass through is called a *high-pass filter*. A high-pass filter will remove slowly changing trends from the signal. Finally, a signal that lets through a range of frequencies between two specified frequencies, say, W_1 and W_2, is called a *band-pass filter*. The bandwidth of this filter is said to be $W_2 - W_1$ Hz. The magnitude of the transfer functions of an ideal high-pass filter and an ideal band-pass filter with bandwidth W are shown in Figure 11.6. In all the ideal filter characteristics, there is a sharp transition between the *passband* of the filter (the range of frequencies that are not attenuated) and the *stopband* of the filter (those frequency intervals where the signal is completely attenuated). Real filters do not have such sharp transitions, or *cutoffs*. The magnitude characteristics of a more realistic low-pass filter are shown in Figure 11.7. Notice the more gentle rolloff. But when the cutoff between stopband and passband is not sharp, how do we define the band-

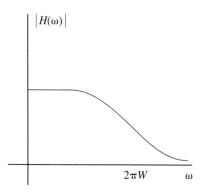

FIGURE 11.7   **Magnitude of the transfer functions of a realistic low-pass filter.**

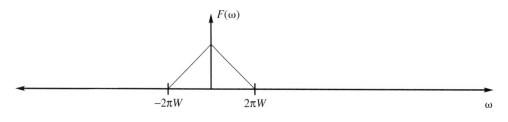

FIGURE 11.8   **A function F(ω).**

width? There are several different ways of defining the bandwidth. The most common way is to define the frequency at which the magnitude of the transfer function is $1/\sqrt{2}$ of its maximum value (or the magnitude squared is 1/2 of its maximum value) as the cutoff frequency.

11.7 Sampling

In 1928 Harry Nyquist at Bell Laboratories showed that if we have a signal whose Fourier transform is zero above some frequency W Hz, it can be accurately represented using $2W$ equally spaced samples per second. This very important result, known as the *sampling theorem*, is at the heart of our ability to transmit analog waveforms such as speech and video using digital means. There are several ways to prove this result. We will use the results presented in the previous section to do so.

11.7.1 Ideal Sampling—Frequency Domain View

Let us suppose we have a function $f(t)$ with Fourier transform $F(\omega)$, shown in Figure 11.8, which is zero for ω greater than $2\pi W$. Define the periodic extension of $F(\omega)$ as

$$F_P(\omega) = \sum_{n=-\infty}^{\infty} F(\omega - n\sigma_0), \qquad \sigma_0 = 4\pi W. \qquad (11.37)$$

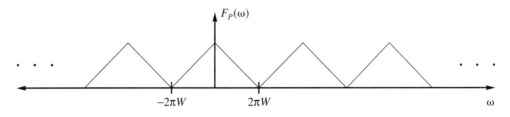

FIGURE 11.9   **The periodic extension $F_P(\omega)$.**

The periodic extension is shown in Figure 11.9. As $F_P(\omega)$ is periodic, we can express it in terms of a Fourier series expansion:

$$F_P(\omega) = \sum_{n=-\infty}^{\infty} c_n e^{jn\frac{1}{2W}\omega}. \tag{11.38}$$

The coefficients of the expansion $\{c_n\}_{n=-\infty}^{\infty}$ are then given by

$$c_n = \frac{1}{4\pi W} \int_{-2\pi W}^{2\pi W} F_P(\omega) e^{-jn\frac{1}{2W}\omega} d\omega. \tag{11.39}$$

However, in the interval $(-2\pi W, 2\pi W)$, $F(\omega)$ is identical to $F_P(\omega)$; therefore,

$$c_n = \frac{1}{4\pi W} \int_{-2\pi W}^{2\pi W} F(\omega) e^{-jn\frac{1}{2W}\omega} d\omega. \tag{11.40}$$

The function $F(\omega)$ is zero outside the interval $(-2\pi W, 2\pi W)$, so we can extend the limits to infinity without changing the result:

$$c_n = \frac{1}{2W} \left[\frac{1}{2\pi} \int_{-\infty}^{\infty} F(\omega) e^{-jn\frac{1}{2W}\omega} d\omega \right]. \tag{11.41}$$

The expression in brackets is simply the inverse Fourier transform evaluated at $t = \frac{n}{2W}$; therefore,

$$c_n = \frac{1}{2W} f\left(\frac{n}{2W}\right). \tag{11.42}$$

Knowing $\{c_n\}_{n=-\infty}^{\infty}$ and the value of W, we can reconstruct $F_P(\omega)$. Because $F_P(\omega)$ and $F(\omega)$ are identical in the interval $(-2\pi W, 2\pi W)$, therefore knowing $\{c_n\}_{n=-\infty}^{\infty}$, we can also reconstruct $F(\omega)$ in this interval. But $\{c_n\}_{n=-\infty}^{\infty}$ are simply the samples of $f(t)$ every $\frac{1}{2W}$ seconds, and $F(\omega)$ is zero outside this interval. Therefore, given the samples of a function $f(t)$ obtained at a rate of $2W$ samples per second, we should be able to exactly reconstruct the function $f(t)$.

Let us see how we can do this:

$$f(t) = \frac{1}{2\pi} \int_{-\infty}^{\infty} F(\omega) e^{-j\omega t} d\omega \tag{11.43}$$

$$= \frac{1}{2\pi} \int_{-2\pi W}^{2\pi W} F(\omega)e^{-j\omega t} d\omega \tag{11.44}$$

$$= \frac{1}{2\pi} \int_{-2\pi W}^{2\pi W} F_P(\omega)e^{-j\omega t} d\omega \tag{11.45}$$

$$= \frac{1}{2\pi} \int_{-2\pi W}^{2\pi W} \sum_{n=-\infty}^{\infty} c_n e^{jn\frac{1}{2W}\omega} e^{-j\omega t} d\omega \tag{11.46}$$

$$= \frac{1}{2\pi} \sum_{n=-\infty}^{\infty} c_n \int_{-2\pi W}^{2\pi W} e^{jw(t-\frac{n}{2W})} d\omega. \tag{11.47}$$

Evaluating the integral and substituting for c_n from Equation (11.42), we obtain

$$f(t) = \sum_{n=-\infty}^{\infty} f\left(\frac{n}{2W}\right) \text{Sinc}\left[2W\left(t - \frac{n}{2W}\right)\right] \tag{11.48}$$

where

$$\text{Sinc}[x] = \frac{\sin(\pi x)}{\pi x}. \tag{11.49}$$

Thus, given samples of $f(t)$ taken every $\frac{1}{2W}$ seconds, or, in other words, samples of $f(t)$ obtained at a rate of $2W$ samples per second, we can reconstruct $f(t)$ by interpolating between the samples using the Sinc function.

11.7.2 Ideal Sampling—Time Domain View

Let us look at this process from a slightly different point of view, starting with the sampling operation. Mathematically, we can represent the sampling operation by multiplying the function $f(t)$ with a train of impulses to obtain the sampled function $f_S(t)$:

$$f_S(t) = f(t) \sum_{n=-\infty}^{\infty} \delta(t - nT), \qquad T < \frac{1}{2W}. \tag{11.50}$$

To obtain the Fourier transform of the sampled function, we use the convolution theorem:

$$\mathcal{F}\left[f(t) \sum_{n=-\infty}^{\infty} \delta(t - nT)\right] = \mathcal{F}\left[f(t)\right] \otimes \mathcal{F}\left[\sum_{n=-\infty}^{\infty} \delta(t - nT)\right]. \tag{11.51}$$

Let us denote the Fourier transform of $f(t)$ by $F(\omega)$. The Fourier transform of a train of impulses in the time domain is a train of impulses in the frequency domain (Problem 5):

$$\mathcal{F}\left[\sum_{n=-\infty}^{\infty} \delta(t - nT)\right] = \sigma_0 \sum_{n=-\infty}^{\infty} \delta(w - n\sigma_0) \qquad \sigma_0 = \frac{2\pi}{T}. \tag{11.52}$$

FIGURE 11.10   **Fourier transform of the sampled function.**

Thus, the Fourier transform of $f_S(t)$ is

$$F_S(\omega) = F(\omega) \otimes \sum_{n=-\infty}^{\infty} \delta(w - n\sigma_0) \qquad (11.53)$$

$$= \sum_{n=-\infty}^{\infty} F(\omega) \otimes \delta(w - n\sigma_0) \qquad (11.54)$$

$$= \sum_{n=-\infty}^{\infty} F(\omega - n\sigma_0) \qquad (11.55)$$

where the last equality is due to the sifting property of the delta function.

Pictorially, for $F(\omega)$ as shown in Figure 11.8, $F_S(\omega)$ is shown in Figure 11.10. Note that if T is less than $\frac{1}{2W}$, σ_0 is greater than $4\pi W$, and as long as σ_0 is greater than $4\pi W$, we can recover $F(\omega)$ by passing $F_S(\omega)$ through an ideal low-pass filter with bandwidth W Hz ($2\pi W$ radians).

What happens if we do sample at a rate less than $2W$ samples per second (that is, σ_0 is less than $4\pi W$)? Again we can see the results most easily in a pictorial fashion. The result for σ_0 equal to $3\pi W$ is shown in Figure 11.11. Filtering this signal through an ideal low-pass filter, we get the distorted signal shown in Figure 11.12. Therefore, if σ_0 is less than $4\pi W$, we can no longer recover the signal $f(t)$ from its samples. This distortion is known as *aliasing*. In order to prevent aliasing, it is useful to filter the signal prior to sampling using a low-pass filter with a bandwidth less than half the sampling frequency.

Once we have the samples of a signal, sometimes the actual times they were sampled at are not important. In these situations we can normalize the sampling frequency to unity. This means that the highest frequency component in the signal is at 0.5 Hz, or π radians. Thus, when dealing with sampled signals, we will often talk about frequency ranges of $-\pi$ to π.

11.8 Discrete Fourier Transform

The procedures that we gave for obtaining the Fourier series and transform were based on the assumption that the signal we were examining could be represented as a continuous function of time. However, for the applications that we will be interested in, we will primarily be dealing with samples of a signal. To obtain the Fourier transform of nonperiodic signals, we started from the Fourier series and modified it to take into account the nonperiodic nature of

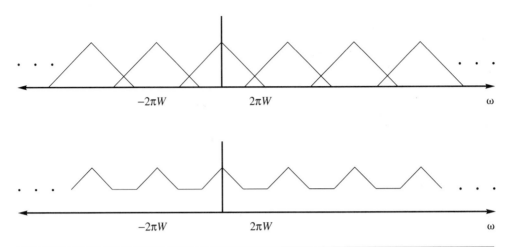

FIGURE 1 1 . 1 1   **Effect of sampling at a rate less than 2W samples per second.**

$-2\pi W$ $2\pi W$ ω

FIGURE 1 1 . 1 2   **Aliased reconstruction.**

the signal. To obtain the discrete Fourier transform (DFT), we again start from the Fourier series. We begin with the Fourier series representation of a sampled function, the discrete Fourier series.

Recall that the Fourier series coefficients of a periodic function $f(t)$ with period T is given by

$$c_k = \frac{1}{T} \int_0^T f(t) e^{jkw_0 t}\, dt. \tag{11.56}$$

Suppose instead of a continuous function, we have a function sampled N times during each period T. We can obtain the coefficients of the Fourier series representation of this sampled function as

$$F_k = \frac{1}{T} \int_0^T f(t) \sum_{n=0}^{N-1} \delta\left(t - \frac{n}{N}T\right) e^{jkw_0 t}\, dt \tag{11.57}$$

$$= \frac{1}{T} \sum_{n=0}^{N-1} f\left(\frac{n}{N}T\right) e^{j\frac{2\pi k n}{N}} \tag{11.58}$$

where we have used the fact that $w_0 = \frac{2\pi}{T}$, and we have replaced c_k by F_k. Taking $T = 1$ for convenience and defining

$$f_n = f\left(\frac{n}{N}\right),$$

we get the coefficients for the discrete Fourier series (DFS) representation:

$$F_k = \sum_{n=0}^{N-1} f_n e^{j\frac{2\pi kn}{N}}. \tag{11.59}$$

Notice that the sequence of coefficients $\{F_k\}$ is periodic with period N.

The Fourier series representation was given by

$$f(t) = \sum_{k=-\infty}^{\infty} c_k e^{jn\omega_0 t}. \tag{11.60}$$

Evaluating this for $t = \frac{n}{N}T$, we get

$$f_n = f(\frac{n}{N}T) = \sum_{k=-\infty}^{\infty} c_k e^{j\frac{2\pi kn}{N}}. \tag{11.61}$$

Let us write this in a slightly different form:

$$f_n = \sum_{k=0}^{N-1} \sum_{l=-\infty}^{\infty} c_{k+lN} e^{j\frac{2\pi n(k+lN)}{N}} \tag{11.62}$$

but

$$e^{j\frac{2\pi n(k+lN)}{N}} = e^{j\frac{2\pi kn}{N}} e^{j2\pi nl} \tag{11.63}$$

$$= e^{j\frac{2\pi kn}{N}}. \tag{11.64}$$

Therefore,

$$f_n = \sum_{k=0}^{N-1} e^{j\frac{2\pi kn}{N}} \sum_{l=-\infty}^{\infty} c_{k+lN}. \tag{11.65}$$

Define

$$\bar{c}_k = \sum_{l=-\infty}^{\infty} c_{k+lN}. \tag{11.66}$$

Clearly, $\bar{c}_k$ is periodic with period N. In fact, we can show that $\bar{c}_k = \frac{1}{N} F_k$ and

$$f_n = \frac{1}{N} \sum_{k=0}^{N-1} F_k e^{j\frac{2\pi kn}{N}}. \tag{11.67}$$

Obtaining the discrete Fourier transform from the discrete Fourier series is simply a matter of interpretation. We are generally interested in the discrete Fourier transform of a finite-length sequence. If we assume that the finite-length sequence is one period of a periodic sequence, then we can use the DFS equations to represent this sequence. The only difference is that the expressions are only valid for one "period" of the "periodic" sequence.

The DFT is an especially powerful tool because of the existence of a fast algorithm, called appropriately the *fast Fourier transform* (FFT), that can be used to compute it.

11.9 Z-Transform

In the previous section we saw how to extend the Fourier series to use with sampled functions. We can also do the same with the Fourier transform. Recall that the Fourier transform was given by the equation

$$F(\omega) = \int_{-\infty}^{\infty} f(t)e^{-j\omega t}dt. \tag{11.68}$$

Replacing $f(t)$ with its sampled version, we get

$$F(\omega) = \int_{-\infty}^{\infty} f(t) \sum_{n=-\infty}^{\infty} \delta(t - nT)e^{-j\omega t}dt \tag{11.69}$$

$$= \sum_{n=-\infty}^{\infty} f_n e^{-j\omega nT} \tag{11.70}$$

where $f_n = f(nT)$. This is called the discrete time Fourier transform. The Z-transform of the sequence $\{f_n\}$ is a generalization of the discrete time Fourier transform and is given by

$$F(z) = \sum_{n=-\infty}^{\infty} f_n z^{-n} \tag{11.71}$$

where

$$z = e^{\sigma T + jwT}. \tag{11.72}$$

Notice that if we let σ equal zero, we get the original expression for the Fourier transform of a discrete time sequence. We denote the Z-transform of a sequence by

$$F(z) = \mathcal{Z}[f_n].$$

We can express this another way. Notice that the magnitude of z is given by

$$|z| = e^{\sigma T}.$$

Thus, when σ equals zero, the magnitude of z is one. Because z is a complex number, the magnitude of z is equal to one on the unit circle in the complex plane. Therefore, we can say that the Fourier transform of a sequence can be obtained by evaluating the Z-transform of the sequence on the unit circle. Notice that the Fourier transform thus obtained will be periodic, which we expect because we are dealing with a sampled function. Further, if we assume T to be one, ω varies from $-\pi$ to π, which corresponds to a frequency range of -0.5 to 0.5 Hz.

This makes sense because, by the sampling theorem, if the sampling rate is one sample per second, the highest frequency component that can be recovered is 0.5 Hz.

For the Z-transform to exist—in other words, for the power series to converge—we need to have

$$\sum_{n=-\infty}^{\infty} \left| f_n z^{-n} \right| < \infty.$$

Whether this inequality holds will depend on the sequence itself and the value of z. The values of z for which the series converges are called the *region of convergence* of the Z-transform. From our earlier discussion, we can see that for the Fourier transform of the sequence to exist, the region of convergence should include the unit circle. Let us look at a simple example.

Example 11.9.1:

Given the sequence

$$f_n = a^n u[n]$$

where $u[n]$ is the unit step function

$$u[n] = \begin{cases} 1 & n \geq 0 \\ 0 & n < 0 \end{cases} \tag{11.73}$$

the Z-transform is given by

$$F(z) = \sum_{n=0}^{\infty} a^n z^{-n} \tag{11.74}$$

$$= \sum_{n=0}^{\infty} (az^{-1})^n. \tag{11.75}$$

This is simply the sum of a geometric series. As we confront this kind of sum quite often, let us briefly digress and obtain the formula for the sum of a geometric series.

Suppose we have a sum

$$S_{mn} = \sum_{k=m}^{n} x^k = x^m + x^{m+1} + \cdots + x^n \tag{11.76}$$

then

$$x S_{mn} = x^{m+1} + x^{m+2} + \cdots + x^{n+1}. \tag{11.77}$$

Subtracting Equation (11.77) from Equation (11.76), we get

$$(1 - x) S_{mn} = x^m - x^{n+1}$$

and

$$S_{mn} = \frac{x^m - x^{n+1}}{1 - x}.$$

If the upper limit of the sum is infinity, we take the limit as n goes to infinity. This limit exists only when $|x| < 1$.

Using this formula, we get the Z-transform of the $\{f_n\}$ sequence as

$$F(z) = \frac{1}{1 - az^{-1}}, \qquad |az^{-1}| < 1 \tag{11.78}$$

$$= \frac{z}{z - a}, \qquad |z| > |a|. \tag{11.79}$$

◆

In this example the region of convergence is the region $|z| > a$. For the Fourier transform to exist, we need to include the unit circle in the region of convergence. In order for this to happen, a has to be less than one.

Using this example, we can get some other Z-transforms that will be useful to us.

Example 11.9.2:

In the previous example we found that

$$\sum_{n=0}^{\infty} a^n z^{-n} = \frac{z}{z - a}, \qquad |z| > |a|. \tag{11.80}$$

If we take the derivative of both sides of the equation with respect to a, we get

$$\sum_{n=0}^{\infty} na^{n-1} z^{-n} = \frac{z}{(z - a)^2}, \qquad |z| > |a|. \tag{11.81}$$

Thus,

$$\mathcal{Z}[na^{n-1}u[n]] = \frac{z}{(z - a)^2}, \qquad |z| > |a|.$$

If we differentiate Equation (11.80) m times, we get

$$\sum_{n=0}^{\infty} n(n - 1) \cdots (n - m + 1) a^{n-m} = \frac{m!z}{(z - a)^{m+1}}.$$

In other words,

$$\mathcal{Z}\left[\binom{n}{m} a^{n-m} u[n]\right] = \frac{z}{(z - a)^{m+1}}. \tag{11.82}$$

◆

In these examples the Z-transform is a ratio of polynomials in z. For sequences of interest to us, this will generally be the case, and the Z-transform will be of the form

$$F(z) = \frac{N(z)}{D(z)}.$$

TABLE 11.1   Some Z-transform pairs.

$\{f_n\}$	$F(z)$
$a^n u[n]$	$\frac{z}{z-a}$
$nTu[n]$	$\frac{Tz^{-1}}{(1-z^{-1})^2}$
$\sin(\alpha nT)$	$\frac{(\sin \alpha nT)z^{-1}}{1-2\cos(\alpha T)z^{-1}+z^{-2}}$
$\cos(\alpha nT)$	$\frac{(\cos \alpha nT)z^{-1}}{1-2\cos(\alpha T)z^{-1}+z^{-2}}$

The values of z for which $F(z)$ is zero are called the *zeros* of $F(z)$; the values for which $F(z)$ is infinity are called the *poles* of $F(z)$. For finite values of z, the poles will occur at the roots of the polynomial $D(z)$.

The inverse Z-transform is formally given by the contour integral

$$\frac{1}{2\pi j} \oint_C F(z)z^{n-1}dz$$

where the integral is over the counterclockwise contour C, and C lies in the region of convergence. This integral can be difficult to evaluate directly; therefore, in most cases we use alternative methods for finding the inverse Z-transform.

11.9.1 Tabular Method

The inverse Z-transform has been tabulated for a number of interesting cases (see Table 11.1). If we can write $F(z)$ as a sum of these functions

$$F(z) = \sum \alpha_i F_i(z)$$

then the inverse Z-transform is given by

$$f_n = \sum \alpha_i f_{i,n}$$

where $F_i(z) = \mathcal{Z}[\{f_{i,n}\}]$.

Example 11.9.3:

$$F(z) = \frac{z}{z-0.5} + \frac{2z}{z-0.3}$$

From our earlier example we know the inverse Z-transform of $z/(z-a)$. Using that, the inverse Z-transform of $F(z)$ is

$$f_n = 0.5^n u[n] + 2(0.3)^n u[n].$$ ◆

11.9.2 Partial Fraction Expansion

In order to use the tabular method, we need to be able to decompose the function of interest to us as a sum of simpler terms. The partial fraction expansion approach does exactly that when the function is a ratio of polynomials in z.

Suppose $F(z)$ can be written as a ratio of polynomials $N(z)$ and $D(z)$. For the moment let us assume that the degree of $D(z)$ is greater than the degree of $N(z)$, and that all the roots of $D(z)$ are distinct (distinct roots are referred to as simple roots); that is,

$$F(z) = \frac{N(z)}{(z - z_1)(z - z_2) \cdots (z - z_L)}. \tag{11.83}$$

Then we can write $F(z)/z$ as

$$\frac{F(z)}{z} = \sum_{i=1}^{L} \frac{A_i}{z - z_i}. \tag{11.84}$$

If we can find the coefficients A_i, then we can write $F(z)$ as

$$F(z) = \sum_{i=1}^{L} \frac{A_i z}{z - z_i}$$

and the inverse Z-transform will be given by

$$f_n = \sum_{i=1}^{L} A_i z_i^n u[n].$$

The question then becomes one of finding the value of the coefficients A_i. This can be simply done as follows: Suppose we want to find the coefficient A_k. Multiply both sides of Equation (11.84) by $(z - z_k)$. Simplifying this we obtain

$$\frac{F(z)(z - z_k)}{z} = \sum_{i=1}^{L} \frac{A_i(z - z_k)}{z - z_i} \tag{11.85}$$

$$= A_k + \sum_{\substack{i=1 \\ i \neq k}}^{L} \frac{A_i(z - z_k)}{z - z_i}. \tag{11.86}$$

Evaluating this equation at $z = z_k$, all the terms in the summation go to zero and

$$A_k = \frac{F(z)(z - z_k)}{z} \bigg|_{z = z_k}. \tag{11.87}$$

Example 11.9.4:

Let us use the partial fraction expansion method to find the inverse Z-transform of

$$F(z) = \frac{6z^2 - 9z}{z^2 - 2.5z + 1}.$$

Then

$$\frac{F(z)}{z} = \frac{1}{z} \frac{6z^2 - 9z}{z^2 - 2.5z + 1} \tag{11.88}$$

$$= \frac{6z - 9}{(z - 0.5)(z - 2)}. \tag{11.89}$$

We want to write $F(z)/z$ in the form

$$\frac{F(z)}{z} = \frac{A_1}{z - 0.5} + \frac{A_2}{z - 2}.$$

Using the approach described above, we obtain

$$A_1 = \frac{(6z - 9)(z - 0.5)}{(z - 0.5)(z - 2)}\bigg|_{z=0.5} \tag{11.90}$$

$$= 4 \tag{11.91}$$

$$A_2 = \frac{(6z - 9)(z - 2)}{(z - 0.5)(z - 2)}\bigg|_{z=2} \tag{11.92}$$

$$= 2. \tag{11.93}$$

Therefore,

$$F(z) = \frac{4z}{z - 0.5} + \frac{2z}{z - 2}$$

and

$$f_n = [4(0.5)^n + 2(2)^n]u[n]. \qquad \blacklozenge$$

The procedure becomes slightly more complicated when we have repeated roots of $D(z)$. Suppose we have a function

$$F(z) = \frac{N(z)}{(z - z_1)(z - z_2)^2}.$$

The partial fraction expansion of this function is

$$\frac{F(z)}{z} = \frac{A_1}{z - z_1} + \frac{A_2}{z - z_2} + \frac{A_3}{(z - z_2)^2}.$$

The values of A_1 and A_3 can be found as shown previously:

$$A_1 = \frac{F(z)(z - z_1)}{z}\bigg|_{z=z_1} \tag{11.94}$$

$$A_3 = \frac{F(z)(z - z_2)^2}{z}\bigg|_{z=z_2}. \tag{11.95}$$

However, we run into problems when we try to evaluate A_2. Let's see what happens when we multiply both sides by $(z - z_2)$:

$$\frac{F(z)(z - z_2)}{z} = \frac{A_1(z - z_2)}{z - z_1} + A_2 + \frac{A_3}{z - z_2}. \tag{11.96}$$

If we now evaluate this equation at $z = z_2$, the third term on the right-hand side becomes undefined. In order to avoid this problem, we first multiply both sides by $(z - z_2)^2$ and take the derivative with respect to z prior to evaluating the equation at $z = z_2$:

$$\frac{F(z)(z - z_2)^2}{z} = \frac{A_1(z - z_2)^2}{z - z_1} + A_2(z - z_2) + A_3. \tag{11.97}$$

Taking the derivative of both sides with respect to z, we get

$$\frac{d}{dz} \frac{F(z)(z - z_2)^2}{z} = \frac{2A_1(z - z_2)(z - z_1) - A_1(z - z_2)^2}{(z - z_1)^2} + A_2. \tag{11.98}$$

If we now evaluate the expression at $z = z_2$, we get

$$A_2 = \frac{d}{dz} \frac{F(z)(z - z_2)^2}{z} \bigg|_{z=z_2}. \tag{11.99}$$

Generalizing this approach, we can show that if $D(z)$ has a root of order m at some z_k, that portion of the partial fraction expansion can be written as

$$\frac{F(z)}{z} = \frac{A_1}{z - z_k} + \frac{A_2}{(z - z_k)^2} + \cdots + \frac{A_m}{(z - z_k)^m} \tag{11.100}$$

and the lth coefficient can be obtained as

$$A_l = \frac{1}{(m - l)!} \frac{d^{(m-l)}}{dz^{(m-l)}} \frac{F(z)(z - z^k)^m}{z} \bigg|_{z=z_k}. \tag{11.101}$$

Finally, let us drop the requirement that the degree of $D(z)$ be greater or equal to the degree of $N(z)$. When the degree of $N(z)$ is greater than the degree of $D(z)$, we can simply divide $N(z)$ by $D(z)$ to obtain

$$F(z) = \frac{N(z)}{D(z)} = Q(z) + \frac{R(z)}{D(z)} \tag{11.102}$$

where $Q(z)$ is the quotient and $R(z)$ is the remainder of the division operation. Clearly, $R(z)$ will have degree less than $D(z)$.

To see how all this works together, consider the following example.

Example 11.9.5:

Let us find the inverse Z-transform of the function

$$F(z) = \frac{2z^4 + 1}{2z^3 - 5z^2 + 4z - 1}. \tag{11.103}$$

The degree of the numerator is greater than the degree of the denominator, so we divide once to obtain

$$F(z) = z + \frac{5z^3 - 4z^2 + z + 1}{2z^3 - 5z^2 + 4z - 1}. \tag{11.104}$$

The inverse Z-transform of z is δ_{n-1}, where δ_n is the discrete delta function defined as

$$\delta_n = \begin{cases} 1 & n = 0 \\ 0 & \text{otherwise.} \end{cases} \tag{11.105}$$

Let us call the remaining ratio of polynomials $F_1(z)$. We find the roots of the denominator of $F_1(z)$ as

$$F_1(z) = \frac{5z^3 - 4z^2 + z + 1}{2(z - 0.5)(z - 1)^2}. \tag{11.106}$$

Then

$$\frac{F_1(z)}{z} = \frac{5z^3 - 4z^2 + z + 1}{2z(z - 0.5)(z - 1)^2} \tag{11.107}$$

$$= \frac{A_1}{z} + \frac{A_2}{z - 0.5} + \frac{A_3}{z - 1} + \frac{A_4}{(z - 1)^2}. \tag{11.108}$$

Then

$$A_1 = \left. \frac{5z^3 - 4z^2 + z + 1}{2(z - 0.5)(z - 1)^2} \right|_{z=0} = -1 \tag{11.109}$$

$$A_2 = \left. \frac{5z^3 - 4z^2 + z + 1}{2z(z - 1)^2} \right|_{z=0.5} = 4.5 \tag{11.110}$$

$$A_4 = \left. \frac{5z^3 - 4z^2 + z + 1}{2z(z - 0.5)} \right|_{z=1} = 3. \tag{11.111}$$

To find A_3, we take the derivative with respect to z, then set $z = 1$:

$$A_3 = \left. \frac{d}{dz} \left[\frac{5z^3 - 4z^2 + 2z + 1}{2z(z - 0.5)} \right] \right|_{z=1} = -3. \tag{11.112}$$

Therefore,

$$F_1(z) = -1 + \frac{4.5z}{z - 0.5} - \frac{3z}{z - 1} + \frac{3z}{(z - 1)^2} \tag{11.113}$$

and

$$f_{1,n} = -\delta_n + 4.5(0.5)^n u[n] - 3u[n] + 3nu[n] \tag{11.114}$$

and

$$f_n = \delta_{n-1} - \delta_n + 4.5(0.5)^n u[n] - (3 - 3n)u[n]. \tag{11.115}$$

$\blacklozenge$

11.9.3 Long Division

If we could write $F(z)$ as a power series, then from the Z-transform expression the coefficients of z^{-n} would be the sequence values f_n.

Example 11.9.6:

Let's find the inverse z-transform of

$$F(z) = \frac{z}{z-a}.$$

Dividing the numerator by the denominator we get the following:

$$
\begin{array}{r}
1 \quad + \quad az^{-1} \quad + \quad a^2z^{-2} \quad \cdots \\
\hline
z-a \overline{)\; z } \\
z \quad - \quad a \\
\hline
a \\
a \quad - \quad a^2z^{-1} \\
\hline
a^2z^{-1}
\end{array}
$$

Thus, the quotient is

$$1 + az^{-1} + a^2z^{-2} + \cdots = \sum_{n=0}^{\infty} a^n z^{-n}.$$

We can easily see that the sequence for which $F(z)$ is the Z-transform is

$$f_n = a^n u[n]. \qquad \qquad \blacklozenge$$

11.9.4 Z-Transform Properties

Analogous to the continuous linear systems, we can define the transfer function of a discrete linear system as a function of z that relates the Z-transform of the input to the Z-transform of the output. Let $\{f_n\}_{n=-\infty}^{\infty}$ be the input to a discrete linear time-invariant system, and $\{g_n\}_{n=-\infty}^{\infty}$ be the output. If $F(z)$ is the Z-transform of the input sequence, and $G(z)$ is the Z-transform of the output sequence, then these are related to each other by

$$G(z) = H(z)F(z) \qquad (11.116)$$

and $H(z)$ is the transfer function of the discrete linear time-invariant system.

If the input sequence $\{f_n\}_{n=-\infty}^{\infty}$ had a Z-transform of one, then $G(z)$ would be equal to $H(z)$. It is an easy matter to find the requisite sequence:

$$F(z) = \sum_{n=-\infty}^{\infty} f_n z^{-n} = 1 \Rightarrow f_n = \begin{cases} 1 & n = 0 \\ 0 & \text{otherwise.} \end{cases} \qquad (11.117)$$

This particular sequence is called the *discrete delta function*. The response of the system to the discrete delta function is called the impulse response of the system. Obviously, the transfer function $H(z)$ is the Z-transform of the impulse response.

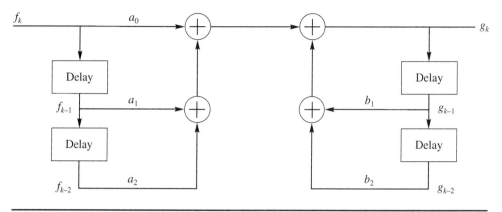

FIGURE 11.13 **A discrete system.**

11.9.5 Discrete Convolution

In the continuous time case, the output of the linear time-invariant system was a convolution of the input with the impulse response. Does the analogy hold in the discrete case? We can check this out easily by explicitly writing out the Z-transforms in Equation (11.116). For simplicity let us assume the sequences are all one-sided; that is, they are only nonzero for nonnegative values of the subscript:

$$\sum_{n=0}^{\infty} g_n z^{-n} = \sum_{n=0}^{\infty} h_n z^{-n} \sum_{m=0}^{\infty} f_m z^{-m}. \tag{11.118}$$

Equating like powers of z:

$$g_0 = h_0 f_0$$
$$g_1 = f_0 h_1 + f_1 h_0$$
$$g_2 = f_0 h_2 + f_1 h_1 + f_2 h_0$$
$$\vdots$$
$$g_n = \sum_{m=0}^{n} f_m h_{n-m}.$$

Thus, the output sequence is a result of the discrete convolution of the input sequence with the impulse response.

Most of the discrete linear systems we will be dealing with will be made up of delay elements, and their input-output relations can be written as constant coefficient difference equations. For example, for the system shown in Figure 11.13, the input-output relationship can be written in the form of the following difference equation:

$$g_k = a_0 f_k + a_1 f_{k-1} + a_2 f_{k-2} + b_1 g_{k-1} + b_2 g_{k-2}. \tag{11.119}$$

The transfer function of this system can be easily found by using the *shifting theorem*. The shifting theorem states that if the Z-transform of a sequence $\{f_n\}$ is $F(z)$, then the Z-transform of the sequence shifted by some integer number of samples n_0 is $z^{-n_0} F(z)$.

The theorem is easy to prove. Suppose we have a sequence $\{f_n\}$ with Z-transform $F(z)$. Let us look at the Z-transform of the sequence $\{f_{n-n_0}\}$:

$$\mathcal{Z}[\{f_{n-n_0}\}] = \sum_{n=-\infty}^{\infty} f_{n-n_0} z^{-n} \tag{11.120}$$

$$= \sum_{m=-\infty}^{\infty} f_m z^{-m-n_0} \tag{11.121}$$

$$= z^{-n_0} \sum_{m=-\infty}^{\infty} f_m z^{-m} \tag{11.122}$$

$$= z^{-n_0} F(z). \tag{11.123}$$

Assuming $G(z)$ is the Z-transform of $\{g_n\}$ and $F(z)$ is the Z-transform of $\{f_n\}$, we can take the Z-transform of both sides of the difference equation (11.119):

$$G(z) = a_0 F(z) + a_1 z^{-1} F(z) + a_2 z^{-2} F(z) + b_1 z^{-1} G(z) + b_2 z^{-2} G(z) \tag{11.124}$$

from which we get the relationship between $G(z)$ and $F(z)$ as

$$G(z) = \frac{a_0 + a_1 z^{-1} + a_2 z^{-2}}{1 - b_1 z^{-1} - b_2 z^{-2}} F(z). \tag{11.125}$$

By definition the transfer function $H(z)$ is therefore

$$H(z) = \frac{G(z)}{F(z)} \tag{11.126}$$

$$= \frac{a_0 + a_1 z^{-1} + a_2 z^{-2}}{1 - b_1 z^{-1} - b_2 z^{-2}}. \tag{11.127}$$

11.10 Summary

In this chapter we have reviewed some of the mathematical tools we will be using throughout the remainder of this book. We started with a review of vector space concepts, followed by a look at a number of ways we can represent a signal, including the Fourier series, the Fourier transform, the discrete Fourier series, the discrete Fourier transform, and the Z-transform. We also looked at the operation of sampling and the conditions necessary for the recovery of the continuous representation of the signal from its samples.

Further Reading

1. There are a large number of books that provide a much more detailed look at the concepts described in this chapter. A nice one is *Signal Processing and Linear Systems*, by B.P. Lathi [134].

2. For a thorough treatment of the fast Fourier transform (FFT), see *Numerical Recipes in C*, by W.H. Press, S.A. Teukolsky, W.T. Vetterling, and B.J. Flannery [183].

11.11   Projects and Problems

1. Let X be a set of N linearly independent vectors, and let V be the collection of vectors obtained using all linear combinations of the vectors in X.

   (a) Show that given any two vectors in V, the sum of these vectors is also an element of V.

   (b) Show that V contains an additive identity.

   (c) Show that for every $\mathbf{x}$ in V, there exists a $(-\mathbf{x})$ in V such that their sum is the additive identity.

2. Prove Parseval's theorem for the Fourier transform.

3. Prove the modulation property of the Fourier transform.

4. Prove the convolution theorem for the Fourier transform.

5. Show that the Fourier transform of a train of impulses in the time domain is a train of impulses in the frequency domain:

$$\mathcal{F}\left[\sum_{n=-\infty}^{\infty} \delta(t - nT)\right] = \sigma_0 \sum_{n=-\infty}^{\infty} \delta(w - n\sigma_0) \qquad \sigma_0 = \frac{2\pi}{T}. \qquad (11.128)$$

6. Find the Z-transform for the following sequences:

   (a) $h_n = 2^{-n}u[n]$, where $u[n]$ is the unit step function.

   (b) $h_n = (n^2 - n)3^{-n}u[n]$.

   (c) $h_n = (n2^{-n} + (0.6)^n)u[n]$.

7. Given the following input-output relationship:

$$y_n = 0.6y_{n-1} + 0.5x_n + 0.2x_{n-1}$$

   (a) Find the transfer function $H(z)$.

   (b) Find the impulse response $\{h_n\}$.

8. Find the inverse Z-transform of the following:

   (a) $H(z) = \frac{5}{z-2}$.

   (b) $H(z) = \frac{z}{z^2 - 0.25}$.

   (c) $H(z) = \frac{z}{z - 0.5}$.

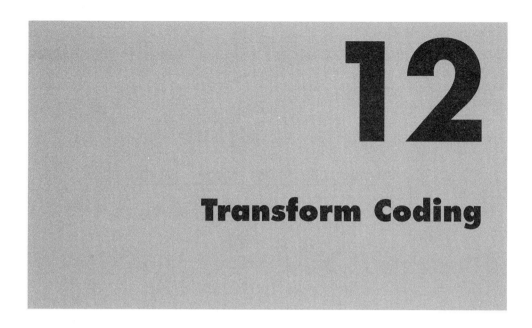

Transform Coding

12.1 Overview

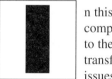n this chapter we will describe a technique in which the source output is decomposed, or transformed, into components that are then coded according to their individual characteristics. We will then look at a number of different transforms, including the popular discrete cosine transform, and discuss the issues of quantization and coding of the transformed coefficients. This chapter concludes with a description of the baseline sequential JPEG image-coding algorithm and some of the issues involved with transform coding of audio signals.

12.2 Introduction

In the previous chapter we developed a number of tools that can be used to transform a given sequence into different representations. If we take a sequence of inputs and transform them into another sequence in which most of the information is contained in only a few elements, we can then encode and transmit those elements, along with their location in the new sequence, resulting in data compression. In our discussion, we will use the terms "variance" and "information" interchangeably. The justification for this is shown in the results in Chapter 7. For example, recall that for a Gaussian source the differential entropy is given as $\frac{1}{2} \log 2\pi e\sigma^2$. Thus, an increase in the variance results in an increase in the entropy, which is a measure of the information contained in the source output.

To begin our discussion of transform coding, consider the following example.

Example 12.2.1:

Let's revisit Example 7.5.1. In Example 7.5.1, we studied the encoding of the output of a
source that consisted of a sequence of pairs of numbers. Each pair of numbers corresponds
to the height and weight of an individual. In particular, let's look at the sequence of outputs
shown in Table 12.1.

If we look at the height and weight as the coordinates of a point in two-dimensional space,
the sequence can be shown graphically as in Figure 12.1. Notice that the output values tend to

TABLE 12.1   Original sequence.

Height	Weight
65	170
75	188
60	150
70	170
56	130
80	203
68	160
50	110
40	80
50	153
69	148
62	140
76	164
64	120

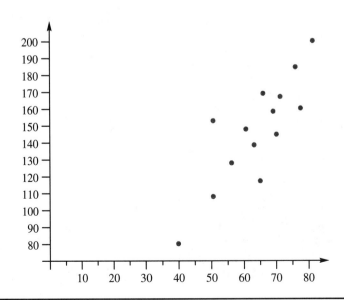

FIGURE 12.1   Source output sequence.

TABLE 12.2   **Transformed sequence.**

First Coordinate	Second Coordinate
182	3
202	0
162	0
184	−2
141	−4
218	1
174	−4
121	−6
90	−7
161	10
163	−9
153	−6
181	−9
135	−15

cluster around the line $y = 2.5x$. We can rotate this set of values by the transformation

$$\theta = \mathbf{A}\mathbf{x} \tag{12.1}$$

where $\mathbf{x}$ is the two-dimensional source output vector

$$\mathbf{x} = \begin{bmatrix} x_0 \\ x_1 \end{bmatrix} \tag{12.2}$$

x_0 corresponds to height and x_1 corresponds to weight, A is the rotation matrix

$$\mathbf{A} = \begin{bmatrix} \cos\phi & \sin\phi \\ -\sin\phi & \cos\phi \end{bmatrix} \tag{12.3}$$

ϕ is the angle between the x-axis and the $y = 2.5x$ line, and

$$\theta = \begin{bmatrix} \theta_0 \\ \theta_1 \end{bmatrix} \tag{12.4}$$

is the rotated or transformed set of values. For this particular case the matrix $\mathbf{A}$ is

$$\mathbf{A} = \begin{bmatrix} 0.37139068 & 0.92847669 \\ -0.92847669 & 0.37139068 \end{bmatrix} \tag{12.5}$$

and the transformed sequence (rounded to the nearest integer) is shown in Table 12.2. (For a brief review of matrix concepts, see Appendix B.)

Notice that for each pair of values, almost all the energy is compacted into the first element of the pair, while the second element of the pair is significantly smaller. If we plot this sequence in pairs, we get the result shown in Figure 12.2. Note that we have rotated the original values by an angle of approximately 68 degrees ($\arctan 2.5$).

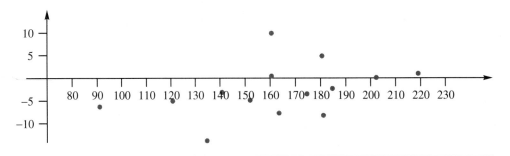

FIGURE 1 2 . 2   The transformed sequence.

TABLE 1 2 . 3   Reconstructed sequence.

Height	Weight
68	169
75	188
60	150
68	171
53	131
81	203
65	162
45	112
34	84
60	150
61	151
57	142
67	168
50	125

Suppose we set all the second elements of the transformation to zero, that is, the second coordinates of the sequence shown in Table 12.2. This reduces the number of elements that need to be encoded by half. What is the effect of throwing away half the elements of the sequence? We can find that out by taking the inverse transform of the reduced sequence. The inverse transform consists of reversing the rotation. We can do this by multiplying the blocks of two of the transformed sequence with the second element in each block set to zero with the matrix

$$\mathbf{A}^{-1} = \begin{bmatrix} \cos\phi & -\sin\phi \\ \sin\phi & \cos\phi \end{bmatrix} \qquad (12.6)$$

and obtain the reconstructed sequence shown in Table 12.3. Comparing this to the original sequence in Table 12.1, we see that, even though we transmitted only half the number of elements present in the original sequence, this "reconstructed" sequence is very close to the original. The reason there is so little error introduced in the sequence $\{x_n\}$ is that for this particular transformation the error introduced into the $\{x_n\}$ sequence is equal to the error introduced into the $\{\theta_n\}$ sequence. That is,

$$\sum_{i=0}^{N-1}(x_i - \hat{x}_i)^2 = \sum_{i=0}^{N-1}(\theta_i - \hat{\theta}_i)^2 \qquad (12.7)$$

where $\{\hat{x}_n\}$ is the reconstructed sequence, and

$$\hat{\theta}_i = \begin{cases} \theta_i & i = 0, 2, 4, \ldots \\ 0 & \text{otherwise} \end{cases} \qquad (12.8)$$

(see Problem 1). The error introduced in the $\{\theta_n\}$ sequence is the sum of squares of the θ_ns that are set to zero. The magnitudes of these elements are quite small, and therefore the total error introduced into the reconstructed sequence is quite small also. ◆

We could reduce the number of samples we needed to code because most of the information contained in each pair of values was put into one element of each pair. As the other element of the pair contained very little information, we could discard it without a significant effect on the fidelity of the reconstructed sequence. The transform in this case acted on pairs of values; therefore, the maximum reduction in the number of significant samples was a factor of two. We can extend this idea to longer blocks of data. By compacting most of the information in a source output sequence into a few elements of the transformed sequence using a reversible transform, and then discarding the elements of the sequence that do not contain much information, we can get a large amount of compression. This is the basic idea behind transform coding.

In Example 12.2.1 we have presented a geometric view of the transform process. We can also examine the transform process in terms of the changes in statistics between the original and transformed sequences. It can be shown that we can get the maximum amount of compaction if we use a transform that decorrelates the input sequence; that is, the sample-to-sample correlation of the transformed sequence is zero. The first transform to provide decorrelation for discrete data was presented by Hotelling [104] in the *Journal of Educational Psychology* in 1933. He called his approach the *method of principal components*. The analogous transform for continuous functions was obtained by Karhunen [123] and Loéve [141]. This decorrelation approach was first utilized for compression, in what we now call transform coding, by Kramer and Mathews [128], and Huang and Schultheiss [105].

Transform coding consists of three steps. First, the data sequence $\{x_n\}$ is divided into blocks of size N. Each block is mapped into a transform sequence $\{\theta_n\}$ using a reversible mapping in a manner similar to that described in Example 12.2.1. As shown in the example, different elements of each block of the transformed sequence generally have different statistical properties. In Example 12.2.1, most of the energy of the block of two input values was contained in the first element of the block of two transformed values, while very little of the energy was contained in the second element. This meant that the second element of each block of the transformed sequence would have a small magnitude, while the magnitude of the first element could vary considerably depending on the magnitude of the elements in the input block. The second step consists of quantizing the transformed sequence. The quantization strategy used will depend on three main factors: the desired average bit rate, the statistics of the various elements of the transformed sequence, and the effect of distortion in the transformed coefficients on the reconstructed sequence. In Example 12.2.1, we could take all the bits available to us and use them to quantize the first coefficient. In more complex situations, the strategy used may be very different. In fact, we may use different techniques, such as differential encoding and vector quantization [204], to encode the different coefficients.

Finally, the quantized value needs to be encoded using some binary encoding technique. The binary coding may be as simple as using a fixed-length code or as complex as a combination of run-length coding and Huffman or arithmetic coding. We will see an example of the latter when we describe the JPEG algorithm.

The various quantization and binary coding techniques have been described at some length in previous chapters, so we will spend the next section describing various transforms. We will then discuss quantization and coding strategies in the context of these transforms.

1 2 . 3   The Transform

All the transforms we deal with will be linear transforms; that is, we can get the sequence $\{\theta_n\}$ from the sequence $\{x_n\}$ as

$$\theta_n = \sum_{i=0}^{N-1} x_i a_{n,i}. \tag{12.9}$$

This is referred to as the *forward transform*. For the transforms that we will be considering, a major difference between the transformed sequence $\{\theta_n\}$ and the original sequence $\{x_n\}$ is that the characteristics of the elements of the θ sequence are determined by their position within the sequence. For example, in Example 12.2.1 the first element of each pair of the transformed sequence was more likely to have a large magnitude compared to the second element. In general, we cannot make such statements about the source output sequence $\{x_n\}$. A measure of the differing characteristics of the different elements of the transformed sequence $\{\theta_n\}$ is the variance σ_n^2 of each element. These variances will strongly influence how we encode the transformed sequence. The size of the block N is dictated by practical considerations. In general, the complexity of the transform grows more than linearly with N. Therefore, beyond a certain value of N, the computational costs overwhelm any marginal improvements that might be obtained by increasing N. Furthermore, in most real sources the statistical characteristics of the source output can change abruptly. For example, when we go from a silence period to a voiced period in speech, the statistics change drastically. Similarly, in images, the statistical characteristics of a smooth region of the image can be very different from the statistical characteristics of a busy region of the image. If N is large, the probability that the statistical characteristics change significantly within a block increases. This generally results in a larger number of the transform coefficients with large values, which in turn leads to a reduction in the compression ratio.

The original sequence $\{x_n\}$ can be recovered from the transformed sequence $\{\theta_n\}$ via the *inverse transform*:

$$x_n = \sum_{i=0}^{N-1} \theta_i b_{n,i}. \tag{12.10}$$

The transforms can be written in matrix form as

$$\theta = \mathbf{A}\mathbf{x} \tag{12.11}$$

$$\mathbf{x} = \mathbf{B}\theta \tag{12.12}$$

where $\mathbf{A}$ and $\mathbf{B}$ are $N \times N$ matrices and the (i,j)th element of the matrices is given by

$$[\mathbf{A}]_{i,j} = a_{i,j} \tag{12.13}$$

$$[\mathbf{B}]_{i,j} = b_{i,j}. \tag{12.14}$$

The forward and inverse transform matrices $\mathbf{A}$ and $\mathbf{B}$ are inverses of each other; that is, $\mathbf{AB} = \mathbf{BA} = \mathbf{I}$, where $\mathbf{I}$ is the identity matrix.

Equations (12.9) and (12.10) deal with the transform coding of one-dimensional sequences, such as sampled speech and audio sequences. However, transform coding is one of the most popular methods used for image compression. In order to take advantage of the two-dimensional nature of dependencies in images, we need to look at two-dimensional transforms.

Let $X_{i,j}$ be the (i,j)th pixel in an image. A general linear two-dimensional transform for a block of size $N \times N$ is given as

$$\Theta_{k,l} = \sum_{i=0}^{N-1}\sum_{j=0}^{N-1} X_{i,j} a_{i,j,k,l}. \tag{12.15}$$

All two-dimensional transforms in use today are *separable* transforms; that is, we can take the transform of a two-dimensional block by first taking the transform along one dimension, then repeating the operation along the other direction. In terms of matrices, this involves first taking the (one-dimensional) transform of the rows, and then taking the column-by-column transform of the resulting matrix. We can also reverse the order of the operations, first taking the transform of the columns, and then taking the row-by-row transform of the resulting matrix. The transform operation can be represented as

$$\Theta_{k,l} = \sum_{i=0}^{N-1}\sum_{j=0}^{N-1} a_{k,i} X_{i,j} a_{l,j} \tag{12.16}$$

which in matrix terminology would be given by

$$\Theta = \mathbf{A}\mathbf{X}\mathbf{A}^T. \tag{12.17}$$

The inverse transform is given as

$$\mathbf{X} = \mathbf{B}\Theta\mathbf{B}^T. \tag{12.18}$$

All the transforms we deal with will be *orthonormal transforms*. An orthonormal transform has the property that the inverse of the transform matrix is simply its transpose because the rows of the transform matrix form an orthonormal basis set:

$$\mathbf{B} = \mathbf{A}^{-1} = \mathbf{A}^T. \tag{12.19}$$

For an orthonormal transform, the inverse transform will be given as

$$\mathbf{X} = \mathbf{A}^T \Theta \mathbf{A}. \tag{12.20}$$

Orthonormal transforms are energy preserving; that is, the sum of the squares of the transformed sequence is the same as the sum of the squares of the original sequence. We can see this most easily in the case of the one-dimensional transform:

$$\sum_{i=0}^{N-1} \theta_i^2 = \theta^T \theta \tag{12.21}$$

$$= (\mathbf{A}x)^T \mathbf{A}x \tag{12.22}$$

$$= x^T \mathbf{A}^T \mathbf{A}x. \tag{12.23}$$

If $\mathbf{A}$ is an orthonormal transform, $\mathbf{A}^T \mathbf{A} = \mathbf{A}^{-1} \mathbf{A} = \mathbf{I}$, then

$$x^T \mathbf{A}^T \mathbf{A}x = x^T x \tag{12.24}$$

$$= \sum_{n=0}^{N-1} x_n^2 \tag{12.25}$$

and

$$\sum_{i=0}^{N-1} \theta_i^2 = \sum_{n=0}^{N-1} x_n^2. \tag{12.26}$$

The efficacy of a transform depends on how much energy compaction is provided by the transform. One way of measuring the amount of energy compaction afforded by a particular orthonormal transform is to take a ratio of the arithmetic mean of the variances of the transform coefficient to their geometric means [118]. This ratio is also referred to as the transform coding gain G_{TC}:

$$G_{TC} = \frac{\frac{1}{N} \sum_{i=0}^{N-1} \sigma_i^2}{(\prod_{i=0}^{N-1} \sigma_i^2)^{\frac{1}{N}}} \tag{12.27}$$

where σ_i^2 is the variance of the ith coefficient θ_i.

Transforms can be interpreted in several ways. We have already mentioned a geometric interpretation and a statistical interpretation. We can also interpret them as a decomposition of the signal in terms of a basis set. For example, suppose we have a two-dimensional orthonormal transform $\mathbf{A}$. The inverse transform can be written as

$$\begin{bmatrix} x_0 \\ x_1 \end{bmatrix} = \begin{bmatrix} a_{00} & a_{10} \\ a_{01} & a_{11} \end{bmatrix} \begin{bmatrix} \theta_0 \\ \theta_1 \end{bmatrix} = \theta_0 \begin{bmatrix} a_{00} \\ a_{01} \end{bmatrix} + \theta_1 \begin{bmatrix} a_{10} \\ a_{11} \end{bmatrix} \tag{12.28}$$

We can see that the transformed values are actually the coefficients of an expansion of the input sequence in terms of the rows of the transform matrix. The rows of the transform matrix are often referred to as the basis vectors for the transform because they form an orthonormal basis set, and the elements of the transformed sequence are often called the transform coefficients. By characterizing the basis vectors in physical terms we can get a physical interpretation of the transform coefficients.

Example 12.3.1:

Consider the following transform matrix:

$$\mathbf{A} = \frac{1}{\sqrt{2}} \begin{bmatrix} 1 & 1 \\ 1 & -1 \end{bmatrix} \qquad (12.29)$$

We can verify that this is indeed an orthonormal transform.

Notice that the first row of the matrix would correspond to a "low-pass" signal (no change from one component to the next), while the second row would correspond to a "high-pass" signal. Thus, if we tried to express a sequence in which each element has the same value in terms of these two rows, the second coefficient should be zero. Suppose the original sequence is (α, α). Then

$$\begin{bmatrix} \theta_0 \\ \theta_1 \end{bmatrix} = \frac{1}{\sqrt{2}} \begin{bmatrix} 1 & 1 \\ 1 & -1 \end{bmatrix} \begin{bmatrix} \alpha \\ \alpha \end{bmatrix} = \begin{bmatrix} \sqrt{2}\alpha \\ 0 \end{bmatrix} \qquad (12.30)$$

The "low-pass" coefficient has a value of $\sqrt{2}\alpha$, while the "high-pass" coefficient has a value of 0. The "low-pass" and "high-pass" coefficients are generally referred to as the low-frequency and high-frequency coefficients.

Let us take two sequences in which the components are not the same and the degree of variation is different. Consider the two sequences $(3, 1)$ and $(3, -1)$. In the first sequence the second element differs from the first by 2; in the second sequence, the magnitude of the difference is 4. We could say that the second sequence is more "high pass" than the first sequence. The transform coefficients for the two sequences are $(2\sqrt{2}, \sqrt{2})$ and $(\sqrt{2}, 2\sqrt{2})$, respectively. Notice that the high-frequency coefficient for the sequence in which we see a larger change is twice that of the high-frequency coefficient for the sequence with less change. Thus, the two coefficients do seem to behave like the outputs of a low-pass filter and a high-pass filter.

Finally, notice that in every case the sum of the squares of the original sequence is the same as the sum of the squares of the transform coefficients; that is, the transform is energy preserving, as it must be, since $\mathbf{A}$ is orthonormal. ◆

We can interpret one-dimensional transforms as an expansion in terms of the rows of the transform matrix. Similarly, we can interpret two-dimensional transforms as expansions in terms of matrices that are formed by the outer product of the rows of the transform matrix. Recall that the outer product is given by

$$\mathbf{x}\mathbf{x}^T = \begin{bmatrix} x_0 x_0 & x_0 x_1 & \cdots & x_0 x_{N-1} \\ x_1 x_0 & x_1 x_1 & \cdots & x_1 x_{N-1} \\ \vdots & \vdots & & \vdots \\ x_{N-1} x_0 & x_{N-1} x_1 & \cdots & x_{N-1} x_{N-1} \end{bmatrix} \qquad (12.31)$$

To see this more clearly, let us use the transform introduced in Example 12.3.1 for a two-dimensional transform.

Example 12.3.2:

For an $N \times N$ transform $\mathbf{A}$, let $\alpha_{i,j}$ be the outer product of the ith and jth rows:

$$\alpha_{i,j} = \begin{bmatrix} a_{i0} \\ a_{i1} \\ \vdots \\ a_{iN-1} \end{bmatrix} \begin{bmatrix} a_{j0} & a_{j1} & \cdots & a_{jN-1} \end{bmatrix} \tag{12.32}$$

$$= \begin{bmatrix} a_{i0}a_{j0} & a_{i0}a_{j1} & \cdots & a_{i0}a_{jN-1} \\ a_{i1}a_{j0} & a_{i1}a_{j1} & \cdots & a_{i1}a_{jN-1} \\ \vdots & \vdots & & \vdots \\ a_{iN-1}a_{j0} & a_{iN-1}a_{j1} & \cdots & a_{iN-1}a_{jN-1} \end{bmatrix} \tag{12.33}$$

For the transform of Example 12.3.1, the outer products are

$$\alpha_{0,0} = \frac{1}{2} \begin{bmatrix} 1 & 1 \\ 1 & 1 \end{bmatrix} \quad \alpha_{0,1} = \frac{1}{2} \begin{bmatrix} 1 & -1 \\ 1 & -1 \end{bmatrix} \tag{12.34}$$

$$\alpha_{1,0} = \frac{1}{2} \begin{bmatrix} 1 & 1 \\ -1 & -1 \end{bmatrix} \quad \alpha_{1,1} = \frac{1}{2} \begin{bmatrix} 1 & -1 \\ -1 & 1 \end{bmatrix} \tag{12.35}$$

From (12.20), the inverse transform is given by

$$\begin{bmatrix} x_{01} & x_{01} \\ x_{10} & x_{11} \end{bmatrix} = \frac{1}{2} \begin{bmatrix} 1 & 1 \\ 1 & -1 \end{bmatrix} \begin{bmatrix} \theta_{00} & \theta_{01} \\ \theta_{10} & \theta_{11} \end{bmatrix} \begin{bmatrix} 1 & 1 \\ 1 & -1 \end{bmatrix} \tag{12.36}$$

$$= \frac{1}{2} \begin{bmatrix} \theta_{00} + \theta_{01} + \theta_{10} + \theta_{11} & \theta_{00} - \theta_{01} + \theta_{10} - \theta_{11} \\ \theta_{00} + \theta_{01} - \theta_{10} - \theta_{11} & \theta_{00} - \theta_{01} - \theta_{10} + \theta_{11} \end{bmatrix} \tag{12.37}$$

$$= \theta_{00}\alpha_{0,0} + \theta_{01}\alpha_{0,1} + \theta_{10}\alpha_{1,0} + \theta_{11}\alpha_{1,1}. \tag{12.38}$$

The transform values θ_{ij} can be viewed as the coefficients of the expansion of $\mathbf{x}$ in terms of the matrices $\alpha_{i,j}$. The matrices $\alpha_{i,j}$ are known as the *basis* matrices.

For historical reasons, the coefficient θ_{00}, corresponding to the basis matrix $\alpha_{0,0}$, is called the DC coefficient, while the coefficients corresponding to the other basis matrices are called AC coefficients. DC stands for direct current, which is current that does not change with time. AC stands for alternating current, which does change with time. Notice that all the elements of the basis matrix $\alpha_{0,0}$ are the same, hence the DC designation.   ◆

In the following section we will look at some of the variety of transforms available to us, then at some of the issues involved in quantization and coding. Finally, we will describe in detail two applications, one for image coding and one for audio coding.

1 2 . 4   Transforms of Interest

In Example 12.2.1, we constructed a transform that was specific to the data. In practice, it is generally not feasible to construct a transform for the specific situation, for several reasons.

Unless the characteristics of the source output are stationary over a long interval, the transform needs to be recomputed often, and it is generally burdensome to compute a transform for every different set of data. Furthermore, the overhead required to transmit the transform itself might negate any compression gains. Both of these problems become especially acute when the size of the transform is large. However, there are times when we want to find out the best we can do with transform coding. In these situations, we can use data-dependent transforms to obtain an idea of the best performance available. The best-known data-dependent transform is the discrete Karhunen-Loéve transform (KLT). We will describe this transform in the next section.

12.4.1 Karhunen-Loéve Transform

The rows of the discrete Karhunen-Loéve transform [6], also known as the Hotelling transform, consist of the eigenvectors of the autocorrelation matrix. The autocorrelation matrix for a random process X is a matrix whose (i,j)th element $[R]_{i,j}$ is given by

$$[R]_{i,j} = E[X_n X_{n+|i-j|}]. \tag{12.39}$$

We can show [118] that a transform constructed in this manner will minimize the geometric mean of the variance of the transform coefficients. Hence, the Karhunen-Loéve transform provides the largest transform coding gain of any transform coding method.

If the source output being compressed is nonstationary, the autocorrelation function will change with time. Thus, the autocorrelation matrix will change with time, and the KLT will have to be recomputed. For a transform of any reasonable size, this is a significant amount of computation. Furthermore, as the autocorrelation is computed based on the source output, it is not available to the receiver. Therefore, either the autocorrelation or the transform itself has to be sent to the receiver. The overhead can be significant and remove any advantages to using the optimum transform. However, in applications where the statistics change slowly and the transform size can be kept small, the KLT can be of practical use [198].

Example 12.4.1:

Let us see how to obtain the KLT transform of size two for an arbitrary input sequence. The autocorrelation matrix of size two for a stationary process is

$$\mathbf{R} = \begin{bmatrix} R_{xx}(0) & R_{xx}(1) \\ R_{xx}(1) & R_{xx}(0) \end{bmatrix} \tag{12.40}$$

Solving the equation $|\lambda \mathbf{I} - \mathbf{R}| = 0$, we get the two eigenvalues $\lambda_1 = R_{xx}(0) + R_{xx}(1)$, and $\lambda_2 = R_{xx}(0) - R_{xx}(1)$. The corresponding eigenvectors are

$$V_1 = \begin{bmatrix} \alpha \\ \alpha \end{bmatrix} \qquad V_2 = \begin{bmatrix} \beta \\ -\beta \end{bmatrix} \tag{12.41}$$

where α and β are arbitrary constants. If we now impose the orthonormality condition, which requires the vectors to have a magnitude of 1, we get

$$\alpha = \beta = \frac{1}{\sqrt{2}}$$

and the transform matrix $\mathbf{K}$ is

$$\mathbf{K} = \frac{1}{\sqrt{2}} \begin{bmatrix} 1 & 1 \\ 1 & -1 \end{bmatrix} \tag{12.42}$$

Notice that this matrix is not dependent on the values of $R_{xx}(0)$ and $R_{xx}(1)$. This is only true of the 2×2 KLT. The transform matrices of higher order are functions of the autocorrelation values.   ◆

Although the Karhunen-Loéve transform maximizes the transform coding gain as defined by (12.27), it is not practical in most circumstances. Therefore, we need transforms that do not depend on the data being transformed. We describe some of the more popular transforms in the following sections.

12.4.2 Discrete Cosine Transform

The discrete cosine transform (DCT) gets its name from the fact that the rows of the $N \times N$ transform matrix $\mathbf{C}$ are obtained as a function of cosines.

$$[\mathbf{C}]_{i,j} = \begin{cases} \sqrt{\frac{1}{N}} \cos \frac{(2j+1)i\pi}{2N} & i = 0, j = 0, 1, \ldots, N-1 \\ \sqrt{\frac{2}{N}} \cos \frac{(2j+1)i\pi}{2N} & i = 1, 2, \ldots, N-1, j = 0, 1, \ldots, N-1. \end{cases} \tag{12.43}$$

The rows of the transform matrix are shown in graphical form in Figure 12.3. Notice how the amount of variation increases as we progress down the rows; that is, the frequency of the rows increases as we go from top to bottom.

The outer products of the rows are shown in Figure 12.4. Notice that the basis matrices show increased variation as we go from the top-left matrix, corresponding to the θ_{00} coefficient, to the bottom-right matrix, corresponding to the $\theta_{(N-1)(N-1)}$ coefficient.

The DCT is closely related to the discrete Fourier transform (DFT) mentioned in Chapter 11, and in fact can be obtained from the DFT. However, in terms of compression, the DCT performs better than the DFT.

To see why, recall that when we find the Fourier coefficients for a sequence of length N, we assume that the sequence is periodic with period N. If the original sequence is as shown in Figure 12.5a, the DFT assumes that the sequence outside the interval of interest behaves in the manner shown in Figure 12.5b. This introduces sharp discontinuities, at the beginning and the end of the sequence. In order to represent these sharp discontinuities, the DFT needs nonzero coefficients for the high-frequency components. Because these components are needed only at the two endpoints of the sequence, their effect needs to be canceled out at other points in the sequence. Thus, the DFT adjusts other coefficients accordingly. When we discard the high-frequency coefficients (which should not have been there anyway) during the compression process, the coefficients that were canceling out the high-frequency effect in other parts of the sequence result in the introduction of additional distortion.

The DCT can be obtained using the DFT by mirroring the original N-point sequence to obtain a $2N$-point sequence, as shown in Figure 12.6b. The DCT is simply the first N points of the resulting $2N$-point DFT. When we take the DFT of the $2N$-point mirrored sequence,

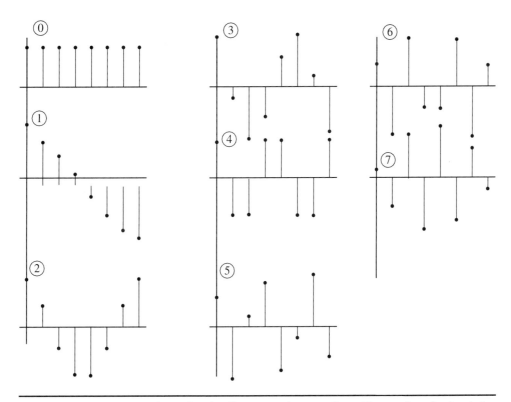

FIGURE 12.3   **Basis set for the discrete cosine transform. The numbers in the circles correspond to the row of the transform matrix.**

we again have to assume periodicity. However, as we can see from Figure 12.6c, this does not introduce any sharp discontinuities at the edges.

The DCT is substantially better at energy compaction for most correlated sources when compared to the DFT [118]. In fact, for Markov sources with high correlation coefficient ρ,

$$\rho = \frac{E[x_n x_{n+1}]}{E[x_n^2]}, \tag{12.44}$$

the compaction ability of the DCT is very close to that of the KLT. As many sources can be modeled as Markov sources with high values for ρ, this superior compaction ability has made the DCT the most popular transform. It is a part of many international standards, including JPEG, MPEG, and CCITT H.261, among others.

12.4.3 Discrete Sine Transform

The discrete sine transform (DST) is a complementary transform to the DCT. Where the DCT provides performance close to the optimum KLT when the correlation coefficient ρ is large, the DST performs close to the optimum KLT in terms of compaction when the magnitude of

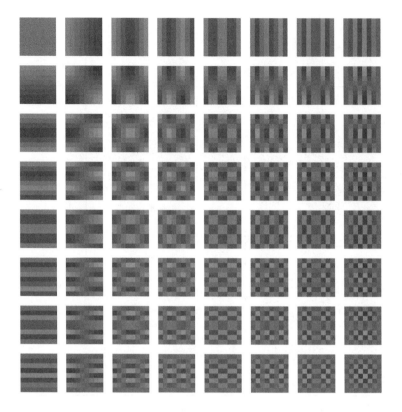

FIGURE 1 2 . 4   The basis matrices for the DCT.

ρ is small. Because of this property, it is often used as the complementary transform to DCT in image [72] and audio [26] coding applications.

The elements of the transform matrix for an $N \times N$ DST are

$$[\mathbf{S}]_{ij} = \sqrt{\frac{2}{N+1}} \sin \frac{\pi(i+1)(j+1)}{N+1} \qquad i, j = 0, 1, \ldots, N-1. \tag{12.45}$$

1 2 . 4 . 4   Discrete Walsh-Hadamard Transform

A transform that is especially simple to implement is the discrete Walsh-Hadamard transform (DWHT). The DWHT transform matrices are rearrangements of discrete Hadamard matrices, which are of particular importance in coding theory [144]. A Hadamard matrix of order N is defined as an $N \times N$ matrix H, with the property that $HH^T = NI$, where I is the $N \times N$ identity matrix. Hadamard matrices whose dimensions are a power of two can be constructed in the following manner:

$$H_{2N} = \begin{bmatrix} H_N & H_N \\ H_N & -H_N \end{bmatrix} \tag{12.46}$$

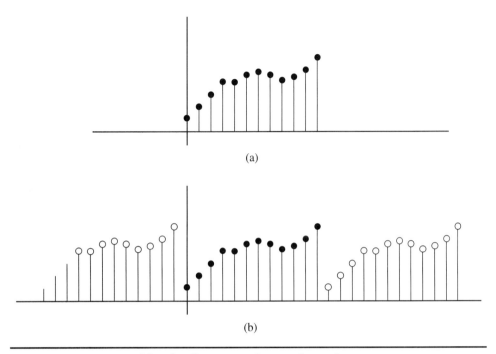

(a)

(b)

FIGURE 12.5   **Taking the discrete Fourier transform of a sequence.**

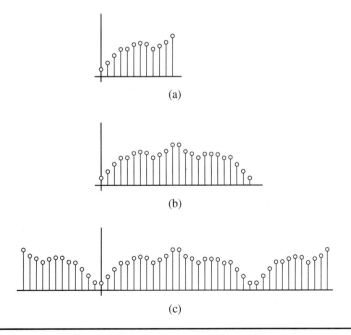

(a)

(b)

(c)

FIGURE 12.6   **Taking the discrete cosine transform of a sequence.**

with $H_1 = [1]$. Therefore,

$$H_2 = \begin{bmatrix} H_1 & H_1 \\ H_1 & -H_1 \end{bmatrix} = \begin{bmatrix} 1 & 1 \\ 1 & -1 \end{bmatrix} \tag{12.47}$$

$$H_4 = \begin{bmatrix} H_2 & H_2 \\ H_2 & -H_2 \end{bmatrix} = \begin{bmatrix} 1 & 1 & 1 & 1 \\ 1 & -1 & 1 & -1 \\ 1 & 1 & -1 & -1 \\ 1 & -1 & -1 & 1 \end{bmatrix} \tag{12.48}$$

$$H_8 = \begin{bmatrix} H_4 & H_4 \\ H_4 & -H_4 \end{bmatrix} = \begin{bmatrix} 1 & 1 & 1 & 1 & 1 & 1 & 1 & 1 \\ 1 & -1 & 1 & -1 & 1 & -1 & 1 & -1 \\ 1 & 1 & -1 & -1 & 1 & 1 & -1 & -1 \\ 1 & -1 & -1 & 1 & 1 & -1 & -1 & 1 \\ 1 & 1 & 1 & 1 & -1 & -1 & -1 & -1 \\ 1 & -1 & 1 & -1 & -1 & 1 & -1 & 1 \\ 1 & 1 & -1 & -1 & -1 & -1 & 1 & 1 \\ 1 & -1 & -1 & 1 & -1 & 1 & 1 & -1 \end{bmatrix} \tag{12.49}$$

The DWHT transform matrix H can be obtained from the Hadamard matrix by multiplying it by a normalizing factor so that $HH^T = I$ instead of NI, and by reordering the rows in increasing *sequency* order. The sequency of a row is half the number of sign changes in that row. In H_8 the first row has sequency 0, the second row has sequency $7/2$, the third row has sequency $3/2$, and so on. Normalization involves multiplying the matrix by $\frac{1}{\sqrt{N}}$. Reordering the H_8 matrix in increasing sequency order, we get

$$H = \frac{1}{\sqrt{8}} \begin{bmatrix} 1 & 1 & 1 & 1 & 1 & 1 & 1 & 1 \\ 1 & 1 & 1 & 1 & -1 & -1 & -1 & -1 \\ 1 & 1 & -1 & -1 & -1 & -1 & 1 & 1 \\ 1 & 1 & -1 & -1 & 1 & 1 & -1 & -1 \\ 1 & -1 & -1 & 1 & 1 & -1 & -1 & 1 \\ 1 & -1 & -1 & 1 & -1 & 1 & 1 & -1 \\ 1 & -1 & 1 & -1 & -1 & 1 & -1 & 1 \\ 1 & -1 & 1 & -1 & 1 & -1 & 1 & -1 \end{bmatrix} \tag{12.50}$$

Because the matrix without the scaling factor consists of ± 1, the transform operation consists simply of addition and subtraction. For this reason, this transform is useful in situations where minimizing the amount of computations is very important. However, the amount of energy compaction obtained with this transform is substantially less than the compaction obtained by the use of the DCT. Therefore, where sufficient computational power is available, DCT is the transform of choice.

12.5   Quantization and Coding of Transform Coefficients

If the amount of information conveyed by each coefficient is different, it makes sense to assign differing numbers of bits to the different coefficients. There are two approaches to assigning bits. One approach relies on the average properties of the transform coefficients, while the other approach assigns bits as needed by individual transform coefficients.

In the first approach, we first obtain an estimate of the variances of the transform coefficients. These estimates can be used by one of two algorithms to assign the number of bits used to quantize each of the coefficients. We assume that the relative variance of the coefficients corresponds to the amount of information contained in each coefficient. Thus, coefficients with higher variance are assigned more bits than coefficients with smaller variance.

Let us find an expression for the distortion, then find the bit allocation that minimizes the distortion. To perform the minimization we will use the method of Lagrange [59]. If the average number of bits per sample to be used by the transform coding system is R, and the average number of bits per sample used by the kth coefficient is R_k, then

$$R = \frac{1}{M} \sum_{k=1}^{M} R_k \tag{12.51}$$

where M is the number of transform coefficients. The reconstruction error variance for the kth quantizer $\sigma_{r_k}^2$ is related to the kth quantizer input variance $\sigma_{\theta_k}^2$ by the following:

$$\sigma_{r_k}^2 = \alpha_k 2^{-2R_k} \sigma_{\theta_k}^2 \tag{12.52}$$

where α_k is a factor that depends on the input distribution and the quantizer.

The total reconstruction error is given by

$$\sigma_r^2 = \sum_{k=1}^{M} \alpha_k 2^{-2R_k} \sigma_{\theta_k}^2. \tag{12.53}$$

The objective of the bit allocation procedure is to find R_k to minimize (12.53) subject to the constraint of (12.51). If we assume that α_k is a constant α for all k, we can set up the minimization problem in terms of Lagrange multipliers as

$$J = \alpha \sum_{k=1}^{M} 2^{-2R_k} \sigma_{\theta_k}^2 - \lambda \left(R - \frac{1}{M} \sum_{k=1}^{M} R_k \right). \tag{12.54}$$

Taking the derivative of J with respect to R_k and setting it equal to zero, we can obtain this expression for R_k:

$$R_k = \frac{1}{2} \log_2 (2\alpha \ln 2 \sigma_{\theta_k}^2) - \frac{1}{2} \log_2 \lambda. \tag{12.55}$$

Substituting this expression for R_k in (12.51), we get a value for λ:

$$\lambda = \prod_{k=1}^{M} (2\alpha \ln 2 \sigma_{\theta_k}^2)^{\frac{1}{M}} 2^{-2R}. \tag{12.56}$$

TABLE 12.4   Bit allocation map for an 8 × 8 transform.

8	7	5	3	1	1	0	0
7	5	3	2	1	0	0	0
4	3	2	1	1	0	0	0
3	3	2	1	1	0	0	0
2	1	1	1	0	0	0	0
1	1	0	0	0	0	0	0
1	0	0	0	0	0	0	0
0	0	0	0	0	0	0	0

Substituting this expression for λ in (12.55), we finally obtain the individual bit allocations:

$$R_k = R + \frac{1}{2} \log_2 \frac{\sigma_{\theta_k}^2}{\prod_{k=1}^{M}(\sigma_{\theta_k}^2)^{\frac{1}{M}}}. \qquad (12.57)$$

Although these values of R_k will minimize (12.53), they are not guaranteed to be integers, or even positive. The standard approach at this point is to set the negative R_ks to zero. This will increase the average bit rate above the constraint. Therefore, the nonzero R_ks are uniformly reduced until the average rate is equal to R.

The second algorithm that uses estimates of the variance is a recursive algorithm and functions as follows:

1. Compute $\sigma_{\theta_k}^2$ for each coefficient.

2. Set $R_k = 0$ for all k and set $R_b = MR$, where R_b is the total number of bits available for distribution.

3. Sort the variances $\{\sigma_{\theta_k}^2\}$. Suppose $\sigma_{\theta_1}^2$ is the maximum.

4. Increment R_l by 1, and divide $\sigma_{\theta_1}^2$ by 2.

5. Decrement R_b by 1. If $R_b = 0$, then stop; otherwise, go to 3.

If we follow this procedure, we end up allocating more bits to the coefficients with higher variance.

This form of bit allocation is called *zonal sampling*. The reason for this name can be seen from the example of a bit allocation map for the 8 × 8 DCT of an image shown in Table 12.4. Notice that there is a zone of coefficients that roughly comprises the right lower diagonal of the bit map that has been assigned zero bits. In other words, these coefficients are to be discarded. The advantage to this approach is its simplicity. Once the bit allocation has been obtained, every coefficient at a particular location is always quantized using the same number of bits. The disadvantage is that, because the bit allocations are performed based on average value, variations that occur on the local level are not reconstructed properly. For example, consider an image of an object with sharp edges in front of a relatively plain background. The number of pixels that occur on edges is quite small compared to the total number of pixels. Therefore, if we allocate bits based on average variances, the coefficients that are important for representing edges (the high-frequency coefficients) will get few or no bits assigned to

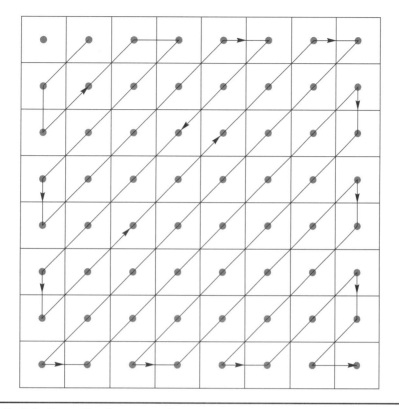

FIGURE 12.7   **The zigzag scanning pattern for an 8 × 8 transform.**

them. This means that the reconstructed image will not contain a very good representation of the edges.

This problem can be avoided by using a different approach to bit allocation known as *threshold coding* [240, 182, 44]. In this approach, which coefficient to keep and which to discard is not decided a priori. In the simplest form of threshold coding, we specify a threshold value. Coefficients with magnitude below this threshold are discarded, while the other coefficients are quantized and transmitted. The information about which coefficients have been retained is sent to the receiver as side information. A simple approach described by Pratt [182] is to code the first coefficient on each line regardless of the magnitude. After this, when we encounter a coefficient with a magnitude above the threshold value, we send two codewords: one for the quantized value of the coefficient, and one for the count of the number of coefficients since the last coefficient with magnitude greater than the threshold. For the two-dimensional case, the block size is usually small, and each "line" of the transform is very short. Thus, this approach would be quite expensive. Chen and Pratt [44] suggest scanning the block of transformed coefficients in a zigzag fashion, as shown in Figure 12.7. If we scan an 8 × 8 block of quantized transform coefficients in this manner, we will find that in general a large section of the tail end of the scan will consist of zeros. This is because generally the higher-order coefficients have smaller amplitude. This is reflected in the bit allocation table shown in

T A B L E   1 2 . 5   An 8 × 8 block from the Sena image.

124	125	122	120	122	119	117	118
121	121	120	119	119	120	120	118
126	124	123	122	121	121	120	120
124	124	125	125	126	125	124	124
127	127	128	129	130	128	127	125
143	142	143	142	140	139	139	139
150	148	152	152	152	152	150	151
156	159	158	155	158	158	157	156

Table 12.4. As we shall see later, if we use midtread quantizers (quantizers with a zero output level), combined with the fact that the step sizes for the higher-order coefficients are generally chosen to be quite large, this means that many of these coefficients will be quantized to zero. Therefore, there is a high probability that after a few coefficients along the zigzag scan, all coefficients will be zero. In this situation, Chen and Pratt suggest the transmission of a special *end-of-block* (EOB) symbol. Upon reception of the EOB signal, the receiver would automatically set all remaining coefficients along the zigzag scan to zero.

The algorithm developed by the Joint Photographic Experts Group (JPEG), described in the next section, uses a rather clever variation of this approach.

1 2 . 6   Application to Image Compression—JPEG

The JPEG standard is one of the most widely known standards for lossy image compression. It is a result of the collaboration of the International Standards Organization (ISO), which is a private organization, and what was the CCITT (now ITU-T), a part of the United Nations. The approach recommended by JPEG is a transform coding approach using the DCT. The approach is a modification of the scheme proposed by Chen and Pratt [44]. In this section we will briefly describe the baseline JPEG algorithm. In order to illustrate the various components of the algorithm, we will use an 8 × 8 block of the Sena image, shown in Table 12.5. For more details, see [178].

1 2 . 6 . 1   The Transform

The transform used in the JPEG scheme is the DCT transform described earlier. The input image is first "level shifted" by 2^{P-1}; that is, we subtract 2^{P-1} from each pixel value, where P is the number of bits used to represent each pixel. Thus, if we are dealing with 8-bit images whose pixels take on values between 0 and 255, we would subtract 128 from each pixel so that the value of the pixel varies between -128 and 127. The image is divided into blocks of size 8 × 8, which are then transformed using an 8 × 8 forward DCT. If any dimension of the image is not a multiple of eight, the encoder replicates the last column or row until the final size is a multiple of eight. These additional rows or columns are removed during the decoding process. If we take the 8 × 8 block of pixels shown in Table 12.5, subtract 128 from it, and take the DCT of this level-shifted block, we obtain the DCT coefficients shown in Table 12.6. Notice

TABLE 12.6 The DCT coefficients corresponding to the block of data from the Sena image after level shift.

39.88	6.56	−2.24	1.22	−0.37	−1.08	0.79	1.13
−102.43	4.56	2.26	1.12	0.35	−0.63	−1.05	−0.48
37.77	1.31	1.77	0.25	−1.50	−2.21	−0.10	0.23
−5.67	2.24	−1.32	−0.81	1.41	0.22	−0.13	0.17
−3.37	−0.74	−1.75	0.77	−0.62	−2.65	−1.30	0.76
5.98	−0.13	−0.45	−0.77	1.99	−0.26	1.46	0.00
3.97	5.52	2.39	−0.55	−0.051	−0.84	−0.52	−0.13
−3.43	0.51	−1.07	0.87	0.96	0.09	0.33	0.01

TABLE 12.7 Sample quantization table.

16	11	10	16	24	40	51	61
12	12	14	19	26	58	60	55
14	13	16	24	40	57	69	56
14	17	22	29	51	87	80	62
18	22	37	56	68	109	103	77
24	35	55	64	81	104	113	92
49	64	78	87	103	121	120	101
72	92	95	98	112	100	103	99

that the lower-frequency coefficients in the top-left corner of the table have larger values than the higher-frequency coefficients. This is generally the case, except for situations in which there is substantial activity in the image block.

12.6.2 Quantization

The JPEG algorithm uses uniform midtread quantization to quantize the various coefficients. The quantizer step sizes are organized in a table called the *quantization table* and can be viewed as the fixed part of the quantization. An example of a quantization table from the JPEG recommendation [178] is shown in Table 12.7. Each quantized value is represented by a label. The label corresponding to the quantized value of the transform coefficient θ_{ij} is obtained as

$$l_{ij} = \left\lfloor \frac{\theta_{ij}}{Q_{ij}} + 0.5 \right\rfloor \tag{12.58}$$

where Q_{ij} is the (i,j)th element of the quantization table, and $\lfloor x \rfloor$ is the largest integer smaller than x. Consider the θ_{00} coefficient from Table 12.6. The value of θ_{00} is 39.88. From Table 12.7, Q_{00} is 16. Therefore,

$$l_{00} = \left\lfloor \frac{39.88}{16} + 0.5 \right\rfloor = \lfloor 2.9925 \rfloor = 2. \tag{12.59}$$

The reconstructed value is obtained from the label by multiplying the label with the corresponding entry in the quantization table. Therefore, the reconstructed value of θ_{00} would be

TABLE 12.8 **The quantizer labels obtained by using the quantization table on the coefficients.**

2	1	0	0	0	0	0	0
-9	0	0	0	0	0	0	0
3	0	0	0	0	0	0	0
0	0	0	0	0	0	0	0
0	0	0	0	0	0	0	0
0	0	0	0	0	0	0	0
0	0	0	0	0	0	0	0
0	0	0	0	0	0	0	0

$l_{00} \times Q_{00}$, which is $2 \times 16 = 32$. The quantization error in this case is $39.88 - 32 = -7.88$. Similarly, from Tables 12.6 and 12.7, θ_{01} is 6.56 and Q_{01} is 11. Therefore,

$$l_{01} = \left\lfloor \frac{6.56}{11} + 0.5 \right\rfloor = \lfloor 1.096 \rfloor = 1. \tag{12.60}$$

The reconstructed value is 11, and the quantization error is $11 - 6.56 = 4.44$. Continuing in this fashion, we obtain the labels shown in Table 12.8.

From the sample quantization table shown in Table 12.7, we can see that the step size generally increases as we move from the DC coefficient to the higher-order coefficients. Because the quantization error is an increasing function of the step size, more quantization error will be introduced in the higher-frequency coefficients than in the lower-frequency coefficients. The decision on the relative size of the step sizes is based on how errors in these coefficients will be perceived by the human visual system. Different coefficients in the transform have widely different perceptual importance. Quantization errors in the DC and lower AC coefficients are more easily detectable than the quantization error in the higher AC coefficients. Therefore, we use larger step sizes for perceptually less important coefficients.

Because the quantizers are all midtread quantizers (that is, they all have a zero output level), the quantization process also functions as the thresholding operation. All coefficients with magnitudes less than half the corresponding step size will be set to zero. Because the step sizes at the tail end of the zigzag scan are larger, the probability of finding a long run of zeros increases at the end of the scan. This is the case for the 8×8 block of labels shown in Table 12.8. The entire run of zeros at the tail end of the scan can be coded with an EOB code after the last nonzero label, resulting in substantial compression.

Furthermore, this effect also provides us with a method to vary the rate. By making the step sizes larger, we can reduce the number of nonzero values that need to be transmitted, which translates to a reduction in the number of bits that need to be transmitted.

12.6.3 Coding

Chen and Pratt [44] used separate Huffman codes for encoding the label for each coefficient and the number of coefficients since the last nonzero label. The JPEG approach is somewhat more complex but results in higher compression. In the JPEG approach, the labels for the DC and AC coefficients are coded differently.

From Figure 12.4 we can see that the basis matrix corresponding to the DC coefficient is a constant matrix. Thus, the DC coefficient is some multiple of the average value in the 8×8 block. The average pixel value in any 8×8 block will not differ substantially from the average value in the neighboring 8×8 block; therefore, the DC coefficient values will be quite close. Given that the labels are obtained by dividing the coefficients with the corresponding entry in the quantization table, the labels corresponding to these coefficients will be closer still. Therefore, it makes sense to encode the differences between neighboring labels rather than to encode the labels themselves.

Depending on the number of bits used to encode the pixel values, the number of values that the labels, and hence the differences, can take on may become quite large. A Huffman code for such a large alphabet would be quite unmanageable. The JPEG recommendation resolves this problem by partitioning the possible values that the differences can take on into categories. The size of these categories grows as a power of two. Thus, category 0 has only one member (0), category 1 has two members (-1 and 1), category 2 has four members (-3, -2, 2, and 3), and so on. The category numbers are then Huffman coded. The number of codewords in the Huffman code is equal to the base two logarithm of the number of possible values that the label differences can take on. If the differences can take on 4096 possible values, the size of the Huffman code is $\log_2 4096 = 12$. The elements within each category are specified by tacking on extra bits to the end of the Huffman code for that category. As the categories are different sizes, we need a differing number of bits to identify the value in each category. For example, because category 0 contains only one element, we need no additional bits to specify the value. Category 1 contains two elements, so we need 1 bit tacked on to the end of the Huffman code for category 1 to specify the particular element in that category. Similarly, we need 2 bits to specify the element in category 2, 3 bits for category 3, and n bits for category n.

The categories and the corresponding difference values are shown in Table 12.9. For example, if the difference between two labels was 6, we would send the Huffman code for category 3. As category 3 contains the eight values $\{-7, -6, -5, -4, 4, 5, 6, 7\}$, the Huffman code for category 3 would be followed by 3 bits that would specify which of the eight values in category 3 was being transmitted.

The binary code for the AC coefficients is generated in a slightly different manner. The category C that a nonzero label falls in and the number of zero-valued labels Z since the last nonzero label form a pointer to a specific Huffman code as shown in Table 12.10. Thus, if the label being encoded falls in category 3, and there have been 15 zero-valued labels prior to this nonzero label in the zigzag scan, then we form the pointer $F/3$, which points to the codeword 1111111111110111. Because the label falls in category 3, we follow this codeword with 3 bits that indicate which of the eight possible values in category 3 is the value that the label takes on.

There are two special codes shown in Table 12.10. The first is for the end-of-block (EOB). This is used in the same way as in the Chen and Pratt [44] algorithm; that is, if a particular label value is the last nonzero value along the zigzag scan, the code for it is immediately followed by the EOB code. The other code is the ZRL code, which is used when the number of consecutive zero values along the zigzag scan exceeds 15.

To see how all of this fits together, let's encode the labels in Table 12.8. The label corresponding to the DC coefficient is coded by first taking the difference between the value of

TABLE 1 2 . 9   Coding of the differences of the DC labels.

0			0			
1			−1	1		
2		−3	−2	2	3	
3	−7	. . .	−4	4	. . .	7
4	−15	. . .	−8	8	. . .	15
5	−31	. . .	−16	16	. . .	31
6	−63	. . .	−32	32	. . .	63
7	−127	. . .	−64	64	. . .	127
8	−255	. . .	−128	128	. . .	255
9	−511	. . .	−256	256	. . .	511
10	−1,023	. . .	−512	512	. . .	1,023
11	−2,047	. . .	−1,024	1,024	. . .	2,047
12	−4,095	. . .	−2,048	2,048	. . .	4,095
13	−8,191	. . .	−4,096	4,096	. . .	8,191
14	−16,383	. . .	−8,192	8,192	. . .	16,383
15	−32,767	. . .	−16,384	16,384	. . .	32,767
16			32,768			

TABLE 1 2 . 1 0 Sample table for obtaining the Huffman code for a given label value and run length. The values of Z are represented in hexadecimal.

Z/C	Codeword	Z/C	Codeword	. . .	Z/C	Codeword
0/0 (EOB)	1010			. . .	F/0 (ZRL)	11111111001
0/1	00	1/1	1100	. . .	F/1	1111111111110101
0/2	01	1/2	11011	. . .	F/2	1111111111110110
0/3	100	1/3	1111001	. . .	F/3	1111111111110111
0/4	1011	1/4	111110110	. . .	F/4	1111111111111000
0/5	11010	1/5	11111110110	. . .	F/5	1111111111111001
⋮	⋮	⋮	⋮		⋮	

the quantized label in this block and the quantized label in the previous block. If we assume that the corresponding label in the previous block was −1, then the difference would be 3. From Table 12.9 we can see that this value falls in category 2. Therefore, we would send the Huffman code for category 2 followed by the 2-bit sequence 11 to indicate that the value in category 2 being encoded was 3, and not −3, −2, or 2. To encode the AC coefficients, we first order them using the zigzag scan. We obtain the sequence

$$1 \; -9 \; 3 \; 0 \; 0 \; 0 \cdots 0$$

The first value, 1, belongs to category 1. Because there are no zeros preceding it, we transmit the Huffman code corresponding to 0/1, which from Table 12.10 is 00. We then follow this by a single bit 1 to indicate that the value being transmitted is 1 and not −1. Similarly, −9 is the seventh element in category 4. Therefore, we send the binary string 1011, which is the Huffman code for 0/4, followed by 0110 to indicate that −9 is the seventh element in category 4. The next label is 3, which belongs to category 2, so we send the Huffman code

TABLE 12.11 The quantized values of the coefficients.

32	11	0	0	0	0	0	0
−108	0	0	0	0	0	0	0
42	0	0	0	0	0	0	0
0	0	0	0	0	0	0	0
0	0	0	0	0	0	0	0
0	0	0	0	0	0	0	0
0	0	0	0	0	0	0	0
0	0	0	0	0	0	0	0

TABLE 12.12 The reconstructed block.

123	122	122	121	120	120	119	119
121	121	121	120	119	118	118	118
121	121	120	119	119	118	117	117
124	124	123	122	122	121	120	120
130	130	129	129	128	128	128	127
141	141	140	140	139	138	138	137
152	152	151	151	150	149	149	148
159	159	158	157	157	156	155	155

01 corresponding to 0/2, followed by the 2 bits 11. All the labels after this point are 0, so we send the EOB Huffman code, which in this case is 1010. If we assume that the Huffman code for the DC coefficient was 2 bits long, we have sent a grand total of 21 bits to represent this 8×8 block. This translates to an average $\frac{21}{64}$ bits per pixel.

To obtain a reconstruction of the original block, we perform the dequantization, which simply consists of multiplying the labels in Table 12.8 with the corresponding values in Table 12.7. Taking the inverse transform of the quantized coefficients shown in Table 12.11 and adding 128, we get the reconstructed block shown in Table 12.12. We can see that in spite of going from 8 bits per pixel to $\frac{21}{64}$ bits per pixel, the reproduction is remarkably close to the original.

If we wanted an even more accurate reproduction, we could do so at the cost of increased bit rate by multiplying the step sizes in the quantization table by one-half and using these values as the new step sizes. Using the same assumptions as before, we can show that this will result in an increase in the number of bits transmitted. We can go in the other direction by multiplying the step sizes with a number greater than one. This will result in a reduction in bit rate at the cost of increased distortion.

Finally, we present some examples of JPEG-coded images in Figures 12.8 and 12.9. These were coded using shareware generated by the Independent JPEG Group (organizer, Dr. Thomas G. Lane). Notice the high degree of "blockiness" in the lower-rate image (Figure 12.8). This is a standard problem of most block-based techniques, and specifically of the transform coding approach. A number of solutions have been suggested for removing this blockiness, including postfiltering at the block edges as well as transforms that overlap the block boundaries. Each approach has its own drawbacks. The filtering approaches tend to

F I G U R E   1 2 . 8   Sinan image coded at 0.5 bits per pixel using the JPEG algorithm.

F I G U R E   1 2 . 9   Sinan image coded at 0.25 bits per pixel using the JPEG algorithm.

reduce the resolution of the reconstructions, while the overlapped approaches increase the complexity.

12.7 Application to Audio Compression

Transform coding has been widely applied to high-quality audio coding. Applications include the ATRAC algorithm used in the MiniDisc system from Sony [226], Dolby AC-2 and AC-3 algorithms, and the MPEG Layer III algorithm. In this section, we look at some of the ways in which the basic transform coding algorithm has been modified to take advantage of the characteristics of human audio perception. Some of these properties were briefly described in Chapter 7.

Recall that central to models of human audio perception is the notion of *masking*. Masking can be spectral—a tone at one frequency masks the tone at another frequency. Or it can be temporal—a tone at one time can mask the tone at another time. Temporal masking can be backward, forward, or simultaneous, depending on whether the sound being masked occurs before, during, or after the sound that does the masking. All these various types of maskings can be used to reduce the bit rate in a compression scheme. For example, the goal in the selection of the step size of a quantizer in a coding scheme is twofold: reduction of bit rate, which generally translates to larger step size, and reduction of the perceptibility of quantization noise, which means a smaller step size. If the signal being encoded has some large values that will mask certain components of the sound below a certain threshold, then the step size of the quantizer used to encode those components can be increased to take advantage of this fact.

A further modification is introduced because of the presence of sudden sharp increases in the signal value in different types of audio material. Consider the signal shown in Figure 12.10. The sequence consists of 128 samples, the first 118 of which are 0, followed by a sharp increase in value. The 128-point DCT of this sequence is shown in Figure 12.11. Notice that many of these coefficients are quite large. If we were to send all these coefficients, we would have data expansion instead of data compression. If we only keep the 10 largest coefficients, the reconstructed signal is shown in Figure 12.12. Notice that not only are the nonzero signal values not well represented, there is also error in the samples prior to the change in value of the signal. If this were an audio signal and the large values had occurred at the beginning of the sequence, the forward masking effect would have reduced the perceptibility of the quantization error. In the situation shown in Figure 12.12, backward masking will mask some of the quantization error. However, masking occurs for only a short duration prior to the masking sound. Therefore, if the length of the block in question is longer than the masking interval, the distortion will be evident to the listener.

The ATRAC algorithm used in the MiniDisc as well as algorithms used in other systems [226, 26] avoid this problem by using two different modes in the transform stage: a long mode, in which 11.6 milliseconds worth of data are presented to the transform, and a short mode, in which only 2.9 milliseconds worth of data are presented to the transform.

A preprocessor analyzes each block of data prior to the transform. In situations like those described above, the length of the transform is decreased from 11.6 milliseconds worth of data to 2.9 milliseconds worth of data.

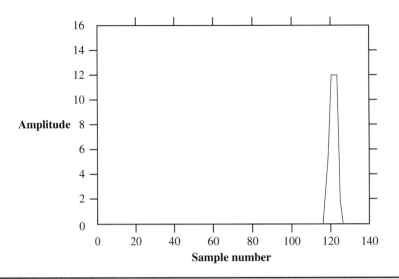

FIGURE   12.10   Source output sequence.

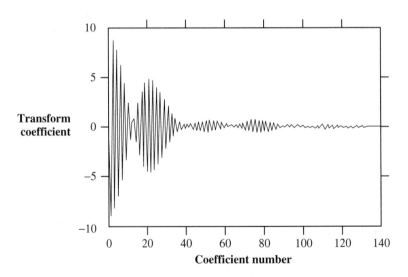

FIGURE   12.11   Transformed sequence.

One of the problems with low-rate transform coding of audio is the blocking effect, where block boundaries can be perceived by the listener. A popular approach used in Dolby AC-2 and AC-3 to get around this problem is based on a subband coding-like algorithm developed by Princen and Bradley [184]. In this approach, the input sequence is divided into overlapping blocks. The overlap allows for a continuity between the various blocks. Thus, the first block may consist of the 1st through the 124th sample, the second block may consist of the 65th through the 192nd sample, the third block may contain the 129th through the 256th sample,

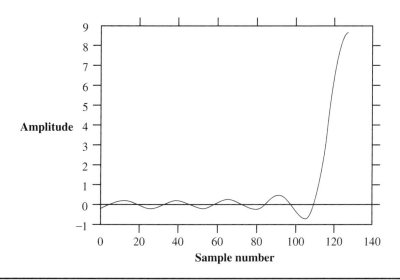

FIGURE 12.12   **Reconstructed sequence.**

and so on. If we took the transform of these blocks and transmitted the transformed sequence, we would end up sending twice as many samples as in the original sequence. However, Princen and Bradley have shown that if we alternately use modified forms of the DCT and DST, we can decimate the transformed sequence so that we end up with the same number of elements as the original sequence without incurring any distortion in the reconstructed sequence. This is analogous to the subband case, except that in the case of subband coding the sequences are decimated in time. In this particular case, the sequences are decimated in the transform domain. Because we are coding overlapping blocks, this approach removes the problem of discontinuities at the block boundaries.

12.8 Summary

In this chapter we have described the concept of transform coding and provided some of the details needed for the investigation of this compression scheme. The basic encoding scheme works as follows:

- Divide the source output into blocks. In the case of speech or audio data, they will be one-dimensional blocks. In the case of images, they will be two-dimensional blocks. In image coding, a typical block size is 8×8.

- Take the transform of this block. In the case of one-dimensional data, this involves premultiplying the N vector of source output samples by the transform matrix. In the case of image data, for the transforms we have looked at, this involves premultiplying the $N \times N$ block by the transform matrix and postmultiplying the result with the transpose of the transform matrix. Fast algorithms exist for performing the transforms described in this chapter (see [66]).

■ Quantize the coefficients. Various techniques exist for the quantization of these coefficients. We have described the approach used by JPEG.

■ Encode the quantized value. The quantized value can be encoded using a fixed-length code or any of the different variable-length codes described in earlier chapters. We have described the approach taken by JPEG.

The decoding scheme is the inverse of the encoding scheme.

The basic approach can be modified depending on the particular characteristics of the data. We have described some of the modifications used by various commercial algorithms for transform coding of audio signals.

Further Reading

1. For detailed information about the JPEG standard, *JPEG Still Image Data Compression Standard*, by W.B. Pennebaker and J.M. Mitchell [178], is an invaluable reference. This book also contains the entire text of the official draft JPEG recommendation, ISO DIS 10918-1 and ISO DIS 10918-2.

2. Chapter 12 in *Digital Coding of Waveforms*, by N.S. Jayant and P. Noll [118], provides a more mathematical treatment of the subject of transform coding.

3. A good source for information about transforms is *Fundamentals of Digital Image Processing*, by A.K. Jain [114]. Another one is *Digital Image Processing*, by R.C. Gonzales and R.E. Wood [96]. This book has an especially nice discussion of the Hotelling transform.

4. The bit allocation problem and its solutions are described in *Vector Quantization for Signal Compression*, by A. Gersho and R.M. Gray [86].

5. A very readable description of transform coding of images is presented in *Digital Image Compression Techniques*, by M. Rabbani and P.W. Jones [185].

6. *The Data Compression Book*, by M. Nelson and J.-L. Gailly [167], provides a very readable discussion of the JPEG algorithm.

1 2 . 9   P r o j e c t s   a n d   P r o b l e m s

1. A square matrix $\mathbf{A}$ has the property that $\mathbf{A}^T\mathbf{A} = \mathbf{A}\mathbf{A}^T = \mathbf{I}$, where $\mathbf{I}$ is the identity matrix. If X_1 and X_2 are two N-dimensional vectors and

$$\Theta_1 = \mathbf{A}X_1$$
$$\Theta_2 = \mathbf{A}X_2$$

then show that

$$|X_1 - X_2|^2 = |\Theta_1 - \Theta_2|^2 \qquad (12.61)$$

2. Consider the following sequence of values:

$$\begin{array}{cccccccc} 10 & 11 & 12 & 11 & 12 & 13 & 12 & 11 \\ 10 & -10 & 8 & -7 & 8 & -8 & 7 & -7 \end{array}$$

(a) Transform each row separately using an eight-point DCT. Plot the resulting 16 transform coefficients.

(b) Combine all 16 numbers into a single vector and transform it using a 16-point DCT. Plot the 16 transform coefficients.

(c) Compare the results of (a) and (b). For this particular case would you suggest a block size of 8 or 16 for greater compression? Justify your answer.

3. Consider the following "image":

$$\begin{array}{cccc} 4 & 3 & 2 & 1 \\ 3 & 2 & 1 & 1 \\ 2 & 1 & 1 & 1 \\ 1 & 1 & 1 & 1 \end{array}$$

(a) Obtain the two-dimensional DWHT transform by first taking the one-dimensional transform of the rows, then taking the column-by-column transform of the resulting matrix.

(b) Obtain the two-dimensional DWHT transform by first taking the one-dimensional transform of the columns, then taking the row-by-row transform of the resulting matrix.

(c) Compare and comment on the results of (a) and (b).

4. (This problem was suggested by P.F. Swaszek.) Let us compare the energy compaction properties of the DCT and the DWHT transforms.

(a) For the Sena image, compute the mean squared value of each of the 64 coefficients using the DCT. Plot these values.

(b) For the Sena image, compute the mean squared value of each of the 64 coefficients using the DWHT. Plot these values.

(c) Compare the results of (a) and (b). Which transform provides more energy compaction? Justify your answer.

5. Implement the transform and quantization portions of the JPEG standard. For coding the labels use an arithmetic coder instead of the modified Huffman code described in this chapter.

(a) Encode the Sena image using this transform coder at rates of (approximately) 0.25, 0.5, and 0.75 bits per pixel. Compute the mean squared error at each rate and plot the rate versus the mse.

(b) Repeat part (a) using one of the public domain implementations of JPEG.

(c) Compare the plots obtained using the two coders and comment on the relative performance of the coders.

6. One of the extensions to the JPEG standard allows for the use of multiple quantization matrices. Investigate the issues involved in designing a set of quantization matrices. Should the quantization matrices be similar or dissimilar? How would you measure their similarity? Given a particular block, do you need to quantize it with each quantization matrix to select the best? Or is there a computationally more efficient approach? Describe your findings in a report.

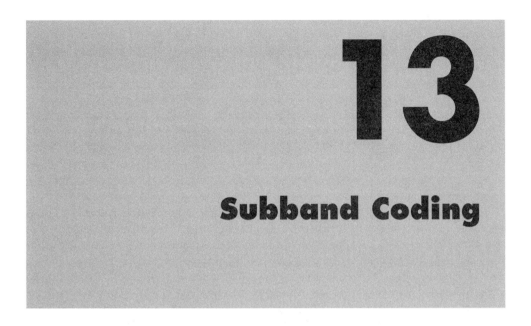

Subband Coding

13.1 Overview

n this chapter we present the second of three approaches to compression in which the source output is decomposed into constituent parts. Each constituent part is encoded using one or more of the methods that have been described previously. The approach described in this chapter, known as subband coding, relies on separating the source output into different bands of frequencies using digital filters. We provide a general description of the subband coding system and, for those readers with some knowledge of Z-transforms, a more mathematical analysis of the system. The sections containing the mathematical analysis are not essential to understanding the rest of the chapter and are marked with a ⋆. If you are not interested in the mathematical analysis, you should skip these sections. This is followed by a description of a popular approach to bit allocation. We conclude the chapter with applications to audio and image compression.

13.2 Introduction

In previous chapters we looked at a number of different compression schemes. Each of these schemes is most efficient when the data have certain characteristics. A vector quantization scheme is most effective if blocks of the source output show a high degree of clustering. A differential encoding scheme is most effective when the sample-to-sample difference is small. If the source output is truly random, it is best to use scalar quantization or lattice vector quantization. Thus, if a source exhibited certain well-defined characteristics, we could choose a compression scheme most suited to that characteristic. Unfortunately, most source outputs

FIGURE 13.1   **A rapidly changing source output that contains a long-term component with slow variations.**

exhibit a combination of characteristics, which makes it difficult to select a compression scheme exactly suited to the source output.

In the last chapter we looked at techniques for decomposing the source output into different frequency bands using block transforms. The transform coefficients had differing statistics and differing perceptual importance. We made use of these differences in allocating bits for encoding the different coefficients. This variable bit allocation resulted in a decrease in the average number of bits required to encode the source output. One of the drawbacks of transform coding is the artificial division of the source output into blocks, which results in the generation of coding artifacts at the block edges, or blocking. One approach to avoiding this blocking is the lapped orthogonal transform (LOT) [147]. In this chapter we look at a popular approach to decomposing the image into different frequency bands without the imposition of an arbitrary block structure. After the input has been decomposed into its constituents, we can use the coding technique best suited to each constituent to improve compression performance. Furthermore, each component of the source output may have different perceptual characteristics. For example, quantization error that is perceptually objectionable in one component may be acceptable in a different component of the source output. Therefore, a coarser quantizer that uses fewer bits can be used to encode the component that is perceptually less important.

Consider the sequence $\{x_n\}$ plotted in Figure 13.1. We can see that, while there is a significant amount of sample-to-sample variation, there is also an underlying long-term trend shown by the dotted line that varies slowly.

One way to extract this trend is to average the sample values in a moving window. The averaging operation smooths out the rapid variations, making the slow variations more evident. Let's pick a window of size two and generate a new sequence $\{y_n\}$ by averaging neighboring values of x_n:

$$y_n = \frac{x_n + x_{n-1}}{2}. \tag{13.1}$$

The consecutive values of y_n will be closer to each other than the consecutive values of x_n. Therefore, the sequence $\{y_n\}$ can be coded more efficiently using differential encoding than we could encode the sequence $\{x_n\}$. However, we want to encode the sequence $\{x_n\}$, not the sequence $\{y_n\}$. Therefore, we follow the encoding of the averaged sequence $\{y_n\}$ by the difference sequence $\{z_n\}$:

$$z_n = x_n - y_n = x_n - \frac{x_n + x_{n-1}}{2} = \frac{x_n - x_{n-1}}{2}. \tag{13.2}$$

The sequences $\{y_n\}$ and $\{z_n\}$ can be coded independently of each other. This way we can use the compression schemes that are best suited for each sequence.

E x a m p l e   1 3 . 2 . 1 :

Suppose we want to encode the following sequence of values $\{x_n\}$:

$$10 \quad 14 \quad 10 \quad 12 \quad 14 \quad 8 \quad 14 \quad 12 \quad 10 \quad 8 \quad 10 \quad 12$$

There is a significant amount of sample-to-sample correlation, so we might consider using a DPCM scheme to compress this sequence. In order to get an idea of the requirements on the quantizer in a DPCM scheme, let us take a look at the sample-to-sample differences $x_n - x_{n-1}$:

$$10 \quad 4 \quad -4 \quad 2 \quad 2 \quad -6 \quad 6 \quad -2 \quad -2 \quad -2 \quad 2 \quad 2$$

Ignoring the first value, the dynamic range of the differences is from -6 to 6. Suppose we want to quantize these values using m bits per sample. This means we could use a quantizer with $M = 2^m$ levels or reconstruction values. If we choose a uniform quantizer, the size of each quantization interval, Δ, is the range of possible input values divided by the total number of reconstruction values. Therefore,

$$\Delta = \frac{12}{M}$$

which would give us a maximum quantization error of $\frac{\Delta}{2}$ or $\frac{6}{M}$.

Now let's generate two new sequences $\{y_n\}$ and $\{z_n\}$ according to (13.1) and (13.2). All three sequences are plotted in Figure 13.2. Notice that given y_n and z_n, we can always recover x_n:

$$x_n = y_n + z_n. \tag{13.3}$$

Let's try to encode each of these sequences. The sequence $\{y_n\}$ is

$$10 \quad 12 \quad 12 \quad 11 \quad 13 \quad 11 \quad 11 \quad 13 \quad 11 \quad 10 \quad 9 \quad 11$$

Notice that the $\{y_n\}$ sequence is "smoother" than the $\{x_n\}$ sequence—the sample-to-sample variation is much smaller. This becomes evident when we look at the sample-to-sample differences:

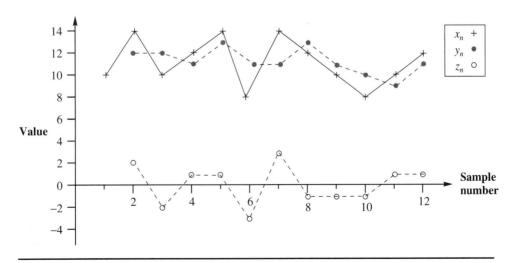

F I G U R E   1 3 . 2   **Original set of samples and the two components.**

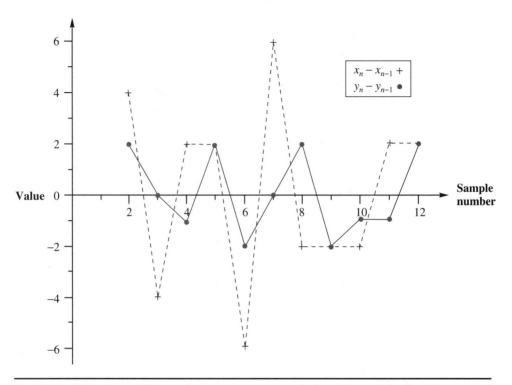

FIGURE 13.3   **Difference sequences generated from the original and averaged sequences.**

$$10 \quad 2 \quad 0 \quad -1 \quad 2 \quad -2 \quad 0 \quad 2 \quad -2 \quad -1 \quad -1 \quad 2$$

The difference sequences $\{x_n - x_{n-1}\}$ and $\{y_n - y_{n-1}\}$ are plotted in Figure 13.3. Again, ignoring the first difference, the dynamic range of the differences $y_n - y_{n-1}$ is 4. If we take the dynamic range of these differences as a measure of the range of the quantizer, then for an M-level quantizer, the step size of the quantizer is $\frac{4}{M}$ and the maximum quantization error is $\frac{2}{M}$. This maximum quantization error is one-third the maximum quantization error incurred when the $\{x_n\}$ sequence is quantized using an M-level quantizer. However, in order to reconstruct $\{x_n\}$, we also need to transmit $\{z_n\}$. The $\{z_n\}$ sequence is

$$0 \quad 2 \quad -2 \quad 1 \quad 1 \quad -3 \quad 3 \quad -1 \quad -1 \quad -1 \quad 1 \quad 1$$

The dynamic range for z_n is 6, half the dynamic range of the difference sequence for $\{x_n\}$. (We could have inferred this directly from the definition of z_n.) The sample-to-sample difference varies more than the actual values. Therefore, instead of differentially encoding this sequence, we quantize each individual sample. For an M-level quantizer, the required step size would be $\frac{6}{M}$, giving a maximum quantization error of $\frac{3}{M}$.

For the same number of bits per sample, we can code both y_n and z_n and incur less distortion. At the receiver, we add y_n and z_n to get the original sequence x_n back. The maximum possible quantization error in the reconstructed sequence would be $\frac{5}{M}$, which is less than the maximum error we would incur if we encoded the $\{x_n\}$ sequence directly.

Although we use the same number of bits for each value of y_n and z_n, the number of elements in each of the $\{y_n\}$ and $\{z_n\}$ sequences is the same as the number of elements in the original $\{x_n\}$ sequence. Although we are using the same number of bits per sample, we are transmitting twice as many samples and, in effect, doubling the bit rate.

We can avoid this by sending every other value of y_n and z_n. Let's divide the sequence $\{y_n\}$ into subsequences $\{y_{2n}\}$ and $\{y_{2n-1}\}$—that is, a subsequence containing only the odd-numbered elements $\{y_1, y_3, \ldots\}$, and a subsequence containing only the even-numbered elements $\{y_2, y_4, \ldots\}$. Similarly, we divide the $\{z_n\}$ sequence into subsequences $\{z_{2n}\}$ and $\{z_{2n-1}\}$. If we transmit either the even-numbered subsequences or the odd-numbered subsequences, we would transmit only as many elements as in the original sequence. To see how we recover the sequence $\{x_n\}$ from these subsequences, suppose we only transmitted the subsequences $\{y_{2n}\}$ and $\{z_{2n}\}$:

$$y_{2n} = \frac{x_{2n} + x_{2n-1}}{2}$$

$$z_{2n} = \frac{x_{2n} - x_{2n-1}}{2}.$$

To recover the even-numbered elements of the $\{x_n\}$ sequence, we add the two subsequences. In order to obtain the odd-numbered members of the $\{x_n\}$ sequence, we take the difference:

$$y_{2n} + z_{2n} = x_{2n} \tag{13.4}$$

$$y_{2n} - z_{2n} = x_{2n-1}. \tag{13.5}$$

Thus, we can recover the entire original sequence $\{x_n\}$, sending only as many bits as required to transmit the original sequence while incurring less distortion.

Is the last part of the previous statement still true? In our original scheme we proposed to transmit the sequence $\{y_n\}$ by transmitting the differences $y_n - y_{n-1}$. As we now need to transmit the subsequence $\{y_{2n}\}$, we will be transmitting the differences $y_{2n} - y_{2n-2}$ instead. In order for our original statement about reduction in distortion to hold, the dynamic range of this new sequence of differences should be less than or equal to the dynamic range of the original difference. A quick check of the $\{y_n\}$ shows us that the dynamic range of the new differences is still 4, and our claim of incurring less distortion still holds. ◆

There are several things we can see from this example. First, the number of different values that we transmit is the same, whether we send the original sequence $\{x_n\}$ or the two subsequences $\{y_n\}$ and $\{z_n\}$. Decomposing the $\{x_n\}$ sequence into subsequences did not result in any increase in the number of values that we need to transmit. Second, the two subsequences had distinctly different characteristics, which led to our use of different techniques to encode the different sequences. If we had not split the $\{x_n\}$ sequence, we would have been using essentially the same approach to compress both subsequences. Finally, we could have used the same decomposition approach to decompose the two constituent sequences, which then could be decomposed further still.

While this example was specific to a particular set of values, we can see that decomposing a signal can lead to different ways of looking at the problem of compression. This added flexibility can lead to improved compression performance.

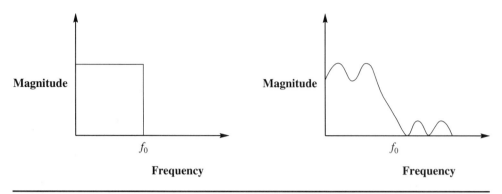

FIGURE   13.4   Ideal and realistic low-pass filter characteristics.

Before we leave this example let us formalize the process of decomposing or *analysis*, and recomposing or *synthesis*. In our example, we decomposed the input sequence $\{x_n\}$ into two subsequences $\{y_n\}$ and $\{z_n\}$ by the operations

$$y_n = \frac{x_n + x_{n-1}}{2} \tag{13.6}$$

$$z_n = \frac{x_n - x_{n-1}}{2}. \tag{13.7}$$

We can implement these operations using discrete time filters. We briefly considered discrete time filters in Chapter 11. We take a slightly more detailed look at filters in the next section.

13.3 Filters

A system that isolates certain frequency components is called a *filter*. The analogy here with mechanical filters such as coffee filters is obvious. A coffee filter or a filter in a water purification system blocks coarse particles and allows only the finer-grained components of the input to pass through. The analogy is not complete, however, because mechanical filters always block the coarser components of the input, while the filters we are discussing can selectively let through or block any range of frequencies. Filters that only let through components below a certain frequency f_0 are called low-pass filters; filters that block all frequency components below a certain value f_0 are called high-pass filters. The frequency f_0 is called the *cutoff frequency*. Filters that let through components that have frequency content above some frequency f_1 but below frequency f_2 are called band-pass filters.

One way to characterize filters is by their *magnitude transfer function*—the ratio of the magnitude of the input and output of the filter as a function of frequency. In Figure 13.4 we show the magnitude transfer function for an ideal low-pass filter and a more realistic low-pass filter, both with a cutoff frequency of f_0. In the ideal case, all components of the input signal with frequencies below f_0 are unaffected except for a constant amount of amplification. All frequencies above f_0 are blocked. In other words, the cutoff is sharp. In the case of the more realistic filter, the cutoff is more gradual. Also, the amplification for the components with frequency less than f_0 is not constant, and components with frequencies above f_0 are not totally blocked. This phenomenon is referred to as *ripple* in the passband and stopband.

The filters we will discuss are digital filters, which operate on a sequence of numbers that are usually samples of a continuously varying signal. We have discussed sampling in Chapter 11. For those of you who skipped that chapter, let us take a brief look at the sampling operation.

How often does a signal have to be sampled in order to reconstruct the signal from the samples? If one signal changes more rapidly than another, it is reasonable to assume that we would need to sample the more rapidly varying signal more often than the slowly varying signal in order to achieve an accurate representation. In fact, it can be shown mathematically that if the highest frequency component of a signal is f_0, then we need to sample the signal at more than $2f_0$ times per second. This result is known as the *Nyquist theorem* or *Nyquist rule* after Harry Nyquist, a famous mathematician from Bell Laboratories. His pioneering work laid the groundwork for much of digital communication. The Nyquist rule can also be extended to signals that only have frequency components between two frequencies f_1 and f_2. If f_1 and f_2 satisfy certain criteria, then we can show that in order to recover the signal exactly, we need to sample the signal at a rate of at least $2(f_2 - f_1)$ samples per second [118].

What would happen if we violated the Nyquist rule and sampled at less than twice the highest frequency? In Chapter 11 we showed that it would be impossible to recover the original signal from the sample. Components with frequencies higher than half the sampling rate show up at lower frequencies. This process is called *aliasing*. In order to prevent aliasing, most systems that require sampling will contain an "anti-aliasing filter" that restricts the input to the sampler to be less than half the sampling frequency. If the signal contains components at more than half the sampling frequency, we will introduce distortion by filtering out these components. However, the distortion due to aliasing is generally more severe than the distortion we introduce due to filtering.

Digital filtering involves taking a weighted sum of current and past inputs to the filter and, in some cases, the past outputs of the filter. The general form of the input-output relationships of the filter is given by

$$y_n = \sum_{i=0}^{N} a_i x_{n-i} + \sum_{i=1}^{M} b_i y_{n-i} \tag{13.8}$$

where the sequence $\{x_n\}$ is the input to the filter, the sequence $\{y_n\}$ is the output from the filter, and the values $\{a_i\}$ and $\{b_i\}$ are called the *filter coefficients*.

If the input sequence is a single 1 followed by all 0s, the output sequence is called the impulse response of the filter. Notice that if the b_i are all 0, then the impulse response will die out after N samples. These filters are called *finite impulse response* (FIR) filters. The number N is sometimes called the number of *taps* in the filter. If any of the b_i have nonzero values, the impulse response can, in theory, continue forever. Filters with nonzero values for some of the b_i are called *infinite impulse response* (IIR) filters.

Example 13.3.1:

Suppose we have a filter with $a_0 = 1.25$ and $a_1 = 0.5$. If the input sequence $\{x_n\}$ is given by

$$x_n = \begin{cases} 1 & n = 0 \\ 0 & n \neq 0, \end{cases} \tag{13.9}$$

then the output is given by

$$y_0 = a_0 x_0 + a_1 x_{-1} = 1.25$$
$$y_1 = a_0 x_1 + a_1 x_0 = 0.5$$
$$y_n = 0 \qquad n < 0 \text{ or } n > 1.$$

This output is called the impulse response of the filter. The impulse response sequence is usually represented by $\{h_n\}$. Therefore, for this filter we would say that

$$h_n = \begin{cases} 1.25 & n = 0 \\ 0.5 & n = 1 \\ 0 & \text{otherwise.} \end{cases} \qquad (13.10)$$

Notice that if we know the impulse response we also know the values of a_i. Knowledge of the impulse response completely specifies the filter. Furthermore, because the impulse response goes to zero after a finite number of samples (two in this case), the filter is an FIR filter.

The filters we used in Example 13.2.1 are both two-tap FIR filters with impulse responses

$$h_n = \begin{cases} \frac{1}{2} & n = 0 \\ \frac{1}{2} & n = 1 \\ 0 & \text{otherwise} \end{cases} \qquad (13.11)$$

for the "averaging" or low-pass filter, and

$$h_n = \begin{cases} \frac{1}{2} & n = 0 \\ -\frac{1}{2} & n = 1 \\ 0 & \text{otherwise} \end{cases} \qquad (13.12)$$

for the "difference" or high-pass filter.

Now let's consider a different filter with $a_0 = 1$ and $b_1 = 0.9$. For the same input as above, the output is given by

$$y_0 = a_0 x_0 + b_1 y_{-1} = 1(1) + 0.9(0) = 1 \qquad (13.13)$$
$$y_1 = a_0 x_1 + b_1 y_0 = 1(0) + 0.9(1) = 0.9 \qquad (13.14)$$
$$y_2 = a_0 x_2 + b_1 y_1 = 1(0) + 0.9(0.9) = 0.81 \qquad (13.15)$$
$$\vdots \quad \vdots$$
$$y_n = (0.9)^n. \qquad (13.16)$$

The impulse response can be written more compactly as

$$h_n = \begin{cases} 0 & n < 0 \\ (0.9)^n & n \geq 0. \end{cases} \qquad (13.17)$$

Notice that the impulse response is nonzero for all $n \geq 0$, which makes this an IIR filter.   ◆

Although it is not as clear in the IIR case as it was in the FIR case, the impulse response completely specifies the filter. Once we know the impulse response of the filter, we know the relationship between the input and output of the filter. If $\{x_n\}$ and $\{y_n\}$ are the input and output, respectively, of a filter with impulse response $\{h_n\}_{n=0}^{M}$, then $\{y_n\}$ can be obtained from $\{x_n\}$ and $\{h_n\}$ via the following relationship:

$$y_n = \sum_{k=0}^{M} h_k x_{n-k},$$

(13.18)

where M is finite for an FIR filter and infinite for an IIR filter. The relationship, shown in (13.18), is known as *convolution* and can be easily obtained through the use of the properties of linearity and shift invariance (see Problem 1).

Because FIR filters are simply weighted averages, they are always stable. When we say a filter is stable we mean that as long as the input is bounded, the output will also be bounded. This is not true of IIR filters. Certain IIR filters can give an unbounded output even when the input is bounded.

Example 13.3.2:

Consider a filter with $a_0 = 1$ and $b_1 = 2$. Suppose the input sequence is a single 1 followed by 0s. Then the output is

$$y_0 = a_0 x_0 + b_1 y_{-1} = 1(1) + 2(0) = 1$$ (13.19)
$$y_1 = a_0 x_0 + b_1 y_0 = 1(0) + 2(1) = 2$$ (13.20)
$$y_2 = a_0 x_1 + b_1 y_1 = 1(0) + 2(2) = 4$$ (13.21)

$$\vdots \quad \vdots$$

$$y_n = 2^n.$$ (13.22)

Even though the input contained a single 1, the output at time $n = 30$ is 2^{30}, or more than a billion! ◆

Although IIR filters can become unstable, they can also provide better performance, in terms of sharper cutoffs and less ripple in the passband and stopband for a fewer number of coefficients.

The study of design and analysis of digital filters is a fascinating and important subject. We provide some of the details in Sections 13.5—13.8. If you are not interested in these topics, you can take a more utilitarian approach and make use of the literature to select the necessary filters rather than design them. In the following section we briefly describe some of the families of filters used to generate the examples in this chapter. We also provide filter coefficients that you can use for experiment.

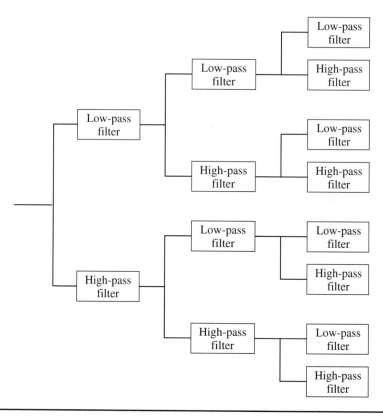

FIGURE 13.5   An eight-band filter bank.

13.3.1 Some Filters Used in Subband Coding

The most frequently used filter banks in subband coding consist of a cascade of stages, where each stage consists of a low-pass filter and a high-pass filter, as shown in Figure 13.5. The most popular among these filters are the *quadrature mirror filters* (QMF), which were first proposed by Croisier, Esteban, and Galand [56]. These filters have the property that if the impulse response of the low-pass filter is given by $\{h_n\}$, then the high-pass impulse response is given by $\{(-1)^n h_{N-1-n}\}$. The QMF filters designed by Johnston [121] are widely used in a number of applications. The filter coefficients for 8-, 16-, and 32-tap filters are given in Tables 13.1—13.3. Notice that the filters are symmetric; that is,

$$h_{N-1-n} = h_n \qquad n = 0, 1, \ldots, \frac{N}{2} - 1. \tag{13.23}$$

As we shall see later, the filters with fewer taps are less efficient in their decomposition than the filters with more taps. However, from Equation (13.18) we can see that the number of taps dictates the number of multiply-add operations necessary to generate the filter outputs. Thus, if we want to obtain more efficient decompositions, we do so by increasing the amount of computation.

TABLE 13.1   Coefficients for the 8-tap Johnston low-pass filter.

h_0, h_7	0.00938715
h_1, h_6	0.06942827
h_2, h_5	-0.07065183
h_3, h_4	0.48998080

TABLE 13.2   Coefficients for the 16-tap Johnston low-pass filter.

h_0, h_{15}	0.002898163
h_1, h_{14}	-0.009972252
h_2, h_{13}	-0.001920936
h_3, h_{12}	0.03596853
h_4, h_{11}	-0.01611869
h_5, h_{10}	-0.09530234
h_6, h_9	0.1067987
h_7, h_8	0.4773469

TABLE 13.3   Coefficients for the 32-tap Johnston low-pass filter.

h_0, h_{31}	0.0022551390
h_1, h_{30}	-0.0039715520
h_2, h_{29}	-0.0019696720
h_3, h_{28}	0.0081819410
h_4, h_{27}	0.00084268330
h_5, h_{26}	-0.014228990
h_6, h_{25}	0.0020694700
h_7, h_{24}	0.022704150
h_8, h_{23}	-0.0079617310
h_9, h_{22}	-0.034964400
h_{10}, h_{21}	0.019472180
h_{11}, h_{20}	0.054812130
h_{12}, h_{19}	-0.044524230
h_{13}, h_{18}	-0.099338590
h_{14}, h_{17}	0.13297250
h_{15}, h_{16}	0.46367410

Another popular set of filters are the Smith-Barnwell filters [215], some of which are shown in Tables 13.4 and 13.5.

These families of filters differ in a number of ways. For example, consider the Johnston eight-tap filter and the Smith-Barnwell eight-tap filter. The magnitude transfer functions for these two filters are plotted in Figure 13.6. Notice that the cutoff for the Smith-Barnwell filter is much sharper than the cutoff for the Johnston filter. This means that the separation provided

TABLE   13.4   Coefficients for the eight-tap Smith-Barnwell low-pass filter.

h_0	0.0348975582178515
h_1	−0.01098301946252854
h_2	−0.06286453934951963
h_3	0.223907720892568
h_4	0.556856993531445
h_5	0.357976304997285
h_6	−0.02390027056113145
h_7	−0.07594096379188282

TABLE   13.5   Coefficients for the 16-tap Smith-Barnwell low-pass filter.

h_0	0.02193598203004352
h_1	0.001578616497663704
h_2	−0.06025449102875281
h_3	−0.0118906596205391
h_4	0.137537915636625
h_5	0.05745450056390939
h_6	−0.321670296165893
h_7	−0.528720271545339
h_8	−0.295779674500919
h_9	0.0002043110845170894
h_{10}	0.02906699789446796
h_{11}	−0.03533486088708146
h_{12}	−0.006821045322743358
h_{13}	0.02606678468264118
h_{14}	0.001033363491944126
h_{15}	−0.01435930957477529

by the eight-tap Johnston filter is not as good as that provided by the eight-tap Smith-Barnwell filter. We will see the effect of this when we look at image compression later in this chapter.

These filters are examples of some of the more popular filters. Many more filters exist in the literature, and more are being discovered.

13.4   The Basic Subband Coding Algorithm

The basic subband coding system is shown in Figure 13.7.

13.4.1   Analysis

The source output is passed through a bank of filters, called the analysis filter bank, which covers the range of frequencies that make up the source output. The passbands of the filters

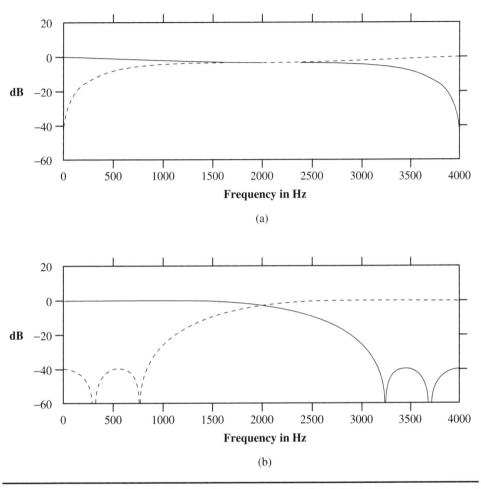

FIGURE 13.6   **Magnitude transfer functions of the (a) eight-tap Johnston and (b) eight-tap Smith-Barnwell filters.**

can be nonoverlapping or overlapping. Nonoverlapping and overlapping filter banks are shown in Figure 13.8. The outputs of the filters are then subsampled.

The justification for the subsampling is the Nyquist rule and its generalization, which tells us that we only need twice as many samples per second as the range of frequencies. This means that we can reduce the number of samples at the output of the filter because the range of frequencies at the output of the filter is less than the range of frequencies at the input to the filter. This process of reducing the number of samples is called *decimation*,[1] or *downsampling*. The amount of decimation depends on the ratio of the bandwidth of the filter

---

[1] The word *decimation* has a rather bloody origin. During the time of the Roman empire, if a legion broke ranks and ran during battle, its members were lined up and every tenth person was killed. This process was called decimation.

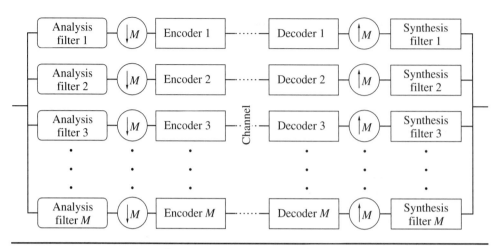

FIGURE 13.7   **Block diagram of the subband coding system.**

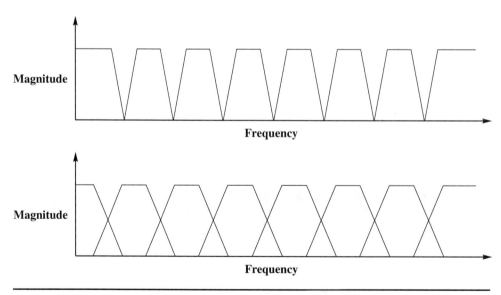

FIGURE 13.8   **Nonoverlapping and overlapping filter banks.**

output to the filter input. If the bandwidth at the output of the filter is $1/M$ of the bandwidth at the input to the filter, we would decimate the output by a factor of M by keeping every Mth sample. The symbol $M \downarrow$ is used to denote this decimation.

Once the output of the filters has been decimated, the output is encoded using one of several encoding schemes, including ADPCM, PCM, and vector quantization.

1 3 . 4 . 2 Q u a n t i z a t i o n a n d C o d i n g

Along with the selection of the compression scheme, the allocation of bits between the subbands is an important design parameter. Different subbands contain differing amounts of information. Therefore, we need to allocate the available bits among the subbands according to some measure of the information content. There are a number of different ways we could distribute the available bits. For example, suppose we were decomposing the source output into four bands and we wanted a coding rate of 1 bit per sample. We could accomplish this by using 1 bit per sample for each of the four bands. On the other hand, we could simply discard the output of two of the bands and use 2 bits per sample for the two remaining bands. Or, we could discard the output of three of the four filters and use 4 bits per sample to encode the output of the remaining filter.

This *bit allocation* procedure can have a significant impact on the quality of the final reconstruction, especially when the information content of different bands is very different.

If we use the variance of the output of each filter as a measure of information, and assume that the compression scheme is scalar quantization, we can arrive at several simple bit allocation schemes (see Section 12.5). If we use a slightly more sophisticated model for the outputs of the filters, we can arrive at significantly better bit allocation procedures (see Section 13.9).

1 3 . 4 . 3 S y n t h e s i s

The quantized and coded coefficients are used to reconstruct a representation of the original signal at the decoder. First, the encoded samples from each subband are decoded at the receiver. These decoded values are then upsampled by inserting an appropriate number of 0s between samples. Once the number of samples per second has been brought back to the original rate, the upsampled signals are passed through a bank of reconstruction filters. The outputs of the reconstruction filters are added to give the final reconstructed outputs.

We can see that the basic subband system is simple. The three major components of this system are the *analysis and synthesis filters*, the *bit allocation* scheme, and the *encoding* scheme. A substantial amount of research has focused on each of these components. Various filter bank structures have been studied in order to find filters that are simple to implement and provide good separation between the frequency bands. In the next section we briefly look at some of the techniques used in the design of filter banks, but our descriptions are necessarily limited. For a (much) more detailed look, see the excellent book by P.P. Vaidyanathan [228].

The bit allocation procedures have also been extensively studied in the contexts of subband coding, wavelet-based coding, and transform coding. We have already described some bit allocation schemes in Section 12.5, and we describe a different approach in Section 13.9. There are also some bit allocation procedures that have been developed in the context of wavelets, which we describe in the next chapter.

The separation of the source output according to frequency also opens up the possibility for innovative ways to use compression algorithms. The decomposition of the source output in this manner provides inputs for the compression algorithms, each of which has more clearly defined characteristics than the original source output. We can use these characteristics to select separate compression schemes appropriate to each of the different inputs.

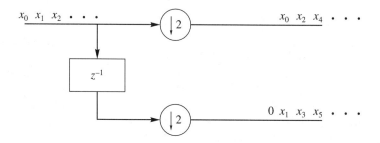

FIGURE 13.9   **Decomposition of an input sequence into its odd and even components.**

Human perception of audio and video inputs is frequency dependent. We can use this fact to design our compression schemes so that the frequency bands that are most important to perception are reconstructed most accurately. Whatever distortion there has to be is introduced in the frequency bands to which humans are least sensitive. We describe some applications to the coding of speech, audio, and images later in this chapter.

Before we proceed to bit allocation procedures and implementations, we provide a more mathematical analysis of the subband coding system. We also look at some approaches to the design of filter banks for subband coding. The analysis relies heavily on the Z-transform concepts introduced in Chapter 11 and will primarily be of interest to readers with an electrical engineering background. The material is not essential to understanding the rest of the chapter; if you are not interested in these details, you should skip these sections and go directly to Section 13.9.

13.5 Design of Filter Banks ★

In this and the following starred section we will take a closer look at the analysis, downsampling, upsampling, and synthesis operations. Our approach follows that of [36]. We assume familiarity with the Z-transform concepts of Chapter 11. We begin with some notation. Suppose we have a sequence $x_0, x_1, x_2, \ldots$. We can divide this sequence into two subsequences: $x_0, x_2, x_4, \ldots$ and $x_1, x_3, x_5, \ldots$ using the scheme shown in Figure 13.9, where z^{-1} corresponds to a delay of one sample and $\downarrow M$ denotes a subsampling by a factor of M. This subsampling process is called *downsampling* or *decimation*.

The original sequence can be recovered from the two downsampled sequences by inserting 0s between consecutive samples of the subsequences, delaying the top branch by one sample and adding the two together. Adding 0s between consecutive samples is called *upsampling* and is denoted by $\uparrow M$. The reconstruction process is shown in Figure 13.10.

While we have decomposed the source output sequence into two subsequences, there is no reason for the statistical and spectral properties of these subsequences to be different. As our objective is to decompose the source output sequences into subsequences with differing characteristics, there is much more yet to be done.

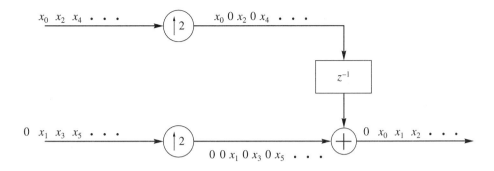

FIGURE 13.10   Reconstructing the input sequence from its odd and even components.

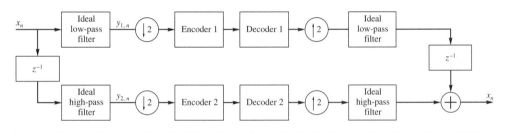

FIGURE 13.11   Decomposition into two bands using ideal filters.

Generalizing this, we obtain the system shown in Figure 13.11. The source output sequence is fed to an ideal low-pass filter and an ideal high-pass filter, each with a bandwidth of $\pi/2$. We assume that the source output sequence had a bandwidth of π. If the original source signal was sampled at the Nyquist rate, as the output of the two filters have bandwidths half that of the original sequence, the filter outputs are actually oversampled by a factor of two. We can, therefore, subsample these signals by a factor of two without any loss of information. The two bands now have different characteristics and can be encoded differently. For the moment let's assume that the encoding is performed in a lossless manner so that the reconstructed sequence exactly matches the source output sequence.

Let us look at how this system operates in the frequency domain. We begin by looking at the downsampling operation.

13.5.1   Downsampling   ★

To see the effects of downsampling, we will obtain the Z-transform of the downsampled sequence in terms of the original source sequence. Because it is easier to understand what is going on if we can visualize the process, we will use the example of a source sequence that has the frequence profile shown in Figure 13.12. For this sequence the output of the ideal filters will have the shape shown in Figure 13.13.

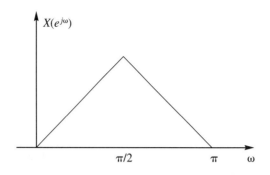

FIGURE 13.12   **Spectrum of the source output.**

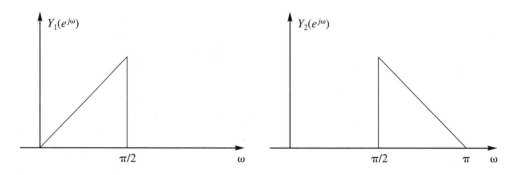

FIGURE 13.13   **Spectrum of the outputs of the ideal filters.**

Let's represent the downsampled sequence as $\{w_{i,n}\}$. The Z-transform $W_1(z)$ of the downsampled sequence $w_{1,n}$ is

$$W_1(z) = \sum w_{1,n}z^{-n}. \tag{13.24}$$

The downsampling operation means that

$$w_{1,n} = y_{1,2n}. \tag{13.25}$$

In order to find the Z-transform of this sequence, we go through a two-step process. Define the sequence

$$y'_{1,n} = \frac{1}{2}(1 + e^{jn\pi})y_{1,n} \tag{13.26}$$

$$= \begin{cases} y_{1,n} & n \text{ even} \\ 0 & \text{otherwise.} \end{cases} \tag{13.27}$$

We could also have written Equation (13.26) as

$$y'_{1,n} = \frac{1}{2}(1 + (-1)^n)y_{1,n}$$

however, writing the relationship as in Equation (13.26) makes it easier to extend this development to the case where we divide the source output into more than two bands.

The Z-transform of $y'_{1,n}$ is given as

$$Y'_1(z) = \sum_{n=-\infty}^{\infty} \frac{1}{2}(1 + e^{jn\pi})y_{1,n}z^{-n}. \tag{13.28}$$

Assuming all summations converge,

$$Y'_1(z) = \frac{1}{2}\sum_{n=-\infty}^{\infty} y_{1,n}z^{-n} + \frac{1}{2}\sum_{n=-\infty}^{\infty} y_{1,n}(ze^{-j\pi})^{-n} \tag{13.29}$$

$$= \frac{1}{2}Y_1(z) + \frac{1}{2}Y_1(-z) \tag{13.30}$$

where we have used the fact that

$$e^{-j\pi} = \cos(\pi) - j\sin\pi = -1.$$

Noting that

$$w_{1,n} = y'_{1,2n} \tag{13.31}$$

$$W_1(z) = \sum_{n=-\infty}^{\infty} w_{1,n}z^{-n} = \sum_{-\infty}^{\infty} y'_{1,2n}z^{-n}. \tag{13.32}$$

Substituting $m = 2n$,

$$W_1(z) = \sum_{-\infty}^{\infty} y'_{1,m}z^{\frac{-m}{2}} \tag{13.33}$$

$$= Y'_1(z^{\frac{1}{2}}) \tag{13.34}$$

$$= \frac{1}{2}Y_1(z^{\frac{1}{2}}) + \frac{1}{2}Y_1(-z^{\frac{1}{2}}). \tag{13.35}$$

Why didn't we simply write the Z-transform of $w_{1,n}$ directly in terms of $y_{1,n}$ and use the substitution $m = 2n$? If we had, the equivalent equation to (13.33) would contain the odd indexed terms of $y_{1,n}$, which we know do not appear at the output of the downsampler. In Equation (13.33), we also get the odd indexed terms of $y'_{1,n}$; however, as these terms are all zero (see Equation (13.26)), they do not contribute to the Z-transform.

Substituting $z = e^{j\omega}$ we get

$$W_1(e^{j\omega}) = \frac{1}{2}Y_1(e^{j\frac{\omega}{2}}) + \frac{1}{2}Y(-e^{j\frac{\omega}{2}}). \tag{13.36}$$

Plotting this for the $Y_1(e^{j\omega})$ of Figure 13.13, we get the spectral shape shown in Figure 13.14; that is, the spectral shape of the downsampled signal is a stretched version of the spectral shape of the original signal. A similar situation exists for the downsampled signal $w_{2,n}$.

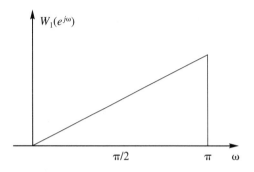

FIGURE 13.14   **Spectrum of the downsampled low-pass filter output.**

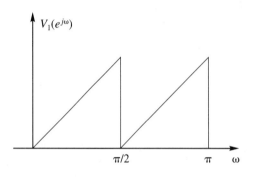

FIGURE 13.15   **Spectrum of the upsampled signal.**

13.5.2 Upsampling ★

Let's take a look now at what happens after the upsampling. The upsampled sequence $v_{1,n}$ can be written as

$$v_{1,n} = \begin{cases} w_{1,\frac{n}{2}} & n \text{ even} \\ 0 & n \text{ odd.} \end{cases} \tag{13.37}$$

The Z-transform $V_1(z)$ is thus

$$V_1(z) = \sum_{n=-\infty}^{\infty} v_{1,n} z^{-n} \tag{13.38}$$

$$= \sum_{n=-\infty}^{\infty} w_{1,\frac{n}{2}} z^{-n} \qquad n \text{ even} \tag{13.39}$$

$$= \sum_{m=-\infty}^{\infty} w_{1,m} z^{-2m} \tag{13.40}$$

$$= W_1(z^2). \tag{13.41}$$

The spectrum is sketched in Figure 13.15. The "stretching" of the sequence in the time domain has led to a compression in the frequency domain. This compression has also resulted in a replication of the spectrum in the $[0, \pi]$ interval. This replication effect is called *imaging*. We remove the images by using an ideal low-pass filter in the top branch and an ideal high-pass filter in the bottom branch.

Because the use of the filters prior to sampling reduces the bandwidth, which in turn allows the downsampling operation to proceed without aliasing, these filters are called *anti-aliasing* filters. Because they decompose the source output into components, they are also called *analysis* filters. The filters after the upsampling operation are used to recompose the original signal; therefore, they are called *synthesis* filters. We can also view these filters as interpolating between nonzero values to recover the signal at the point that we have inserted zeros. Therefore, these filters are also called *interpolation* filters.

Although the use of ideal filters would give us perfect reconstruction of the source output, in practice we do not have ideal filters available. When we use more realistic filters in place of the ideal filters, we end up introducing distortion. In the next section we look at this situation and discuss how we can reduce or remove this distortion.

13.6 Perfect Reconstruction Using Two-Channel Filter Banks ★

Suppose we replace the ideal low-pass filter in Figure 13.11 with a more realistic filter with the magnitude response shown in Figure 13.4. The spectrum of the output of the low-pass filter is shown in Figure 13.16. Notice that we now have nonzero values for frequencies above $\frac{\pi}{2}$. If we now subsample by two, we will end up sampling at *less* than twice the highest frequency, or in other words, we will be sampling at below the Nyquist rate. This will result in the introduction of aliasing distortion, which will show up in the reconstruction. A similar situation will occur when we replace the ideal high-pass filter with a realistic high-pass filter.

In order to get perfect reconstruction after synthesis, we need to somehow get rid of the aliasing and imaging effects. Let us look at the conditions we need to impose upon the filters $H_1(z)$, $H_2(z)$, $K_1(z)$, and $K_2(z)$ in order to accomplish this. These conditions are called *perfect reconstruction* (PR) conditions.

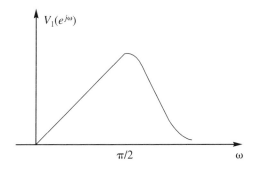

FIGURE 13.16   Output of the low-pass filter.

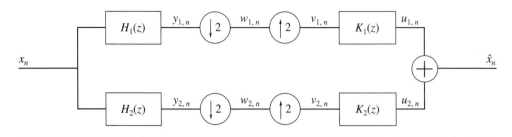

FIGURE 13.17   **Two-channel subband decimation and interpolation.**

Consider Figure 13.17. Let's obtain an expression for $\hat{X}(z)$ in terms of $H_1(z), H_2(z), K_1(z)$, and $K_2(z)$. We start with the reconstruction:

$$\hat{X}(z) = U_1(z) + U_2(z) \tag{13.42}$$
$$= V_1(z)K_1(z) + V_2(z)K_2(z). \tag{13.43}$$

Therefore, we need to find $V_1(z)$ and $V_2(z)$. The sequence $v_{1,n}$ is obtained by upsampling $w_{1,n}$. Therefore, from Equation (13.41),

$$V_1(z) = W_1(z^2). \tag{13.44}$$

The sequence $w_{1,n}$ is obtained by downsampling $y_{1,n}$,

$$Y_1(z) = X(z)H_1(z).$$

Therefore, from Equation (13.35),

$$W_1(z) = \frac{1}{2}\left[X(z^{\frac{1}{2}})H_1(z^{\frac{1}{2}}) + X(-z^{\frac{1}{2}})H_1(-z^{\frac{1}{2}})\right] \tag{13.45}$$

and

$$V_1(z) = \frac{1}{2}[X(z)H_1(z) + X(-z)H_1(-z)]. \tag{13.46}$$

Similarly, we can also show that

$$V_2(z) = \frac{1}{2}[X(z)H_2(z) + X(-z)H_2(-z)]. \tag{13.47}$$

Substituting the expressions for $V_1(z)$ and $V_2(z)$ into Equation (13.43) we obtain

$$\hat{X}(z) = \frac{1}{2}\left[H_1(z)K_1(z) + H_2(z)K_2(z)\right]X(z)$$
$$+ \frac{1}{2}\left[H_1(-z)K_1(z) + H_2(-z)K_2(z)\right]X(-z). \tag{13.48}$$

For perfect reconstruction we would like $\hat{X}(z)$ to be a delayed and perhaps amplitude-scaled version of $X(z)$; that is,

$$\hat{X}(z) = cX(z)z^{-n_0}. \tag{13.49}$$

In order for this to be true, we need to impose conditions on $H_1(z)$, $H_2(z)$, $K_1(z)$, and $K_2(z)$. There are several ways we can do this, with each approach providing a different solution. One approach involves writing Equation (13.48) in matrix form as

$$\hat{X}(z) = \frac{1}{2} \begin{bmatrix} K_1(z) & K_2(z) \end{bmatrix} \begin{bmatrix} H_1(z) & H_1(-z) \\ H_2(z) & H_2(-z) \end{bmatrix} \begin{bmatrix} X(z) \\ X(-z) \end{bmatrix} \tag{13.50}$$

For perfect reconstruction, we need

$$\begin{bmatrix} K_1(z) & K_2(z) \end{bmatrix} \begin{bmatrix} H_1(z) & H_1(-z) \\ H_2(z) & H_2(-z) \end{bmatrix} = \begin{bmatrix} cz^{-n_0} & 0 \end{bmatrix} \tag{13.51}$$

where we have absorbed the factor of $\frac{1}{2}$ into the constant c. This means that the synthesis filters $K_1(z)$ and $K_2(z)$ satisfy

$$\begin{bmatrix} K_1(z) & K_2(z) \end{bmatrix} = \frac{cz^{-n_0}}{\det[\mathcal{H}(z)]} \begin{bmatrix} H_2(-z) & -H_1(-z) \end{bmatrix} \tag{13.52}$$

where

$$\mathcal{H}(z) = \begin{bmatrix} H_1(z) & H_1(-z) \\ H_2(z) & H_2(-z) \end{bmatrix} \tag{13.53}$$

If $H_1(z)$ and/or $H_2(z)$ are IIR filters, the reconstruction filters can become quite complex. Therefore, we would like to have both the analysis and synthesis filters be FIR filters. If we select the analysis filters to be FIR, then in order to guarantee that the synthesis filters are also FIR we need

$$\det[\mathcal{H}(z)] = \gamma z^{-n_1}$$

where γ is a constant. Examining $\det[\mathcal{H}(z)]$

$$\begin{aligned} \det[\mathcal{H}(z)] &= H_1(z)H_2(-z) - H_1(-z)H_2(z) \\ &= P(z) - P(-z) = \gamma z^{-n_1} \end{aligned} \tag{13.54}$$

where $P(z) = H_1(z)H_2(-z)$. If we examine Equation (13.54), we can see that n_1 has to be odd because all terms containing even powers of z in $P(z)$ will be canceled out by the corresponding terms in $P(-z)$. Thus, $P(z)$ can have an arbitrary number of even-indexed coefficients (as they will get canceled out), but there must be only one nonzero coefficient of an odd power of z. By choosing any valid factorization of the form

$$P(z) = P_1(z)P_2(z) \tag{13.55}$$

we can obtain many possible solutions of perfect reconstruction FIR filter banks with

$$H_1(z) = P_1(z) \tag{13.56}$$

and

$$H_2(z) = P_2(-z). \tag{13.57}$$

Although these filters are perfect reconstruction filters, for applications in data compression they suffer from one significant drawback. Because these filters may be of unequal bandwidth, the output of the larger bandwidth filter suffers from severe aliasing. If the output of both bands is available to the receiver, this is not a problem because the aliasing is canceled out in the reconstruction process. However, in many compression applications we discard the subband containing the least amount of energy, which will generally be the output of the filter with the smaller bandwidth. In this case the reconstruction will contain a large amount of aliasing distortion. In order to avoid this problem for compression applications, we generally wish to minimize the amount of aliasing in each subband. A class of filters that is useful in this situation is the *quadrature mirror filters* (QMF). We look at these filters in the next section.

13.6.1   Two-Channel PR Quadrature Mirror Filters ⋆

Before we introduce the quadrature mirror filters, let's rewrite Equation (13.48) as

$$\hat{X}(z) = T(z)X(z) + S(z)X(-z) \tag{13.58}$$

where

$$T(z) = \frac{1}{2}[H_1(z)K_1(z) + H_2(z)K_2(z)] \tag{13.59}$$

$$S(z) = \frac{1}{2}[H_1(-z)K_1(z) + H_2(-z)K_2(z)]. \tag{13.60}$$

In order for the reconstruction of the input sequence $\{x_n\}$ to be a delayed, and perhaps scaled, version of $\{x_n\}$, we need to get rid of the aliasing term $X(-z)$ and have $T(z)$ be a pure delay. To get rid of the aliasing term, we need

$$S(z) = 0, \qquad \forall z.$$

From Equation (13.60), this will happen if

$$K_1(z) = H_2(-z) \tag{13.61}$$
$$K_2(z) = -H_1(-z). \tag{13.62}$$

After removing the aliasing distortion, a delayed version of the input will be available at the output if

$$T(z) = cz^{-n_0} \qquad c \text{ is a constant.} \tag{13.63}$$

Replacing z by $e^{j\omega}$, this means that we want

$$|T(e^{j\omega})| = \text{constant} \tag{13.64}$$
$$\arg(T(e^{j\omega})) = Kw \qquad K \text{ constant.} \tag{13.65}$$

The first requirement eliminates amplitude distortion, while the second, the linear phase requirement, is necessary to eliminate phase distortion. If these requirements are satisfied,

$$\hat{x}(n) = cx(n - n_0). \tag{13.66}$$

That is, the reconstructed signal is a delayed version of input signal $x(n)$. However, meeting both requirements simultaneously is not a trivial task.

Consider the problem of designing $T(z)$ to have linear phase. Substituting (13.61) and (13.62) into Equation (13.59), we obtain

$$T(z) = \frac{1}{2}[H_1(z)H_2(-z) - H_1(-z)H_2(z)].$$ (13.67)

Therefore, if we choose $H_1(z)$ and $H_2(z)$ to be linear phase FIR, $T(z)$ will also be a linear phase FIR filter. In the QMF approach, we first select the low-pass filter $H_1(z)$, then define the high-pass filter $H_2(z)$ to be a mirror image of the low-pass filter:

$$H_2(z) = H_1(-z).$$ (13.68)

This is referred to as a *mirror* condition and is the original reason for the name of the QMF filters [228]. We can see that this condition will force both filters to have equal bandwidth.

Given the mirror condition and $H_1(z)$, a linear phase FIR filter, we will have linear phase and

$$T(z) = \frac{1}{2}[H_1^2(z) - H_1^2(-z)].$$ (13.69)

It is not clear that $\left|T(e^{j\omega})\right|$ is a constant. In fact, we will show in Section 13.8 that a linear phase two-channel FIR QMF bank with the filters chosen as in Equation (13.68) can have PR property if and only if $H_1(z)$ is in the simple two-tap form

$$H_1(z) = h_0 z^{-2k_0} + h_1 z^{-(2k_1+1)}.$$ (13.70)

Then, $T(z)$ is given by

$$T(z) = 2h_0 h_1 z^{-(2k_0+2k_1+1)}$$ (13.71)

which is of the desired form cz^{-n_0}. However, if we look at the magnitude characteristics of the two filters, we see that they have poor cutoff characteristics. The magnitude of the low-pass filter is given by

$$\left|H_1(e^{j\omega})\right|^2 = h_0^2 + h_1^2 + 2h_0 h_1 \cos(2k_0 - 2k_1 - 1)\omega$$ (13.72)

and the high-pass filter is given by

$$\left|H_2(e^{j\omega})\right|^2 = h_0^2 + h_1^2 - 2h_0 h_1 \cos(2k_0 - 2k_1 - 1)\omega.$$ (13.73)

For $h_0 = h_1 = k_0 = k_1 = 1$, the magnitude responses are plotted in Figure 13.18. Notice the poor cutoff characteristics of these two filters.

Thus, for perfect reconstruction with no aliasing and no amplitude or phase distortion, the mirror condition does not seem like such a good idea. However, if we slightly relax these rather strict conditions, we can obtain some very nice designs. For example, instead of attempting to eliminate all phase and amplitude distortion, we could elect to eliminate only the phase distortion and *minimize* the amplitude distortion. We can optimize the coefficients of $H_1(z)$ such that $\left|T(e^{j\omega})\right|$ is made as close to a constant as possible, while minimizing the stopband energy of $H_1(z)$ in order to have a good low-pass characteristic. Such an optimization has been suggested by Johnston [121] and Jain and Crochiere [115]. They construct the objective function

$$J = \alpha \int_{\omega_s}^{\pi} \left| H_1(e^{j\omega}) \right|^2 d\omega + (1 - \alpha) \int_0^{\pi} (1 - \left| T(e^{j\omega}) \right|^2) d\omega \qquad (13.74)$$

which has to be minimized to obtain $H_1(z)$ and $T_1(z)$, where ω_s is the cutoff frequency of the filter.

We can also go the other way and eliminate the amplitude distortion, then attempt to minimize the phase distortion. A review of these approaches can be found in [36, 228].

13.6.2   Power Symmetric FIR Filters ★

Another approach, independently discovered by Smith and Barnwell [215] and Mintzer [158], can be used to design a two-channel filter bank in which aliasing, amplitude distortion, and phase distortion can be completely eliminated. As discussed earlier, choosing

$$K_1(z) = -H_2(-z)$$
$$K_2(z) = H_1(-z) \qquad (13.75)$$

eliminates aliasing. This leaves us with

$$T(z) = \frac{1}{2}[H_1(-z)H_2(z) - H_1(z)H_2(-z)].$$

In the approach due to Smith and Barnwell [215] and Mintzer [158], with N an odd integer, we select

$$H_2(z) = z^{-N}H_1(-z^{-1}) \tag{13.76}$$

so that

$$T(z) = \frac{1}{2}z^{-N}[H_1(z)H_1(z^{-1}) + H_1(-z)H_1(-z^{-1})]. \tag{13.77}$$

Therefore, the perfect reconstruction requirement reduces to finding a prototype low-pass filter $H(z) = H_1(z)$ such that

$$Q(z) = H(z)H(z^{-1}) + H(-z)H(-z^{-1}) = \text{constant}. \tag{13.78}$$

Defining

$$R(z) = H(z)H(z^{-1}), \tag{13.79}$$

the perfect reconstruction requirement becomes

$$Q(z) = R(z) + R(-z) = \text{constant}. \tag{13.80}$$

But $R(z)$ is simply the Z-transform of the autocorrelation sequence of $h(n)$. The autocorrelation sequence $\rho(n)$ is given by

$$\rho(n) = \sum_{k=0}^{N} h_k h_{k+n}. \tag{13.81}$$

The Z-transform of $\rho(n)$ is given by

$$R(z) = \mathcal{Z}[\rho(n)] = \mathcal{Z}\left[\sum_{k=0}^{N} h_k h_{k+n}\right]. \tag{13.82}$$

We can express the sum $\sum_{k=0}^{N} h_k h_{k+n}$ as a convolution:

$$h_n \otimes h_{-n} = \sum_{k=0}^{N} h_k h_{k+n}. \tag{13.83}$$

Using the fact that the Z-transform of a convolution of two sequences is the product of the Z-transforms of the individual sequences, we obtain

$$R(z) = \mathcal{Z}[h_n]\mathcal{Z}[h_{-n}] = H(z)H(z^{-1}). \tag{13.84}$$

Writing out $R(z)$ as the Z-transform of the sequence $\{\rho(n)\}$ we obtain

$$R(z) = \rho(N)z^N + \rho(N-1)z^{N-1} + \cdots + \rho(0) + \cdots + \rho(N-1)z^{-(N-1)} + \rho(N)z^{-N}. \tag{13.85}$$

Then $R(-z)$ is

$$R(-z) = -\rho(N)z^N + \rho(N-1)z^{N-1} - \cdots + \rho(0) - \cdots + \rho(N-1)z^{-(N-1)} - \rho(N)z^{-N}. \quad (13.86)$$

Adding $R(z)$ and $R(-z)$, we obtain $Q(z)$ as

$$Q(z) = 2\rho(N-1)z^{N-1} + 2\rho(N-3)z^{N-3} + \cdots + 2\rho(0) + \cdots + 2\rho(N-1)z^{-(N-1)}. \quad (13.87)$$

Notice that the terms containing the odd powers of z got canceled out. Thus, for $Q(z)$ to be a constant all we need is that for even values of the lag n (except for $n = 0$), $\rho(n)$ be zero. In other words,

$$\rho(2n) = \sum_{k=0}^{N} h_k h_{k+2n} = 0, \qquad n \neq 0. \quad (13.88)$$

Writing this requirement in terms of the impulse response:

$$\sum_{k=0}^{N} h_k h_{k+2n} = \begin{cases} 0 & n \neq 0 \\ \rho(0) & n = 0 . \end{cases} \quad (13.89)$$

If we now normalize the impulse response,

$$\sum_{k=0}^{N} |h_k|^2 = 1 \quad (13.90)$$

we obtain the perfect reconstruction requirement

$$\sum_{k=0}^{N} h_k h_{k+2n} = \delta_n. \quad (13.91)$$

In other words, for perfect reconstruction, the impulse response of the prototype filter is orthogonal to the twice-shifted version of itself.

13.7 M-Band QMF Filter Banks ★

We have looked at how we can decompose an input signal into two bands. In many applications it is necessary to divide the input into multiple bands. We can do this by using a recursive two-band splitting as shown in Figure 13.19, or we can obtain banks of filters that directly split the input into multiple bands. Given that we have good filters that provide two-band splitting, it would seem that using a recursive splitting, as shown in Figure 13.19, would be an efficient way of obtaining an M-band split. Unfortunately, even when the spectral characteristics of the filters used for the two-band split are quite good, when we employ them in the tree structure shown in Figure 13.19, the spectral characteristics may not be very good. For example, consider the four-tap filter with filter coefficients shown in Table 13.6. In Figure 13.20 we show what happens to the spectral characteristics when we look at the two-band split (at point **A** in Figure 13.19), the four-band split (at point **B** in Figure 13.19), and the eight-band split (at

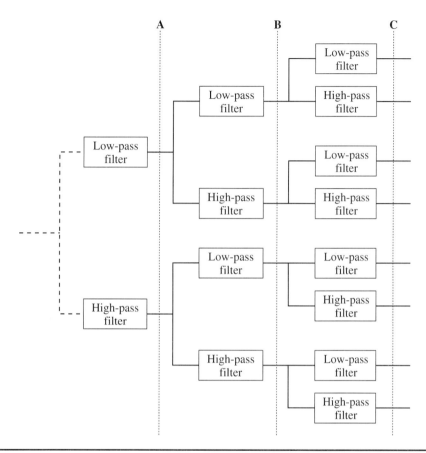

FIGURE 13.19   Decomposition of an input sequence into multiple bands by
recursively using a two-band split.

**TABLE 13.6   Coefficients for the four-tap
Daubechies low-pass filter.**

h_0	0.4829629131445341
h_1	0.8365163037378079
h_2	0.2241438680420134
h_3	−0.1294095225512604

point **C** in Figure 13.19). For a two-band split the magnitude characteristic is flat, with some
aliasing. When we employ these same filters to obtain a four-band split from the two-band
split, there is an increase in the aliasing. When we go one step further to obtain an eight-band
split, the magnitude characteristics deteriorate substantially, as evidenced by Figure 13.20.
The various bands are no longer clearly distinct. There is significant overlap between the
bands, and hence there will be a significant amount of aliasing in each band.

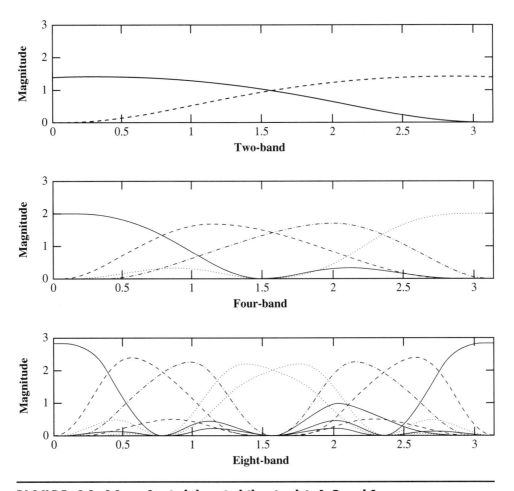

FIGURE 13.20   **Spectral characteristics at points A, B, and C.**

In order to see why there is an increase in distortion, let us follow the top branch of the tree. The path followed by the signal is shown in Figure 13.21a. As we will show later (Section 13.8), the three filters and downsamplers can be replaced by a single filter and downsampler as shown in Figure 13.21b, where

$$\mathbf{A}(z) = H_L(z)H_L(z^2)H_L(z^4). \tag{13.92}$$

If $H_L(z)$ corresponds to a 4-tap filter, then $\mathbf{A}(z)$ corresponds to a $3 \times 6 \times 12 = 216$-tap filter! However, this is a severely constrained filter because it was generated using only four coefficients. If we had set out to design a 216-tap filter from scratch, we would have had significantly more freedom in selecting the coefficients. This is a strong motivation for designing filters directly for the M-band case.

An M-band filter bank has two sets of filters that are arranged as shown in Figure 13.7. The input signal $x(n)$ is split into M frequency bands using an analysis bank of M filters of

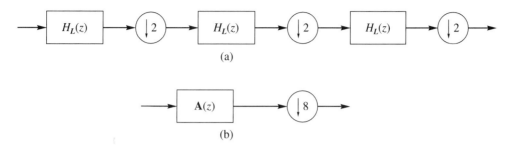

FIGURE 13.21   *Equivalent structures for recursive filtering using a two-band split.*

bandwidth π/M. The signal in any of these M channels is then downsampled by a factor L. This constitutes the analysis bank. The subband signals $y_k(n)$ are encoded and transmitted. At the synthesis stage the subband signals are then decoded, upsampled by a factor of L by interlacing adjacent samples with $L-1$ zeros, and then passed through the synthesis or interpolation filters. The output of all these synthesis filters is added together to obtain the reconstructed signal. This constitutes the synthesis filter bank. Thus, the analysis and synthesis filter banks together take an input signal $x(n)$ and produce an output signal $\hat{x}(n)$. These filters could be any combination of FIR and IIR filters.

Depending on whether M is less than, equal to, or greater than L, the filter bank is called an *underdecimated, critically (maximally) decimated,* or *overdecimated* filter bank. For most practical applications, maximal decimation or "critical subsampling" is used.

A detailed study of M-band filters is beyond the scope of this chapter. Suffice it to say that in broad outline much of what we said about two-band filters can be generalized to M-band filters. (For more on this subject, see [228].)

13.8 The Polyphase Decomposition ★

A major problem with representing the combination of filters and downsamplers is the time-varying nature of the up- and downsamplers. An elegant way of solving this problem is with the use of *polyphase decomposition*. In order to demonstrate this concept, let us first consider the simple case of two-band splitting. We will first consider the analysis portion of the system shown in Figure 13.22. Suppose the analysis filter $H_1(z)$ is given by

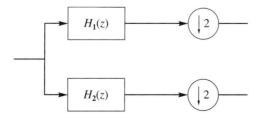

FIGURE 13.22   **Analysis portion of a two-band subband coder.**

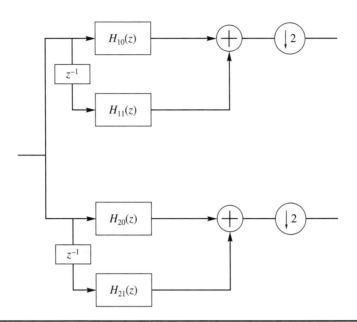

FIGURE 1 3 . 2 3   **Alternative representation of the analysis portion of a two-band subband coder.**

$$H_1(z) = h_0 + h_1 z^{-1} + h_2 z^{-2} + h_3 z^{-3} + \cdots. \tag{13.93}$$

By grouping the odd and even terms together, we can write this as

$$H_1(z) = (h_0 + h_2 z^{-2} + h_4 z^{-4} + \cdots) + z^{-1}(h_1 + h_3 z^{-2} + h_5 z^{-4} + \cdots). \tag{13.94}$$

Define

$$H_{10}(z) = h_0 + h_2 z^{-1} + h_4 z^{-2} + \cdots \tag{13.95}$$

$$H_{11}(z) = h_1 + h_3 z^{-1} + h_5 z^{-2} + \cdots \tag{13.96}$$

Then $H_1(z) = H_{10}(z^2) + z^{-1}H_{11}(z^2)$. Similarly, we can decompose the filter $H_2(z)$ into components $H_{20}(z)$ and $H_{21}(z)$, and we can represent the system of Figure 13.22 as shown in Figure 13.23. The filters $H_{10}(z)$, $H_{11}(z)$ and $H_{20}(z)$, $H_{21}(z)$ are called the polyphase components of $H_1(z)$ and $H_2(z)$.

Let's take the inverse Z-transform of the polyphase components of $H_1(z)$:

$$h_{10}(n) = h_{2n} \qquad n = 0, 1, \ldots \tag{13.97}$$

$$h_{11}(n) = h_{2n+1} \qquad n = 0, 1, \ldots. \tag{13.98}$$

Thus, $h_{10}(n)$ and $h_{11}(n)$ are simply the impulse response h_n downsampled by two. Consider the output of the downsampler for a given input $X(z)$. The input to the downsampler is $X(z)H_1(z)$; thus, the output from Equation (13.35) is

$$Y_1(z) = \frac{1}{2}X(z^{\frac{1}{2}})H_1(z^{\frac{1}{2}}) + \frac{1}{2}X(-z^{\frac{1}{2}})H_1(-z^{\frac{1}{2}}). \tag{13.99}$$

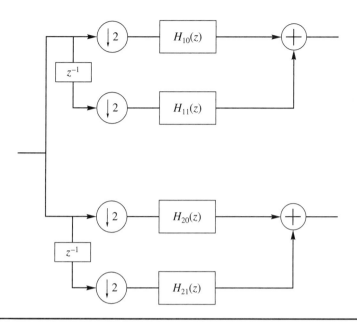

FIGURE 13.24   **Polyphase representation of the analysis portion of a two-band subband coder.**

Replacing $H_1(z)$ with its polyphase representation, we get

$$Y_1(z) = \frac{1}{2}X(z^{\frac{1}{2}})[H_{10}(z) + z^{-\frac{1}{2}}H_{11}(z)] + \frac{1}{2}X(-z^{\frac{1}{2}})[H_{10}(z) - z^{-\frac{1}{2}}H_{11}(z)] \qquad (13.100)$$

$$= H_{10}(z)\left[\frac{1}{2}X(z^{\frac{1}{2}}) + \frac{1}{2}X(-z^{\frac{1}{2}})\right] + H_{11}(z)\left[\frac{1}{2}z^{-\frac{1}{2}}X(z^{\frac{1}{2}}) - \frac{1}{2}z^{-\frac{1}{2}}X(-z^{\frac{1}{2}})\right] (13.101)$$

Note that the first expression in square brackets is the output of a downsampler whose input is $X(z)$, while the quantity in the second set of square brackets is the output of a downsampler whose input is $z^{-1}X(z)$. Therefore, we could implement this system as shown in Figure 13.24.

Now let us consider the synthesis portion of the two-band system shown in Figure 13.25. As in the case of the analysis portion, we can write the transfer functions in terms of their polyphase representation. Thus,

$$G_1(z) = G_{10}(z^2) + z^{-1}G_{11}(z^2) \qquad (13.102)$$
$$G_2(z) = G_{20}(z^2) + z^{-1}G_{21}(z^2). \qquad (13.103)$$

Consider the output of the synthesis filter $G_1(z)$ given an input $Y_1(z)$. From Equation (13.41), the output of the upsampler is

$$U_1(z) = Y_1(z^2) \qquad (13.104)$$

and the output of $G_1(z)$ is

$$V_1(z) = Y_1(z^2)G_1(z) \qquad (13.105)$$
$$= Y_1(z^2)G_{10}(z^2) + z^{-1}Y_1(z^2)G_{11}(z^2). \qquad (13.106)$$

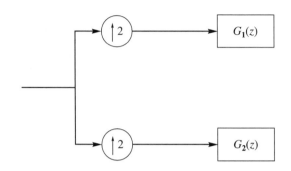

FIGURE 13.25   The synthesis portion of a two-band subband coder.

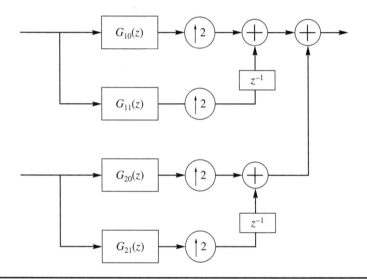

FIGURE 13.26   Polyphase representation of the synthesis portion of a two-band subband coder.

The first term in the equation above is the output of an upsampler that *follows* a filter with transfer function $G_{10}(z)$ with input $Y(z)$. Similarly, $Y_1(z^2)G_{11}(z^2)$ is the output of an upsampler that follows a filter with transfer function $G_{11}(z)$ with input $Y(z)$. Thus, this system can be represented as shown in Figure 13.26.

Putting the polyphase representations of the analysis and synthesis portions together, we get the system shown in Figure 13.27. Looking at the portion in the dashed box, we can see that this is a completely linear time-invariant system.

The polyphase representation can be a very useful tool for the design and analysis of filters. While many of its uses are beyond the scope of this chapter, we can use this representation to prove our statement about the two-band perfect reconstruction QMF filters.

Recall that we want

$$T(z) = \frac{1}{2}[H_1(z)H_2(-z) - H_1(-z)H_2(z)] = cz^{-n_0}.$$

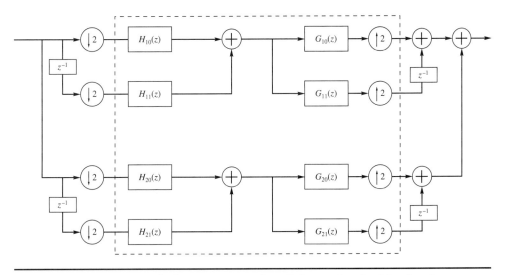

FIGURE 13.27   **Polyphase representation of the two-band subband coder.**

If we impose the mirror condition $H_2(z) = H_1(-z)$, $T(z)$ becomes

$$T(z) = \frac{1}{2}[H_1^2(z) - H_1^2(-z)].\tag{13.107}$$

The polyphase decomposition of $H_1(z)$ is

$$H_1(z) = H_{10}(z^2) + z^{-1}H_{11}(z^2).$$

Substituting this into Equation (13.107) for $H_1(z)$ and

$$H_1(-z) = H_{10}(z^2) - z^{-1}H_{11}(z^2)$$

for $H_1(-z)$, we obtain

$$T(z) = 2z^{-1}H_{10}(z^2)H_{11}(z^2).\tag{13.108}$$

Clearly, the only way $T(z)$ can have the form cz^{-n_0} is if both $H_{10}(z)$ and $H_{11}(z)$ are simple delays; that is,

$$H_{10}(z) = h_0z^{-k_0}\tag{13.109}$$
$$H_{11}(z) = h_1z^{-k_1}.\tag{13.110}$$

This results in

$$T(z) = 2h_0h_1z^{-(2k_0+2k_1+1)}\tag{13.111}$$

which is of the form cz^{-n_0} as desired. The resulting filters have the transfer functions

$$H_1(z) = h_0z^{-2k_0} + h_1z^{-(2k_1+1)}\tag{13.112}$$
$$H_2(z) = h_0z^{-2k_0} - h_1z^{-(2k_1+1)}.\tag{13.113}$$

13.9 Bit Allocation

Once we have separated the source output into the constituent sequences, we need to decide how much of the coding resource should be used to encode the output of each synthesis filter. In other words, we need to allocate the available bits between the subband sequences. In the previous chapter we described a bit allocation procedure that uses the variances of the transform coefficient. In this section we describe a bit allocation approach that attempts to use as much information about the subbands as possible to distribute the bits.

Let's begin with some notation. We have a total of B_T bits that we need to distribute among M subbands. Suppose R corresponds to the average rate in bits per sample for the overall system, and R_k is the average rate for subband k. Let's begin with the case where the input is decomposed into M equal bands, each of which is decimated by a factor of M. Finally, let's assume that we know the rate distortion function for each band. (If you recall from Chapter 7, this is a rather strong assumption and we will relax it shortly.) We also assume that the distortion measure is such that the total distortion is the sum of the distortion contribution of each band.

We want to find the bit allocation R_k such that

$$R = \frac{1}{M} \sum_{k=1}^{M} R_k \tag{13.114}$$

and the reconstruction error is minimized. Each value of R_k corresponds to a point on the rate distortion curve. The question is where on the rate distortion curve for each subband should we operate to minimize the average distortion. There is a trade-off between rate and distortion. If we decrease the rate (that is, move down the rate distortion curve), we will increase the distortion. Similarly, if we want to move to the left on the rate distortion curve and minimize the distortion, we end up increasing the rate. We need a formulation that incorporates both rate and distortion and the trade-off involved. The formulation we use is based on a landmark paper in 1988 by Yaacov Shoham and Allen Gersho [213]. Let's define a functional J_k:

$$J_k = D_k + \lambda R_k \tag{13.115}$$

where D_k is the distortion contribution from the kth subband and λ is a Lagrangian parameter. This is the quantity we wish to minimize. In this expression the parameter λ in some sense specifies the trade-off. If we are primarily interested in minimizing the distortion, we can set λ to a small value. If our primary interest is in minimizing the rate, we keep the value of λ large. We can show that the values of D_k and R_k that minimize J_k occur where the slope of the rate distortion curve is λ. Thus, given a value of λ and the rate distortion function, we can immediately identify the values of R_k and D_k. So what should the value of λ be, and how should it vary between subbands?

Let's take the second question first. We would like to allocate bits in such a way that any increase in any of the rates will have the same impact on the distortion. This will happen when we pick R_k in such a way that the slopes of the rate distortion functions for the different subbands are the same; that is, we want to use the same λ for each subband. Let's see what happens if we do not. Consider the two rate distortion functions shown in Figure 13.28. Suppose the points marked **x** on the rate distortion functions correspond to the selected rates.

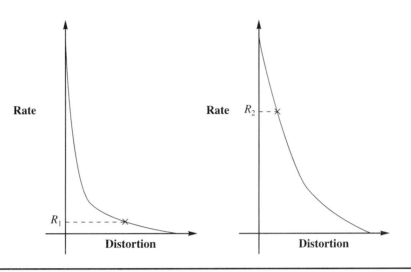

FIGURE 13.28   Two rate distortion functions.

Obviously, the slopes, and hence the values of λ, are different in the two cases. Because of the differences in the slope, an increase by ΔR in the rate R_1 will result in a much larger decrease in the distortion than the increase in distortion if we decreased R_2 by ΔR. Because the total distortion is the sum of the individual distortions, we can therefore reduce the overall distortions by increasing R_1 and decreasing R_2. We will be able to keep doing this until the slope corresponding to the rates are the same in both cases. Thus, the answer to our second question is that we want to use the same value of λ for all the subbands.

Given a set of rate distortion functions and a value of λ, we automatically get a set of rates R_k. We can then compute the average and check if it satisfieies our constraint on the total number of bits we can spend. If it does not, we modify the value of λ until we get a set of rates that satisfies our rate constraint.

However, generally we do not have rate distortion functions available. In these cases we use whatever is available. For some cases we might have *operational* rate distortion curves available. By "operational" we mean performance curves for particular types of encoders operating on specific types of sources. For example, if we knew we were going to be using *pdf*-optimized nonuniform quantizers with entropy coding, we could estimate the distribution of the subband and use the performance curve for *pdf*-optimized nonuniform quantizers for that distribution. We might only have the performance of the particular encoding scheme for a limited number of rates. In this case we need to have some way of obtaining the slope from a few points. We could estimate this numerically from these points. Or we could fit the points to a curve and estimate the slope from the curve. In these cases we might not be able to get exactly the average rate we wanted.

Finally, we have been talking about a situation where the number of samples in each subband is exactly the same, and therefore the total rate is simply the sum of the individual rates. If this is not true, we need to weight the rates of the individual subbands. The functional to be minimized becomes

$$J = \sum D_k + \lambda \sum \beta_k R_k \qquad (13.116)$$

where β_k is the weight reflecting the relative length of the sequence generated by the kth filter. The distortion contribution from each subband might not be equally relevant, perhaps because of the filter construction or because of the perceptual weight attached to those frequencies [243]. In these cases we can modify our functional still further to include the unequal weighting of the distortion:

$$J = \sum w_k D_k + \lambda \sum \beta_k R_k. \qquad (13.117)$$

13.10 Application to Speech Coding—G.722

The ITU-T recommendation G.722 provides a technique for wideband coding of speech signals that is based on subband coding. The basic objective of this recommendation is to provide high-quality speech at 64 kbits per second (kbps). The recommendation also contains two other modes that encode the input at 56 and 48 kbps. These two modes are used when an auxiliary channel is needed. The first mode provides for an auxiliary channel of 8 kbps; the second mode, for an auxiliary channel of 16 kbps.

The speech output or audio signal is filtered to 7 kHz to prevent aliasing, then sampled at 16,000 samples per second. Notice that the cutoff frequency for the anti-aliasing filter is 7 kHz, not 8 kHz, even though we are sampling at 16,000 samples per second. One reason for this is that the cutoff for the anti-aliasing filter is not going to be sharp like that of the ideal low-pass filter. Therefore, the highest frequency component in the filter output will be greater than 7 kHz. Each sample is encoded using a 14-bit uniform quantizer. This 14-bit input is passed through a bank of two 24-coefficient FIR filters. The coefficients of the low-pass QMF filter are shown in Table 13.7.

The coefficients for the high-pass QMF filter can be obtained by the relationship

$$h_{HP,n} = (-1)^n h_{LP,n}. \qquad (13.118)$$

TABLE 13.7   Transmit and receive QMF coefficient values.

h_0, h_{23}	3.66211×10^{-4}
h_1, h_{22}	-1.34277×10^{-3}
h_2, h_{21}	-1.34277×10^{-3}
h_3, h_{20}	6.46973×10^{-3}
h_4, h_{19}	1.46484×10^{-3}
h_5, h_{18}	-1.90430×10^{-2}
h_6, h_{17}	3.90625×10^{-3}
h_7, h_{16}	4.41895×10^{-2}
h_8, h_{15}	-2.56348×10^{-2}
h_9, h_{14}	-9.82666×10^{-2}
h_{10}, h_{13}	1.16089×10^{-1}
h_{11}, h_{12}	4.73145×10^{-1}

The low-pass filter passes all frequency components in the range of 0 to 4 kHz, while the high-pass filter passes all remaining frequencies. The output of the filters is downsampled by a factor of two. The downsampled sequences are encoded using adaptive differential PCM (ADPCM) systems.

The ADPCM system that encodes the downsampled output of the low-frequency filter uses 6 bits per sample, with the option of dropping 1 or 2 least significant bits in order to provide room for the auxiliary channel. The output of the high-pass filter is encoded using 2 bits per sample. Because the 2 least significant bits of the quantizer output of the low-pass ADPCM system could be dropped and then not available to the receiver, the adaptation and prediction at both the transmitter and receiver are performed using only the 4 most significant bits of the quantizer output.

If all 6 bits are used in the encoding of the low-frequency subband, we end up with a rate of 48 kbps for the low band. Since the high band is encoded at 2 bits per sample, the output rate for the high subband is 16 kbps. Therefore, the total output rate for the subband-ADPCM system is 64 kbps.

The quantizer is adapted using a variation of the Jayant algorithm [117]. Both ADPCM systems use the past two reconstructed values and the past six quantizer outputs to predict the next sample, in the same way as the predictor for recommendation G.726 described in Chapter 10. The predictor is adapted in the same manner as the predictor used in the G.726 algorithm.

At the receiver, after being decoded by the ADPCM decoder, each output signal is upsampled by the insertion of a zero after each sample. The upsampled signals are passed through the reconstruction filters. These filters are identical to the filters used for decomposing the signal. The low-pass reconstruction filter coefficients are given in Table 13.7, and the coefficients for the high-pass filter can be obtained using Equation (13.118).

13.11 Application to Audio Coding—MPEG Audio

The Moving Picture Experts Group (MPEG) has proposed an audio coding scheme that is based in part on subband coding. Actually, MPEG has proposed three coding schemes, called Layer 1, Layer 2, and Layer 3 coding. Each is more complex than the previous and provides higher compression. The coders are also "upward" compatible; a Layer N decoder is able to decode the bitstream generated by the Layer $N - 1$ encoder. In this section we will look primarily at the Layer 1 and Layer 2 coders.

The Layer 1 and Layer 2 coders both use a bank of 32 filters, splitting the input into 32 bands, each with a bandwidth of $f_s/64$, where f_s is the sampling frequency. Allowable sampling frequencies are 32,000 samples per second, 44,100 samples per second, and 48,000 samples per second.

The output of the subbands is quantized using a uniform quantizer with a variable number of bits. The number of bits assigned to code each subband is determined by a psychoacoustic model that takes advantage of the masking properties of the human ear to reduce the number of bits. Recall in Chapter 7 when we studied human perception, if we have a large amplitude signal at one frequency, it affects the audibility of signals at other frequencies. In particular, a loud signal at one frequency may make quantization noise at other frequencies inaudible. Therefore, if we have a large signal in one of the subbands, we can tolerate more quantization error in the neighboring subbands and use fewer bits. There may be large components in a number of subbands, and since the masking effect is cumulative, the encoder obtains the masking effect using an iterative procedure. There is no way to know in advance how many different masking signals there may be, and the encoder simply continues computing until it runs out of time. Most of the complexity in the encoder results from this calculation and the bit allocations.

The masking effects are computed on a frame-by-frame basis. In Layers 1 and 2, each frame consists of 384 and 1152 samples, respectively. From time to time, there may be a dramatic change in the value of the signal within a frame. Because the masking computation is done based on the peak value of the signal in each frame, small amplitude signals in a frame may not be reproduced very well. This problem is solved in Layer 3 by taking a smaller analysis frame.

13.12 Application to Image Compression

We have discussed how to separate a sequence into its components. However, all the examples we have used are one-dimensional sequences. What do we do when the sequences contain two-dimensional dependencies such as images? The obvious answer is that we need two-dimensional filters that separate the source output into components based on both the horizontal and vertical frequencies. Fortunately, in most cases, this two-dimensional filter can be implemented as two one-dimensional filters, which can be applied first in one dimension, then in the other. Filters that have this property are called *separable* filters. Two-dimensional nonseparable filters do exist [230]; however, the gains are offset by the increase in complexity.

Generally, for subband coding of images we filter each row of the image separately using a high-pass and low-pass filter. The output of the filters is decimated by a factor of two. Assume that the images were of size $N \times N$. After this first stage, we will have two images of size $N \times \frac{N}{2}$. We then filter each column of the two subimages, decimating the outputs of the filters again by a factor of two. This results in four images of size $\frac{N}{2} \times \frac{N}{2}$. We can stop at this point or continue the decomposition process with one or more of the four subimages, resulting in 7, 10, 13, or 16 images. Generally, of the four original subimages, only one or two are further decomposed. The reason for not decomposing the other subimages is that many of the pixel values in the high-frequency subimages are close to zero. Thus, there is little reason to spend computational power to decompose these subimages.

Example 13.12.1:

Let's take the "image" in Table 13.8 and decompose it using the low-pass and high-pass filters of Example 13.2.1. After filtering each row with the low-pass filter, the output is decimated by a factor of two. Each output from the filter depends on the current input and the past input. For the very first input (that is, the pixels at the left edge of the image), we will assume that the past values of the input were zero. The decimated output of the low-pass and high-pass filters is shown in Table 13.9.

We take each of these subimages and filter them column by column using the low-pass and high-pass filters and decimate the outputs by two. In this case, the first input to the filters

TABLE 13.8   A sample "image."

10	14	10	12	14	8	14	12
10	12	8	12	10	6	10	12
12	10	8	6	8	10	12	14
8	6	4	6	4	6	8	10
14	12	10	8	6	4	6	8
12	8	12	10	6	6	6	6
12	10	6	6	6	6	6	6
6	6	6	6	6	6	6	6

TABLE 13.9   Filtered and decimated output.

Decimated Low-Pass Output				Decimated High-Pass Output			
5	12	13	11	5	−2	1	3
5	10	11	8	5	−2	−1	2
6	9	7	11	6	−1	1	1
4	5	5	7	4	−1	−1	1
7	11	7	5	7	−1	−1	1
6	10	8	6	6	2	−2	0
6	8	6	6	6	−2	0	0
3	6	6	6	3	0	0	0

TABLE 13.10 Four subimages.

Low-Low Image				Low-High Image			
2.5	6	6.5	5.5	2.5	6	6.5	5.5
5.5	9.5	9	9.5	0.5	−0.5	−2	1.5
5.5	8	6	6	1.5	3	1	−1
6	9	7	6	0	−1	−1	0

High-Low Image				High-High Image			
2.5	−1	0.5	1.5	2.5	−1	0.5	1.5
5.5	−1.5	0	1.5	0.5	0.5	1	−0.5
5.5	−1	−1	1	1.5	0	0	0
6	0	−1	0	0	−2	1	0

is the top element in each row. We assume that there is a zero row of pixels right above this row in order to provide the filter with "past" values. After filtering and decimation, we get four subimages (Table 13.10). The subimage obtained by low-pass filtering of the columns of the subimage (which was the output of the row low-pass filtering) is called the low-low (LL) image. Similarly, the other images are called the low-high (LH), high-low (HL), and high-high (HH) images.

◆

TABLE 1 3 . 1 1 **Alternate four subimages.**

Low-Low Image				Low-High Image			
10	12	13	11	0	0	−0.5	−0.5
11	9.5	9	9.5	1	−0.5	−2	1.5
11	8	6	6	3	3	1	−1
12	9	7	6	0	−1	−1	0

High-Low Image				High-High Image			
0	−2	1	3	0	0	0	0
0	−1.5	0	1.5	0	0.5	1	−0.5
0	−1	−1	1	0	0	0	0
0	0	−1	0	0	−2	1	0

If we look closely at the final set of subimages in the previous example, we notice that there is a difference in the characteristics of the values in the left or top row and the interiors of some of the subimages. For example, in the high-low subimage, the values in the first column are significantly larger than the other values in the subimage. Similarly, in the low-high subimage, the values in the first row are generally very different than the other values in the subimage. The reason for this variance is our assumption that the "past" of the image above the first row and to the left of the column was zero. The difference between zero and the image values was much larger than the normal pixel-to-pixel differences. Therefore, we ended up adding some spurious structure to the image reflected in the subimages. Generally, this is undesirable because it is easier to select appropriate compression schemes when the characteristics of the subimages are as uniform as possible. For example, if we did not have the relatively large values in the first column of the high-low subimage, we could choose a quantizer with a smaller step size.

In this example, this effect was limited to a single row or column because the filters used a single past value. However, most filters use a substantially larger number of past values in the filtering operation, and a larger portion of the subimage is affected.

We can avoid this problem by assuming a different "past." There are a number of ways this can be done. A simple method that works well is to reflect the values of the pixels at the boundary. For example, for the sequence 6 9 5 4 7 2 $\cdots$, which was to be filtered with a three-tap filter, we would assume the past as $\boxed{9\ 6}$ 6 9 5 4 7 2 $\cdots$. If we use this approach for the image in Example 13.12.1, the four subimages would be as shown in Table 13.11.

Notice how much sparser each image is, except for the low-low image. Most of the energy in the original image has been compacted into the low-low image. Since the other subimages have very few values that need to be encoded, we can devote most of our resources to the low-low subimage.

13.12.1 Decomposing an Image

Earlier a set of filters was provided to be used in one-dimensional subband coding. We can use those same filters to decompose an image into its subbands.

Example 13.12.2:

FIGURE 13.29   **Decomposition of Sinan image using the eight-tap Johnston filter.**

Let's use the eight-tap Johnston filter to decompose the Sinan image into four subbands. The results of the decomposition are shown in Figure 13.29. Notice that, as in the case of the image in Example 13.12.1, most of the signal energy is concentrated in the low-low subimage. However, there remains a substantial amount of energy in the higher bands. To see this more clearly, let's look at the decomposition using the 16-tap Johnston filter. The results are shown in Figure 13.30. Notice how much less energy there is in the higher subbands. In fact, the high-high subband seems completely empty. As we shall see later, this difference in *energy compaction* can have a drastic effect on the reconstruction.

Increasing the size of the filter is not necessarily the only way of improving the energy compaction. Figure 13.31 shows the decomposition obtained using the eight-tap Smith-Barnwell filter. The results are almost identical to the 16-tap Johnston filter. Therefore, rather than increase the computational load by going to a 16-tap filter, we can keep the same computational load and simply use a different filter.

◆

13.12.2 Coding the Subbands

Once we have decomposed an image into subbands, we need to find the best encoding scheme to use with each subband. The coding schemes we have studied to date are scalar quantization,

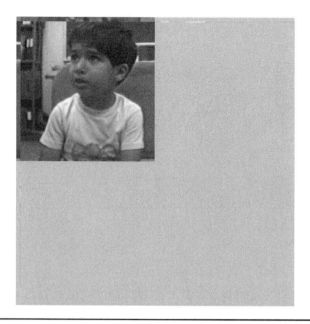

FIGURE 13.30   Decomposition of Sinan image using the 16-tap Johnston filter.

FIGURE 13.31   Decomposition of Sinan image using the the eight-tap Smith-Barnwell filter.

vector quantization, and differential encoding. Let us encode some of the decomposed images from the previous section using two of the coding schemes we have studied earlier, scalar quantization and differential encoding.

Example 13.12.3:

In the previous example we noted the fact that the eight-tap Johnston filter did not compact the energy as well as the 16-tap Johnston filter or the eight-tap Smith-Barnwell filter. Let's see how this affects the encoding of the decomposed images.

When we encode these images at an average rate of 0.5 bits per pixel, there are $4 \times 0.5 = 2$ bits available to encode four values, one value from each of the four subbands. If we use the recursive bit allocation procedure on the eight-tap Johnston filter outputs, we end up allocating 1 bit to the low-low band and 1 bit to the high-low band. As the pixel-to-pixel difference in the low-low band is quite small, we use a DPCM encoder for the low-low band. The high-low band does not show this behavior, which means we can simply use scalar quantization for the high-low band. As there are no bits available to encode the other two bands, these bands can be discarded. This results in the image shown in Figure 13.32, which is far from pleasing. However, if we use the same compression approach with the image decomposed using the eight-tap Smith-Barnwell filter, the result is Figure 13.33, which is much more pleasing.

FIGURE 13.32   Sinan image coded at 0.5 bits per pixel using the eight-tap Johnston filter.

FIGURE 13.33   Sinan image coded at 0.5 bits per pixel using the eight-tap Smith-Barnwell filter.

To understand why we get such different results from using the two filters, we need to look at the way the bits were allocated to the different bands. In this implementation, we used the recursive bit allocation algorithm. In the image decomposed using the Johnston filter, there was significant energy in the high-low band. The algorithm allocated 1 bit to the low-low band and 1 bit to the high-low band. This resulted in poor encoding for both, and subsequently poor reconstruction. There was very little signal content in any of the bands other than the low-low band for the image decomposed using the Smith-Barnwell filter. Therefore, the bit allocation algorithm assigned both bits to the low-low band, which provided a reasonable reconstruction.

If the problem with the encoding of the image decomposed by the Johnston filter is an insufficient number of bits for encoding the low-low band, why not simply assign both bits to the low-low band? The problem is that the bit allocation scheme assigned a bit to the high-low band because there was a significant amount of information in that band. If both bits were assigned to the low-low band, we would have no bits left for use in encoding the high-low band, and we would end up throwing away information necessary for the reconstruction.   ◆

The issue of energy compaction becomes a very important factor in reconstruction quality. Filters that allow for more energy compaction permit the allocation of bits to a smaller number of subbands. This in turn results in a better reconstruction.

The coding schemes used in this example were DPCM and scalar quantization, the techniques generally preferred in subband coding. The advantage provided by subband coding is readily apparent if we compare the result shown in Figure 13.33 to results in the previous chapters where we used either DPCM or scalar quantization without prior decomposition.

It would appear that the subband approach lends itself naturally to vector quantization. After decomposing an image into subbands, we could design separate codebooks for each subband to reflect the characteristics of that particular subband. The only problem with this idea is that the low-low subband generally requires a large number of bits per pixel. As we mentioned in Chapter 9, it is generally not feasible to operate the nonstructured vector quantizers at high rates. Therefore, when vector quantizers are used, they are generally used only for encoding the higher frequency bands. This may change as vector quantization algorithms that operate at higher rates are developed.

13.13 Summary

In this chapter we introduced another approach to the decomposition of signals. In subband coding we decompose the source output into components. Each of these components can then be encoded using one of the techniques described in the previous chapters. The general subband encoding procedure can be summarized as follows:

- Select a set of filters for decomposing the source. We have provided a number of filters in this chapter. Many more filters can be obtained from the published literature (we give some references below).

- Using the filters, obtain the subband signals $\{y_{k,n}\}$:

$$y_{k,n} = \sum_{i=0}^{N-1} h_{k,i} x_{n-i} \qquad (13.119)$$

where $\{h_{k,n}\}$ are the coefficients of the kth filter.

- Decimate the output of the filters.

- Encode the decimated output.

The decoding procedure is the inverse of the encoding procedure. When encoding images the filtering and decimation operations have to be performed twice, once along the rows and once along the columns. Care should be taken to avoid problems at edges, as described in Section 13.12.

Further Reading

1. *Handbook for Digital Signal Processing*, edited by S.K. Mitra and J.F. Kaiser [162], is an excellent source of information about digital filters.

2. *Multirate Systems and Filter Banks*, by P.P. Vaidyanathan [228], provides detailed information on QMF filters, as well as the relationship between wavelets and filter banks and much more.

3. The topic of subband coding is also covered in *Digital Coding of Waveforms*, by N.S. Jayant and P. Noll [118].

4. The MPEG-1 audio coding algorithm is described in "ISO-MPEG-1 Audio: A Generic Standard for Coding of High-Quality Digital Audio," by K. Brandenburg and G. Stoll [28], in the October 1994 issue of the *Journal of the Audio Engineering Society*.

5. A review of the rate distortion method of bit allocation is provided in "Rate Distortion Methods for Image and Video Compression," by A. Ortega and K. Ramachandran, in the November 1998 issue of *IEEE Signal Processing Magazine* [169].

13.14 Projects and Problems

1. A linear shift invariant system has the following properties:

- If for a given input sequence $\{x_n\}$ the output of the system is the sequence $\{y_n\}$, then if we delay the input sequence by k units to obtain the sequence $\{x_{n-k}\}$, the corresponding output will be the sequence $\{y_n\}$ delayed by k units.

- If the output corresponding to the sequence $\{x_n^{(1)}\}$ is $\{y_n^{(1)}\}$, and the output corresponding to the sequence $\{x_n^{(2)}\}$ is $\{y_n^{(2)}\}$, then the output corresponding to the sequence $\{\alpha x_n^{(1)} + \beta x_n^{(2)}\}$ is $\{\alpha y_n^{(1)} + \beta y_n^{(2)}\}$.

Use these two properties to show the convolution property given in Equation (13.18).

2. Let's design a set of simple four-tap filters that satisfies the perfect reconstruction condition.

(a) We begin with the low-pass filter. Assume that the impulse response of the filter is given by $\{h_{1,k}\}_{k=0}^{k=3}$. Further assume that

$$|h_{1,k}| = |h_{1,j}| \qquad \forall j, k.$$

Find a set of values for $\{h_{i,j}\}$ that satisfies Equation (13.91).

(b) Plot the magnitude of the transfer function $H_1(z)$.

(c) Using Equation (13.23), find the high-pass filter coefficients $\{h_{2,k}\}$.

(d) Find the magnitude of the transfer function $H_2(z)$.

3. Given an input sequence

$$x_n = \begin{cases} (-1)^n & n = 0, 1, 2, \ldots \\ 0 & \text{otherwise} \end{cases}$$

(a) Find the output sequence y_n if the filter impulse response is

$$h_n = \begin{cases} \frac{1}{\sqrt{2}} & n = 0, 1 \\ 0 & \text{otherwise.} \end{cases}$$

(b) Find the output sequence w_n if the impulse response of the filter is

$$h_n = \begin{cases} \frac{1}{\sqrt{2}} & n = 0 \\ -\frac{1}{\sqrt{2}} & n = 1 \\ 0 & \text{otherwise.} \end{cases}$$

(c) Looking at the sequences y_n and w_n, what can you say about the sequence x_n?

4. Given an input sequence

$$x_n = \begin{cases} 1 & n = 0, 1, 2, \ldots \\ 0 & \text{otherwise} \end{cases}$$

(a) Find the output sequence y_n if the filter impulse response is

$$h_n = \begin{cases} \frac{1}{\sqrt{2}} & n = 0, 1 \\ 0 & \text{otherwise.} \end{cases}$$

(b) Find the output sequence w_n if the impulse response of the filter is

$$h_n = \begin{cases} \frac{1}{\sqrt{2}} & n = 0 \\ -\frac{1}{\sqrt{2}} & n = 1 \\ 0 & \text{otherwise.} \end{cases}$$

(c) Looking at the sequences y_n and w_n, what can you say about the sequence x_n?

5. Write a program to perform the analysis and downsampling operations and another to perform the upsampling and synthesis operations for an image compression application. The programs should read the filter parameters from a file. The synthesis program should read the output of the analysis program and write out the reconstructed images. The analysis program should also write out the subimages scaled so that they can be displayed. Test your program using the Johnston eight-tap filter and the Sena image.

6. In this problem we look at some of the many ways we can encode the subimages obtained after subsampling. Use the eight-tap Johnston filter to decompose the Sena image into four subimages.

(a) Encode the low-low band using an adptive delta modulator (CFDM or CVSD). Encode all other bands using a 1-bit scalar quantizer.

(b) Encode the low-low band using a 2-bit adaptive DPCM system. Encode the low-high and high-low bands using a 1-bit scalar quantizer.

(c) Encode the low-low band using a 3-bit adaptive DPCM system. Encode the low-high and high-low band using a 0.5 bit/pixel vector quantizer.

(d) Compare the reconstructions obtained using the different schemes.

14 Wavelet-Based Compression

14.1 Overview

n this chapter we introduce the concept of wavelets and describe how to use wavelet-based decompositions in compression schemes. We begin with an introduction to wavelets and multiresolution analysis and then describe how we can implement a wavelet decomposition using filters. We then examine the implementations of several wavelet-based compression schemes.

14.2 Introduction

In the previous two chapters we looked at a number of ways to decompose a signal. In this chapter we look at another approach to decompose a signal that has become increasingly popular in recent years: the use of wavelets. Wavelets are being used in a number of different applications. Depending on the application, different aspects of wavelets can be emphasized. As our particular application is compression, we will emphasize those aspects of wavelets that are important in the design of compression algorithms. You should be aware that there is much more to wavelets than is presented in this chapter. At the end of the chapter we suggest options if you want to delve more deeply into this subject.

The practical implementation of wavelet compression schemes is very similar to that of subband coding schemes. As in the case of subband coding, we decompose the signal (analysis) using filter banks. The outputs of the filter banks are downsampled, quantized, and encoded. The decoder decodes the coded representations, upsamples, and recomposes the signal using a synthesis filter bank.

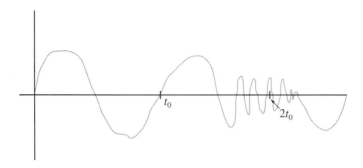

FIGURE 14.1   A nonstationary signal.

In the next several sections we will briefly examine the construction of wavelets and describe how we can obtain a decomposition of a signal using multiresolution analysis. We will then describe some of the currently popular schemes for image compression. If you are primarily interested at this time in implementation of wavelet-based compression schemes, you should skip the next few sections and go directly to Section 14.5.

In the last two chapters we have described several ways of decomposing signals. Why do we need another one? To answer this question, let's begin with our standard tool for analysis, the Fourier transform. Given a function $f(t)$, we can find the Fourier transform $F(\omega)$ as

$$F(\omega) = \int_{-\infty}^{\infty} f(t)e^{j\omega t}dt.$$

Integration is an averaging operation; therefore, the analysis we obtain, using the Fourier transform, is in some sense an "average" analysis, where the averaging interval is all of time. Thus, by looking at a particular Fourier transform, we can say, for example, that there is a large component of frequency 10 kHz in a signal, but we cannot tell when in time this component occurred. Another way of saying this is that Fourier analysis provides excellent localization in frequency and none in time. The converse is true for the time function $f(t)$, which provides exact information about the value of the function at each instant of time but does not directly provide spectral information. It should be noted that both $f(t)$ and $F(\omega)$ represent the same function, and all the information is present in each representation. However, each representation makes different kinds of information easily accessible.

If we have a very nonstationary signal, like the one shown in Figure 14.1, we would like to know not only the frequency components but when in time the particular frequency components occurred. One way to obtain this information is via the *short-term Fourier transform* (STFT). With the STFT, we break the time signal $f(t)$ into pieces of length T and apply Fourier analysis to each piece. This way we can say, for example, that a component at 10 kHz occurred in the third piece—that is, between time $2T$ and time $3T$. Thus, we obtain an analysis that is a function of both time and frequency. If we simply chopped the function into pieces, we could get distortion in the form of boundary effects (see Problem 1). In order to reduce the boundary effects, we *window* each piece before we take the Fourier transform. If the window shape is

FIGURE 14.2 **The first three STFT basis functions for the first time interval.**

given by $g(t)$, the STFT is formally given by

$$F(\omega, \tau) = \int_{-\infty}^{\infty} f(t)g^*(t - \tau)e^{j\omega t}dt. \tag{14.1}$$

If the window function $g(t)$ is a Gaussian, the STFT is called the *Gabor transform*.

The problem with the STFT is the fixed window size. Consider Figure 14.1. In order to obtain the low-pass component at the beginning of the function, the window size should be at least t_0 so that the window will contain at least one cycle of the low-frequency component. However, a window size of t_0 or greater means that we will not be able to accurately localize the high-frequency spurt. A large window in the time domain corresponds to a narrow filter in the frequency domain, which is what we want for the low-frequency components—and what we do not want for the high-frequency components. This dilemma is formalized in the uncertainty principle, which states that for a given window $g(t)$, the product of the time spread σ_t^2 and the frequency spread σ_ω^2 is lower bounded by $\sqrt{1/2}$, where

$$\sigma_t^2 = \frac{\int t^2 |g(t)|^2 dt}{\int |g(t)|^2 dt} \tag{14.2}$$

$$\sigma_\omega^2 = \frac{\int \omega^2 |G(\omega)|^2 d\omega}{\int |G(\omega)|^2 d\omega}. \tag{14.3}$$

Thus, if we wish to have finer resolution in time, that is, reduce σ_t^2, we end up with an increase in σ_ω^2, or a lower resolution in the frequency domain. How do we get around this problem?

Let's take a look at the discrete STFT in terms of basis expansion, and for the moment, let's look at just one interval:

$$F(m, 0) = \int_{-\infty}^{\infty} f(t)g^*(t)e^{-jm\omega_0 t}dt. \tag{14.4}$$

The basis functions are $g(t)$, $g(t)e^{j\omega_o t}$, $g(t)e^{j2\omega_o t}$, and so on. The first three basis functions are shown in Figure 14.2. We can see that we have a window with constant size, and within this window, we have sinusoids with an increasing number of cycles. Let's conjure up a different set of functions in which the number of cycles is constant, but the size of the window keeps changing, as shown in Figure 14.3. Notice that although the number of cycles of the sinusoid in each window is the same, as the size of the window gets smaller, these cycles occur in a smaller time interval; that is, the frequency of the sinusoid increases. Furthermore, the lower frequency functions cover a longer time interval, while the higher frequency functions cover a shorter time interval, thus avoiding the problem that we had with the STFT. If we can write our function in terms of these functions and their translates, we have a representation that

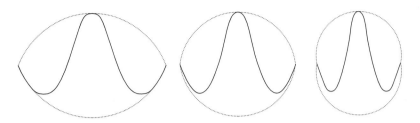

FIGURE 14.3 **Three wavelet basis functions.**

gives us time and frequency localization and can provide high frequency resolution at low frequencies (longer time window) and high time resolution at high frequencies (shorter time window). This, crudely speaking, is the basic idea behind wavelets.

In the following section we will formalize the concept of wavelets. Then we will discuss how to get from a wavelet basis set to an implementation. If you wish to move directly to implementation issues, you should skip to Section 14.5.

14.3 Wavelets

In the example at the end of the previous section, we started out with a single function. All other functions were obtained by changing the size of the function or *scaling* and translating this single function. This function is called the *mother wavelet*. Mathematically, we can scale a function $f(t)$ by replacing t with t/a, where the parameter a governs the amount of scaling. For example, consider the function

$$f(t) = \begin{cases} \cos(\pi t) & -1 \leq t \leq 1 \\ 0 & \text{otherwise.} \end{cases}$$

We have plotted this function in Figure 14.4. To scale this function by 0.5, we replace t by $t/0.5$:

$$f\left(\frac{t}{0.5}\right) = \begin{cases} \cos(\pi \frac{t}{0.5}) & -1 \leq \frac{t}{0.5} \leq 1 \\ 0 & \text{otherwise} \end{cases}$$
$$= \begin{cases} \cos(2\pi t) & -\frac{1}{2} \leq t \leq \frac{1}{2} \\ 0 & \text{otherwise.} \end{cases}$$

We have plotted the scaled function in Figure 14.5. If we define the norm of a function $f(t)$ by

$$\|f(t)\|^2 = \int_{-\infty}^{\infty} f^2(t)dt$$

scaling obviously changes the norm of the function:

$$\left\|f\left(\frac{t}{a}\right)\right\|^2 = \int_{-\infty}^{\infty} f^2\left(\frac{t}{a}\right)dt$$
$$= a \int_{-\infty}^{\infty} f^2(x)dx$$

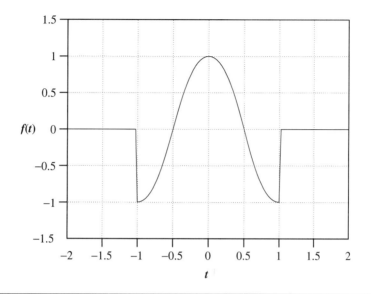

FIGURE 14.4   A function f(t).

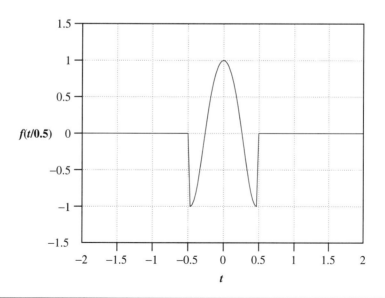

FIGURE 14.5   The function $f(\frac{t}{0.5})$.

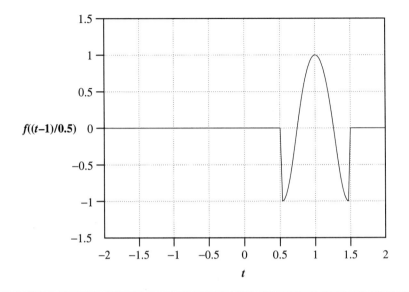

FIGURE 14.6   A scaled and translated function.

where we have used the substitution $x = t/a$. Thus,

$$\left\| f\left(\frac{t}{a}\right) \right\|^2 = a \, \|f(t)\|^2 .$$

If we want the scaled function to have the same norm as the original function, we need to multiply it by $1/\sqrt{a}$.

Mathematically, we can represent the translation of a function to the right or left by an amount b by replacing t by $t - b$ or $t + b$. For example, if we want to translate the scaled function shown in Figure 14.5 by one, we have

$$f\left(\frac{t-1}{0.5}\right) = \begin{cases} \cos(2\pi(t-1)) & -\frac{1}{2} \le t - 1 \le \frac{1}{2} \\ 0 & \text{otherwise} \end{cases}$$

$$= \begin{cases} \cos(2\pi(t-1)) & \frac{1}{2} \le t \le \frac{3}{2} \\ 0 & \text{otherwise.} \end{cases}$$

The scaled and translated function is shown in Figure 14.6. Thus, given a *mother wavelet* $\psi(t)$, the remaining functions are obtained as

$$\psi_{a,b}(t) = \frac{1}{\sqrt{a}} \psi\left(\frac{t-b}{a}\right) \tag{14.5}$$

with Fourier transforms

$$\Psi(\omega) = \mathcal{F}[\psi(t)]$$
$$\Psi_{a,b}(\omega) = \mathcal{F}[\psi_{a,b}(t)]. \tag{14.6}$$

Our expansion using coefficients with respect to these functions is obtained from the inner product of $f(t)$ with the wavelet functions:

$$w_{a,b} = \langle \psi_{a,b}(t), f(t) \rangle = \int_{-\infty}^{\infty} \psi_{a,b}(t) f(t) dt. \qquad (14.7)$$

We can recover the function $f(t)$ from the $w_{a,b}$ by

$$f(t) = \frac{1}{C_\psi} \int_{-\infty}^{\infty} \int_{-\infty}^{\infty} w_{a,b} \psi_{a,b}(t) \frac{da db}{a^2} \qquad (14.8)$$

where

$$C_\psi = \int_0^\infty \frac{|\Psi(\omega)|^2}{\omega} d\omega. \qquad (14.9)$$

For integral (14.8) to exist, we need C_ψ to be finite. For C_ψ to be finite, we need $\Psi(0) = 0$. Otherwise, we have a singularity in the integrand of (14.9). Note that $\Psi(0)$ is the average value of $\psi(t)$; therefore, a requirement on the mother wavelet is that it have zero mean. The condition that C_ψ be finite is often called the *admissibility condition*. We would also like the wavelets to have finite energy; that is, we want the wavelets to belong to the vector space L_2 (see Example 11.3.1). Using Parseval's relationship, we can write this requirement as

$$\int_{-\infty}^{\infty} |\Psi(\omega)|^2 d\omega < \infty.$$

For this to happen, $|\Psi(\omega)|^2$ has to decay as ω goes to infinity. These requirements mean that the energy in $\Psi(\omega)$ is concentrated in a narrow frequency band, which gives the wavelet its frequency localization capability.

If a and b are continuous, then $w_{a,b}$ is called the *continuous wavelet transform* (CWT). Just as with other transforms, we will be more interested in the discrete version of this transform. We first obtain a series representation where the basis functions are continuous functions of time with discrete scaling and translating parameters a and b. The discrete versions of the scaling and translating parameters have to be related to each other because if the scale is such that the basis functions are narrow, the translation step should be correspondingly small and vice versa. There are a number of ways we can choose these parameters. The most popular approach is to select a and b according to

$$a = a_0^{-m}, \qquad b = n b_0 a_0^{-m} \qquad (14.10)$$

where m and n are integers, a_0 is selected to be 2, and b_0 has a value of 1. This gives us the wavelet set

$$\psi_{m,n}(t) = a_0^{m/2} \psi(a_0^m t - n b_0), \qquad m, n \in Z. \qquad (14.11)$$

For $a_0 = 2$ and $b_0 = 1$, we have

$$\psi_{m,n}(t) = 2^{m/2} \psi(2^m t - n). \qquad (14.12)$$

(Note that these are the most commonly used choices, but they are not the only choices.) If this set is *complete*, then $\{\psi_{m,n}(t)\}$ are called *affine* wavelets. The wavelet coefficients are given by

$$w_{m,n} = \langle f(t), \psi_{m,n}(t)\rangle \tag{14.13}$$

$$= a_0^{m/2} \int f(t)\psi(a_0^m t - nb_0)dt. \tag{14.14}$$

The function $f(t)$ can be reconstructed from the wavelet coefficients by

$$f(t) = \sum_m \sum_n w_{m,n}\psi_{m,n}(t). \tag{14.15}$$

Wavelets come in many shapes. We will look at some of the more popular ones later in this chapter. One of the simplest wavelets is the Haar wavelet, which we will use to explore the various aspects of wavelets. The Haar wavelet is given by

$$\psi(t) = \begin{cases} 1 & 0 \le t < \frac{1}{2} \\ -1 & \frac{1}{2} \le t < 1. \end{cases} \tag{14.16}$$

By translating and scaling this mother wavelet, we can synthesize a variety of functions.

This version of the transform, where $f(t)$ is a continuous function while the transform consists of discrete values, is a wavelet series analogous to the Fourier series. It is also called the *discrete time wavelet transform* (DTWT). We have moved from the continuous wavelet transform, where both the time function $f(t)$ and its transform $w_{a,b}$ were continuous functions of their arguments, to the wavelet series, where the time function is continuous but the time-scale wavelet representation is discrete. Given that in data compression we are generally dealing with sampled functions that are discrete in time, we would like both the time and frequency representations to be discrete. This is called the *discrete wavelet transform* (DWT). However, before we get to that, let's look into one additional concept—multiresolution analysis.

14.4 Multiresolution Analysis and the Scaling Function

The idea behind multiresolution analysis is fairly simple. Let's define a function $\phi(t)$ that we call a *scaling* function. We will later see that the scaling function is closely related to the mother wavelet. By taking linear combinations of the scaling function and its translates we can generate a large number of functions

$$f(t) = \sum_k a_k\phi(t - k). \tag{14.17}$$

The scaling function has the property that a function that can be represented by the scaling function can also be represented by the dilated versions of the scaling function.

For example, one of the simplest scaling functions is the Haar scaling function:

$$\phi(t) = \begin{cases} 1 & 0 \le t < 1 \\ 0 & \text{otherwise.} \end{cases} \tag{14.18}$$

Then $f(t)$ can be any piecewise continuous function that is constant in the interval $[k, k+1)$ for all k.

Let's define

$$\phi_k(t) = \phi(t - k). \tag{14.19}$$

The set of all functions that can be obtained using a linear combination of the set $\{\phi_k(t)\}$

$$f(t) = \sum_k a_k \phi_k(t) \tag{14.20}$$

is called the *span* of the set $\{\phi_k(t)\}$, or $\text{Span}\{\phi_k(t)\}$. If we now add all functions that are limits of sequences of functions in $\text{Span}\{\phi_k(t)\}$, this is referred to as the closure of $\text{Span}\{\phi_k(t)\}$ and denoted by $\overline{\text{Span}\{\phi_k(t)\}}$. Let's call this set V_0.

If we want to generate functions at a higher resolution, say, functions that are required to be constant over only half a unit interval, we can use a dilated version of the "mother" scaling function. In fact, we can obtain scaling functions at different resolutions in a manner similar to the procedure used for wavelets:

$$\phi_{j,k}(t) = 2^{j/2} \phi(2^j t - k). \tag{14.21}$$

The indexing scheme is the same as that used for wavelets, with the first index referring to the resolution while the second index denotes the translation. For the Haar example,

$$\phi_{1,0}(t) = \begin{cases} \sqrt{2} & 0 \le t < \frac{1}{2} \\ 0 & \text{otherwise.} \end{cases} \tag{14.22}$$

We can use translates of $\phi_{1,0}(t)$ to represent all functions that are constant over intervals $[k/2, (k+1)/2)$ for all k. Notice that in general any function that can be represented by the translates of $\phi(t)$ can also be represented by a linear combination of translates of $\phi_{1,0}(t)$. The converse, however, is not true. Defining

$$V_1 = \overline{\text{Span}\{\phi_{1,k}(t)\}} \tag{14.23}$$

we can see that $V_0 \subset V_1$. Similarly, we can show that $V_1 \subset V_2$, and so on.

Example 14.4.1:

Consider the function shown in Figure 14.7. We can approximate this function using translates of the Haar scaling function $\phi(t)$. The approximation is shown in Figure 14.8a. If we call this approximation $\phi_f^{(0)}(t)$, then

$$\phi_f^{(0)}(t) = \sum_k c_{0,k} \phi_k(t) \tag{14.24}$$

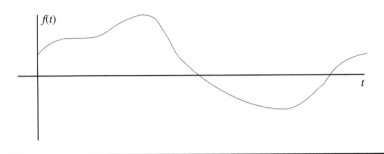

FIGURE 14.7   A sample function.

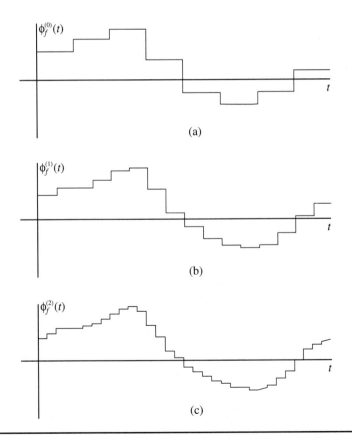

(a)

(b)

(c)

FIGURE 14.8   Approximations of the function shown Figure 14.7.

where

$$c_{0,k} = \int_{k}^{k+1} f(t)\phi_k(t)dt. \tag{14.25}$$

We can obtain a more refined approximation, or an approximation at a higher resolution, $\phi_f^{(1)}(t)$, shown in Figure 14.8b, if we use the set $\{\phi_{1,k}(t)\}$:

$$\phi_f^{(1)}(t) = \sum_k c_{1,k}\phi_{1,k}(t). \tag{14.26}$$

Notice that we need twice as many coefficients at this resolution compared to the previous resolution. The coefficients at the two resolutions are related by

$$c_{0,k} = \frac{1}{\sqrt{2}}(c_{1,2k} + c_{1,2k+1}). \tag{14.27}$$

Continuing in this manner (Figure 14.8c), we can get higher and higher resolution approximations of $f(t)$ with

$$\phi_f^{(m)}(t) = \sum_k c_{m,k}\phi_{m,k}(t). \tag{14.28}$$

Recall that, according to the Nyquist rule, if the highest frequency component of a signal is at f_0 Hz, we need $2f_0$ samples per second to accurately represent it. Therefore, we could obtain an accurate representation of $f(t)$ using the set of translates $\{\phi_{j,k}(t)\}$, where $2^{-j} < \frac{1}{2f_0}$.
As

$$c_{j,k} = 2^{j/2} \int_{\frac{k}{2^j}}^{\frac{k+1}{2^j}} f(t)dt, \tag{14.29}$$

by the mean value theorem of calculus, $c_{j,k}$ is equal to a sample value of $f(t)$ in the interval $[k2^{-j}, (k+1)2^{-j})$. Therefore, the function $\phi_f^{(j)}(t)$ would represent more than $2f_0$ samples per second of $f(t)$. ◆

We said earlier that a scaling function has the property that any function that can be represented exactly by an expansion at some resolution j can also be represented by dilations of the scaling function at resolution $j + 1$. In particular, this means that the scaling function itself can be represented by its dilations at a higher resolution:

$$\phi(t) = \sum_k h_k\phi_{1,k}(t). \tag{14.30}$$

Substituting $\phi_{1,k}(t) = \sqrt{2}\phi(2t - k)$, we obtain the *multiresolution analysis* (MRA) equation:

$$\phi(t) = \sum_k h_k\sqrt{2}\phi(2t - k). \tag{14.31}$$

This equation will be of great importance to us when we begin looking at ways of implementing the wavelet transform.

Example 14.4.2:

Consider the Haar scaling function. Picking

$$h_0 = h_1 = \frac{1}{\sqrt{2}}$$

and

$$h_k = 0 \qquad \text{for } k > 1$$

satisfies the recursion equation.   ◆

Example 14.4.3:

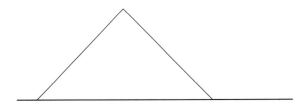

FIGURE 14.9   **Triangular scaling function.**

Consider the triangle scaling function shown in Figure 14.9. For this function

$$h_0 = \frac{1}{2\sqrt{2}}, \quad h_1 = \frac{1}{\sqrt{2}}, \quad h_2 = \frac{1}{2\sqrt{2}}$$

satisfies the recursion equation.   ◆

  While both the Haar scaling function and the triangle scaling functions are valid scaling functions, there is an important difference between the two. The Haar function is orthogonal to its translates; that is,

$$\int \phi(t)\phi(t - m)dt = \delta_m.$$

This is obviously not true of the triangle function. In this chapter we will be principally concerned with scaling functions that are orthogonal because they give rise to orthonormal transforms that, as we have previously seen, are very useful in compression.
  How about the Haar wavelet? Can it be used as a scaling function? Some reflection will show that we cannot obtain the Haar wavelet from a linear combination of its dilated versions.
  So, where do wavelets come into the picture? Let's continue with our example using the Haar scaling function. Let us assume for the moment that there is a function $g(t)$ that can be exactly represented by $\phi_g^{(1)}(t)$; that is, $g(t)$ is a function in the set V_1. We can decompose

$\phi_g^{(1)}(t)$ into the sum of a lower-resolution version of itself, namely, $\phi_g^{(0)}(t)$, and the difference $\phi_g^{(1)}(t) - \phi_g^{(0)}(t)$. Let's examine this difference over an arbitrary unit interval $[k, k+1)$:

$$\phi_g^{(1)}(t) - \phi_g^{(0)}(t) = \begin{cases} c_{0,k} - \sqrt{2}c_{1,2k} & k \leq t < k + \frac{1}{2} \\ c_{0,k} - \sqrt{2}c_{1,2k+1} & k + \frac{1}{2} \leq t < k+1 \,. \end{cases} \tag{14.32}$$

Substituting for $c_{0,k}$ from (14.27), we obtain

$$\phi_g^{(1)}(t) - \phi_g^{(0)}(t) = \begin{cases} -\frac{1}{\sqrt{2}}c_{1,2k} + \frac{1}{\sqrt{2}}c_{1,2k+1} & k \leq t < k + \frac{1}{2} \\ \frac{1}{\sqrt{2}}c_{1,2k} - \frac{1}{\sqrt{2}}c_{1,2k+1} & k + \frac{1}{2} \leq t < k+1 \,. \end{cases} \tag{14.33}$$

Defining

$$d_{0,k} = -\frac{1}{\sqrt{2}}c_{1,2k} + \frac{1}{\sqrt{2}}c_{1,2k+1}$$

over the arbitrary interval $[k, k+1)$,

$$\phi_g^{(1)}(t) - \phi_g^{(0)}(t) = d_{0,k}\psi_{0,k}(t) \tag{14.34}$$

where

$$\psi_{0,k}(t) = \begin{cases} 1 & k \leq t < k + \frac{1}{2} \\ -1 & k + \frac{1}{2} \leq t < k+1 \,. \end{cases} \tag{14.35}$$

But this is simply the kth translate of the Haar wavelet. Thus, for this particular case the function can be represented as the sum of a scaling function and a wavelet at the same resolution:

$$\phi_g^{(1)}(t) = \sum_k c_{0,k}\phi_{0,k}(t) + \sum_k d_{0,k}\psi_{0,k}(t). \tag{14.36}$$

In fact, we can show that this decomposition is not limited to this particular example. A function in V_1 can be decomposed into a function in V_0—that is, a function that is a linear combination of the scaling function at resolution 0, and a function that is a linear combination of translates of a mother wavelet. Denoting the set of functions that can be obtained by a linear combination of the translates of the mother wavelet as W_0, we can write this symbolically as

$$V_1 = V_0 \oplus W_0. \tag{14.37}$$

In other words, any function in V_1 can be represented using functions in V_0 and W_0.

Obviously, once a scaling function is selected, the choice of the wavelet function cannot be arbitrary. The wavelet that generates the set W_0 and the scaling function that generates the sets V_0 and V_1 are intrinsically related. In fact, from (14.37), $W_0 \subset V_1$, and therefore any function in W_0 can be represented by a linear combination of $\{\phi_{1,k}\}$. In particular, we can write the mother wavelet $\psi(t)$ as

$$\psi(t) = \sum_k w_k\phi_{1,k}(t) \tag{14.38}$$

or

$$\psi(t) = \sum_k w_k \sqrt{2}\phi(2t - k).$$ (14.39)

This is the counterpart of the multiresolution analysis equation for the wavelet function and will be of primary importance in the implementation of the decomposition.

All of this development has been for a function in V_1. What if the function can only be accurately represented at resolution $j + 1$? If we define W_j as the closure of the span of $\psi_{j,k}(t)$, we can show that

$$V_{j+1} = V_j \oplus W_j.$$ (14.40)

But, as j is arbitrary,

$$V_j = V_{j-1} \oplus W_{j-1}$$ (14.41)

and

$$V_{j+1} = V_{j-1} \oplus W_{j-1} \oplus W_j.$$ (14.42)

Continuing in this manner, we can see that for any $k \leq j$

$$V_{j+1} = V_k \oplus W_k \oplus W_{k+1} \oplus \cdots \oplus W_j.$$ (14.43)

In other words, if we have a function that belongs to V_{j+1} (i.e., that can be exactly represented by the scaling function at resolution $j + 1$), we can decompose it into a sum of functions starting with a lower-resolution approximation followed by a sequence of functions generated by dilations of the wavelet that represent the leftover details. This is very much like what we did in subband coding. A major difference is that, while the subband decomposition is in terms of sines and cosines, the decomposition in this case can use a variety of scaling functions and wavelets. Thus, we can adapt the decomposition to the signal being decomposed by selecting the scaling function and wavelet.

14.5 Implementation Using Filters

One of the most popular approaches to implementing the decomposition discussed in the previous section is using a hierarchical filter structure similar to the one used in subband coding. In this section we will look at how to obtain the structure and the filter coefficients.

We start with the MRA equation

$$\phi(t) = \sum_k h_k \sqrt{2}\phi(2t - k).$$ (14.44)

Substituting $t = 2^j t - m$, we obtain the equation for an arbitrary dilation and translation:

$$\phi(2^j t - m) = \sum_k h_k \sqrt{2}\phi(2(2^j t - m) - k)$$ (14.45)

$$= \sum_k h_k \sqrt{2}\phi(2^{j+1} t - 2m - k)$$ (14.46)

$$= \sum_l h_{l-2m} \sqrt{2}\phi(2^{j+1} t - l)$$ (14.47)

where in the last equation we have used the substitution $l = 2m + k$. Suppose we have a function $f(t)$ that can be accurately represented at resolution $j + 1$ by some scaling function $\phi(t)$. We assume that the scaling function and its dilations and translations form an orthonormal set. The coefficients c_{j+1} can be obtained by

$$c_{j+1,k} = \int f(t)\phi_{j+1,k}dt. \qquad (14.48)$$

If we can represent $f(t)$ accurately at resolution $j + 1$ with a linear combination of $\phi_{j+1,k}(t)$, then from the previous section we can decompose it into two functions: one in terms of $\phi_{j,k}(t)$ and one in terms of the jth dilation of the corresponding wavelet $\{\psi_{j,k}(t)\}$. The coefficients $c_{j,k}$ are given by

$$c_{j,k} = \int f(t)\phi_{j,k}(t)dt \qquad (14.49)$$

$$= \int f(t)2^{\frac{j}{2}}\phi(2^{j}t - k)dt. \qquad (14.50)$$

Substituting for $\phi(2^{j}t - k)$ from (14.47), we get

$$c_{j,l} = \int f(t)2^{\frac{j}{2}}\sum_{l} h_{l-2k}\sqrt{2}\phi(2^{j+1}t - l)dt. \qquad (14.51)$$

Interchanging the order of summation and integration, we get

$$c_{j,l} = \sum_{l} h_{l-2k}\int f(t)2^{\frac{j}{2}}\sqrt{2}\phi(2^{j+1}t - l)dt. \qquad (14.52)$$

But the integral is simply $c_{j+1,k}$. Therefore,

$$c_{j,k} = \sum_{k} h_{k-2m}c_{j+1,k}. \qquad (14.53)$$

We have encountered this relationship before in the context of the Haar function. Equation (14.27) provides the relationship between coefficients of the Haar expansion at two resolution levels. In a more general setting, the coefficients $\{h_j\}$ provide a link between the coefficients $\{c_{j,k}\}$ at different resolutions. Thus, given the coefficients at resolution level $j + 1$, we can obtain the coefficients at all other resolution levels. But how do we start the process? Recall that $f(t)$ can be accurately represented at resolution $j + 1$. Therefore, we can replace $c_{j+1,k}$ by the samples of $f(t)$. Let's represent these samples by x_k. Then the coefficients of the low-resolution expansion are given by

$$c_{j,k} = \sum_{k} h_{k-2m}x_k. \qquad (14.54)$$

In Chapter 11, we introduced the input-output relationship of a linear filter as

$$y_m = \sum_{k} h_k x_{m-k} = \sum_{k} h_{m-k}x_k. \qquad (14.55)$$

Replacing m by $2m$, we get every other sample of the output

$$y_{2m} = \sum_k h_{2m-k} x_k. \tag{14.56}$$

Comparing (14.56) with (14.54), we can see that the coefficients of the low-resolution approximation are every other output of a linear filter whose impulse response is h_{-k}. Recall that $\{h_k\}$ are the coefficients that satisfy the MRA equation. Using the terminology of subband coding, the coefficients $c_{j,k}$ are the downsampled output of the linear filter with impulse response $\{h_{-k}\}$.

The detail portion of the representation is obtained in a similar manner. Again we start from the recursion relationship. This time we use the recursion relationship for the wavelet function as our starting point:

$$\psi(t) = \sum_k w_k \sqrt{2} \phi(2t - k). \tag{14.57}$$

Again substituting $t = 2^j t - m$ and using the same simplifications, we get

$$\psi(2^j t - m) = \sum_k w_{k-2m} \sqrt{2} \phi(2^{j+1} t - k). \tag{14.58}$$

Using the fact that the dilated and translated wavelets form an orthonormal basis, we can obtain the detail coefficients $d_{j,k}$ by

$$d_{j,k} = \int f(t) \psi_{j,k}(t) dt \tag{14.59}$$

$$= \int f(t) 2^{\frac{j}{2}} \psi(2^j t - k) dt \tag{14.60}$$

$$= \int f(t) 2^{\frac{j}{2}} \sum_l w_{l-2k} \sqrt{2} \phi(2^{j+1} t - l) dt \tag{14.61}$$

$$= \sum_l w_{l-2k} \int f(t) 2^{\frac{j+1}{2}} \phi(2^{j+1} t - l) dt \tag{14.62}$$

$$= \sum_l w_{l-2k} c_{j+1,l}. \tag{14.63}$$

Thus, the detail coefficients are the decimated outputs of a filter with impulse response $\{w_{-k}\}$.

At this point we can use exactly the same arguments to further decompose the coefficients $\{c_j\}$.

In order to retrieve $\{c_{j+1,k}\}$ from $\{c_{j,k}\}$ and $\{d_{j,k}\}$, we upsample the lower resolution coefficients and filter, using filters with impulse response $\{h_k\}$ and $\{w_k\}$

$$c_{j+1,k} = \sum_l c_{j,l} b_{k-2l} \sum_l d_{j,l} w_{k-2l}.$$

14.5.1 Scaling and Wavelet Coefficients

In order to implement the wavelet decomposition, the coefficients $\{h_k\}$ and $\{w_k\}$ are of primary importance. In this section we look at some of the properties of these coefficients that will help us in finding different decompositions.

We start with the MRA equation. Integrating both sides of the equation over all t, we obtain

$$\int_{-\infty}^{\infty} \phi(t)dt = \int_{-\infty}^{\infty} \sum_k h_k \sqrt{2}\phi(2t - k)dt. \tag{14.64}$$

Interchanging the summation and integration on the right-hand side of the equation, we get

$$\int_{-\infty}^{\infty} \phi(t)dt = \sum_k h_k \sqrt{2} \int_{-\infty}^{\infty} \phi(2t - k)dt. \tag{14.65}$$

Substituting $x = 2t - k$ with $dx = 2dt$ in the right-hand side of the equation, we get

$$\int_{-\infty}^{\infty} \phi(t)dt = \sum_k h_k \sqrt{2} \int_{-\infty}^{\infty} \phi(x)\frac{1}{2}dx \tag{14.66}$$

$$= \sum_k h_k \frac{1}{\sqrt{2}} \int_{-\infty}^{\infty} \phi(x)dx. \tag{14.67}$$

Assuming that the average value of the scaling function is not zero, we can divide both sides by the integral and we get

$$\sum_k h_k = \sqrt{2}. \tag{14.68}$$

If we normalize the scaling function to have a magnitude of one, we can use the orthogonality condition on the scaling function to get another condition on $\{h_k\}$:

$$\int |\phi(t)|^2 dt = \int \sum_k h_k \sqrt{2}\phi(2t - k) \sum_m h_m \sqrt{2}\phi(2t - m)dt \tag{14.69}$$

$$= \sum_k \sum_m h_k h_m 2 \int \phi(2t - k)\phi(2t - m)dt \tag{14.70}$$

$$= \sum_k \sum_m h_k h_m \int \phi(x - k)\phi(x - m)dx \tag{14.71}$$

where in the last equation we have used the substitution $x = 2t$. The integral on the right-hand side is zero except when $k = m$. When $k = m$, the integral is unity and we obtain

$$\sum_k h_k^2 = 1. \tag{14.72}$$

We can actually get a more general property by using the orthogonality of the translates of the scaling function

$$\int \phi(t)\phi(t - m)dt = \delta_m. \tag{14.73}$$

Rewriting this using the MRA equation to substitute for $\phi(t)$ and $\phi(t - m)$, we obtain

$$\int \left[\sum_k h_k \sqrt{2} \phi(2t - k) \right] \left[\sum_l h_l \sqrt{2} \phi(2t - 2m - l) \right] dt$$

$$= \sum_k \sum_l h_k h_l 2 \int \phi(2t - k) \phi(2t - 2m - l) dt. \qquad (14.74)$$

Substituting $x = 2t$, we get

$$\int \phi(t) \phi(t - m) dt = \sum_k \sum_l h_k h_l \int \phi(x - k) \phi(x - 2m - l) dx \qquad (14.75)$$

$$= \sum_k \sum_l h_k h_l \delta_{k - (2m+l)} \qquad (14.76)$$

$$= \sum_k h_k h_{k-2m}. \qquad (14.77)$$

Therefore, we have

$$\sum_k h_k h_{k-2m} = \delta_m \qquad (14.78)$$

Notice that this is the same relationship we had to satisfy for perfect reconstruction in the previous chapter.

Using these relationships, we can generate scaling coefficients for filters of various lengths.

Example 14.5.1:

For $k = 2$, we have from (14.68) and (14.72)

$$h_0 + h_1 = \sqrt{2} \qquad (14.79)$$
$$h_0^2 + h_1^2 = 1. \qquad (14.80)$$

These equations are uniquely satisfied by

$$h_0 = h_1 = \frac{1}{\sqrt{2}},$$

which is the Haar scaling function.   ◆

An orthogonal expansion does not exist for all lengths. In the following example, we consider the case of $k = 3$.

Example 14.5.2:

For $k = 3$, from the three conditions (14.68), (14.72), and (14.78), we have

$$h_0 + h_1 + h_2 = \sqrt{2} \qquad (14.81)$$
$$h_0^2 + h_1^2 + h_2^2 = 1 \qquad (14.82)$$
$$h_0 h_2 = 0 \qquad (14.83)$$

The last condition can only be satisfied if $h_0 = 0$ or $h_2 = 0$. In either case we will be left with the two-coefficient filter for the Haar scaling function. ◆

In fact, we can see that for k odd, we will always end up with a condition that will force one of the coefficients to zero, thus leaving an even number of coefficients. When the number of coefficients gets larger than the number of conditions, we end up with an infinite number of solutions.

Example 14.5.3:

Consider the case when $k = 4$. The three conditions give us the following three equations:

$$h_0 + h_1 + h_2 + h_3 = \sqrt{2} \tag{14.84}$$
$$h_0^2 + h_1^2 + h_2^2 + h_3^2 = 1 \tag{14.85}$$
$$h_0 h_2 + h_1 h_3 = 0 \tag{14.86}$$

We have three equations and four unknowns; that is, we have one degree of freedom. We can use this degree of freedom to impose further conditions on the solution. The solutions to these equations include the Daubechies four-tap solution:

$$h_0 = \frac{1 + \sqrt{3}}{4\sqrt{2}}, \quad h_1 = \frac{3 + \sqrt{3}}{4\sqrt{2}}, \quad h_2 = \frac{3 - \sqrt{3}}{4\sqrt{2}}, \quad h_3 = \frac{1 - \sqrt{3}}{4\sqrt{2}}. \qquad ◆$$

Given the close relationship between the scaling function and the wavelet, it seems reasonable that we should be able to obtain the coefficients for the wavelet filter from the coefficients of the scaling filter. In fact, if the wavelet function is orthogonal to the scaling function at the same scale

$$\int \phi(t - k)\psi(t - m)dt = 0, \tag{14.87}$$

then

$$w_k = \pm(-1)^k h_{N-k} \tag{14.88}$$

and

$$\sum_k h_k w_{n-2k} = 0. \tag{14.89}$$

Furthermore,

$$\sum_k w_k = 0. \tag{14.90}$$

The proof of these relationships is somewhat involved [33].

14.5.2 Families of Wavelets

Let's move to the more practical aspects of compression using wavelets. We have said that there is an infinite number of possible wavelets. Which one is best depends on the application.

TABLE 14.1 **Coefficients for the 4-tap Daubechies low-pass filter.**

h_0	0.4829629131445341
h_1	0.8365163037378079
h_2	0.2241438680420134
h_3	−0.1294095225512604

TABLE 14.2 **Coefficients for the 12-tap Daubechies low-pass filter.**

h_0	0.111540743350
h_1	0.494623890398
h_2	0.751133908021
h_3	0.315250351709
h_4	−0.226264693965
h_5	−0.129766867567
h_6	0.097501605587
h_7	0.027522865530
h_8	−0.031582039318
h_9	0.000553842201
h_{10}	0.004777257511
h_{11}	−0.001077301085

In this section we list different wavelets and their corresponding filters. You are encouraged to experiment with these to find those best suited to your application.

The 4-tap, 12-tap, and 20-tap Daubechies filters are shown in Tables 14.1–14.3. The 6-tap, 12-tap, and 18-tap Coiflet filters are shown in Tables 14.4–14.6.

14.6 Image Compression

One of the most popular applications of wavelets has been to image compression. The JPEG 2000 standard, which is designed to update and replace the current JPEG standard, will use wavelets instead of the DCT to perform decomposition of the image. During our discussion we have always referred to the signal to be decomposed as a one-dimensional signal; however, images are two-dimensional signals. There are two approaches to the subband decomposition of two-dimensional signals: using two-dimensional filters, or using separable transforms that can be implemented using one-dimensional filters on the rows first and then on the columns (or vice versa). Most approaches, including the JPEG 2000 verification model, use the second approach.

In Figure 14.10 we show how an image can be decomposed using subband decomposition. We begin with an $N \times M$ image. We filter each row and then downsample to obtain two $N \times \frac{M}{2}$ images. We then filter each column and subsample the filter output to obtain four $\frac{N}{2} \times \frac{M}{2}$ images. Of the four subimages, the one obtained by low-pass filtering the rows and columns is referred to as the LL image; the one obtained by low-pass filtering the rows and

TABLE 14.3 Coefficients for the 20-tap Daubechies low-pass filter.

h_0	0.026670057901
h_1	0.188176800078
h_2	0.527201188932
h_3	0.688459039454
h_4	0.281172343661
h_5	−0.249846424327
h_6	−0.195946274377
h_7	0.127369340336
h_8	0.093057364604
h_9	−0.071394147166
h_{10}	−0.029457536822
h_{11}	0.033212674059
h_{12}	0.003606553567
h_{13}	−0.010733175483
h_{14}	0.001395351747
h_{15}	0.001992405295
h_{16}	−0.000685856695
h_{17}	−0.000116466855
h_{18}	0.000093588670
h_{19}	−0.000013264203

TABLE 14.4 Coefficients for the 6-tap Coiflet low-pass filter.

h_0	−0.051429728471
h_1	0.238929728471
h_2	0.602859456942
h_3	0.272140543058
h_4	−0.051429972847
h_5	−0.011070271529

TABLE 14.5 Coefficients for the 12-tap Coiflet low-pass filter.

h_0	0.011587596739
h_1	−0.029320137980
h_2	−0.047639590310
h_3	0.273021046535
h_4	0.574682393857
h_5	0.294867193696
h_6	−0.054085607092
h_7	−0.042026480461
h_8	0.016744410163
h_9	0.003967883613
h_{10}	−0.001289203356
h_{11}	−0.000509505539

TABLE 14.6   Coefficients for the 18-tap Coiflet low-pass filter.

h_0	−0.002682418671
h_1	0.005503126709
h_2	0.016583560479
h_3	−0.046507764479
h_4	−0.043220763560
h_5	0.286503335274
h_6	0.561285256870
h_7	0.302983571773
h_8	−0.050770140755
h_9	−0.058196250762
h_{10}	0.024434094321
h_{11}	0.011229240962
h_{12}	−0.006369601011
h_{13}	−0.001820458916
h_{14}	0.000790205101
h_{15}	0.000329665174
h_{16}	−0.000050192775
h_{17}	−0.000024465734

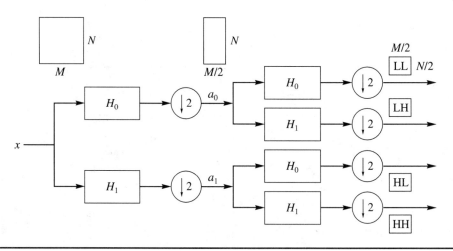

FIGURE 14.10   Subband decomposition of an $N \times M$ image.

FIGURE 14.11   First-level decomposition.

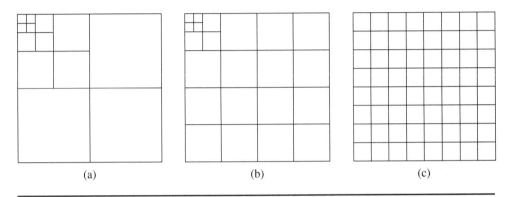

(a)   (b)   (c)

FIGURE 14.12   Three popular subband structures.

high-pass filtering the columns is referred to as the LH image; the one obtained by high-pass filtering the rows and low-pass filtering the columns is called the HL image; and the subimage obtained by high-pass filtering the rows and columns is referred to as the HH image. This decomposition is sometimes represented as shown in Figure 14.11. Each of the subimages obtained in this fashion can then be filtered and subsampled to obtain four more subimages. This process can be continued until the desired subband structure is obtained. Three popular structures are shown in Figure 14.12. In the structure in Figure 14.12a, the LL subimage has been decomposed after each decomposition into four more subimages, resulting in a total of 10 subimages. This is one of the more popular decompositions.

Example 14.6.1:

Let's use the Daubechies wavelet filter to repeat what we did in Examples 13.12.2 and 13.12.3 using the Johnston and the Smith-Barnwell filters. If we use the 4-tap Daubechies filter, we obtain the decomposition shown in Figure 14.13. Notice that even though we are only using a 4-tap filter, we get results comparable to the 16-tap Johnston filter and the 8-tap Smith-Barnwell filters.

If we now encode this image at the rate of 0.5 bits per pixel, we get the reconstructed image shown in Figure 14.14. Notice that the quality is comparable to that obtained using filters requiring two or four times as much computation.

FIGURE   14.13   Decomposition of Sinan image using the four-tap Daubechies filter.

FIGURE   14.14   Reconstruction of Sinan image encoded using 0.5 bits per pixel and
                            the four-tap Daubechies filter.   ◆

In this example we used a simple scalar quantizer for quantization of the coefficients. However, if we use strategies that are motivated by the properties of the coefficients themselves, we can obtain significant performance improvements. In the next sections we examine two popular quantization strategies developed specifically for wavelets.

14.7 Embedded Zerotree Coder

The embedded zerotree wavelet (EZW) coder was introduced by Shapiro [212]. It is a quantization and coding strategy that incorporates some characteristics of the wavelet decomposition. Just as the quantization and coding approach used in the JPEG standard, which were motivated by the characteristics of the coefficients, were superior to the generic zonal coding algorithms, the EZW approach and its descendants significantly outperform some of the generic approaches. The particular characteristic used by the EZW algorithm is that there are wavelet coefficients in different subbands that represent the same spatial location in the image. If the decomposition is such that the size of the different subbands is different (the first two decompositions in Figure 14.12), then a single coefficient in the smaller subband may represent the same spatial location as multiple coefficients in the other subbands.

In order to put our discussion on more solid ground, consider the 10-band decomposition shown in Figure 14.15. The coefficient a in the upper-left corner of band I represents the same spatial location as coefficients a_1 in band II, a_2 in band III, and a_3 in band IV. In turn, the coefficient a_1 represents the same spatial location as coefficients a_{11}, a_{12}, a_{13}, and a_{14} in band V. Each of these pixels represents the same spatial location as four pixels in band VIII, and so on. In fact, we can visualize the relationships of these coefficients in the form of a tree: The coefficient a forms the root of the tree with three descendants a_1, a_2, and a_3. The coefficient a_1 has descendants a_{11}, a_{12}, a_{13}, and a_{14}. The coefficient a_2 has descendants $a_{21}, a_{22}, a_{23}, a_{24}$, and the coefficient a_3 has descendants a_{31}, a_{32}, a_{33}, and a_{34}. Each of these coefficients in turn has four descendants, making a total of 64 coefficients in this tree. A pictorial representation of the tree is shown in Figure 14.16.

Recall that when natural images are decomposed in this manner most of the energy is compacted into the lower bands. Thus, in many cases the coefficients closer to the root of the tree have higher magnitudes than coefficients further away from the root. This means that often if a coefficient has a magnitude less than a given threshold, all its descendants will have magnitudes less than that threshold. In a scalar quantizer, the outer levels of the quantizer correspond to larger magnitudes. Consider the 3-bit quantizer shown in Figure 14.17. If we determine that all coefficients arising from a particular root have magnitudes smaller than T_0 and we inform the decoder of this situation, then for all coefficients in that tree we need only use 2 bits per sample, while getting the same performance as we would have obtained using the 3-bit quantizer. If the binary coding scheme used in Figure 14.17 is used, in which the first bit is the sign bit and the next bit is the most significant bit of the magnitude, then the information that a set of coefficients has value less than T_0 is the same as saying that the most significant bit of the magnitude is 0. If there are N coefficients in the tree, this is a savings of N bits minus however many bits are needed to inform the decoder of this situation.

Before we describe the EZW algorithm, we need to introduce some terminology. Given a threshold T, if a given coefficient has a magnitude greater than T, it is called a *significant*

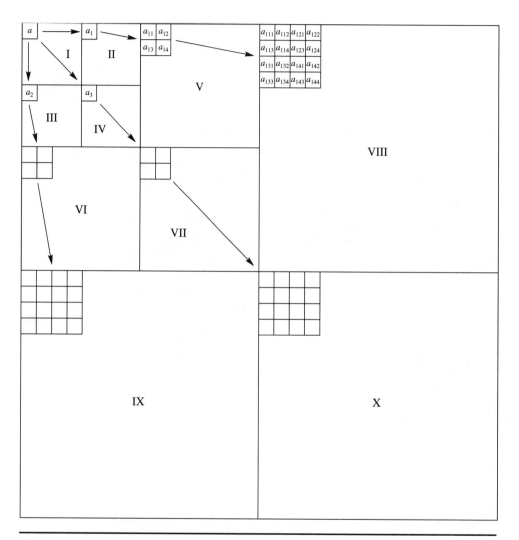

FIGURE 14.15   A 10-band wavelet decomposition.

coefficient at level T. If the magnitude of the coefficient is less than T (it is insignificant), and all its descendants have magnitudes less than T, then the coefficient is called a *zerotree root*. Finally, it might happen that the coefficient itself is less than T but some of its descendants have a value greater than T. Such a coefficient is called an *isolated zero*.

The EZW algorithm is a multiple-pass algorithm, with each pass consisting of two steps: *significance map encoding* or the *dominant pass*, and *refinement* or the *subordinate pass*. If $c_{\max}$ is the value of the largest coefficient, the initial value of the threshold T_0 is given by

$$T_0 = 2^{\lfloor \log_2 c_{\max} \rfloor}.$$

(14.91)

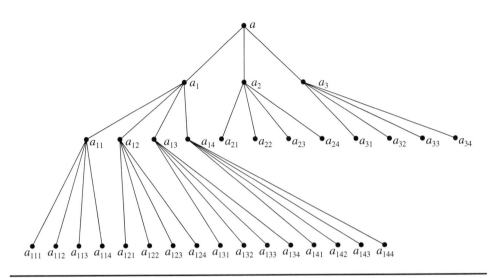

FIGURE 14.16 Data structure used in the EZW coder.

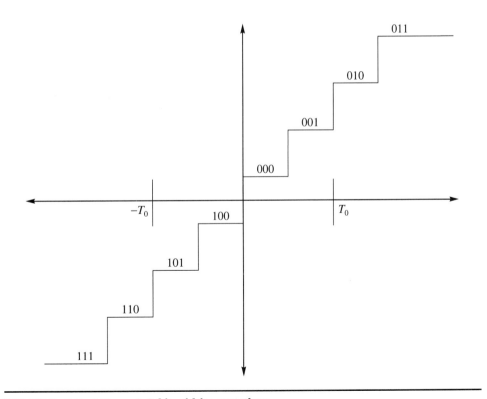

FIGURE 14.17 A 3-bit midrise quantizer.

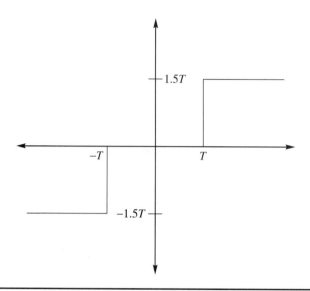

FIGURE 1 4 . 1 8   A three-level midtread quantizer.

This selection guarantees that the largest coefficient will lie in the interval $[T_0, 2T_0)$. In each pass, the threshold T_i is reduced to half the value it had in the previous pass:

$$T_i = \frac{1}{2}T_{i-1}. \tag{14.92}$$

For a given value of T_i, we assign one of four possible labels to the coefficients: *significant positive (sp), significant negative (sn), zerotree root (zr),* and *isolated zero (iz).* If we used a fixed-length code, we would need 2 bits to represent each of the labels. Note that when a coefficient has been labeled a zerotree root, we do not need to label its descendants. This assignment is referred to as *significance map coding.*

We can view the significance map coding in part as quantization using a three-level midtread quantizer. This situation is shown in Figure 14.18. The coefficients labeled *significant* are simply those that fall in the outer levels of the quantizer and are assigned an initial reconstructed value of $1.5T_i$ or $-1.5T_i$, depending on whether the coefficient is positive or negative. Note that selecting T_i according to (14.91) and (14.92) guarantees the significant co-efficients will lie in the interval $[T, 2T)$. Once a determination of significance has been made, the significant coefficients are included in a list for further refinement in the refinement or subordinate passes. In the refinement pass, we determine whether the coefficient lies in the upper or lower half of the interval $[T, 2T)$. In successive refinement passes, as the value of T is reduced, the interval containing the significant coefficient is narrowed still further and the reconstruction is updated accordingly. An easy way to perform the refinement is to take the difference between the coefficient value and its reconstruction and quantize it using a two-level quantizer with reconstruction values $\pm T/4$. This quantized value is then added on to the current reconstruction value as a correction term.

The wavelet coefficients that have not been previously determined significant are scanned in the manner depicted in Figure 14.19, with each parent node in a tree scanned before its

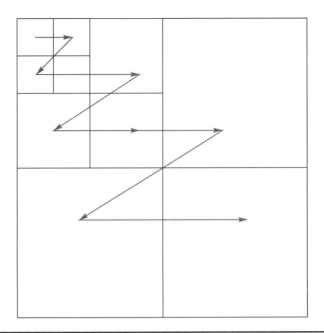

FIGURE 14.19 **Scanning of wavelet coefficients for encoding using the EZW algorithm.**

offspring. This makes sense because if the parent is determined to be a zerotree root, we would not need to encode the offspring.

Although this may sound confusing, in order to see how simple the encoding procedure actually is, let's use an example.

Example 14.7.1:

Let's use the seven-level decomposition shown below to demonstrate the various steps of EZW:

26	6	13	10
−7	7	6	4
4	−4	4	−3
2	−2	−2	0

To obtain the initial threshold value T_0, we find the maximum magnitude coefficient, which in this case is 26. Then

$$T_0 = 2^{\lfloor \log_2 26 \rfloor} = 16.$$

Comparing the coefficients against 16, we find 26 is greater than 16 so we send sp. The next coefficient in the scan is 6, which is less than 16. Furthermore, its descendants (13, 10, 6, and 4) are all less than 16. Therefore, 6 is a zerotree root, and we encode this entire set with the label zr. The next coefficient in the scan is −7, which is also a zerotree root, as is 7, the final element in the scan. We do not need to encode the rest of the coefficients separately because they have already been encoded as part of the various zerotrees. The sequence of labels to be transmitted at this point is

$$sp \quad zr \quad zr \quad zr$$

Since each label requires 2 bits (for fixed-length encoding), we have used up 8 bits from our bit budget. The only significant coefficient in this pass is the coefficient with a value of 26. We include this coefficient in our list to be refined in the subordinate pass. Calling the subordinate list L_S, we have

$$L_S = \{26\}.$$

The reconstructed value of this coefficient is $1.5T_0 = 24$, and the reconstructed bands look like this:

24	0	0	0
0	0	0	0
0	0	0	0
0	0	0	0

The next step is the subordinate pass, in which we obtain a correction term for the reconstruction value of the significant coefficients. In this case, the list L_S contains only one element. The difference between this element and its reconstructed value is $26 - 24 = 2$. Quantizing this with a two-level quantizer with reconstruction levels $\pm T_0/4$, we obtain a correction term of 4. Thus, the reconstruction becomes $24 + 4 = 28$. Transmitting the correction term costs a single bit, therefore at the end of the first pass we have used up 9 bits. Using only these 9 bits, we would obtain the following reconstruction:

28	0	0	0
0	0	0	0
0	0	0	0
0	0	0	0

We now reduce the value of the threshold by a factor of two and repeat the process. The value of T_1 is 8. We rescan the coefficients that have not yet been deemed significant. To emphasize the fact that we do not consider the coefficients that have been deemed significant in the previous pass, we replace them with $\star$:

$\star$	6	13	10
-7	7	6	4
4	-4	4	-3
2	-2	-2	0

The first coefficient we encounter has a value of 6. This is less than the threshold value of 8; however, the descendants of this coefficient include coefficients with values of 13 and 10. Therefore, this coefficient cannot be classified as a zerotree root. This is an example of what we defined as an isolated zero. The next two coefficients in the scan are -7 and 7. Both of these coefficients have magnitudes less than the threshold value of 8. Furthermore, all their descendants also have magnitudes less than 8. Therefore, these two coefficients are coded as *zr*. The next two elements in the scan are 13 and 10, which are both coded as *sp*. The final two elements in the scan are 6 and 4. These are both less than the threshold, but they do not have any descendants. We code these coefficients as *iz*. Thus, this dominant pass is coded as

$$iz \ zr \ zr \ sp \ sp \ iz \ iz$$

which requires 14 bits, bringing the total number of bits used to 23. The significant coefficients are reconstructed with values $1.5T_1 = 12$. Thus, the reconstruction at this point is

28	0	12	12
0	0	0	0
0	0	0	0
0	0	0	0

We add the new significant coefficients to the subordinate list:

$$L_S = \{26, 13, 10\}.$$

In the subordinate pass, we take the difference between the coefficients and their reconstructions and quantize these to obtain the correction or refinement values for these coefficients. The possible values for the correction terms are $\pm T_1/4 = \pm 2$:

$$26 - 28 = -2 \Rightarrow \text{Correction term} = -2$$
$$13 - 12 = 1 \Rightarrow \text{Correction term} = 2 \qquad (14.93)$$
$$10 - 12 = -2 \Rightarrow \text{Correction term} = -2$$

Each correction requires a single bit, bringing the total number of bits used to 26. With these corrections, the reconstruction at this stage is

26	0	14	10
0	0	0	0
0	0	0	0
0	0	0	0

If we go through one more pass, we reduce the threshold value to 4. The coefficients to be scanned are

$\star$	6	$\star$	$\star$
-7	7	6	4
4	-4	4	-3
2	-2	-2	0

The dominant pass results in the following coded sequence:

$$sp \ sn \ sp \ sp \ sp \ sp \ sn \ iz \ iz \ sp \ iz \ iz \ iz$$

This pass cost 26 bits, equal to the total number of bits used previous to this pass. The reconstruction upon decoding of the dominant pass is

26	6	14	10
−6	6	6	6
6	−6	6	0
0	0	0	0

The subordinate list is

$$L_S = \{26, 13, 10, 6, -7, 7, 6, 4, 4, -4, 4\}$$

By now it should be reasonably clear how the algorithm works. We continue encoding until we have exhausted our bit budget or until some other criterion is satisfied.   ◆

There are several observations we can make from this example. Notice that the encoding process is geared to provide the most bang for the bit at each step. At each step the bits are used to provide the maximum reduction in the reconstruction error. If at any time the encoding is interrupted, the reconstruction using this (interrupted) encoding is the best that the algorithm could have provided using this many bits. The encoding improves as more bits are transmitted. This form of coding is called *embedded coding*. In order to enhance this aspect of the algorithm, we can also sort the subordinate list at the end of each pass using information available to both encoder and decoder. This would increase the likelihood of larger coefficients being encoded first, thus providing for a greater reduction in the reconstruction error.

Finally, in the example we determined the number of bits used by assuming fixed-length encoding. In practice, arithmetic coding is used, providing a further reduction in rate.

14.8 Set Partitioning in Hierarchical Trees

The SPIHT (Set Partitioning in Hierarchical Trees) algorithm is a generalization of the EZW algorithm and was proposed by Amir Said and William Pearlman [199]. Recall that in EZW we transmit a lot of information for little cost when we declare an entire subtree to be insignificant and represent all the coefficients in it with a zerotree root label zr. The SPIHT algorithm uses a partitioning of the trees (which in SPIHT are called *spatial orientation trees*) in a manner that tends to keep insignificant coefficients together in larger subsets. The partitioning decisions are binary decisions that are transmitted to the decoder, providing a significance map encoding that is more efficient than EZW. In fact, the efficiency of the significance map encoding in SPIHT is such that arithmetic coding of the binary decisions provides very little gain. The thresholds used for checking significance are powers of two, so in essence the SPIHT algorithm sends the binary representation of the integer value of the wavelet coefficients. As in EZW, the significance map encoding, or set partitioning and ordering step, is followed by a refinement step in which the representations of the significant coefficients are refined.

Let's briefly describe the algorithm and then look at some examples of its operation. However, before we do that we need to get familiar with some notation. The data structure used by the SPIHT algorithm is similar to that used by the EZW algorithm—although not the same. The wavelet coefficients are again divided into trees originating from the lowest resolution

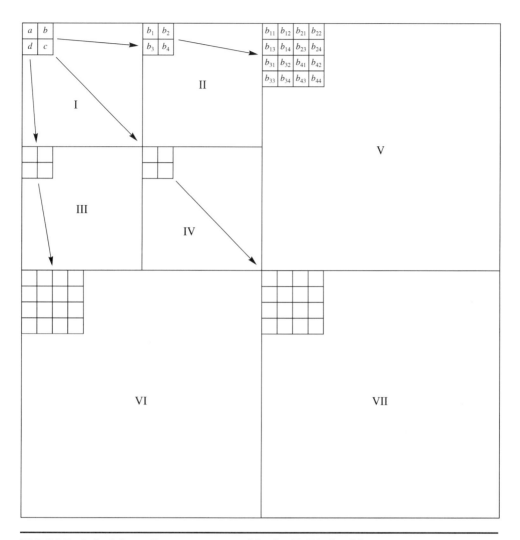

FIGURE 14.20   Data structure used in the SPIHT algorithm.

band (band I in our case). The coefficients are grouped into 2×2 arrays that, except for the coefficients in band I, are offsprings of a coefficient of a lower resolution band. The coefficients in the lowest resolution band are also divided into 2×2 arrays. However, unlike the EZW case, all but one of them are root nodes. The coefficient in the top-left corner of the array does not have any offsprings. The data structure is shown pictorially in Figure 14.20 for a seven-band decomposition.

The trees are further partitioned into four types of sets, which are sets of coordinates of the coefficients:

- $\mathcal{O}(i,j)$ This is the set of coordinates of the offsprings of the wavelet coefficient at location (i,j). As each node can either have four offsprings or none, the size of $\mathcal{O}(i,j)$ is either zero or four. For example, in Figure 14.20 the set $\mathcal{O}(0,1)$ consists of the coordinates of the coefficients b_1, b_2, b_3, and b_4.

- $\mathcal{D}(i,j)$ This is the set of all descendants of the coefficient at location (i,j). Descendants include the offsprings, the offsprings of the offsprings, and so on. For example, in Figure 14.20 the set $\mathcal{D}(0,1)$ consists of the coordinates of the coefficients $b_1, \ldots, b_4, b_{11}$, $\ldots, b_{14}, \ldots, b_{44}$. Because the number of offsprings can either be zero or four, the size of $\mathcal{D}(i,j)$ is either zero or a sum of powers of four.

- $\mathcal{H}$ This is the set of all root nodes—essentially band I in the case of Figure 14.20.

- $\mathcal{L}(i,j)$ This is the set of coordinates of all the descendants of the coefficient at location (i,j) except for the immediate offsprings of the coefficient at location (i,j). In other words,

$$\mathcal{L}(i,j) = \mathcal{D}(i,j) - \mathcal{O}(i,j).$$

In Figure 14.20 the set $\mathcal{L}(0,1)$ consists of the coordinates of the coefficients $b_{11}, \ldots, b_{14}, \ldots, b_{44}$.

A set $\mathcal{D}(i,j)$ or $\mathcal{L}(i,j)$ is said to be significant if any coefficient in the set has a magnitude greater than the threshold. Finally, thresholds used for checking significance are powers of two, so in essence the SPIHT algorithm sends the binary representation of the integer value of the wavelet coefficients. The bits are numbered with the least significant bit being the zeroth bit, the next bit being the first significant bit, and the kth bit being referred to as the $k-1$ most significant bit.

With these definitions under our belt, let us now describe the algorithm. The algorithm makes use of three lists: the *list of insignificant pixels* (LIP), the *list of significant pixels* (LSP), and the *list of insignificant sets* (LIS). The LSP and LIP lists will contain the coordinates of coefficients, while the LIS will contain the coordinates of the roots of sets of type $\mathcal{D}$ or $\mathcal{L}$. We start by determining the initial value of the threshold. We do this by calculating

$$n = \lfloor \log_2 c_{\max} \rfloor$$

where $c_{\max}$ is the maximum magnitude of the coefficients to be encoded. The LIP list is initialized with the set $\mathcal{H}$. Those elements of $\mathcal{H}$ that have descendants are also placed in LIS as type $\mathcal{D}$ entries. The LSP list is initially empty.

In each pass, we will first process the members of LIP, then the members of LIS. This is essentially the significance map encoding step. We then process the elements of LSP in the refinement step.

We begin by examining each coordinate contained in LIP. If the coefficient at that coordinate is significant (that is, it is greater than 2^n), we transmit a 1 followed by a bit representing the sign of the coefficient (we will assume 1 for positive, 0 for negative). We then move that coefficient to the LSP list. If the coefficient at that coordinate is not significant, we transmit a 0.

After examining each coordinate in LIP, we begin examining the sets in LIS. If the set at coordinate (i,j) is not significant, we transmit a 0. If the set is significant, we transmit a 1. What we do after that depends on whether the set is of type $\mathcal{D}$ or $\mathcal{L}$.

If the set is of type $\mathcal{D}$, we check each of the offsprings of the coefficient at that coordinate. In other words, we check the four coefficients whose coordinates are in $\mathcal{O}(i,j)$. For each coefficient that is significant, we transmit a 1, the sign of the coefficient, and then move the coefficient to the LSP. For the rest we transmit a 0 and add their coordinates to the LIP. Now that we have removed the coordinates of $\mathcal{O}(i,j)$ from the set, what is left is simply the set $\mathcal{L}(i,j)$. If this set is not empty, we move it to the end of the LIS and mark it to be of type $\mathcal{L}$. Note that this new entry into the LIS has to be examined during *this* pass. If the set is empty, we remove the coordinate (i,j) from the list.

If the set is of type $\mathcal{L}$, we add each coordinate in $\mathcal{O}(i,j)$ to the end of the LIS as the root of a set of type $\mathcal{D}$. Again, note that these new entries in the LIS have to be examined during this pass. We then remove (i,j) from the LIS.

Once we have processed each of the sets in the LIS (including the newly formed ones), we proceed to the refinement step. In the refinement step we examine each coefficient that was in the LSP *prior to the current pass* and output the nth most significant bit of $|c_{i,j}|$. We ignore the coefficients that have been added to the list in this pass because, by declaring them significant at this particular level, we have already informed the decoder of the value of the nth most significant bit.

This completes one pass. Depending on the availability of more bits or external factors, if we decide to continue with the coding process, we decrement n by one and continue. Let's see the functioning of this algorithm on an example.

Example 14.8.1:

Let's use the same example we used for demonstrating the EZW algorithm:

26	6	13	10
−7	7	6	4
4	−4	4	−3
2	−2	−2	0

We will go through three passes at the encoder and generate the transmitted bitstream, then decode this bitstream.

First Pass: The value for n in this case is 4. The three lists at the encoder are

$$\text{LIP: } \{(0,0) \to 26, (0,1) \to 6, (1,0) \to -7, (1,1) \to 7\}$$
$$\text{LIS: } \{(0,1)\mathcal{D}, (1,0)\mathcal{D}, (1,1)\mathcal{D}\}$$
$$\text{LSP: } \{\}$$

In the listing for LIP, we have included the $\to \#$ to make it easier to follow the example. Beginning our algorithm, we examine the contents of LIP. The coefficient at location $(0,1)$ is greater than 16. In other words, it is significant; therefore, we transmit a 1, then a 0 to indicate the coefficient is positive and move the coordinate to LSP. The next three coefficients are all insignificant at this value of the threshold; therefore, we transmit a 0 for each coefficient and leave them in LIP. The next step is to examine the contents of LIS. Looking at the descendants of the coefficient at location $(0, 1)$ (13, 10, 6, and 4), we see that none of them are significant at this value of the threshold so we transmit a 0. Looking at the descendants of c_{10} and c_{11}, we can see that none of these are significant at this value of the threshold. Therefore, we transmit a 0 for each set. As this is the first pass, there are no elements from the previous pass in LSP; therefore, we do not do anything in the refinement pass. We have transmitted a total of 8 bits at the end of this pass (10000000), and the situation of the three lists is as follows:

$$\text{LIP: } \{(0, 1) \rightarrow 6, (1, 0) \rightarrow -7, (1, 1) \rightarrow 7\}$$
$$\text{LIS: } \{(0, 1)\mathcal{D}, (1, 0)\mathcal{D}, (1, 1)\mathcal{D}\}$$
$$\text{LSP: } \{(0, 0) \rightarrow 26\}$$

Second Pass: For the second pass we decrement n by 1 to 3, which corresponds to a threshold value of 8. Again, we begin our pass by examining the contents of LIP. There are three elements in LIP. Each is insignificant at this threshold so we transmit three 0s. The next step is to examine the contents of LIS. The first element of LIS is the set containing the descendants of the coefficient at location $(0, 1)$. Of this set, both 13 and 10 are significant at this value of the threshold; in other words, the set $\mathcal{D}(0, 1)$ is significant. We signal this by sending a 1 and examine the offsprings of c_{01}. The first offspring has a value of 13, which is significant and positive, so we send a 1 followed by a 0. The same is true for the second offspring, which has a value of 10. So we send another 1 followed by a 0. We move the coordinates of these two to the LSP. The next two offsprings are both insignificant at this level; therefore, we move these to LIP and transmit a 0 for each. As $\mathcal{L}(0, 1) = \{\}$, we remove $(0, 1)\mathcal{D}$ from LIS. Looking at the other elements of LIS, we can clearly see that both of these are insignificant at this level; therefore, we send a 0 for each. In the refinement pass we examine the contents of LSP from the previous pass. There is only one element in there that is not from the current sorting pass, and it has a value of 26. The third MSB of 26 is 1; therefore, we transmit a 1 and complete this pass. In the second pass we have transmitted 13 bits: 0001101000001. The condition of the lists at the end of the second pass is as follows:

$$\text{LIP: } \{(0, 1) \rightarrow 6, (1, 0) \rightarrow -7, (1, 1) \rightarrow 7(1, 2) \rightarrow 6, (1, 3) \rightarrow 4\}$$
$$\text{LIS: } \{(1, 0)\mathcal{D}, (1, 1)\mathcal{D}\}$$
$$\text{LSP: } \{(0, 0) \rightarrow 26, (0, 2) \rightarrow 13, (0, 3) \rightarrow 10\}$$

Third Pass: The third pass proceeds with $n = 2$. As the threshold is now smaller, there are significantly more coefficients that are deemed significant, and we end up sending 26 bits. You can easily verify for yourself that the transmitted bitstream for the third pass is 10111010101101100110000010. The condition of the lists at the end of the third pass is as follows:

$$\text{LIP: } \{(3, 0) \rightarrow 2, (3, 1) \rightarrow -2, (2, 3) \rightarrow -3, (3, 2) \rightarrow -2, (3, 3) \rightarrow 0\}$$
$$\text{LIS: } \{\}$$
$$\text{LSP: } \{(0, 0) \rightarrow 26, (0, 2) \rightarrow 13, (0, 3) \rightarrow 10, (0, 1) \rightarrow 6, (1, 0) \rightarrow -7, (1, 1) \rightarrow 7,$$
$$(1, 2) \rightarrow 6, (1, 3) \rightarrow 4(2, 0) \rightarrow 4, (2, 1) \rightarrow -4, (2, 2) \rightarrow 4\}$$

Now for decoding this sequence. At the decoder we also start out with the same lists as the encoder:

$$\text{LIP: } \{(0,0), (0,1), (1,0), (1,1)\}$$
$$\text{LIS: } \{(0,1)\mathcal{D}, (1,0)\mathcal{D}, (1,1)\mathcal{D}\}$$
$$\text{LSP: } \{\}$$

We assume that the initial value of n is transmitted to the decoder. This allows us to set the threshold value at 16. Upon receiving the results of the first pass (10000000), we can see that the first element of LIP is significant and positive and no other coefficient is significant at this level. Using the same reconstruction procedure as in EZW, we can reconstruct the coefficients at this stage as

24	0	0	0
0	0	0	0
0	0	0	0
0	0	0	0

and, following the same procedure as at the encoder, the lists can be updated as

$$\text{LIP: } \{(0,1), (1,0), (1,1)\}$$
$$\text{LIS: } \{(0,1)\mathcal{D}, (1,0)\mathcal{D}, (1,1)\mathcal{D}\}$$
$$\text{LSP: } \{(0,0)\}$$

For the second pass we decrement n by one and examine the transmitted bitstream: 0001101000001. Since the first 3 bits are 0 and there are only three entries in LIP, all the entries in LIP are still insignificant. The next 9 bits give us information about the sets in LIS. The fourth bit of the received bitstream is 1. This means that the set with root at coordinate $(0,1)$ is significant. Since this set is of type $\mathcal{D}$, the next bits relate to its offsprings. The 101000 sequence indicates that the first two offsprings are significant at this level and positive and the last two are insignificant. Therefore, we move the first two offsprings to LSP and the last two to LIP. We can also approximate these two significant coefficients in our reconstruction by $1.5 \times 2^3 = 12$. We also remove $(0,1)\mathcal{D}$ from LIS. The next two bits are both 0, indicating that the two remaining sets are still insignificant. The final bit corresponds to the refinement pass. It is a 1, so we update the reconstruction of the $(0,0)$ coefficient to $24 + 8/2 = 28$. The reconstruction at this stage is

28	0	12	12
0	0	0	0
0	0	0	0
0	0	0	0

and the lists are as follows:

$$\text{LIP: } \{(0,1), (1,0), (1,1), (1,2), (1,3)\}$$
$$\text{LIS: } \{(1,0)\mathcal{D}, (1,1)\mathcal{D}\}$$
$$\text{LSP: } \{(0,0), (0,2), (0,3)\}$$

For the third pass we again decrement n, which is now 2, giving a threshold value of 4. Decoding the bitstream generated during the third pass (1011101010110110011000010), we update our reconstruction to

26	6	14	10
−6	6	6	6
6	−6	6	0
0	0	0	0

and our lists become

LIP: $\{3,0),(3,1)\}$

LIS: $\{\}$

LSP: $\{(0,0),(0,2),(0,3),(0,1),(1,0),(1,1),(1,2),(2,0),(2,1),(3,2)\}$

At this stage we do not have any sets left in LIS and we simply update the values of the coefficients.   ◆

Finally, let's look at an example of an image coded using SPIHT. The image shown in Figure 14.21 is the reconstruction obtained from a compressed representation that used 0.5 bits per pixel. (The programs used to generate this image were obtained from the following website: *http://ipl.rpi.edu/SPIHT*.) Comparing this with Figure 14.14, we can see a definite improvement in the quality.

Wavelet decomposition has been finding its way into various standards. The earliest example was the FBI fingerprint image compression standard. The latest is the new image compression being developed by the JPEG committee, commonly referred to as JPEG 2000. We take a brief look at the current status of JPEG 2000.

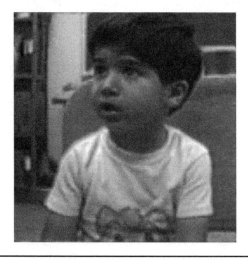

FIGURE 14.21   **Reconstruction of Sinan image encoded using SPIHT at 0.5 bits per pixel.**

14.9 JPEG 2000

The current JPEG standard provides excellent performance at rates above 0.25 bits per pixel. However, at lower rates there is a sharp degradation in the quality of the reconstructed image. To correct this and other shortcomings, the JPEG committee initiated work on another standard, commonly known as JPEG 2000. While there is much about JPEG 2000 that is yet to be determined, there are some aspects that are relatively certain. One is that the standard will be based on wavelet decomposition.

There are actually two types of wavelet filters that are included in the standard. One type is the wavelet filters we have been discussing in this chapter. Another type consists of filters that generate integer coefficients; this type is particularly useful when the wavelet decomposition is part of a lossless compression scheme.

The coding scheme being considered by the JPEG committee is based on a scheme, originally proposed by Taubman [224] and Taubman and Zakhor [225], known as EBCOT. The acronym EBCOT stands for "Embedded Block Coding with Optimized Truncation," which nicely summarizes the technique. It is a block coding scheme that generates an embedded bitstream. The block coding is independently performed on nonoverlapping blocks within individual subbands. Within a subband all blocks that do not lie on the right or lower boundaries are required to have the same dimensions. A dimension cannot exceed 256.

Embedding and independent block coding seem inherently contradictory. The way EBCOT resolves this contradiction is to organize the bitstream in a succession of layers. Each layer corresponds to a certain distortion level. Within each layer each block is coded with a variable number of bits (which could be zero). The partitioning of bits between blocks is obtained using a Lagrangian optimization that dictates the partitioning or truncation points. The quality of the reproduction is proportional to the numbers of layers received.

The embedded coding scheme is similar in philosophy to the EZW and SPIHT algorithms; however, the data structures used are different. The EZW and SPIHT algorithms used trees of coefficients from the same spatial location across different bands. In the case of the EBCOT algorithm, each block resides entirely within a subband, and each block is coded independently of other blocks, which precludes the use of trees of the type used by EZW and SPIHT. Instead, the EBCOT algorithm uses a quadtree data structure. At the lowest level, we have a 2×2 set of blocks of coefficients. These are, in turn, organized into sets of 2×2 *quads*, and so on. A node in this tree is said to be significant at level n if any of its descendants are significant at that level. A coefficient c_{ij} is said to be significant at level n if $|c_{ij}| \geq 2^n$. As in the case of EZW and SPIHT, the algorithm makes multiple passes, including significance map encoding passes and a magnitude refinement pass. The bits generated during these procedures are encoded using arithmetic coding.

14.10 Summary

In this chapter we have introduced the concepts of wavelets and multiresolution analysis, and we have seen how we can use wavelets to provide an efficient decomposition of signals prior to compression. We have also described several compression techniques based on wavelet decomposition. Wavelets and their applications are currently areas of intensive research.

Further Reading

1. There are a number of excellent introductory books on wavelets. The one I found most accessible was *Introduction to Wavelets and Wavelet Transforms—A Primer*, by C.S. Burrus, R.A. Gopinath, and H. Guo [33].

2. Probably the best mathematical source on wavelets is the book *Ten Lectures on Wavelets*, by I. Daubechies [58].

3. There are a number of tutorials on wavelets available on the Internet. The best source for all matters related to wavelets (and more) on the Internet is "The Wavelet Digest" (*http://www.wavelet.org*). This site includes pointers to many other interesting and useful sites dealing with different applications of wavelets.

14.11 Projects and Problems

1. In this problem we consider the boundary effects encountered when using the short-term Fourier transform. Given the signal

$$f(t) = \sin(2t)$$

(a) Find the Fourier transform $F(\omega)$ of $f(t)$.

(b) Find the STFT $F_1(\omega)$ of $f(t)$ using a rectangular window

$$g(t) = \begin{cases} 1 & -2 \le t \le 2 \\ 0 & \text{otherwise} \end{cases}$$

for the interval $[-2, 2]$.

(c) Find the STFT $F_2(\omega)$ of $f(t)$ using a window

$$g(t) = \begin{cases} 1 + \cos(\frac{\pi}{2}t) & -2 \le t \le 2 \\ 0 & \text{otherwise.} \end{cases}$$

(d) Plot $|F(\omega)|$, $|F_1(\omega)|$, and $|F_2(\omega)|$. Comment on the effect of using different window functions.

2. For the function

$$f(t) = \begin{cases} 1 + \sin(2t) & 0 \le t \le 1 \\ \sin(2t) & \text{otherwise} \end{cases}$$

using the Haar wavelet find and plot the coefficients $\{c_{j,k}\}, j = 0, 1, 2; k = 0, \ldots, 10$.

3. For the seven-level decomposition shown below:

21	6	15	12
−6	3	6	3
3	−3	0	−3
3	0	0	0

(a) Find the bitstream generated by the EZW coder.

(b) Decode the bitstream generated in the previous step. Verify that you get the original coefficient values.

4. Using the coefficients from the seven-level decomposition in the previous problem:

(a) Find the bitstream generated by the SPIHT coder.

(b) Decode the bitstream generated in the previous step. Verify that you get the original coefficient values.

15

Analysis/Synthesis Schemes

15.1 Overview

nalysis/synthesis schemes rely on the availability of a parametric model of the source output generation. When such a model exists, the transmitter analyzes the source output and extracts the model parameters, which are transmitted to the receiver. The receiver uses the model along with the transmitted parameters to synthesize an approximation to the source output. The difference between this approach and the techniques we have looked at in previous chapters is that what is transmitted is not a direct representation of the samples of the source output; instead, the transmitter informs the receiver how to go about regenerating those outputs. For this approach to work, a good model for the source has to be available. Since good models for speech production exist, this approach has been widely used for the low-rate coding of speech. We describe several different analysis/synthesis techniques for speech compression. In recent years the fractal approach to image compression has been gaining in popularity. Because this approach is also one in which the receiver regenerates the source output using "instructions" from the transmitter, we describe it in this chapter.

15.2 Introduction

In the previous chapters we have presented a number of lossy compression schemes that provide an estimate of each source output value to the receiver. Historically, an earlier approach towards lossy compression is to model the source output and send the model parameters to the source instead of the estimates of the source output. The receiver tries to synthesize the source output based on the received model parameters.

Consider an image transmission system that works as follows. At the transmitter, we have a person who examines the image to be transmitted and comes up with a description of the image. At the receiver, we have another person who then proceeds to create that image. For example, suppose the image we wish to transmit is a picture of a field of sunflowers. Instead of trying to send the picture, we simply send the words "field of sunflowers." The person at the receiver paints a picture of a field of sunflowers on a piece of paper and gives it to the user. Thus, an image of an object is transmitted from the transmitter to the receiver in a highly compressed form. This approach towards compression should be familiar to listeners of sports broadcasts on radio. It requires that both transmitter and receiver work with the same model. In terms of sports broadcasting, this means that the viewer has a mental picture of the sports arena, and both the broadcaster and listener attach the same meaning to the same terminology.

This approach works for sports broadcasting because the source being modeled functions under very restrictive rules. In a basketball game, when the referee calls a dribbling foul, listeners generally don't picture a drooling chicken. If the source violates the rules, the reconstruction would suffer. If the basketball players suddenly decided to put on a ballet performance, the transmitter (sportscaster) would be hard pressed to represent the scene accurately to the receiver. Therefore, it seems that this approach to compression can only be used for artificial activities that function according to man-made rules. Of the sources that we are interested in, only text fits this description, and the rules that govern the generation of text are complex and differ widely from language to language.

Fortunately, while natural sources may not follow man-made rules, they are subject to the laws of physics, which can prove to be quite restrictive. This is particularly true of speech. No matter what language is being spoken, the speech is generated using machinery that is not very different from person to person. Moreover, this machinery has to obey certain physical laws that substantially limit the behavior of outputs. Therefore, speech can be analyzed in terms of a model, and the model parameters can be extracted and transmitted to the receiver. At the receiver the speech can be synthesized using the model. This analysis/synthesis approach was first employed by Homer Dudley at Bell Laboratories, who developed what is known as the channel vocoder (described in the next section). Actually, the synthesis portion had been attempted even earlier by Kempelen Farkas Lovag (1734–1804). He developed a "speaking machine" in which the vocal tract was modeled by a flexible tube whose shape could be modified by an operator. Sound was produced by forcing air through this tube using bellows [62].

Unlike speech, images are generated in a variety of different ways; therefore, the analysis/synthesis approach does not seem very useful for image or video compression. However, if we restrict the class of images to "talking heads" of the type we would encounter in a video-conferencing situation, we might be able to satisfy the conditions required for this approach. When we talk, our facial gestures are restricted by the way our faces are constructed and by the physics of motion. This realization has led to the new field of model-based video coding (see Chapter 16).

A totally different approach to image compression based on the properties of self-similarity is the *fractal coding* approach. While this approach does not explicitly depend on some physical limitations, it fits in with the techniques described in this chapter; that is, what is stored or transmitted is not the samples of the source output, but a method for synthesizing the output. We will study this approach in Section 15.4.1.

FIGURE 15.1   **A model for speech synthesis.**

15.3 Speech Compression

A very simplified model of speech synthesis is shown in Figure 15.1. As we described in Chapter 7, speech is produced by forcing air first through an elastic opening, the vocal cords, and then through the laryngeal, oral, nasal, and pharynx passages, and finally through the mouth and the nasal cavity. Everything past the vocal cords is generally referred to as the vocal tract. The first action generates the sound, which is then modulated into speech as it traverses through the vocal tract.

In Figure 15.1, the excitation source corresponds to the sound generation, and the vocal tract filter models the vocal tract. As we mentioned in Chapter 7, there are several different sound inputs that can be generated by different conformations of the vocal cords and the associated cartilages.

Therefore, in order to generate a specific fragment of speech, we have to generate a sequence of sound inputs or excitation signals and the corresponding sequence of appropriate vocal tract approximations.

At the transmitter, the speech is divided into segments. Each segment is analyzed to determine an excitation signal and the parameters of the vocal tract filter. In some of the schemes, a model for the excitation signal is transmitted to the receiver. The excitation signal is then synthesized at the receiver and used to drive the vocal tract filter. In other schemes, the excitation signal itself is obtained using an analysis-by-synthesis approach. This signal is then used by the vocal tract filter to generate the speech signal.

Over the years many different analysis/synthesis speech compression schemes have been developed, and substantial research into the development of new approaches and the improvement of existing schemes continues. Given the large amount of information, we can only sample some of the more popular approaches in this chapter. See [83, 13, 78, 127] for more detailed coverage and pointers to the vast literature on the subject.

The approaches we will describe in this chapter include *channel vocoders*, which are of special historical interest; the *linear predictive coder*, which is the U.S. Government standard at the rate of 2.4 kbps; *code excited linear prediction* (CELP) based schemes; *sinusoidal coders*, which provide excellent performance at rates of 4.8 kbps and higher and are also a part of several national and international standards; and *mixed excitation linear prediction*, which is to be the new 2.4 kbps federal standard speech coder. In our description of these approaches, we will use the various national and international standards as examples.

15.3.1 The Channel Vocoder

In the channel vocoder [61], each segment of input speech is analyzed using a bank of band-pass filters called the *analysis filters*. The energy at the output of each filter is estimated at fixed intervals and transmitted to the receiver. In a digital implementation, the energy estimate

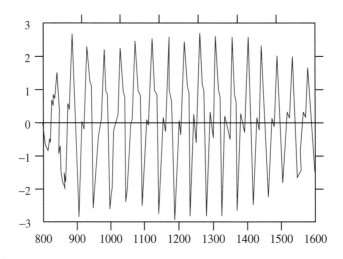

FIGURE 15.2   *The sound /e/ in* test.

may be the average squared value of the filter output. In analog implementations, this is the sampled output of an envelope detector. Generally, an estimate is generated 50 times every second. Along with the estimate of the filter output, a decision is made as to whether the speech in that segment is voiced, as in the case of the sounds /a/ /e/ /o/, or unvoiced, as in the case for the sounds /s/ /ff/. Voiced sounds tend to have a pseudoperiodic structure, as seen in Figure 15.2, which is a plot of the /e/ part of a male voice saying the word *test*. The period of the fundamental harmonic is called the *pitch* period. The transmitter also forms an estimate of the pitch period, which is transmitted to the receiver.

Unvoiced sounds tend to have a noiselike structure, as seen in Figure 15.3, which is the /s/ sound in the word *test*.

At the receiver, the vocal tract filter is implemented by a bank of band-pass filters. The bank of filters at the receiver, known as the *synthesis filters*, is identical to the bank of analysis filters. Based on whether the speech segment was deemed to be voiced or unvoiced, either a pseudonoise source or a periodic pulse generator is used as the input to the synthesis filter bank. The period of the pulse input is determined by the pitch estimate obtained for the segment being synthesized at the transmitter. The input is scaled by the energy estimate at the output of the analysis filters. A block diagram of the synthesis portion of the channel vocoder is shown in Figure 15.4.

Since the introduction of the channel vocoder, a number of variations have been developed. The channel vocoder matches the frequency profile of the input speech. There is no attempt to reproduce the speech samples per se. However, not all frequency components of speech are equally important. In fact, as the vocal tract is a tube of nonuniform cross section, it resonates at a number of different frequencies. These frequencies are known as *formants* [173]. The formant values change with different sounds; however, we can identify ranges in which they occur. For example, the first formant occurs in the range 200–800 Hz for a male speaker, and in the range 250–1000 Hz for a female speaker. The importance of these formants has led to the development of *formant vocoders*, which transmit an estimate of the formant values

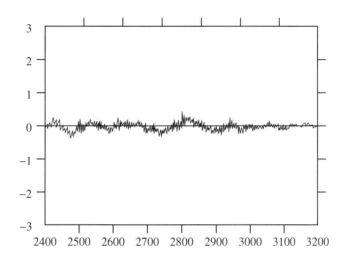

FIGURE 15.3   *The sound /s/ in test.*

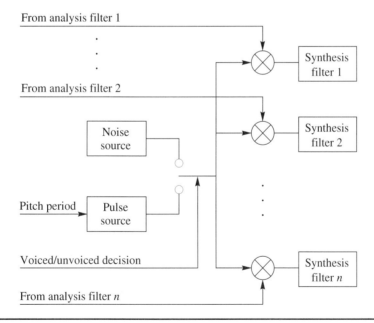

FIGURE 15.4   *The channel vocoder receiver.*

(usually four formants are considered sufficient) and an estimate of the bandwidth of each formant. At the receiver the excitation signal is passed through tunable filters that are tuned to the formant frequency and bandwidth.

An important development in the history of the vocoders was an understanding of the importance of the excitation signal. Schemes that require the synthesis of the excitation signal

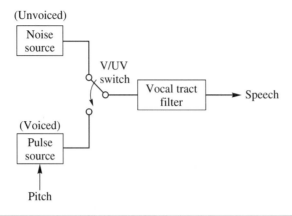

FIGURE 15.5   A model for speech synthesis.

at the receiver spend a considerable amount of computational resources to obtain accurate voicing information and accurate pitch periods. This expense can be avoided through the use of voice excitation. In the voice-excited channel vocoder, the voice is first filtered using a narrow-band low-pass filter. The output of the low-pass filter is sampled and transmitted to the receiver. At the receiver, this low-pass signal is passed through a nonlinearity to generate higher-order harmonics that, together with the low-pass signal, are used as the excitation signal. Voice excitation removes the problem of pitch extraction. It also removes the necessity for declaring every segment either voiced or unvoiced. As there are usually quite a few segments that are neither totally voiced or unvoiced, this can result in a substantial increase in quality. Unfortunately, the increase in quality is reflected in the high cost of transmitting the low-pass filtered speech signal.

The channel vocoder, although historically the first approach to analysis/synthesis—indeed the first approach to speech compression—is not as popular as some of the other schemes described here. However, all the different schemes can be viewed as descendants of the channel vocoder.

15.3.2   The Linear Predictive Coder (Government Standard LPC-10)

Of the many descendants of the channel vocoder, the most well-known is the linear predictive coder (LPC). Instead of the vocal tract being modeled by a bank of filters, in the linear predictive coder the vocal tract is modeled as a single linear filter whose output y_n is related to the input ϵ_n by

$$y_n = \sum_{i=1}^{M} b_i y_{n-i} + G\epsilon_n \tag{15.1}$$

where G is called the gain of the filter. As in the case of the channel vocoder, the input to the vocal tract filter is either the output of a random noise generator or a periodic pulse generator. A block diagram of the LPC receiver is shown in Figure 15.5.

At the transmitter, a segment of speech is analyzed. The parameters obtained include a decision as to whether the segment of speech is voiced or unvoiced, the pitch period if the segment is declared voiced, and the parameters of the vocal tract filter. In this section, we will take a somewhat detailed look at the various components that make up the linear predictive coder. As an example, we will use the specifications for the 2.4-kbit U.S. Government Standard LPC-10.

The input speech is generally sampled at 8000 samples per second. In the LPC-10 standard, the speech is broken into 180 sample segments, corresponding to 22.5 milliseconds of speech per segment.

The Voiced/Unvoiced Decision

If we compare Figures 15.2 and 15.3, we can see there are two major differences. Notice that the samples of the voiced speech have larger amplitude; that is, there is more energy in the voiced speech. Also, the unvoiced speech contains higher frequencies. As both speech segments have average values close to zero, this means that the unvoiced speech waveform crosses the $x = 0$ line more often than the voiced speech sample. Therefore, we can get a fairly good idea about whether the speech is voiced or unvoiced based on the energy in the segment relative to background noise and the number of zero crossings within a specified window. In the LPC-10 algorithm, the speech segment is first low-pass filtered using a filter with a bandwidth of 1 kHz. The energy at the output relative to the background noise is used to obtain a tentative decision about whether the signal in the segment should be declared voiced or unvoiced. The estimate of the background noise is basically the energy in the unvoiced speech segments. This tentative decision is further refined by counting the number of zero crossings and checking the magnitude of the coefficients of the vocal tract filter. We will talk more about this latter point later in this section. Finally, it can be perceptually annoying to have a single voiced frame sandwiched between unvoiced frames. The voicing decision of the neighboring frames is considered in order to prevent this from happening.

Estimating the Pitch Period

Estimating the pitch period is one of the most computationally intensive steps of the analysis process. Over the years a number of different algorithms for pitch extraction have been developed. In Figure 15.2, it would appear that obtaining a good estimate of the pitch should be relatively easy. However, we should keep in mind that the segment shown in Figure 15.2 consists of 800 samples, which is considerably more than the samples available to the analysis algorithm. Furthermore, the segment shown here is noise-free and consists entirely of a voiced input. For a machine to extract the pitch from a short noisy segment, which may contain both voiced and unvoiced components, can be a difficult undertaking.

Several algorithms make use of the fact that the autocorrelation of a periodic function $R_{xx}(k)$ will have a maximum when k is equal to the pitch period. Coupled with the fact that the estimation of the autocorrelation function generally leads to a smoothing out of the noise, this makes the autocorrelation function a useful tool for obtaining the pitch period. Unfortunately, there are also some problems with the use of the autocorrelation. Voiced speech is not exactly periodic, which makes the maximum lower than we would expect from a periodic signal.

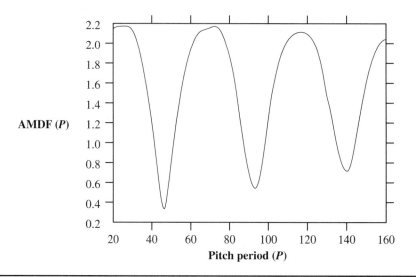

FIGURE 15.6   **AMDF function for the sound /e/ in *test*.**

Generally, a maximum is detected by checking the autocorrelation value against a threshold; if the value is greater than the threshold, a maximum is declared to have occurred. When there is uncertainty about the magnitude of the maximum value, it is difficult to select a value for the threshold. Another problem occurs because of the interference due to other resonances in the vocal tract. There are a number of algorithms that resolve these problems in different ways. (see [127, 173, 186] for details).

In this section, we will describe a closely related technique, employed in the LPC-10 algorithm, that uses the average magnitude difference function (AMDF). The AMDF is defined as

$$AMDF(P) = \frac{1}{N} \sum_{i=k_0+1}^{k_0+N} |y_i - y_{i-P}| \tag{15.2}$$

If a sequence $\{y_n\}$ is periodic with period P_0, samples that are P_0 apart in the $\{y_n\}$ sequence will have values close to each other, and therefore the AMDF will have a minimum at P_0. If we evaluate this function using the /e/ and /s/ sequences, we get the results shown in Figures 15.6 and 15.7. Notice that not only do we have a minimum when P equals the pitch period, but any spurious minimums we may obtain in the unvoiced segments are very shallow; that is, the difference between the minimum and average values is quite small. Therefore, the AMDF can serve a dual purpose: it can be used to identify the pitch period as well as the voicing condition.

The job of pitch extraction is simplified by the fact that the pitch period in humans tends to fall in a limited range. Thus, we do not have to evaluate the AMDF for all possible values of P. For example, the LPC-10 algorithm assumes that the pitch period is between 2.5 and 19.5 milliseconds. Assuming a sampling rate of 8000 samples a second, this means that P is between 20 and 160.

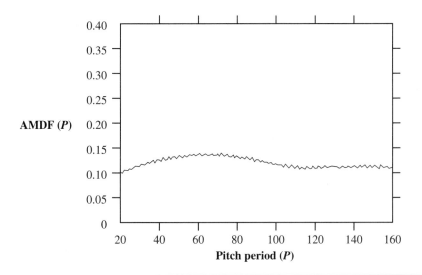

FIGURE 15.7   AMDF function for the sound /s/ in *test.*

Obtaining the Vocal Tract Filter

In linear predictive coding, the vocal tract is modeled by a linear filter with the input-output relationship shown in Equation (15.1). At the transmitter, during the analysis phase we obtain the filter coefficients that best match the segment being analyzed in a mean squared error sense. That is, if $\{y_n\}$ are the speech samples in that particular segment, then we want to choose $\{a_i\}$ to minimize the average value of e_n^2 where

$$e_n^2 = \left(y_n - \sum_{i=1}^{M} a_i y_{n-i} - G\epsilon_n \right)^2 . \tag{15.3}$$

If we take the derivative of the expected value of e_n^2 with respect to the coefficients $\{a_j\}$, we get a set of M equations:

$$\frac{\delta}{\delta a_j} E \left[\left(y_n - \sum_{i=1}^{M} a_i y_{n-i} - G\epsilon_n \right)^2 \right] = 0 \tag{15.4}$$

$$\Rightarrow -2E \left[\left(y_n - \sum_{i=1}^{M} a_i y_{n-i} - G\epsilon_n \right) y_{n-j} \right] = 0 \tag{15.5}$$

$$\Rightarrow \sum_{i=1}^{M} a_i E\left[y_{n-i} y_{n-j} \right] = E\left[y_n y_{n-j} \right] \tag{15.6}$$

where in the last step we have made use of the fact that $E[\epsilon_n y_{n-j}]$ is zero for $j \neq 0$. In order to solve (15.6) for the filter coefficients, we need to be able to estimate $E[y_{n-i} y_{n-j}]$. There are two different approaches for estimating these values, called the *autocorrelation* approach and the *autocovariance* approach, each leading to a different algorithm. In the autocorrelation approach, we assume that the $\{y_n\}$ sequence is stationary and therefore

$$E\left[y_{n-1}y_{n-j}\right] = R_{yy}(|i - j|) \tag{15.7}$$

Furthermore, we assume that the $\{y_n\}$ sequence is zero outside the segment for which we are calculating the filter parameters. Therefore, the autocorrelation function is estimated as

$$R_{yy}(k) = \sum_{n=n_0+1+k}^{n_0+N} y_n y_{n-k} \tag{15.8}$$

and the M equations of the form of (15.6) can be written in matrix form as

$$\mathbf{R}A = P \tag{15.9}$$

where

$$\mathbf{R} = \begin{bmatrix} R_y y(0) & R_{yy}(1) & R_{yy}(2) & \cdots & R_{yy}(M-1) \\ R_{yy}(1) & R_{yy}(0) & R_{yy}(1) & \cdots & R_{yy}(M-2) \\ R_{yy}(2) & R_{yy}(1) & R_{yy}(0) & \cdots & R_{yy}(M-3) \\ \vdots & \vdots & \vdots & & \vdots \\ R_{yy}(M-1) & R_{yy}(M-2) & R_{yy}(M-3) & \cdots & R_{yy}(0) \end{bmatrix} \tag{15.10}$$

$$A = \begin{bmatrix} a_1 \\ a_2 \\ a_3 \\ \vdots \\ a_M \end{bmatrix} \tag{15.11}$$

and

$$P = \begin{bmatrix} R_{yy}(1) \\ R_{yy}(2) \\ R_{yy}(3) \\ \vdots \\ R_{yy}(M) \end{bmatrix} \tag{15.12}$$

This matrix equation can be solved directly to find the filter coefficients

$$A = \mathbf{R}^{-1}P. \tag{15.13}$$

However, the special form of the matrix $\mathbf{R}$ obviates the need for computing $\mathbf{R}^{-1}$. Note that not only is $\mathbf{R}$ symmetric, but also each diagonal of $\mathbf{R}$ consists of the same element. For example, the main diagonal contains only the element $R_{yy}(0)$, while the diagonals above and below the main diagonal contain only the element $R_{yy}(1)$. This special type of matrix is called a *Toeplitz matrix*, and there are a number of efficient algorithms available for the inversion of Toeplitz matrices [71]. Because $\mathbf{R}$ is Toeplitz, we can obtain a recursive solution to (15.9) that is computationally very efficient and that has an added attractive feature from the point of view of compression. This algorithm is known as the Levinson-Durbin algorithm [137, 63]. We describe the algorithm without derivation. For details of the derivation, see [171, 173].

In order to compute the filter coefficients of an Mth-order filter, the Levinson-Durbin algorithm requires the computation of all filters of order less than M. Furthermore, during the computation of the filter coefficients, the algorithm generates a set of constants k_i known as the *reflection* coefficients, or *partial correlation* (PARCOR) coefficients. In the algorithm description below, we denote the order of the filter using superscripts. Thus, the coefficients of the fifth-order filter would be denoted by $\{a_i^{(5)}\}$. The algorithm also requires the computation of the estimate of the average error $E[e_n^2]$. We will denote the average error using an mth-order filter by E_m. The algorithm proceeds as follows:

1. Set $E_0 = R_{yy}(0)$, $i = 0$.

2. Increment i by one.

3. Calculate $k_i = (\sum_{j=1}^{i-1} a_j^{(i-1)} R_{yy}(i-j+1) - R_{yy}(i))/E_{i-1}$.

4. Set $a_i^{(i)} = k_i$.

5. Calculate $a_j^{(i)} = a_j^{(i-1)} + k_i a_{i-j}^{i-1}$ for $j = 1, 2, \ldots, i-1$.

6. Calculate $E_i = (1 - k_i^2)E_{i-1}$.

7. If $i < M$, go to step 2.

In order to get an effective reconstruction of the voiced segment, the order of the vocal tract filter needs to be sufficiently high. Generally, the order of the filter is 10 or more. Because the filter is an IIR filter, error in the coefficients can lead to instability, especially for the high orders necessary in linear predictive coding. As the filter coefficients are to be transmitted to the receiver, they need to be quantized. This means that quantization error is introduced into the value of the coefficients, and that can lead to instability.

This problem can be avoided by noticing that if we know the PARCOR coefficients, we can obtain the filter coefficients from them. Furthermore, PARCOR coefficients have the property that as long as the magnitudes of the coefficients are less than one, the filter obtained from them is guaranteed to be stable. Therefore, instead of quantizing the coefficients $\{a_i\}$ and transmitting them, the transmitter quantizes and transmits the coefficients $\{k_i\}$. As long as we make sure that all the reconstruction values for the quantizer have magnitudes less than one, it is possible to use relatively high-order filters in the analysis/synthesis schemes.

The assumption of stationarity that was used to obtain (15.6) is not really valid for speech signals. If we discard this assumption, the equations to obtain the filter coefficients change. The term $E[y_{n-i}y_{n-j}]$ is now a function of both i and j. Defining

$$c_{ij} = E[y_{n-i}y_{n-j}] \tag{15.14}$$

we get the equation

$$CA = S \tag{15.15}$$

where

$$
\mathbf{C} = \begin{bmatrix}
c_{11} & c_{12} & c_{13} & \cdots & c_{1M} \\
c_{21} & c_{22} & c_{23} & \cdots & c_{2M} \\
\vdots & \vdots & \vdots & & \vdots \\
c_{M1} & c_{M2} & c_{M3} & \cdots & c_{MM}
\end{bmatrix}
\tag{15.16}
$$

and

$$
S = \begin{bmatrix}
c_{10} \\
c_{20} \\
c_{30} \\
\vdots \\
c_{M0}
\end{bmatrix}
\tag{15.17}
$$

The elements c_{ij} are estimated as

$$
c_{ij} = \sum_{n=n_0+1}^{n_0+N} y_{n-i}y_{n-j}.
\tag{15.18}
$$

Notice that we no longer assume that the values of y_n outside of the segment under consideration are zero. This means that in calculating the $\mathbf{C}$ matrix for a particular segment, we use samples from previous segments. This method of computing the filter coefficients is called the *covariance method*.

The $\mathbf{C}$ matrix is symmetric but no longer Toeplitz, so we can't use the Levinson-Durbin recursion to solve for the filter coefficients. The equations are generally solved using a technique called the *Cholesky decomposition*. We will not describe the solution technique here. (You can find it in most texts on numerical techniques; an especially good source is [183].) For an in-depth study of the relationship between the Cholesky decomposition and the reflection coefficients, see [88].

The LPC-10 algorithm uses the covariance method to obtain the reflection coefficients. It also uses the PARCOR coefficients to update the voicing decision. In general, for voiced signals the first two PARCOR coefficients have values close to one. Therefore, if both the first two PARCOR coefficients have very small values, the algorithm sets the voicing decision to unvoiced.

Transmitting the Parameters

Once the various parameters have been obtained, they need to be coded and transmitted to the receiver. There are a variety of ways this can be done. Let us look at how the LPC-10 algorithm handles this task.

The parameters that need to be transmitted include the voicing decision, the pitch period, and the vocal tract filter parameters. One bit suffices to transmit the voicing information. The pitch is quantized to 1 of 60 different values using a log-companded quantizer. The LPC-10 algorithm uses a 10th-order filter for voiced speech and a 4th-order filter for unvoiced speech. Thus, we have to send 11 values (10 reflection coefficients and the gain) for voiced speech and 5 for unvoiced speech.

The vocal tract filter is especially sensitive to errors in reflection coefficients that have magnitudes close to one. As the first few coefficients are most likely to have values close to one, the LPC-10 algorithm specifies the use of nonuniform quantization for k_1 and k_2. The nonuniform quantization is implemented by first generating the coefficients

$$g_i = \frac{1 + k_i}{1 - k_i} \qquad (15.19)$$

which are then quantized using a 5-bit uniform quantizer. The coefficients k_3 and k_4 are both quantized using a 5-bit uniform quantizer. In the voiced segments, coefficients k_5 through k_8 are quantized using a 4-bit uniform quantizer, k_9 is quantized using a 3-bit uniform quantizer, and k_{10} is quantized using a 2-bit uniform quantizer. In the unvoiced segments, the 21 bits used to quantize k_5 through k_{10} in the voiced segments are used for error protection.

The gain G is obtained by finding the root mean squared (rms) value of the segment and quantized using 5-bit log-companded quantization. Including an additional bit for synchronization, we end up with a total of 54 bits per frame. Multiplying this by the total number of frames per second gives us the target rate of 2400 bits per second.

Synthesis

At the receiver, the voiced frames are generated by exciting the received vocal tract filter by a locally stored waveform. This waveform is 40 samples long. It is truncated or padded with zeros depending on the pitch period. If the frame is unvoiced, the vocal tract is excited by a pseudorandom number generator.

The LPC-10 coder provides intelligible reproduction at 2.4 kbits. The use of only two kinds of excitation signals gives an artificial quality to the voice. This approach also suffers when used in noisy environments. The encoder can be fooled into declaring segments of speech unvoiced because of background noise. When this happens, the speech information gets lost.

15.3.3 Code Excited Linear Predicton (CELP)

As we mentioned earlier, one of the most important factors in generating natural-sounding speech is the excitation signal. As the human ear is especially sensitive to pitch errors, a great deal of effort has been devoted to the development of accurate pitch detection algorithms. However, no matter how accurate the pitch is in a system using the LPC vocal tract filter, the use of a periodic pulse excitation that consists of a single pulse per pitch period leads to a "buzzy twang" [207]. In 1982, Atal and Remde [14] introduced the idea of multipulse linear predictive coding (MP-LPC), in which several pulses were used during each segment. The spacing of these pulses is determined by evaluating a number of different patterns from a codebook of patterns.

A codebook of excitation patterns is constructed. Each entry in this codebook is an excitation sequence that consists of a few nonzero values separated by zeros. Given a segment from the speech sequence to be encoded, the encoder obtains the vocal tract filter using the LPC analysis described previously. The encoder then excites the vocal tract filter with the entries of the codebook. The difference between the original speech segment and the synthesized speech is fed to a perceptual weighting filter, which weights the error using a perceptual weighting criterion. The codebook entry that generates the minimum average weighted error is declared to be the best match. The index of the best-match entry is sent to the receiver along with the parameters for the vocal tract filter.

This approach was improved upon by Atal and Schroeder in 1984 with the introduction of the system that is commonly known as *code excited linear prediction* (CELP). In CELP, instead of having a codebook of pulse patterns, we allow a variety of excitation signals. For each segment the encoder finds the excitation vector that generates synthesized speech that best matches the speech segment being encoded. This approach is closer in a strict sense to a waveform coding technique such as DPCM than to the analysis/synthesis schemes. However, as the ideas behind CELP are similar to those behind LPC, we included CELP in this chapter. The main components of the CELP coder include the LPC analysis, the excitation codebook, and the perceptual weighting filter. Each component of the CELP coder has been investigated in great detail by a large number of researchers. For a survey of some of the results, see [83]. In the rest of the section, we give two examples of very different kinds of CELP coders. The first algorithm is the U.S. Government Standard 1016, a 4.8 kbps coder; the other is the CCITT (now ITU-T) G.728 standard, a low-delay 16 kbps coder.

Besides CELP, the MP-LPC algorithm had another descendant that has become a standard. In 1986, Kroon, Deprettere, and Sluyter [130] developed a modification of the MP-LPC algorithm. Instead of using excitation vectors in which the nonzero values are separated by an arbitrary number of zero values, they forced the nonzero values to occur at regularly spaced intervals. Furthermore, they allowed the nonzero values to take on a number of different values. They called this scheme *regular pulse excitation* (RPE) coding. A variation of RPE, called *regular pulse excitation with long-term prediction* (RPE-LTP) [102], was adopted as a standard for digital cellular telephony by the Group Speciale Mobile (GSM) subcommittee of the European Telecommunications Standards Institute at the rate of 13 kbps.

Federal Standard 1016

The vocal tract filter used by the CELP coder in FS 1016 is given by

$$y_n = \sum_{i=1}^{10} b_i y_{n-i} + \beta y_{n-P} + G\epsilon_n \qquad (15.20)$$

where P is the pitch period and the term βy_{n-P} is the contribution due to the pitch periodicity. The input speech is sampled at 8000 samples per second and divided into 30-millisecond frames containing 240 samples. Each frame is divided into four subframes of length 7.5 millisecond [39]. The coefficients $\{b_i\}$ for the 10th-order short-term filter are obtained using the autocorrelation method.

The pitch period P is calculated once every subframe. In order to reduce the computational load, the pitch value is assumed to lie between between 20 and 147 every odd subframe. In every even subframe, the pitch value is assumed to lie within 32 samples of the pitch value in the previous frame.

The FS 1016 algorithm uses two codebooks [38], a stochastic codebook and an adaptive codebook. An excitation sequence is generated for each subframe by adding one scaled element from the stochastic codebook and one scaled element from the adaptive codebook. The scale factors and indices are selected to minimize the perceptual error between the input and synthesized speech.

The stochastic codebook contains 512 entries. These entries are generated using a Gaussian random number generator, the output of which is quantized to -1, 0, or 1. If the input is less than -1.2, it is quantized to -1; if it is greater than 1.2, it is quantized to 1; and if it lies between -1.2 and 1.2, it is quantized to 0. The codebook entries are adjusted so that each entry differs from the preceding entry in only two places. This structure helps reduce the search complexity.

The adaptive codebook consists of the excitation vectors from the previous frame. Each time a new excitation vector is obtained, it is added to the codebook. In this manner, the codebook adapts to local statistics.

The FS 1016 coder has been shown to provide excellent reproductions in both quiet and noisy environments at rates of 4.8 kbps and above [38]. Because of the richness of the excitation signals, the reproduction does not suffer from the problem of sounding artificial. The lack of a voicing decision makes it more robust to background noise. The quality of the reproduction of this coder at 4.8 kbps has been shown to be equivalent to a delta modulator operating at 32 kbps [38]. The price for this quality is much higher complexity and a much longer coding delay. We will address this last point in the next section.

CCITT G.728 Speech Standard

By their nature, the schemes described in this chapter have some coding delay built into them. By "coding delay," we mean the time between when a speech sample is encoded to when it is decoded if the encoder and decoder were connected back-to-back (i.e., there were no transmission delays). In the schemes we have studied, a segment of speech is first stored in a buffer. We do not start extracting the various parameters until a complete segment of speech is available to us. Once the segment is completely available, it is processed. If the processing is real time, this means another segment's worth of delay. Finally, once the parameters have been obtained, coded, and transmitted, the receiver has to wait until at least a significant part of the information is available before it can start decoding the first sample. Therefore, if a segment contains 20 milliseconds' worth of data, the coding delay would be approximately somewhere between 40 to 60 milliseconds. This kind of delay may be acceptable for some applications; however, there are other applications where such long delays are not acceptable. For example, in some situations there are several intermediate tandem connections between the initial transmitter and the final receiver. In such situations, the total delay would be a multiple of the coding delay of a single connection. The size of the delay would depend on the number of tandem connections and could rapidly become quite large.

For such applications, CCITT approved recommendation G.728, a CELP coder with a coder delay of 2 milliseconds operating at 16 kbps. As the input speech is sampled at 8000 samples per second, this rate corresponds to an average rate of 2 bits per sample.

In order to lower the coding delay, the size of each segment has to be reduced significantly because the coding delay will be some multiple of the size of the segment. The G.728

recommendation uses a segment size of five samples. With five samples and a rate of 2 bits per sample, we only have 10 bits available to us. Using only 10 bits, it would be impossible to encode the parameters of the vocal tract filter as well as the excitation vector. Therefore, the algorithm obtains the vocal tract filter parameters in a backward adaptive manner; that is, the vocal tract filter coefficients to be used to synthesize the current segment are obtained by analyzing the previous decoded segments. The CCITT requirements for G.728 included the requirement that the algorithm operate under noisy channel conditions. It would be extremely difficult to extract the pitch period from speech corrupted by channel errors. Therefore, the G.728 algorithm does away with the pitch filter. Instead, the algorithm uses a 50th-order vocal tract filter. The order of the filter is large enough to model the pitch of most female speakers. Not being able to use pitch information for male speakers does not cause much degradation [42]. The vocal tract filter is updated every fourth frame, which is once every 20 samples or 2.5 milliseconds. The autocorrelation method is used to obtain the vocal tract parameters.

As the vocal tract filter is completely determined in a backward adaptive manner, we have all 10 bits available to encode the excitation sequence. Ten bits would be able to index 1024 excitation sequences. However, to examine 1024 excitation sequences every 0.625 milliseconds is a rather large computational load. In order to reduce this load, the G.728 algorithm uses a product codebook where each excitation sequence is represented by a normalized sequence and a gain term. The final excitation sequence is a product of the normalized excitation sequence and the gain. Of the 10 bits, 3 bits are used to encode the gain using a predictive encoding scheme, while the remaining 7 bits form the index to a codebook containing 127 sequences.

Block diagrams of the encoder and decoder for the CCITT G.728 coder are shown in Figure 15.8. The low-delay CCITT G.728 CELP coder operating at 16 kbps provides reconstructed speech quality superior to the 32 kbps CCITT G.726 ADPCM algorithm described in Chapter 10. Various efforts are under way to reduce the bit rate for this algorithm without compromising too much on quality and delay.

15.3.4 Sinusoidal Coders

A competing approach to CELP in the low-rate region is a relatively new form of coder called the sinusoidal coder [83]. Recall that the main problem with the LPC coder was the paucity of excitation signals. The CELP coder resolved this problem by using a codebook of excitation signals. The sinusoidal coders solve this problem by using an excitation signal that is the sum of sine waves of arbitrary amplitudes, frequencies, and phases. Thus, the excitation signal is of the form

$$e_n = \sum_{l=1}^{L} a_l \cos(n\omega_l + \psi_l) \tag{15.21}$$

where the number of sinusoids L required for each frame depends on the contents of the frame. If the input to a linear system is a sinusoid with frequency ω_l, the output will also be a sinusoid with frequency ω_l, albeit with different amplitude and phase. The vocal tract filter is a linear system. Therefore, if the excitation signal is of the form of (15.21), the synthesized speech

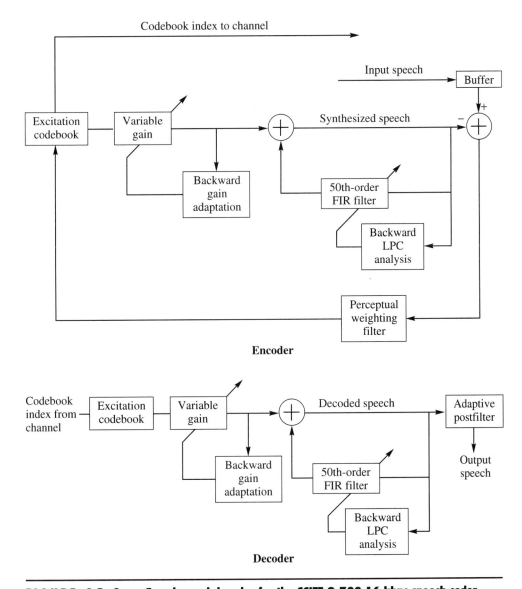

FIGURE 15.8   **Encoder and decoder for the CCITT G.728 16 kbps speech coder.**

$\{s_n\}$ will be of the form

$$s_n = \sum_{i=1}^{L} A_l \cos(n\omega_l + \phi_l). \tag{15.22}$$

Thus, each frame is characterized by a set of spectral amplitudes A_l, frequencies ω_l, and phase terms ϕ_l. The number of parameters required to represent the excitation sequence is the same as the number of parameters required to represent the synthesized speech. Therefore, rather than estimate and transmit the parameters of both the excitation signal and vocal tract filter and then synthesize the speech at the receiver by passing the excitation signal through the vocal tract filter, the sinusoidal coders directly estimate the parameters required to synthesize the speech at the receiver.

Just like the coders discussed previously, the sinusoidal coders divide the input speech into frames and obtain the parameters of the speech separately for each frame. If we synthesized the speech segment in each frame independent of the other frames, we would get synthetic speech that is discontinuous at the frame boundaries. These discontinuities severely degrade the quality of the synthetic speech. Therefore, the sinusoidal coders use different interpolation algorithms to smooth the transition from one frame to another.

Transmitting all the separate frequencies ω_l would require significant transmission resources, so the sinusoidal coders obtain a fundamental frequency w_0 for which the approximation

$$\hat{y}_n = \sum_{k=1}^{K(\omega_0)} \hat{A}(k\omega_0) \cos(nk\omega_0 + \phi_k) \tag{15.23}$$

is close to the speech sequence y_n. Because this is a harmonic approximation, the approximate sequence $\{\hat{y}_n\}$ will be most different from the speech sequence $\{y_n\}$ when the segment of speech being encoded is unvoiced. Therefore, this difference can be used to decide whether the frame or some subset of it is unvoiced.

The two most popular sinusoidal coding techniques today are represented by the sinusoidal transform coder (STC) [154] and the multiband excitation coder (MBE) [99]. While the STC and MBE are similar in many respects, they differ in how they handle unvoiced speech. In the MBE coder, the frequency range is divided into bands, each consisting of several harmonics of the fundamental frequency ω_0. Each band is checked to see if it is unvoiced or voiced. The voiced bands are synthesized using a sum of sinusoids, while the unvoiced bands are obtained using a random number generator. The voiced and unvoiced bands are synthesized separately and then added together.

In the STC, the proportion of the frame that contains a voiced signal is measured using a "voicing probability" P_v. The voicing probability is a function of how well the harmonic model matches the speech segment. Where the harmonic model is close to the speech signal, the voicing probability is taken to be unity. The sine wave frequencies are then generated by

$$w_k = \begin{cases} kw_0 & \text{for } kw_0 \leq w_c P_v \\ k^* w_0 + (k - k^*) w_u & \text{for } kw_0 > w_c P_v \end{cases} \tag{15.24}$$

where w_c corresponds to the cutoff frequency (4 kHz), w_u is the unvoiced pitch corresponding to 100 Hz, and k^* is the largest value of k for which $k^* w_0 \leq w_c P_v$. The speech is then synthesized as

$$\hat{y}_n = \sum_{k=1}^{K} \hat{A}(w_k) \cos(nw_k + \phi_k). \tag{15.25}$$

Both the STC and the MBE coders have been shown to perform well at low rates. A version of the MBE coder known as the improved MBE (IMBE) coder has been approved by the Association of Police Communications Officers (APCO) as the standard for law enforcement.

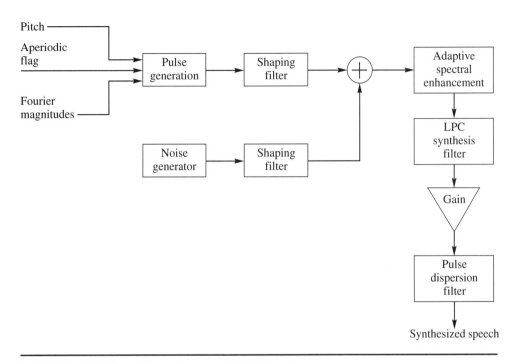

FIGURE   15.9   Block diagram of MELP decoder.

15.3.5 Mixed Excitation Linear Prediction (MELP)

The mixed excitation linear prediction (MELP) coder was selected to be the new federal standard for speech coding at 2.4 kbps by the Defense Department Voice Processing Consortium (DDVPC). The MELP algorithm uses the same LPC filter to model the vocal tract. However, it uses a much more complex approach to the generation of the excitation signal.

A block diagram of the decoder for the MELP system is shown in Figure 15.9. As evident from the figure, the excitation signal for the synthesis filter is no longer simply noise or a periodic pulse but a multiband mixed excitation. The mixed excitation contains both a filtered signal from a noise generator as well as a contribution that depends directly on the input signal.

The first step in constructing the excitation signal is pitch extraction. The MELP algorithm obtains the pitch period using a multistep approach. In the first step an integer pitch value P_1 is obtained by

1. first filtering the input using a low-pass filter with a cutoff of 1 kHz

2. computing the normalized autocorrelation for lags between 40 and 160

The normalized autocorrelation $r(\tau)$ is defined as

$$r(\tau) = \frac{c_\tau(0,\tau)}{\sqrt{c_\tau(0,0)c_\tau(\tau,\tau)}}$$

where

$$c_\tau(m, n) = \sum_{-\lfloor \tau/2 \rfloor - 80}^{-\lfloor \tau/2 \rfloor + 79} y_{k+m} y_{k+n}.$$

The first estimate of the pitch P_1 is obtained as the value of τ that maximizes the normalized autocorrelation function. This value is refined by looking at the signal filtered using a filter with passband in the 0–500 Hz range. This stage uses two values of P_1, one from the current frame and one from the previous frame, as candidates. The normalized autocorrelation values are obtained for lags from five samples less to five samples more than the candidate P_1 values. The lags that provide the maximum normalized autocorrelation value for each candidate are used for *fractional pitch refinement*. The idea behind fractional pitch refinement is that if the maximum value of $r(\tau)$ is found for some $\tau = T$, then the maximum could be in the interval $(T - 1, T]$ or $[T, T + 1)$. The fractional offset is computed using

$$\Delta = \frac{c_T(0, T + 1)c_T(T, T) - c_T(0, T)c_T(T, T + 1)}{c_T(0, T + 1)[c_T(T, T) - c_T(T, T + 1)] + c_T(0, T)[c_T(T + 1, T + 1) - c_T(T, T + 1)]}. \tag{15.26}$$

The normalized autocorrelation at the fractional pitch values are given by

$$r(T+\Delta) = \frac{(1 - \Delta)c_T(0, T) + \Delta c_T(0, T + 1)}{\sqrt{c_T(0, 0)[(1 - \Delta)^2 c_T(T, T) + 2\Delta(1 - \Delta)c_T(T, T + 1) + \Delta^2 c_T(T + 1, T + 1)]}}. \tag{15.27}$$

The fractional estimate that gives the higher autocorrelation is selected as the refined pitch value P_2.

The final refinements of the pitch value are obtained using the linear prediction residuals. The residual sequence is generated by filtering the input speech signal with the filter obtained using the LPC analysis. For the purposes of pitch refinement the residual signal is filtered using a low-pass filter with a cutoff of 1 kHz. The normalized autocorrelation function is computed for this filtered residual signal for lags from five samples less to five samples more than the candidate P_2 value, and a candidate value of P_3 is obtained. If $r(P_3) \geq 0.6$, we check to make sure that P_3 is not a multiple of the actual pitch. If $r(P_3) < 0.6$, we do another fractional pitch refinement around P_2 using the input speech signal. If in the end $r(P_3) < 0.55$, we replace P_3 with a long-term average value of the pitch. The final pitch value is quantized on a logarithmic scale using a 99-level uniform quantizer.

The input is also subjected to a multiband voicing analysis using five filters with passbands 0–500, 500–1000, 1000–2000, 2000–3000, and 3000–4000 Hz. The goal of the analysis is to obtain the voicing strengths Vbp_i for each band used in the shaping filters. Noting that P_2 was obtained using the output of the lowest band filter, $r(P_2)$ is assigned as the lowest band voicing strength Vbp_1. For the other bands, Vbp_i is the larger of $r(P_2)$ for that band and the correlation of the envelope of the band-pass signal. If the value of Vbp_1 is small, this indicates a lack of low-frequency structure, which in turn indicates an unvoiced or transition input. Thus, if $Vbp_1 < 0.5$, the pulse component of the excitation signal is selected to be aperiodic, and this decision is communicated to the decoder by setting the aperiodic flag to 1. When $Vbp_1 > 0.6$, the values of the other voicing strengths are quantized to 1 if their value is greater than 0.6, and to 0 otherwise. In this way signal energy in the different bands is turned on or off depending on the voicing strength. There are several exceptions to this quantization rule. If Vbp_2, Vbp_3, and Vbp_4 all have magnitudes less than 0.6 and Vbp_5 has a value greater than 0.6, they are all (including Vbp_5) quantized to 0. Also, if the residual signal contains a few large values, indicating sudden transitions in the input signal, the voicing strengths are adjusted. In particular, the *peakiness* is defined as

$$\text{peakiness} = \frac{\sqrt{\frac{1}{160} \sum_{n=1}^{160} d_n^2}}{\frac{1}{160} \sum_{n=1}^{160} |d_n|}. \tag{15.28}$$

If this value exceeds 1.34, Vbp_1 is forced to 1. If the peakiness value exceeds 1.6, Vbp_1, Vbp_2, and Vbp_3 are all set to 1.

In order to generate the pulse input, the algorithm measures the magnitude of the discrete Fourier transform coefficients corresponding to the first 10 harmonics of the pitch. The prediction residual is generated using the quantized predictor coefficients. The algorithm searches in a window of width $\lfloor 512/\hat{P}_3 \rfloor$ samples around the initial estimates of the pitch harmonics for the actual harmonics where $\hat{P}_3$ is the quantized value of P_3. The magnitudes of the harmonics are quantized using a vector quantizer with a codebook size of 256. The codebook is searched using a weighted Euclidean distance that emphasizes lower frequencies over higher frequencies.

At the decoder, using the magnitudes of the harmonics and information about the periodicity of the pulse train, the algorithm generates one excitation signal. Another signal is generated using a random number generator. Both are shaped by the multiband shaping filter before being combined. This mixture signal is then processed through an *adaptive spectral enhancement filter*, which is based on the LPC coefficients, to form the final excitation signal. Note that in order to preserve continuity from frame to frame, the parameters used for generating the excitation signal are adjusted based on their corresponding values in neighboring frames.

15.4 Image Compression

Although there have been a number of attempts to mimic the linear predictive coding approach for image compression, they have not been overly successful. A major reason for this is that while speech can be modeled as the output of a linear filter, most images cannot. However, a totally different analysis/synthesis approach, conceived in the mid-1980s, has found some degree of success—fractal compression.

15.4.1 Fractal Compression

There are several different ways to approach the topic of fractal compression. Our approach is to use the idea of fixed-point transformation. A function $f(\cdot)$ is said to have a fixed point x_0 if $f(x_0) = x_0$. Suppose we restrict the function $f(\cdot)$ to be of the form $ax + b$. Then, except for when $a = 1$, this equation always has a fixed point:

$$ax_0 + b = x_o$$

$$\Rightarrow x_0 = \frac{b}{1-a}. \tag{15.29}$$

This means that if we wanted to transmit the value of x_0, we could instead transmit the values of a and b and obtain x_0 at the receiver using (15.29). We do not have to solve this equation to obtain x_0. Instead, we could take a guess at what x_0 should be and then refine the guess using the recursion

$$x_0^{(n+1)} = ax_0^{(n)} + b. \tag{15.30}$$

Example 15.4.1:

Suppose that instead of sending the value $x_0 = 2$, we sent the values of a and b as 0.5 and 1.0. The receiver starts out with a guess for x_0 as $x_0^{(0)} = 1$. Then

$$
\begin{aligned}
x_0^{(1)} &= ax_0^{(0)} + b = 1.5 \\
x_0^{(2)} &= ax_0^{(1)} + b = 1.75 \\
x_0^{(3)} &= ax_0^{(2)} + b = 1.875 \\
x_0^{(4)} &= ax_0^{(3)} + b = 1.9375 \\
x_0^{(5)} &= ax_0^{(4)} + b = 1.96875 \\
x_0^{(6)} &= ax_0^{(5)} + b = 1.984375
\end{aligned}
\tag{15.31}
$$

and so on. As we can see, with each iteration we come closer and closer to the actual x_0 value of 2. This would be true no matter what our initial guess was. ◆

Thus, the value of x_0 is accurately specified by specifying the fixed-point equation. The receiver can retrieve the value either by the solution of (15.29) or via the recursion (15.30).

Let us generalize this idea. Suppose that for a given image $\mathcal{I}$ (treated as an array of integers), there exists a function $f(\cdot)$ such that $f(\mathcal{I}) = \mathcal{I}$. If it was cheaper in terms of bits to represent $f(\cdot)$ than it was to represent $\mathcal{I}$, we could treat $f(\cdot)$ as the compressed representation of $\mathcal{I}$.

This idea was first proposed by Michael Barnsley and Alan Sloan [18] based on the idea of self-similarity. Barnsley and Sloan noted that certain natural-looking objects can be obtained as the fixed point of a certain type of function. If an image can be obtained as a fixed point of some function, can we then solve the *inverse* problem? That is, given an image, can we find the function for which the image is the fixed point? The first practical public answer to this came from Arnaud Jacquin in his Ph.D. dissertation [112] in 1989. The technique we describe in this section is from Jacquin's 1992 paper [113].

Instead of generating a single function directly for which the given image is a fixed point, we partition the image into blocks R_k, called *range* blocks, and obtain a transformation f_k for each block. The transformations f_k are not fixed-point transformations since they do not satisfy the equation

$$f_k(R_k) = R_k. \tag{15.32}$$

Range blocks

Domain blocks

FIGURE 15.10   Range blocks and examples of domain blocks.

Instead, they are a mapping from a block of pixels D_k from some other part of the image. While each individual mapping f_k is not a fixed-point mapping, we will see later that we can combine all these mappings to generate a fixed-point mapping. The image blocks D_k are called *domain* blocks, and they are chosen to be larger than the range blocks. In [113], the domain blocks are obtained by sliding a $K \times K$ window over the image in steps of $K/2$ or $K/4$ pixels. As long as the window remains within the boundaries of the image, each $K \times K$ block thus encountered is entered into the domain pool. The set of all domain blocks does not have to partition the image. In Figure 15.10 we show the range blocks and two possible domain blocks.

The transformations f_k are composed of a *geometric* transformation g_k and a *massic* transformation m_k. The geometric transformation consists of moving the domain block to the location of the range block and adjusting the size of the domain block to match the size of the range block. The massic transformation adjusts the intensity and orientation of the pixels in the domain block after it has been operated on by the geometric transform. Thus,

$$\hat{R}_k = f_k(D_k) = m_k(g_k(D_k)). \tag{15.33}$$

We have used $\hat{R}_k$ instead of R_k on the left-hand side of (15.33) because it is generally not possible to find an exact functional relationship between domain and range blocks. Therefore, we have to settle for some degree of loss of information. Generally, this loss is measured in terms of mean squared error.

The effect of all these functions together can be represented as the transformation $f(\cdot)$. Mathematically, this transformation can be viewed as a union of the transformations f_k:

$$f = \bigcup_k f_k. \qquad (15.34)$$

Notice that while each transformation f_k maps a block of different size and location to the location of R_k, looking at it from the point of view of the entire image, it is a mapping from the image to the image. As the union of R_k is the image itself, we could represent all the transformations as

$$\hat{\mathcal{I}} = f(\hat{\mathcal{I}}) \qquad (15.35)$$

where we have used $\hat{\mathcal{I}}$ instead of $\mathcal{I}$ to account for the fact that the reconstructed image is an approximation to the original.

We can now pose the encoding problem as that of obtaining D_k, g_k, and m_k such that the difference $d(R_k, \hat{R}_k)$ is minimized, where $d(R_k, \hat{R}_k)$ can be the mean squared error between the blocks R_k and $\hat{R}_k$.

Let us first look at how we would obtain g_k and m_k assuming that we already know which domain block D_k we are going to use. We will then return to the question of selecting D_k.

Knowing which domain block we are using for a given range block automatically specifies the amount of displacement required. If the range blocks R_k are of size $M \times M$, then the domain blocks are usually taken to be of size $2M \times 2M$. In order to adjust the size of D_k to be the same as that of R_k, we generally replace each 2×2 block of pixels with their average value. Once the range block has been selected, the geometric transformation is easily obtained.

Let's define $T_k = g_k(D_k)$, and t_{ij} as the ijth pixel in T_k $i, j = 0, 1, \ldots, M - 1$. The massic transformation m_k is then given by

$$m_k(t_{ij}) = i(\alpha_k t_{ij} + \Delta_k) \qquad (15.36)$$

where $i(\cdot)$ denotes a shuffling or rearrangement of the pixels with the block. Possible rearrangements (or *isometries*) include the following:

1. Rotation by 90 degrees, $i(t_{ij}) = t_{j(M-1-i)}$

2. Rotation by 180 degrees, $i(t_{ij}) = t_{(M-1-i)(M-1-j)}$

3. Rotation by -90 degrees, $i(t_{ij}) = t_{(M-1-i)j}$

4. Reflection about midvertical axis, $i(t_{ij}) = t_{i(M-1-j)}$

5. Reflection about midhorizontal axis, $i(t_{ij}) = t_{(M-1-i)j}$

6. Reflection about diagonal, $i(t_{ij}) = t_{ji}$

7. Reflection about cross diagonal, $i(t_{ij}) = t_{(M-1-j)(M-1-i)}$

8. Identity mapping, $i(t_{ij}) = t_{ij}$

Therefore, for each massic transformation m_k, we need to find values of α_k, Δ_k, and an isometry. For a given range block R_k, in order to find the mapping that gives us the closest approximation $\hat{R}_k$, we can try all possible combinations of transformations and domain blocks—a massive computation. In order to reduce the computations, we can restrict the number of domain blocks to search. However, in order to get the best possible approximation, we would like the pool of domain blocks to be as large as possible. Jacquin [113] resolves this situation in the following manner. First, he generates a relatively large pool of domain blocks by the method described earlier. The elements of the domain pool are then divided into *shade blocks, edge blocks*, and *midrange blocks*. The shade blocks are those in which the variance of pixel values within the block is small. The edge block, as the name implies, contains those blocks that have a sharp change of intensity values. The midrange blocks are those that fit into neither category—not too smooth but with no well-defined edges. The shade blocks are then removed from the domain pool. The reason is that, given the transformations we have described, a shade domain block can only generate a shade range block. If the range block is a shade block, it is much more cost effective simply to send the average value of the block rather than attempt any more complicated transformations.

The encoding procedure proceeds as follows. A range block is first classified into one of the three categories described above. If it is a shade block, we simply send the average value of the block. If it is a midrange block, the massic transformation is of the form $\alpha_k t_{ij} + \Delta_k$. The isometry is assumed to be the identity isometry. First α_k is selected from a small set of values—Jacquin [113] uses the values $(0.7, 0.8, 0.9, 1.0)$—such that $d(R_k, \alpha_k T_k)$ is minimized. Thus, we have to search over the possible values of α and the midrange domain blocks in the domain pool in order to find the (α_k, D_k) pair that will minimize $d(R_k, \alpha_k T_k)$. The value of Δ_k is then selected as the difference of the average values of R_k and $\alpha_k T_k$.

If the range block R_k is classified as an edge block, selection of the massic transformation is a somewhat more complicated process. The block is first divided into a bright and a dark region. The dynamic range of the block $r_d(R_k)$ is then computed as the difference of the average values of the light and dark regions. For a given domain block, this is then used to compute the value of α_k by

$$\alpha_k = \min\left\{ \frac{r_d(R_k)}{r_d(T_j)}, \alpha_{\max} \right\} \tag{15.37}$$

where $\alpha_{\max}$ is an upper bound on the scaling factor. The value of α_k obtained in this manner is then quantized to one of a small set of values. Once the value of α_k has been obtained, Δ_k is obtained as the difference of either the average values of the bright regions or the average values of the dark regions, depending on whether we have more pixels in the dark regions or the light regions. Finally, each of the isometries is tried out to find the one that gives the closest match between the transformed domain block and the range block.

Once the transformations have been obtained, they are communicated to the receiver in terms of the following parameters: the location of the selected domain block and a single bit denoting whether the block is a shade block or not. If it is a shade block, the average intensity value is transmitted; if it is not, the quantized scale factor and offset are transmitted along with the label of the isometry used.

The receiver starts out with some arbitrary initial image $\mathcal{I}_0$. The transformations are then applied for each of the range blocks to obtain the first approximation. Then the transformations are applied to the first approximation to get the second approximation, and so on. Let us see an example of the decoding process.

Example 15.4.2:

FIGURE   15.11   Original Elif image.

The image Elif, shown in Figure 15.11, was encoded using the fractal approach. The original image was of size 256 × 256, and each pixel was coded using 8 bits. Therefore, the storage space required was 65,536 bytes. The compressed image consisted of the transformations described above. The transformations required a total of 4,580 bytes, which translates to an average rate of 0.56 bits per pixel. The decoding process started with the transformations being applied to an all-zero image. The first six iterations of the decoding process are shown in Figure 15.12. The process converged in nine iterations. The final image is shown in Figure 15.13. Notice the difference in this reconstructed image and the low-rate reconstructed image obtained using the DCT. The blocking artifacts are for the most part gone. However, this does not mean that the reconstruction is free of distortions and artifacts. They are especially visible in the chin and neck region.   ◆

In our discussion (and illustration) we have assumed that the size of the range blocks is constant. If so, how large should we pick the range block? If we pick the size of the range block to be large, we will have to send fewer transformations, thus improving the compression.

FIGURE 15.12   The first six iterations of the fractal decoding process.

FIGURE 1 5 . 1 3   **Final reconstructed Elif image.**

However, if the size of the range block is large, it becomes more difficult to find a domain block that, after appropriate transformation, will be close to the range block, which in turn will increase the distortion in the reconstructed image. One compromise between picking a large or small value for the size of the range block is to start out with a large size and, if a good enough match is not found, to progressively reduce the size of the range block until we have either found a good match or reached a minimum size. We could also compute a weighted sum of the rate and distortion

$$J = D + \beta R$$

where D is a measure of the distortion, and R represents the number of bits required to represent the block. We could then either subdivide or not depending on the value of J.

We can also start out with range blocks that have the minimum size (also called the *atomic blocks*) and obtain larger blocks via merging smaller blocks.

There are a number of ways in which we can perform the subdivision. The most commonly known approach is *quadtree partitioning*, initially introduced by Samet [201]. In quadtree partitioning we start by dividing up the image into the maximum-size range blocks. If a particular block does not have a satisfactory reconstruction, we can divide it up into four blocks. These blocks in turn can also, if needed, be divided into four blocks. An example of quadtree partitioning can be seen in Figure 15.14. In this particular case there are three possible sizes for the range blocks. Generally, we would like to keep the minimum size of the range block small if fine detail in the image is of greater importance [76]. Since we have multiple sizes for the range blocks, we also need multiple sizes for the domain blocks.

Quadtree partitioning is not the only method of partitioning available. Another popular method of partitioning is the HV method. In this method we allow the use of rectangular

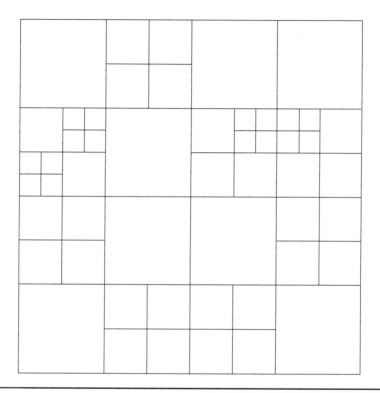

FIGURE 15.14 **An example of quadtree partitioning.**

regions. Instead of dividing a square region into four more square regions, rectangular regions are divided either vertically or horizontally in order to generate more homogeneous regions. In particular, if there are vertical or horizontal edges in a block, it is partitioned along these edges. One way to obtain the locations of partitions for a given $M \times N$ range block is to calculate the biased vertical and horizontal differences:

$$v_i = \frac{\min(i, N - i - 1)}{N - 1} \left(\sum_j \mathcal{I}_{i,j} - \sum_j \mathcal{I}_{i+1,j} \right)$$

$$h_j = \frac{\min(j, M - j - 1)}{M - 1} \left(\sum_j \mathcal{I}_{i,j} - \sum_j \mathcal{I}_{i,j+1} \right).$$

The values of i and j for which $|v_i|$ and $|h_j|$ are the largest indicate the row and column for which there is maximum difference between two halves of the block. Depending on whether $|v_i|$ or $|h_j|$ is larger, we can divide the rectangle either vertically or horizontally.

Finally, partitioning does not have to be rectangular, or even regular. People have experimented with triangle partitions as well as irregular-shaped partitions [203].

The fractal approach is a novel way of looking at image compression. At present the quality of the reconstructions using the fractal approach is about the same as the quality of the reconstruction using the DCT approach employed in JPEG. However, the fractal technique is relatively new, and further research may bring significant improvements. The fractal approach has one significant advantage: decoding is simple and fast. This makes it especially useful in applications where compression is performed once and decompression is performed many times.

15.5 Summary

We have looked at two very different ways of using the analysis/synthesis approach. In speech coding the approach works because of the availability of a mathematical model for the speech generation process. We have seen how this model can be used in a number of different ways, depending on the constraints of the problem. Where the primary objective is to achieve intelligible communication at the lowest rate possible, the LPC algorithm provides a very nice solution. If we also want the quality of the speech to be high, CELP and the different sinusoidal techniques provide higher quality at the cost of more complexity and processing delay. If delay also needs to be kept below a threshold, one particular solution is the low-delay CELP algorithm in the G.728 recommendation. For images, fractal coding provides a very different way to look at the problem. Instead of using the physical structure of the system to generate the source output, it uses a more abstract view to obtain an analysis/synthesis technique.

Further Reading

1. For information about various aspects of speech processing, *Voice and Speech Processing,* by T. Parsons [173], is a very readable source.

2. The classic tutorial on linear prediction is "Linear Prediction," by J. Makhoul [145], which appeared in the April 1975 issue of the *Proceedings of the IEEE.*

3. For a thorough review of recent activity in speech compression, see "Advances in Speech and Audio Compression," by A. Gersho [83], which appeared in the June 1994 issue of the *Proceedings of the IEEE.*

4. An excellent source for information about speech coders is *Digital Speech: Coding for Low Bit Rate Communication Systems*, by A. Kondoz [127].

5. An excellent description of the G.728 algorithm can be found in "A Low Delay CELP Coder for the CCITT 16 kb/s Speech Coding Standard," by J.-H. Chen, R.V. Cox, Y.-C. Lin, N. Jayant, and M.J. Melchner [42], in the June 1992 issue of the *IEEE Journal on Selected Areas of Communications.*

6. A good introduction to fractal image compression is *Fractal Image Compression: Theory and Application*, Y. Fisher (ed.) [76], New York: Springer-Verlag, 1995.

7. The October 1993 issue of the *Proceedings of the IEEE* contains a special section on fractals with a tutorial on fractal image compression by A. Jacquin.

15.6 Projects and Problems

1. Write a program for the detection of voiced and unvoiced segments using the AMDF function. Test your algorithm on the `test.snd` sound file.

2. The `testf.raw` file is a female voice saying the word *test*. Isolate 10 voiced and unvoiced segments from the `testm.raw` file and the `testf.snd` file. (Try to pick the same segments in the two files.) Compute the number of zero crossings in each segment and compare your results for the two files.

3. (a) Select a voiced segment from the `testf.raw` file. Find the fourth-, sixth-, and tenth-order LPC filters for this segment using the Levinson-Durbin algorithm.

(b) Pick the corresponding segment from the `testf.snd` file. Find the fourth-, sixth-, and tenth-order LPC filters for this segment using the Levinson-Durbin algorithm.

(c) Compare the results of (a) and (b).

4. Select a voiced segment from the `test.raw` file. Find the fourth-, sixth-, and tenth-order LPC filters for this segment using the Levinson-Durbin algorithm. For each of the filters, find the multipulse sequence that results in the closest approximation to the voiced signal.

16

Video Compression

16.1 Overview

Video compression can be viewed as image compression with a temporal component since video consists of a time sequence of images. From this point of view, the only "new" technique introduced in this chapter is a strategy to take advantage of this temporal correlation. However, there are different situations in which video compression becomes necessary, each requiring a solution specific to its peculiar conditions. In this chapter we briefly look at video compression algorithms and standards developed for three different situations: videoconferencing, applications such as broadcast video, and video over packet-switched networks.

16.2 Introduction

Of all the different sources of data, perhaps the one that produces the largest amount of data is video. Consider a video sequence generated using the CCIR 601 format (Section 16.4). Each image frame is made up of more than a quarter million pixels. At the rate of 30 frames per second and 16 bits per pixel, this corresponds to a data rate of about 21 Mbytes or 168 Mbits per second. This is certainly a change from the data rates of 2.4, 4.8, and 16 kbits per second that are the targets for speech coding systems discussed in Chapter 15.

Video compression can be viewed as the compression of a sequence of images; in other words, image compression with a temporal component. This is essentially the approach we will take in this chapter. However, there are limitations to this approach. We do not perceive motion video in the same manner as we perceive still images. Motion video may mask coding artifacts that would be visible in still images. On the other hand, artifacts that may not be visible in reconstructed still images can be very annoying in reconstructed motion video sequences. For example, consider a compression scheme that introduces a modest random amount of change in the average intensity of the pixels in the image. Unless a reconstructed still image was being compared side by side with the original image, this artifact may go totally unnoticed. However, in a motion video sequence, especially one with low activity, random intensity changes can be quite annoying. As another example, poor reproduction of edges can be a serious problem in the compression of still images. However, if there is some temporal activity in the video sequence, errors in the reconstruction of edges may go unnoticed.

Although a more holistic approach might lead to better compression schemes, it is more convenient to view video as a sequence of correlated images. Most of the video compression algorithms make use of the temporal correlation to remove redundancy. The previous reconstructed frame is used to generate a prediction for the current frame. The difference between the prediction and the current frame, the prediction error or residual, is encoded and transmitted to the receiver. The previous reconstructed frame is also available at the receiver. Therefore, if the receiver knows the manner in which the prediction was performed, it can use this information to generate the prediction values and add them to the prediction error to generate the reconstruction. The prediction operation in video coding has to take into account motion of the objects in the frame, which is known as motion compensation (described in the next section).

We will also describe a number of different video compression algorithms. For the most part, we restrict ourselves to discussions of techniques that have found their way into international standards. Because there are a significant number of products that use proprietary video compression algorithms, it is difficult to find or include descriptions of them.

We have classified the algorithms based on the application area. While attempts have been made to develop standards that are "generic," the application requirements play a large part in determining the features to be used and the values of parameters. When the compression algorithm is being designed for two-way communication, it is necessary for the coding delay to be minimal. Furthermore, compression and decompression should have about the same level of complexity. The complexity can be unbalanced in a broadcast application, where there is one transmitter and many receivers, and the communication is essentially one-way. In this case, the encoder can be much more complex than the receiver. There is also more tolerance for encoding delays. In applications where the video is to be decoded on workstations and personal computers, the decoding complexity has to be extremely low in order for the decoder to decode a sufficient number of images to give the illusion of motion. However, as the encoding is generally not done in real time, the encoder can be quite complex. When the video is to be transmitted over packet networks, the effects of packet loss have to be taken into account when designing the compression algorithm. Thus, each application will present its own unique requirements and demand a solution that fits those requirements.

We will assume that you are familiar with the particular image compression technique being used. For example, when discussing transform-based video compression techniques, we assume that you have reviewed Chapter 12 and are familiar with the descriptions of transforms and the JPEG algorithm contained in that chapter.

16.3 Motion Compensation

In most video sequences there is little change in the contents of the image from one frame to the next. Even in sequences that depict a great deal of activity, there are significant portions of the image that do not change from one frame to the next. Most video compression schemes take advantage of this redundancy by using the previous frame to generate a prediction for the current frame. We have used prediction previously when we studied differential encoding schemes. If we try to apply those techniques blindly to video compression by predicting the value of each pixel by the value of the pixel at the same location in the previous frame, we will run into trouble because we would not be taking into account the fact that objects tend to move between frames. Thus, the object in one frame that was providing the pixel at a certain location (i_0, j_0) with its intensity value might be providing the same intensity value in the next frame to a pixel at location (i_1, j_1). If we don't take this into account, we can actually increase the amount of information that needs to be transmitted.

Example 16.3.1:

Consider the two frames of a motion video sequence shown in Figure 16.1. The only differences between the two frames are that the devious looking individual has moved slightly downward and to the right of the frame, while the triangular object has moved to the left. The differences between the two frames are so slight, you would think that if the first frame was available to both the transmitter and receiver, not much information would need to be transmitted to the receiver in order to reconstruct the second frame. However, if we simply take the difference between the two frames, as shown in Figure 16.2, the displacement of the objects in the frame results in an image that contains more detail than the original image. In

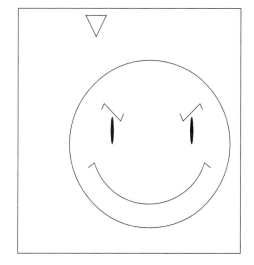

FIGURE 16.1   Two frames of a video sequence.

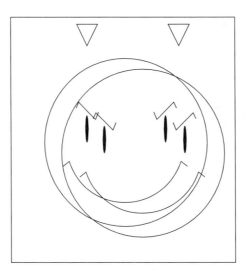

FIGURE 16.2   Difference between the two frames.

other words, instead of the differencing operation reducing the information, there is actually
more information that needs to be transmitted.   ◆

In order to use a previous frame to predict the pixel values in the frame being encoded, we
have to take the motion of objects in the image into account. Although a number of approaches
have been investigated, the method that has worked best in practice is a simple approach called
block-based motion compensation. In this approach, the frame being encoded is divided into
blocks of size $M \times M$. For each block, we search the previous reconstructed frame for the
block of size $M \times M$ that most closely matches the block being encoded. We can measure
the closeness of a match, or distance, between two blocks by the sum of absolute differences
between corresponding pixels in the two blocks. We would obtain the same results if we used
the sum of squared differences between the corresponding pixels as a measure of distance.
Generally, if the distance from the block being encoded to the closest block in the previous
reconstructed frame is greater than some prespecified threshold, the block is declared uncom-
pensable and is encoded without the benefit of prediction. This decision is also transmitted to
the receiver. If the distance is below the threshold, then a *motion vector* is transmitted to the
receiver. The motion vector is the relative location of the block to be used for prediction obtained by subtracting the coordinates of the upper-left corner pixel of the block being encoded
from the coordinates of the upper-left corner pixel of the block being used for prediction.

Suppose the block being encoded is an 8×8 block between pixel locations $(24, 40)$ and
$(31, 47)$; that is, the upper-left corner pixel of the 8×8 block is at location $(24, 40)$. If the
block that best matches it in the previous frame is located between pixels at location $(21, 43)$
and $(28, 50)$, then the motion vector would be $(-3, 3)$. The motion vector was obtained by
subtracting the location of the upper-left corner of the block being encoded from the location
of the upper-left corner of the best matching block. Note that the blocks are numbered starting

from the top-left corner. Therefore, a positive x component means that the best matching block in the previous frame is to the right of the location of the block being encoded. Similarly, a positive y component means that the best matching block is at a location below that of the location of the block being encoded.

Example 16.3.2:

Let us again try to predict the second frame of Example 16.3.1 using motion compensation. We divide the image into blocks and then predict the second frame from the first in the manner described above. Figure 16.3 shows the blocks in the previous frame that were used to predict some of the blocks in the current frame.

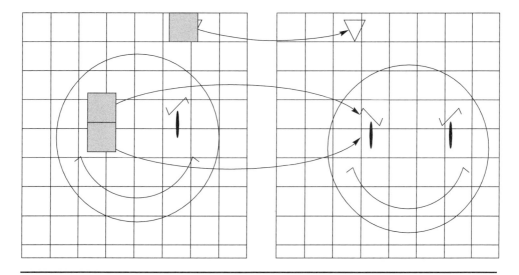

FIGURE 16.3   Motion-compensated prediction.

Notice that in this case all that needs to be transmitted to the receiver are the motion vectors. The current frame is completely predicted by the previous frame.   ◆

We have been describing motion compensation where the displacement between the block being encoded and the best matching block is an integer number of pixels in the horizontal and vertical directions. There are algorithms in which the displacement is measured in half pixels. In order to do this, pixels of the coded frame being searched are interpolated to obtain twice as many pixels as in the original frame. This "doubled" image is then searched for the best matching block.

The doubled image is obtained as follows: Consider Table 16.1. In this image A, B, C, and D are the pixels of the original frame. The pixels h_1, h_2, v_1, and v_2 are obtained by interpolating

TABLE 16.1   "Doubled" image.

A	h_1	B
v_1	c	v_2
C	h_2	D

between the two neighboring pixels:

$$h_1 = \left\lfloor \frac{A+B}{2} + 0.5 \right\rfloor$$

$$h_2 = \left\lfloor \frac{C+D}{2} + 0.5 \right\rfloor$$

$$v_1 = \left\lfloor \frac{A+C}{2} + 0.5 \right\rfloor$$

$$v_2 = \left\lfloor \frac{B+D}{2} + 0.5 \right\rfloor \tag{16.1}$$

while the pixel c is obtained as the average of the four neighboring pixels from the coded original:

$$c = \left\lfloor \frac{A+B+C+D}{4} + 0.5 \right\rfloor .$$

We have described motion compensation in very general terms in this section. The various schemes in this chapter use specific motion compensation schemes that differ from each other. The differences generally involve the region of search for the matching block and the search procedure. We will look at the details with the study of the compression schemes. But before we begin our study of compression schemes, we briefly discuss how video signals are represented in the next section.

16.4 Video Signal Representation

The development of different representations of video signals has depended a great deal on past history. We will also take a historical view, starting with black-and-white television proceeding to digital video formats. The history of the development of analog video signal formats for the United States has been different than for Europe. Although we will show the development using the formats used in the United States, the basic ideas are the same for all formats.

A black-and-white television picture is generated by exciting the phosphor on the television screen using an electron beam whose intensity is modulated to generate the image we see. The path that the modulated electron beam traces is shown in Figure 16.4. The line created by the horizontal traversal of the electron beam is called a line of the image. In order to trace a second line, the electron beam has to be deflected back to the left of the screen. During this period, the gun is turned off in order to prevent the retrace from becoming visible. The image generated by the traversal of the electron gun has to be updated rapidly enough for

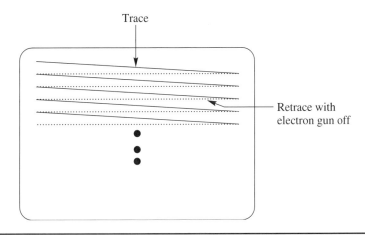

FIGURE 16.4   The path traversed by the electron beam in a television.

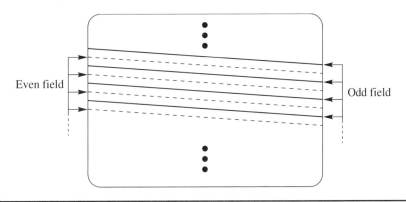

FIGURE 16.5   A frame and its constituent fields.

persistence of vision to make the image appear stable. However, higher rates of information transfer require higher bandwidths, which translate to higher costs.

In order to keep the cost of bandwidth low it was decided to send 525 lines 30 times a second. These 525 lines are said to constitute a *frame*. However, a thirtieth of a second between frames is long enough for the image to appear to flicker. To avoid the flicker, it was decided to divide the image into two interlaced fields. A field is sent once every sixtieth of a second. First, one field consisting of 262.5 lines is traced by the electron beam. Then, the second field consisting of the remaining 262.5 lines is traced *between* the lines of the first field. The situation is shown schematically in Figure 16.5. The first field is shown with solid lines while the second field is shown with dashed lines. The first field begins on a full line and ends on a half line while the second field begins on a half line and ends on a full line. Not all 525 lines are displayed on the screen. Some are lost due to the time required for the electron gun to position the beam from the bottom to the top of the screen. We actually see about 486 lines per frame.

In a color television, instead of a single electron gun, we have three electron guns that act in unison. These guns excite red, green, and blue phosphor dots embedded in the screen. The beam from each gun strikes only one kind of phosphor, and the gun is named according to the color of the phosphor it excites. Thus, the red gun strikes only the red phosphor, the blue gun strikes only the blue phosphor, and the green gun strikes only the green phosphor. (Each gun is prevented from hitting a different type of phosphor by an aperture mask.)

In order to control the three guns we need three signals: a red signal, a blue signal, and a green signal. If we transmitted each of these separately, we would need three times the bandwidth. With the advent of color television, there was also the problem of backward compatibility. Most people had black-and-white television sets, and television stations did not want to broadcast using a format that most of the viewing audience could not see on their existing sets. Both issues were resolved with the creation of a composite color signal. In the United States, the specifications for the composite signal were created by the National Television Systems Committee, and the composite signal is often called an NTSC signal. The corresponding signals in Europe are PAL (Phase Alternating Lines), developed in Germany, and SECAM (Séquential Coleur avec Mémoire), developed in France. There is some (hopefully) good-natured rivalry between proponents of the different systems. Some problems with color reproduction in the NTSC signal have led to the name *Never Twice the Same Color*, while the ideosyncracies of the SECAM system have led to the name *Systéme Essentiallement Contre les Américains* (system essentially against the Americans).

The composite color signal consists of a *luminance* component, corresponding to the black-and-white television signal, and two *chrominance* components. The luminance component is denoted by Y:

$$Y = 0.299R + 0.587G + 0.114B \qquad (16.2)$$

where R is the red component, G is the green component, and B is the blue component. The weighting of the three components was obtained through extensive testing with human observers. The two chrominance signals are obtained as

$$C_b = B - Y \qquad (16.3)$$
$$C_r = R - Y. \qquad (16.4)$$

These three signals can be used by the color television set to generate the red, blue, and green signals needed to control the electron guns. The luminance signal can be used directly by the black-and-white televisions.

Because the eye is much less sensitive to changes of the chrominance in an image, the chrominance signal does not need to have higher frequency components. Thus, lower bandwidth of the chrominance signals along with a clever use of modulation techniques permits all three signals to be encoded without need of any bandwidth expansion. (A simple and readable explanation of television systems can be found in [5].)

The early efforts toward digitization of the video signal were devoted to sampling the composite signal, and in the United States the Society of Motion Picture and Television Engineers developed a standard that required sampling the NTSC signal at a little more than 14 million times a second. In Europe, the efforts at standardization of video were centered around the characteristics of the PAL signal. Because of the differences between NTSC and PAL, this would have resulted in different "standards." In the late 1970s, this approach was dropped in

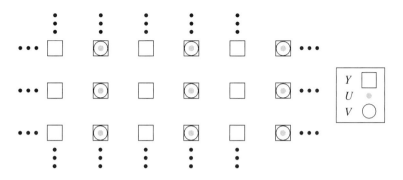

FIGURE 16.6 **Recommendation 601 4:2:2 sampling format.**

favor of sampling the components and the development of a worldwide standard. This standard was developed under the auspices of the International Consultative Committee on Radio (CCIR) and was called CCIR recommendation 601-2. CCIR is now known as ITU-R, and the recommendation is officially known as ITU-R recommendation BT.601-2. However, the standard is generally referred to as recommendation 601 or CCIR 601.

The standard proposes a family of sampling rates based on the sampling frequency of 3.725 MHz (3.725 million samples per second). Multiples of this sampling frequency permit samples on each line to line up vertically, thus generating the rectangular array of pixels necessary for digital processing. Each component can be sampled at an integer multiple of 3.725 MHz, up to a maximum of four times this frequency. The sampling rate is represented as a triple of integers, with the first integer corresponding to the sampling of the luminance component and the remaining two corresponding to the chrominance components. Thus, 4:4:4 sampling means that all components were sampled at 13.5 MHz. The most popular sampling format is the 4:2:2 format, in which the luminance signal is sampled at 13.5 MHz, while the lower-bandwidth chrominance signals are sampled at 6.75 MHz. If we ignore the samples of the portion of the signal that do not correspond to active video, the sampling rate translates to 720 samples per line for the luminance signal and 360 samples per line for the chrominance signal. The sampling format is shown in Figure 16.6. The luminance component of the digital video signal is also denoted by Y, while the chrominance components are denoted by U and V. The sampled analog values are converted to digital values as follows. The sampled values of YC_bC_r are normalized so that the sampled Y values, Y_s, take on values between 0 and 1, and the sampled chrominance values, C_{rs} and C_{bs}, take on values between $\frac{-1}{2}$ and $\frac{1}{2}$. These normalized values are converted to 8-bit numbers according to the transformations

$$Y = 219Y_s + 16 \tag{16.5}$$
$$U = 224C_{bs} + 128 \tag{16.6}$$
$$V = 224C_{rs} + 128. \tag{16.7}$$

Thus, the Y component takes on values between 16 and 235, and the U and V components take on values between 16 and 240.

An example of the Y component of a CCIR 601 frame is shown in Figure 16.7. In the top image we show the fields separately, while in the bottom image the fields have been

FIGURE 16.7   Top: Fields of a CCIR 601 frame. Bottom: An interlaced CCIR 601 frame.

FIGURE 16.8   Generation of an SIF frame.

interlaced. Notice that in the interlaced image the smaller figure looks blurred. This is because the individual moved in the sixtieth of a second between the two fields. (This is also proof—if any was needed—that a three-year-old cannot remain still, even for a sixtieth of a second!)

The *YUV* data can also be arranged in other formats. In the Common Interchange Format (CIF), which is used for videoconferencing, the luminance of the image is represented by an array of 288×352 pixels, and the two chrominance signals are represented by two arrays consisting of 144×176 pixels. In the QCIF (Quarter CIF) format, we have half the number of pixels in both the rows and columns.

The MPEG-1 algorithm, which was developed for encoding video at rates up to 1.5 Mbits per second, uses a different subsampling of the CCIR 601 format to obtain the MPEG-SIF format. Starting from a 4:2:2, 480-line CCIR 601 format, the vertical resolution is first reduced by taking only the odd field for both the luminance and the chrominance components. The horizontal resolution is then reduced by filtering (to prevent aliasing) and then subsampling by a factor of two in the horizontal direction. This results in 360×240 samples of Y and 180×240 samples each of U and V. The vertical resolution of the chrominance samples is further reduced by filtering and subsampling in the vertical direction by a factor of two to obtain 180×120 samples for each of the chrominance signals. The process is shown in Figure 16.8, and the resulting format is shown in Figure 16.9.

16.5   Algorithms for Videoconferencing and Videophones

Videoconferencing applications require compression techniques that do not have excess coding delay. In these systems, there is no particular advantage to shifting the complexity onto either the encoder or the decoder because each user of the system will require both

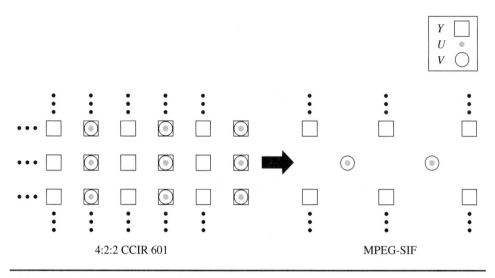

FIGURE 16.9   CCIR 601 to MPEG-SIF.

encoding and decoding capabilities. As in the case of image compression, most of the standards for video compression are based on the discrete cosine transform (DCT). The standard for teleconferencing applications, ITU-T recommendation H.261, is no exception. Most systems currently in use for videoconferencing use proprietary compression algorithms. However, in order for the equipment from different manufacturers to communicate with each other, these systems also offer the option of using H.261. We will describe the compression algorithm used in the H.261 standard in this section.

We will also describe a new approach towards compression of video for videophone applications called three-dimensional model-based coding. This approach is far from maturity, and our description will be rather cursory. The reason for including it here is the great promise it holds for the future.

16.5.1   ITU-T Recommendation H.261

The earliest DCT-based video coding standard is the ITU-T H.261 standard. This algorithm assumes one of two formats, CIF and QCIF. A block diagram of the H.261 video coder is shown in Figure 16.10. The basic idea is simple. An input image is divided into blocks of 8×8 pixels. For a given 8×8 block, we subtract the prediction generated using the previous frame. (If there is no previous frame or the previous frame is very different from the current frame, the prediction might be zero.) The difference between the block being encoded and the prediction is transformed using a DCT. The transform coefficients are quantized and the quantization label encoded using a variable-length code. In the following discussion, we will take a more detailed look at the various components of the compression algorithm.

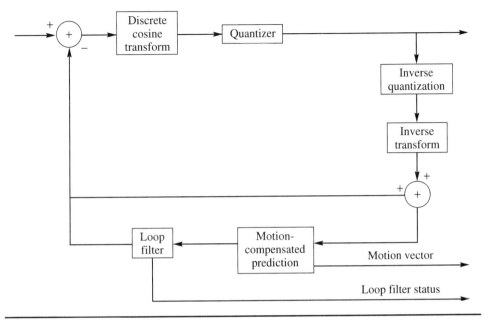

FIGURE 16.10 **Block diagram of the ITU-T H.261 encoder.**

Motion Compensation

Motion compensation requires a large amount of computation. Consider finding a matching block for an 8 × 8 block. Each comparison requires taking 64 differences and then computing the sum of the absolute value of the differences. If we assume that the closest block in the previous frame is located within 20 pixels in either the horizontal or vertical direction of the block to be encoded, we need to perform 1681 comparisons. There are several ways we can reduce the total number of computations.

One way is to increase the size of the block. Increasing the size of the block means more computations per comparison. However, it also means that we will have fewer blocks per frame, so the number of times we have to perform the motion compensation will decrease. However, different objects in a frame may be moving in different directions. The drawback to increasing the size of the block is that the probability that a block will contain objects moving in different directions increases with size. Consider the two images in Figure 16.11. If we use blocks that are made up of 2 × 2 squares, we can find a block that exactly matches the 2 × 2 block that contains the circle. However, if we increase the size of the block to 4 × 4 squares, the block that contains the circle also contains the upper part of the octagon. We cannot find a similar 4 × 4 block in the previous frame. Thus, there is a trade-off involved. Larger blocks reduce the amount of computation; however, they can also result in poor prediction, which in turn can lead to poor compression performance.

Another way we can reduce the number of computations is by reducing the search space. If we reduce the size of the region in which we search for a match, the number of computations

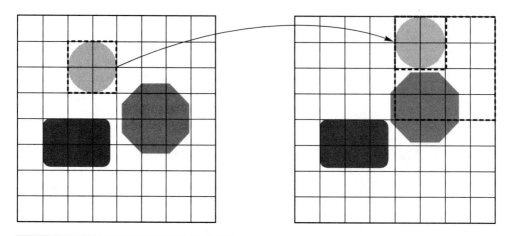

FIGURE 16.11   **Effect of block size on motion compensation.**

will be reduced. However, reducing the search region also increases the probability of missing a match. Again, we have a trade-off between computation and the amount of compression.

The H.261 standard has balanced the trade-offs in the following manner. The 8×8 blocks of luminance and chrominance pixels are organized into *macroblocks*, which consist of four luminance blocks, and one each of the two types of chrominance blocks. The motion-compensated prediction (or motion compensation) operation is performed on the macroblock level. For each macroblock, we search the previous reconstructed frame for the macroblock that most closely matches the macroblock being encoded. In order to further reduce the amount of computations, only the luminance blocks are considered in this matching operation. The motion vector for the prediction of the chrominance blocks is obtained by halving the component values of the motion vector for the luminance macroblock. Therefore, if the motion vector for the luminance blocks was $(-3, 10)$, then the motion vector for the chrominance blocks would be $(-1, 5)$.

The search area is restricted to ± 15 pixels of the macroblock being encoded in the horizontal and vertical directions. That is, if the upper-left corner pixel of the block being encoded is (x_c, y_c), and the upper-left corner of the best matching macroblock is (x_p, y_p), then (x_c, y_c) and (x_p, y_p) have to satisfy the constraints $|x_c - x_p| < 15$ and $|y_c - y_p| < 15$.

The Loop Filter

Sometimes sharp edges in the block used for prediction can result in the generation of sharp changes in the prediction error. This in turn can cause high values for the high-frequency coefficients in the transforms, which can increase the transmission rate. To avoid this, prior to taking the difference, the prediction block can be smoothed by using a two-dimensional spatial filter. The filter is separable; it can be implemented as a one-dimensional filter that first operates on the rows, then on the columns. The filter coefficients are $\frac{1}{4}, \frac{1}{2}, \frac{1}{4}$, except at block boundaries where one of the filter taps would fall outside the block. To prevent this from happening, the block boundaries remain unchanged by the filtering operation.

Example 16.5.1:

TABLE 16.2 Original block of pixels.

110	218	116	112
108	210	110	114
110	218	210	112
112	108	110	116

TABLE 16.3 After filtering the rows.

110	165	140	112
108	159	135	114
110	188	187	112
112	109	111	116

TABLE 16.4 Final block.

110	165	140	112
108	167	148	113
110	161	154	113
112	109	111	116

Let's filter the 4×4 block of pixel values shown in Table 16.2 using the filter specified for the H.261 algorithm. From the pixel values we can see that this is a gray square with a white L in it. (Recall that small pixel values correspond to darker pixels and large pixel values correspond to lighter pixels, with 0 corresponding to black and 255 corresponding to white.)

Let's filter the first row. We leave the first pixel value the same. The second value becomes

$$\frac{1}{4} \times 110 + \frac{1}{2} \times 218 + \frac{1}{4} \times 116 = 165$$

where we have assumed integer division. The third filtered value becomes

$$\frac{1}{4} \times 218 + \frac{1}{2} \times 116 + \frac{1}{4} \times 112 = 140.$$

The final element in the first row of the filtered block remains unchanged. Continuing in this fashion with all four rows, we get the 4×4 block shown in Table 16.3.

Now repeat the filtering operation along the columns. The final 4×4 block is shown in Table 16.4. Notice how much more homogeneous this last block is compared to the original block. This means that it will most likely not introduce any sharp variations in the difference block, and the high-frequency coefficients in the transform will be closer to zero, leading to compression. ◆

This filter is either switched on or off for each macroblock. The conditions for turning the filter on or off are not specified by the recommendations.

The Transform

The transform operation is performed with a DCT on an 8×8 block of pixels or pixel differences. If the motion compensation operation does not provide a close match, then the transform operation is performed on an 8×8 block of pixels. If the transform operation is performed on a block level, either a block or the difference between the block and its predicted value is quantized and transmitted to the receiver. The receiver performs the inverse operations to reconstruct the image. The receiver operation is also simulated at the transmitter, where the reconstructed images are obtained and stored in a frame store. The encoder is said to be in *intra* mode if it operates directly on the input image without the use of motion compensation. Otherwise, it is said to be in *inter* mode.

Quantization and Coding

Depending on how good or poor the prediction is, we can get a wide variation in the characteristics of the coefficients that are to be quantized. In the case of an intra block, the DC coefficients will take on much larger values than the other coefficients. Where there is little motion from frame to frame, the difference between the block being encoded and the prediction will be small, leading to small values for the coefficients.

In order to deal with this wide variation, we need a quantization strategy that can be rapidly adapted to the current situation. The H.261 algorithm does this by switching between 32 different quantizers, possibly from one macroblock to the next. One quantizer is reserved for the intra DC coefficient, while the remaining 31 quantizers are used for the other coefficients. The intra DC quantizer is a uniform midrise quantizer with a step size of 8. The other quantizers are midtread quantizers with a step size of an even value between 2 and 62. Given a particular block of coefficients, if we use a quantizer with smaller step size, we are likely to get a larger number of nonzero coefficients. Because of the manner in which the labels are encoded, the number of bits that will need to be transmitted will increase. Therefore, the availability of transmission resources will have a major impact on the quantizer selection. We will discuss this aspect further when we talk about the transmission buffer. Once a quantizer is selected, the receiver has to be informed about the selection. In H.261, this is done in one of two ways. Each macroblock is preceded by a header. The quantizer being used can be identified as part of this header. When the amount of activity or motion in the sequence is relatively constant, it is reasonable to expect that the same quantizer will be used for a large number of macroblocks. In this case, it would be wasteful to identify the quantizer being used with each macroblock. The macroblocks are organized into *groups of blocks* (GOBs), each of which consist of three rows of 11 macroblocks. This hierarchical arrangement is shown in Figure 16.12. Only the luminance blocks are shown. The header preceding each GOB contains a 5-bit field for identifying the quantizer. Once a quantizer has been identified in the GOB header, the receiver assumes that quantizer is being used, unless this choice is overridden using the macroblock header.

Macroblock

FIGURE 16.12 **A GOB consisting of 33 macroblocks.**

The quantization labels are encoded in a manner similar to, but not exactly the same as, JPEG. The labels are scanned in a zigzag fashion like JPEG. The nonzero labels are coded along with the number, or run, of coefficients quantized to zero. The 20 most commonly occurring combinations of (run, label) are coded with a single variable-length codeword. All other combinations of (run, label) are coded with a 20-bit word, made up of a 6-bit escape sequence, a 6-bit code denoting the run, and an 8-bit code for the label.

In order to avoid transmitting blocks that have no nonzero quantized coefficient, the header preceding each macroblock can contain a variable-length code called the *coded block pattern* (CBP) that indicates which of the six blocks contain nonzero labels. The CBP can take on one of 64 different pattern numbers, which are then encoded by a variable-length code. The pattern number is given by

$$\text{CBP} = 32P_1 + 16P_2 + 8P_3 + 4P_4 + 2P_5 + P_6$$

where P_1 through P_6 correspond to the six different blocks in the macroblock, and is one if the corresponding block has a nonzero quantized coefficient and zero otherwise.

Rate Control

The binary codewords generated by the transform coder form the input to a transmission buffer. The function of the transmission buffer is to keep the output rate of the encoder fixed. If the buffer starts filling up faster than the transmission rate, it sends a message back to the transform coder to reduce the output from the quantization. If the buffer is in danger of becoming emptied because the transform coder is providing bits at a rate lower than the transmission rate, the transmission buffer can request a higher rate from the transform coder. This operation is called *rate control*.

The change in rate can be affected in two different ways. First, the quantizer being used will affect the rate. If a quantizer with a large step size is used, a larger number of coefficients will be quantized to zero. Also, there is a higher probability that those not quantized to zero will be one of the those values that have a shorter variable-length codeword. Therefore, if a higher rate is required, the transform coder selects a quantizer with a smaller step size, and if a lower rate is required, the transform coder selects a quantizer with a larger step size. The quantizer step size is set at the beginning of each GOB, but can be changed at the beginning of any macroblock. If the rate cannot be lowered enough and there is a danger of buffer overflow, the more drastic option of dropping frames from transmission is used.

The ITU-T H.261 algorithm was primarily designed for videophone and videoconferencing applications. Therefore, the algorithm had to operate with minimal coding delay (less than 150 milliseconds). Furthermore, for videophone applications, the algorithm had to operate at very low bit rates. In fact, the title for the recommendation is "Video Codec for Audiovisual Services at $p \times 64$ kbit/s," where p takes on values from 1 to 30. A p value of 2 corresponds to a total transmission rate of 128 kbps, which is the same as two voice-band telephone channels. These are very low rates for video, and the ITU-T H.261 recommendations perform relatively well at these rates.

16.5.2   Model-Based Coding

In speech coding, a major decrease in rate is realized when we go from coding waveforms to an analysis/synthesis approach. An attempt at doing the same for video coding is described in the next section. A technique that has not yet reached maturity but shows great promise for use in videophone applications is an analysis/synthesis technique. The analysis/synthesis approach requires that the transmitter and receiver agree on a model for the information to be transmitted. The transmitter then analyzes the information to be transmitted and extracts the model parameters, which are transmitted to the receiver. The receiver uses these parameters to synthesize the source information. While this approach has been successfully used for speech compression for a long time (see Chapter 15), the same has not been true for images. In a delightful book, *Signals, Systems, and Noise—The Nature and Process of Communications*, published in 1961, J.R. Pierce [180] described his "dream" of an analysis/synthesis scheme for what we would now call a videoconferencing system:

> Imagine that we had at the receiver a sort of rubbery model of the human face. Or we might have a description of such a model stored in the memory of a huge electronic computer.... Then, as the person before the transmitter talked, the transmitter would have to follow the movements of his eyes, lips, and jaws, and other muscular movements and transmit these so that the model at the receiver could do likewise.

Pierce's dream is a reasonably accurate description of a three-dimensional model-based approach to the compression of facial image sequences. In this approach, a generic wireframe model, such as the one shown in Figure 16.13, is constructed using triangles. When encoding the movements of a specific human face, the model is adjusted to the face by matching features and the outer contour of the face. The image textures are then mapped onto this wireframe model to synthesize the face. Once this model is available to both transmitter and receiver, only changes in the face are transmitted to the receiver. These changes can be classified as *global motion* or *local motion* [47]. Global motion involves movement of the head, while local motion involves changes in the features—in other words, changes in facial expressions. The global motion can be modeled in terms of movements of rigid bodies. The facial expressions can be represented in terms of relative movements of the vertices of the triangles in the

FIGURE 16.13   **Generic wireframe model.**

wireframe model. In practice, separating a movement into global and local components can be difficult because most points on the face will be affected by both the changing position of the head and the movement due to changes in facial expression. Different approaches have been proposed to separate these effects [138, 47, 27].

The global movements can be described in terms of rotations and translations. The local motions, or facial expressions, can be described as a sum of *action units* (AU), which are a set of 44 descriptions of basic facial expressions [64]. For example, AU1 corresponds to the raising of the inner brow and AU2 corresponds to the raising of the outer brow; therefore, AU1 + AU2 would mean raising the brow.

Although the synthesis portion of this algorithm is relatively straightforward, the analysis portion is far from simple. Detecting changes in features, which tend to be rather subtle, is a very difficult task. There is a substantial amount of research in this area, and if this problem is resolved, this approach promises rates comparable to the rates of the analysis/synthesis voice coding schemes. A good starting point for exploring this fascinating area is [7].

16.6   Asymmetric Applications

There are a number of applications in which it is cost effective to shift more of the computational burden to the encoder. For example, in multimedia applications where a video sequence is stored on a CD-ROM, the decompression will be performed many times and has to be performed in real time. However, the compression is performed only once, and there is no need for it to be in real time. Thus, the encoding algorithms can be significantly more complex. A similar situation arises in broadcast applications, where for each transmitter there might be thousands of receivers. In this section we will look at the standards developed for such asymmetric applications. These standards have been developed by a joint committee of the International Standards Organization (ISO) and the International Electrotechnical Society (IEC), which is best known as MPEG (Moving Picture Experts Group). MPEG was initially set up in 1988 to develop a set of standard algorithms, at different rates, for applications that required storage of video and audio on digital storage media. Originally, the committee had three work items, nicknamed MPEG-1, MPEG-2, and MPEG-3, targeted at rates of 1.5, 10, and 40 Mbits per second, respectively. Later, it became clear that the algorithms developed for MPEG-2 would accommodate the MPEG-3 rates, and the third work item was dropped [46]. The MPEG-1 work item resulted in a set of standards, ISO/IEC IS 11172, "Information Technology—Coding of Moving Pictures and Associated Audio for Digital Storage Media Up to about 1.5 Mbit/s" [109]. During the development of the standard, the committee felt that the restriction to digital storage media was not necessary, and the set of standards developed under the second work item, ISO/IEC 13818 or MPEG-2, has been issued under the title "Information Technology—Generic Coding of Moving Pictures and Associated Audio Information" [110]. We have examined the audio standard in Chapter 13. In this section we briefly look at the video standards. In July of 1993 the MPEG committee began working on MPEG-4, the third and most ambitious of its standards. The goal of MPEG-4 was to provide an object-oriented framework for the encoding of multimedia. It took two years for the committee to arrive at a satisfactory definition of the scope of MPEG-4, and the call for proposals was finally issued in 1996. The standard ISO/IEC 14496 was finalized in 1998 and approved as an international standard in 1999. The final MPEG standard still under development at the time of this writing is MPEG-7. This work item was started in October 1996 and will specify a standard set of descriptors that can be used to identify content and permit search for particular content in multimedia information.

16.6.1   The MPEG-1 Video Standard

The basic structure of the compression algorithm proposed by MPEG is very similar to that of ITU-T H.261. Blocks (8×8 in size) of either an original frame or the difference between a frame and the motion-compensated prediction are transformed using the DCT. The blocks are organized in macroblocks, which are defined in the same manner as in the H.261 algorithm, and the motion compensation is performed at the macroblock level. The transform coefficients are quantized and transmitted to the receiver. A buffer is used to smooth delivery of bits from the encoder and also for rate control.

The basic structure of the MPEG-1 compression scheme may be viewed as very similar to that of the ITU-T H.261 video compression scheme; however, there are significant differences in the details of this structure. The H.261 standard has videophone and videoconferencing as the main application areas; the MPEG standard at least initially had applications that require digital storage and retrieval as a major focus. This does not mean that use of either algorithm is precluded in applications outside its focus, but simply that the features of the algorithm may be better understood if we keep in mind the target application areas. In videoconferencing a call is set up, conducted, and then terminated. This set of events always occurs together and in sequence. When accessing video from a storage medium, we do not always want to access the video sequence starting from the first frame. We want the ability to view the video sequence starting at, or close to, some arbitrary point in the sequence. A similar situation exists in broadcast situations. Viewers do not necessarily tune into a program at the beginning. They may do so at any random point in time. In H.261 each frame, after the first frame, may contain blocks that are coded using prediction from the previous frame. Therefore, to decode a particular frame in the sequence, it is possible that we may have to decode the sequence starting at the first frame. One of the major contributions of MPEG-1 was the provision of a random access capability. This capability is provided rather simply by requiring that there be frames periodically that are coded without any reference to past frames. These frames are referred to as **I** frames.

In order to avoid a long delay between the time a viewer switches on the TV to the time a reasonable picture appears on the screen, or between the frame that a user is looking for and the frame at which decoding starts, the **I** frames should occur quite frequently. However, because the **I** frames do not use temporal correlation, the compression rate is quite low compared to the frames that make use of the temporal correlations for prediction. Thus, the number of frames between two consecutive **I** frames is a trade-off between compression efficiency and convenience.

In order to improve compression efficiency, the MPEG-1 algorithm contains two other kinds of frames, the *predictive coded* (**P**) frames and the *bidirectionally predictive coded* (**B**) frames. The **P** frames are coded using motion-compensated prediction from the last **I** or **P** frame, whichever happens to be closest. Generally, the compression efficiency of **P** frames is substantially higher than **I** frames. The **I** and **P** frames are sometimes called *anchor* frames, for reasons that will become obvious.

To compensate for the reduction in the amount of compression due to the frequent use of **I** frames, the MPEG standard introduced **B** frames. The **B** frames achieve a high level of compression by using motion-compensated prediction from the most recent anchor frame and the closest future anchor frame. By using both past and future frames for prediction, generally we can get better compression than if we only used prediction based on the past. For example, consider a video sequence in which there is a sudden change between one frame and the next. This is a common occurrence in TV advertisements. In this situation, prediction based on the past frames may be useless. However, predictions based on future frames would have a high probability of being accurate. Note that a **B** frame can only be generated after the future anchor frame has been generated. Furthermore, the **B** frame is not used for predicting any

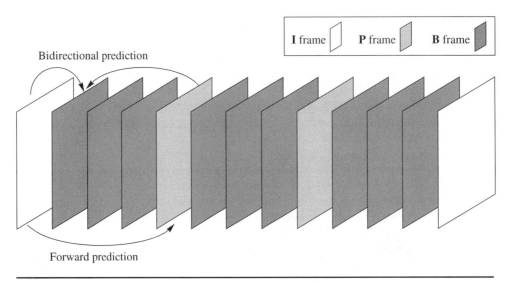

FIGURE   16.14   **A possible arrangement for a group of pictures.**

TABLE   16.5   **A typical sequence of frames in display order.**

I	B	B	P	B	B	P	B	B	P	B	B	I
1	2	3	4	5	6	7	8	9	10	11	12	13

other frame. This means that **B** frames can tolerate more error because this error will not be propagated by the prediction process.

The different frames are organized together in a *group of pictures* (GOP). A GOP is the smallest random access unit in the video sequence. The GOP structure is set up as a trade-off between the high compression efficiency of motion-compensated coding and the fast picture acquisition capability of periodic intra-only processing. As might be expected, a GOP has to contain at least one **I** frame. Furthermore, the first **I** frame in a GOP is either the first frame of the GOP, or is preceded by **B** frames that use motion-compensated prediction only from this **I** frame. A possible GOP is shown in Figure 16.14.

Because of the reliance of the **B** frame on future anchor frames, there are two different sequence orders. The *display order* is the sequence in which the video sequence is displayed to the user. A typical display order is shown in Table 16.5. Let us see how this sequence was generated. The first frame is an **I** frame, which is compressed without reference to any previous frame. The next frame to be compressed is the fourth frame. This frame is compressed using motion-compensated prediction from the first frame. Then we compress frame two, which is compressed using motion-compensated prediction from frame one and frame four. The third frame is also compressed using motion-compensated prediction from the first and fourth frames. The next frame to be compressed is frame seven, which uses motion-

TABLE 16.6   A typical sequence of frames in bitstream order.

I	P	B	B	P	B	B	P	B	B	I	B	B
1	4	2	3	7	5	6	10	8	9	13	11	12

compensated prediction from frame four. This is followed by frames five and six, which are compressed using motion-compensated predictions from frames four and seven. Thus, there is a processing order that is quite different from the display order. The MPEG document calls this the *bitstream order*. The bitstream order for the sequence shown in Table 16.5 is given in Table 16.6. In terms of the bitstream order, the first frame in a GOP is always the **I** frame.

As we can see, unlike the ITU-T H.261 algorithm, the frame being predicted and the frame upon which the prediction is based are not necessarily adjacent. In fact, the number of frames between the frame being encoded and the frame upon which the prediction is based is variable. When searching for the best matching block in a neighboring frame, the region of search depends on assumptions about the amount of motion. More motion will lead to larger search areas than a small amount of motion. When the frame being predicted is always adjacent to the frame upon which the prediction is based, we can fix the search area based on our assumption about the amount of motion. When the number of frames between the frame being encoded and the prediction frame is variable, we make the search area a function of the distance between the two frames. While the MPEG standard does not specify the method used for motion compensation, it does recommend using a search area that grows with the distance between the frame being coded and the frame being used for prediction.

Once motion compensation has been performed, the block of prediction errors is transformed using the DCT and quantized, and the quantization labels are encoded. This procedure is the same as that recommended in the JPEG standard and is described in Chapter 12. The quantization tables used for the different frames are different and can be changed during the encoding process.

Rate control in the MPEG standard can be performed at the sequence level or at the level of individual frames. At the sequence level, any reduction in bit rate first occurs with the **B** frames because they are not essential for the encoding of other frames. At the level of the individual frames, rate control takes place in two steps. First, as in the case of the H.261 algorithm, the quantizer step sizes are increased. If this is not sufficient, then the higher-order frequency coefficients are dropped until the need for rate reduction is past.

The format for MPEG is very flexible. However, the MPEG committee has provided some suggested values for the various parameters. For MPEG-1 these suggested values are called the *constrained parameter bitstream* (CPB). The horizontal picture size is constrained to be less than or equal to 768 pixels, and the vertical size is constrained to be less than or equal to 576 pixels. More importantly, the pixel rate is constrained to be less than 396 macroblocks per frame if the frame rate is 25 frames per second or less, and 330 macroblocks per frame if the frame rate is 30 frames per second or less. The definition of a macroblock is the same as in the ITU-T H.261 recommendations. Therefore, this corresponds to a frame size of 352×288 pixels at the 25-frames-per-second rate, or a frame size of 352×240 pixels at the 30-frames-per-second rate. Keeping the frame at this size allows the algorithm to achieve bit rates of between 1 and 1.5 Mbits per second. When referring to MPEG-1 parameters, most people are actually referring to the CPB.

The MPEG-1 algorithm provides reconstructed images of VHS quality for moderate- to low-motion video sequences, and worse than VHS quality for high-motion sequences at rates of around 1.2 Mbits per second. As the algorithm was targeted to applications such as CD-ROM, there is no consideration of interlaced video. In order to expand the applicability of the basic MPEG algorithm to interlaced video, the MPEG committee provided some additional recommendations, the MPEG-2 recommendations.

16.6.2 The MPEG-2 Video Standard

While MPEG-1 was specifically proposed for digital storage media, the idea behind MPEG-2 was to provide a generic, application-independent standard. To this end, MPEG-2 takes a "tool kit" approach, providing a number of subsets, each containing different options from the set of all possible options contained in the standard. For a particular application, the user can select from a set of *profiles* and *levels*. The profiles define the algorithms to be used, while the levels define the constraints on the parameters. There are five profiles: *simple, main, snr-scalable* (where *snr* stands for signal-to-noise ratio), *spatially scalable*, and *high*. There is an ordering of the profiles; each higher profile is capable of decoding video encoded using all profiles up to and including that profile. For example, a decoder designed for profile *snr-scalable* could decode video that was encoded using profiles *simple, main*, and *snr-scalable*. The *simple* profile eschews the use of **B** frames. Recall that the **B** frames require the most computation to generate (forward and backward prediction), require memory to store the coded frames needed for prediction, and increase the coding delay because of the need to wait for "future" frames for both generation and reconstruction. Therefore, removal of the **B** frames makes the requirements simpler. The *main* profile is very much the algorithm we have discussed in the previous section. The *snr-scalable, spatially scalable*, and *high* profiles may use more than one bitstream to encode the video. The base bitstream is a lower-rate encoding of the video sequence. This bitstream could be decoded by itself to provide a reconstruction of the video sequence. The other bitstream is used to enhance the quality of the reconstruction. This layered approach is useful when transmitting video over a network, where some connections may only permit a lower rate. The base bitstream can be provided to these connections while providing the base and enhancement layers for a higher-quality reproduction over the links that can accommodate the higher bit rate. To understand the concept of layers, consider the following example.

Example 16.6.1:

Suppose after the transform we obtain a set of coefficients, the first eight of which are

$$29.75 \quad 6.1 \quad -6.03 \quad 1.93 \quad -2.01 \quad 1.23 \quad -0.95 \quad 2.11$$

Let us suppose we quantize this set of coefficients using a step size of 4. For simplicity we will use the same step size for all coefficients. Recall that the quantizer label is given by

$$l_{ij} = \left\lfloor \frac{\theta_{ij}}{Q_{ij}^t} + 0.5 \right\rfloor \tag{16.8}$$

and the reconstructed value is given by

$$\hat{\theta}_{ij} = l_{ij} \times Q^t_{ij}. \tag{16.9}$$

Using these equations and the fact that $Q^t_{ij} = 4$, the reconstructed values of the coefficients are

| 28 | 8 | −8 | 0 | −4 | 0 | −0 | 4 |

The error in the reconstruction is

| 1.75 | −1.9 | 1.97 | 1.93 | 1.99 | 1.23 | −0.95 | −1.89 |

Now suppose we have some additional bandwidth made available to us. We can quantize the difference and send that to enhance the reconstruction. Suppose we used a step size of 2 to quantize the difference. The reconstructed values for this enhancement sequence would be

| 2 | −2 | 2 | 2 | 2 | 2 | 0 | −2 |

Adding this to the previous base-level reconstruction, we get an enhanced reconstruction of

| 30 | 6 | −6 | 2 | −2 | 2 | 0 | 2 |

which results in an error of

| −0.25 | 0.1 | −0.03 | −0.07 | −0.01 | −0.77 | −0.95 | 0.11 |

The layered approach allows us to increase the accuracy of the reconstruction when bandwidth is available, while at the same time permitting a lower-quality reconstruction when there is not sufficient bandwidth for the enhancement. In other words, the quality is *scalable*. In this particular case, the error between the original and reconstruction decreases because of the enhancement. Because the signal-to-noise ratio is a measure of error, this can be called *snr-scalable*. If the enhancement layer contained a coded bitstream corresponding to frames that would occur between frames of the base layer, the system could be called *temporally scalable*. If the enhancement allowed an upsampling of the base layer, the system is *spatially scalable*.   ◆

The levels are *low, main, high 1440*, and *high*. The *low* level corresponds to a frame size of 352×240, the *main* level corresponds to a frame size of 720×480, the *high 1440* level corresponds to a frame size of 1440×1152, and the *high* level corresponds to a frame size of 1920×1080. All levels are defined for a frame rate of 30 frames per second. There are many possible combinations of profiles and levels, not all of which are allowed in the MPEG-2 standard. Table 16.7 shows the allowable combinations [46]. A particular profile-level combination is denoted by *XX@YY* where *XX* is the two-letter abbreviation for the profile and *YY* is the two-letter abbreviation for the level. There are a large number of issues, such as bounds on parameters and decodability between different profile-level combinations, that we have not addressed here because they do not pertain to our main focus, compression (see the international standard [110] for these details).

The most important addition from the point of view of compression in MPEG-2 is the addition of several new motion-compensated prediction modes: the field prediction and the

TABLE 16.7   **Allowable profile-level combinations in MPEG-2.**

	Simple Profile	Main Profile	SNR-Scalable Profile	Spatially Scalable Profile	High Profile
High Level		Allowed			Allowed
High 1440		Allowed		Allowed	Allowed
Main Level	Allowed	Allowed	Allowed		Allowed
Low Level		Allowed	Allowed		

dual prime prediction modes. MPEG-1 did not allow interlaced video. Therefore, there was no need for motion compensation algorithms based on fields. In the **P** frames, field predictions are obtained using one of the two most recently decoded fields. When the first field in a frame is being encoded, the prediction is based on the two fields from the previous frame. However, when the second field is being encoded, the prediction is based on the second field from the previous frame and the first field from the current frame. Information about which field is to be used for prediction is transmitted to the receiver. The field predictions are performed in a manner analogous to the motion-compensated prediction described earlier.

In addition to the regular frame and field prediction, MPEG-2 also contains two additional modes of prediction. One is the 16×8 motion compensation. In this mode, two predictions are generated for each macroblock, one for the top half and one for the bottom half. The other is called the dual prime motion compensation. In this technique, two predictions are formed for each field from the two recent fields. These predictions are averaged to obtain the final prediction.

The Grand Alliance HDTV Proposal

When the Federal Communications Commission (FCC) requested proposals for the HDTV standard, they received four proposals for digital HDTV from four consortia. After the evaluation phase, the FCC declined to pick a winner among the four, and instead suggested that all these consortia join forces and produce a single proposal. The resulting partnership has the exalted title of the "Grand Alliance." Currently, the specifications for the digital HDTV system use MPEG-2 as the compression algorithm. The Grand Alliance system uses the *main* profile of the MPEG-2 standard implemented at the *high* level.

16.6.3 MPEG-4

The MPEG-4 standard provides a more abstract approach to the coding of multimedia. The standard views a multimedia "scene" as a collection of objects. These objects can be visual, such as a still background or a talking head, or aural, such as speech, music, background noise, and so on. Each of these objects can be coded independently using different techniques to generate separate elementary bitstreams. These bitstreams are multiplexed along with a scene description. A language called the Binary Format for Scenes (BIFS) based on the Virtual Reality Modeling Language (VRML) has been developed by MPEG for scene descriptions. The decoder can use the scene description and additional input from the user to combine or

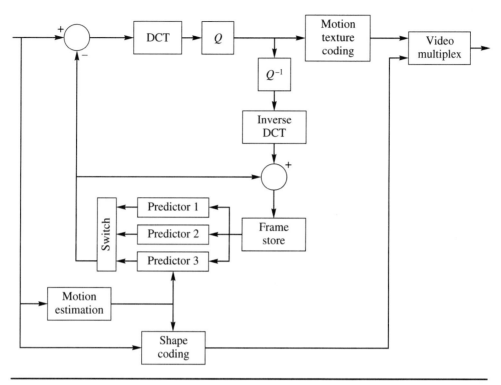

FIGURE 16.15   A block diagram for video coding.

compose the objects to reconstruct the original scene or create a variation on it. The protocol for managing the elementary streams and their multiplexed version, called the Delivery
Multimedia Integration Framework (DMIF), is an important part of MPEG-4. However, as
our focus in this book is on compression, we will not discuss the protocol (for details, see the
standard [111]).

A block diagram for the basic video coding algorithm is shown in Figure 16.15. Although
shape coding occupies a very small portion of the diagram, it is a major part of the algorithm. The different objects that make up the scene are coded and sent to the multiplexer. The
information about the presence of these objects is also provided to the motion-compensated
predictor, which can use object-based motion compensation algorithms to improve the compression efficiency. What is left after the prediction can be transmitted using a DCT-based
coder. The video coding algorithm can also use a background "sprite"—generally a large
panoramic still image that forms the background for the video sequence. The sprite is transmitted once, and the moving foreground video objects are placed in front of different portions
of the sprite based on the information about the background provided by the encoder.

The MPEG-4 standard also envisions the use of model-based coding, where a triangular mesh representing the moving object is transmitted followed by texture information for
covering the mesh. Information about movement of the mesh nodes can then be transmitted
to animate the video object. The texture coding technique suggested by the standard is the

embedded zerotree wavelet (EZW) algorithm. In particular, the standard envisions the use of a facial animation object to render an animated face. The shape, texture, and expressions of the face are controlled using facial definition parameters (FDPs) and facial action parameters (FAPs). BIFS provides features to support custom models and specialized interpretation of FAPs. The MPEG-4 version 2 will also contain features for body animation.

The MPEG-2 standard allows for SNR and spatial scalability. The MPEG-4 standard also allows for object scalability, in which certain objects may not be sent in order to reduce the bandwidth requirement.

We have been mentioning all the things that MPEG-4 "envisions" and "allows." However, considerable work needs to be done in developing object-based compression schemes before we can use the full capability of this standard.

16.6.4 MPEG-7

The scope of the MPEG-7 activities that focus on the development of a multmedia content description interface seems to be somewhat removed from the study of data compression. However, in some sense these activities relate to the core principles of data compression, which is the development of compact descriptions of information. Whether the standard will actually take such a broad view remains to be seen. The call for proposals for MPEG-7 was issued in October 1998, and at this writing the standard is in the process of development.

16.7 Packet Video

The increasing popularity of communication over networks has led to increased interest in the development of compression schemes for use over networks. In this section we look at some of the issues involved in developing video compression schemes for use over networks.

16.7.1 ATM Networks

With the explosion of information, we have also seen the development of new ways of transmitting the information. One of the most efficient ways of transferring information among a large number of users is the use of asynchronous transfer mode (ATM) technology. In the past, communication has usually taken place over dedicated channels; that is, in order to communicate between two points, a channel was dedicated only to transferring information between those two points. Even if there was no information transfer going on during a particular period, the channel could not be used by anyone else. Because of the inefficiency of this approach, there is an increasing movement away from it. In an ATM network, the users divide their information into packets, which are transmitted over channels that can be used by more than one user.

We could draw an analogy between the movement of packets over a communication network and the movement of automobiles over a road network. If we break up a message into packets, then the movement of the message over the network is like the movement of a number of cars on a highway system going from one point to the other. Although two cars may not occupy the same position at the same time, they can occupy the same road at the same time. Thus, more than one group of cars can use the road at any given time. Furthermore, not all the cars in the group have to take the same route. Depending on the amount of traffic on the various roads that run between the origin of the traffic and the destination, different cars can take different routes. This is a more efficient utilization of the road than if the entire road was blocked off until the first group of cars completed its traversal of the road.

Using this analogy, we can see that the availability of transmission capacity, that is, the number of bits per second that we can transmit, is affected by factors that are outside our control. If at a given time there is very little traffic on the network, the available capacity will be high. On the other hand, if there is congestion on the network, the available capacity will be low. Furthermore, the ability to take alternate routes through the network also means that some of the packets may encounter congestion, leading to a variable amount of delay through the network. In order to prevent congestion from impeding the flow of vital traffic, networks will prioritize the traffic, with higher-priority traffic being permitted to move ahead of lower-priority traffic. Users can negotiate with the network for a fixed amount of guaranteed traffic. Of course, such guarantees tend to be expensive, so it is important that the user have some idea about how much high-priority traffic they will be transmitting over the network.

16.7.2 Compression Issues in ATM Networks

In video coding, this situation provides both opportunities and challenges. In the video compression algorithms discussed previously, there is a buffer that smooths the output of the compression algorithm. Thus, if we encounter a high-activity region of the video and generate more than the average number of bits per second, in order to prevent the buffer from overflowing, this period has to be followed by a period in which we generate fewer bits per second than the average. Sometimes this may happen naturally, with periods of low activity following periods of high activity. However, it is quite likely that this would not happen, in which case we have to reduce the quality by increasing the step size or dropping coefficients, or maybe even entire frames.

The ATM network, if it is not congested, will accommodate the variable rate generated by the compression algorithm. But if the network is congested, the compression algorithm will have to operate at a reduced rate. If the network is well designed, the latter situation will not happen too often, and the video coder can function in a manner that provides uniform quality. However, when the network is congested, it may remain so for a relatively long period. Therefore, the compression scheme should have the ability to operate for significant periods of time at a reduced rate. Furthermore, congestion might cause such long delays that some packets arrive after they can be of any use; that is, the frame they were supposed to be a part of might have already been reconstructed.

In order to deal with these problems, it is useful if the video compression algorithm provides information in a layered fashion, with a low-rate high-priority layer that can be used to reconstruct the video, even though the reconstruction may be poor, and low-priority enhancement layers that enhance the quality of the reconstruction. This is similar to the idea of progressive transmission, in which we first send a crude but low-rate representation of the image, followed by higher-rate enhancements. It is also useful if the bit rate required for the high-priority layer does not vary too much.

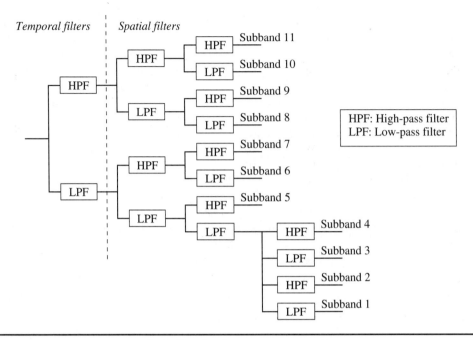

FIGURE   16.16   Analysis filter bank.

16.7.3   Compression   Algorithms   for   Packet   Video

Almost any compression algorithm can be modified to perform in the ATM environment, but some approaches seem more suited to this environment. We briefly present two approaches (see the original papers for more details).

One compression scheme that functions in an inherently layered manner is subband coding. In subband coding, the lower-frequency bands can be used to provide the basic reconstruction, with the higher-frequency bands providing the enhancement. As an example, consider the compression scheme proposed for packet video by Karlsson and Vetterli [124]. In their scheme, the video is divided into 11 bands. First, the video signal is divided into two temporal bands. Each band is then split into four spatial bands. The low-low band of the temporal low-frequency band is then split into four spatial bands. A graphical representation of this splitting is shown in Figure 16.16. The subband denoted 1 in the figure contains the basic information about the video sequence. Therefore, it is transmitted with the highest priority. If the data in all the other subbands are lost, it will still be possible to reconstruct the video using only the information in this subband. We can also prioritize the output of the other bands, and if the network starts getting congested and we are required to reduce our rate, we can do so by not transmitting the information in the lower-priority subbands. Subband 1 also generates the least variable data rate. This is very helpful when negotiating with the network for the amount of priority traffic.

Given the similarity of the ideas behind progressive transmission and subband coding, it should be possible to use progressive transmission algorithms as a starting point in the design of layered compression schemes for packet video. Chen, Sayood, and Nelson [45] use a DCT-based progressive transmission scheme [196] to develop a compression algorithm for packet video. In their scheme, they first encode the difference between the current frame and the prediction for the current frame using a 16×16 DCT. They only transmit the DC coefficient and the three lowest-order AC coefficients to the receiver. The coded coefficients make up the highest-priority layer.

The reconstructed frame is then subtracted from the original. The sum of squared errors is calculated for each 16×16 block. Blocks with squared error greater than a prescribed threshold are subdivided into four 8×8 blocks, and the coding process is repeated using an 8×8 DCT. The coded coefficients make up the next layer. Because only blocks that fail to meet the threshold test are subdivided, information about which blocks are subdivided is transmitted to the receiver as side information.

The process is repeated with 4×4 blocks, which make up the third layer, and 2×2 blocks, which make up the fourth layer. Although this algorithm is a variable-rate coding scheme, the rate for the first layer is constant. Therefore, the user can negotiate with the network for a fixed amount of high-priority traffic. In order to remove the effect of delayed packets from the prediction, only the reconstruction from the higher-priority layers is used for prediction.

This idea can be used with many different progressive transmission algorithms to make them suitable for use over ATM networks.

16.8 Summary

In this chapter we described a number of different video compression algorithms. The only new information in terms of compression algorithms was the description of motion-compensated prediction. While the compression algorithms themselves have already been studied in previous chapters, we looked at how these algorithms are used under different requirements. The three scenarios that we looked at are teleconferencing, asymmetric applications such as broadcast video, and video over packet networks. Each application has slightly different requirements, leading to different ways of using the compression algorithms. We have by no means attempted to cover the entire area of video compression. However, by now you should have sufficient background to explore the subject further using the following list as a starting point.

Further Reading

1. An excellent source for information about the technical issues involved with digital video is the book *The Art of Digital Video*, by J. Watkinson [235].

2. The MPEG-1 standards document [109], "Information Technology—Coding of Moving Pictures and Associated Audio for Digital Storage Media Up to about 1.5 Mbit/s," has an excellent description of the video compression algorithm.

3. Detailed information about the MPEG-1 and MPEG-2 video standards can also be found in *MPEG Video Compression Standard*, by J.L. Mitchell, W.B. Pennebaker, C.E. Fogg, and D.J. LeGall [160].

4. To find more on model-based coding, see "Model Based Image Coding: Advanced Video Coding Techniques for Very Low Bit-Rate Applications," by K. Aizawa and T.S. Huang [7], in the February 1995 issue of the *Proceedings of the IEEE*.

5. A good place to begin exploring the various areas of research in packet video is the June 1989 issue of the *IEEE Journal on Selected Areas of Communication*.

16.9 Projects and Problems

1. **(a)** Take the DCT of the Sinan image and plot the average squared value of each coefficient.

(b) Circularly shift each line of the image by eight pixels. That is, $new\_image[i,j] = old\_image[i, j+8 \ (\text{mod } 256)]$. Take the DCT of the difference and plot the average squared value of each coefficient.

(c) Compare the results in parts (a) and (b) above. Comment on the differences.

Probability and Random Processes

n this appendix we will look at some of the concepts relating to probability and random processes that are important in the study of systems. Our coverage will be highly selective and somewhat superficial, but enough to use probability and random processes as a tool in understanding data compression systems.

A.1 Probability

There are several different ways of defining and thinking about probability. Each approach has some merit; perhaps the best approach is the one that provides the most insight into the problem being studied.

A.1.1 Frequency of Occurrence

The most common way that most people think about probability is in terms of outcomes, or sets of outcomes, of an experiment. Let us suppose we conduct an experiment E that has N possible outcomes. We conduct the experiment n_T times. If the outcome ω_i occurs n_i times, we say that the frequency of occurrence of the outcome ω_i is $\frac{n_i}{n_T}$. We can then define the probability of occurrence of the outcome ω_i as

$$P(\omega_i) = \lim_{n_T \to \infty} \frac{n_i}{n_T}.$$

In practice we do not have the ability to repeat an experiment an infinite number of times, so we often use the frequency of occurrence as an approximation to the probability. To make this more concrete consider a specific experiment. Suppose we turn on a television 1,000,000 times. Of these times, 800,000 times we turn the television on during a commercial and 200,000 times we turn it on and we don't get a commercial. We could say the frequency of occurrence, or the estimate of the probability, of turning on a television set in the middle of a commercial is 0.8. Our experiment E here is the turning on a television set, and the outcomes are *commercial* and *no commercial*. We could have been more careful with noting what was on when we turned on the television set and noticed whether the program was a news program (2000 times), a newslike program (20,000 times), a comedy program (40,000 times), an adventure program (18,000 times), a variety show (20,000 times), a talk show (90,000 times), or a movie (10,000 times), and whether the commercial was for products or services. In this case the outcomes would be *product commercial, service commercial, comedy, adventure, news, pseudonews, variety, talk show*, and *movie*. We could then define an *event* as a set of outcomes. The event *commercial* would consist of the outcomes *product commercial, service commercial*; the event *no commercial* would consist of the outcomes *comedy, adventure, news, pseudonews, variety, talk show, movie*. We could also define other events such as *programs that may contain news*. This set would contain the outcomes *news, pseudonews*, and *talk shows*, and the frequency of occurrence of this set is 0.112.

Formally, when we define an experiment E, associated with the experiment we also define a *sample space S* that consists of the *outcomes* $\{\omega_i\}$. We can then combine these outcomes into sets that are called *events*, and assign probabilities to these events. The largest subset of S (event) is S itself, and the probability of the event S is simply the probability that the experiment will have an outcome. The way we have defined things, this probability is one; that is, $P(S) = 1$.

A.1.2 A Measure of Belief

Sometimes the idea that the probability of an event is obtained through the repetitions of an experiment runs into trouble. What, for example, is the probability of your getting from Logan Airport to a specific address in Boston in a specified period of time? The answer depends on a lot of different factors, including your knowledge of the area, the time of day, the condition of your transport, and so on. You cannot conduct an experiment and get your answer because the moment you conduct the experiment, the conditions have changed, and the answer will now be different. We deal with this situation by defining a priori and a posteriori probabilities. The a priori probability is what you think or believe the probability to be before certain information is received or certain events take place; the a posteriori probability is the probability after you have received further information. Probability is no longer as rigidly defined as in the frequency of occurrence approach but is a somewhat more fluid quantity, the value of which changes with changing experience. For this approach to be useful we have to have a way of describing how the probability evolves with changing information. This is done through the use of *Bayes' rule*, named after the person who first described it. If $P(A)$ is the a priori probability of the event A and $P(A|B)$ is the a posteriori probability of the event A given that the event B has occurred, then

$$P(A|B) = \frac{P(A, B)}{P(B)} \qquad \text{(A.1)}$$

where $P(A, B)$ is the probability of the event A *and* the event B occurring. Similarly,

$$P(B|A) = \frac{P(A, B)}{P(A)}. \tag{A.2}$$

Combining (A.1) and (A.2) we get

$$P(A|B) = \frac{P(B|A)P(A)}{P(B)}. \tag{A.3}$$

If the events A and B do not provide any information about each other, it would be reasonable to assume that

$$P(A|B) = P(A)$$

and therefore from (A.1),

$$P(A, B) = P(A)P(B). \tag{A.4}$$

Whenever (A.4) is satisfied, the events A and B are said to be *statistically independent*, or simply *independent*.

Example A.1.1:

A very common channel model used in digital communication is the *binary symmetric channel*. In this model the input is a random experiment with outcomes 0 and 1. The output of the channel is another random event with two outcomes 0 and 1. Obviously, the two outcomes are connected in some way. To see how, let us first define some events:

A: Input is 0
B: Input is 1
C: Output is 0
D: Output is 1

Let's suppose the input is equally likely to be a 1 or a 0. So $P(A) = P(B) = 0.5$. If the channel was perfect, that is, you got out of the channel what you put in, then we would have

$$P(C|A) = P(D|B) = 1$$

and

$$P(C|B) = P(D|A) = 0.$$

With most real channels this system is seldom encountered, and generally there is a small probability ϵ that the transmitted bit will be received in error. In this case, our probabilities would be

$$P(C|A) = P(D|B) = 1 - \epsilon$$
$$P(C|B) = P(D|A) = \epsilon.$$

How do we interpret $P(C)$ and $P(D)$? These are simply the probability that at any given time the output is a 0 or a 1. How would we go about computing these probabilities given the available information? Using (A.1) we can obtain $P(A, C)$ and $P(B, C)$ from $P(C|A)$, $P(C|B)$, $P(A)$, and $P(B)$. These are the probabilities that the input is 0 and the output is 1, and the input is 1 and the output is 1. The event C—that is, the output is 1—will occur only when one of the two *joint* events occurs, therefore,

$$P(C) = P(A, C) + P(B, C).$$

Similarly,

$$P(D) = P(A, D) + P(B, D).$$

Numerically, this comes out to be

$$P(C) = P(D) = 0.5. \qquad \blacklozenge$$

A.1.3 The Axiomatic Approach

Finally, there is an approach that simply defines probability as a measure, without much regard for physical interpretation. We are very familiar with measures in our daily lives. We talk about getting a 9-foot cable or a pound of cheese. Just as length and width measure the extent of certain physical quantities, probability measures the extent of an abstract quantity, a set. The thing that probability measures is the "size" of the event set. The probability measure follows similar rules to those followed by other measures. Just as the length of a physical object is always greater than or equal to zero, the probability of an event is always greater than or equal to zero. If we measure the length of two objects that have no overlap, then the combined length of the two objects is simply the sum of the lengths of the individual objects. In a similar manner the probability of the union of two events that do not have any outcomes in common is simply the sum of the probability of the individual events. So as to keep this definition of probability in line with the other definitions, we normalize this quantity by assigning the largest set, which is the sample space S, the size of 1. Thus, the probability of an event always lies between 0 and 1. Formally, we can write these rules down as the three *axioms* of probability.

Given a sample space S:

■ *Axiom 1:* If A is an event in S, then $P(A) \geq 0$.

■ *Axiom 2:* The probability of the sample space is 1; that is, $P(S) = 1$.

■ *Axiom 3:* If A and B are two events in S and $A \cap B = \phi$, then $P(A \cup B) = P(A) + P(B)$.

Given these three axioms we can come up with all the other rules we need. For example, suppose A^c is the complement of A. What is the probability of A^c? We can get the answer by using Axiom 2 and Axiom 3. We know that

$$A^c \cup A = S$$

and Axiom 2 tells us that $P(S) = 1$, therefore,

$$P(A^c \cup A) = 1. \qquad \text{(A.5)}$$

We also know that $A^c \cap A = \phi$, therefore, from Axiom 3

$$P(A^c \cup A) = P(A^c) + P(A). \qquad (A.6)$$

Combining equations (A.5) and (A.6), we get

$$P(A^c) = 1 - P(A). \qquad (A.7)$$

Similarly, we can use the three axioms to obtain the probability of $A \cup B$ when $A \cap B \neq \phi$ as

$$P(A \cup B) = P(A) + P(B) - P(A \cap B). \qquad (A.8)$$

In all of the above we have been using two events A and B. We can easily extend these rules to more events.

Example A.1.2:

Find $P(A \cup B \cup C)$ when $A \cap B = A \cap C = \phi$, and $B \cap C \neq \phi$.
   Let

$$D = B \cup C.$$

Then

$$A \cap C = \phi, \quad A \cap B = \phi \quad \Rightarrow \quad A \cap D = \phi.$$

Therefore, from Axiom 3,

$$P(A \cup D) = P(A) + P(D)$$

and using (A.8)

$$P(D) = P(B) + P(C) - P(B \cup C).$$

Combining everything, we get

$$P(A \cup B \cup C) = P(A) + P(B) + P(C) - P(B \cap C). \qquad \blacklozenge$$

The axiomatic approach is especially useful when an experiment does not have discrete outcomes. For example, if we are looking at the voltage on a telephone line, the probability of any specific value of the voltage is zero because there are an uncountably infinite number of different values that the voltage can take, and we can assign nonzero values to only a countably infinite number. Using the axiomatic approach, we can view the sample space as the range of voltages, and events as subsets of this range.
   We have given three different interpretations of probability, and in the process described some rules by which probabilities can be manipulated. The rules described here (such as Bayes' rule, the three axioms, and the other rules we came up with) work the same way regardless of which interpretation you hold dear. The purpose of providing you with three different interpretations was to provide you with a variety of perspectives with which to view a given situation. For example, if someone says that the probability of a head when you flip a coin is 0.5, you might interpret that number in terms of repeated experiments (*if I flipped the coin 1000 times, I would expect to get 500 heads*). However, if someone tells you that

the probability of your getting killed while crossing a particular street is 0.1, you might wish to interpret this information in a more subjective manner. The idea is to use the interpretation that gives you the most insight into a particular problem, while remembering that your interpretation will not change the mathematics of the situation.

Now that have expended a lot of verbiage to say what probability is, let's spend a few lines saying what it is not. Probability does not imply certainty. When we say that the probability of an event is one, this does not mean that event *will* happen. On the other hand, when we say that the probability of an event is zero, that does not mean that event *won't* happen. Remember, mathematics only models reality, it is *not* reality.

A.2 Random Variables

When we are trying to mathematically describe an experiment and its outcomes, it is much more convenient if the outcomes are numbers. A simple way to do this is to define a mapping or function that assigns a number to each outcome. This mapping or function is called a *random variable*. To put that more formally:

> *Definition:* Let S be a sample space with outcomes $\{\omega_i\}$. Then the random variable X is a mapping
>
> $$X : S \to \mathcal{R} \qquad\qquad (A.9)$$
>
> where $\mathcal{R}$ denotes the real number line. Another way of saying the same thing is
>
> $$X(\omega) = x; \qquad \omega \in S,\ x \in \mathcal{R}. \qquad\qquad (A.10)$$

The random variable is generally represented by an uppercase letter, and this is the convention we will follow. The value that the random variable takes on is called the *realization* of the random variable and is represented by a lowercase letter.

Example A.2.1:

Let's take our television example and rewrite it in terms of a random variable X:

$$X(product\ commercial) = 0$$
$$X(service\ commercial) = 1$$
$$X(news) = 2$$
$$X(pseudonews) = 3$$
$$X(talk\ show) = 4$$
$$X(variety) = 5$$
$$X(comedy) = 6$$
$$X(adventure) = 7$$
$$X(movie) = 8$$

Now, instead of talking about the probability of certain programs, we can talk about the probability of the random variable X taking on certain values or ranges of values. For example, $P(X(\omega) \leq 1)$ is the probability of seeing a commercial when the television is turned on (generally, we drop the argument and simply write this as $P(X \leq 1)$). Similarly, the $P(programs\ that\ may\ contain\ news)$ could be written as $P(1 < X \leq 4)$, which is substantially less cumbersome. ◆

A.3 Distribution Functions

Defining the random variable in the way that we did allows us to define a special probability $P(X \leq x)$. This probability is called the *cumulative distribution function (cdf)* and is denoted by $F_X(x)$, where the random variable is the subscript and the realization is the argument. One of the primary uses of probability is the modeling of physical processes, and we will find the cumulative distribution function very useful when we try to describe or model different random processes. We will see more on this later.

For now, let us look at some of the properties of the *cdf*:

Property 1: $0 \leq F_X(x) \leq 1$. This follows from the definition of the *cdf*.

Property 2: The *cdf* is a monotonically nondecreasing function. That is,

$$x_1 \geq x_2 \quad \Rightarrow \quad F_X(x_1) \geq F_X(x_2).$$

To show this simply write the *cdf* as the sum of two probabilities:

$$F_X(x_1) = P(X \leq x_1) = P(X \leq x_2) + P(x_2 < X \leq x_1)$$
$$= F_X(x_2) + P(x_1 < X \leq x_2) \geq F_X(x_2)$$

Property 3:

$$\lim_{n \to \infty} F_X(x) = 1.$$

Property 4:

$$\lim_{n \to -\infty} F_X(x) = 0.$$

Property 5: If we define

$$F_X(x^-) = P(X < x)$$

then

$$P(X = x) = F_X(x) - F_X(x^-).$$

Example A.3.1:

Assuming that the frequency of occurrence was an accurate estimate of the probabilities, let us obtain the *cdf* for our television example:

$$F_X(x) = \begin{cases} 0 & x < 0 \\ 0.4 & 0 \le x < 1 \\ 0.8 & 1 \le x < 2 \\ 0.802 & 2 \le x < 3 \\ 0.822 & 3 \le x < 4 \\ 0.912 & 4 \le x < 5 \\ 0.932 & 5 \le x < 6 \\ 0.972 & 6 \le x < 7 \\ 0.99 & 7 \le x < 8 \\ 1.00 & 8 \le x \end{cases}$$

◆

Notice a few things about this *cdf*. First, the *cdf* consists of step functions. This is characteristic of discrete random variables. Second, the function is continuous from the right. This is due to the way the *cdf* is defined.

The *cdf* is somewhat different when the random variable is a continuous random variable. For example, if we sampled a speech signal and then took differences of the samples, the resulting random process would have a *cdf* that would look something like this:

$$F_X(x) = \begin{cases} \frac{1}{2}e^{2x} & x \le 0 \\ 1 - \frac{1}{2}e^{-2x} & x > 0. \end{cases}$$

The thing to notice in this case is that because $F_X(x)$ is continuous

$$P(X = x) = F_X(x) - F_X(x^-) = 0.$$

We can also have processes that have distributions that are continuous over some ranges and discrete over others.

Along with the cumulative distribution function, another function that also comes in very handy is the *probability density function (pdf)*. The *pdf* corresponding to the *cdf* $F_X(x)$ is written as $f_X(x)$. For continuous *cdf*s, the *pdf* is simply the derivative of the *cdf*. For the discrete random variables, taking the derivative of the *cdf* would introduce delta functions, which have problems of their own. So in the discrete case, we obtain the *pdf* through differencing. It is somewhat awkward to have different procedures for obtaining the same function for different types of random variables. It is possible to define a rigorous unified procedure for getting the *pdf* from the *cdf* for all kinds of random variables. However, in order to do so, we need some familiarity with measure theory, which is beyond the scope of this appendix. Let us look at some examples of *pdf*s.

Example A.3.2:

For our television scenario:

$$
f_X(x) = \begin{cases}
0.4 & \text{if } X = 0 \\
0.4 & \text{if } X = 1 \\
0.002 & \text{if } X = 2 \\
0.02 & \text{if } X = 3 \\
0.09 & \text{if } X = 4 \\
0.02 & \text{if } X = 5 \\
0.04 & \text{if } X = 6 \\
0.018 & \text{if } X = 7 \\
0.01 & \text{if } X = 8 \\
0 & \text{otherwise}
\end{cases}
$$

$\blacklozenge$

Example A.3.3:

For our speech example, the *pdf* is given by

$$
f_X(x) = \frac{1}{2}e^{-2|x|}.
$$

$\blacklozenge$

A.4   Expectation

When dealing with random processes, we often deal with average quantities, like the signal power and noise power in communication systems, and the mean time between failures in various design problems. To obtain these average quantities, we use something called an *expectation operator*. Formally, the expectation operator $E[\ ]$ is defined as follows:

> *Definition:* The *expected value* of a random variable X is given by

$$
E[X] = \sum_i x_i P(X = x_i) \tag{A.11}
$$

> when X is a discrete random variable with realizations $\{x_i\}$ and by

$$
E[X] = \int_{-\infty}^{\infty} x f_X(x) dx \tag{A.12}
$$

> where $f_X(x)$ is the *pdf* of X.

The expected value is very much like the average value and, if the frequency of occurrence is an accurate estimate of the probability, is identical to the average value. Consider the following example:

Example A.4.1:

Suppose in a class of 10 students the grades on the first test were

$$10, 9, 8, 8, 7, 7, 7, 6, 6, 2$$

The average value is $\frac{70}{10}$, or 7. Now let's use the frequency of occurrence approach to estimate the probabilities of the various grades. (Notice in this case the random variable is an identity mapping, i.e., $X(\omega) = \omega$.) The probability estimate of the various values the random variable can take on are

$$P(10) = P(9) = P(2) = 0.1, \quad P(8) = P(6) = 0.2, \quad P(7) = 0.3,$$
$$P(6) = P(5) = P(4) = P(3) = P(1) = P(0) = 0$$

The expected value is therefore given by

$$E[X] = (0)(0) + (0)(1) + (0.1)(2) + (0)(3) + (0)(4) + (0)(5) + (0.2)(6)$$
$$+ (0.3)(7) + (0.2)(8) + (0.1)(9) + (0.1)(10) = 7.$$ ◆

It seems that the expected value and the average value *are* exactly the same! But we have made a rather major assumption about the accuracy of our probability estimate. In general the relative frequency is not exactly the same as the probability, and the average expected values are different. To emphasize this difference and similarity, the expected value is sometimes referred to as the *statistical average*, while our everyday average value is referred to as the *sample average*.

We said at the beginning of this section that we are often interested in things such as signal power. The average signal power is often defined as the average of the signal squared. If we say that the random variable is the signal value, then this means that we have to find the expected value of the square of the random variable. There are two ways of doing this. We could define a new random variable $Y = X^2$, then find $f_Y(y)$ and use (A.12) to find $E[Y]$. An easier approach is to use the *fundamental theorem of expectation*, which is

$$E[g(X)] = \sum_i g(x_i)P(X = x_i) \tag{A.13}$$

for the discrete case, and

$$E[g(X)] = \int_{-\infty}^{\infty} g(x)f_X(x)dx \tag{A.14}$$

for the continuous case.

The expected value, because of the way it is defined, is a linear operator. That is,

$$E[\alpha X + \beta Y] = \alpha E[X] + \beta E[Y], \qquad \alpha \text{ and } \beta \text{ are constants.}$$

You are invited to verify this for yourself.

There are several functions $g()$ whose expectations are used so often that they have been given special names.

A.4.1 Mean

The simplest and most obvious function is the identity mapping $g(X) = X$. The expected value $E(X)$ is referred to as the *mean* and is symbolically referred to as μ_X. If we take a random variable X and add a constant value to it, the mean of the new random process is simply the old mean plus the constant. Let

$$Y = X + a$$

where a is a constant value. Then

$$\mu_Y = E[Y] = E[X + a] = E[X] + E[a] = \mu_X + a.$$

A.4.2 Second Moment

If the random variable X is an electrical signal, the total power in this signal is given by $E[X^2]$, which is why we are often interested in it. This value is called the *second moment* of the random variable.

A.4.3 Variance

If X is a random variable with mean μ_X, then the quantity $E[(X - \mu_X)^2]$ is called the *variance* and is denoted by σ_X^2. The square root of this value is called the *standard deviation* and is denoted by σ. The variance and the standard deviation can be viewed as a measure of the "spread" of the random variable. We can show that

$$\sigma_X^2 = E[X^2] - \mu_X^2.$$

If $E[X^2]$ is the total power in a signal, then the variance is also referred to as the total AC power.

A.5 Types of Distribution

There are several specific distributions that are very useful when describing or modeling various processes.

A.5.1 Uniform Distribution

This is the distribution of ignorance. If we want to model data about which we know nothing except its range, this is the distribution of choice. This is not to say that there are not times when the uniform distribution is a good match for the data. The *pdf* of the uniform distribution is given by

$$f_X(x) = \begin{cases} \frac{1}{b-a} & \text{for } a \leq X \leq b \\ 0 & \text{otherwise.} \end{cases} \tag{A.15}$$

The mean of the uniform distribution can be obtained as

$$\mu_X = \int_a^b x \frac{1}{b-a} dx = \frac{b+a}{2}.$$

Similarly, the variance of the uniform distribution can be obtained as

$$\sigma_X^2 = \frac{(b-a)^2}{12}.$$

Details are left as an exercise.

A.5.2 Gaussian Distribution

This is the distribution of choice in terms of mathematical tractability. Because of its form, it is especially useful with the squared error distortion measure. The probability density function for a random variable with a Gaussian distribution, and mean μ and variance σ^2, is

$$f_X(x) = \frac{1}{\sqrt{2\pi\sigma^2}} \exp -\frac{(x-\mu)^2}{2\sigma^2} \tag{A.16}$$

where the mean of the distribution is μ and the variance is σ^2.

A.5.3 Laplacian Distribution

Many sources that we will deal with will have probability density functions that are quite peaked at zero. For example, speech consists mainly of silence; therefore, samples of speech will be zero or close to zero with high probability. Image pixels themselves do not have any attraction to small values. However, there is a high degree of correlation among pixels. Therefore, a large number of the pixel-to-pixel differences will have values close to zero. In these situations, a Gaussian distribution is not a very close match to the data. A closer match is the Laplacian distribution, which has a *pdf* that is peaked at zero. The density function for a zero mean random variable with Laplacian distribution and variance σ^2 is

$$f_X(x) = \frac{1}{\sqrt{2\sigma^2}} \exp \frac{-\sqrt{2}\,|x|}{\sigma}. \tag{A.17}$$

A.5.4 Gamma Distribution

A distribution with a *pdf* that is even more peaked, though considerably less tractable than the Laplacian distribution, is the Gamma distribution. The density function for a Gamma distributed random variable with zero mean and variance σ^2 is given by

$$f_X(x) = \frac{\sqrt[4]{3}}{\sqrt{8\pi\sigma\,|x|}} \exp \frac{-\sqrt{3}\,|x|}{2\sigma}. \tag{A.18}$$

A.6 Stochastic Process

We are often interested in experiments whose outcomes are a function of time. For example, we might be interested in designing a system that encodes speech. The outcomes are particular patterns of speech that will be encountered by the speech coder. We can mathematically describe this situation by extending our definition of a random variable. Instead of the random variable mapping an outcome of an experiment to a number, we map it to a function of time.

> *Definition:* Let S be a sample space with outcomes $\{\omega_i\}$. Then the random or stochastic process X is a mapping

$$X : S \to \mathcal{F} \tag{A.19}$$

> where $\mathcal{F}$ denotes the set of functions on the real number line. In other words,

$$X(\omega) = x(t); \qquad \omega \in S, \; x \in \mathcal{F}, \; -\infty < t < \infty. \tag{A.20}$$

The functions $x(t)$ are called the *realizations* of the random process, and the collection of functions $\{x_\omega(t)\}$ indexed by the outcomes ω is called the *ensemble* of the stochastic process. We can define the mean and variance of the ensemble as

$$\mu(t) = E[X(t)] \tag{A.21}$$
$$\sigma^2(t) = E[(X(t) - \mu(t))^2]. \tag{A.22}$$

If we sample the ensemble at some time t_0, we get a set of numbers $\{x_\omega(t_0)\}$ indexed by the outcomes ω, which by definition is a random variable. By sampling the ensemble at different times t_i, we get different random variables $\{x_\omega(t_i)\}$. For simplicity we often drop the ω and t and simply refer to these random variables as $\{x_i\}$.

Associated with each of these random variables, we will have a distribution function. We can also define a joint distribution function for two or more of these random variables:

> *Definition:* Given a set of random variables $\{x_1, x_2, \ldots, x_N\}$, the *joint* cumulative distribution function is defined as

$$F_{X_1 X_2 \cdots X_N}(x_1, x_2, \ldots, x_N) = P(X_1 < x_1, X_2 < x_2, \ldots, X_N < x_N) \tag{A.23}$$

> Unless it is clear from the context what we are talking about, we will refer to the *cdf* of the individual random variables X_i as the *marginal cdf* of X_i.

We can also define the joint probability density function for these random variables $f_{X_1 X_2 \cdots X_N}(x_1, x_2, \ldots, x_N)$ in the same manner as we defined the *pdf* in the case of the single random variable. We can classify the relationships between these random variables in a number of different ways. In the following we define some relationships between two random variables. The concepts are easily extended to more than two random variables.

> *Definition:* Two random variables X_1 and X_2 are said to be *independent* if their joint distribution function can be written as the product of the marginal distribution functions of each random variable; that is,

$$F_{X_1 X_2}(x_1, x_2) = F_{X_1}(x_1) F_{X_2}(x_2). \tag{A.24}$$

This also implies that

$$f_{X_1 X_2}(x_1, x_2) = f_{X_1}(x_1) f_{X_2}(x_2). \tag{A.25}$$

If all the random variables $X_1, X_2, \ldots$ are independent and they have the same distribution, they are said to be *independent, identically distributed* (*iid*).

Definition: Two random variables X_1 and X_2 are said to be *orthogonal* if

$$E[X_1 X_2] = 0. \tag{A.26}$$

Definition: Two random variables X_1 and X_2 are said to be *uncorrelated* if

$$E[(X_1 - \mu_1)(X_2 - \mu_2)] = 0 \tag{A.27}$$

where $\mu_1 = E[X_1]$ and $\mu_2 = E[X_2]$.

Definition: The *autocorrelation function* of a random process is defined as

$$R_{xx}(t_i, t_2) = E[X_1 X_2]. \tag{A.28}$$

Definition: For a given value of N, suppose we sample the stochastic process at N times $\{t_i\}$ to get the N random variables $\{X_i\}$ with *cdf* $F_{X_1 X_2 \cdots X_N}(x_1, x_2, \ldots, x_N)$, and another N times $\{t_i + T\}$ to get the random variables $\{X_i'\}$ with *cdf* $F_{X_1' X_2' \cdots X_N'}(x_1', x_2', \ldots, x_N')$. If

$$F_{X_1 X_2 \cdots X_N}(x_1, x_2, \ldots, x_N) = F_{X_1' X_2' \cdots X_N'}(x_1', x_2', \ldots, x_N') \tag{A.29}$$

for all N and T, the process is said to be *stationary*.

The assumption of stationarity is a rather important assumption because it is a statement that the statistical characteristics of the process under investigation do not change with time. Thus, if we design a system for an input based on the statistical characteristics of the input today, the system will still be useful tomorrow because the input will not change its characteristics. The assumption of stationarity is also a very strong assumption, and we can usually make do quite well with a weaker condition, *wide sense* or *weak sense* stationarity.

Definition: A stochastic process is said to be wide sense or weak sense stationary if it satisfies the following conditions:

1. The mean is constant; that is, $\mu(t) = \mu$ for all t.

2. The variance is finite.

3. The autocorrelation function $R_{xx}(t_1, t_2)$ is a function only of the difference between t_1 and t_2, and not of the individual values of t_1 and t_2; that is,

$$R_{xx}(t_1, t_2) = R_{xx}(t_1 - t_2) = R_{xx}(t_2 - t_1). \tag{A.30}$$

Further Reading

1. The classic books on probability are the two-volume set *An Introduction to Probability Theory and Its Applications,* by W. Feller [74].

2. A commonly used text for an introductory course on probability and random processes is *Probability, Random Variables, and Stochastic Processes*, by A. Papoulis [172].

A.7 Projects and Problems

1. If $A \cap B \neq \phi$, show that

$$P(A \cup B) = P(A) + P(B) - P(A \cap B).$$

2. Show that expectation is a linear operator in both the discrete and the continuous case.

3. If a is a constant, show that $E[a] = a$.

4. Show that for a random variable X,

$$\sigma_X^2 = E[X^2] - \mu_X^2.$$

5. Show that the variance of the uniform distribution is given by

$$\sigma_X^2 = \frac{(b-a)^2}{12}.$$

B

A Brief Review
of Matrix Concepts

 n this appendix we will look at some of the basic concepts of matrix algebra. Our intent is simply to familiarize you with some basic matrix operations that we will need in our study of compression. Matrices are very useful for representing linear systems of equations, and matrix theory is a powerful tool for the study of linear operators. In our study of compression techniques we will use matrices both in the solution of systems of equations and in our study of linear transforms.

B.1   A Matrix

A collection of real or complex elements arranged in M rows and N columns is called a matrix of order $M \times N$

$$\mathbf{A} = \begin{bmatrix} a_{00} & a_{01} & \cdots & a_{0N-1} \\ a_{10} & a_{11} & \cdots & a_{1N-1} \\ \vdots & \vdots & & \vdots \\ a_{(M-1)0} & a_{(M-1)1} & \cdots & a_{M-1N-1} \end{bmatrix} \tag{B.1}$$

where the first subscript denotes the row that an element belongs to and the second subscript denotes the column. For example, the element a_{02} belongs in row 0 and column 2, and the element a_{32} belongs in row 3 and column 2. The generic ijth element of a matrix $\mathbf{A}$ is sometimes represented as $[\mathbf{A}]_{ij}$. If the number of rows is equal to the number of columns ($N = M$), then the matrix is called a *square matrix*. A special square matrix that we will be using is the *identity matrix* $\mathbf{I}$, in which the elements on the diagonal of the matrix are 1 and all other elements are 0:

$$[\mathbf{I}]_{ij} = \begin{cases} 1 & i = j \\ 0 & i \neq j. \end{cases} \tag{B.2}$$

If a matrix consists of a single column ($N = 1$), it is called a *column matrix* or *vector* of dimension M. If it consists of a single row ($M = 1$), it is called a *row matrix* or *vector* of dimension N.

The *transpose* $\mathbf{A}^T$ of a matrix $\mathbf{A}$ is the $N \times M$ matrix obtained by writing the rows of the matrix as columns and the columns as rows:

$$\mathbf{A}^T = \begin{bmatrix} a_{00} & a_{10} & \cdots & a_{(M-1)0} \\ a_{01} & a_{11} & \cdots & a_{(M-1)1} \\ \vdots & \vdots & & \vdots \\ a_{0(N-1)} & a_{1(N-1)} & \cdots & a_{M-1N-1} \end{bmatrix} \tag{B.3}$$

The transpose of a column matrix is a row matrix and vice versa.

Two matrices $\mathbf{A}$ and $\mathbf{B}$ are said to be equal if they are of the same order and their corresponding elements are equal; that is,

$$\mathbf{A} = \mathbf{B} \quad \Leftrightarrow \quad a_{ij} = b_{ij}, \; i = 0, 1, \dots M - 1; \; j = 0, 1, \dots N - 1. \tag{B.4}$$

B.2 Matrix Operations

You can add, subtract, and multiply matrices, but since matrices come in all shapes and sizes, there are some restrictions as to what operations you can perform with what kind of matrices. In order to add or subtract two matrices, their dimensions have to be identical—same number of rows and same number of columns. In order to multiply two matrices, the order in which they are multiplied is important. In general $\mathbf{A} \times \mathbf{B}$ is not equal to $\mathbf{B} \times \mathbf{A}$. Multiplication is only defined for the case where the number of columns of the first matrix is equal to the number of rows of the second matrix. The reasons for these restrictions will become apparent when we look at how the operations are defined.

When we add two matrices, the resultant matrix consists of elements that are the sum of the corresponding entries in the matrices being added. Let us add two matrices $\mathbf{A}$ and $\mathbf{B}$ where

$$\mathbf{A} = \begin{bmatrix} a_{00} & a_{01} & a_{02} \\ a_{10} & a_{11} & a_{12} \end{bmatrix} \tag{B.5}$$

and

$$\mathbf{B} = \begin{bmatrix} b_{00} & b_{01} & b_{02} \\ b_{10} & b_{11} & b_{12} \end{bmatrix} \tag{B.6}$$

The sum of the two matrices, $\mathbf{C}$, is given by

$$\mathbf{C} = \begin{bmatrix} c_{00} & c_{12} & c_{13} \\ c_{21} & c_{22} & c_{23} \end{bmatrix} = \begin{bmatrix} a_{00} + b_{00} & a_{01} + b_{01} & a_{02} + b_{02} \\ a_{10} + b_{10} & a_{11} + b_{11} & a_{12} + b_{12} \end{bmatrix} \tag{B.7}$$

Notice that each element of the resulting matrix $\mathbf{C}$ is the sum of corresponding elements of the matrices $\mathbf{A}$ and $\mathbf{B}$. In order for the two matrices to have corresponding elements, the dimension of the two matrices has to be the same. Therefore, addition is only defined for matrices with identical dimensions (i.e., same number of rows and same number of columns).

Subtraction is defined in a similar manner. The elements of the difference matrix are made up of term-by-term subtraction of the matrices being subtracted.

We could have generalized matrix addition and matrix subtraction from our knowledge of addition and subtraction of numbers. Multiplication of matrices is another kettle of fish entirely. It is easiest to describe matrix multiplication with an example. Suppose we have two different matrices $\mathbf{A}$ and $\mathbf{B}$ where

$$\mathbf{A} = \begin{bmatrix} a_{00} & a_{01} & a_{02} \\ a_{10} & a_{11} & a_{12} \end{bmatrix} \tag{B.8}$$

and

$$\mathbf{B} = \begin{bmatrix} b_{00} & b_{01} \\ b_{10} & b_{11} \\ b_{20} & b_{21} \end{bmatrix} \tag{B.9}$$

The product is given by

$$\mathbf{C} = \mathbf{AB} = \begin{bmatrix} c_{00} & c_{01} \\ c_{10} & c_{11} \end{bmatrix} = \begin{bmatrix} a_{00}b_{00} + a_{01}b_{10} + a_{02}b_{20} & a_{00}b_{01} + a_{01}b_{11} + a_{02}b_{21} \\ a_{10}b_{00} + a_{11}b_{10} + a_{12}b_{20} & a_{10}b_{01} + a_{11}b_{11} + a_{12}b_{21} \end{bmatrix}$$
$$\tag{B.10}$$

You can see that the i, j element of the product is obtained by adding term by term the product of elements in the ith row of the first matrix with those of the jth column of the second matrix. Thus, the element c_{10} in the matrix $\mathbf{C}$ is obtained by summing the term-by-term products of row 1 of the first matrix $\mathbf{A}$ with column 0 of the matrix $\mathbf{B}$. We can also see that the resulting matrix will have as many rows as the matrix to the left and as many columns as the matrix to the right.

What happens if we reverse the order of the multiplication? By the rules above we will end up with a matrix with three rows and three columns.

$$\begin{bmatrix} b_{00}a_{00} + b_{01}a_{10} & b_{00}a_{01} + +b_{01}a_{11} & b_{00}a_{02} + b_{01}a_{12} \\ b_{10}a_{00} + b_{11}a_{10} & b_{10}a_{01} + +b_{11}a_{11} & b_{10}a_{02} + b_{11}a_{12} \\ b_{20}a_{00} + b_{21}a_{10} & b_{20}a_{01} + +b_{21}a_{11} & b_{20}a_{02} + b_{21}a_{12} \end{bmatrix} \tag{B.11}$$

The elements of the two product matrices are different as are the dimensions.

As we can see, multiplication between matrices follows some rather different rules than multiplication between real numbers. The sizes have to match up—the number of columns of the first matrix has to be equal to the number of rows of the second matrix, and the order of multiplication is important. Because of the latter fact we often talk about premultiplying or postmultiplying. Premultiplying $\mathbf{B}$ by $\mathbf{A}$ results in the product $\mathbf{AB}$, while postmultiplying $\mathbf{B}$ by $\mathbf{A}$ results in the product $\mathbf{BA}$.

We have three of the four elementary operations. What about the fourth elementary operation, division? The easiest way to present division in matrices is to look at the formal definition of division when we are talking about real numbers. In the real number system, for every number a different from zero, there exists an inverse, denoted by $1/a$ or a^{-1}, such that the product of a with its inverse is one. When we talk about a number b divided by a number a, this is the same as the *multiplication* of b with the inverse of a. Therefore, we could define division by a matrix as the multiplication with the inverse of the matrix. $\mathbf{A}/\mathbf{B}$ would be given by $\mathbf{AB}^{-1}$. Once we have the definition of an inverse of a matrix, the rules of multiplication apply.

So how do we define the inverse of a matrix? Following the definition for real numbers, in order to define the inverse of a matrix we need to have the matrix counterpart of 1. In matrices this counterpart is called the *identity matrix*. The identity matrix is a square matrix with diagonal elements being 1 and off-diagonal elements being 0. For example, a 3×3 identity matrix is given by

$$\mathbf{I} = \begin{bmatrix} 1 & 0 & 0 \\ 0 & 1 & 0 \\ 0 & 0 & 1 \end{bmatrix} \tag{B.12}$$

The identity matrix behaves like the number one in the matrix world. If we multiply any matrix with the identity matrix (of appropriate dimension), we get the original matrix back. Given a square matrix $\mathbf{A}$, we define its inverse, $\mathbf{A}^{-1}$, as the matrix that when premultiplied or postmultiplied by $\mathbf{A}$ results in the identity matrix. For example, consider the matrix

$$\mathbf{A} = \begin{bmatrix} 3 & 4 \\ 1 & 2 \end{bmatrix} \tag{B.13}$$

The inverse matrix is given by

$$\mathbf{A}^{-1} = \begin{bmatrix} 1 & -2 \\ -0.5 & 1.5 \end{bmatrix} \tag{B.14}$$

To check that this is indeed the inverse matrix, let us multiply them:

$$\begin{bmatrix} 3 & 4 \\ 1 & 2 \end{bmatrix} \begin{bmatrix} 1 & -2 \\ -0.5 & 1.5 \end{bmatrix} = \begin{bmatrix} 1 & 0 \\ 0 & 1 \end{bmatrix} \tag{B.15}$$

and

$$\begin{bmatrix} 1 & -2 \\ -0.5 & 1.5 \end{bmatrix} \begin{bmatrix} 3 & 4 \\ 1 & 2 \end{bmatrix} = \begin{bmatrix} 1 & 0 \\ 0 & 1 \end{bmatrix} \tag{B.16}$$

If $\mathbf{A}$ is a vector of dimension M, we can define two specific kinds of products. If $\mathbf{A}$ is a column matrix, then the *inner product* or *dot product* is defined as

$$\mathbf{A}^T \mathbf{A} = \sum_{i=0}^{M-1} a_{i0}^2 \tag{B.17}$$

and the *outer product* or *cross product* is defined as

$$\mathbf{A}\mathbf{A}^T = \begin{bmatrix} a_{00}a_{00} & a_{00}a_{10} & \cdots & a_{00}a_{(M-1)0} \\ a_{10}a_{00} & a_{10}a_{10} & \cdots & a_{10}a_{(M-1)0} \\ \vdots & \vdots & & \vdots \\ a_{(M-1)0}a_{00} & a_{\{(M-1)1\}}a_{10} & \cdots & a_{(M-1)0}a_{(M-1)0} \end{bmatrix} \tag{B.18}$$

Notice that the inner product results in a scalar, while the outer product results in a matrix.

In order to find the inverse of a matrix, we need the concepts of determinant and cofactor. Associated with each square matrix is a scalar value called the *determinant* of the matrix. The determinant of a matrix $\mathbf{A}$ is denoted as $|\mathbf{A}|$. To see how to obtain the determinant of an $N \times N$ matrix, we start with a 2×2 matrix. The determinant of a 2×2 matrix is given as

$$|\mathbf{A}| = \begin{vmatrix} a_{00} & a_{01} \\ a_{10} & a_{11} \end{vmatrix} = a_{00}a_{11} - a_{01}a_{10}. \tag{B.19}$$

Finding the determinant of a 2×2 matrix is easy. To explain how to get the determinants of larger matrices, we need to define some terms.

The *minor* of an element a_{ij} of an $N \times N$ matrix is defined to be the determinant of the $N - 1 \times N - 1$ matrix obtained by deleting the row and column containing a_{ij}. For example, if $\mathbf{A}$ is a 4×4 matrix

$$\mathbf{A} = \begin{bmatrix} a_{00} & a_{01} & a_{02} & a_{03} \\ a_{10} & a_{11} & a_{12} & a_{13} \\ a_{20} & a_{21} & a_{22} & a_{23} \\ a_{30} & a_{31} & a_{32} & a_{33} \end{bmatrix} \tag{B.20}$$

then the minor of the element a_{12}, denoted by M_{12}, is the determinant

$$M_{12} = \begin{vmatrix} a_{00} & a_{01} & a_{03} \\ a_{20} & a_{21} & a_{23} \\ a_{30} & a_{31} & a_{33} \end{vmatrix} \tag{B.21}$$

The cofactor of a_{ij} denoted by $\mathbf{A}_{ij}$ is given by

$$\mathbf{A}_{ij} = (-1)^{i+j} M_{ij}. \tag{B.22}$$

Armed with these definitions we can write an expression for the determinant of an $N \times N$ matrix as

$$|\mathbf{A}| = \sum_{i=0}^{N-1} a_{ij} \mathbf{A}_{ij} \tag{B.23}$$

or

$$|\mathbf{A}| = \sum_{j=0}^{N-1} a_{ij} \mathbf{A}_{ij} \tag{B.24}$$

where the a_{ij} are taken from a single row or a single column. If the matrix has a particular row or column that has a large number of zeros in it, we would need fewer computations if we picked that particular row or column.

Equations (B.23) and (B.24) express the determinant of an $N \times N$ matrix in terms of determinants of $N-1 \times N-1$ matrices. We can express each of the $N-1 \times N-1$ determinants in terms of $N - 2 \times N - 2$ determinants, continuing in this fashion until we have everything expressed in terms of 2×2 determinants, which can be evaluated using (B.19).

Now that we know how to compute a determinant, we need one more definition before we can define the inverse of a matrix. The *adjoint* of a matrix $\mathbf{A}$, denoted by $adj(\mathbf{A})$, is a matrix whose ijth element is the cofactor $\mathbf{A}_{ji}$. The inverse of a matrix $\mathbf{A}$, denoted by $\mathbf{A}^{-1}$, is given by

$$\mathbf{A}^{-1} = \frac{1}{|\mathbf{A}|}\, adj(\mathbf{A}). \tag{B.25}$$

Notice that for the inverse to exist the determinant has to be nonzero. If the determinant for a matrix is zero, the matrix is said to be singular. The method we have described here works well with small matrices; however, it is highly inefficient if N becomes greater than 4. There are a number of efficient methods for inverting matrices; see the books in the Further Reading section for details.

Corresponding to a square matrix $\mathbf{A}$ of size $N \times N$ are N scalar values called the *eigenvalues* of $\mathbf{A}$. The eigenvalues are the N solutions of the equation $|\lambda\mathbf{I} - \mathbf{A}| = 0$. This equation is called the *characteristic equation*.

Example B.2.1:

Let us find the eigenvalues of the matrix

$$\begin{bmatrix} 4 & 5 \\ 2 & 1 \end{bmatrix}$$

$$|\lambda\mathbf{I} - \mathbf{A}| = 0$$

$$\left| \begin{bmatrix} \lambda & 0 \\ 0 & \lambda \end{bmatrix} - \begin{bmatrix} 4 & 5 \\ 2 & 1 \end{bmatrix} \right| = 0$$

$$(\lambda - 4)(\lambda - 1) - 10 = 0$$

$$\lambda_1 = -1 \quad \lambda_2 = 6 \tag{B.26}$$

◆

The eigenvectors V_k of an $N \times N$ matrix are the N vectors of dimension N that satisfy the equation

$$\mathbf{A}V_k = \lambda_k V_k. \tag{B.27}$$

Further Reading

1. The subject of matrices is covered at an introductory level in a number of textbooks. A good one is *Advanced Engineering Mathematics*, by E. Kreyszig [129].

2. Numerical methods for manipulating matrices (and a good deal more) are presented in *Numerical Recipes in C*, by W.H. Press, S.A. Teukolsky, W.T. Vetterling, and B.P. Flannery [183].

The Root Lattices

efine $\mathbf{e}_i^L$ to be a vector in L dimensions whose ith component is 1 and all other components are 0. Some of the root systems that are used in lattice vector quantization are given as follows:

$$
\begin{array}{lll}
D_L & \pm\mathbf{e}_i^L \pm \mathbf{e}_j^L, & i \neq j, i,j = 1,2,\ldots,L \\
A_L & \pm(\mathbf{e}_i^{L+1} - \mathbf{e}_j^{L+1}), & i \neq j, i,j = 1,2,\ldots,L \\
E_L & \pm\mathbf{e}_i^L \pm \mathbf{e}_j^L, & i \neq j, i,j = 1,2,\ldots,L-1, \\
& \frac{1}{2}(\pm\mathbf{e}_1 \pm \mathbf{e}_2 \cdots \pm \mathbf{e}_{L-1} \pm \sqrt{2 - \frac{(L-1)}{4}}\,\mathbf{e}_L) & L = 6,7,8
\end{array}
$$

Let us look at each of these definitions a bit closer and see how they can be used to generate lattices.

D_L: Let us start with the D_L lattice. For $L = 2$, the four roots of the D_2 algebra are $\mathbf{e}_1^2 + \mathbf{e}_2^2$, $\mathbf{e}_1^2 - \mathbf{e}_2^2$, $-\mathbf{e}_1^2 + \mathbf{e}_2^2$, and $-\mathbf{e}_1^2 - \mathbf{e}_2^2$, or $(1,1)$, $(1,-1)$, $(-1,1)$, and $(-1,-1)$. We can pick any two independent vectors from among these four to form the basis set for the D_2 lattice. Suppose we picked $(1,1)$ and $(1,-1)$. Then any integral combination of these vectors is a lattice point. The resulting lattice is shown in Figure 9.24 in Chapter 9. Notice that the sum of the coordinates are all even numbers. This makes finding the closest lattice point to an input a relatively simple exercise.

A_L: The roots of the A_L lattices are described using $L + 1$-dimensional vectors. However, if we select any L independent vectors from this set, we will find that the points that are generated all lie in an L-dimensional slice of the $L + 1$-dimensional space. This can be seen from Figure C.1.

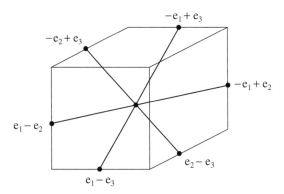

We can obtain an L-dimensional basis set from this using a simple algorithm described in [205]. In two dimensions, this results in the generation of the vectors $(1, 0)$ and $(-\frac{1}{2}, \frac{\sqrt{3}}{2})$. The resulting lattice is shown in Figure 9.25 in Chapter 9. To find the closest point to the A_L lattice, we use the fact that in the embedding of the lattice in $L + 1$ dimensions, the sum of the coordinates is always zero. The exact procedure can be found in [51, 91].

E_L: As we can see from the definition, the E_L lattices go up to a maximum dimension of 8. Each of these lattices can be written as unions of the A_L and D_L lattices and their translated version. For example, the E_8 lattice is the union of the D_8 lattice and the D_8 lattice translated by the vector $(\frac{1}{2}, \frac{1}{2}, \frac{1}{2}, \frac{1}{2}, \frac{1}{2}, \frac{1}{2}, \frac{1}{2}, \frac{1}{2})$. Therefore, to find the closest E_8 point to an input $\mathbf{x}$, we find the closest point of D_8 to $\mathbf{x}$, and the closest point of D_8 to $\mathbf{x} - (\frac{1}{2}, \frac{1}{2}, \frac{1}{2}, \frac{1}{2}, \frac{1}{2}, \frac{1}{2}, \frac{1}{2}, \frac{1}{2})$, and pick the one that is closest to $\mathbf{x}$.

There are several advantages to using lattices as vector quantizers. There is no need to store the codebook, and finding the closest lattice point to a given input is a rather simple operation. However, the quantizer codebook is only a subset of the lattice. How do we know when we have wandered out of this subset, and what do we do about it? Furthermore, how do we generate a binary codeword for each of the lattice points that lie within the boundary? The first problem is easy to solve. Earlier we discussed the selection of a boundary to reduce the effect of the overload error. We can check the location of the lattice point to see if it is within this boundary. If not, we are outside the subset. The other questions are more difficult to resolve. Conway and Sloane [53] have developed a technique that functions by first defining the boundary as one of the quantization regions (expanded many times) of the root lattices. The technique is not very complicated, but it takes some time to set up, so we will not describe it here (see [53] for details).

We have given a sketchy description of lattice quantizers. For a more detailed tutorial review, see [91]. A more theoretical review and overview can be found in [68].

Bibliography

[1] E.F. Abaya and G.L. Wise. On the Existence of Optimal Quantizers. *IEEE Transactions on Information Theory*, IT-28:937–940, November 1982.

[2] N. Abramson. *Information Theory and Coding*. New York: McGraw-Hill, 1963.

[3] H. Abut, editor. *Vector Quantization*. Piscataway, NJ: IEEE Press, 1990.

[4] W.C. Adams, Jr., and C.E. Geisler. Quantizing Characteristics for Signals Having Laplacian Amplitude Probability Density Function. *IEEE Transactions on Communications*, COM-26:1295–1297, August 1978.

[5] T. Adamson. *Electronic Communications*. Albany, NY: Delmar, 1988.

[6] N. Ahmed and K.R. Rao. *Orthogonal Transforms for Digital Signal Processing*. New York: Springer-Verlag, 1975.

[7] K. Aizawa and T.S. Huang. Model-Based Image Coding: Advanced Video Coding Techniques for Very Low Bit-Rate Applications. *Proceedings of the IEEE*, 83:259–271, February 1995.

[8] A.G. Al-Araj. *Recursively Indexed Vector Quantization*. Ph.D. thesis, University of Nebraska–Lincoln, 1994.

[9] A.G. Al-Araj and K. Sayood. Vector Quantization of Nonstationary Sources. In *Proceedings International Conference on Telecommunications—1994*, pages 92–95. Piscataway, NJ: IEEE Press, 1994.

[10] S. Arimoto. An Algorithm for Computing the Capacity of Arbitrary Discrete Memoryless Channels. *IEEE Transactions on Information Theory*, IT-18:14–20, January 1972.

[11] R.B. Arps and T.K. Truong. Comparison of International Standards for Lossless Still Image Compression. *Proceedings of the IEEE*, 82:889–899, June 1994.

[12] R.B. Ash. *Information Theory*. Mineola, NY: Dover, 1990. (Originally published by Interscience Publishers in 1965.)

[13] B.S. Atal, V. Cuperman, and A. Gersho. *Speech and Audio Coding for Wireless and Network Applications*. Norwell, MA: Kluwer Academic Publishers, 1993.

[14] B.S. Atal and J.R. Remde. A New Model of LPC Excitation for Producing Natural Sounding Speech at Low Bit Rates. In *Proceedings IEEE International Conference on Acoustics, Speech, and Signal Processing*, pages 614–617. Piscataway, NJ: IEEE Press, 1982.

[15] R.L. Auger, M.W. Glancy, M.M. Goutmann, and A.L. Kirsch. The Space Shuttle Ground Terminal Delta Modulation System. *IEEE Transactions on Communications*, COM-26:1660–1670, November 1978. Part I of two parts.

[16] C.F. Barnes and R.L. Frost. Residual Vector Quantizers with Jointly Optimized Code Books. In *Advances in Electronics and Electron Physics*, pages 1–59. Amsterdam: Elsevier, 1992.

[17] C.F. Barnes and R.L. Frost. Vector Quantizers with Direct Sum Codebooks. *IEEE Transactions on Information Theory*, 39:565–580, March 1993.

[18] M.F. Barnsley and A.D. Sloan. Chaotic Compression. *Computer Graphics World*, November 1987.

[19] T.C. Bell. Better OPM/L Text Compression. *IEEE Transactions on Communications*, COM-34:1176–1182, December 1986.

[20] T.C. Bell, J.G. Cleary, and I.H. Witten. *Text Compression*. Advanced Reference Series. Englewood Cliffs, NJ: Prentice Hall, 1990.

[21] T.C. Bell, I.H. Witten, and J.G. Cleary. Modeling for Text Compression. *ACM Computing Surveys*, 21:557–591, December 1989.

[22] W.R. Bennett. Spectra of Quantized Signals. *Bell System Technical Journal*, 27:446–472, July 1948.

[23] T. Berger. *Rate Distortion Theory: A Mathematical Basis for Data Compression*. Englewood Cliffs, NJ: Prentice Hall, 1971.

[24] T. Berger, F. Jelinek, and J. Wolf. Permutation Codes for Sources. *IEEE Transactionss on Information Theory*, IT-18:166–169, January 1972.

[25] R.E. Blahut. Computation of Channel Capacity and Rate Distortion Functions. *IEEE Transactions on Information Theory*, IT-18:460–473, July 1972.

[26] M. Bosi and G. Davidson. High Quality, Low Rate Audio Transform Coding for Transmission and Multimedia Application. In *Preprint 3365, Audio Engineering Society*. New York: AES, October 1992.

[27] G. Bozdaği, A.M. Tekalp, and L. Onural. 3-D Motion Estimation and Wireframe Adaptation Including Photometric Effects for Model-Based Coding of Facial Image Sequences. *IEEE Transactions on Circuits and Systems for Video Technology*, 4:246–256, June 1994.

[28] K. Brandenburg and G. Stoll. ISO-MPEG-1 Audio: A Generic Standard for Coding of High-Quality Digital Audio. *Journal of the Audio Engineering Society*, 42:780–792, October 1994.

[29] L. Breiman, J.H. Freidman, R.A. Olshen, and C.J. Stone. *Classification and Regression Trees*. Belmont, CA: Wadsworth, 1984.

[30] J.A. Bucklew and N.C. Gallagher, Jr. A Note on Optimal Quantization. *IEEE Transactions on Information Theory*, IT-25:365–366, May 1979.

[31] J.A. Bucklew and N.C. Gallagher, Jr. Some Properties of Uniform Step Size Quantizers. *IEEE Transactions on Information Theory*, IT-26:610–613, September 1980.

[32] M. Burrows and D.J. Wheeler. A Block Sorting Data Compression Algorithm. Technical Report SRC 124, Digital Systems Research Center, 1994.

[33] C.S. Burrus, R.A. Gopinath, and H. Guo. *Introduction to Wavelets and Wavelet Transforms*. Englewood Cliffs, NJ: Prentice Hall, 1998.

[34] P.J. Burt and E.H. Adelson. The Laplacian Pyramid as a Compact Image Code. *IEEE Transactions on Communications*, COM-31:532–540, April 1983.

[35] A. Buzo, A.H. Gray, R.M. Gray, and J.D. Markel. Speech Coding Based upon Vector Quantization. *IEEE Transactions on Acoustics, Speech, and Signal Processing*, ASSP-28:562–574, October 1980.

[36] H. Caglar. *A Generalized Parametric PR-QMF/Wavelet Transform Design Approach for Multiresolution Signal Decomposition*. Ph.D. thesis, New Jersey Institute of Technology, May 1992.

[37] F.W. Campbell. The Human Eye as an Optical Filter. *Proceedings of the IEEE*, 56:1009–1014, June 1968.

[38] J.P. Campbell, Jr., T.E. Tremain, and V.C. Welch. The DOD 4.8 KBPS Standard (Proposed Federal Standard 1016). In B.S. Atal, V. Cuperman, and A. Gersho, editors, *Advances in Speech Coding*, pages 121–133. Norwell, MA: Kluwer, 1991.

[39] J.P. Campbell, V.C. Welch, and T.E. Tremain. An Expandable Error Protected 4800 bps CELP Coder (US Federal Standard 4800 bps Voice Coder). In *Proceedings International Conference on Acoustics, Speech, and Signal Processing*, pages 735–738. Piscataway, NJ: IEEE Press, 1989.

[40] J. Capon. A Probabilistic Model for Run-Length Coding of Pictures. *IRE Transactions on Information Theory*, pages 157–163, 1959.

[41] CCITT Blue Book. Terminal Equipment and Protocols for Telematic Services—Recommendations t.0–t.63. Geneva: International Telecommunications Union, 1989.

[42] J.-H. Chen, R.V. Cox, Y.-C. Lin, N. Jayant, and M. Melchner. A Low-Delay CELP Coder for the CCITT 16 kb/s Speech Coding Standard. *IEEE Journal on Selected Areas in Communications*, 10:830–849, 1992.

[43] O.T.-C. Chen, Z. Zhang, and B.J. Shen. An Adaptive High-Speed Lossy Data Compression. In *Proceedings Data Compression Conference '92*, pages 349–355. Los Alamitos, CA: IEEE Computer Society Press, 1992.

[44] W.-H. Chen and W.K. Pratt. Scene Adaptive Coder. *IEEE Transactions on Communications*, COM-32:225–232, March 1984.

[45] Y.-C. Chen, K. Sayood, and D.J. Nelson. A Robust Coding Scheme for Packet Video. *IEEE Transactions on Communications*, 40:1491–1501, September 1992.

[46] L. Chiariglione. The Development of an Integrated Audiovisual Coding Standard: MPEG. *Proceedings of the IEEE*, 83:151–157, February 1995.

[47] C.S. Choi, K. Aizawa, H. Harashima, and T. Takebe. Analysis and Synthesis of Facial Image Sequences in Model-Based Image Coding. *IEEE Transactions on Circuits and Systems for Video Technology*, 4:257–275, June 1994.

[48] P.A. Chou, T. Lookabaugh, and R.M. Gray. Optimal Pruning with Applications to Tree-Structured Source Coding and Modeling. *IEEE Transactions on Information Theory*, 35:31–42, January 1989.

[49] J.G. Cleary and W.J. Teahan. Unbounded Length Contexts for PPM. *The Computer Journal*, 40:30–74, February 1997.

[50] J.G. Cleary and I.H. Witten. Data Compression Using Adaptive Coding and Partial String Matching. *IEEE Transactions on Communications*, 32(4):396–402, 1984.

[51] J.H. Conway and N.J.A. Sloane. Fast Quantizing and Decoding Algorithms for Lattice Quantizers and Codes. *IEEE Transactions on Information Theory*, IT-28:227–232, March 1982.

[52] J.H. Conway and N.J.A. Sloane. Voronoi Regions of Lattices, Second Moments of Polytopes and Quantization. *IEEE Transactions on Information Theory*, IT-28:211–226, March 1982.

[53] J.H. Conway and N.J.A. Sloane. A Fast Encoding Method for Lattice Codes and Quantizers. *IEEE Transactions on Information Theory*, IT-29:820–824, November 1983.

[54] G.V. Cormack and R.N.S. Horspool. Data Compression Using Dynamic Markov Modelling. *The Computer Journal*, 30:541–550, June 1987.

[55] T.M. Cover and J.A. Thomas. *Elements of Information Theory*. Wiley Series in Telecommunications. New York: John Wiley and Sons, 1991.

[56] A. Croisier, D. Esteban, and C. Galand. Perfect Channel Splitting by Use of Interpolation/Decimation Techniques. In *Proceedings International Conference on Information Science and Systems*. Piscataway, NJ: IEEE Press, 1976.

[57] C.C. Cutler. Differential Quantization for Television Signals. U.S. Patent 2,605,361. July 29, 1952.

[58] I. Daubechies. *Ten Lectures on Wavelets*. Philadelphia: SIAM, 1992.

[59] M.M. Denn. *Optimization by Variational Methods*. New York: McGraw-Hill, 1969.

[60] H. Dreizen. Content-Driven Progressive Transmission of Grey-Scale Images. *IEEE Transactions on Communications*, COM-35:289–296, March 1987.

[61] H. Dudley. Remaking Speech. *Journal of the Acoustical Society of America*, 11:169–177, 1939.

[62] H. Dudley and T.H. Tarnoczy. Speaking Machine of Wolfgang Von Kempelen. *Journal of the Acoustical Society of America*, 22:151–166, March 1950.

[63] J. Durbin. The Fitting of Time Series Models. *Review of the Institute Inter. Statist.*, 28:233–243, 1960.

[64] P. Ekman and W.V. Friesen. *Facial Action Coding System*. Palo Alto, CA: Consulting Psychologists Press, 1977.

[65] P. Elias. Universal Codeword Sets and Representations of the Integers. *IEEE Transactions on Information Theory*, 21:194–203, 1975.

[66] D.F. Elliot and K.R. Rao. *Fast Transforms—Algorithms, Analysis, Applications*. San Diego, CA: Academic Press, 1982.

[67] W.H. Equitz. A New Vector Quantization Clustering Algorithm. *IEEE Transactions on Acoustics, Speech, and Signal Processing*, 37:1568–1575, October 1989.

[68] M.V. Eyuboglu and G.D. Forney, Jr. Lattice and Trellis Quantization with Lattice and Trellis Bounded Codebooks—High Rate Theory for Memoryless Sources. *IEEE Transactions on Information Theory*, IT-39, January 1993.

[69] N. Faller. An Adaptive System for Data Compression. In *Record of the 7th Asilomar Conference on Circuits, Systems, and Computers*, pages 593–597. Piscataway, NJ: IEEE Press, 1973.

[70] R.M. Fano. *Transmission of Information*. Cambridge, MA: MIT Press, 1961.

[71] D.C. Farden. Solution of a Toeplitz Set of Linear Equations. *IEEE Transactions on Antennas and Propagation*, AP-24:906–907, November 1976.

[72] P.M. Farrelle and A.K. Jain. Recursive Block Coding—A New Approach to Transform Coding. *IEEE Transactions on Communications*, COM-34:161–179, February 1986.

[73] N. Farvardin and J.W. Modestino. Optimum Quantizer Performance for a Class of Non-Gaussian Memoryless Sources. *IEEE Transactions on Information Theory*, IT-30:485–497, May 1984.

[74] W. Feller. *An Introduction to Probability Theory and Its Applications*. New York: John Wiley and Sons, third edition, 1968.

[75] T.R. Fischer. A Pyramid Vector Quantizer. *IEEE Transactions on Information Theory*, IT-32:568–583, July 1986.

[76] Y. Fisher, editor. *Fractal Image Compression*. New York: Springer-Verlag, 1995.

[77] H. Fletcher and W.A. Munson. Loudness, Its Measurement, Definition, and Calculation. *Journal of the Acoustical Society of America*, 5:82–108, 1933.

[78] S. Furui and M.M. Sondhi. *Advances in Speech Signal Processing*. New York: Marcel Dekker, 1991.

[79] R.G. Gallagher. *Information Theory and Reliable Communication*. New York: John Wiley and Sons, 1968.

[80] R.G. Gallagher. Variations on a Theme by Huffman. *IEEE Transactions on Information Theory*, IT-24(6):668–674, November 1978.

[81] N.L. Gerr and S. Cambanis. Analysis of Adaptive Differential PCM of a Stationary Gauss-Markov Input. *IEEE Transactions on Information Theory*, IT-33:350–359, May 1987.

[82] A. Gersho. Quantization. *IEEE Communications Magazine*, 15:16–29, September 1977.

[83] A. Gersho. Advances in Speech and Audio Compression. *Proceedings of the IEEE*, 82:900–918, June 1994.

[84] A. Gersho and V. Cuperman. A Pattern Matching Technique for Speech Coding. *IEEE Communications Magazine*, 21:15–21, December 1983.

[85] A. Gersho and D.J. Goodman. A Training Mode Adaptive Quantizer. *IEEE Transactions on Information Theory*, IT-20:746–749, November 1974.

[86] A. Gersho and R.M. Gray. *Vector Quantization and Signal Compression*. Norwell, MA: Kluwer Academic Publishers, 1991.

[87] A. Gersho and M. Yano. Adaptive Vector Quantization by Progressive Codevector Replacement. In *Proceedings IEEE International Conference on Acoustics, Speech, and Signal Processing*, pages 113–136. Piscataway, NJ: IEEE Press, 1985.

[88] J.D. Gibson. On Reflection Coefficients and the Cholesky Decomposition. *IEEE Transactions on Acoustics, Speech, and Signal Processing*, ASSP-25:93–96, February 1977.

[89] J.D. Gibson. Adaptive Prediction in Speech Differential Encoding Systems. *Proceedings of the IEEE*, 68:488–525, April 1980.

[90] J.D. Gibson, S.K. Jones, and J.L. Melsa. Sequentially Adaptive Prediction and Coding of Speech Signals. *IEEE Transactions on Communications*, COM-22:1789–1797, November 1974.

[91] J.D. Gibson and K. Sayood. Lattice Quantization. In P.W. Hawkes, editor, *Advances in Electronics and Electron Physics*, 72:259–328. San Diego, CA: Academic Press, 1990.

[92] H. Gish and J.N. Pierce. Asymptotically Efficient Quantization. *IEEE Transactions on Information Theory*, IT-14:676–683, September 1968.

[93] A.V. Goldberg and M. Sipser. Compression and Ranking. *SIAM Journal of Computing*, 20(3):524–536, June 1991.

[94] M. Goldberg and H. Sun. Image Sequence Coding. *IEEE Transactions on Communications*, COM-34:703–710, July 1986.

[95] S.W. Golomb. Run-Length Encodings. *IEEE Transactions on Information Theory*, IT-12:399–401, July 1966.

[96] R.C. Gonzales and R.E. Wood. *Digital Image Processing*. Reading, MA: Addison-Wesley, 1992.

[97] R.M. Gray. Vector Quantization. *IEEE Transactions on Acoustics, Speech, and Signal Processing*, 1:4–29, April 1984.

[98] R.M. Gray. *Entropy and Information Theory*. New York: Springer-Verlag, 1990.

[99] D.W. Griffin and J.S. Lim. Multi-Band Excitation Vocoder. *IEEE Transactions on Acoustics, Speech, and Signal Processing*, 36:1223–1235, August 1988.

[100] R.W. Hamming. *Coding and Information Theory*. Englewood Cliffs, NJ: Prentice Hall, second edition, 1986.

[101] G. Held and T.R. Marshall. *Data Compression*. New York: John Wiley and Sons, third edition, 1991.

[102] K. Hellwig, P. Vary, D. Massaloux, and J.P. Petit. Speech Codec for European Mobile Radio System. In *Conference Record, IEEE Global Telecommunications Conference*, pages 1065–1069. Piscataway, NJ: IEEE Press, 1989.

[103] E.E. Hilbert. Cluster Compression Algorithm—A Joint Clustering Data Compression Concept. Technical Report. JPL Publication 77-43. Washington, DC: NASA, 1977.

[104] H. Hotelling. Analysis of a Complex of Statistical Variables into Principal Components. *Journal of Educational Psychology*, 24:417–441, 498–520, 1933.

[105] J.-Y. Huang and P.M. Schultheiss. Block Quantization of Correlated Gaussian Random Variables. *IEEE Transactions on Communication Systems*, CS-11:289–296, September 1963.

[106] B.B. Hubbard. *The World According to Wavelets*. Series in Decision and Control. Wellesley, MA: A K Peters, 1996.

[107] D.A. Huffman. A Method for the Construction of Minimum Redundancy Codes. *Proceedings of the IRE*, 40:1098–1101, 1951.

[108] R. Hunter and A.H. Robinson. International Digital Facsimile Coding Standards. *IEEE Proceedings*, 68:854–867, July 1980.

[109] ISO/IEC IS 11172. Information Technology—Coding of Moving Pictures and Associated Audio for Digital Storage Media Up to about 1.5 Mbits/s.

[110] ISO/IEC IS 13818. Information Technology—Generic Coding of Moving Pictures and Associated Audio Information.

[111] ISO/IEC IS 14496. Coding of Moving Pictures and Audio.

[112] A.E. Jacquin. *A Fractal Theory of Iterated Markov Operators with Applications to Digital Image Coding*. Ph.D. thesis, Georgia Institute of Technology, August 1989.

[113] A.E. Jacquin. Image Coding Based on a Fractal Theory of Iterated Contractive Image Transformations. *IEEE Transactions on Image Processing*, 1:18–30, January 1992.

[114] A.K. Jain. *Fundamentals of Digital Image Processing*. Englewood Cliffs, NJ: Prentice Hall, 1989.

[115] A.K. Jain and R.E. Crochiere. Quadrature Mirror Filter Design in the Time Domain. *IEEE Transactions on Acoustics, Speech, and Signal Processing*, 32:353–361, April 1984.

[116] N.S. Jayant. Adaptive Delta Modulation with One-Bit Memory. *Bell System Technical Journal*, 49:321–342, March 1970.

[117] N.S. Jayant. Adaptive Quantization with One Word Memory. *Bell System Technical Journal*, 52:1119–1144, September 1973.

[118] N.S. Jayant and P. Noll. *Digital Coding of Waveforms*. Englewood Cliffs, NJ: Prentice Hall, 1984.

[119] N.S. Jayant and L. Rabiner. The Application of Dither to the Quantization of Speech Signals. *Bell System Technical Journal*, 51:1293–1304, June 1972.

[120] F. Jelinek. *Probabilistic Information Theory*. New York: McGraw-Hill, 1968.

[121] J.D. Johnston. A Filter Family Designed for Use in Quadrature Mirror Filter Banks. In *Proceedings IEEE International Conference on Acoustics, Speech, and Signal Processing*, pages 291–294. Piscataway, NJ: IEEE Press, April 1980.

[122] B.H. Juang and A.H. Gray. Multiple Stage Vector Quantization for Speech Coding. In *Proceedings IEEE International Conference on Acoustics, Speech, and Signal Processing*, pages 597–600. Piscataway, NJ: IEEE Press, April 1982.

[123] H. Karhunen. Über Lineare Methoden in der Wahrscheinlich-Keitsrechunung. *Annales Academiae Fennicae, Series A*, 1947.

[124] G. Karlsson and M. Vetterli. Packet Video and Its Integration into the Network Architecture. *IEEE Journal on Selected Areas in Communications*, 7:739–751, June 1989.

[125] K. Knowlton. Progressive Transmission of Grey-Scale and Binary Pictures by Simple, Efficient, and Lossless Encoding Schemes. *Proceedings of the IEEE*, 68:885–896, July 1980.

[126] D.E. Knuth. Dynamic Huffman coding. *Journal of Algorithms*, 6:163–180, 1985.

[127] A. Kondoz. *Digital Speech: Coding for Low Bit Rate Communication Systems*. New York: John Wiley and Sons, 1995.

[128] H.P. Kramer and M.V. Mathews. A Linear Encoding for Transmitting a Set of Correlated Signals. *IRE Transactions on Information Theory*, IT-2:41–46, September 1956.

[129] E. Kreyszig. *Advanced Engineering Mathematics*. New York: John Wiley and Sons, seventh edition, 1993.

[130] P. Kroon, E.F. Deprettere, and R.J. Sluyter. Regular-Pulse Excitation—A Novel Approach to Effective and Efficient Multipulse Coding of Speech. *IEEE Transactions on Acoustics, Speech, and Signal Processing*, ASSP-34:1054–1063, October 1986.

[131] G.G. Langdon, Jr. An Introduction to Arithmetic Coding. *IBM Journal of Research and Development*, 28:135–149, March 1984.

[132] G.G. Langdon and J.J. Rissanen. Compression of Black-White Images with Arithmetic Coding. *IEEE Transactions on Communications*, 29(6):858–867, 1981.

[133] G.G. Langdon, Jr., and J.J. Rissanen. A Simple General Binary Source Code. *IEEE Transactions on Information Theory*, IT-28:800–803, September 1982.

[134] B.P. Lathi. *Signal Processing and Linear Systems*. Berkeley Cambridge Press, 1998.

[135] A.M. Law and W.D. Kelton. *Simulation Modeling and Analysis*. New York: McGraw-Hill, 1982.

[136] D.A. Lelewer and D.S. Hirschberg. Data Compression. *ACM Computing Surveys*, 9:261–296, September 1987.

[137] N. Levinson. The Weiner RMS Error Criterion in Filter Design and Prediction. *Journal of Mathematical Physics*, 25:261–278, 1947.

[138] H. Li and R. Forchheimer. Two-View Facial Movement Estimation. *IEEE Transactions on Circuits and Systems for Video Technology*, 4:276–287, June 1994.

[139] Y. Linde, A. Buzo, and R.M. Gray. An Algorithm for Vector Quantization Design. *IEEE Transactions on Communications*, COM-28:84–95, January 1980.

[140] S.P. Lloyd. Least Squares Quantization in PCM. *IEEE Transactions on Information Theory*, IT-28:127–135, March 1982.

[141] M. Loéve. Fonctions Aléatoires de Seconde Ordre. In P. Lévy, editor, *Processus Stochastiques et Mouvement Brownien*. Paris: Hermann, 1948.

[142] D.G. Luenberger. *Optimization by Vector Space Methods.* Series in Decision and Control. New York: John Wiley and Sons, 1969.

[143] J. Lukaszewicz and H. Steinhaus. On Measuring by Comparison. *Zastos. Mat.*, pages 225–231, 1955. (In Polish.)

[144] F.J. MacWilliams and N.J.A. Sloane. *The Theory of Error Correcting Codes.* Amsterdam: North-Holland, 1977.

[145] J. Makhoul. Linear Prediction: A Tutorial Review. *Proceedings of the IEEE*, 63:561–580, April 1975.

[146] J. Makhoul, S. Roucos, and H. Gish. Vector Quantization in Speech Coding. *Proceedings of the IEEE*, 73:1551–1588, 1985.

[147] H.S. Malvar. *Signal Processing with Lapped Transforms.* Norwood, MA: Artech House, 1992.

[148] J.L. Mannos and D.J. Sakrison. The Effect of a Visual Fidelity Criterion on the Encoding of Images. *IEEE Transactions on Information Theory*, IT-20:525–536, July 1974.

[149] M. Mansuripur. *Introduction to Information Theory.* Englewood Cliffs, NJ: Prentice Hall, 1987.

[150] P.A. Maragos, R.W. Schafer, and R.M. Mersereau. Two Dimensional Linear Prediction and Its Application to Adaptive Predictive Coding of Images. *IEEE Transactions on Acoustics, Speech, and Signal Processing*, ASSP-32:1213–1229, December 1984.

[151] S.A. Martucci. Reversible Compression of HDTV Images Using Median Adaptive Prediction and Arithmetic Coding. In *IEEE International Symposium on Circuits and Systems*, pages 1310–1313. Piscataway, NJ: IEEE Press, 1990.

[152] W. Mauersberger. Experimental Results on the Performance of Mismatched Quantizers. *IEEE Transactions on Information Theory*, IT-25:381–386, July 1979.

[153] J. Max. Quantizing for Minimum Distortion. *IRE Transactions on Information Theory*, IT-6:7–12, January 1960.

[154] R.J. McAulay and T.F. Quatieri. Low-Rate Speech Coding Based on the Sinusoidal Model. In S. Furui and M.M. Sondhi, editors, *Advances in Speech Signal Processing*, Chapter 6, pages 165–208. New York: Marcel Dekker, 1992.

[155] R.J. McEliece. *The Theory of Information and Coding*, volume 3 of *Encyclopedia of Mathematics and Its Application*. Reading, MA: Addison-Wesley, 1977.

[156] N.D. Memon and K. Sayood. Lossless Image Compression: A Comparative Study. In *Proceedings of the SPIE Conference on Electronic Imaging*. Bellingham, WA: SPIE, 1995.

[157] N.D. Memon and X. Wu. Recent Developments in Context-Based Predictive Techniques for Lossless Image Compression. *The Computer Journal*, 40:127–136, 1997.

[158] F. Mintzer. Filters for Distortion-Free Two-Band Multirate Filter Banks. *IEEE Transactions on Acoustics, Speech, and Signal Processing*, ASSP-33:626–630, June 1985.

[159] J.L. Mitchell and W.B. Pennebaker. Optimal Hardware and Software Arithmetic Coding Procedures for the Q-Coder. *IBM Journal of Research and Development*, 32:727–736, November 1988.

[160] J.L. Mitchell, W.B. Pennebaker, C.E. Fogg, and D.J. LeGall. *MPEG Video Compression Standard*. New York: Chapman and Hall, 1997.

[161] D. Mitra. Mathematical Analysis of an Adaptive Quantizer. *Bell Systems Technical Journal*, pages 867–898, May–June 1974.

[162] S.K. Mitra and J.F. Kaiser, editors. *Handbook for Digital Signal Processing*. New York: John Wiley and Sons, 1993.

[163] A. Moffat. Implementing the PPM Data Compression Scheme. *IEEE Transactions on Communications*, COM-38:1917–1921, November 1990.

[164] B.C.J. Moore. *An Introduction to the Psychology of Hearing*. San Diego, CA: Academic Press, third edition, 1989.

[165] S. Na and K. Sayood. Recursive Indexing Preserves the Entropy of a Memoryless Geometric Source. Unpublished, 1996.

[166] N.M. Nasrabadi and R.A. King. Image Coding Using Vector Quantization. *IEEE Transactions on Communications*, COM-36:957–971, August 1988.

[167] M. Nelson and J.-L. Gailly. *The Data Compression Book*. New York: M&T Books, 1996.

[168] D.J. Newman. The Hexagon Theorem. *IEEE Transactions on Information Theory*, IT-28:137–139, March 1982.

[169] A. Ortega and K. Ramachandran. Rate-Distortion Methods for Image and Video Compression. *IEEE Signal Processing Magazine*, pages 23–50, November 1998.

[170] S. Panchanathan and M. Goldberg. Adaptive Algorithm for Image Coding Using Vector Quantization. *Signal Processing: Image Communication*, 4:81–92, 1991.

[171] P.E. Papamichalis. *Practical Approaches to Speech Coding*. Englewood Cliffs, NJ: Prentice Hall, 1987.

[172] A. Papoulis. *Probability, Random Variables, and Stochastic Processes*. New York: McGraw-Hill, third edition, 1991.

[173] T. Parsons. *Voice and Speech Processing*. New York: McGraw-Hill, 1987.

[174] R. Pasco. *Source Coding Algorithms for Fast Data Compression*. Ph.D. thesis, Stanford University, 1976.

[175] D. Paul. A 500–800 bps Adaptive Vector Quantization Vocoder Using a Perceptually Motivated Distortion Measure. In *Conference Record, IEEE Globecom*, pages 1079–1082. Piscataway, NJ: IEEE Press, 1982.

[176] W.A. Pearlman. Polar Quantization of a Complex Gaussian Random Variable. *IEEE Transactions on Communications*, COM-27:892–899, June 1979.

[177] W.B. Pennebaker and J.L. Mitchell. Probability Estimation for the Q-Coder. *IBM Journal of Research and Development*, 32:737–752, November 1988.

[178] W.B. Pennebaker and J.L. Mitchell. *JPEG Still Image Data Compression Standard*. New York: Van Nostrand Reinhold, 1993.

[179] W.B. Pennebaker, J.L. Mitchell, G.G. Langdon, Jr., and R.B. Arps. An Overview of the Basic Principles of the Q-Coder Adaptive Binary Arithmetic Coder. *IBM Journal of Research and Development*, 32:717–726, November 1988.

[180] J.R. Pierce. *Symbols, Signals, and Noise—The Nature and Process of Communications*. New York: Harper, 1961.

[181] S. Pigeon and Y. Bengio. A Memory-Efficient Adaptive Huffman Coding Algorithm for Very Large Sets of Symbols. In J. Storer and M. Cohn, editors, *Proceedings of the 1998 Data Compression Conference*, page 568. Los Alamitos, CA: IEEE Computer Society Press, 1998.

[182] W.K. Pratt. *Digital Image Processing*. New York: Wiley-Interscience, 1978.

[183] W.H. Press, S.A. Teukolsky, W.T. Vetterling, and B.P. Flannery. *Numerical Recipes in C*. New York: Cambridge University Press, second edition, 1992.

[184] J.P. Princen and A.P. Bradley. Analysis/Synthesis Filter Design Based on Time Domain Aliasing Cancellation. *IEEE Transactions on Acoustics, Speech, and Signal Processing*, ASSP-34:1153–1161, October 1986.

[185] M. Rabbani and P.W Jones. *Digital Image Compression Techniques*, volume TT7 of *Tutorial Texts Series*. Bellingham, WA: SPIE Optical Engineering Press, 1991.

[186] L.R. Rabiner and R.W. Schafer. *Digital Processing of Speech Signals*. Signal Processing. Englewood Cliffs, NJ: Prentice Hall, 1978.

[187] V. Ramamoorthy and K. Sayood. A Hybrid LBG/Lattice Vector Quantizer for High Quality Image Coding. In E. Arikan, editor, *Proceedings 1990 Bilkent International Conference on New Trends in Communication, Control, and Signal Processing*. Amsterdam: Elsevier, 1990.

[188] B. Ramamurthi and A. Gersho. Classified Vector Quantization of Images. *IEEE Transactions on Communications*, COM-34:1105–1115, November 1986.

[189] R.F. Rice. Some Practical Universal Noiseless Coding Techniques. Technical Report. JPL Publication 79-22. Pasadena, CA: Jet Propulsion Laboratory, March 1979.

[190] R.F. Rice, P.S. Yeh, and W. Miller. Algorithms for a Very High Speed Universal Noiseless Coding Module. Technical Report 91-1, Jet Propulsion Laboratory. Pasadena, CA: California Institute of Technology, February 1991.

[191] E.A. Riskin. Pruned Tree Structured Vector Quantization in Image Coding. In *Proceedings International Conference on Acoustics, Speech, and Signal Processing*, pages 1735–1737. Piscataway, NJ: IEEE Press, 1989.

[192] J.J. Rissanen. Generalized Kraft Inequality and Arithmetic Coding. *IBM Journal of Research and Development*, 20:198–203, May 1976.

[193] J.J. Rissanen and G.G. Langdon. Arithmetic Coding. *IBM Journal of Research and Development*, 23(2):149–162, March 1979.

[194] J.J. Rissanen and G.G. Langdon. Universal Modeling and Coding. *IEEE Transactions on Information Theory*, IT-27(1):12–22, 1981.

[195] J.J. Rissanen and K.M. Mohiuddin. A Multiplication-Free Multialphabet Arithmetic Code. *IEEE Transactions on Communications*, 37:93–98, February 1989.

[196] M.C. Rost and K. Sayood. A Progressive Data Compression Scheme Based on Adaptive Transform Coding. In *Proceedings 31st Midwest Symposium on Circuits and Systems*, pages 912–915. Amsterdam: Elsevier, 1988.

[197] M.J. Sabin and R.M. Gray. Product Code Vector Quantizers for Waveform and Voice Coding. *IEEE Transactions on Acoustics, Speech, and Signal Processing*, ASSP-32:474–488, June 1984.

[198] J.A. Saghri, A.J. Tescher, and J.T. Reagan. Terrain Adaptive Transform Coding of Multispectral Data. In *Proceedings International Conference on Geosciences and Remote Sensing*, pages 313–316. Piscataway, NJ: IEEE Press, 1994.

[199] A. Said and W.A. Pearlman. A New Fast and Efficient Coder Based on Set Partitioning in Hierarchical Trees. *IEEE Transactions on Circuits and Systems for Video Technologies*, pages 243–250, June 1996.

[200] D.J. Sakrison. A Geometric Treatment of the Source Encoding of a Gaussian Random Variable. *IEEE Transactions on Information Theory*, IT-14:481–486, May 1968.

[201] H. Samet. *The Design and Analysis of Spatial Data Structures*. Reading, MA: Addison-Wesley, 1990.

[202] A.A. Sardinas and G.W. Patterson. A Necessary and Sufficient Condition for the Unique Decomposition of Coded Messages. In *IRE Convention Records*, pages 104–108, 1953.

[203] D. Saupe, M. Ruhl, R. Hamzaoui, L. Grandi, and D. Marini. Optimal Hierarchical Partitions for Fractal Image Compression. In *Proceedings IEEE International Conference on Image Processing*, 1998.

[204] K. Sayood and J.D. Gibson. Explicit Additive Noise Models for Uniform and Nonuniform MMSE Quantization. *Signal Processing*, 7:407–414, 1984.

[205] K. Sayood, J.D. Gibson, and M.C. Rost. An Algorithm for Uniform Vector Quantizer Design. *IEEE Transactions on Information Theory*, IT-30:805–814, November 1984.

[206] K. Sayood and S. Na. Recursively Indexed Quantization of Memoryless Sources. *IEEE Transactions on Information Theory*, IT-38:1602–1609, November 1992.

[207] M.R. Schroeder. Linear Predictive Coding of Speech: Review and Current Directions. *IEEE Communications Magazine*, 23:54–61, August 1985.

[208] M.J. Shalkhauser and W.A. Whyte, Jr. Digital Codec for Real-Time Processing of Broadcast Quality Video Signals at 1.8 Bits/Pixel. In *Proceedings Global Telecommunications Conference*, November 1989. Also NASA Technical Memorandum 102325.

[209] C.E. Shannon. A Mathematical Theory of Communication. *Bell System Technical Journal*, 27:379–423, 623–656, 1948.

[210] C.E. Shannon. Prediction and Entropy of Printed English. *Bell System Technical Journal*, 30:50–64, January 1951.

[211] C.E. Shannon. Coding Theorems for a Discrete Source with a Fidelity Criterion. *IRE International Convention Records*, vol. 7, part 4, pages 142–163, 1959.

[212] J.M. Shapiro. Embedded Image Coding Using Zerotrees of Wavelet Coefficients. *IEEE Transactions on Signal Processing*, SP-41:3445–3462, December 1993.

[213] Y. Shoham and A. Gersho. Efficient Bit Allocation for an Arbitrary Set of Quantizers. *IEEE Transactions on Acoustics, Speech, and Signal Processing*, ASSP-36:1445–1453, September 1988.

[214] K.R. Sloan, Jr., and S.L. Tanimoto. Progressive Refinement of Raster Images. *IEEE Transactions on Computers*, C-28:871–874, November 1979.

[215] M.J.T. Smith and T.P. Barnwell III. A Procedure for Designing Exact Reconstruction Filter Banks for Tree Structured Subband Coders. In *Proceedings IEEE International Conference on Acoustics, Speech, and Signal Processing*. Piscataway, NJ: IEEE Press, 1984.

[216] H. Stark and J.W. Woods. *Probability, Random Processes, and Estimation Theory for Engineers*. Englewood Cliffs, NJ: Prentice Hall, second edition, 1994.

[217] R. Steele. *Delta Modulation Systems*. New York: Halstead Press, 1975.

[218] S.S. Stevens and H. Davis. *Hearing—Its Psychology and Physiology*. Woodbury, NY: American Institute of Physics, 1938.

[219] J.A. Storer. *Data Compression—Methods and Theory*. New York: Computer Science Press, 1988.

[220] J.A. Storer and T.G. Syzmanski. Data Compression via Textual Substitution. *Journal of the ACM*, 29:928–951, 1982.

[221] P.F. Swaszek. Vector Quantization. In I.F. Blake and H.V. Poor, editors, *Communications and Networks: A Survey of Recent Advances*, pages 362–389. New York: Springer-Verlag, 1986.

[222] P.F. Swaszek and J.B. Thomas. Multidimensional Spherical Coordinates Quantization. *IEEE Transactions on Information Theory*, IT-29:570–575, July 1983.

[223] S.L. Tanimoto. Image Transmission with Gross Information First. *Computer Graphics and Image Processing*, 9:72–76, January 1979.

[224] D. Taubman. *Directionality and Scalability in Image and Video Compression*. Ph.D. thesis, University of California–Berkeley, May 1994.

[225] D. Taubman and A. Zakhor. Multirate 3-D Subband Coding with Motion Compensation. *IEEE Transactions on Image Processing*, IP-3:572–588, September 1994.

[226] K. Tsutsui, H. Suzuki, O. Shimoyoshi, M. Sonohara, K. Agagiri, and R.M. Heddle. ATRAC: Adaptive Transform Acoustic Coding for MiniDisc. In *Conference Records Audio Engineering Society Convention*. New York: AES, October 1992.

[227] B.P. Tunstall. *Synthesis of Noiseless Compression Codes*. Ph.D. thesis, Georgia Institute of Technology, September 1967.

[228] P.P. Vaidyanathan. *Multirate Systems and Filter Banks*. Englewood Cliffs, NJ: Prentice Hall, 1993.

[229] B.L. van der Waerden. *A History of Algebra*. New York: Springer-Verlag, 1985.

[230] M. Vetterli. Multirate Filterbanks for Subband Coding. In J.W. Woods, editor, *Subband Image Coding*, pages 43–100. Norwell, MA: Kluwer Academic Publishers, 1991.

[231] A.J. Viterbi and J.K. Omura. *Principles of Digital Communications and Coding*. New York: McGraw-Hill, 1979.

[232] J.S. Vitter. Design and Analysis of Dynamic Huffman Codes. *Journal of ACM*, 34(4):825–845, October 1987.

[233] G.K. Wallace. The JPEG Still Picture Compression Standard. *Communications of the ACM*, 34:31–44, April 1991.

[234] X. Wang, S.M. Shende, and K. Sayood. Online Compression of Video Sequences Using Adaptive Vector Quantization. In *Proceedings Data Compression Conference 1994*, pages 185–194. Los Alamitos, CA: IEEE Computer Society Press, 1994.

[235] J. Watkinson. *The Art of Digital Video*. Stoneham, MA: Focal Press, 1990.

[236] M. Weinberger, G. Seroussi, and G. Sapiro. The LOCO-I Lossless Image Compression Algorithm: Principles and Standardization into JPEG-LS. Hewlett-Packard Laboratories Technical Report No. HPL-98-193, November 1998.

[237] T.A. Welch. A Technique for High-Performance Data Compression. *IEEE Computer*, pages 8–19, June 1984.

[238] B. Widrow, J.M. McCool, M.G. Larimore, and C.R. Johnson, Jr. Stationary and Non-stationary Learning Characteristics of the LMS Adaptive Filter. *Proceedings of the IEEE*, 64:1151–1162, August 1976.

[239] S.G. Wilson. Magnitude Phase Quantization of Independent Gaussian Variates. *IEEE Transactions on Communications*, COM-28:1924–1929, November 1980.

[240] P.A. Wintz. Transform Picture Coding. *Proceedings of the IEEE*, 60:809–820, July 1972.

[241] I.H. Witten, A. Moffat, and T.C. Bell. *Managing Gigabytes: Compressing and Indexing Documents and Images*. New York: Van Nostrand Reinhold, 1994.

[242] I.H. Witten, R. Neal, and J.G. Cleary. Arithmetic Coding for Data Compression. *Communications of the Association for Computing Machinery*, 30:520–540, June 1987.

[243] J.W. Woods and T. Naveen. A Filter Based Bit Allocation Scheme for Subband Compression of HDTV. *IEEE Transactions on Image Processing*, IP-1:436–440, July 1992.

[244] X. Wu and N.D. Memon. CALIC—A Context Based Adaptive Lossless Image Coding Scheme. *IEEE Transactions on Communications*, 45:437–444, May 1996.

[245] X. Wu, N.D. Memon, and K. Sayood. A Context Based Adaptive Lossless/Nearly-Lossless Coding Scheme for Continuous Tone Images. ISO Working Document. ISO/IEC SC29/WG1/N256, 1995.

[246] Y. Yasuda. Overview of Digital Facsimile Coding Techniques in Japan. *IEEE Proceedings*, 68:830–845, July 1980.

[247] P.S. Yeh, R.F. Rice, and W. Miller. On the Optimality of Code Options for a Universal Noiseless Coder. Technical Report 91-2, Jet Propulsion Laboratory. Pasadena, CA: California Institute of Technology, February 1991.

[248] J. Ziv and A. Lempel. A Universal Algorithm for Data Compression. *IEEE Transactions on Information Theory*, IT-23(3):337–343, May 1977.

[249] J. Ziv and A. Lempel. Compression of Individual Sequences via Variable-Rate Coding. *IEEE Transactions on Information Theory*, IT-24(5):530–536, September 1978.

Index